CompTIA® Network+ Guide to Networks

Seventh Edition

Jill West

Tamara Dean

Jean Andrews

CENGAGE
Learning·

Australia • Brazil • Mexico • Singapore • United Kingdom • United States

CENGAGE
Learning·

CompTIA® Network+ Guide to Networks, Seventh Edition
Jill West, Tamara Dean, Jean Andrews

SVP, GM Skills & Global Product Management: Dawn Gerrain

Product Director: Kathleen McMahon

Product Team Manager: Kristin McNary

Senior Director, Development:
Marah Bellegarde

Product Development Manager:
Leigh Hefferon

Senior Content Developer:
Michelle Ruelos Cannistraci

Developmental Editor: Ann Shaffer

Product Assistant: Abigail Pufpaff

Vice President, Marketing Services:
Jennifer Ann Baker

Senior Marketing Manager: Eric LaScola

Senior Production Director: Wendy Troeger

Production Director: Patty Stephan

Senior Content Project Manager:
Brooke Greenhouse

Senior Art Director: Jack Pendleton

Cover Image: © vovan/Shutterstock.com

For product information and technology assistance, contact us at
Cengage Learning Customer & Sales Support, 1-800-354-9706

For permission to use material from this text or product,
submit all requests online at **www.cengage.com/permissions**
Further permissions questions can be e-mailed to
permissionrequest@cengage.com

Library of Congress Control Number: 2015936128

ISBN: 978-1-305-09094-1

Cengage Learning
20 Channel Center Street
Boston, MA 02210
USA

Cengage Learning is a leading provider of customized learning solutions with employees residing in nearly 40 different countries and sales in more than 125 countries around the world. Find your local representative at **www.cengage.com**

Cengage Learning products are represented in Canada by Nelson Education, Ltd.

To learn more about Cengage Learning, visit **www.cengage.com**

Purchase any of our products at your local college store or at our preferred online store **www.cengagebrain.com**

Notice to the Reader

Publisher does not warrant or guarantee any of the products described herein or perform any independent analysis in connection with any of the product information contained herein. Publisher does not assume, and expressly disclaims, any obligation to obtain and include information other than that provided to it by the manufacturer. The reader is expressly warned to consider and adopt all safety precautions that might be indicated by the activities described herein and to avoid all potential hazards. By following the instructions contained herein, the reader willingly assumes all risks in connection with such instructions. The publisher makes no representations or warranties of any kind, including but not limited to, the warranties of fitness for particular purpose or merchantability, nor are any such representations implied with respect to the material set forth herein, and the publisher takes no responsibility with respect to such material. The publisher shall not be liable for any special, consequential, or exemplary damages resulting, in whole or part, from the readers' use of, or reliance upon, this material.

Printed in the United States of America
Print Number: 02   Print Year: 2016

Brief Table of Contents

Table of Contents

CHAPTER 5
Network Cabling **209**

CHAPTER 6
Wireless Networking **275**

Preface

Knowing how to install, configure, and troubleshoot a computer network is a highly marketable and exciting skill. This book first introduces the fundamental building blocks that form a modern network, such as protocols, media, topologies, and hardware. It then provides in-depth coverage of the most important concepts in contemporary networking, such as TCP/IP, Ethernet, wireless transmission, virtual networks, security, and troubleshooting. After reading this book and completing the end-of-chapter exercises, you will be prepared to select the best network design, hardware, and software for your environment. You will also have the skills to build a network from scratch and maintain, upgrade, troubleshoot, and manage an existing network. Finally, you will be well-prepared to pass CompTIA's Network+ N10-006 certification exam.

This book explains technical concepts logically and in a clear, approachable style. In addition, concepts are reinforced by real-world examples of networking issues from a professional's standpoint. Each chapter opens with an "On the Job" story from a network engineer, technician, or administrator. These real-world examples, along with Applying Concepts activities, Hands-On Projects, and Case Projects in each chapter, make this book a practical learning tool. The numerous tables and illustrations, along with the glossaries, appendices, and study questions, make the book a valuable reference for any networking professional.

Intended Audience

This book is intended to serve the needs of students and professionals who are interested in mastering fundamental, vendor-independent networking concepts. No previous networking experience is necessary to begin learning from this book, although knowledge of basic computer principles is helpful. Those seeking to pass CompTIA's Network+ certification exam will find the text's content, approach, and numerous study questions especially helpful. For more information on CompTIA® Network+ certification, visit CompTIA's Web site at *comptia.org*.

The book's pedagogical features are designed to provide a truly interactive learning experience, preparing you for the challenges of the highly dynamic networking industry. In addition to the information presented in the text, each chapter includes Applying Concepts activities and Hands-On Projects that guide you through software and hardware configuration in a step-by-step fashion. At the end of each chapter, you will also find Case Projects that place you in the role of problem solver, requiring you to apply concepts presented in the chapter to achieve a successful solution.

Chapter Descriptions

The following list summarizes the topics covered in each chapter of this book:

Chapter 1, "Introduction to Networking," begins by answering the question "What is a network?" Next, it presents the fundamental types of networks and describes the devices and topologies that create a network. This chapter also introduces the OSI model, best practices for safety when working with networks, and the seven-step troubleshooting model.

Chapter 2, "How Computers Find Each Other on Networks," describes addressing standards used by devices on a network and explains how host names and domain names work. It also discusses ports and sockets at the Transport layer and IP addresses at the Network layer. The chapter concludes with an introduction to commands used in troubleshooting networks.

Chapter 3, "How Data Is Transported Over Networks," describes the functions of the core TCP/IP protocols, as well as common IPv4 and IPv6 routing protocols. It also explains multiple TCP/IP utilities used for network discovery and troubleshooting.

Chapter 4, "Structured Cabling and Networking Elements," introduces best practices for managing network and cabling equipment, and explains issues related to managing power and the environment in which networking equipment operates. This chapter also describes characteristics of NIC and Ethernet interfaces, and explains how to create a network map that can be used in network troubleshooting.

Chapter 5, "Network Cabling," discusses basic data transmission concepts, including signaling, data modulation, multiplexing, bandwidth, baseband, and broadband. Next, it describes several Ethernet standards and compares the benefits and limitations of different networking media. The chapter explores connectors, converters, and couplers for each cabling type, and concludes with an examination of common cable problems and the tools used for troubleshooting those problems.

Chapter 6, "Wireless Networking," examines how nodes exchange wireless signals and identifies potential obstacles to successful wireless transmission. It describes WLAN (wireless LAN) architecture and specifies the characteristics of popular WLAN transmission methods. In Chapter 6, you will also learn how to install and configure wireless access points and clients, manage wireless security concerns, and evaluate common problems experienced with wireless networks.

Chapter 7, "Cloud Computing and Remote Access," identifies features and benefits of cloud computing and explains methods for remotely connecting to a network. It covers VPNs and their protocols as well as methods of encryption and user authentication. This chapter also helps you recognize symptoms of connectivity and security problems commonly encountered with remote connections.

Chapter 8, "Network Risk Management," covers common security needs and vulnerabilities of a network, including risks associated with people, hardware, software, and Internet access. Here you'll also learn the elements of an effective security policy and how to apply appropriate security measures and devices when designing a network. Finally, this chapter teaches you how to prevent and respond to malware infections.

Chapter 9, "Unified Communications and Network Performance Management," presents basic network management concepts and describes how to utilize system and event logs to evaluate, monitor, and manage network performance. It explores how unified communications, such as voice and video transmissions, affect a network's performance, and related quality of service issues. The chapter concludes with a discussion of network availability issues and options for network redundancy.

Chapter 10, "Network Segmentation and Virtualization," explores advanced concepts related to TCP/IP-based networking, such as subnetting, CIDR (Classless Interdomain Routing), and supernetting. It also explains virtualization and identifies characteristics of virtual network components. It describes techniques for incorporating virtual components into VLANs and explains advanced features of switches, including VLAN management. Chapter 10 concludes with a discussion on methods of combining VM and VLAN technologies.

Chapter 11, "Wide Area Networks," expands on your knowledge of networks by examining WAN (wide area network) topologies and characteristics, as well as connection and transmission methods, such as T-carriers, ISDN, DSL, broadband cable, and Metro Ethernet. It discusses wireless WAN technologies, such as WiMAX, HSPA+, LTE, and satellite communications, and concludes with an exploration of common problems with WAN connections.

Chapter 12, "Industrial and Enterprise Networking," describes significant components of an industrial control system or SCADA system. You'll also learn how to inventory and manage network assets, identify significant business documents, and create and follow appropriate change management procedures in an enterprise network environment. The chapter presents significant physical security controls, and then concludes by describing components of a reliable disaster recovery plan and a defensible incident response plan.

The four appendices at the end of this book serve as references for the networking professional:

Appendix A, "CompTIA Network+ N10-006 Certification Exam Objectives," provides a complete list of the latest CompTIA Network+ certification exam objectives, including the percentage of the exam's content that each domain represents and which chapters in the book cover material associated with each objective.

Appendix B, "Numbering Systems," teaches you step-by-step processes for manually converting between various numbering systems, as well as shortcut procedures for these conversions.

Appendix C, "Visual Guide to Connectors," provides a visual connector reference chart for quick identification of connectors and receptacles used in contemporary networking.

Appendix D, "CompTIA Network+ Practice Exam," offers a practice exam containing 100 questions similar in content and presentation to those you will find on CompTIA's Network+ examination.

New to This Edition

- Content maps completely to CompTIA's Network+ N10-006 exam for productive exam preparation.

- New arrangement of content consolidates similar concepts for efficient coverage, allowing for deeper investigation of particularly rich concepts and skills that are emphasized in the latest CompTIA Network+ N10-006 exam, including a stronger emphasis on security, troubleshooting, and virtualization, with added coverage of VLANs, industrial and enterprise networks, and fiber-optic technology.

- Interactive learning features throughout each chapter make essential information easily accessible and help in visualizing high-level concepts with insightful diagrams, useful tables for quick reference, and bulleted lists that present condensed information in easy-to-digest chunks.

- Applying Concepts activities embedded in each chapter help solidify concepts as you read through the chapter and provide immediate practice of relevant skills.

- OSI layer icons provide visual reinforcement of the link between concepts and the relevant layers of the OSI model.

- New and updated skills-based projects encourage hands-on exploration of chapter concepts.

Features

To aid you in fully understanding networking concepts, this book includes many features designed to enhance your learning experience.

Chapter Objectives—Each chapter begins with a list of the concepts to be mastered within that chapter. This list provides you with both a quick reference to the chapter's contents and a useful study aid.

On the Job stories—Each chapter begins with a story in a real-world context for the technology and concepts presented, giving you insight into a variety of modern computing environments from the various perspectives of many different professionals in the IT industry.

Applying Concepts activities—Embedded within each chapter are activities with step-by-step instructions to help you apply concepts as you learn them.

Illustrations, photos, tables, and bullet lists—Numerous full-color illustrations and photos of network media, methods of signaling, protocol behavior, hardware, topology, software screens, peripherals, and components help you visualize common network elements, theories, and concepts. In addition, the many tables and bulleted lists provide details and comparisons of both practical and theoretical information.

CompTIA Network+ Exam Tips and Notes—Each chapter's content is supplemented with Note features that provide additional insight and understanding, while CompTIA Network+ Exam Tips guide you in your preparations for taking the CompTIA Network+ certification exam.

Legacy Networking features—Older technology covered by the CompTIA Network+ exam provides historical reference to current technology.

Chapter Summaries—Each chapter's text is followed by a summary of the concepts introduced in that chapter. These summaries provide a helpful way to revisit the ideas covered in each chapter.

Review Questions—The end-of-chapter assessment begins with a set of review questions that reinforce the ideas introduced in each chapter. Many questions are situational. Rather than simply asking you to repeat what you've learned, these questions help you evaluate and apply the material you learned. Answering these questions will ensure that you have mastered the important concepts and provide valuable practice for taking CompTIA's Network+ exam.

Hands-On Projects—Although it is important to understand the theory behind networking technology, nothing can improve upon real-world experience. To this end, each chapter provides several Hands-On Projects aimed at providing you with practical software and hardware implementation experience as well as practice in applying critical thinking skills to the concepts learned throughout the chapter.

Case Projects—Each chapter concludes with two in-depth projects where you implement the skills and knowledge gained in the chapter through real design and implementation scenarios in a variety of computing environments. The Case Projects introduce you to a multitude of real-world software, hardware, and other solutions that increase your familiarity with these products in preparation for addressing workforce challenges.

Text and Graphic Conventions

Wherever appropriate, additional information and exercises have been added to this book to help you better understand the topic at hand. The following icons are used throughout the text to alert you to additional materials:

The Note icon draws your attention to helpful material related to the subject being described.

The CompTIA Network+ Exam Tip icon provides helpful pointers when studying for the exam.

OSI model icons highlight the specific layers of the OSI model being discussed, and indicate when the layers of interest change throughout the chapter.

Each Hands-On Project in this book is preceded by both the Hands-On icon and a description of the project.

Case Project icons mark case projects, which are more in-depth assignments that require a higher level of concept application.

Network+

All of the content that relates to CompTIA's Network+ certification exam, whether it is a page or a sentence, is highlighted with a Network+ icon and the relevant objective number in the margin. This unique feature highlights the important information at a glance, so you can pay extra attention to areas of the certification material that you most need to study.

State of the Information Technology (IT) Field

Organizations depend on computers and information technology to thrive and grow. Globalization, or connecting with customers and suppliers around the world, is a direct result of the widespread use of the Internet. Rapidly changing technology further affects how companies do business and keeps the demand for skilled and certified IT workers strong across industries. Every sector of the economy requires IT professionals who can establish, maintain, troubleshoot, and extend their business systems.

Despite the economic downturn that began in 2007, employment in IT rebounded early and with vigor. The latest *Occupational Outlook Handbook* from the Bureau of Labor Statistics (part of the U.S. Department of Labor) reports that there were more than 365,000 network and computer systems administrator positions in 2012, the most recent year for which this information is available, with a predicted increase of 12 percent between 2012 and 2022 and the highest growth rate in positions related to cloud computing technology. Median pay for jobs in this sector is almost $73,000.

In any industry, a skilled workforce is important for continually driving business. Finding highly skilled IT workers can be a struggle for employers, given that technologies change approximately every two years. With such a quick product life cycle, IT workers must strive to keep up with these changes to continually bring value to their employers.

Certifications

Different levels of education are required for the many jobs in the IT industry. Additionally, the level of education and type of training required varies from employer to employer, but the need for qualified technicians remains a constant. As technology changes and advances in the industry evolve, many employers prefer candidates who already have the skills to implement these new technologies. Traditional degrees and diplomas do not identify the skills that a job applicant possesses. Companies are relying increasingly on technical certifications to adequately identify the quality and skill qualifications of a job applicant, and these certifications can offer job seekers a competitive edge over their competition.

Certifications fall into one of two categories: vendor-neutral and vendor-specific. Vendor-neutral certifications are those that test for the skills and knowledge required in specific industry job roles and do not subscribe to a vendor's specific technology solutions. Some examples of vendor-neutral certifications include all of the CompTIA certifications, Project Management Institute's certifications, and ISACA's certifications. Vendor-specific certifications validate the skills and knowledge necessary to be successful while utilizing a specific vendor's technology solution. Some examples of vendor-specific certifications include those offered by Microsoft, Red Hat, Oracle, and Cisco.

As employers struggle to fill open IT positions with qualified candidates, certifications are a means of validating the skill sets necessary to be successful within organizations. In most careers, salary and compensation are determined by experience and education, but in the IT field, the number and type of certifications an employee earns also determine salary and wage increases. For example, according to CompTIA, companies such as Dell, HP, Ricoh, Sharp, and Xerox recommend or require their networking technicians achieve CompTIA Network+ certification.

Certification provides job applicants with more than just a competitive edge over their noncertified counterparts competing for the same IT positions. Some institutions of higher education grant college credit to students who successfully pass certification exams, moving them further along in their degree programs. Certification also gives individuals who are interested in careers in the military the ability to move into higher positions more quickly. And many advanced certification programs accept, and sometimes require, entry-level certifications as part of their exams. For example, Apple accepts the CompTIA Network+ certification as part of one optional path for joining their Apple Consultants Network.

Career Planning

Finding a career that fits a person's personality, skill set, and lifestyle is challenging and fulfilling, but can often be difficult. What are the steps individuals should take to find that dream career? Is IT interesting to you? Chances are, that if you are reading this book, this question has already been answered. What is it about IT that you like? The world of work in the IT industry is vast. Some questions to ask yourself: Are you a person who likes to work alone, or do you like to work in a group? Do you like speaking directly with customers, or do you prefer to stay behind the scenes? Does your lifestyle encourage a lot of travel, or do you need to stay in one location? All of these factors influence your job decision. Inventory assessments are a good first step to learning more about you, your interests, work values, and abilities. A variety of Web sites can offer assistance with career planning and assessments.

What's New with CompTIA Network+ Certification

With its N10-006 Network+ exam, CompTIA has emphasized more hands-on experience and expanded the scope of the exam to include the latest network technologies. Objectives that used to require only identifying protocols, devices, and standards now require demonstrating an ability to install and configure connectivity devices or to apply protocols and standards. There's a stronger emphasis on security, virtualization, and troubleshooting. Some objectives have been added or expanded, such as coverage of fiber-optic technology, VLANs, and enterprise networks. A few older technologies have been dropped from the objectives. However, bear in mind that some legacy protocols and standards appear in the objectives' list of acronyms, and the CompTIA Network+ exam could refer to them.

As with the previous Network+ exam, the N10-006 version includes many scenario-based questions. Mastering, rather than simply memorizing, the material in this book will help you succeed on the exam and on the job.

Here are the domains covered on the new CompTIA Network+ exam:

Domain	% of Examination
Domain 1.0 Network architecture	22%
Domain 2.0 Network operations	20%
Domain 3.0 Network security	18%
Domain 4.0 Troubleshooting	24%
Domain 5.0 Industry standards, practices, and network theory	16%

How to Become CompTIA Certified

To become CompTIA certified, you must:

1. Select a testing center and a certification exam provider. For more information, visit the following Web site: *http://certification.comptia.org/getCertified/steps_to_certification.aspx*

2. Register for and schedule a time to take the CompTIA certification exam at a convenient location.

3. Take and pass the CompTIA certification exam.

For more information about CompTIA's certifications, please visit *http://certification.comptia.org/getCertified.aspx*

CompTIA is a nonprofit information technology (IT) trade association.

To contact CompTIA with any questions or comments, call 866-835-8020 or visit *http://certification.comptia.org/contact.aspx*. The Computing Technology Industry Association (CompTIA) is the voice of the world's information technology (IT) industry. Its members are the companies at the forefront of innovation and the professionals responsible for maximizing the benefits organizations receive from their investments in technology.

CompTIA is dedicated to advancing industry growth through its educational programs, market research, networking events, professional certifications, and public policy advocacy.

CompTIA is a not-for-profit information technology (IT) trade association. CompTIA's certifications are designed by subject matter experts from across the IT industry. Each CompTIA certification is vendor-neutral, covers multiple technologies, and requires demonstration of skills and knowledge widely sought after by the IT industry.

CompTIA.

Becoming a CompTIA Certified IT Professional is Easy

It's also the best way to reach greater professional opportunities and rewards.

Why Get CompTIA Certified?

Growing Demand

Labor estimates predict some technology fields will experience growth of over 20% by the year 2020.* CompTIA certification qualifies the skills required to join this workforce.

Higher Salaries

IT professionals with certifications on their resume command better jobs, earn higher salaries and have more doors open to new multi-industry opportunities.

Verified Strengths

91% of hiring managers indicate CompTIA certifications are valuable in validating IT expertise, making certification the best way to demonstrate your competency and knowledge to employers.**

Universal Skills

CompTIA certifications are vendor neutral—which means that certified professionals can proficiently work with an extensive variety of hardware and software found in most organizations.

 **Learn** >  **Certify** >  **Work**

Learn more about what the exam covers by reviewing the following:	Purchase a voucher at a Pearson VUE testing center or at CompTIAstore.com.	Congratulations on your CompTIA certification!
• Exam objectives for key study points. • Sample questions for a general overview of what to expect on the exam and examples of question format. • Visit online forums, like LinkedIn, to see what other IT professionals say about CompTIA exams.	• Register for your exam at a Pearson VUE testing center: • Visit pearsonvue.com/CompTIA to find the closest testing center to you. • Schedule the exam online. You will be required to enter your voucher number or provide payment information at registration. • Take your certification exam.	• Make sure to add your certification to your resume. • Check out the CompTIA Certification Roadmap to plan your next career move.

Learn more: Certification.CompTIA.org/networkplus

* Source: CompTIA 9th Annual Information Security Trends study: 500 U.S. IT and Business Executives Responsible for Security
** Source: CompTIA Employer Perceptions of IT Training and Certification
*** Source: 2013 IT Skills and Salary Report by CompTIA Authorized Partner

The CompTIA Marks are the proprietary trademarks and/or service marks of CompTIA Properties, LLC used under license from CompTIA Certifications, LLC through participation in the CompTIA Authorized Partner Program. More information about the program can be found at *http://www.comptia.org/certifications.capp/login.aspx.*

CompTIA Network+ Test Preparation Materials

CompTIA Network+ Guide to Networks, Seventh Edition is packed with tools to help students prepare for CompTIA's N10-006 Network+ exam, released in 2015. This book includes the Network+ icon in the margins highlighting relevant content, a table in Appendix A explaining where each exam objective is covered in the book, and a 100-question practice exam in Appendix D.

Instructor's Materials

Everything you need for your course is in one place! This collection of book-specific lecture and class tools is available online. Please visit *login.cengage.com* and log on to access instructor-specific resources on the Instructor Companion Site, which includes the Instructor's Manual, Solutions Manual, test creation tools, PowerPoint Presentations, Syllabus, and figure files.

- *Electronic Instructor's Manual*—The Instructor's Manual that accompanies this textbook includes additional instructional material to assist in class preparation, including suggestions for lecture topics.

- *Solutions Manual*—The instructor's resources include solutions to all end-of-chapter material, including Review Questions and Case Projects.

- *Cengage Learning Testing Powered by Cognero*—This flexible, online system allows you to do the following:

  - Author, edit, and manage test bank content from multiple Cengage Learning solutions.

  - Create multiple test versions in an instant.

  - Deliver tests from your LMS, your classroom, or wherever you want.

PowerPoint Presentations

This book comes with a set of Microsoft PowerPoint slides for each chapter. These slides are meant to be used as a teaching aid for classroom presentations, to be made available to students on the network for chapter review, or to be printed for classroom distribution. Instructors are also at liberty to add their own slides for other topics introduced.

Figure Files

All of the figures and tables in the book are reproduced. Similar to PowerPoint presentations, these are included as a teaching aid for classroom presentation, to make available to students for review, or to be printed for classroom distribution.

Total Solutions for CompTIA Network+

To access additional course materials, please visit *www.cengagebrain.com*. At the *CengageBrain.com* home page, search for the ISBN of your title (from the back cover of your book) using the search box at the top of the page. This will take you to the product page where these resources can be found. Additional resources include a MindTap, Lab Manual, CourseNotes, assessment, and digital labs.

Lab Manual for CompTIA Network+ Guide to Networks, Seventh Edition

This Lab Manual contains over 70 labs to provide students with additional hands-on experience and to help prepare for the CompTIA Network+ exam. The Lab Manual includes lab activities, objectives, materials lists, step-by-step procedures, illustrations, and review questions.

CourseNotes

This laminated quick reference card reinforces critical knowledge for the CompTIA Network+ exam in a visual and user-friendly format. CourseNotes serves as a useful study aid, as a supplement to the textbook, or as a quick reference tool during the course and afterward.

MindTap

MindTap is a personalized teaching experience with relevant assignments that guide students to analyze, apply, and improve thinking, allowing you to measure skills and outcomes with ease.

- *Personalized teaching*—Personalize your teaching with a Learning Path that is built with key student objectives. Control what students see and when they see it. Use it as is or match to your syllabus exactly—hide, rearrange, add, and create your own content.

- *Guide students*—Guide students with a unique Learning Path of relevant readings, multimedia, and activities that moves students up the learning taxonomy from basic knowledge and comprehension to analysis and application.

- *Promote better outcomes*—Empower instructors and motivate students with analytics and reports that provide a snapshot of class progress, time in course, engagement, and completion rates.

LabConnection

LabConnection provides powerful computer-based exercises, simulations, and demonstrations for hands-on, skills courses. It can be used as both a virtual lab and as a homework assignment tool, and provides automatic grading and student record maintenance. LabConnection maps directly to the textbook and provides remediation to the text and to the CompTIA Network+ certification exam. It includes the following features:

- *Enhanced comprehension*—Through LabConnection's guidance in the virtual lab environment, learners develop skills that are accurate and consistently effective.

- *Exercises*—LabConnection includes dozens of exercises that assess and prepare the learner for the virtual labs, establishing and solidifying the skills and knowledge required to complete the lab.

- *Virtual labs*—Labs consist of end-to-end procedures performed in a simulated environment where the student can practice the skills required of professionals.

- *Guided learning*—LabConnection allows learners to make mistakes but alerts them to errors made before they can move on to the next step, sometimes offering demonstrations as well.

- *Video demonstrations*—Video demonstrations guide the learners step-by-step through the labs, while providing additional insights to solidify the concepts.

- *Grades and record keeping*—LabConnection grades the exercises and records the completion status of the lab portion, easily porting to, and compatible with, distance learning platforms.

ExamConnection

The online testing system, ExamConnection, automatically grades students and keeps class and student records. ExamConnection tests against Cengage's textbook as well as against the CompTIA Network+ certification exam, including a quiz for each chapter in the book along with a midterm and final exam. ExamConnection is managed by the classroom instructor, who has 100 percent control, 100 percent of the time. It is hosted and maintained by dtiPublishing.

Web-Based Labs

Using a real lab environment over the Internet, students can log on anywhere, anytime via a Web browser to gain essential hands-on experience in networking using labs from *CompTIA® Network+ Guide to Networks, Seventh Edition*.

About the Authors

Jean Andrews has more than 30 years of experience in the computer industry, including more than 13 years in the college classroom. She has worked in a variety of businesses and corporations designing, writing, and supporting application software; managing a PC repair help desk; and troubleshooting wide area networks. She has written numerous books on software, hardware, and the Internet, including the best-selling *CompTIA A+ Comprehensive Guide to Managing and Maintaining Your PC, Eighth Edition, CompTIA A+ Guide to Hardware, Sixth Edition*, and *CompTIA A+ Guide to Software: Managing, Maintaining and Troubleshooting, Sixth Edition*. She lives in north Georgia.

Jill West brings a unique cross-section of experience in business, writing, and education to the development of innovative educational materials. She has taught multiple ages and content areas using a flipped classroom approach, distance learning, and educational counseling. Jill was instrumental in piloting a flipped classroom program for learning support courses at

North Georgia Technical College, and she has over a decade's experience working with Jean Andrews in textbook development. Jill and her husband Mike live in northwest Georgia where they homeschool their four children.

Tamara Dean has worked in the field of networking for nearly 20 years, most recently as a networking consultant, and before that, as the manager of Internet services and data center operations for a regional ISP. She has managed LANs at the University of Wisconsin and at a pharmaceutical firm, worked as a telecommunications analyst for the FCC, and cofounded a local radio station. Well published in networking, Ms. Dean also authored *Guide to Telecommunications Technology* for Cengage Learning.

Acknowledgments

What an incredible experience this has been, and what an amazing team we have been privileged to work with. The level of professionalism from everyone involved in this project clearly evidences their commitment to quality. Special thanks to Kristin McNary, Product Team Manager, for your fine leadership. Thank you, Michelle Ruelos Cannistraci, Senior Content Developer, and Ann Shaffer, Developmental Editor. The project ran smoothly under your steady intendance and dedication to excellence. Thank you to all of the following for your attention to detail, resourceful solutions, and creative ideas: Kristin McNary, Product Team Manager; Serge Palladino, Technical Editor; Karen Annett, Copy Editor; Brooke Baker, Senior Content Project Manager; Aravinda Doss, Senior Project Manager; Christian Kunciw, QA Leader; Kathy Kucharek and Amber Hosea, Permissions; and Danielle Shaw, Technical Editor. Working with each of you on this project has truly been a pleasurable experience.

Many more people contributed time, expertise, and advice during the course of this revision. Every contribution has made this book better than it would have been without your help. Thank you to Robert Wilson and all the IT guys at McCallie School for allowing Jill to hang out with you and be fascinated by the work you do every day. Thank you to each of the reviewers who, driven by your dedication to high-quality education for your students, contributed a great deal of expertise, constantly challenging us to higher levels of insight, accuracy, and clarity. Specifically, thank you to:

Jonathan S. Weissman, Finger Lakes Community College

Jane Perschbach, Central Texas College

Richard Smolenski, Westwood College

Darlene Wood, Fayetteville Technical Community College

Gregg Tennefoss, Tidewater Community College

Jake Mihevc, Mohawk Valley Community College

To the instructors and learners who use this book, we invite and encourage you to send suggestions or corrections for future editions. Please write to us at *jill.west@cengage.com*. We never ignore a good idea! And to instructors, if you have ideas for how to make a class in CompTIA Network+ preparation a success, please share your ideas with other instructors!

Dedication

This book is dedicated to the covenant of God with man on earth.

Jean Andrews, Ph.D.

Jill West

I'd like to say a personal thank you to the people in my life who make this work possible. To my children, Jessica, Sarah, Daniel, and Zack: Thank you for your patience and your hugs and kisses during the long work hours. To my husband, Mike: You mean the world to me. This is your accomplishment, too.

Jill West

Read This Before You Begin

The Applying Concepts activities, Hands-On Projects, and Case Projects in this book help you to apply what you have learned about computer networking. Although some modern networking components can be expensive, the projects aim to use widely available and moderately priced hardware and software. The following section lists the minimum hardware and software requirements that allow you to complete all the projects in this book. In addition to the following requirements, students must have administrator privileges on their workstations and, for some projects, on a second workstation, to successfully complete the projects.

Hardware Lab Requirements

- Each student workstation computer requires at least 1 GB of RAM, an Intel Pentium or compatible processor running at 500 MHz or faster, and a minimum of 500 MB of free space on the hard disk. Many projects also require workstations to have at least one installed NIC.

- Some projects require the use of a second workstation computer in order to create a network connection between computers. The second computer has the same minimum requirements as the first one.

- For installing computer equipment, students need a computer repair toolkit that includes a static mat and wrist guard, both flathead and Phillips screwdrivers, and a utility knife.

- For working with computer connectivity, each student needs a removable Ethernet NIC capable of 100-Mbps or faster throughput.

- For projects with physical transmission media, students require a workstation with a free PCI slot and a PCI NIC, plus a networking toolkit that includes the following cable-making supplies: at least 30 feet of Cat 5 or better cabling, at least six RJ-45 plugs, a wire cutter, a cable stripper, and a crimping tool.

- For configuring VLANs on a Cisco router, each class should have a router that runs the Cisco IOS or access to an emulator program and IOS image of a Cisco switch.

- For projects with wireless transmission, each class should have a wireless access point capable of 802.11g or 802.11n transmission and compatible wireless NICs for each student workstation.

- For implementing a basic client-server network, a class requires at least two Ethernet switches, each capable of 100-Mbps or faster throughput, and four or more Cat 5 or better straight-through patch cables that are each at least 3 feet long.

Software Lab Requirements

Most projects are written for workstations running either Windows 7, Windows 8.1, or a Linux operating system. Many include instructions for modifying the steps to work with computers running a different operating system than the one specified in that project. Software requirements include:

- Windows 7 or Windows 8.1 updated with the most current service packs for each student workstation
- The latest version of Ubuntu Desktop, which will be installed in a virtual environment
- Ubuntu Server operating system, which will be installed in a virtual environment
- The latest version of Chrome, Firefox, or Internet Explorer Web browser
- The latest version of WinZip file compression and expansion software
- The latest version of Adobe Acrobat Reader

To complete the virtual machine Case Projects, students will need Hyper-V on Windows 8.1 Professional, 64-bit version, or they can use Oracle VirtualBox on a Windows 7 or Windows 8.1 machine.

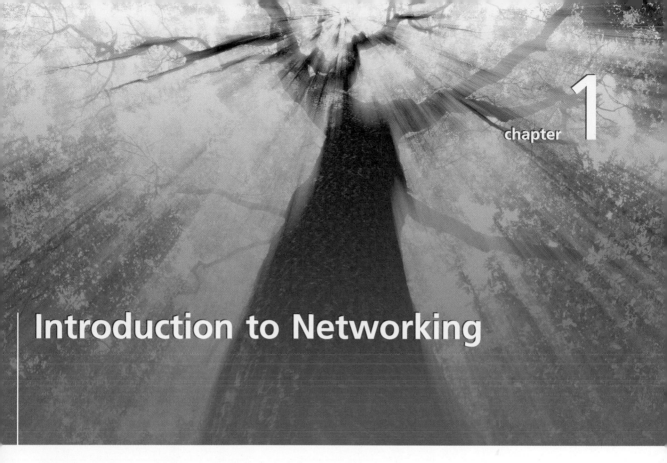

## chapter 1

Introduction to Networking

After reading this chapter and completing the exercises, you will be able to:

- Identify types of applications and protocols used on a network
- Distinguish between the client-server and peer-to-peer models used to control access to a network
- Describe various networking hardware devices and the most common physical topologies
- Describe the seven layers of the OSI model
- Explore best practices for safety when working with networks and computers
- Describe the seven-step troubleshooting model for solving a networking problem

On the Job

This story is about a client who visited our PC Clinic, a free service offered by our students to the community. Mrs. Jones is an elderly woman who had visited our PC Clinic several times with a variety of PC issues. This visit, she came in with a brand new Dell mini desktop PC.

At home, Mrs. Jones had hooked up all of the cables. Everything worked except her Internet connection. When she called Dell, the technician said she needed a device that cost $40. When it arrived in the mail, she plugged the USB end into her computer. She then tried to plug her phone line into the other end of the device but it didn't fit.

We took a look at the device, or dongle, as a small piece of hardware is sometimes called. It was designed to create an Ethernet connection via USB, with a USB connector on one end and an RJ-45 port on the other. Mrs. Jones's PC also had a wireless card built into the motherboard, but she said that her home network was not wireless.

Next we asked her, "Which Internet service provider do you have?" She said, "I pay AT&T." "Ok, you have a DSL connection with AT&T," we explained. "Do you plug your phone line into the computer?" "No," she said. "When I do that, my phone doesn't work." "Do you have a dial-up service?" "No," she replied. "I use AOL."

Aha! Mrs. Jones had a dial-up service which required an RJ-11 connection, not an RJ-45 connection! And her new desktop PC contained no modem, which is necessary to access dial-up service.

After searching Dell's Web site, we were able to locate an External V.92 56K USB Fax/Modem, a modem that connects to the PC through a USB connection. Mrs. Jones was very grateful, and looking forward to being "connected" again.

June West
Program Director, Computer Technology
Spartanburg Community College

Loosely defined, a network is a group of computers and other devices (such as printers) that are connected by some type of transmission media. Variations on the elements of a network and the way it is designed, however, are nearly infinite. A network can be as small as two computers connected by a cable in a home office or the largest network of all, the Internet, made up of millions of computers connected across the world via a combination of cable, phone lines, and wireless links. Networks might link cell phones, personal computers, mainframe computers, printers, plotters, fax machines, and corporate phone systems. They might communicate through copper wires, fiber-optic cable, or radio waves. This chapter introduces you to the fundamentals of networks and how technicians support them.

How Networks Are Used

Network+
1.6
1.10
5.10

The resources a network makes available to its users include applications and the data provided by these applications. Collectively, these resources are usually referred to as network services. Let's quickly survey several types of applications that are typically found on most networks.

Client-Server Applications

A **client-server application** involves two computers. The first, a client computer, requests data or a service from the second computer, called the server. For example, in Figure 1-1, someone uses a Web browser to request a Web page from a Web server. How does the client know how to make the request in a way the server can understand and respond to? These networked devices use methods and rules for communication known as **protocols**. To handle the request for a Web page, the client computer must first find the Web server. Then, the client and server must agree on the protocols they will use to communicate. Finally, the client makes the request and the server sends its response, in the form of a Web page. Hardware, the operating system, and the applications on both computers are all involved in this process.

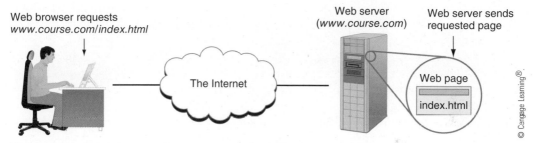

Web browser requests
www.course.com/index.html

Web server
(*www.course.com*)

Web server sends
requested page

The Internet

Web page

index.html

Figure 1-1   A Web browser (client application) requests a Web page from a Web server (server application); the Web server returns the requested data to the client

Here's a brief list of several popular client-server applications used on networks and the Internet:

- *Web service*—A Web server serves up Web pages to clients. Many corporations have their own Web servers, which are available privately on the corporate network. Other Web servers are public, accessible from anywhere on the Internet. The primary protocol used by Web servers and browsers (clients) is **HTTP (Hypertext Transfer Protocol)**. When HTTP is layered on top of an encryption protocol, such as **SSL (Secure Sockets Layer)** or **TLS (Transport Layer Security)**, the result is **HTTPS (HTTP Secure)**, which gives a secure transmission. The most popular Web server application is Apache (see *apache.org*), which primarily runs on UNIX systems, and the second most popular is Internet Information Services (IIS), which is embedded in the Windows Server operating system.

NOTE

To verify that a Web-based transmission is secure, look for "https" in the URL in the browser address box, as in *https://www.wellsfargo.com*.

- *email services*—Email is a client-server application that involves two servers. The client uses **SMTP (Simple Mail Transfer Protocol)** to send an email message to the first server, which is sometimes called the SMTP server (see Figure 1-2). The first server sends the message on to the receiver's mail server, where it's stored until the recipient requests delivery. The recipient's mail server delivers the message to the receiving client using one of two protocols: **POP3 (Post Office Protocol, version 3)** or **IMAP4 (Internet Message Access Protocol, version 4)**. Using POP3, email is downloaded to the client computer. Using IMAP4, the client application manages the email stored on the server. An example of a popular email server application is Microsoft Exchange Server. Outlook, an application in the Microsoft Office suite of applications, is a popular email client application.

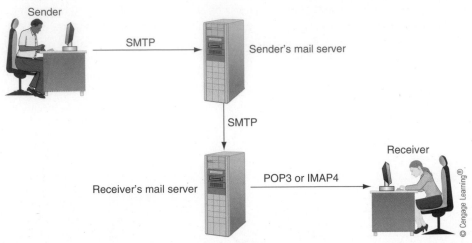

Figure 1-2   SMTP is used to send email to a recipient's email server, and POP3 or IMAP4 is used by the client to receive email

- *FTP service*—FTP is a client-server application that transfers files between two computers, and it primarily uses **FTP (File Transfer Protocol)**. FTP does not provide encryption and is, therefore, not secure. Web browsers can be FTP clients, although dedicated FTP client applications, such as CuteFTP by GlobalSCAPE (*cuteftp.com*), offer more features for file transfer than does a browser.

An encrypted and secure version of FTP is SFTP (Secure File Transfer Protocol). In later chapters, you'll learn to set up an FTP server and client and an SFTP server and client.

- *Telnet service*—The **Telnet** protocol is used by the Telnet client-server command-line application to allow an administrator or other user to "remote in" or control a computer remotely. Telnet is included in many operating systems, but transmissions in Telnet are not encrypted, which has caused Telnet to be largely replaced by other more secure programs, such as the ssh command in the Linux operating system.

The ssh command in Linux uses the Secure Shell (SSH) protocol, which creates a secure channel or tunnel between two computers.

- *Remote Desktop*—In Windows operating systems, the Windows **Remote Desktop** application uses **RDP (Remote Desktop Protocol)** to provide secure, encrypted transmissions that allow a technician to remote in—that is, to access a remote computer from the technician's local computer, as shown in Figure 1-3. For example, when a vendor supports software on your corporate network, the vendor's support technician at the vendor's site can use Remote Desktop to connect to a computer on your corporate network to troubleshoot problems with the vendor's software. The corporate computer serves up its Windows desktop from which the technician can access any resources on your corporate network. In this situation, the vendor's computer is running Remote Desktop as a client and the corporate computer is running Remote Desktop as a server or host.

Desktop of the remote (host) computer

Drive C of the remote computer

Drive C of the local (client) computer

Figure 1-3 Using Remote Desktop, you can access the desktop of the remote computer on your local computer

Source: Microsoft LLC

Because they can be accessed from outside the local network, remote access servers necessitate strict security measures.

NOTE

- *remote applications*—A remote application is an application that is installed and executed on a server and is presented to a user working at a client computer. Windows Server 2008 and later include Remote Desktop Services to manage remote applications, and versions of Windows Server prior to 2008 provided Terminal Services. Both use RDP to present the remote application and its data to the client. Remote applications are becoming popular because most of the computing power (memory and CPU speed) and technical support (for application installations and updates and for backing up data) are focused on the server in a centralized location, which means the client computers require less computing power and desk-side support.

File and Print Services

Network+
1.6

The term file services refers to a server's ability to share data files and disk storage space. A computer that provides file services is called a file server, and serves up data to users, in contrast to users keeping copies of the data on their workstations. Data stored at a central location is typically more secure because a network administrator can take charge of backing up this data, rather than relying on individual users to make their own backups.

Using print services to share printers across a network saves time and money. A high-capacity printer can cost thousands of dollars, but can handle the printing tasks of an entire department, thereby eliminating the need to buy a desktop printer for each employee. With one printer, less time is spent on maintenance and management. If a shared printer fails, the network administrator can sometimes diagnose and solve the problem from a workstation anywhere on the network.

Communications Services

Using the same network to deliver multiple types of communications services, such as video, voice, and fax, is known as convergence. A similar term, unified communications (UC), refers to the centralized management of multiple network-based communications. For example, a company might use one software program to manage intraoffice phone calls, long-distance phone calls, cell phone calls, voice mail, faxes, and text messaging for all the users on your network.

Let's consider three types of communication services your network might support and the protocols and models they use:

- *conversational voice*—VoIP (Voice over IP) allows two or more people to have voice conversations over a network. VoIP voice is fast replacing traditional telephone service in homes and businesses. For conversational voice, VoIP applications, such as Skype and Google Talk, use a point-to-point model rather than a client-server model, which means that each computer involved is independent of the other computers. Additionally, computers engaged in a conference call would use a point-to-multipoint model, which involves one transmitter and multiple receivers.

- *streaming live audio and video*—A video teleconference (VTC) application, such as Skype or Google Talk, allows people to communicate in video and voice, primarily using the point-to-point model. On the other hand, when you watch a live sports event on your computer, the application is using a client-server model with one server and many clients, called a multicast distribution. The Session layer protocol that is specifically designed to transmit audio and video and that works in conjunction with VoIP is RTP (Real-time Transport Protocol).

- *streaming stored audio and video*—When you watch a video on Youtube.com, you're using a client-server model, as the movie stored on the *Youtube.com* server is streamed to your client computer.

Voice and video transmissions are delay-sensitive, meaning you don't want to hear breaks in your conversation or see a buffering message when you watch a movie over the Internet. On the other hand, occasional loss of data (skipping video frames, for example) can be tolerated; for that reason, voice and video transmissions are considered loss-tolerant. Network administrators must pay attention to the quality of service (QoS) a network provides for voice and video.

Network administrators must be aware of the applications used on a network, including the application protocols they use and the amount of bandwidth they require. Bandwidth, as the term is used here, means the amount of traffic, or data transmission activity, on the network.

Another important consideration for administrators is the methods used to control access to the network.

Controlling Network Access

 A topology describes how the parts of a whole work together. When studying networking, you need to understand both the physical topology and the logical topology:

- The term physical topology, or network topology, mostly applies to hardware and describes how computers, other devices, and cables fit together to form the physical network.

- The term logical topology has to do with software and describes how access to the network is controlled, including how users and programs initially gain access to the network and how specific resources, such as applications and databases, are shared on the network.

In this part of the chapter, you learn about controlling network access. Later in the chapter, you'll learn about the physical topologies.

Controlling how users and programs get access to the resources on a network is a function of the operating systems used on the network. Each operating system (OS) is configured to use one of two models to connect to network resources: the peer-to-peer model or the client-server model. The peer-to-peer model can be achieved using any assortment of desktop, mobile devices, or tablet operating systems, but the client-server model requires one or more network operating systems (NOSs), which controls access to the entire network. Examples of NOSs are Windows Server 2012 R2, Ubuntu Server, and Red Hat (Ubuntu and Red Hat are versions of Linux).

 The peer-to-peer model and the client-server model are sometimes referred to as the peer-to-peer topology and the client-server topology. The CompTIA Network+ exam expects you to know how to use the word *topology*.

Peer-to-Peer Network Model

Using a peer-to-peer (P2P) network model, the operating system of each computer on the network is responsible for controlling access to its resources without centralized control. The computers, called nodes or hosts on the network, form a logical group of computers and users that share resources (see Figure 1-4). Administration, resources, and security on a computer are controlled by that computer.

 When looking at the diagrams in Figure 1-4 and later in Figure 1-5, keep in mind that the connecting lines describe the logical arrangement or topology of the group of computers, as opposed to the physical arrangement. The physical arrangement in both diagrams may be the same, but the model the OSs use to logically connect differs.

Examples of operating systems that might be installed on computers in a peer-to-peer network are Windows 7, Windows 8.1, Linux, and Mac OS X on desktop and laptop computers and iOS, Android, and BlackBerry on mobile devices.

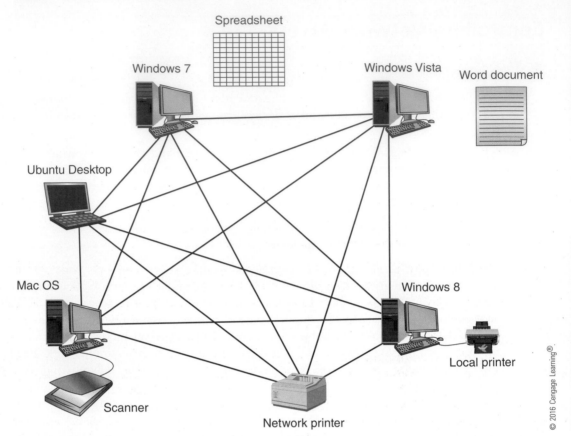

Figure 1-4 In a peer-to-peer network, no computer has more authority than another; each computer controls its own resources, and communicates directly with other computers

If all computers in a peer-to-peer network are running a Windows operating system, each computer user has a Windows **local account** that works only on that one computer. Resources can be shared in these ways:

- Using Windows folder and file sharing, each computer maintains a list of users and their rights on that particular PC. Windows allows a user on the network to access local resources based on these assigned rights.

- Using a homegroup, each computer shares files, folders, libraries, and printers with other computers in the homegroup. A homegroup limits how sharing can be controlled for individual users because any user of any computer in the homegroup can access homegroup resources.

You can also use a combination of folder and file sharing and homegroups on the same network and even using the same computers. That can get confusing, so it's best to stick with one method or the other.

This book assumes you are already aware of the knowledge and skills covered in the CompTIA A+ certification objectives. Using and supporting homegroups and sharing folders and files are part of this content. If you need to learn how homegroups and folder and file sharing are configured and supported, see *CompTIA A+ Guide to Managing and Maintaining Your PC*, by Jean Andrews.

Generally, if the network supports fewer than 15 computers, a peer-to-peer network is the way to go. The following are advantages of using peer-to-peer networks:

- They are simple to configure. For this reason, they may be used in environments in which time or technical expertise is scarce.

- They are often less expensive to set up and maintain than other types of networks. A network operating system, such as Windows Server 2012 R2, is much more expensive than a desktop operating system, such as Windows 8.1 Professional.

The following are disadvantages of using traditional peer-to-peer networks:

- They are not scalable, which means, as a peer-to-peer network grows larger, adding or changing significant elements of the network may be difficult.

- They are not necessarily secure—meaning that in simple installations, data and other resources shared by network users can be easily discovered and used by unauthorized people.

- They are not practical for connecting more than a few computers because it becomes too time consuming to manage the resources on the network. For example, suppose you set up a file server with a folder named \SharedDocs and create 12 local accounts on the file server, one for each of 12 users who need access to the folder. Then you must set up the workstations with the same local accounts, and the password to each local account on the workstation must match the password for the matching local account on the file server. It can be an organizational nightmare to keep it all straight! If you need to manage that many users and shared resources, it's probably best to implement Windows Server or another NOS.

Client-Server Network Model

In the client-server network model (which is sometimes called the client-server architecture or client-server topology), resources are managed by the NOS via a centralized directory database. The database can be managed by one or more servers, so long as they each have a similar NOS installed (see Figure 1-5).

When Windows Server controls network access to a group of computers, this logical group is called a Windows domain. The centralized directory database that contains user account information and security for the entire group of computers is called Active Directory (AD). Each user on the network has his own domain-level account called a global account, also called a global username or network ID, which is assigned by the network administrator and is kept in Active Directory. A user can sign on to the network from any computer on the network and get access to the resources that Active Directory allows. The process is managed by Active Directory Domain Services (AD DS).

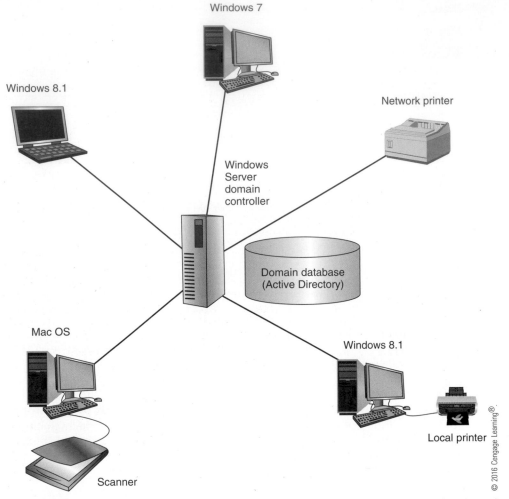

Figure 1-5 A Windows domain uses the client-server model to control access to the network, where security on each computer or device is controlled by a centralized database on a domain controller

Clients on a client-server network can run applications installed on the desktop and store their own data on local storage devices. Clients don't share their resources directly with each other; instead, access is controlled by entries in the centralized domain database. A client computer accesses resources on another computer by way of the servers controlling this database.

In summary, the NOS (for example, Windows Server 2012 R2, Ubuntu Server, or Red Hat Linux) is responsible for:

- Managing data and other resources for a number of clients
- Ensuring that only authorized users access the network
- Controlling which types of files a user can open and read
- Restricting when and from where users can access the network

- Dictating which rules computers will use to communicate

- In some situations, supplying applications and data files to clients

Servers that have a NOS installed require more memory, processing power, and storage capacity than clients because servers are called on to handle heavy processing loads and requests from multiple clients. For example, a server might use a RAID (redundant array of independent disks) configuration of hard drives, so that if one hard drive fails, another hard drive automatically takes its place.

Although client-server networks are typically more complex in their design and maintenance than peer-to-peer networks, they offer many advantages over peer-to-peer networks, including:

- User accounts and passwords to the network are assigned in one place.

- Access to multiple shared resources (such as data files or printers) can be centrally granted to a single user or groups of users.

- Problems on the network can be monitored, diagnosed, and often fixed from one location.

- Client-server networks are also more scalable than peer-to-peer networks. In other words, it's easier to add computers and other devices to a client-server network.

Regardless of the logical topology or the OSs used, the OSs on a network are able to communicate with each other via the protocols they have in common. The two primary protocols are TCP (Transmission Control Protocol) and IP (Internet Protocol) and the suite of all the protocols an OS uses for communication on a network is the TCP/IP suite of protocols.

You can think of applications and their data as the payload traveling on a network and the operating systems as the traffic controllers managing the traffic. The road system itself is the hardware on which the traffic flows. Let's now look at the basics of networking hardware and the physical topologies they use.

Networking Hardware and Physical Topologies

Two computers connected by an ad hoc Wi-Fi connection are technically a network; however, let's start our discussion of networking hardware with the slightly more complex network shown in Figure 1-6. Keep in mind that every host or node on a network needs a network address so that other hosts or nodes can find it.

Notice the two printers in Figure 1-6. A network printer has a network port and connects directly to the switch. A local printer connects directly to a computer on the network.

LANs and Their Hardware

The network in Figure 1-6 is a local area network (LAN) because each node on the network can communicate directly with others on the network. LANs are usually contained

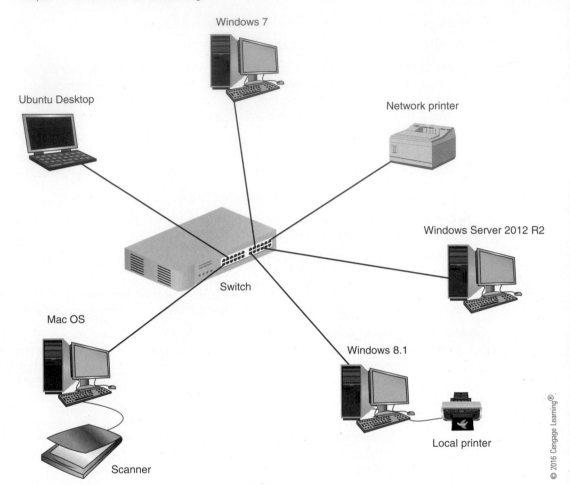

Figure 1-6 This LAN has five computers, a network printer, a local printer, a scanner, and a switch, and is using a star topology

in a small space, such as an office or building. The five computers and a network printer all connect to the switch by way of wired connections. A **switch** (see Figure 1-7) receives incoming data from one of its ports and redirects (switches) it to another port or multiple ports that will send the data to its intended destination(s). The physical topology used by the network is called a **star topology** because all devices connect to one central device, the switch.

Computers, network printers, switches, and other network devices have network ports into which you plug a network cable. A network port can be an **onboard network port** embedded in the computer's motherboard, such as the port on the laptop in Figure 1-8. Another type of port is provided by a **network interface card (NIC)**, also called a **network adapter**, installed in an expansion slot on the motherboard (see Figure 1-9).

A LAN can have several switches. For example, the network in Figure 1-10 has three switches daisy-chained together. The two yellow lines in the figure connecting the three

Courtesy of Juniper Networks, Inc

Figure 1-7 Industrial-grade and consumer-grade switches

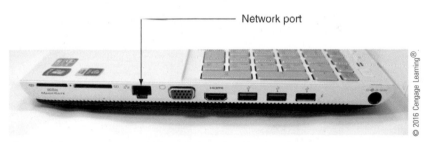

Network port

Figure 1-8 A laptop provides an onboard network port to connect to a wired network

switches represent the backbone of this network. A backbone is a central conduit that connects the segments (pieces) of a network and is sometimes referred to as "a network of networks." The backbone might use higher transmission speeds and different cabling than network cables connected to computers because of the heavier traffic and the longer distances it might span.

Because the three switches are daisy-chained together in a single line, the network is said to use a bus topology. However, each switch is connected to its computers via a star topology. Therefore, the topology of the network in Figure 1-10 is said to be a star-bus topology. A topology that combines topologies in this way is known as a hybrid topology.

Figure 1-9 This Intel Gigabit Ethernet adapter, also called a network interface card or NIC, uses a PCIe x1 slot on a motherboard

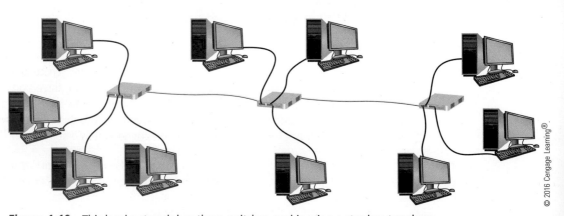

Figure 1-10 This local network has three switches, and is using a star-bus topology

Legacy Networking
Ring Topology

In addition to the bus, star, and hybrid topologies, the CompTIA Network+ exam expects you to know about the ring topology, which is seldom used today. In a **ring topology**, nodes are connected in a ring, with one node connecting only to its two neighboring nodes (see Figure 1-11). A node can put data on the ring only when it holds a token, which is a small group of bits passed around the ring. This is similar to saying "I hold the token, so I get to talk now." The ring topology is rarely used today primarily because of its slow speed.

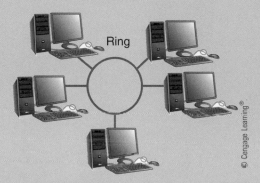

Figure 1-11 Using a ring topology, a computer connects to the two computers adjacent to it in the ring

A LAN needs a way to communicate with other networks, and that's the purpose of a router. A **router** is a device that manages traffic between two or more networks and can help find the best path for traffic to get from one network to another. In small home networks, a consumer-grade router is used to connect the LAN to the Internet (see Figure 1-12a).

A home network might use a combo device, which is both a router and a switch, and perhaps a wireless access point that creates a Wi-Fi hot spot. For example, the device may provide three network ports and a Wi-Fi hot spot that are part of the local network and one network port to connect to the Internet service provider (ISP) and on to the Internet. In this situation (see Figure 1-12b), the three ports are provided by a switch embedded in the device. The home router belongs to the home's local network and the ISP's local network. Don't confuse this combo device with an industrial-grade router in which each port connects to a different LAN.

Industrial-grade routers can have several network ports, one for each of the networks it connects to. In that case, the router belongs to each of these networks. For example, in Figure 1-13, the router connects three LANs and has a network address that belongs to Network A, another network address that belongs to Network B, and a third network address for Network C.

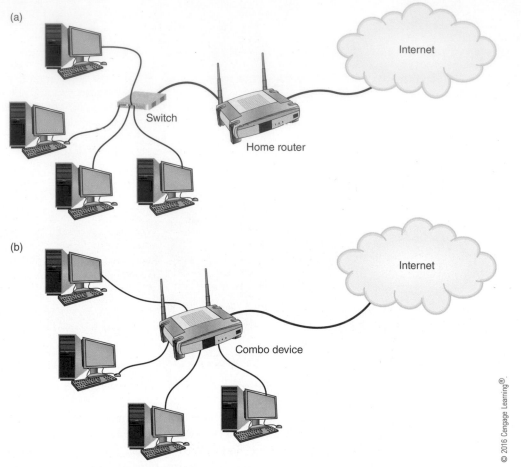

Figure 1-12 (a) A router stands between the LAN and the Internet, connecting the two networks; (b) home networks often use a combo device that works as both a switch and a router

The fundamental difference between a switch and a router is that a switch belongs only to its local network and a router belongs to two or more local networks. Recall that nodes on a local network communicate directly with one another. However, a host on one LAN cannot communicate with a host on another LAN without a router to manage that communication and stand as a gateway between the networks.

Let's make the distinction now between the two terms, *host* and *node*. A host is any computer on a network that hosts a resource such as an application or data, and a node is any computer or device on a network that can be addressed on the local network. A client computer or server is both a node and a host, but a router or switch does not normally host resources and is, therefore, merely a node on the network.

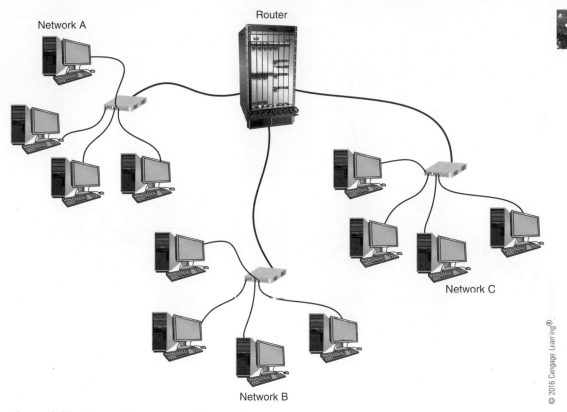

Figure 1-13   Three LANs connected by a router

As you might have already guessed, networked hardware devices such as NICs, switches, and routers can communicate with each other because of the protocols they have in common. In Chapters 3 and 4, you'll learn about the protocols used by NICs, switches, and routers.

MANs and WANs

A group of connected LANs in the same geographical area—for example, a handful of government offices surrounding a state capitol building—is known as a MAN (metropolitan area network) or CAN (campus area network). A group of LANs that spread over a wide geographical area is called a WAN (wide area network). MANs and WANs often use different transmission methods and media than LANs. The Internet is the largest and most varied WAN in the world. The smallest network is a PAN (personal area network), which is a network of personal devices, such as the network you use when you sync your cell phone and your computer.

Figure 1-14 shows a WAN link between two local networks bound by routers. For example, a corporation might have an office in San Francisco and another in Philadelphia. Each office has a LAN, and a WAN link connects the two LANs. The WAN link is most likely provided by a third-party service provider.

You've just learned how applications, operating systems, and hardware create, manage, and use a network. Now let's see, from a bird's-eye view, how they all work together.

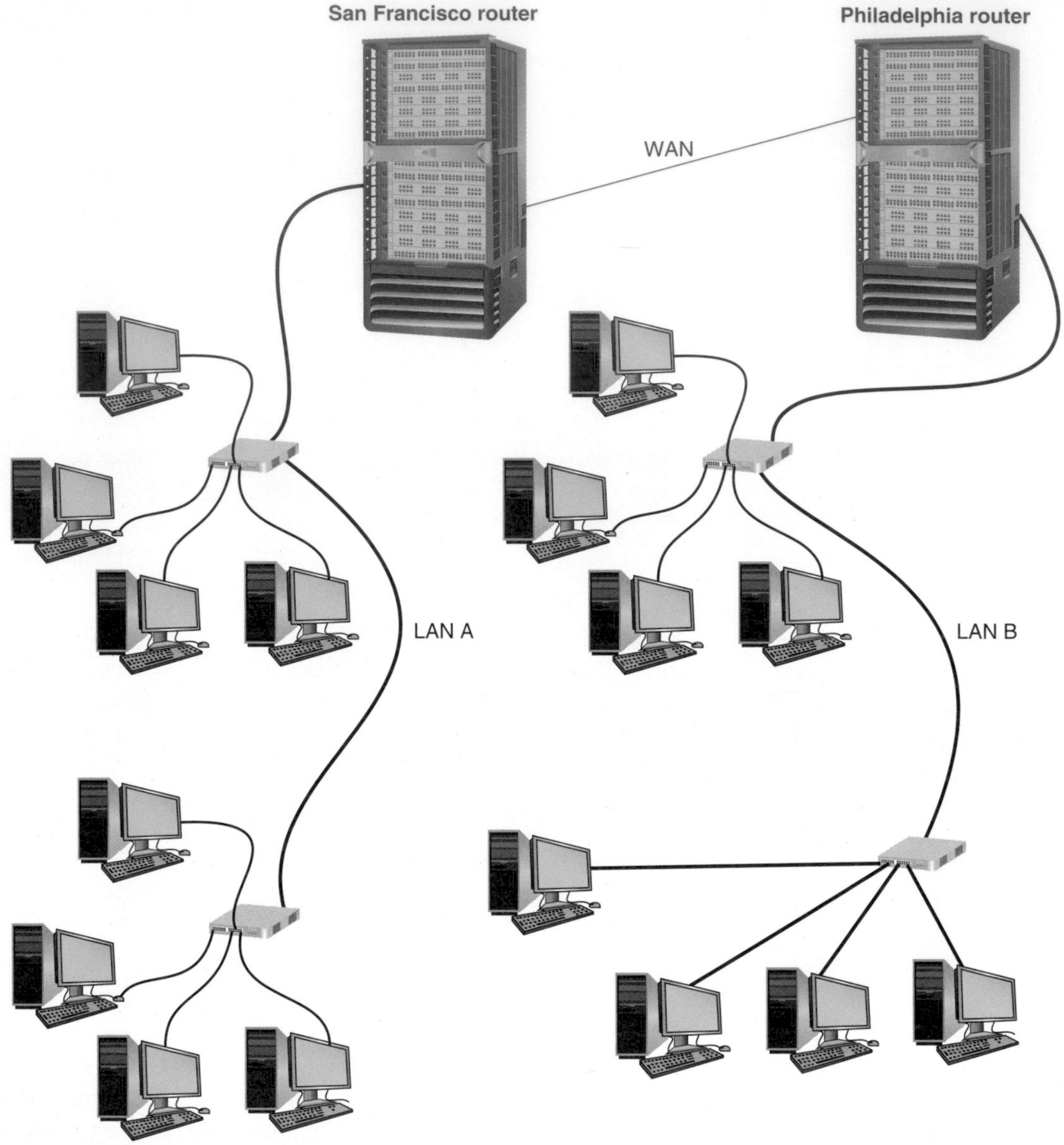
San Francisco router
Philadelphia router
WAN
LAN A
LAN B

Figure 1-14 A WAN connects two LANs in different geographical areas

The Seven-Layer OSI Model

Network+ 2.5 5.1 5.2 5.9

Recall that an application, such as a browser, depends on the operating system to communicate across the network. Operating systems, meanwhile, depend on hardware to communicate across the network (see the left side of Figure 1-15). Throughout the entire process, protocols govern each layer of communication.

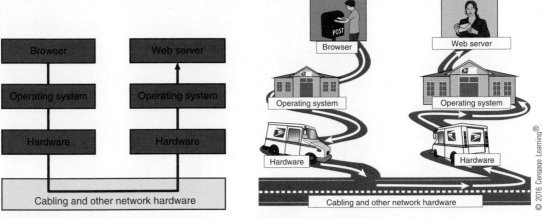

Figure 1-15 A browser and Web server communicate by way of the operating system and hardware, similar to the way a letter is sent through the mail using the U.S. Postal Service and the road system

To get a better sense of how this works, it's helpful to think of a different type of communication: two people communicating by way of the U.S. Postal Service (see the right side of Figure 1-15). The sender depends on the mailbox to hold her letter until a postal worker picks it up and takes it to the post office. The people at the post office, in turn, depend on truck drivers to transport the letter to the correct city. The truck drivers, for their part, depend on the road system. Throughout the entire process, various protocols govern how people behave. For example, the sender follows basic rules for writing business letters, the mail carriers follow U.S. Postal Service regulations for processing the mail, and the truck drivers follow traffic laws. Think of how complex it might be to explain to someone all the different rules or protocols involved if you were not able to separate or categorize these activities into layers.

Early in the evolution of networking, a seven-layer model was developed to categorize the layers of communication. This model, which is called the OSI (Open Systems Interconnection) reference model, is illustrated on the left side of Figure 1-16. It was first developed by the International Organization for Standardization, also called the ISO. (Its shortened name, *ISO*, is derived from a Greek word meaning *equal*.) Network engineers, hardware technicians, programmers, and network administrators still use the layers of the OSI model to communicate about networking technologies. In this book, you'll learn to use the OSI model to help you understand networking protocols and troubleshoot network problems.

The CompTIA Network+ exam expects you to know how to apply the OSI model when troubleshooting network problems.

As you study various protocols used in networking, it will help tremendously to map each protocol onto the OSI model. By doing so, you'll better understand the logistics of which

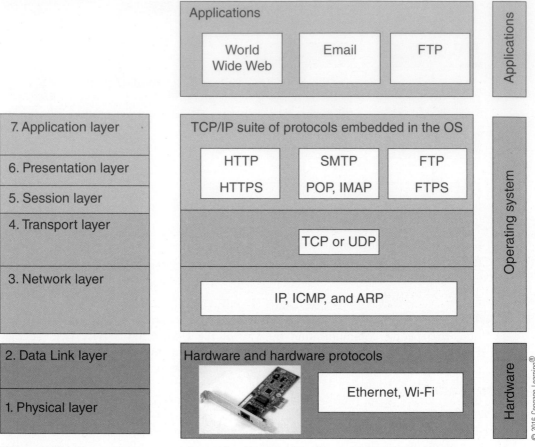

Figure 1-16   How software, protocols, and hardware map to the seven-layer OSI model

software program or device is initiating and/or receiving the protocol or data and how other protocols are relating to it.

Now let's take a brief look at each layer in the OSI model. The layers are numbered in descending order, starting with Layer 7, the Application layer, at the top. Figure 1-16 guides you through the layers.

> You need to memorize the seven layers of the OSI model. Here's a seven-word mnemonic that can help: **A**ll **P**eople **S**eem **T**o **N**eed **D**ata **P**rocessing.

Network+
5.1
5.2

Layer 7: Application Layer

The **Application layer** in the OSI model describes the interface between two applications, each on separate computers. Earlier in this chapter, you learned about several protocols used at this layer, including HTTP, SMTP, POP3, IMAP4, FTP, Telnet, and RDP. Application layer protocols are used by programs that fall into two categories:

- Application programs that provide services to a user, such as a browser and Web server using the HTTP Application layer protocol

- Utility programs that provide services to the system, such as SNMP (Simple Network Management Protocol) programs that monitor and gather information about network traffic and can alert network administrators about adverse conditions that need attention

Data that is passed between applications or utility programs and the operating system is called a **payload** and includes control information. The two end-system computers that initiate sending and receiving data are called hosts.

Layer 6: Presentation Layer

In the OSI model, the Presentation layer is responsible for reformatting, compressing, and/or encrypting data in a way that the application on the receiving end can read. For example, an email message can be encrypted at the Presentation layer by the email client or by the operating system.

Layer 5: Session Layer

The Session layer of the OSI model describes how data between applications is synced and recovered if messages don't arrive intact at the receiving application. For example, the Skype application works with the operating system to establish and maintain a session between two end points for as long as a voice conversation or video conference is in progress.

The Application, Presentation, and Session layers are so intertwined that, in practice, it's often difficult to distinguish between them. Also, tasks for each layer may be performed by the operating system or the application. Most tasks are performed by the OS when an application makes an API call to the OS. In general, an API (application programming interface) call is the method an application uses when it makes a request of the OS.

Layer 4: Transport Layer

The Transport layer is responsible for transporting Application layer payloads from one application to another. The two main Transport layer protocols are TCP, which guarantees delivery, and UDP, which does not:

- *TCP (Transmission Control Protocol)*—Makes a connection with the end host, checks whether the data is received, and resends it if it is not. TCP is, therefore, called a **connection-oriented protocol**. TCP is used by applications such as Web browsers and email. Guaranteed delivery takes longer and is used when it is important to know that the data reached its destination.

- *UDP (User Datagram Protocol)*—Does not guarantee delivery by first connecting and checking whether data is received; thus, UDP is called a **connectionless protocol** or **best-effort protocol**. UDP is used for broadcasting, such as streaming video or audio over the Web, where guaranteed delivery is not as important as fast transmission. UDP is also used to monitor network traffic.

The protocols add their own control information in an area at the beginning of the payload called the **header** to create a message ready to be transmitted to the Network layer. The process of adding a header to the data inherited from the layer above is called **encapsulation**. The Transport layer header addresses the receiving application by a number called a **port number**. If the message is too large to transport on the network, TCP divides it into smaller messages called **segments**. In UDP, the message is called a **datagram**.

In our Post Office analogy, you can think of a message as a letter. The sender puts the letter in an envelope and adds the name of the sender and receiver, similar to how the Transport layer encapsulates the payload into a segment or datagram that identifies both the sending and destination applications.

Layer 3: Network Layer

The **Network layer**, sometimes called the Internet layer, is responsible for moving messages from one node to another until they reach the destination host. The principal protocol used by the Network layer is **IP (Internet Protocol)**. IP adds its own Network layer header to the segment or datagram, and the entire Network layer message is now called a **packet**. The Network layer header identifies the sending and receiving hosts by their IP addresses. An **IP address** is an address assigned to each node on a network, which the Network layer uses to uniquely identify them on the network. In our Post Office analogy, the Network layer would be the trucking system used by the Post Office and the IP addresses would be the full return and destination addresses written on the envelope.

IP relies on several routing protocols to find the best route for a packet when traversing several networks on its way to its destination. These routing protocols include **ICMP (Internet Control Message Protocol)** and **ARP (Address Resolution Protocol)**.

Along the way, if a Network layer protocol is aware that a packet is larger than the maximum size for its network, it will divide the packet into smaller packets in a process called **fragmentation**.

Layer 2: Data Link Layer

Layers 2 and 1 are responsible for interfacing with the physical hardware only on the local network. The protocols at these layers are programmed into the firmware of a computer's NIC and other networking hardware. Layer 2, the **Data Link layer**, is more commonly called the **Link layer**. The type of networking hardware or technology used on a network determines the Link layer protocol used. Examples of Link layer protocols are Ethernet and Wi-Fi. (Ethernet works on wired networks and Wi-Fi is wireless.) As you'll learn in later chapters, several types of switches exist. The least intelligent (nonprogrammable) switches, which are called **Link layer switches** or **Layer 2 switches**, operate at this layer.

The term *firmware* refers to programs embedded into hardware devices and that do not change unless a firmware upgrade is performed.

The Link layer puts its own control information in a Link layer header and also attaches control information to the end of the packet in a trailer. The entire Link layer message is then called a frame. The frame header contains the hardware addresses of the source and destination NICs. This address is called a MAC (Media Access Control) address, physical address, hardware address, or Data Link layer address and is embedded on every network adapter on the globe (refer back to Figure 1-9). The physical addresses are short-range addresses that can only find nodes on the local network.

In our Post Office analogy, a truck might travel from one post office to the next en route to its final destination. The address of a post office along the route would be similar to the physical address of a NIC that a frame reaches as it traverses only one LAN on its way to its destination.

Layer 1: Physical Layer

Layer 1, the Physical layer, is the simplest layer of all and is responsible only for sending bits via a wired or wireless transmission. These bits can be transmitted as wavelengths in the air (for example, Wi-Fi), voltage on a copper wire (for example, Ethernet with twisted-pair cabling), or light (for example, Ethernet with fiber-optic cabling).

It's interesting to consider that the top layers of the OSI model work the same for both wired and wireless transmissions. In fact, the only layers that must deal with the details of wired versus wireless transmissions are the Link layer and Physical layer on the firmware of the NIC. Finally, in our Post Office analogy, the Link layer and Physical layer compare with the various road systems a truck might use, each with its own speed limits and traffic rules.

Protocol Data Unit or PDU

There are several different names for a group of bits as it moves from one layer to the next and from one LAN to the next. Although technicians loosely call this group of bits a message or a transmission, the technical name is a protocol data unit (PDU). Table 1-1 can help you keep all these names straight.

Memorize the details of Table 1-1. You'll need them for the CompTIA Network+ exam.

Table 1-1   Names for a PDU or message as it moves from one layer to another

OSI model	Name	Extremely technical name
Layer 7, Application layer Layer 6, Presentation layer Layer 5, Session layer	Payload or data	L7PDU
Layer 4, Transport layer	Segment (TCP) or datagram (UDP)	L4PDU
Layer 3, Network layer	Packet	L3PDU
Layer 2, Data Link layer	Frame	L2PDU
Layer 1, Physical layer	Bit	L1PDU

Summary of How the Layers Work Together

Now let's tie the layers together, as shown in Figure 1-17. This transmission involves a browser and Web server on their respective hosts, a switch, and a router. As you follow the red line from browser to Web server, notice the sending host encapsulates the payload in headers and a trailer before sending it, much like an assistant would place the boss's business letter in an envelope before putting it in the mail.

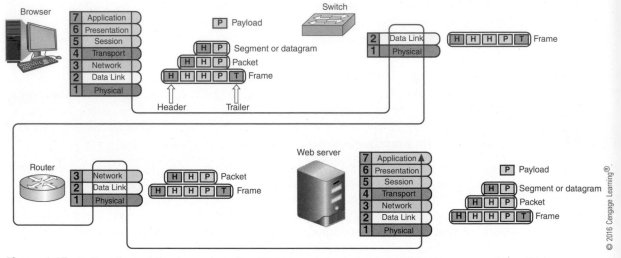

Figure 1-17 Follow the red line to see how the OSI layers work when a browser makes a request to a Web server

In the reverse order, the receiving host removes the headers and trailer before the message reaches the Web server application, just as the receiver's assistant would remove the letter from the envelope before handing it to the receiver. Removing a header and trailer from a layer below is called **decapsulation**.

In conceptual drawings and network maps, symbols are used for switches and routers. In the figure, notice the square symbol representing a switch, and the round symbol, which stands for a router.

The steps listed in Table 1-2 summarize the process illustrated in Figure 1-17.

A four-layer model similar to the OSI model is the TCP/IP model. Using the TCP/IP model, the Application, Presentation, and Session layers are wrapped together and called the Application layer. The Physical layer is so simple, it's ignored, which makes for four layers: Application layer, Transport layer, Internet layer (the Network layer in the OSI model), and Network Interface layer (the Data Link layer in the OSI model).

So now you have the big picture of networking and how it works. Let's turn our attention to staying safe when working around networks and computers.

Table 1-2   Steps through the OSI layers during a browser-to-Web server transmission

Sending host	1. The browser, involving the Application, Presentation, and Session layers, creates an HTTP message or payload on its source computer and passes it down to the Transport layer.
	2. The Transport layer (TCP, which is part of the OS) encapsulates the payload by adding its own header and passes the segment down to the Network layer.
	3. IP at the Network layer in the OS receives the segment (depicted as two yellow boxes in the figure), adds its header, and passes the packet down to the Data Link layer.
	4. The Data Link layer on the NIC firmware receives the packet (depicted as three yellow boxes in the figure), adds its header and trailer, and passes the frame to the Physical layer.
	5. The Physical layer on the NIC hardware puts bits on the network.
Switch	6. The network transmission is received by a Data Link layer switch, which passes the frame up to the Data Link layer (firmware on the switch), which looks at the destination MAC address to decide where to send the frame.
	7. The pass-through frame is sent to the correct port on the switch and on to the router.
Router	8. The router has two NICs, one for each of the two networks to which it belongs. The Physical layer of the first NIC receives the frame and passes it up to the Data Link layer (NIC firmware), which removes the frame header and trailer and passes the packet up to IP at the Network layer (firmware program or other software) on the router.
	9. This Network layer IP program looks at the destination IP address and determines the next node en route for the packet and passes the packet back down to the Data Link layer on the second NIC. The Data Link layer adds a new frame header and trailer appropriate for this second NIC's LAN, including the MAC address of the next destination node. It passes the frame to its Physical layer (NIC hardware), which sends the bits on their way.
Destination host	10. When the frame reaches the destination host NIC, the Data Link layer NIC firmware receives it, removes the frame header and trailer, and passes the packet up to IP at the Network layer, which removes its header and passes the segment up to TCP at the Transport layer.
	11. TCP removes its header and passes the payload up to HTTP at the Application layer. HTTP presents the message to the Web server.

© 2016 Cengage Learning®

Staying Safe When Working with Networks and Computers

 As a network and computer technician, you need to know how to protect yourself and sensitive electronic components as you work. Let's look at some best practices for safety.

Emergency Procedures

In case of an emergency, such as a fire alert, you'll need to know the best escape route or emergency exit for you and others around you. Look in the lobby and hallways at your place of work for a posted building layout and fire escape plan so that you are prepared in an emergency. You also need to be aware of emergency exit doors, which are usually labeled with battery-powered, lighted Exit signs and clearly marked on the posted building layout.

Fire Suppression Systems A company is likely to have a fire suppression system in its data center that includes the following:

- *emergency alert system* —These systems vary, but they typically generate loud noise and flashing lights. Some send text and voice message alerts to key personnel, and post alerts by email, network messages, and other means.

- *portable fire extinguishers*—Note that electrical fires require a Class C fire extinguisher, as shown in Figure 1-18.

- *emergency power-off switch*—Don't use a power-off switch unless you really need to; improper shutdowns are hard on computers and their data.

- *suppression agent*—This can consist of a foaming chemical, gas, or water that sprays everywhere to put out the fire.

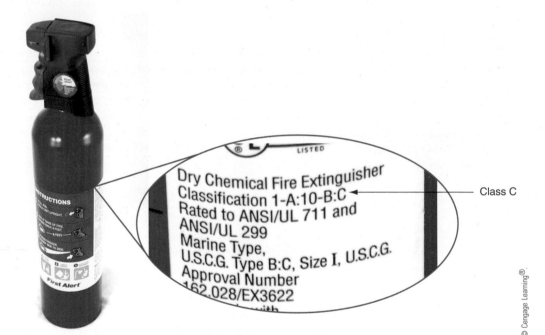

Class C

Figure 1-18 A Class C fire extinguisher is rated to put out electrical fires

NOTE In the United States, the national Emergency Alert System can only be activated by the president at the national level. It requires TV, radio, cable TV, satellite, and cellular service providers to broadcast the alert. The system can also be used at the state and local level to alert about missing children (AMBER alert) and dangerous weather conditions.

Fail Open or Fail Close What happens to security when a system responsible for security fails? Does the system allow access during the failure (**fail open**) or deny access during the failure (**fail close**)? For example, during a fire alert, using a fail-open policy, all exit doors stay unlocked so that people can safely leave the building and firefighters can enter the building, even though this might present a security risk for thieves entering the building. On the other hand, if firewall software protecting access to a database of customer credit card numbers fails, it might be configured to fail close and to deny access to the database until the software is back up.

A fail-open policy is often based on common sense so as to ensure that, in an emergency, no one is harmed when a system is not working. A fail-close policy is usually based on the need for security to protect private data or other resources.

The term *open* or *close* takes on the opposite meaning when talking about electrical circuits. When a circuit breaker fails, there is a break in the circuit and the circuit is said to be open. The breaker opens the circuit to protect it from out-of-control electricity. Although this sounds like double-talk, an open circuit is, therefore, a fail-close system.

Material Safety Data Sheet (MSDS) You might need to use cleaning solutions to clean optical discs, tapes and tape drivers, and other devices. Most of these cleaning solutions contain flammable and poisonous materials. Take care when using them so that they don't get on your skin or in your eyes. To find out what to do if you are accidentally exposed to a dangerous solution, look on the instructions printed on the can or check out the material safety data sheet (see Figure 1-19). A material safety data sheet (MSDS) explains how to properly handle substances such as chemical solvents and how to dispose of them.

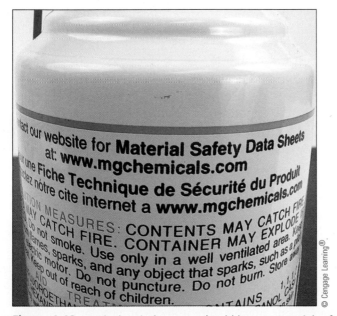

Figure 1-19 Each chemical you use should have a material safety data sheet available

An MSDS includes information such as physical data, toxicity, health effects, first aid, storage, shipping, disposal, and spill procedures. It typically comes packaged with the chemical, but if you can't locate it, you can order one from the manufacturer, or you can find one on the Web (see *ilpi.com/msds*).

HVAC Systems

The **heating, ventilation, and air conditioning (HVAC) system** controls the environment in a data center, including the temperature, humidity, airflow, and air filtering. The HVAC system must provide acceptable temperature and humidity ranges for devices that might overheat or fail due to high humidity. HVAC systems and network cabling often occupy the space above the ceiling or below the floor in a data center; this space is called the **plenum**. For older buildings that don't have structured plenums, the data center might instead have a raised floor.

It's important that the HVAC system and fire suppression system are compatible. For example, the fluid used in the HVAC system should not be a type that can trigger a false alert by the fire suppression system if the fluid leaks.

Protecting Against Static Electricity

Computer components are grounded inside a computer case, and computer power cables all use a three-prong plug for this purpose. The third prong is grounded. **Grounding** means that a device is connected directly to the earth, so that, in the event of a short, the electricity flows into the earth, rather than out of control through the device and back to the power station, which can cause an electrical fire.

In addition, sensitive electronic components (for example, a NIC, motherboard, and memory modules) can be damaged by **electrostatic discharge (ESD)**, commonly known as **static electricity**. Static electricity is an electrical charge at rest. When your body and a component have different static charges and you touch the component, you can discharge up to 1500 volts of static electricity without seeing a spark or feeling the discharge. However, it only takes 10 volts to damage the component.

Static electricity can cause two types of damage in an electronic component: catastrophic failure and upset failure. A **catastrophic failure** destroys the component beyond use. An **upset failure** can shorten the life of a component and/or cause intermittent errors. Before touching a component, first ground yourself using one of these methods:

- Wear an ESD strap around your wrist that clips onto the chassis or computer case, which eliminates any ESD between you and the chassis and its components (see Figure 1-20).

- If you don't have an ESD strap handy, be sure to at least touch the case before you touch any component inside the case. This is not as effective as wearing an ESD strap, but can reduce the risk of ESD.

- To protect a sensitive component, always store it inside an antistatic bag when it's not in use.

In addition to protecting against ESD, always shut down and unplug a computer before working inside it.

Figure 1-20 An ESD strap, which protects computer components from ESD, can clip to the side of the computer chassis and eliminate ESD between you and the chassis

 Installation Safety

When installing equipment, you need to pay special attention to protecting yourself and the equipment.

Lifting Heavy Objects Back injury, caused by lifting heavy objects, is one of the most common injuries that happen at work. Whenever possible, put heavy objects, such as a large laser printer, on a cart to move them. If you do need to lift a heavy object, follow these guidelines to keep from injuring your back:

1. Decide which side of the object to face so that the load is the most balanced.

2. Stand close to the object with your feet apart.

3. Keeping your back straight, bend your knees and grip the load.

4. Lift with your legs, arms, and shoulders, and not with your back or stomach.

5. Keep the load close to your body and avoid twisting your body while you're holding it.

6. To put the object down, keep your back as straight as you can and lower the object by bending your knees.

Don't try to lift an object that is too heavy for you. Because there are no exact guidelines for when heavy is too heavy, use your best judgment as to when to ask for help.

Rack Installations Switches, routers, servers, and patch panels (a panel, such as the one shown in Figure 1-21, where cables converge in one location) can be installed in a data center in racks, which can be open all around or enclosed in cabinets (see Figure 1-22). When selecting racks and installing devices in racks, it's important to follow the device manufacturer's guidelines for the requirements for the rack and the directions for installation.

Figure 1-21 This patch panel can be installed in a rack and is used where cables converge.
Courtesy of Siemon

Figure 1-22 Open racks on the left and an enclosed cabinet on the right

Here are some general directions for safely installing rack-mountable devices, such as a rack-mountable server, router, or switch:

- Some racks have wheels. Before you begin the installation, engage the brakes on the rack wheels so the rack doesn't roll.

- To protect against ESD, be sure to wear an ESD strap during the installation.

- Place the device in the rack for good airflow to help keep it cool. It's best for the front of a device to face the colder aisle in the data center. Also, keep in mind that you must be able to access the device from the front and the rear.

- The device must be well grounded, following the manufacturer's directions.

- Pay attention to your tools as you work so they don't accidentally fall into a rack of expensive equipment. For example, remove that little screwdriver from your shirt pocket.

- Some rack-mountable devices that generate a lot of heat have fan trays that install in the rack slot under the device to provide extra airflow. Be sure to install the fan tray oriented in the rack so that air flows in the same direction as the fans inside the device, which are part of the device's power supply.

Figure 1-23 shows one step in the installation: attaching brackets and sliders to the side of the device before sliding it into the rack. After an industrial-grade switch or router has been installed in a rack, the next steps are to use network cables to connect it to the network, power it up, and configure it. Most often, you can configure the device by using a computer on the network to access a utility program in the device's firmware. In Chapter 10, you'll learn how to configure an industrial-grade switch. Configuring and programming routers is beyond the scope of this book.

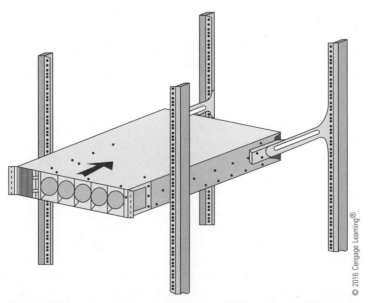

Figure 1-23   This switch uses brackets and sliders to install in a rack

Electrical and Tool Safety in Data Centers

Electrical and tool safety in workplaces is generally regulated by **OSHA (Occupational Safety and Health Administration)**, which is the main federal agency charged with safety and health in the workplace. See *osha.gov*.

OSHA regulations for electrical safety require that electrical devices be turned off and the electrical supply locked out before employees work near these devices. For example, OSHA requires that all devices in a data center cabinet, rack, or panel be turned off and the power locked out before employees work inside of or with these units.

Following are some general OSHA guidelines when using power (electric) tools or other hand tools in the workplace. Your employer can give you more details specific to your work environment:

- Wear **personal protective equipment (PPE)** to protect yourself as you work. For example, wear eye protection where dust or fumes are generated by power tools.

- Keep all tools in good condition and properly store tools not in use. Examine a tool for damage before you use it.

- Use the right tool for the job and operate the tool according to the manufacturer's instructions and guidelines. Don't work with a tool unless you are trained and authorized to use it.

- Watch out for **trip hazards**, so you and others don't stumble on a tool or cord. For example, keep power tool electrical extension cords out from underfoot, and don't leave hand tools lying around unattended.

Troubleshooting Network Problems

 As a network technician, you'll be called on to troubleshoot problems with networking hardware, operating systems, applications that use the network, and other network resources. The flowchart in Figure 1-24 illustrates the method used by most expert networking troubleshooters to solve networking problems.

Here are the steps:

Step 1: Identify the problem and its symptoms—As you gather information about the problem, begin by identifying the symptoms, questioning the user, finding out what has recently changed, and determining the scope of the problem. If possible, duplicate the problem. For multiple problems, approach each problem individually. Solve it before moving on to the next.

Step 2: Establish a theory of probable cause—As you observe the extent of the problem, make your best guess as to the source of the problem. Troubleshooters generally follow the bottom-to-top OSI model by first suspecting and eliminating hardware (for example, a loose cable or failed NIC), before moving on to software as the cause of a problem. As you question the obvious and check simple things first, such as a loose network cable, you might solve the problem right on the spot.

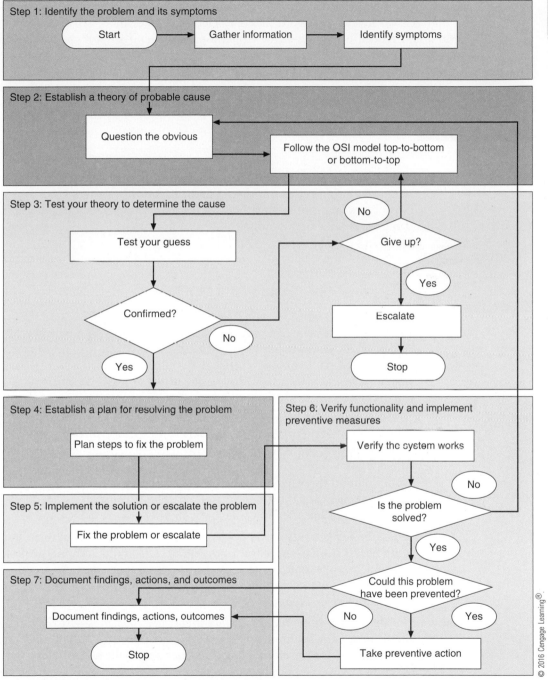

Figure 1-24   General approach to solving network problems

Some situations are obviously software related, such as when a user cannot log on to the network and gets an invalid password message. Here, it makes more sense to follow the top-to-bottom OSI model, beginning at the Application layer, and suspect the user has forgotten his or her password.

As you work, use a divide-and-conquer approach by eliminating parts of the whole until you zero in on the source of the problem.

Step 3: *Test your theory to determine the cause*—For more complicated or expensive solutions, test your theory to assure yourself that it will indeed solve the problem before you implement the solution. If your test proves your theory is wrong, move on to another guess or escalate the problem to the next tier of support in your organization.

As with any computer-related troubleshooting, be sure you choose the least invasive and least expensive solution first before moving on to more drastic or expensive changes to a computer or the network.

Step 4: *Establish a plan for resolving the problem*—Changes to a network have the potential for disrupting a lot of people's work. Before you implement a fix, consider the scope of your change, especially how it will affect users, their applications, and their data. Unless the problem poses an emergency, make your changes when the least number of users are on the network.

Step 5: *Implement the solution or escalate the problem*—Before you make the change, be sure to alert all affected users in advance, create backups of software and data as needed, and save or write down current settings before you change them. Keep good notes as you work, so you can backtrack as necessary. Test your solution thoroughly, and clean up after yourself when you're done. For major changes, it's often best to roll out changes in stages so as to make sure all is working for a few users before you affect many users.

For complex problems, you might need to escalate the problem to someone with access to more technical resources or with more authority to test or implement a solution. An organization might require that major changes to a network be documented in a change management system. You learn about these systems in Chapter 12.

Step 6: *Verify functionality and implement preventive measures*—At the time you implement your solution, you'll test the system for full system functionality. It's also a good idea to return a few days later and make sure all is working as you expected. Also consider what you can do to make sure the problem doesn't reappear. For example, is more preventive maintenance required? Do you need to implement network monitoring software?

Step 7: *Document findings, actions, and outcomes*—Most organizations use a call tracking system (also called help desk software) to document problems and their resolutions. Your organization is likely to expect you to document the name, department, and contact information of the person who originated the call for help; when the call first came in; information about the problem; the symptoms of the problem; the resolution of the problem; the name of the technician who handled the problem; and perhaps the amount of time spent resolving the problem. Your company may also require you to document unique or insightful solutions to problems in your company's knowledge base for you and others to draw from in the future. A knowledge base is a collection of accumulated insights and solutions to the problems encountered on a particular network.

Applying Concepts
Troubleshoot a Failed Network Connection

Suppose your computer cannot connect to the Internet. Here's a simple process for troubleshooting this problem that demonstrates all seven steps in the troubleshooting model:

Step 1: Identify the problem and its symptoms—You open your browser on your desktop computer and discover you can't reach any Web site and you see an error message on the browser screen. You open Windows Explorer or File Explorer and find that you can't navigate to resources normally available on your local network.

Step 2: Establish a theory of probable cause—Because a network technician was working near your desk when you left the evening before, you suspect your network cable might have been left unplugged. In the OSI model, you've started at the bottom by suspecting the problem is hardware related.

Step 3: Test your theory to determine the cause—You check the cable and discover it is lying on the floor, not connected to your desktop.

Step 4: Establish a plan for resolving the problem—You decide to plug in the network cable. This is a very simple resolution that does not affect other users. In other situations, your plan might involve informing coworkers of what is about to happen.

Step 5: Implement the solution or escalate the problem—You plug in the cable.

Step 6: Verify functionality and implement preventive measures—You open your browser and find you can surf the Web. You verify local network resources are available from Windows Explorer or File Explorer.

Step 7: Document findings, actions, and outcomes—This simple problem and solution doesn't require documentation. However, network technicians are generally expected to document troubleshooting tasks and solutions.

In almost every chapter in this book, you'll build your network troubleshooting skills. Many times, the resolution of a problem boils down to the question of where your company's network begins and ends. For most situations, the demarcation point (or demarc) is the device that marks where a telecommunications service provider's network ends and the organization's network begins. For example, an Internet service provider might be responsible for fiber-optic cable to your building to connect to your LAN. The device where the WAN ends and the LAN begins is the demarc. The service provider is responsible for its network beyond the demarc.

Chapter Summary

How Networks Are Used

- Networks provide a wide range of network services, including client-server applications, such as Web services, email services, FTP services, Telnet services, Remote Desktop, remote applications, file and print services, and communication services, such as conversational voice and streaming audio and video.

- Web servers and browsers primarily use HTTP and HTTPS for communication. Email services primarily use SMTP, POP3, and IMAP4 for communication. FTP services use the FTP protocol, and Telnet uses the Telnet protocol. Remote Desktop and Windows Remote Applications use the RDP protocol.

- File and print services enable multiple users to share data, storage areas, and printers.

- Streaming voice and video can use a point-to-point communication model or a multicast distribution model. The RTP protocol is used with multicast distribution. Video and voice is delay-sensitive and loss-tolerant.

Controlling Network Access

- The peer-to-peer model for controlling access to a network allows every computer to share resources directly with every other computer. By default, no computer on a peer-to-peer network has more authority than another. However, each computer can be configured to share only some of its resources, while keeping other resources inaccessible.

- Traditional peer-to-peer networks are usually simple and inexpensive to set up. However, they are not necessarily scalable or secure.

- The client-server model for access control relies on a centrally administered server (or servers) using a network operating system (NOS) that manages shared resources for multiple clients. In a Windows NOS, the group of networked computers is called a domain and the directory database that contains user account information is called Active Directory.

- Client-server networks are more complex and expensive to install than peer-to-peer networks. However, they are more easily managed, more scalable, and typically more secure. They are by far the most popular type of network access control in use today.

- Servers require more processing power, hard disk space, and memory than client computers.

Networking Hardware and Physical Topologies

- A LAN (local area network) is a network of computers and other devices that can directly address all other nodes. A LAN is typically confined to a relatively small space, such as one building or one floor in a large building.

- In a star topology, all computers and network devices connect to one central device, which is likely to be a switch.

- A computer or other device connects to a wired network via a network port and a network cable. The port is provided by a network interface card (NIC) or is an onboard port embedded in the device's motherboard.

- A backbone is a central conduit that connects parts of a network and might use the bus topology, in which devices are daisy-chained together in a single line.

- A star-bus topology is a type of hybrid typology that contains elements of both the star and bus topologies.

- A router manages traffic between two or more LANs and belongs to each network to which it directly connects.

- A MAN is made up of several LANs that cover multiple buildings in the same geographical area.

- LANs can be interconnected to form WANs (wide area networks), which traverse longer distances in two or more geographical areas and may use different transmission methods and media than LANs. The Internet is the largest example of a WAN.

The Seven-Layer OSI Model

- The seven layers of the OSI model are the Application (Layer 7), Presentation (Layer 6), Session (Layer 5), Transport (Layer 4), Network (Layer 3), Data Link (Layer 2), and Physical (Layer 1).

- At Layers 7, 6, and 5, a transmission of data and its control information is known as the payload.

- A message at the Transport layer is called a segment in TCP and a datagram in UDP.

- IP is the primary protocol used at the Network layer, although several routing protocols are also used. An IP transmission is called a packet.

- A message at the Data Link layer is called a frame. The protocol used depends on the technology of the networking hardware, for example, Ethernet or Wi-Fi.

- Some switches operate at the Data Link layer and routers operate at the Network layer.

Staying Safe When Working with Networks and Computers

- Emergency procedures can include designated emergency exits, building layouts, and fire escape plans to help aid people in an emergency alert.

- A fire suppression system can include an emergency alert system, portable fire extinguishers, an emergency power-off switch, and suppression agents.

- To ensure a system's security, it's important to have a fail-open or fail-close policy that determines how security is handled when the system fails.

- A material safety data sheet (MSDS) explains how to properly handle substances that can be destructive to humans.

- A heating, ventilation, and air conditioning (HVAC) system is responsible for controlling humidity and temperature in a data center, and is necessary to protect equipment.

- When working with sensitive components, you can protect against ESD by using an electrostatic discharge (ESD) strap.

- For rack installations, protect against ESD, ground the device, place it in the rack for good airflow, and pay attention to tool safety as you work.

Troubleshooting Network Problems

- The seven troubleshooting steps used in networking are: (1) Identify the problem and its symptoms, (2) establish a theory of probable cause, (3) test your theory, (4) establish a plan to fix the problem, (5) implement the solution or escalate the problem, (6) verify functionality and implement preventive measures, and (7) document findings, actions, and outcomes.

- Troubleshooting can follow the top-to-bottom OSI model or the bottom-to-top OSI model, depending on the nature of the problem.

- Troubleshooting problems and their solutions are documented in a call tracking system. An organization might require that major changes to a network be documented in a change management system.

Key Terms

For definitions of key terms, see the Glossary near the end of the book.

Active Directory (AD)

Active Directory Domain Services (AD DS)

API (application programming interface) call

Application layer

ARP (Address Resolution Protocol)

backbone

bandwidth

best-effort protocol

bus topology

call tracking system

CAN (campus area network)

catastrophic failure

client-server applications

client-server network model

connectionless protocol

connection-oriented protocol

convergence

Data Link layer

Data Link layer address

datagram

decapsulation

delay-sensitive

demarc

demarcation point

domain

electrostatic discharge (ESD)

emergency alert system

encapsulation

fail close

fail open

file server

file services

fire suppression system

fragmentation

frame

FTP (File Transfer Protocol)

global account

grounding

hardware address

header

heating, ventilation, and air conditioning (HVAC) system

host

HTTP (Hypertext Transfer Protocol)

HTTPS (HTTP Secure)

hybrid topology

ICMP (Internet Control Message Protocol)

IMAP4 (Internet Message Access Protocol, version 4)

IP (Internet Protocol)

IP address

knowledge base

Layer 2 switch

Link layer

Link layer switch

local account

local area network (LAN)

logical topology

loss-tolerant

MAC (Media Access Control) address

MAN (metropolitan area network)

material safety data sheet (MSDS)

multicast distribution

network

network adapter

network interface card (NIC)

Network layer

network operating system (NOS)

network services

node

onboard network port

OSHA (Occupational Safety and Health Administration)

OSI (Open Systems Interconnection) reference model

Packet

PAN (personal area network)

patch panel

payload

peer-to-peer (P2P) network model

personal protective equipment (PPE)

physical address

Physical layer

physical topology

plenum

point-to-multipoint model

point-to-point model

POP3 (Post Office Protocol, version 3)

port number

Presentation layer

print services

protocol

protocol data unit (PDU)

quality of service (QoS)

rack

RDP (Remote Desktop Protocol)

remote application

Remote Desktop

Remote Desktop Services

ring topology

router

RTP (Real-time Transport Protocol)

scalable

Secure Shell (SSH)

segment

Session layer

SFTP (Secure File Transfer Protocol)

SMTP (Simple Mail Transfer Protocol)

SSL (Secure Sockets Layer)

star topology

star-bus topology

static electricity

switch

TCP (Transmission Control Protocol)

TCP/IP

Telnet

Terminal Services

TLS (Transport Layer Security)

topology

trailer

Transport layer

trip hazard

UDP (User Datagram Protocol)

unified communications (UC)

upset failure

video teleconference (VTC)

VoIP (Voice over IP)

WAN (wide area network)

Review Questions

1. In the client-server model, what is the primary protocol used for communication between a browser and Web server?

   a. FTP

   b. TCP

   c. HTTP

   d. SSL

2. Which two encryption protocols might be used to provide secure transmissions for browser and Web server communications?

   a. HTTP and HTTPS

   b. SSL and TLS

   c. SSL and HTTP

   d. TCP and UDP

3. Apache is a popular example of what type of networking software?

   a. Web server

   b. Browser

    c. Email server

    d. Email client

4. Which email protocol allows an email client to download email messages to the local computer?

    a. IMAP4

    b. SMTP

    c. TCP

    d. POP3

5. Which email protocol allows an email client to read mail stored on the mail server?

    a. IMAP4

    b. SMTP

    c. TCP

    d. POP3

6. Which client-server application allows an administrator to control a remote computer, but does not encrypt or secure the communication between client and server?

    a. Telnet

    b. Remote Desktop

    c. FTP

    d. SSH

7. Which application embedded in Windows operating systems allows remote control of a computer and uses the RDP secure protocol for transmissions?

    a. Telnet

    b. Remote Desktop

    c. FTP

    d. SSH

8. What service provided by Windows Server 2012 R2 allows a computer to serve up applications to other computers on the network?

    a. Remote Desktop Services

    b. Windows 8.1

    c. File Transfer Protocol

    d. Active Directory

9. List three types of services a network might support that are considered part of unified communications or convergence.

    a. File transfers, print services, and conversational voice

    b. User authentication, streaming live audio and video, and print services

c. Web services, email services, and file services

   d. Conversational voice, streaming live audio and voice, and streaming stored audio and voice

10. Which Session layer protocol is a streaming live video teleconference likely to use on the network?

   a. UDP

   b. SMTP

   c. RTP

   d. TCP

11. A network consists of 10 computers, all running Windows 7 Professional. One computer acts as a file server and serves up data to other computers on the network. Which networking model does the network use?

12. In Question 11, suppose one computer is upgraded from Windows 7 Professional to Windows Server 2012 R2. Which networking model can the network now support that it could not support without the upgrade?

13. What is the name of the domain controller database that Windows Server 2012 R2 uses to store data about user access and resources on the network?

14. A network consists of seven computers and a network printer all connected directly to one switch. Which network topology does this network use?

15. In Question 14, suppose a new switch is connected to the first switch by way of a network cable and three computers are connected to the new switch. Which network topology is now used?

16. What is the fundamental distinction between a Layer 2 switch and a router?

17. What is the fundamental distinction between a node and a host?

18. What is the fundamental distinction between a MAN and a WAN?

19. What is a message called that is delivered by TCP? What is a message called that is delivered by UDP? At which layer do the two protocols work?

20. Which type of address is used at the Transport layer to identify the receiving application?

21. Is TCP or UDP normally used when streaming live video? Why?

22. At the Network layer, what is a message called?

23. What is the primary protocol used at the Network layer?

24. At the Network layer, what type of address is used to identify the receiving host?

25. What is a PDU called at the Link layer?

26. At the Link layer, which type of network address is used to identify the receiving node?

27. Why is it important to wear an ESD strap when installing a server in a rack?

28. A computer is unable to access the network. When you check the LED lights near the computer's network port, you discover the lights are not lit. Which layer of the OSI model are you using to troubleshoot this problem? At which two layers does the network adapter work?

29. A user complains that he cannot access a particular Web site, although he is able to access other Web sites. At which layer of the OSI model should you begin troubleshooting the problem?

30. A user complains that Skype drops her videoconference calls and she must reconnect. At which layer of the OSI model should you begin troubleshooting? Which OSI layer is responsible for not dropping the Skype connection?

Hands-On Projects

Project 1-1: Set Up a Small Network

For this project, you'll need two Windows 7 or Windows 8.1 computers, a small consumer-grade switch (one that does not require its firmware to be configured), and two regular network cables (a regular network cable is also called a straight-through cable or patch cable). Do the following to set up a small network:

1. Use the network cables to connect each computer to the switch. Make sure the switch has power. Verify the LED lights on the network ports of the computers and switch are lit and/or blinking to verify network connectivity and activity.

2. Open the Network and Sharing Center of each computer to verify that Windows sees the computer connected to the network. (In Windows 7, click **Start, Control Panel**, and make sure Control Panel is set to **Small icons** view. Then click **Network and Sharing Center**. In Windows 8.1, to open Control Panel, right-click the **Start** button and click **Control Panel**.)

3. If you don't see connectivity, reset the connection by restarting the computer. In Chapter 2, you'll learn about easier methods to verify and reset a network connection.

4. Open Windows Explorer or File Explorer and look in the Network group in the navigation pane. You should see the other computer listed. You won't be able to access resources on the other computer unless you share these resources in a homegroup or share a specific folder or file.

5. Answer the following questions:

    a. Does your network use a client-server or peer-to-peer model?

    b. What is the topology of your network?

    c. If the lights on the switch ports were not lit or blinking, what is the best theory of probable cause? At what layer of the OSI model would this theory be?

As you work your way through this book, you will continue to build your small network and its resources.

Project 1-2: Guidelines for Installing a Switch

While working as an intern in a corporate data center, you are asked to research the guidelines for installing a Cisco Nexus 5000 series switch in a rack. Search the Cisco Web site and other sites and answer the following questions:

1. Find a photo of any Nexus 5000 series switch. How much does the switch cost? Create a screenshot showing a photo of the switch and its price.

2. What are the two types of racks Cisco recommends for the switch? Find a rack of each type that meets these qualifications. Create screenshots showing a photo of each rack, its manufacturer, and price.

3. Create a screenshot showing the required equipment for installing the switch.

4. Create a screenshot showing the additional items needed to ground the switch.

5. Why does Cisco recommend you keep the shipping container?

6. Which installs first, the brackets or the sliders?

7. Create a document and insert into it the screenshots you made and the answers to the questions. Include in the document your name and course information and email the document to your instructor.

Project 1-3: Research Network Operating Systems

The client-server network at Scoops, a chain of ice cream stores, currently depends on one server machine running Windows Server 2008 as its NOS. However, the system was installed five years ago, and the chain is growing. The company's general manager has heard a lot of good things about Linux operating systems—in particular, a type of Linux called Fedora. He asks you to find out how these two NOSs differ in their file sharing, remote access, and mail service capabilities. Also, he wonders how the two compare in their ease of use, reliability, and support. He remarks that he doesn't want to spend a lot of time looking after the server, and reminds you that he is not a technical expert. After some research, what can you tell him about the similarities and differences between these two NOSs? Do you advise the Scoops chain to change its server's NOS to Linux? Why or why not?

Project 1-4: IT and Networking Certifications

This book prepares you to take the CompTIA Network+ N10-006 exam, which is considered a fundamental benchmark toward a career in IT. Many other IT certifications apply to IT and networking. Use the Web to research and answer the following questions:

1. Which certification does CompTIA recommend a candidate for the CompTIA Network+ exam already have?

2. How long does CompTIA recommend you work in networking before you take the CompTIA Network+ exam?

3. Cisco offers a full range of certifications focused on all aspects of networking. How long does Cisco recommend you work in networking before you take the CCNA Routing and Switching exam for certification?

4. How long does Cisco recommend you work in networking before you take the CCIE Routing and Switching exam?

5. Microsoft offers a group of certifications collectively called the Microsoft Certified Solutions Expert (MCSE). What are the eight MCSE certifications?

6. Search online for a job opening in IT networking in your geographical area and save or print the job description and requirements. (Excellent sites that post IT jobs are Indeed.com and Monster.com.) Answer the following questions about the job:

   a. Which degrees are required or recommended?

   b. What types of skills are required or recommended?

   c. Which IT certifications are required or recommended?

Case Projects

In Case Project 1-1, you set up a virtual machine (VM) using Client Hyper-V, and in Case Project 1-2, you set up a VM using Oracle VirtualBox. You only need to do one of these case projects. However, you'll need to do one because we'll continue to build your virtual network of VMs in later chapters. Client Hyper-V and VirtualBox are client hypervisors, which is software used to manage VMs installed on a workstation. If you don't want to use Client Hyper-V or VirtualBox as your hypervisor of choice, you can substitute another client hypervisor, such as VMware Player, which can be downloaded free from *vmware.com*. Note that Windows Hyper-V and Oracle VirtualBox don't play well on the same computer, and can cause problems, such as failed network connectivity. For that reason, don't install Hyper-V and VirtualBox on the same computer.

CASE PROJECTS

Case Project 1-1: Set Up a Virtual Machine Using Hyper-V

In this project, you use Hyper-V, which is software embedded in Windows 8.1 Professional, 64-bit version, to create and manage virtual machines (VM) and virtual networks on a single workstation. You'll first enable the workstation BIOS to support virtualization and enable Hyper-V and then create a VM in Hyper-V. Then you will install an OS in the VM. Your instructor will provide access to the Windows operating system installation files used in the VM.

Using a Windows 8.1 Pro, 64-bit version computer, follow these steps to enable virtualization in BIOS, enable Hyper-V, and configure a virtual switch for the virtual network:

1. For Hyper-V to work, hardware-assisted virtualization (HAV) must be enabled in BIOS setup. If you are not sure it is enabled, power down your computer, turn it on, press a key during start-up to access BIOS setup, and make sure hardware-assisted virtualization is enabled. For one system, that's done on the Security BIOS screen shown in Figure 1-25. Also make sure that any subcategory items under HAV are enabled. Save your changes, exit BIOS setup, and allow the system to restart to Windows 8.1.

2. Hyper-V is disabled in Windows 8.1 Pro by default. To enable it, right-click **Start** and click **Programs and Features**. Then click **Turn Windows features on or off**. Check **Hyper-V** and close all windows. You'll need to restart the computer for the change to take effect.

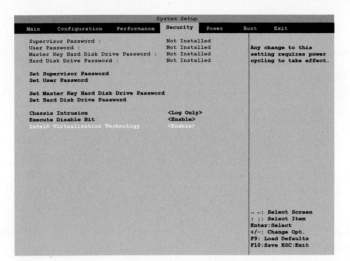

Figure 1-25   Virtualization must be enabled in BIOS setup for Client Hyper-V to work

Source: Jean Andrews

3. Launch the **Hyper-V Manager** application. In the Hyper-V Manager left pane, select the host computer.

4. To make sure your VMs have access to the network or the Internet, you need to first install a virtual switch in Hyper-V. To create a new virtual network switch, click **Virtual Switch Manager** in the Actions pane.

5. In the Virtual Switch Manager dialog box, verify **New virtual network switch** is selected in the left pane. To bind the virtual switch to the physical network adapter so the VMs can access the physical network, select **External** in the right pane. Then click **Create Virtual Switch**. In the next dialog box, make sure **Allow management operating system to share this network adapter** is checked and click **Apply**. Click **Yes**. Your virtual LAN now has a virtual switch. Close the Virtual Switch Manager dialog box.

To create a VM, follow these steps:

6. In the Actions pane, click **New** and then click **Virtual Machine**. The New Virtual Machine Wizard launches. Use these parameters for the new VM:

   - Select a name for your VM, for example VM1 or VM_Lab_B.

   - Make sure **Generation 1** is selected in the Specify Generation box.

   - Set the amount of RAM for the VM. Be sure to specify at least the minimum requirement for the OS you plan to install in the VM.

   - Check **Use Dynamic Memory for this virtual machine**.

   - Specify the VM can use the new virtual switch you created earlier.

   - Specify a new dynamically expanding virtual hard drive.

   - Specify how you will install an OS in the VM, which depends on the method your instructor used to provide you these setup files.

7. After the VM is created, it's listed in the middle pane of the Hyper-V Manager window. When you select it, its thumbnail appears in the middle pane of the Hyper-V Manager window.

Now you're ready to install an OS in the VM. The OS setup files are likely to come bundled in a single ISO file. An ISO file is a Disc Image File, which is a virtual DVD or CD. Follow these steps to mount an ISO file or a physical CD or DVD to the VM's virtual optical drive and install Windows:

8. Select the VM in the middle pane of the Hyper-V Manager window and click **Settings** near the bottom of the Actions pane. In the left pane of the Settings dialog box, select the **DVD Drive**. In the right pane, select **Image file**. Click **Browse** and browse to the ISO file. Select it and click **Open**. Click **OK** to mount the ISO file to the virtual DVD drive.

9. To boot the VM to the DVD drive, select **BIOS** in the left pane of the Settings box to verify the boot priority order of the VM begins with CD. Click **Apply** to apply your changes.

10. To boot up the selected VM, click **Start** in the Actions pane of the Hyper-V Manager window. To see the VM in its own window, double-click the thumbnail, as shown in Figure 1-26, where a Windows 8 installation has begun.

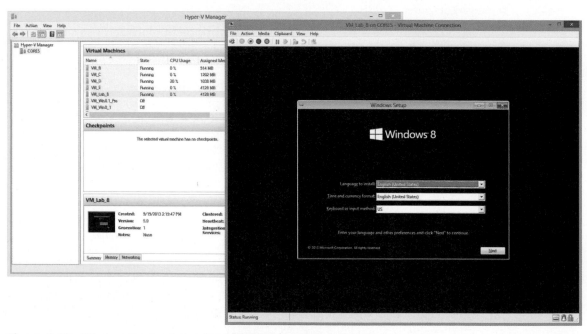

Figure 1-26 Windows 8 setup is running in the VM managed by Hyper-V

Source: Microsoft LLC

11. After you have installed Windows in the VM, open Internet Explorer to confirm the VM has a good Internet connection.

In future chapters, you'll continue to build your virtual network and install resources in the VMs on your network.

Case Project 1-2: Set Up a Virtual Machine Using Oracle VirtualBox

Using Windows 7 or Windows 8.1, you can download and install Oracle VirtualBox and use this free hypervisor to create virtual machines and a virtual network. Have available an ISO file to install the Windows operating system in the VM. Follow these steps:

1. Go to **virtualbox.org/wiki/Downloads** and download **VirtualBox for Windows hosts x86/amd64** to your desktop or other folder on your hard drive. Install the software, accepting default settings during the installation. The Oracle VM VirtualBox Manager window opens (see Figure 1-27).

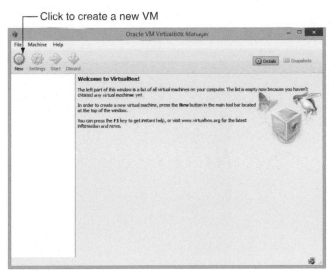

Figure 1-27   Use the VirtualBox Manager to create and manage virtual machines

Source: Oracle VirtualBox

2. To create a virtual machine using VirtualBox, click **New** in the toolbar and follow the wizard to create a VM. Name the virtual machine **VM10** and select the Windows OS you will install in it. You can accept all default settings for the VM.

3. With the VM selected, click **Settings** in the VirtualBox Manager window. In the VM10-Settings box, click **Storage** in the left pane.

4. In the Storage Tree area, to the right of Controller: IDE, click **Add CD/DVD Device**, which is represented by the single CD icon, as shown in Figure 1-28.

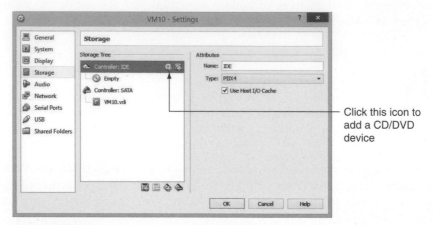

Figure 1-28   Storage Tree options allow you to mount an ISO image as a virtual CD in the VM

Source: Oracle VirtualBox

5. A dialog box appears. Click **Choose disk**. Browse to the location of the ISO file that contains the Windows operating system setup files made available by your instructor, click **Open**, and then click **OK**. You return to the VirtualBox Manager window.

6. Click **Start** on the toolbar. Your VM starts up and begins the process of installing the operating system.

## chapter 2

How Computers Find Each Other on Networks

After reading this chapter and completing the exercises, you will be able to:

- Describe how computers and other devices are addressed on a network
- Explain how host names and domain names work
- Identify how ports and sockets work at the OSI Transport layer
- Demonstrate how IP addresses are assigned and formatted at the OSI Network layer
- Use command-line tools to troubleshoot problems with network addresses

On the Job

While I was working as a junior project manager in the Technology Solutions Department for a large corporation, I was assigned to work on a network infrastructure project. At the time, I had no training as a network engineer, and was instead responsible for small- to medium-sized technology projects as they related to a business unit that spanned five states. For this new project, our goal was to change the network's topology in a way that would allow the network to grow over time for the least amount of money, and to keep the network up to date with the latest trends within the industry.

As with most projects, a budget was set at the beginning. This budget allowed us to hire a professional vendor to complete the wiring and cabling installations. The network engineers who worked for the vendor were experts on everything related to wiring and cabling. However, before they could get very far, our budget was aggressively reduced. Suddenly, we could no longer afford the cabling experts. Instead, senior managers decided that work would be completed by our company's own junior IT technicians, people who were better suited to printer paper jam resolution than recabling an entire network. They knew nothing about hierarchical cable structure, maximum cable distances, or endpoint terminations.

This ignorance of basic networking standards had dire consequences on our project's budget and timeline. But the problem wasn't just that the IT people doing the work lacked the proper knowledge. As the project manager, with no systematic knowledge of networking standards, I was also hampered in my ability to keep things on track.

Part of a successful project manager's job is recognizing the need for subject matter experts, or at least being able to understand where to find key pieces of information related to the project and then interpreting that information as it relates to the project. In my case, a simple understanding of a set of telecommunications standards, or TIA/EIA-568, would have been indispensable in completing the network topology change project.

Our in-house team began the project on a vacant floor that was to become new employee office space. We unknowingly exceeded cable runs, terminated wall outlet connection points incorrectly, and generally did a poor installation job. Only after new client computers were installed and exhibited a variety of connection issues did we realize our installation was most likely the culprit. We soon understood that our lack of prior planning and our ignorance of industry standards were to blame. Through painful trial and error, we gained an in-depth knowledge of telecommunications structured cabling and the tools needed to implement a network topology change, but with the cost of this knowledge was a lot of time on a ladder removing ceiling tiles and working late into the night to ensure clients were able to effectively run their applications at the start of the next workday.

Tom Johnson
Segment Account Manager, Defense Industry

In Chapter 1, you learned that the OSI model can be used to describe just about every aspect of networking. You saw firsthand the usefulness of working your way up or down the seven layers of the OSI model to troubleshoot networking problems. In this chapter, you learn the several methods used to address and find software, computers, and other devices on a network. We'll take a top-down approach to the OSI model as we explore these topics, starting at the Application layer and working our way down to the Data Link layer. (The lowest OSI layer, the Physical layer, does not require a network address.) At the end of this chapter, you learn how to troubleshoot addressing problems by using an OSI top-down or bottom-up approach to solving the problem.

In Chapter 3, you'll take your networking skills to the next level by learning how data is transported over a network. Now let's begin this chapter with an overview of the several ways software and devices are addressed on a network.

Overview of Addressing on Networks

 Network+
1.3
1.8
2.6
4.2

In Chapter 1, you learned that addressing methods operate at the Application, Transport, Network, and Data Link layers of the OSI model so that one host or node can find another on a network.

The organization responsible for tracking the assignments of port numbers, domain names, and IP addresses is the Internet Assigned Numbers Authority (IANA) (pronounced "I–anna"). IANA is a department of the Internet Corporation for Assigned Names and Numbers (ICANN). ICANN is a nonprofit organization charged with setting many policies that guide how the Internet works. For more information, see iana.org and icann.org. At icann.org, you can download helpful white papers that explain how the Internet works.

Here's a quick overview of the four addressing methods, starting at the top of the OSI model:

- *Application layer FQDNs, computer names, and host names*—Every host on a network is assigned a unique character-based name called the fully qualified host name or the fully qualified domain name (FQDN), for example, john.mycompany.com, ftp.mycompany.com, and www.mycompany.com. Collectively, the last two parts of a host name (for example, mycompany.com) are called the domain name, which matches the name of the organization's domain or network. The first part (for example, john, ftp, and www) is the host name, which identifies the individual computer on the network. Ftp is the host name usually given to an FTP server, and www is typically the host name assigned to a computer running a Web server. The FQDN is sometimes called the computer name and, more loosely, it is simply called the host name.

When a techie refers to a host name, you can assume she's actually referring to the FQDN unless stated otherwise.

- *Transport layer port numbers*—Recall that a port number identifies one application among several applications that might be running on a host and is used by the Transport layer to find an application. For example, a Web server application is usually configured to listen for incoming requests at port 80.

- *Network layer IP address*—An IP address is assigned to every interface, which is a network connection made by a node or host on a network. The IP address can be used to find hosts on any computer on the globe if the IP address is public on the Internet. Two types of IP addresses are used on the Internet:

    ○ *IPv4*—Internet Protocol version 4 (IPv4) addresses have 32 bits and are written as four decimal numbers called octets, for example, 92.106.50.200.

    ○ *IPv6*—Internet Protocol version 6 (IPv6) addresses have 128 bits and are written as eight blocks of hexadecimal numbers, for example 2001:0DB8:0B80:0000:0000:00D3:9C5A:00CC.

- *Data Link layer MAC address*—The MAC address, also called the physical address, is embedded on every NIC on the globe and is assumed to be unique to that NIC. Nodes on a LAN find each other using their MAC addresses. However, MAC addresses are not used to find nodes on networks other than the local network.

A hexadecimal number (also called a hex number) is a number written in the base 16 number system, which uses the 16 numerals 0, 1, 2, 3, 4, 5, 6, 7, 8, 9, A, B, C, D, E, and F. The CompTIA Network+ exam expects you to be familiar with the hex number system. To learn how this number system works and how to convert hex numbers to other number systems, see Appendix B.

IP addresses may be stored, retrieved, and tracked in an application, such as when you enter an IP address into your browser. But for routing purposes, an IP address is used only at the Network layer.

MAC Addresses

Network+ 1.8

You can find a network adapter's MAC address (physical address) by examining the NIC. It will be stamped directly onto the NIC's circuit board or on a sticker attached to some part of the NIC, as shown in Figure 2-1. Later in this chapter, you'll learn to use TCP/IP utilities to report the MAC address.

Traditional MAC addresses contain two parts, are 48 bits long, and are written as hexadecimal numbers separated by colons—for example, 00:60:8C:00:54:99. The first 24 bits (six hex characters, such as 00:60:8C in our example) are known as the OUI (Organizationally Unique Identifier) or block ID or company-ID, and identifies the NIC's manufacturer. A manufacturer's OUI is assigned by the Institute of Electrical and Electronics Engineers (IEEE). If you know a computer's MAC address, you can determine which company manufactured its NIC by looking up its block ID. The IEEE maintains a database of block IDs and their manufacturers, which is accessible via the Web. At the time of this writing, the database search page could be found at *http://standards.ieee.org/regauth/oui /index.shtml*.

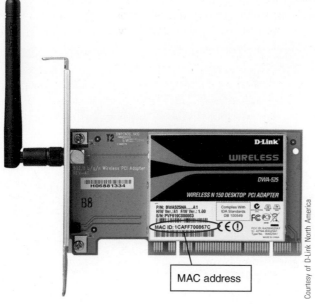

MAC address

Courtesy of D-Link North America

Figure 2-1 NIC with MAC address

Links to Web sites given in this book might become outdated as Web sites change. If a given link doesn't work, try a Google search on the item to find the new link.

NOTE

The last 24 bits make up the extension identifier or device ID and identify the device. Manufacturers assign each NIC a unique extension identifier, based on the NIC's model and manufacture date, so that no two NICs share the same MAC address.

Network+
1.3
1.8
2.6
4.2
Applying Concepts

Explore Addresses on Your Computer

You can permanently assign a static IP address to a computer or device, or you can configure the computer or device to receive (or lease) a dynamic IP address from a DHCP (Dynamic Host Configuration Protocol) server each time it connects to the network and requests an IP address. For Windows 7, follow these steps to configure these TCP/IP settings:

1. In Control Panel, open the **Network and Sharing Center**. Then click **Change adapter settings**. Right-click the network connection and click **Properties**.

2. Using the TCP/IPv4 properties box (see Figure 2-2), you can select **Obtain an IP address automatically** for dynamic IP addressing to be assigned by a DHCP server, or you can manually assign a static IP address, subnet mask, and default gateway. Notice you can also configure TCP/IP to obtain DNS server addresses from the DHCP server, or you can manually assign DNS server addresses.

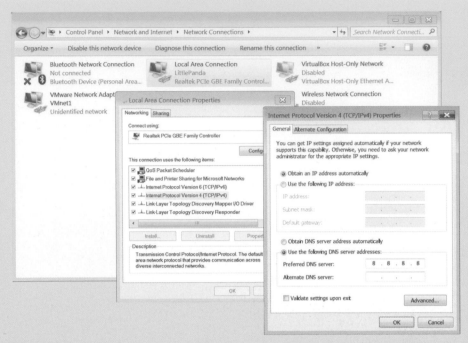

Figure 2-2   Configure TCP/IP for a network interface by using static or dynamic IP addressing

Source: Microsoft LLC

Here's a brief explanation of these settings:

- A **gateway** is a computer, router, or other device that a host uses to access another network. The **default gateway** is the gateway device that nodes on the network turn to first for access to the outside world.

- A **subnet mask** is a 32-bit number that helps one computer find another. The 32 bits are used to indicate what portion of an IP address is the network portion and what part is the host portion. Using this information, a computer can know if a remote computer with a given IP address is on its own or a different network.

- **DNS servers** are responsible for tracking computer names and their IP addresses. When you enter a computer name, such as *www.cengage.com*, in your browser address box, a DNS server is needed to find the IP address of that host.

After the connection to the network is made, you can use the **ipconfig** utility in a Command Prompt window to find out the current TCP/IP settings.

In Windows, commands can be entered at a command-line interface (CLI) that does not provide the Windows graphics normally provided by the graphical user interface (GUI). Network technicians need to be comfortable with the CLI because it is quicker and often more powerful and flexible than a GUI. In Windows, the CLI is provided by a Command Prompt window.

 To open a regular Command Prompt window in Windows 7, click Start, type cmd in the Search programs and files box, and press Enter. To open a Command Prompt window with administrative privileges (called an elevated command prompt window), click Start, type cmd, right-click cmd.exe, and click Run as administrator.

To open a regular Command Prompt window in Windows 8.1, right-click Start and click Command Prompt in the Quick Link menu. To open an elevated Command Prompt window, click Command Prompt (Admin) in the Quick Link menu.

Here are two ways to use the `ipconfig` command. You'll learn more about this command later in this chapter:

1. Open a Command Prompt window and enter the **`ipconfig`** command to view IP configuration information (see Figure 2-3). Which Local Area Connections are available on your computer? Which ones are currently connected? Also locate your connection's IPv4 or IPv6 address, subnet mask, and default gateway.

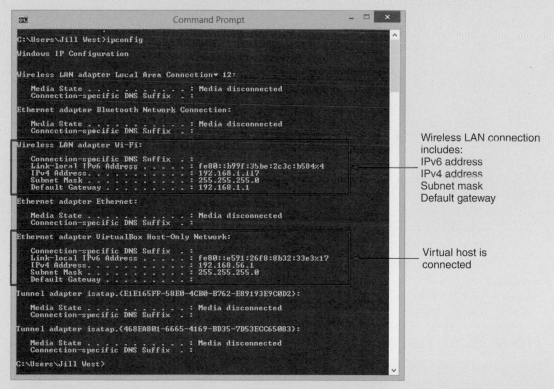

Figure 2-3 This computer is connected to two different network interfaces, one of which is a virtual network inside VirtualBox

Source: Microsoft LLC

2. The `ipconfig` command shows an abbreviated summary of configuration information. To see a more complete summary, use the command **`ipconfig /all`**. See Figure 2-4 for an example.

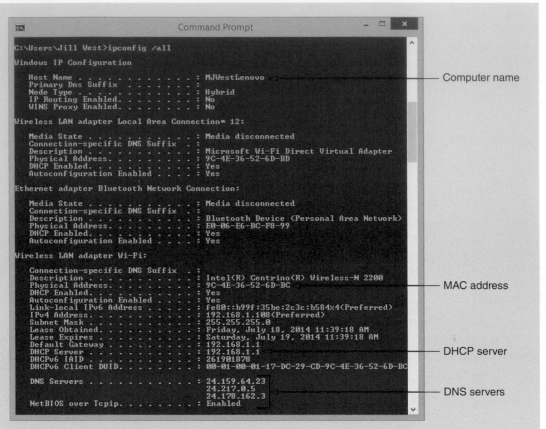

Figure 2-4 `ipconfig /all` gives a great deal more information than `ipconfig` by itself

Source: Microsoft LLC

Now that you have the big picture of how addressing happens at each layer of the OSI model, let's dig into the details of how it all works, beginning with host names and domain names at the top of the model.

How Host Names and Domain Names Work

Host names and domain names were created because character-based names are easier to remember than numeric IP addresses. Recall that an FQDN is a host name and a domain name together, such as *www.cengage.com*. The last part of an FQDN (*com* in our example) is called the **top-level domain** (TLD).

Host names and domain names can include letters, hyphens, and underscores, but no other special characters.

Domain names must be registered with an Internet naming authority that works on behalf of ICANN. Table 2-1 lists some well-known ICANN-approved TLDs. The first eight TLDs listed in this table were established in the mid-1980s. Of these, no restrictions exist on the use of the .com, .org, and .net TLDs, but ICANN does restrict what type of hosts can be associated with the .arpa, .mil, .int, .edu, and .gov TLDs. A complete list of current TLDs can be found at *iana.org/domains/root/db/*.

Table 2-1   Some well-known top-level domains

Domain suffix	Type of organization
ARPA	Reverse lookup domain (special Internet function)
COM	Commercial
EDU	Educational
GOV	Government
ORG	Noncommercial organization (such as a nonprofit agency)
NET	Network (such as an ISP)
INT	International Treaty Organization
MIL	United States military organization
BIZ	Businesses
INFO	Unrestricted use
AERO	Air-transport industry
COOP	Cooperatives

© 2016 Cengage Learning®

Registries and registrars of domain names are organizations with unique functions. A domain name registry operator, also known as a registry, is an organization or country responsible for one or more TLDs and maintains a database or registry of TLD information. A domain name registrar such as *godaddy.com* is an organization accredited by registries and ICANN to lease domain names to companies or individuals, following the guidelines of the TLD registry operators.

In 2011, ICANN decided to loosen its restrictions on TLD names and allow organizations and countries to apply for a new TLD composed of almost any alphanumeric string, including one that uses characters not found in the English language. Applying for a new TLD costs $185,000, and each application undergoes a rigorous evaluation.

You're now ready to learn about **name resolution**, which is the process of discovering the IP address of a host when you know its fully qualified domain name. Before we study name resolution on the Internet, let's see how name resolution can work on a local network.

Legacy Networking
Hosts Files

The first incarnation of the Internet, which was called ARPANET, had fewer than 1000 hosts. The entire network relied on one ASCII text file called HOSTS.TXT to associate computer names with IP addresses. This file was generically known as a hosts file or host table. Growth of the Internet soon made this simple arrangement impossible to maintain. However, when using a peer-to-peer network that doesn't have its own DNS server, you may still encounter this older system of using a text file to associate internal host names with their IP addresses on the local network. For UNIX, Linux, and Windows systems, the filename of a hosts file is hosts with no file extension. In UNIX or Linux, the hosts file is stored in the /etc directory, and on a Windows computer, the hosts file is located in the \Windows\System32\drivers\etc folder.

UNIX or Linux filenames and commands are case sensitive: a Hosts file and a hosts file are considered two different files. Windows, on the other hand, is not case sensitive. The Hosts and hosts filenames in command lines refer to the same file.

Also know that UNIX and Linux use the forward slash in paths to filenames and Windows uses the backslash for this purpose.

Figure 2-5 shows an example of a hosts file. Notice that each host (for example, *www.cengage.com*) is matched by one line identifying the host's name and IP address. In addition, a third field, called an alias, provides a nickname for the host (for example, Web). A line that begins with a hashtag (pound symbol) is called a comment line. Comments are used to document the contents of a file and are not interpreted by a program accessing the file.

```
# Host database
#
# This file contains the mappings of IP addresses to host names and the
# aliases for each host name. In the presence of the domain name service,
# this file may not be consulted.
#
# Comments (such as these) may be inserted on individual lines or
# following the machine name denoted by a '#' symbol.
#
#
# Address     Host name                    Alias

::1           localhost.cengage.com        localhost
127.0.0.1     localhost.cengage.com        localhost


69.32.133.79     www.cengage.com           Web
69.32.134.163    ftp.cengage.com           FTP
69.32.146.63     gale.cengage.com          Gale
69.32.132.117    poweron.cengage.com       TechSupport
```

Figure 2-5 Sample hosts file

Source: The Linux Foundation

To use a hosts file, suppose a user on the cengage.com domain wants to access the Web site provided by the corporate network. He enters the address *www.cengage.com* in his browser address box, and the OS resolves the name to its IP address by searching for *www.cengage.com* in its hosts file. It then can send the browser's request to the correct IP address on the local network.

To set up a hosts file, a network administrator must store the hosts file in the correct directory on all computers on the network and update as necessary. This method might work for a small organization that has a few servers made available for its users. However, it's not sufficient for large organizations, much less for the Internet. Instead, an automated solution is mandatory.

 Web site developers sometimes use hosts files to assign a host name to a new Web site so that the site can be tested on the local network before it's deployed to the Internet.

DNS (Domain Name System)

Network+
1.3

In the mid-1980s, DNS (Domain Name System or Domain Name Service) was designed to associate computer names with IP addresses. DNS is an Application layer client-server system of computers and databases made up of these elements:

- *namespace*—The DNS namespace is the entire collection of computer names and their associated IP addresses stored in databases on DNS name servers around the globe.

- *name servers*—DNS name servers, also called DNS servers, hold these databases, which are organized in a hierarchical structure.

- *resolvers*—A resolver is a DNS client that requests information from DNS name servers.

How Name Servers Are Organized
DNS name servers are organized in the hierarchical structure shown in Figure 2-6. At the root level, 13 clusters of root servers hold information used to locate the top-level domain (TLD) servers. These TLD servers hold information about the authoritative servers, which are the authority on computer names and their IP addresses for computers in their domains.

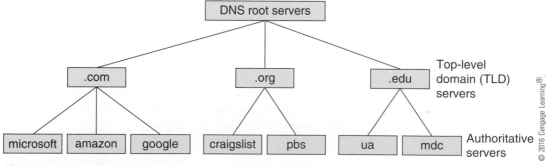

Figure 2-6   Hierarchy of name servers

To understand how the three levels of servers work, let's look at an example. Suppose an employee at Cengage, using a computer in the cengage.com domain, enters www.mdc.edu in her Web browser address box. The browser makes an API call to the DNS resolver, a TCP/IP component in the OS, for the IP address of the *www.mdc.edu* host.

 Recall that an application uses an API call to request the operating system perform a service or task.

Here are the steps to resolve the name, which are also illustrated in Figure 2-7:

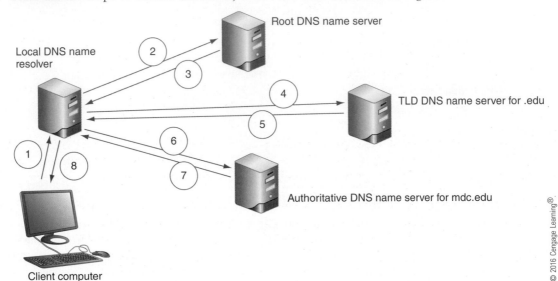

Figure 2-7 Queries for name resolution for *www.mdc.edu*

Step 1—The resolver on the client computer first searches its **DNS cache**, a database stored on the local computer, for the match. If it can't find the information there, the resolver sends a DNS message or query to its local DNS name server. This name server is the authoritative name server for the cengage.com domain. In this example, let's assume it doesn't yet know the IP address of the *www.mdc.edu* host.

 DNS messages are Application layer messages that use UDP at the Transport layer. Communication with DNS servers occur on port 53.

Steps 2 and 3—The local name server queries a root server with the request. The root server responds to the local name server with a list of IP addresses of TLD name servers responsible for the .edu suffix.

Steps 4 and 5—The local name server makes the same request to one of the TLD name servers responsible for the .edu suffix. The TLD name server responds with the IP address of the mdc.edu authoritative server.

Steps 6 and 7—The local name server makes the request to the DNS name server at Miami Dade Community College, which responds to the Cengage name server with the IP address of the *www.mdc.edu* host.

Step 8—The local name server responds to the client resolver with the requested IP address. Both the Cengage name server and the Cengage client computer store the information in their DNS caches, and, therefore, don't need to ask again.

Requests sometimes involve additional name servers. Following are a few ways the process can get more complex:

- The local name server might not be an authoritative name server for its organization. Instead, it might exist merely to resolve names for clients, in which case it is called a caching-only server. In that situation, when it receives a request for information that is not stored in its DNS cache, it will first query the company's authoritative name server.

- Name servers within a company might not have access to root servers. The local name server might query the name server at the company's Internet service provider (ISP), which might query a name server elsewhere on the Internet that acts as the ISP's naming authority. This name server might query a root server; however, if any name server in the process has the requested information, it responds without the involvement of a root server, TLD name server, or authoritarian name server.

- A TLD name server might be aware of an intermediate name server rather than the authoritative name server. When the local name server queries this intermediate name server, it might respond with the IP address of the authoritative name server.

Recursive and Iterative Queries

There are two types of DNS requests: recursive queries and iterative queries. A recursive query is a query that demands a resolution or the answer "It can't be found." For example, the initial request the resolver makes to the local server is a recursive query. In other words, the local server must provide the information requested by the resolver, as in "The buck stops here." When the local server issues queries to other servers, these queries are called iterative queries, which means the other servers only provide information if they have it; iterative queries do not demand a resolution. Although it's possible for a name server to make a recursive query of another server, generally, it doesn't happen.

DNS Zones and Zone Transfers

The records for host names and IP addresses are stored on thousands of servers around the globe, rather than being centralized on a single server or group of servers. In other words, DNS doesn't follow a centralized database model, but rather a distributed database model. Because data is distributed over thousands of servers, DNS will not fail catastrophically if one or a handful of servers experience errors.

Each organization that provides host services (for example, Web sites or email) on the public Internet is responsible for providing and maintaining DNS authoritative servers for public access. An organization will have an authoritative name server (called the primary DNS server) and a backup authoritative name server (called the secondary DNS server), and possibly several caching-only name servers. The domains (for example, cengage.com and course.com) that the organization is responsible for managing are called collectively a DNS zone. A large organization can keep all its domains in a single zone, or it can subdivide its domains into multiple zones to make each zone easier to manage.

The primary DNS server holds the authoritative DNS database for the organization. When a secondary DNS server needs to update its database, it makes the request to the primary server for the update; the process is called a zone transfer. Caching-only DNS servers do not participate in zone transfers, which helps reduce network traffic on slow links in intranets where these servers are often used.

DNS Server Software What software can you run to provide a DNS name server and DNS database? By far, the most popular DNS server software is BIND (Berkeley Internet Name Domain), which is free, open source software that runs on Linux, UNIX, and Windows platforms. Open source is the term for software whose code is publicly available for use and modification. You can download the software from *isc.org*. However, most Linux and UNIX distributions include BIND in the distribution.

Many other DNS server software products exist. For example, the Windows Server operating system has a built-in DNS service called Microsoft DNS Server, which partners closely with Active Directory (AD) services. A wise network administrator knows that DNS authoritative records must be accessible to Internet users, but Active Directory must be highly secured. The solution is to use a split DNS design, also called a split-horizon DNS, in which internal and external DNS queries are handled by different DNS servers or by a single DNS server that is specially configured to keep internal and external DNS zones separate.

In Figure 2-8, you can see two firewalls, one protecting the external DNS server and another one in front of the internal DNS server. A firewall is a device, either a router or a computer running special software, that selectively filters or blocks traffic between networks. All firewalls are porous to some degree in that they always let *some* traffic through; the question is what kind of traffic they let through. The external DNS server is behind a more porous firewall, which allows greater exposure to the Internet so that certain permissible traffic gets through. The internal DNS server is better protected behind the second, more hardened firewall, which is stricter about the types of traffic allowed through. The area between the two firewalls is called a DMZ or demilitarized zone. All DNS requests from the inside network that require external resolution are forwarded to the external DNS server, which also handles incoming queries from the Internet. Internal DNS requests are handled by AD's DNS server, which is kept secure from the Internet.

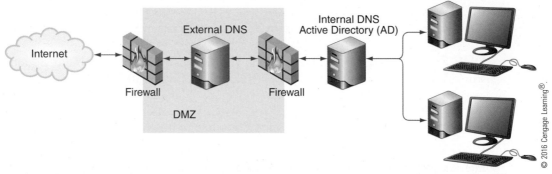

Figure 2-8   DNS services handled by two different servers so that the internal network remains protected

How a Namespace Database Is Organized Now let's see how records in a DNS database are organized. Several types of records, called resource records, are kept in a DNS database:

- An A (Address) record stores the name-to-address mapping for a host. This resource record provides the primary function of DNS—to match host names to IP addresses, using IPv4 addresses.

- An AAAA (Address) record (called a "quad-A record") also holds the name-to-address mapping, but the IP address is an IPv6 type IP address.

- A CNAME (Canonical Name) record holds alternative names for a host.

- A PTR (Pointer) record is used for reverse lookups, to provide a host name when you know its IP address.
- An MX (Mail Exchanger) record identifies a mail server and is used for email traffic.

The CompTIA Network+ exam expects you to know about the five types of DNS resource records listed above.

Each resource record includes a Time to Live field that identifies how long the record should be saved in a cache on a server, and this Time to Live is included in zone transfers. Administrators can set the time to live based on how volatile is the DNS data (in other words, how often the administrator expects the IP addresses to change).

Network+ 1.3

Applying Concepts
Configure a DNS Server

The steps for configuring a DNS server vary, depending on the software. For example, you configure the popular BIND software by creating or editing specific text files called zone files. When the BIND service first starts, it reads the data in the zone files and, as with all DNS servers, it listens for DNS requests at port 53. Table 2-2 lists a few zone file entries. Each line, or record, contains the text *IN* which indicates the record can be used by DNS servers on the Internet.

Table 2-2   Zone file records used to configure a DNS server

Record	Description
www.example.com IN A 92.100.80.40	This A record maps the server named www in the example.com domain to the IP address 92.100.80.40. The name www.example.com is called the canonical name or true name of the server.
40.80.100.92.in-addr-arpa. IN PTR www.example.com	This PTR record is used for reverse lookup—that is, to find the name when you know the IP address. Note the IP address is reversed and *in-addr-arpa* is appended to it.
example.com IN MX 1 panda.horse.com example.com IN MX 2 jack.sally.com example.com IN MX 3 susie.horse.com	These MX records tell mailers the preferred routes to take, ordered by best route, when sending mail to the example.com domain.
ns1.example.com IN CNAME www .example.com	This CNAME (canonical name) record says that the www .example.com host can also be addressed by its alias name ns1.example.com.
www.example.com IN AAAA 2001:db8:cafe:f9::d3	This AAAA record maps a name to an IPv6 address.

© 2016 Cengage Learning®

DDNS (Dynamic DNS) Suppose you want to maintain a Web server and Web site in your home office, but you don't maintain a DNS name server and you don't lease a static IP address from your ISP. How can name resolution to your Web site work without your having a DNS server and a static IP address? The solution is to sign up with a Dynamic DNS provider, such as dynDNS.org or TZO.com, to manage dynamic updates to its DNS records for your domain name. The provider uses monitoring software and the DDNS (Dynamic DNS) protocol to monitor the IP addresses dynamically assigned to your home network by your ISP. The monitoring software reports IP address changes to the DDNS service, which automatically updates DNS records. Home routers sometimes provide the monitoring software embedded in the router firmware (see Figure 2-9).

Figure 2-9   A Cisco home router can enable monitoring the IP address and report changes to dynDNS.org or TZO.com

Source: Cisco Systems, Inc.

Although a DNS record update on an authoritative name server becomes effective throughout the Internet in a matter of hours, the delay is still seen as a negative impact on those accessing your site. For this reason, most organizations are willing to pay more for a statically assigned IP address.

Now we move down to Layer 4 of the OSI model to see how port numbers are used to identify an application when it receives communication from a remote host.

How Ports and Sockets Work

Port numbers ensure that data is transmitted to the correct application among other applications running on a computer. If you compare network addressing with the addressing system used by the postal service, and you equate a host's IP address to the address of a building, then a port number is similar to an apartment number within that building.

A socket consists of a host's IP address and the port number of an application running on the host, with a colon separating the two values. For example, the standard port number for the Telnet service is 23. If a host has an IP address of 10.43.3.87, the socket address for Telnet running on that host is 10.43.3.87:23.

When the host receives a request to communicate on port 23, it establishes or opens a session for communication with the Telnet service and the socket is said to be open. When the TCP session is complete, the socket is closed or dissolved. You can think of a socket as a virtual circuit between a server and client. (See Figure 2-10.)

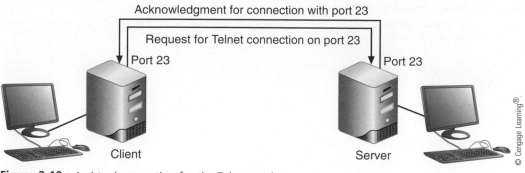

Acknowledgment for connection with port 23

Request for Telnet connection on port 23

Port 23

Port 23

Client

Server

© Cengage Learning®

Figure 2-10   A virtual connection for the Telnet service

Port numbers range from 0 to 65535 and are divided by IANA into three types:

- *well-known ports*—These ports range from 0 to 1023 and are assigned by IANA to widely used and well-known protocols and programs, such as Telnet, FTP, and HTTP. Table 2-3 lists some of these well-known ports used by TCP and/or UDP.

- *registered ports*—These ports range from 1024 to 49151 and can be used by network users and processes that are not considered standard processes. Default assignments of these registered ports must be registered with IANA. For example, port 1109 is registered to the Kerberos authentication protocol, and port 1293 is registered to the IPsec encryption protocol. (Later in this book, you'll learn more about these two protocols.)

- *dynamic and private ports*—These ports range from 49152 to 65535 and are open for use without restriction. A dynamic port is a port number that can be assigned by a client or server as the need arises. For example, if a client program has several open sockets with multiple servers, it can use a different dynamic port number for each socket. A private port number is one assigned by a network administrator that is different from the well-known port number for that service. For example, the administrator might assign a private port number other than the standard port 80 to a Web server on the Internet so that several people can test the site before it's made available to the public. To reach the Web server, a tester must enter the private port number in the browser address box.

To prepare for the CompTIA Network+ exam, you need to memorize all the well-known port numbers listed in Table 2-3. Several of these protocols are discussed in detail in later chapters. We've put them all together in this table for easy reference.

In Chapter 1, you learned about most of the protocols listed in Table 2-3. Here's a brief description of the ones not yet covered:

- **SNMP (Simple Network Management Protocol)** is used to monitor and manage network traffic. You'll learn much more about it in Chapter 9.

- **TFTP (Trivial File Transfer Protocol)** is seldom used by humans. Computers commonly use it as they are booting up to request configuration files from another computer on the local network. TFTP uses the UDP transport protocol, whereas normal FTP uses the TCP transport protocol.

Table 2-3   Well-known TCP and UDP ports

Port number	Process name	Protocol used	Description
20	FTP-DATA	TCP	File transfer—data
21	FTP	TCP	File transfer—control (An FTP server listens at port 21 and sends/receives data at port 20)
22	SSH	TCP	Secure Shell
23	TELNET	TCP	Telnet
25	SMTP	TCP	Simple Mail Transfer Protocol
53	DNS	TCP and UDP	Domain Name System
67	DHCPv4	UDP	Dynamic Host Configuration Protocol for IPv4—client to server
68	DHCPv4	UDP	Dynamic Host Configuration Protocol for IPv4—server to client
69	TFTP	UDP	Trivial File Transfer Protocol
80	HTTP	TCP and UDP	Hypertext Transfer Protocol
110	POP3	TCP	Post Office Protocol, version 3
123	NTP	UDP	Network Time Protocol
137-139	NetBIOS	TCP and UDP	TCP/IP legacy support for the outdated NetBIOS protocols
143	IMAP	TCP	Internet Message Access Protocol
161	SNMP	TCP and UDP	Simple Network Management Protocol
443	HTTPS	TCP	Secure implementation of HTTP
445	SMB	TCP	Server Message Block
546	DHCPv6	UDP	Dynamic Host Configuration Protocol for IPv6—client to server
547	DHCPv6	UDP	Dynamic Host Configuration Protocol for IPv6—server to client
1720	H.323	TCP	Packet-Based Multimedia Communications Systems
2427/2727	MGCP	TCP and UDP	Media Gateway Control Protocol
3389	RDP	TCP	Remote Desktop Protocol
5004	RTP	UDP	Real-time Transport Protocol
5005	RTCP	UDP	Real-time Transport Control Protocol
5060	SIP	UDP	Session Initiation Protocol or SIP, not encrypted
5061	SIP	UDP	Encrypted SIP

- **NTP (Network Time Protocol)** is a simple protocol used to synchronize clocks on computers on a network.

- **SMB (Server Message Block)** was first used by earlier Windows OSs for file sharing on a network. UNIX uses a version of SMB in its **Samba** software, which is used to share files with other operating systems, including Windows systems. The cross-platform version of SMB used between Windows, UNIX, and other operating systems is called the **CIFS (Common Internet File System)** protocol.

- **SIP (Session Initiation Protocol)** is used to make an initial connection between hosts for transferring multimedia data. After the connection is established, another protocol is typically used—for example, VoIP in a video conference. SIP is a type of **signaling protocol**, which is a protocol that makes an initial connection between hosts but that does not actually participate in data exchange. You'll learn more about SIP in Chapter 9.

- **H.323** is another signaling protocol used to make a connection between hosts prior to communicating multimedia data. H.323 has largely been replaced by SIP, which is easier to use.

- **MGCP (Media Gateway Control Protocol)** is yet another signaling protocol used to communicate multimedia data. You'll learn more about it in Chapter 9.

- **NetBIOS over TCP/IP**, also called **NetBT** or simply **NetBIOS**, is a protocol that allows old applications designed for out-of-date NetBIOS networks to work on TCP/IP networks. NetBIOS has its own name resolution service, Windows Internet Name Service (WINS), which uses port 137; a datagram service for connectionless communication, which uses port 138; and connection-oriented communication, which uses port 139. If you find NetBIOS applications on your network, you'll need to enable NetBIOS over TCP/IP to make them work. However, you'll want to replace these out-of-date applications as soon as you can.

You can use a **packet analyzer**, also called a **protocol analyzer**, to collect and examine network messages that use all of these various protocols. You'll install and use the Wireshark protocol analyzer in a project at the end of this chapter.

How IP Addresses Are Formatted and Assigned

Recall that networks may use two types of IP addresses: IPv4 addresses, which have 32 bits, and IPv6 addresses, which have 128 bits. In this part of the chapter, you learn how IPv4 addresses are formatted and assigned. Then you learn how IPv6 addresses are formatted and assigned.

How IPv4 Addresses Are Formatted and Assigned

Recall that a 32-bit IP address is organized into four groups of 8 bits each, which are presented as four decimal numbers separated by periods, such as 72.56.105.12. Each of these four groups is called an octet. The largest possible 8-bit number is 11111111, which is equal to 255 in decimal, so the largest possible IP address in decimal is 255.255.255.255, which in binary is 11111111.11111111.11111111.11111111. Each of the four octets can be any number from 0 to 255, making a total of about 4.3 billion IPv4 addresses ($256{\times}256{\times}256{\times}256$). Some IP addresses are reserved, so these numbers are approximations.

Computers rely on the binary number system, also called the base 2 number system, which uses only two numerals called bits: 0 and 1. The octal number system or base 8 number system has eight numerals (0 through 7). The Comp-TIA Network+ exam expects you to be familiar with the binary and octal number systems. To learn how the binary and octal number systems work and how to convert between number systems, see Appendix B.

Let's begin our discussion of IPv4 addresses by looking at how they are classified.

Classes of IP Addresses IPv4 addresses are divided into five classes: Class A, Class B, Class C, Class D, and Class E. When IPv4 addresses were available from IANA, a company could lease a Class A, Class B, or Class C license, acquiring multiple IP addresses in a class license. As shown in Table 2-4, the first part of an IP address identifies the network, and the last part identifies the host.

Table 2-4 IP address classes

Class	Network octets*	Approximate number of possible networks or licenses	Approximate number of possible IP addresses in each network
A	1.x.y.z to 126.x.y.z	126	16 million
B	128.0.x.y to 191.255.x.y	16,000	65,000
C	192.0.0.x to 223.255.255.x	2 million	254

© 2016 Cengage Learning®

*An x, y, or z in the IP address stands for an octet that is used to identify hosts.

NETWORK+ EXAM TIP The CompTIA Network+ exam expects you to be able to identify the class of any IP address. For the exam, memorize the second column in Table 2-4.

Figure 2-11 shows how each class of IP addresses is divided into the network and host portions.

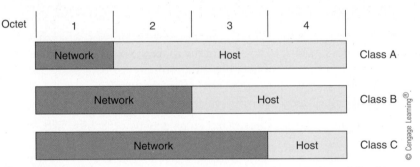

Figure 2-11 The network portion and host portion for each class of IP addresses

When class licenses were available from IANA, here's how Class A, B, and C licenses were leased:

- A Class A license was for a single octet. For example, a company that leased the Class A license 119 acquired 119.0.0.0 through 119.255.255.255 IP addresses.

- A Class B license was for the first two octets. For example, a company that leased the Class B 150.100 license acquired 150.100.0.0 through 150.100.255.255 IP addresses.

- A Class C license was for the first three octets. For example, a company that leased the Class C 200.80.15 license acquired 200.80.15.0 through 200.80.15.255 IP addresses.

Class D and Class E IP addresses are not available for general use. Class D addresses begin with octets 224 through 239 and are used for multicasting, in which one host sends messages to multiple hosts, such as when a host transmits a videoconference over the Internet. Class E addresses, which begin with 240 through 254, are reserved for research. Also, the block of addresses that begin with 127 are reserved for research and loopback addresses.

The IP addresses listed in Table 2-5 are reserved for special use by TCP/IP and should not be assigned to a device on a network.

Table 2-5   Reserved IP addresses

IP address	How it is used
255.255.255.255	Used for broadcast messages by TCP/IP background processes; a broadcast message is read by every node on the network
0.0.0.0	Currently unassigned
127.0.0.1	Indicates your own computer and is called the loopback address

© 2016 Cengage Learning®

NOTE

Later in the chapter, you learn to use the loopback address to verify that TCP/IP is configured correctly on a computer. The computer actually "talks to itself" using the TCP/IP loopback interface, which is the computer's connection with itself. When the computer can "hear itself," you know that TCP/IP is configured correctly.

How a DHCP Server Assigns IP Addresses

Recall that static IP addresses are manually assigned by the network administrator, whereas dynamic IP addresses are automatically assigned by a DHCP server each time a computer connects to the network. Because it's unmanageable to keep up with static IP address assignments, most network administrators choose to use dynamic IP addressing.

If a computer configured to use DHCP first connects to the network and is unable to lease an IPv4 address from the DHCP server, it uses an Automatic Private IP Addressing (APIPA) address in the address range 169.254.0.1 through 169.254.255.254.

Network+
1.3
Applying Concepts
Configure a DHCP Server

Each type of DHCP server software is configured differently. Generally, you define a range of IP addresses, called a DHCP scope, to be assigned to clients when they request an address. For example, Figure 2-12 shows a screen provided by the firmware utility for a home router, which is also a DHCP server. Using this screen, you set the starting IP address (192.168.1.100 in the figure) and the maximum number of IP addresses that can be assigned (50 in the figure). Therefore, the scope or range of IP addresses this DHCP server assigns is 192.168.1.100 to 192.168.1.149.

When other nodes on the network need to know the IP address of a particular client, you can have DHCP assign the client a static IP address. A static IP address assigned by DHCP is called a DHCP reservation. For example, suppose a network printer needs a static IP address so that computers on the network can consistently find it. To make a reservation for the DHCP server shown in Figure 2-12, click DHCP Reservation. This displays the screen shown in Figure 2-13, where you can view the currently assigned IP addresses and reserve addresses. In Figure 2-13, the Canon1719B0 network printer has a reserved IP address of 192.168.1.100.

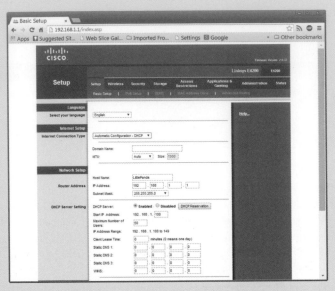

Figure 2-12 Set a range of IP addresses on a DHCP server

Source: Cisco Systems, Inc.

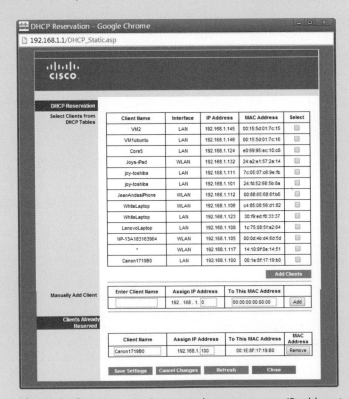

Figure 2-13 Clients on the network can reserve an IP address to be assigned by the DHCP server

Source: Cisco Systems, Inc.

In Linux systems, you configure the DHCP software by editing a text file. For example, the text file for one Linux DHCP server is dhcpd.conf, which is stored in the /etc/dhcp directory. Figure 2-14 shows the text file as it appears in the Linux vim text editor. A # at the beginning of a line identifies the line as a comment line (a line that is not executed). The range of IP addresses that will be assigned to clients in Figure 2-14 is 10.254.239.10 to 10.254.239.20, which is 11 IP addresses.

```
# If this DHCP server is the official DHCP server for the local
# network, the authoritative directive should be uncommented.
authoritative;

# Use this to send dhcp log messages to a different log file (you also
# have to hack syslog.conf to complete the redirection).
log-facility local7;

# No service will be given on this subnet, but declaring it helps the
# DHCP server to understand the network topology.

#subnet 10.152.187.0 netmask 255.255.255.0 {
#}

# This is a very basic subnet declaration.

subnet 10.254.239.0 netmask 255.255.255.224 {
  range 10.254.239.10 10.254.239.20;
  option routers rtr-239-0-1.example.org, rtr-239-0-2.example.org;
}

# This declaration allows BOOTP clients to get dynamic addresses,
# which we don't really recommend.

#subnet 10.254.239.32 netmask 255.255.255.224 {
#  range dynamic-bootp 10.254.239.40 10.254.239.60;
#  option broadcast-address 10.254.239.31;
#  option routers rtr-239-32-1.example.org;
#}
```

DHCP range of IP addresses

Figure 2-14 Edit a text file in Linux to set an IP address range for a DHCP server

Source: Canonical Ltd.

DHCP for IPv4 servers listen at port 67 and DHCPv4 clients receive responses at port 68. When using DHCP for IPv6, DHCP servers listen at port 546 and clients receive responses at port 547.

Public and Private IP Addresses The Class A, B, and C licensed IP addresses are available for use on the Internet and are therefore called public IP addresses. To conserve its public IP addresses, a company can use private IP addresses on its private networks, which are not allowed on the Internet. IEEE recommends that the following IP addresses be used for private networks:

- 10.0.0.0 through 10.255.255.255
- 172.16.0.0 through 172.31.255.255
- 192.168.0.0 through 192.168.255.255

IEEE, a nonprofit organization, is responsible for many Internet standards. Standards are proposed to the networking community in the form of an RFC (Request for Comment). RFC 1918 outlines recommendations for private IP addresses. To view an RFC, visit the Web site *rfc-editor.org*.

Address Translation, NAT, and PAT Network Address Translation (NAT) is a technique designed to conserve the number of public IP addresses needed by a network.

A gateway device or router that stands between a private network and other networks substitutes the private IP addresses used by computers on the private network with its own public IP address when these computers need access to other networks or the Internet. The process is called **address translation**. Besides requiring only a single public IP address for the entire private network, another advantage of NAT is security; the gateway hides the entire private network behind this one address.

What happens when a host on the Internet needs to respond to the local host that sent it a request? You might wonder how the gateway knows which local host is the intended recipient, when several local hosts might have made the request. The gateway uses **Port Address Translation (PAT)** to assign a separate TCP port number to each ongoing conversation, or session, between a local host and an Internet host. See Figure 2-15. When the Internet host responds to the local host, the gateway uses PAT to determine which local host is the intended recipient.

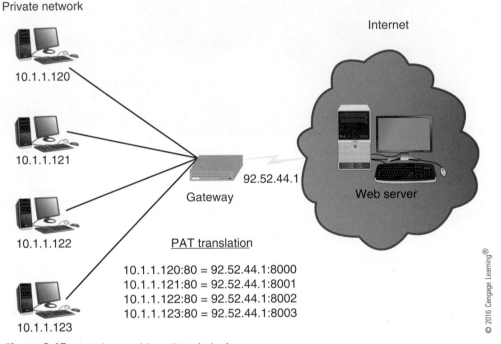

Figure 2-15 PAT (Port Address Translation)

Two variations of NAT you need to be aware of are:

- *SNAT*—Using **Static Network Address Translation (SNAT)**, the gateway assigns the same public IP address to a host each time it makes a request to access the Internet. This method works well when a local host is running a server that is accessed from the Internet. It's used on home networks that have only a single public IP address provided by an ISP.

- *DNAT or Dynamic NAT*—Using **Dynamic Network Address Translation (DNAT)**, the gateway has a pool of public IP addresses that it is free to assign to a local host whenever the local host makes a request to access the Internet. Large organizations that lease many public IP addresses use DNAT.

Applying Concepts
Configure Address Translation Using NAT

For simple default gateways such as a home router, configuring address translation means making sure NAT is turned on. That's about all you can do. However, for more advanced gateways, such as an industrial-grade Cisco router or Linux server, you configure the NAT software by editing NAT translation tables stored on the device.

For example, suppose your network supports a Web server available to the Internet, as shown in Figure 2-16. On the Web, the Web site is known by the public IP address 69.32.208.74. Figure 2-17 shows the sample text file required to set up the translation tables for SNAT to direct traffic to the Web server at private IP address 192.168.10.7. (The lines that begin with ! or exclamation marks are comment lines.) The first group of lines defines the router's outside interface, which connects with the outside network, and is called the serial interface. The second group defines the router's inside Ethernet interface. The last line that is not a comment line says that when clients from the Internet send a request to IP address 69.32.208.74, the request is translated to the IP address 192.168.10.7.

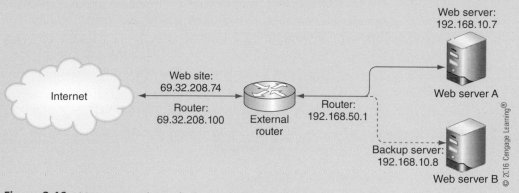

Figure 2-16   Messages to the Web site are being routed to Web server A

```
interface serial 0/0
  ip address 69.32.208.100 255.255.255.0
  ip nat outside

!--- Defines the serial 0/0 interface as the router's NAT outside interface
!--- with an IP address of 69.32.208.100

interface ethernet 1/1
  ip address 192.168.50.1 255.255.255.0
  ip nat inside

!--- Defines the Ethernet 1/1 interface as the router's NAT inside interface
!--- with an IP address of 192.168.50.1


ip nat inside source static 192.168.10.7 69.32.208.74

!--- States that source information about the inside host will be translated
!--- so the host's private IP address (192.168.10.7) will appear as the
!--- public IP address (69.32.208.74). Both ingoing and outgoing traffic
!--- exchanged with the public IP address will be routed to the host at the
!--- private IP address.
```

Figure 2-17   NAT translation table entry in Linux

At the end of this chapter, you'll create your own NAT translation table entry using this example as a template. To help you better understand where the IP address in a translation table entry comes from, answer the following questions about the information in Figures 2-16 and 2-17:

1. What is the router's outside interface IP address?

2. What is the router's inside interface IP address?

3. What is the Web site's public IP address?

4. What is the private IP address of the active Web server?

 ## How IPv6 Addresses Are Formatted and Assigned

The IPv6 standards were developed to improve routing capabilities and speed of communication over the established IPv4 standards and to allow for more public IP addresses on the Internet. Let's begin our discussion of IPv6 by looking at how IPv6 addresses are written and displayed:

- Recall that an IPv6 address has 128 bits that are written as eight blocks (also called quartets) of hexadecimal numbers separated by colons, like this:
  2001:0000:0B80:0000:0000:00D3:9C5A:00CC

- Each block is 16 bits. For example, the first block in the preceding IP address is the hexadecimal number 2001, which can be written as 0010 0000 0000 0001 in binary.

- Leading zeroes in a four-character hex block can be eliminated. This means our sample IP address can be written as 2001:0000:B80:0000:0000:D3:9C5A:CC.

- If blocks contain all zeroes, they can be written as double colons (::). This means our sample IP address can be written two ways:

  ○ 2001::B80:0000:0000:D3:9C5A:CC

  ○ 2001:0000:B80::D3:9C5A:CC

  To avoid confusion, only one set of double colons is used in an IP address. In this example, the preferred method is the second one 2001:0000:B80::D3:9C5A:CC because the address contains the fewest zeroes.

The way computers communicate using IPv6 has changed the terminology used to describe TCP/IP communication. Here are a few terms used in the IPv6 standards:

- A link, sometimes called the local link, is any local area network (LAN) bounded by routers.

- An interface is a node's attachment to a link. The attachment can be a physical attachment using a network adapter or wireless connection or a logical attachment. For example, a logical attachment can be used for tunneling. Tunneling is a method used by IPv6 to transport IPv6 packets through or over an IPv4 network.

- The last 64 bits or four blocks of an IPv6 address identify the interface and are called the interface ID or interface identifier. These 64 bits uniquely identify an interface on the local link.

- Neighbors are two or more nodes on the same link.

Types of IP Addresses IPv6 classifies IP addresses differently than IPv4. IPv6 supports these three types of IP addresses, classified as to how the address is used:

- *unicast address*—This type of address specifies a single node on a network. Two types of unicast addresses are global and link local addresses.

- *multicast address*—Packets are delivered to all nodes in the targeted, multicast group.

- *anycast address*—This type of address can identify multiple destinations, with packets delivered to the closest destination. For example, a DNS name server might send a DNS request to a group of DNS servers that have all been assigned the same anycast address. A router handling the request examines routes to all the DNS servers in the group and routes the request to the closest server.

Recall that with IPv4 broadcasting, messages are sent to every node on a network. However, IPv6 reduces network traffic by eliminating broadcasting. The concepts of broadcasting, multicasting, anycasting, and unicasting are depicted in Figure 2-18.

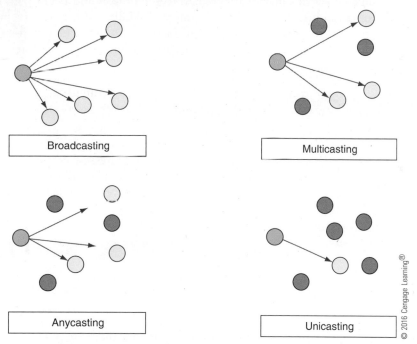

Figure 2-18 Concepts of broadcasting, multicasting, anycasting, and unicasting

Two types of unicast addresses are diagrammed in Figure 2-19 and described next:

- *global addresses*—A global unicast address, also called a global address, can be routed on the Internet. These addresses are similar to public IPv4 addresses. Most global addresses begin with the prefix 2000::/3, although other prefixes are being released. The /3 indicates that the first three bits are fixed and are always 001. Looking at Figure 2-19, notice the 16 bits or one block called the subnet ID, which can be used to identify a subnet on a large corporate network. A subnet is a smaller network within a larger network.

Global address

3 bits	◄───────── 45 bits ─────────►	◄─── 16 bits ───►	◄───────────── 64 bits ─────────────►
001	Global routing prefix	Subnet ID	Interface ID

Link local address

◄─────────────────────── 64 bits ───────────────────────►	◄───────────── 64 bits ─────────────►
1111 1110 1000 0000 0000 0000 0000 .... 0000 FE80::/64	Interface ID

© Cengage Learning®

Figure 2-19 Two types of IPv6 addresses

- *link local addresses*—A link local unicast address, also called a link local address or local address, can be used for communicating with nodes in the same link. These addresses are similar to IPv4's autoconfigured APIPA addresses and begin with FE80::/ 10. This prefix notation means the address begins with FE80, but the first 10 bits of the reserved prefix must be followed by another 54 zeroes to make 64 bits for the network portion of the address. Link local addresses are not allowed on the Internet.

A third type of unicast address is a site local unicast address, which is a hybrid between a global and local unicast address. It was not put to popular use and was deprecated (omitted) from the latest IPv6 standards.

Table 2-6 lists some currently used address prefixes for IPv6 addresses. Notice in the table the unique local unicast addresses, which work on local links and are similar to IPv4 private IP addresses. You can expect more prefixes to be assigned as they are needed.

Table 2-6 Address prefixes for types of IPv6 addresses

IP address type	Address prefix	Notes
Global unicast	2000::/3	First 3 bits are always 001
Link local unicast	FE80::/64	First 64 bits are always 1111 1110 1000 0000 0000 0000 0000
Unique local unicast	FC00::/7	First 7 bits are always 1111 110
	FD00::/8	First 8 bits are always 1111 1101
Multicast	FF00::/8	First 8 bits are always 1111 1111

© 2016 Cengage Learning®

An excellent resource for learning more about IPv6 and how it works is the e-book *TCP/IP Fundamentals for Microsoft Windows*. To download the free PDF, search for it at *microsoft.com/download*.

You can use the `ipconfig` command to view IPv4 and IPv6 addresses assigned to all network connections. For example, in Figure 2-20, four IP addresses have been assigned to the physical connections on a laptop, as follows:

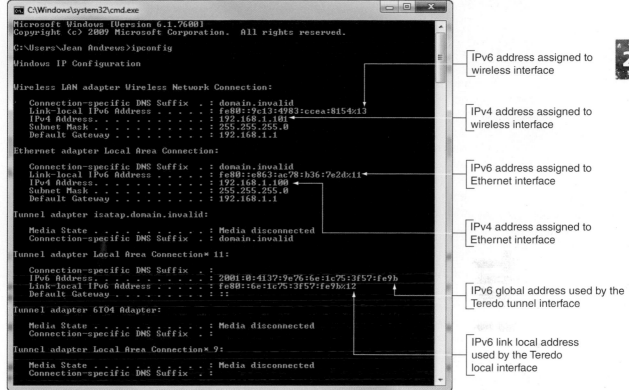

Figure 2-20 The `ipconfig` command shows IPv4 and IPv6 addresses assigned to this computer

Source: Microsoft LLC

- Windows has assigned to the wireless connection two IP addresses, one using IPv4 and one using IPv6.

- The Ethernet LAN connection has also been assigned an IPv4 address and an IPv6 address.

IPv6 addresses are followed by a % sign and a number. For example, %13 follows the first IP address in Figure 2-20. This number, which is called the zone ID or scope ID, is used to identify the link the computer belongs to.

IPv6 Autoconfiguration IPv6 addressing is designed so that a computer can autoconfigure its own link local IP address without the help of a DHCPv6 server. This is similar to how IPv4 uses an APIPA address. Here's what happens with autoconfiguration when a computer using IPv6 first makes a network connection:

Step 1—The computer creates its IPv6 address. It uses FE80::/64 as the first 64 bits or the prefix. Depending on how the OS is configured, the last 64 bits (called the interface ID) can be generated in two ways:

- *The 64 bits are randomly generated*—In this case, the IP address is called a temporary address and is never registered in DNS or used to generate global addresses for use on the Internet. The IP address changes often to help prevent hackers from discovering the computer. This is the default method used by Windows 7 and Windows 8.

- *The 64 bits are generated from the network adapter's MAC address*—MAC addresses consist of 48 bits and must be converted to the 64-bit standard, called the EUI-64 (Extended Unique Identifier-64) standard. To generate the interface ID, the OS takes the 48 bits of the device's MAC address, inserts a fixed 16-bit value in the middle of the 48 bits between the OUI and NIC portions, and inverts the value of the seventh bit.

 **NOTE** The seventh bit of the 48-bit MAC address is always set to 0 if the address was assigned by the IEEE, as verification that the MAC address is, indeed, globally unique. If the seventh bit is set to 1, you know that the MAC address was assigned locally, perhaps by a virtual machine or manually by an administrator, and is therefore not necessarily unique. Either way, the seventh bit's value is reversed when the MAC address is used to generate an IPv6 address.

Step 2—The computer checks to make sure its IP address is unique on the network.

Step 3—The computer asks if a router on the network can provide configuration information. If a router responds with DHCP information, the computer uses whatever information this might be, such as the IP addresses of DNS servers or the network prefix, which will become the first 64 bits of its own IP address. The process is called prefix discovery and the computer uses the prefix to generate its own link local or global IPv6 address by appending its interface ID to the prefix.

Because a computer can generate its own link local or global IP address, a DHCPv6 server, also called a DHCP6 server, usually serves up only global IPv6 addresses to hosts that require static IP addresses. For example, Web servers and DNS name servers can receive their static IPv6 addresses from a DHCP6 server.

Tunneling When a network is configured to use both IPv4 and IPv6 protocols, the network is said to be dual stacked. However, if packets on this network must traverse other networks where dual stacking is not used, the solution is to use tunneling. Because the Internet is not completely dual stacked, tunneling is always used for IPv6 transmission on the Internet. Three tunneling protocols developed for IPv6 packets to travel over or through an IPv4 network are:

- 6to4 is the most common tunneling protocol. IPv6 addresses intended to be used by this protocol always begin with the same 16-bit prefix (called fixed bits), which is 2002 and the prefix is written as 2002::/16. The next 32 bits of the IPv6 address are the 32 bits of the IPv4 address of the sending host.

- ISATAP (pronounced "eye-sa-tap") stands for Intra-Site Automatic Tunnel Addressing Protocol. This protocol works only on a single organization's intranet. By default, ISATAP is enabled in Windows 7 and Windows 8.1.

- Teredo (pronounced "ter-EE-do") is named after the Teredo worm, which bores holes in wood. IPv6 addresses intended to be used by this protocol always begin with 2001 and the prefix is written as 2001::/32. Teredo is enabled by default in Windows 7, but not

Windows 8.1. On UNIX and Linux systems that don't have Teredo installed by default, you can install third-party software such as Miredo to provide the Teredo service.

To run a tunneling protocol, you simply need to enable it. The service is managed by software called the tunnel broker using automatic tunneling. The 6to4 tunneling protocol doesn't work with a tunnel broker and must be manually configured.

One more tunneling example is needed. Suppose you have a rather futuristic network that is set up to use *only* IPv6 protocols and not IPv4. In that case, IPv4 packets could only traverse the network via the 4to6 tunneling protocol. This network would also require static IPv4 routes configured on routers and Layer 3 switches so that 4to6 encapsulated IPv4 packets could arrive, pass through, and leave the network. An example is illustrated in Figure 2-21 where routers A, C, D, and Z are configured to use the 4to6 protocol to tunnel IPv4 packets that arrive from outside the intranet at gateway routers A or Z and are routed through the 4to6 tunnel to the other side of the intranet.

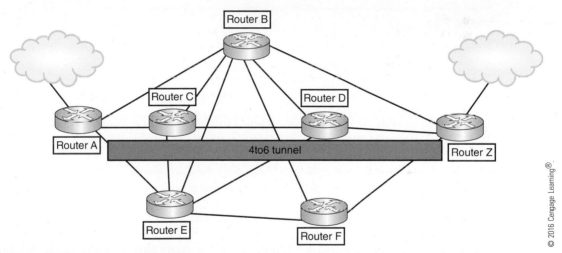

Figure 2-21   A 4to6 tunnel is used to move IPv4 packets through a futuristic IPv6 network that is configured to not use IPv4

© 2016 Cengage Learning®

Tools for Troubleshooting IP Address Problems

Now that you are familiar with the basics of IP addressing, you can learn how to solve problems with IP addresses. Event Viewer is one of the first places to start looking for clues when something goes wrong with a computer. It can provide a lot of valuable information about the problems the computer is experiencing, and may even make suggestions for what to do next. For example, consider the NetBT error shown in Figure 2-22.

When Event Viewer doesn't give the information you need, you might try the command prompt instead. We used the `ipconfig` command in the Command Prompt window earlier

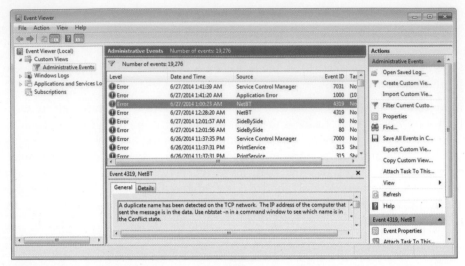

Figure 2-22   Event Viewer provided the diagnosis of a problem and recommended steps to fix the problem
Source: Microsoft LLC

in the chapter. Let's look at a few other tools here, and, in the next chapter, we'll explore a few more. These command-line tools all require a CLI.

> Earlier in the chapter, you learned to access the CLI in Windows. On a Linux system, you'll need to open a shell prompt. The steps for accessing a shell prompt vary depending on the Linux distribution that you're using. For Ubuntu Desktop, click the Dashboard icon at the top of the left sidebar, and, in the Applications group, select Terminal. To close the shell prompt, use the exit command.

ping

Network+
4.2
4.6

The utility **ping** (Packet Internet Groper) is used to verify that TCP/IP is installed, bound to the NIC, configured correctly, and communicating with the network. Think about how a whale sends out a signal and listens for the echo. The nature of the echo can tell the whale a lot of information about the object the original signal bumped into. The ping utility starts by sending out a signal called an echo request to another computer, which is simply a request for a response. The other computer then responds to the request in the form of an echo reply. The process of sending this signal back and forth is known as pinging. The protocol used by the echo request and echo reply is ICMP, a light-weight protocol used to carry error messages and information about the network.

The first tool you should use to test basic connectivity to the network, Internet, and specific hosts is ping. The `ping` command has several options or parameters, and a few of them are listed here:

ping [-a] [-t] [-n] [-?] [IP address] [host name] [/?]

Table 2-7 gives some examples of how these options can be used.

Table 2-7   Options for the `ping` command

Sample `ping` commands	Description
`ping www.google.com`	You can ping a host using its host name to verify you have Internet access and name resolution. Google.com is a reliable site to use for testing. See the results in Figure 2-23.
`ping 8.8.8.8`	Ping an IP address on the Internet to verify you have Internet access. The address 8.8.8.8, which is easy to remember, points to Google's public DNS servers.
`ping -a 8.8.8.8`	Use the `-a` parameter in the command line to test for name resolution and to display the host name to verify DNS is working.
`ping 92.10.11.200`	In this example, `92.10.11.200` is the address of a host on another subnet in your corporate network. This ping shows if you can reach that subnet.
`ping 192.168.1.1`	In this example, `192.168.1.1` is the address of your default gateway. This ping shows if you can reach it.
`ping 127.0.0.1`	Ping the loopback address, 127.0.0.1, to determine whether your workstation's TCP/IP services are running.
`ping localhost`	This is another way of pinging your loopback address.
`ping -?` or `ping /?`	These two commands display the help text for the `ping` command, including its syntax and a full list of parameters.
`ping -t 192.168.1.1`	The `-t` parameter causes pinging to continue until interrupted. To display statistics, press CTRL+Break. To stop pinging, press CTRL+C.
`ping -n 2 192.168.1.1`	The `-n` parameter defines a number of echo requests to send. By default, ping sends four echo requests. In this example, we've limited it to two.

© 2016 Cengage Learning®

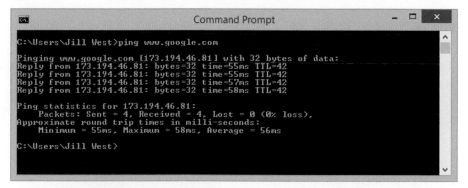

Figure 2-23   Results of a successful `ping`

Source: Microsoft LLC

IPv6 networks use a version of ICMP called **ICMPv6**. Here are two variations of ping for different operating systems, which can be used with IPv6 addresses:

- **ping6**—On Linux computers running IPv6, use `ping6` to verify whether an IPv6 host is available. When you ping a multicast address with `ping6`, you get responses from all IPv6 hosts on that subnet.

- **ping -6**—On Windows computers, use `ping` with the `-6` switch. The `ping -6` command verifies connectivity on IPv6 networks.

In Windows, the -6 parameter is not necessary when pinging an IPv6 address (as opposed to pinging a host name) because the format of the address itself specifies that an IPv6 host is being pinged.

For the ping6 and ping -6 commands to work over the Internet, you must have access to the IPv6 Internet. Your ISP may provide native IPv6 connectivity, or you may be able to use an IPv6 tunnel provided by an IPv6 tunnel broker service, such as Tunnelbroker.net, offered by Hurricane Electric, or SixXS.net. Let's review some sample IPv6 pings. The command ping -6 fe80::20c5:6548:7ba0:b92c pings an IPv6 host on the local subnet using that host's IPv6 address. The results of this ping are shown in Figure 2-24.

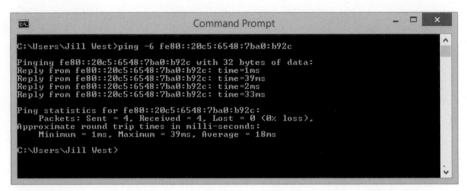

Figure 2-24   An IPv6 `ping` sent to a neighboring computer at the IPv6 address fe80::20c5:6548:7ba0:b92c

Source: Microsoft LLC

In this case, a successful connection shows that the computer issuing the `ping` command does have IPv6 capability, and that the local network supports IPv6 connectivity. Now on your own computer, try pinging Google's IPv6 DNS server, as follows: **ping -6 2001:4860:4860::8888**.

Figure 2-25 shows the results on a computer with an ISP that does not provide access to the IPv6 Internet; the IPv6 ping was unsuccessful.

```
C:\Users\Jill West>ping -6 2001:4860:4860::8888

Pinging 2001:4860:4860::8888 with 32 bytes of data:
Request timed out.
Request timed out.
Request timed out.
Request timed out.

Ping statistics for 2001:4860:4860::8888:
    Packets: Sent = 4, Received = 0, Lost = 4 (100% loss),

C:\Users\Jill West>
```

Figure 2-25   This `ping` failed because the ISP does not provide IPv6 connectivity

Source: Microsoft LLC

As IPv6 connectivity becomes more prevalent, the likelihood of needing to ping an IPv6 host on the open Web increases. The IPv6 address for Google's public DNS servers is relatively easy to remember, if you can remember a couple of simple tips.

The address is **2001:4860:4860::8888**. The IPv6 prefix 2001 is very common—recall that Teredo IP addresses begin with 2001. The next two sections can be typed out on your number pad by rotating clockwise, starting at 4 and ending at 0 (type the 4, 8, and 6 with your first three fingers and the 0 with your thumb), and do this twice. Don't forget the double colon before the next section, which replaces several sections of zeroes, and end with the same 8888 that you memorized for Google's IPv4 address.

ipconfig

You learned about the Windows utility ipconfig earlier in this chapter. Table 2-8 describes some popular parameters for the `ipconfig` command. Notice that, with the `ipconfig` command, you need to type a forward slash (/) before a parameter, rather than a hyphen, as you do with the `ping` command.

Table 2-8   Examples of the `ipconfig` command

`ipconfig` **command**	**Description**
ipconfig /? or ipconfig -?	Displays the help text for the `ipconfig` command, including its syntax and a full list of parameters.
ipconfig /all	Displays TCP/IP configuration information for each network adapter.
ipconfig /release	Releases the IP address when dynamic IP addressing is being used. Releasing the IP address effectively disables the computer's communications with the network until a new IP address is assigned.
ipconfig /release6	Releases an IPv6 IP address.
ipconfig /renew	Leases a new IP address (often the same one you just released) from a DHCP server. To solve problems with duplicate IP addresses, misconfigured DHCP, or misconfigured DNS, reset the TCP/IP connection by using these two commands: ipconfig /release ipconfig /renew
ipconfig /renew6	Leases a new IPv6 IP address from a DHCP IPv6 server.
ipconfig /displaydns	Displays information about name resolutions that Windows currently holds in the DNS resolver cache.
ipconfig /flushdns	Flushes—or clears—the name resolver cache, which might solve a problem when the browser cannot find a host on the Internet or when a misconfigured DNS server has sent wrong information to the resolver cache.

© 2016 Cengage Learning®

ifconfig

On UNIX and Linux systems, use the ifconfig utility to view and manage TCP/IP settings. As with ipconfig on Windows systems, you can use ifconfig to view and modify TCP/IP settings and to release and renew the DHCP configuration.

Remember that Linux and UNIX commands are case sensitive. Be sure to use the `ifconfig` command and not `Ifconfig`.

If your Linux or UNIX system provides a GUI (graphical user interface), first open a shell prompt. At the shell prompt, you can use the `ifconfig` commands listed in Table 2-9.

Table 2-9 Some `ifconfig` commands

`ifconfig` **command**	**Description**
`ifconfig`	Displays basic TCP/IP information and network information, including the MAC address of the NIC.
`ifconfig -a`	Displays TCP/IP information associated with every interface on a Linux device; can be used with other parameters. See Figure 2-26.
`ifconfig down`	Marks the interface, or network connection, as unavailable to the network.
`ifconfig up`	Reinitializes the interface after it has been taken down (via the `ifconfig down` command), so that it is once again available to the network.
`man ifconfig`	Displays the manual pages, called man pages, for the `ifconfig` command, which tells you how to use the command and about command parameters (similar to the `ipconfig /?` command in Windows).

```
                                          Terminal
bill@lab-2 ~ $ ifconfig -a
eth0: flags=4099<UP,BROADCAST,MULTICAST>  mtu 1500  metric 1
         ether 00:21:86:a1:9e:97  txqueuelen 1000  (Ethernet)
         RX packets 840251  bytes 1154908740 (1.0 GiB)
         RX errors 0  dropped 0  overruns 0  frame 0
         TX packets 527337  bytes 52280636 (49.8 MiB)
         TX errors 0  dropped 0 overruns 0  carrier 0  collisions 0
         device interrupt 20  memory 0xfc100000-fc120000

lo: flags=73<UP,LOOPBACK,RUNNING>  mtu 16436  metric 1
         inet 127.0.0.1  netmask 255.0.0.0
         inet6 ::1  prefixlen 128  scopeid 0x10<host>
         loop  txqueuelen 0  (Local Loopback)
         RX packets 517899  bytes 39147630 (37.3 MiB)
         RX errors 0  dropped 0  overruns 0  frame 0
         TX packets 517899  bytes 39147630 (37.3 MiB)
         TX errors 0  dropped 0 overruns 0  carrier 0  collisions 0

sit0: flags=128<NOARP>  mtu 1480  metric 1
         sit  txqueuelen 0  (IPv6-in-IPv4)
         RX packets 0  bytes 0 (0.0 B)
         RX errors 0  dropped 0  overruns 0  frame 0
         TX packets 0  bytes 0 (0.0 B)
         TX errors 0  dropped 0 overruns 0  carrier 0  collisions 0

wlan0: flags=4163<UP,BROADCAST,RUNNING,MULTICAST>  mtu 1500  metric 1
         inet 192.168.1.18  netmask 255.255.255.0  broadcast 192.168.1.255
         inet6 fe80::216:ebff:fe05:86e2  prefixlen 64  scopeid 0x20<link>
         ether 00:16:eb:05:86:e2  txqueuelen 1000  (Ethernet)
         RX packets 572551  bytes 718725120 (685.4 MiB)
         RX errors 0  dropped 0  overruns 0  frame 0
         TX packets 382519  bytes 71994123 (68.6 MiB)
         TX errors 0  dropped 0 overruns 0  carrier 0  collisions 0

bill@lab-2 ~ $ ▮
```

Figure 2-26 Detailed information available through `ifconfig`

Source: The Linux Foundation

NOTE

Other `ifconfig` parameters, such as those that apply to DHCP settings, vary according to the type and version of the UNIX or Linux system you use.

nslookup

The **nslookup** (name space lookup) utility allows you to query the DNS database from any computer on the network and find the host name of a device by specifying its IP address, or vice versa. This is useful for verifying that a host is configured correctly or for troubleshooting DNS resolution problems. For example, if you want to find out whether the host named *www.cengage.com* is operational, enter the command `nslookup www.cengage.com`.

Figure 2-27 shows the result of running a simple `nslookup` command.

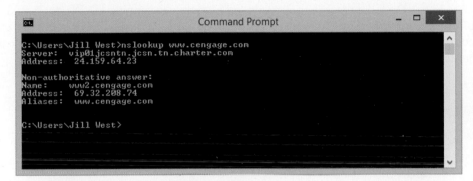

Figure 2-27 `nslookup` shows server and host information

Source: Microsoft LLC

Notice that the command provides the target host's IP address as well as the name and address of the primary DNS server for the local network that provided the information.

To find the host name of a device whose IP address you know, you need to perform a **reverse DNS lookup**: `nslookup 69.32.208.74`. In this case, the response would include the FQDN for the target host and the name and address of the primary DNS server that made the response.

The `nslookup` command is primarily used for troubleshooting DNS servers. If you think your DNS server at IP address 24.159.64.23 is down, you can perform this test: `nslookup 127.0.0.1 24.159.64.23`. This command directs your DNS server at 24.159.64.23 to resolve the identity of the host at 127.0.0.1, which of course is the local host. (See Figure 2-28.)

Figure 2-28 DNS server returns the identity of the local host

Source: Microsoft LLC

The nslookup utility is available in two modes: interactive and noninteractive. So far you've used nslookup in noninteractive mode, which gives a response for a single `nslookup` command. This is fine when you're investigating only one server, or when you're retrieving single items of information at a time. However, to test multiple DNS servers at one time, you'll want to use the nslookup utility in interactive mode, which makes available more of the utility's options. To launch interactive mode, type the `nslookup` command without any parameters and press Enter.

As shown in Figure 2-29, after you enter this command, the command prompt changes to a greater-than symbol (>). You can then use additional commands to find out more about the contents of the DNS database. For example, on a computer running UNIX, you could view a list of all the host name and IP address correlations on a particular DNS server by entering the command `ls`. Or you could specify 5 seconds as the period to wait for a response instead of the default of 10 seconds by entering `timeout=5`.

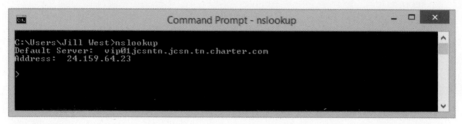

Figure 2-29   Interactive mode of the nslookup utility

Source: Microsoft LLC

You can change DNS servers from within interactive mode with the `server` subcommand and specifying the IP address of the new DNS server. Before using the `server` subcommand, it's helpful to use the `ipconfig /all` command in noninteractive mode to determine what other DNS servers are available. After you pick a DNS server, you can enter nslookup's interactive mode, and then assign a new DNS server with the command: `server 24.217.0.5`. This example, shown in Figure 2-30, assigns a DNS server with the address 24.217.0.5.

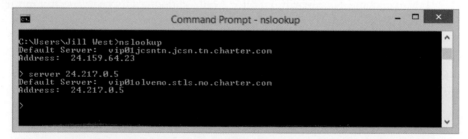

Figure 2-30   The `server` subcommand can be used to change DNS servers

Source: Microsoft LLC

To exit nslookup's interactive mode and return to the normal command prompt, enter `exit`.

Many other nslookup options exist. To see these options on a UNIX or Linux system, use the `man nslookup` command. On a Windows-based system, use the `nslookup ?` command.

Chapter Summary

Overview of Addressing on Networks

■ Hosts on a network are assigned host names, which include the organization's domain name. DNS keeps track of which host name belongs to each IP address.

■ Applications are assigned one or more port numbers to communicate with other applications.

■ IPv4 addresses have 32 bits and are written as four decimal numbers called octets. IPv6 addresses have 128 bits and are written as eight blocks of hexadecimal numbers.

■ Every NIC on the globe is assigned a unique 48-bit MAC address, which is frequently written as 12 hexadecimal numerals separated by colons. The first part of the MAC address is the 24-bit OUI, which identifies the NIC's manufacturer. The second part is the 24-bit device ID, which is based on the NIC's model and manufacture date.

■ You can assign a static IP address to a computer or device, or you can configure a device to receive a dynamic IP address from a DHCP server each time the device connects to the network.

■ Use the `ipconfig` command in the Command Prompt window to view IP configuration information. `ipconfig /all` shows more complete configuration information.

How Host Names and Domain Names Work

■ A fully qualified domain name (FQDN) includes both a host name portion and a domain name portion. The last part of a host name is the top-level domain (TLD).

■ Name resolution is the process of matching an FQDN to its IP address.

■ The hosts file is a text file that contains a list of IP addresses and associated host names. In UNIX or Linux, the hosts file is stored in the /etc directory. On a Windows computer, the hosts file is located in the \Windows\System32\drivers\etc folder.

■ DNS is an automated name resolution service that operates at the Application layer. The DNS namespace is the entire collection of computer names and their associated IP addresses stored in databases around the world. Hierarchical name servers hold these databases, and resolvers request the information from the name servers.

■ DNS root servers hold information used to locate TLD servers. TLD servers hold information about authoritative servers, which maintain authoritative records of computer names and IP addresses in their domains.

■ A resolver on the client computer sends a recursive query, which demands resolution, to a local DNS server; the local server takes responsibility for ensuring that a recursive query is resolved. The local server sends iterative queries to other servers—that is, it sends queries that the other servers respond to with whatever information they have. Iterative queries do not require a resolution.

■ DNS data is spread throughout the globe in a distributed database model. Each hosting organization is responsible for providing DNS authoritative servers for public access to the DNS zone it manages.

- Several DNS server software options are available, the most popular being BIND (Berkeley Internet Name Domain).

- Windows Server includes its own Microsoft DNS Server, which can be configured as an integral part of Active Directory. A split DNS design places a separate DNS server in the DMZ for public access in order to protect Active Directory and the rest of an organization's internal network from the outer Web.

- Five common types of DNS resource records are A (Address) records, AAAA (Address) records, CNAME (Canonical Name) records, PTR (Pointer) records, and MX (Mail Exchanger) records.

- Small organizations may choose to use DDNS (Dynamic DNS) to report on IP address assignment changes to their Web server and Web sites when they don't want to pay for a static IP address.

How Ports and Sockets Work

- An IP address and a port number written together, for example 10.43.3.87:23, is called a socket. During a communication session, the socket is open. When the session is complete, the socket is closed.

- Well-known ports range from 0 to 1023 and are assigned by IANA. Registered ports range from 1024 to 49151; only default assignments of these ports are registered with IANA. Dynamic ports and private ports range from 49152 to 65535 and are open for use without restriction.

- You can use a packet analyzer to collect and examine network messages that use several protocols, including SNMP, SSH, TFTP, NTP, SMB, CIFS, SIP, H.323, and MGCP.

How IP Addresses Are Formatted and Assigned

- Each of the four octets in an IPv4 address can be any number from 0 to 255, making a total of about 4.3 billion possible IPv4 addresses.

- Class A addresses range from 1.x.y.z to 126.x.y.z. Class B addresses range from 128.0.x.y to 191.255.x.y. Class C addresses range from 192.0.0.x to 223.255.255.x. Reserved IPv4 addresses include 255.255.255.255, 0.0.0.0, and 127.0.0.1.

- You can define a range of available IP addresses in DHCP, or assign a static IP address as a DHCP reservation, such as for a network printer.

- Classes A, B, and C IP addresses are available as both public and private addresses. Class A private addresses are 10.0.0.0 through 10.255.255.255. Class B private addresses are 172.16.0.0 through 172.31.255.255. Class C private addresses are 192.168.0.0 through 192.168.255.255.

- NAT (Network Address Translation) is used to allow devices that have private IP addresses access to the Internet and to protect these devices on a private network from direct exposure to the Internet. Translation table entries can be used to configure static NAT assignments.

- According to IPv6 standards, a link is any local area network bounded by routers. An interface is a node's attachment to a link. The last 64 bits of an IPv6 address are the interface identifier. Neighbors are two or more nodes on the same link.

- Tunneling protocols are used to allow IPv6 packets to travel over or through an IPv4 network: ISATAP, Teredo, Miredo, and 6to4. The 4to6 protocol is a futuristic protocol intended to be used to tunnel IPv4 packets over an IPv6 network that does not support IPv4 traffic.

- The three types of IPv6 addresses are unicast, multicast, and anycast addresses. Two types of unicast addresses are global and link local addresses.

- IPv6 addressing is designed so a computer can configure its own link local or global IP address without the help of a DHCPv6 server. The settings for this autoconfiguration feature can be adjusted to generate a random number, or to use the NIC's MAC address to define the last 64 bits of the address.

Tools for Troubleshooting IP Address Problems

- The ping utility uses ICMP to verify that TCP/IP is installed, bound to the NIC, configured correctly, and communicating with the network.

- The ipconfig utility is useful for viewing and adjusting a Windows computer's TCP/IP settings.

- On UNIX and Linux systems, the ifconfig utility is used to view and manage TCP/IP settings, including DHCP configuration.

- The nslookup utility allows you to query the DNS database from any computer on the network. You can use nslookup in interactive mode to test multiple DNS servers at a time and change the DNS server selected for the device.

Key Terms

For definitions of key terms, see the Glossary near the end of the book.

4to6

6to4

A (Address) record

AAAA (Address) record

address translation

alias

anycast address

authoritative server

Automatic Private IP Addressing (APIPA)

base 2 number system

base 8 number system

binary number system

BIND (Berkeley Internet Name Domain)

bit

block ID

caching-only server

canonical name

CIFS (Common Internet File System)

Class A

Class B

Class C

CNAME (Canonical Name) record

command-line interface (CLI)

company-ID

computer name

DDNS (Dynamic DNS)

default gateway

device ID

DHCP (Dynamic Host Configuration Protocol)

DHCP6

DHCPv6

DHCP scope

distributed database model

DMZ (demilitarized zone)

DNS (Domain Name System or Domain Name Service)

DNS cache

DNS server

DNS zone

domain name

dual stacked

dynamic IP address

Dynamic Network Address Translation (DNAT)

dynamic port

elevated command prompt window

EUI-64 (Extended Unique Identifier-64)

extension identifier

firewall

fully qualified domain name (FQDN)

fully qualified host name

gateway

global address

global unicast address

H.323

hex number

hexadecimal number

host name

host table

hosts file

ICMPv6

ifconfig

interface

interface ID

Internet Corporation for Assigned Names and Numbers (ICANN)

Internet Protocol version 4 (IPv4)

Internet Protocol version 6 (IPv6)

ipconfig

ISATAP (Intra-Site Automatic Tunnel Addressing Protocol)

iterative query

link

link local address

link local unicast address

local link

loopback address

loopback interface

MGCP (Media Gateway Control Protocol)

Miredo

multicast address

multicasting

MX (Mail Exchanger) record

name resolution

name server

namespace

neighbor

NetBIOS

NetBT (NetBIOS over TCP/IP)

Network Address Translation (NAT)

nslookup (name space lookup)

NTP (Network Time Protocol)

octal number system

octet

open source

OUI (Organizationally Unique Identifier)

packet analyzer

ping (Packet Internet Groper)

ping -6

ping6

Port Address Translation (PAT)

private IP address

private port

protocol analyzer

PTR (Pointer) record

public IP address

recursive query

registered port

reservation

resolver

resource record

reverse DNS lookup

root server

Samba

scope ID

shell prompt

signaling protocol

SIP (Session Initiation Protocol)

SMB (Server Message Block)

SNMP (Simple Network Management Protocol)

socket

split DNS

split-horizon DNS

static IP address

Static Network Address Translation (SNAT)

subnet

subnet ID

subnet mask

Teredo

TFTP (Trivial File Transfer Protocol)

Time to Live field

top-level domain (TLD)

tunneling

unicast address

vim text editor

well-known port

zone file

zone ID

zone transfer

Review Questions

1. Which part of a MAC address is unique to each manufacturer?

    a. The network identifier

    b. The OUI

    c. The device identifier

    d. The physical address

2. What decimal number corresponds to the binary number 11111111?

   a. 255

   b. 256

   c. 127

   d. 11111111

3. What type of device does a computer turn to first when attempting to make contact with a host on another network?

   a. Default gateway

   b. DNS server

   c. Root server

   d. DHCP server

4. Which statement describes SMTP?

   a. SMTP is a connectionless protocol that uses UDP

   b. SMTP is a connection-based protocol that uses UDP

   c. SMTP is a connectionless protocol that uses TCP

   d. SMTP is a connection-based protocol that uses TCP

5. When your computer first joins an IPv6 network, what is the prefix of the IP address the computer first configures for itself?

   a. FE80::/10

   b. FF00::/8

   c. 2001::/64

   d. 2001::/3

6. You have just brought online a new secondary DNS server and notice your monitoring software reports a significant increase in network traffic. Which two hosts on your network are likely to be causing the increased traffic and why?

   a. The caching and primary DNS servers, because the caching server is requesting zone transfers from the primary server

   b. The secondary and primary DNS servers, because the secondary server is requesting zone transfers from the primary server

   c. The root and primary DNS servers, because the primary server is requesting zone transfers from the root server.

   d. The Web server and primary DNS server, because the Web server is requesting zone transfers from the primary DNS server.

7. Suppose you send data to the 11111111 11111111 11111111 11111111 IP address on an IPv4 network. To which device(s) are you transmitting?

   a. All devices on the Internet

   b. All devices on your local network

   c. The one device with this given IP address

   d. Because no device can have this given IP address, no devices receive the transmission

8. If you are connected to a network that uses DHCP, and you need to terminate your Windows workstation's DHCP lease, which command would you use?

   a. `ipconfig/release`

   b. `ipconfig/renew`

   c. `ifconfig/release`

   d. `ifconfig/new`

9. What computers are the highest authorities in the Domain Name System hierarchy?

   a. Authoritative name servers

   b. Root servers

   c. Top-level domain servers

   d. Primary DNS server

10. What version of SMB can be used across Windows, UNIX, and other operating systems?

   a. SIP (Session Initiation Protocol)

   b. RDP (Remote Desktop Protocol)

   c. CIFS (Common Internet File System)

   d. MGCP (Media Gateway Control Protocol)

11. Suppose you want to change the default port for RDP as a security precaution. What port does RDP use by default, and from what range of numbers should you select a private port number?

12. Which type of DNS record identifies a mail server?

13. How many bits does an IPv6 address contain?

14. On what port is an IPv6 client listening for DHCP messages?

15. The second 64 bits of an autoconfigured IPv6 address may either be random or generated from the computer's MAC address, which contains 48 bits. What standard defines the conversion of the MAC address to the IPv6 64-bit device ID?

16. You issue a transmission from your workstation to the following socket on your LAN: 10.1.1.145:110. Assuming your network uses standard port designations, what Application layer protocol are you using?

17. What protocol does a network gateway use to keep track of which internal client is talking to which external Web server?

18. You are the network manager for a computer training center that allows clients to bring their own laptops to class for learning and taking notes. Clients need access to the Internet, so you have configured your network's DHCP server to issue IP addresses automatically. What DHCP option should you modify to make sure you are not wasting addresses that were used by clients who have left for the day?

19. What is the range of IP addresses that might be assigned by APIPA?

20. While troubleshooting a network connection problem for a coworker, you discover the computer is querying a nonexistent DNS server. What command-line utility can you use to assign the correct DNS server IP address?

21. FTP sometimes uses a random port for data transfer, but an FTP server always, unless programmed otherwise, listens to the same port for session requests from clients. What port is the FTP server listening on?

22. While troubleshooting a network connection problem for a coworker, you discover that the computer has a static IP address and is giving a duplicate IP address error. What command-line utility can you use to find out what other device may already be using that IP address?

23. What is the IPv4 loopback address? What is the IPv6 loopback address?

24. You have just set up a new wireless network in your house, and you want to determine whether your Linux laptop has connected to it and obtained a valid IP address. What command will give you the information you need?

25. You have decided to use SNAT and PAT on your small office network. At minimum, how many IP addresses must you obtain from your ISP for all five clients in your office to be able to access servers on the Internet?

26. If you know that your colleague's TCP/IP host name is JSMITH, and you need to find out his IP address, what command should you type at your shell prompt or command prompt?

27. When determining whether a local network has any NetBIOS traffic, do you use the nslookup utility in interactive mode or a packet analyzer such as Wireshark?

28. List three signaling protocols discussed in the chapter that are used for communicating multimedia data.

29. What version of the ping command do you use in Windows with IPv6 addresses? What version do you use on a Linux system?

30. When running a scan on your computer, you find that a session has been established with a host at the address 208.85.40.44:80. Which protocol is in use for this session? What command-line utility might you use to find out who the host is?

Hands-On Projects

Project 2-1: Create a NAT Translation Table Entry

Your corporation hosts a Web site at the static public IP address 92.110.30.123. A router directs this traffic to a Web server at the private IP address 192.168.11.100. However, the Web server needs a hardware upgrade and will be down for two days. Your network administrator has asked you to configure the router so that requests to the IP address 92.110.30.123 are redirected to the backup server for the Web site, which has the private IP address 192.168.11.110. The router's inside Ethernet interface uses IP address 192.168.11.254 and its outside interface uses the IP address 92.110.30.65. Answer the following questions about the new static route you'll be creating:

1. What is the router's outside interface IP address?

2. What is the router's inside interface IP address?

3. What is the Web site's public IP address?

4. What is the private IP address of the backup Web server?

Use the example given earlier in the chapter as a template to create the NAT translation table entries for the address translation. For the subnet masks, use the default subnet mask for a Class C IP address license. Include appropriate comment lines in your table.

Project 2-2: View and Change IPv6 Autoconfiguration

By default, when configuring an IPv6 address, Windows 8 generates a random number to fill out the bits needed for the NIC portion of the IPv6 address. This security measure helps conceal your device's MAC address, and further protects your privacy by generating a new number every so often. There may be times, however, when you need your system to maintain a static IPv6 address. To do this, you can disable the temporary IPv6 address feature using the Netsh utility in an elevated command prompt window. Do the following:

1. Open an elevated command prompt window.

2. Find your computer's current IPv6 address and MAC address. Carefully compare the two addresses. Are they in any way numerically related?

3. To disable the random IP address generation feature, enter the command:

    `netsh interface ipv6 set global randomizeidentifiers=disabled`

4. To instruct Windows to use the EUI-64 standard instead of the default settings, use this command:

    `netsh interface ipv6 set privacy state=disabled`

5. What is your computer's new IPv6 address? Notice that the fixed value FF FE has been inserted halfway through the MAC address values in the second half of the IPv6 address. Note that the host portion of the IPv6 address may look slightly different because of the way the values are converted for use by IPv6. Recall that the seventh bit of the MAC address is inverted, resulting in a slightly different value.

6. Reenable random IPv6 address generation with these commands:

    `netsh interface ipv6 set global randomizeidentifiers=enabled`
    `netsh interface ipv6 set privacy state=enabled`

Project 2-3: Manage DNS

You have learned that clients as well as name servers store DNS information to associate names with IP addresses. In this project, you view the contents of a local DNS cache, clear it, and view it again after performing some DNS lookups. Then you change DNS servers and view the DNS cache once again.

1. To view the DNS cache, open a command prompt and enter the following command: `ipconfig /displaydns`

2. If this computer has been used to resolve host names with IP addresses—for example, if it has been used to retrieve mail or browse the Web—a list of locally cached resource records appears. Read the file to see what kinds of records have been saved, using the scroll bar if necessary. How many are A records and how many are a different type, such as CNAME?

3. Next clear the DNS cache with this command: `ipconfig /flushdns`

The operating system confirms that the DNS resolver cache has been flushed. One circumstance in which you might want to empty a client's DNS cache is if the client needs to reach a host whose IP address has changed (for example, a Web site whose server was moved to a different hosting company). As long as the DNS information is locally cached, the client will continue to look for the host at the old location. Clearing the cache allows the client to retrieve the new IP address for the host.

4. View the DNS cache again with the command: `ipconfig /displaydns`

Because you just emptied the DNS cache, you will receive a message that indicates that Windows could not display the DNS resolver cache. (See Figure 2-31.)

Figure 2-31   This DNS cache is empty

Source: Microsoft LLC

5. Switch to your browser window and go to **www.cengage.com**. Next go to **www.google.com**. Finally, go to **www.loc.gov**.

6. Return to the Command Prompt window and view the DNS cache once more to see a new list of resource records using this command: `ipconfig /displaydns`

7. Scroll up through the list of resource records and note how many associations were saved in your local DNS cache after visiting just three Web sites. How many hosts are identified for each site you visited? What type of record is most common? Can you think of any situations, other than wanting to reach a host that has moved to a different address, in which you might want to clear your DNS cache?

By default, DHCP supplies the IP addresses of DNS servers when you first connect to a network. When traveling, you can still use your organization's DNS servers, even when they are far away from your laptop. Doing so means you don't have to rely on DNS servers provided by a public hot spot, which might be controlled by hackers.

Follow these steps to view or change the name server information on a Windows 8.1 workstation:

8. Open the Network and Sharing Center and click **Change adapter settings**.

9. Right-click the connection you want to configure, and click **Properties** on the shortcut menu. Respond to the UAC box as necessary.

10. On the Networking tab under "This connection uses the following items," select **Internet Protocol Version 4 (TCP/IPv4)**, and click **Properties**. The Internet Protocol Version 4 (TCP/ IPv4) Properties dialog box opens.

11. To change the default settings and specify the DNS server for your workstation, rather than allowing DHCP to supply the DNS server address, on the General tab, click **Use the following DNS server addresses**.

12. Enter the IP address for your primary DNS server in the Preferred DNS server space and the address for your secondary DNS server in the Alternate DNS server space. For the purposes of this project, if your instructor has not specified another DNS server, you can point to Google's public DNS servers. Use 8.8.8.8 as the Preferred DNS server and 8.8.4.4 as the Alternate DNS server.

13. Now that you have changed your DNS servers, will you still have DNS data stored in your DNS cache? To find out, return to the command prompt and view the DNS cache to see what records are still there. Then close all windows, saving your changes.

Project 2-4: Set Up an FTP Server

In this project, using the small network you created in Chapter 1 in Project 1-1, you install and use FTP, which is a client-server application. Designate one computer as computer A, the server, and the other computer as computer B, the client. Do the following using computer A:

1. Create a folder named **Normal Users** and create a file in the folder named **Normal Users.txt**. Later, any files or folders you want on your FTP site can be stored in this folder.

2. Go to **filezilla-project.org** and download the free FTP FileZilla Server software to your desktop and install the software. As you do so, be sure to not accept other free software the site offers. You might need to restart the installation as you reject other software.

3. When the FileZilla server installs, accept all default settings, which places a shortcut on your desktop and sets the FTP service to start automatically.

4. During the installation, the Connect to Server dialog box appears (see Figure 2-32). Enter an administration password and be sure to write down this password. Because you're running only one FTP server on computer A, check the **Always connect to this server** check box. Also note the Server Address is 127.0.0.1, which is your loopback IP address. When you click OK, the FileZilla Server admin window opens. You can also open the admin window by using the shortcut on your desktop.

5. You're now ready to configure your FTP server. To set up a user group, click **Edit, Groups**. In the right pane under Groups, click **Add**. In the Add user group dialog box, type **Normal Users** and click **OK**.

6. Under Directories, click **Add**. Point to the **Normal Users** folder and click **OK**. The folder is listed under Directories. Under Directories, select the **Normal Users** directory and then click **Set as home dir**. Click **OK**.

7. Next, click **Edit, Users**, and create a new user named **User1**. Put the user in the **Normal Users** group.

Figure 2-32   Enter the admin password used to log on and manage the FileZilla FTP server

Source: Microsoft LLC

8. In the Account settings pane, check **Password** and assign the password **password**. Click **OK**.

9. To verify the service is working, let's use the FTP client commands embedded in Windows. As you work, watch the dialogue recorded in the FileZilla Server window (see Figure 2-33). Open a Command Prompt window and enter the following:

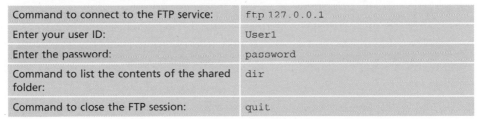

Command to connect to the FTP service:	ftp 127.0.0.1
Enter your user ID:	User1
Enter the password:	password
Command to list the contents of the shared folder:	dir
Command to close the FTP session:	quit

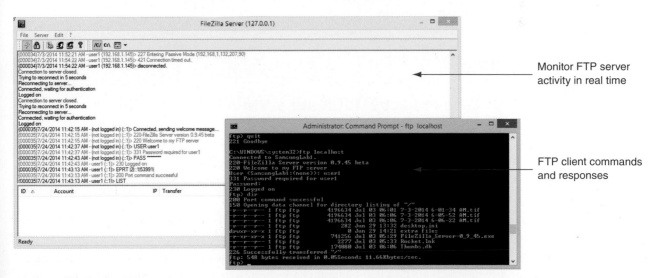

Figure 2-33   Use the FileZilla Server window to monitor real-time activity on the FTP server

Source: Microsoft LLC

10. In the FileZilla Server window, click **Edit, Settings**. Under General settings, note that the server is listening at port 21. You can now close the window.

11. The server software is still running as a background service, listening at port 21 for clients to initiate a session. To see the service running, open the Windows Services console. To do so, right-click **Start**, click **Run**, type **services.msc**, and press **Enter**. In the Services console, verify that the FileZilla service is running and set to start automatically each time the computer starts. Close the Services console.

12. To find out the IP address of computer A, in the Command Prompt window, enter **ipconfig**. What is the IP address?

Using computer B, you're now ready to test the FTP client. Do the following:

13. Open a Command Prompt window and ping computer A. The ping should give replies from computer A, indicating connectivity.

14. Now try the same commands as in step 8 above, using the IP address of computer A in the first command line. Most likely, you will not be able to connect because the firewall on computer A blocks incoming connections on port 21 by default.

On computer A, do the following to open port 21:

15. In the Network and Sharing Center, click **Windows Firewall**. In the Windows Firewall window, click **Advanced settings**. In the left pane, click **Inbound Rules** and then click **New Rule** in the right pane. Create a new rule that opens the TCP local port 21.

On computer B, you should now be able to open an FTP session with computer A. Do the following:

16. Using the entries listed in step 8 and the IP address of computer A, open the session and verify you can see the contents of the shared folder. Quit the session and close the Command Prompt window.

Case Projects

Case Project 2-1: Create a VM and Install Ubuntu Desktop

In the case projects of Chapter 1, you created a virtual machine using Windows 8.1 Client Hyper-V or Oracle VirtualBox. In this case study, you create a second VM in your virtual network and install Ubuntu Desktop in the VM. In the Chapter 3, you'll install Ubuntu Server in your network.

Using the same computer that you used in Case Project 1-1 or 1-2 that has Client Hyper-V or Oracle VirtualBox installed, follow these steps:

1. Go to **ubuntu.com** and download the Ubuntu Desktop OS to your hard drive. The file that downloads is an ISO file. Ubuntu is a well-known version of Linux and offers both desktop and server editions.

2. Open the Oracle VM VirtualBox Manager or Hyper-V Manager. Following the directions in Chapter 1 case projects, create a new VM named VM2. Mount the ISO file that contains the Ubuntu Desktop download to a virtual DVD in your VM.

3. Start up the VM and install Ubuntu Desktop, accepting all default settings (see Figure 2-34). When given the option, don't install any extra software bundled with the OS. You'll need to restart the VM when the installation is done.

Figure 2-34   Ubuntu Desktop is installed in a VM in Windows 8.1 Client Hyper-V

Source: Microsoft LLC

4. To verify you have an Internet connection, open the Mozilla Firefox browser and surf the Web.

Good network technicians must know how to use many operating systems. Poke around in the Ubuntu Desktop interface and get familiar with it. What can you do with the Dashboard icon at the top of the left sidebar? You can also search the Web for tutorials and YouTube videos on how to use Ubuntu Desktop. When you're ready to shut down your VM, click the gear icon in the upper-right corner of the Ubuntu Desktop screen and click **Shut Down** in the menu that appears.

Case Project 2-2: Install and Use Wireshark

Wireshark is a free, open source network protocol analyzer that can help demystify network messages and help make the OSI model a little more tangible. Using Wireshark for the first time can be an epiphany experience for you. You can study the OSI layers, all of the information that is added to every message, and all of the messages that have to go back and forth just to bring up a Web page or even just to connect to the network. It all becomes much more real when you see how many packets Wireshark collects during even a short capture.

We'll install Wireshark in this project and take a first look at how it works. In later chapters, we'll dig deeper into Wireshark's capabilities.

1. To begin, go to the Web site at **wireshark.org**. Download and install the appropriate version for your OS.

You may also need to install WinPcap during the Wireshark installation process. WinPcap is a Windows service that does not come standard in Windows, but is required to capture live network data. You can keep the default setting presented in the Wireshark installer to start WinPcap at boot time, but consider unchecking this option if other, nonadministrative users of the computer should not have access to live network data.

2. To start our first capture, in the Wireshark Network Analyzer window, look in the Capture pane under the Start group and select your network interface. Then click **Start**. While the capture is running, challenge your network a bit by opening a couple of Web pages, sending an email with a local email client, or pinging other hosts on the network.

3. You can adjust the pane sizes by grabbing a border between them and dragging. Expand the top pane so you can see more of the captured packets at one time.

4. Let the capture run for a couple of minutes, and then click **Stop** on the command ribbon.

Take a look at some of the items you might have captured, and start to decode this blur of numbers and letters.

The color highlighting can help you begin to make sense of what's on the screen. Notice in Figure 2-35 that TCP messages are a light gray color, SMB2 packets are a yellowish color, and pnrp packets are a light bluish color. You can see the protocol names in the Protocol column.

No.	Time	Source	Destination	Protocol	Length	Info
387	115.279062	fe80::b99f:35be:2c3	fe80::20c5:6548:7ba	SMB2	342	Create Response File: Jill West\Documents\2015 Net+
388	115.279349	fe80::20c5:6548:7ba	fe80::b99f:35be:2c3	SMB2	174	Notify Request File: Jill West\Documents
389	115.281175	fe80::20c5:6548:7ba	fe80::b99f:35be:2c3	SMB2	280	Find Request File: Jill West\Documents\2015 Net+ SMB2_FIND_ID_E
390	115.281329	fe80::b99f:35be:2c3	fe80::20c5:6548:7ba	TCP	74	microsoft-ds > 51715 [ACK] Seq=1912 Ack=2302 Win=258 Len=0
391	115.283423	fe80::b99f:35be:2c3	fe80::20c5:6548:7ba	TCP	1514	[TCP segment of a reassembled PDU]
392	115.283461	fe80::b99f:35be:2c3	fe80::20c5:6548:7ba	TCP	1514	[TCP segment of a reassembled PDU]
393	115.283491	fe80::b99f:35be:2c3	fe80::20c5:6548:7ba	SMB2	358	Find Response;Find Response, Error: STATUS_NO_MORE_FILES
394	115.287874	fe80::20c5:6548:7ba	fe80::b99f:35be:2c3	TCP	74	51715 > microsoft-ds [ACK] Seq=2302 Ack=4792 Win=258 Len=0
395	115.288260	fe80::20c5:6548:7ba	fe80::b99f:35be:2c3	SMB2	166	Close Request File: Jill West\Documents\2015 Net+
396	115.288611	fe80::b99f:35be:2c3	fe80::20c5:6548:7ba	SMB2	202	Close Response
397	115.289396	fe80::b99f:35be:2c3	fe80::20c5:6548:7ba	SMB2	151	Notify Response, Error: STATUS_PENDING
398	115.291304	fe80::20c5:6548:7ba	fe80::b99f:35be:2c3	TCP	74	51715 > microsoft-ds [ACK] Seq=2394 Ack=5281 Win=256 Len=0
399	115.351788	fe80::b99f:35be:2c3	fe80::20c5:6548:7ba	pnrp	284	PNRP LOOKUP Message
400	115.353860	fe80::20c5:6548:7ba	fe80::b99f:35be:2c3	pnrp	96	PNRP AUTHORITY Message
401	115.354064	fe80::b99f:35be:2c3	fe80::20c5:6548:7ba	pnrp	138	PNRP INQUIRE Message
402	115.358557	fe80::20c5:6548:7ba	fe80::b99f:35be:2c3	pnrp	1278	PNRP AUTHORITY Message [Malformed Packet]
403	115.359264	fe80::20c5:6548:7ba	fe80::b99f:35be:2c3	pnrp	1278	PNRP AUTHORITY Message
404	115.359336	fe80::20c5:6548:7ba	fe80::b99f:35be:2c3	pnrp	1278	PNRP AUTHORITY Message

Figure 2-35   Different highlight colors correspond to different protocols

Source: The Wireshark Foundation

5. To see a list of all colors used for highlighting that are currently assigned and to adjust these assignments, click the **Edit coloring rules** button. Here, you can change the priority for matching protocols to colors (because often more than one protocol is used in a single message), and you can assign colors that are easier to spot. In Figure 2-36, the assigned color for TCP is a bright green.

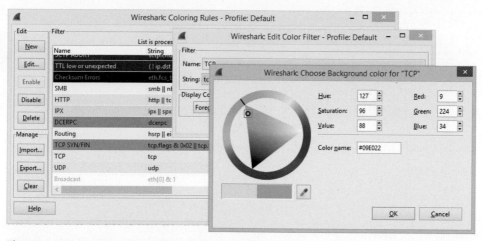

Figure 2-36   Choose colors that are easier to spot

Source: The Wireshark Foundation

6. To filter for a particular kind of packet, type the name of the protocol in the Filter box. Figure 2-37 shows Wireshark filtered for ICMPv6 packets. Try filtering for other protocols discussed earlier in this chapter and see how many different types you can find in your capture. Click **Clear** between searches to return to the complete capture data.

| Filter: | icmpv6 | | | Expression... | Clear | Apply | Save |

No.	Time	Source	Destination	Protocol	Length	Info
17	4.74651800	fe80::b99f:35be:2c3	fe80::20c5:6548:7ba	ICMPv6	86	Neighbor Solicitation for fe
18	4.74866600	fe80::20c5:6548:7ba	fe80::b99f:35be:2c3	ICMPv6	86	Neighbor Advertisement fe80:
31	8.29354000	fe80::ac0d:a107:e19	ff02::1:ff3c:b584	ICMPv6	86	Neighbor Solicitation for fe
32	8.29381900	fe80::b99f:35be:2c3	ff02::1:ff91:a964	ICMPv6	86	Neighbor Solicitation for fe
39	8.40252500	fe80::ac0d:a107:e19	fe80::b99f:35be:2c3	ICMPv6	86	Neighbor Advertisement fe80:

Figure 2-37   Use the filter to narrow your search

Source: The Wireshark Foundation

7. To compare OSI layers represented by each of these protocols, do a slightly more complicated filter where you can see both HTTP packets and ICMPv6 packets in the same search. Enter the following fields into the Filter box: **http or icmpv6**.

8. Look at an ICMPv6 packet and count how many sections of information are available in the middle pane. In Figure 2-38, there are four sections of information, which correspond to Layer 2 (Frame and Ethernet II) and Layer 3 (Internet Protocol Version 6 and Internet Control Message Protocol v6).

9. Examine an HTTP packet (in Figure 2-39, the labeled protocol is SSDP). In Figure 2-39, there are now five sections of information. This time, Layer 7 (Hypertext Transfer Protocol) and Layer 4 (User Datagram Protocol) are represented, in addition to Layer 3 (Internet Protocol Version 4) and Layer 2 (Ethernet II and Frame).

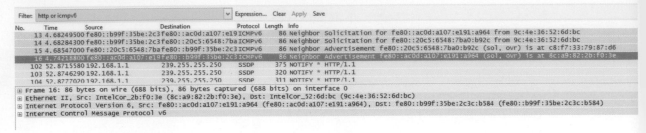

Figure 2-38 Use the middle pane to dig into each layer's headers

Source: The Wireshark Foundation

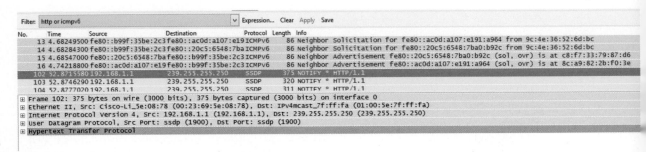

Figure 2-39 This HTTP message is using UDP

Source: The Wireshark Foundation

10. Recall that TCP is a connection-oriented protocol. You can filter a capture to follow a TCP stream so you can see how these messages go back and forth for a single session. Find a TCP packet, right-click it, and select **Follow TCP Stream**. Next, close the Follow TCP Stream window and note that Wireshark has filtered the capture for this stream's packets.

11. Select a TCP message from this filtered data, and explore the middle pane. Click to open each section in that pane. In Figure 2-40, Frame 229 is opened, and the list for the Flags bits is expanded. Notice that the Acknowledgment bit is set, which corresponds to the (ACK) flag on the packet Info in the top pane. You'll learn about these flags in the next chapter.

```
No.     Time        Source              Destination         Protocol Length  Info
      229 90.1321460 fe80::20c5:6548:7ba fe80::b99f:35be:2c3 TCP      86  [TCP Keep-Alive ACK] 51715 > microsoft-ds [ACK] Seq=2 Ack=1 Win=258 Len=0 SLE=0 SRE=1
      354 114.256129 fe80::b99f:35be:2c3 fe80::20c5:6548:7ba SMB2     186 Break Response
      355 114.256263 fe80::b99f:35be:2c3 fe80::20c5:6548:7ba SMB2     180 Notify Response
      356 114.258057 fe80::20c5:6548:7ba fe80::b99f:35be:2c3 SMB2     166 Close Request
⊞ Frame 229: 86 bytes on wire (688 bits), 86 bytes captured (688 bits) on interface 0
⊞ Ethernet II, Src: IntelCor_79:87:d6 (c8:f7:33:79:87:d6), Dst: IntelCor_52:6d:bc (9c:4e:36:52:6d:bc)
⊞ Internet Protocol Version 6, Src: fe80::20c5:6548:7ba0:b92c (fe80::20c5:6548:7ba0:b92c), Dst: fe80::b99f:35be:2c3c:b584 (fe80::b99f:35be:2c3c:b584)
⊟ Transmission Control Protocol, Src Port: 51715 (51715), Dst Port: microsoft-ds (445), Seq: 2, Ack: 1, Len: 0
     Source port: 51715 (51715)
     Destination port: microsoft-ds (445)
     [Stream index: 0]
     Sequence number: 2     (relative sequence number)
     Acknowledgment number: 1     (relative ack number)
     Header length: 32 bytes
  ⊟ Flags: 0x010 (ACK)
       000. .... .... = Reserved: Not set
       ...0 .... .... = Nonce: Not set
       .... 0... .... = Congestion Window Reduced (CWR): Not set
       .... .0.. .... = ECN-Echo: Not set
       .... ..0. .... = Urgent: Not set
       .... ...1 .... = Acknowledgment: Set
       .... .... 0... = Push: Not set
       .... .... .0.. = Reset: Not set
       .... .... ..0. = Syn: Not set
       .... .... ...0 = Fin: Not set
     Window size value: 258
     [Calculated window size: 258]
     [Window size scaling factor: -1 (unknown)]
  ⊞ Checksum: 0x3744 [validation disabled]
  ⊞ Options: (12 bytes), No-Operation (NOP), No-Operation (NOP), SACK
  ⊞ [SEQ/ACK analysis]
```

Figure 2-40 Other TCP segments might have other bits set

Source: The Wireshark Foundation

12. Click **Close this capture file** without saving the file. This returns you to the Wireshark home page, where you can open saved capture files, or you can look through sample captures. Click **Sample Captures** to go to the Wireshark wiki site where you can find samples of many different types of captures. Browse through some of these to become familiar with what to look for when examining different types of messages.

## chapter 3

How Data Is Transported Over Networks

After reading this chapter and completing the exercises, you will be able to:

- Identify and explain the functions of the core TCP/IP protocols
- Explain the purposes and properties of routing and describe common IPv4 and IPv6 routing protocols
- Employ multiple TCP/IP utilities for network discovery and troubleshooting

On the Job

I woke up to a message from an on-call engineer, Bill, saying, "Help, I am out of ideas for DNS troubleshooting!" Twenty minutes later, as I walked into the office, he recited a chaotic list of all the troubleshooting steps he took and every possible problem that could have caused the issue at hand. We took a walk to the vending machines so I could get caffeine and the story.

Dying server hardware forced Bill to move a number of services to new hardware. DNS was scheduled to be last, as the configuration was simple, and moving it was supposed to be a quick and easy task. Everything seemed to work fine, but queries for all of the Internet and a test internal domain were not being answered. The OS configuration and DNS server settings all seemed fine, but no matter what we tweaked, the service did not work right.

Because Bill knew more about DNS than I did, there was little reason for a detailed walk-through of the configurations. I took a quick look, in hope of finding something obvious that he had missed, but the configuration was sound. Because no trivial fix was available, I reverted to basic troubleshooting mode and started to work through a simple list of items to check: "ping localhost, ping the interface, ping the router, and a host beyond it...."

The last check returned "connect: Network is unreachable." A quick glance at the routing table explained the issue: There was no default route. Without a way to forward traffic, no host outside of a few statically defined internal networks were reachable, including all of the root DNS servers.

The fix was simple and, once the service was restored, I helped a bit with moving other services. Another set of eyes is an invaluable asset during late-night work, and I had to work off all that caffeine.

Marcin Antkiewicz

In Chapter 1, you learned that a protocol is a rule that governs how computers on a network exchange data and instructions. In Chapter 2, you learned about how Application and Network layer protocols determine where to send transmitted application data and instructions. You've also learned about the tasks associated with each layer of the OSI model, such as formatting, addressing, and error correction. Recall that these tasks are all governed by protocols.

This chapter focuses on how application data and instructions get from one host to another at the Transport and Network layers. You'll learn how the protocols work at each of these two layers and how routers work at the Network layer. Finally, you'll learn how to troubleshoot routing issues.

TCP/IP Core Protocols

Recall that TCP/IP is a suite of protocols, including TCP, IP (IPv4 and IPv6), UDP, ARP, and many others. TCP/IP is open (a company does not need a license to use it) and routable (routers can determine the best path for directing data over a network). Also remember that TCP/IP protocols add a header to data inherited from the layer before it.

TCP/IP's roots lie with the United States Department of Defense, which developed TCP/IP for its Advanced Research Projects Agency Network (ARPANET) in the late 1960s. ARPANET was the precursor to today's Internet.

In this part of the chapter, we dig into the details of the contents of the headers used at the Transport and Network layers. To begin, let's summarize what you learned in Chapter 1 about headers and trailers as illustrated in Figure 3-1 and described in the following list:

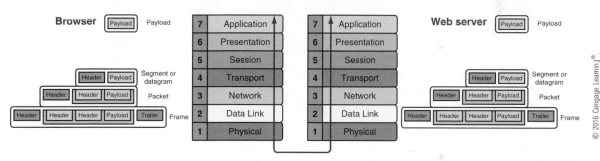

Figure 3-1 Each layer adds its own data and addresses the transmission to the corresponding layer in the destination device

- *Layers 7, 6, and 5*—Data and instructions, known as the payload, are generated by an application running on the source host. For example, in Figure 3-1, the payload is created by the browser as data passes from the highest layer of the OSI model, down on through the next two highest layers.

- *Layer 4*—The Transport layer protocol, usually either TCP or UDP, adds a header to the payload. This header includes a port number to identify the receiving application on the destination host. The entire message then becomes a segment or datagram, depending on the protocol used.

- *Layer 3*—The Network layer adds its own header to the passed-down segment or datagram. This header identifies the IP address of the destination host and the message is called a packet.

- *Layer 2*—The packet is passed to the Data Link layer on the NIC, which encapsulates this data with its own header and trailer, creating a frame. This layer's frame includes physical addresses used to find nodes on the local network.

- *Layer 1*—The Physical layer on the NIC receives the frame and places the actual transmission on the network.

The receiving host de-encapsulates the message at each layer in reverse order and then presents the payload to the receiving application.

In transit, the transmission might pass through any number of connectivity devices, such as switches and routers. Connectivity devices are specialized devices that allow two or more networks or multiple parts of one network to connect and exchange data. A device is known by the topmost OSI layer header it reads and processes, as shown in Figure 3-2. For example, if a switch reads and processes the Data Link layer header but passes the message along without reading higher-layer headers, it is known as a Layer 2 switch. On the other hand, a router that reads and processes the Network layer header and passes along the Transport layer header is known as a Layer 3 device.

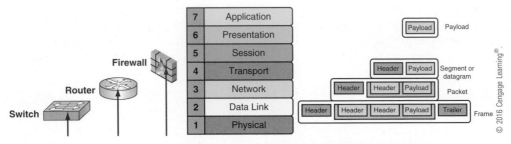

Figure 3-2   Connectivity devices are known by the highest OSI layer they read and process

With our quick review in hand, let's examine the details of the core TCP/IP protocols, beginning with TCP.

TCP (Transmission Control Protocol)

Recall from Chapter 1 that TCP operates in the Transport layer of the OSI model and provides reliable data delivery services. Let's compare TCP to making a phone call, as we look at the three characteristics of TCP in its role as a reliable delivery protocol:

- *connection-oriented protocol*—Before TCP transmits data, it ensures that a connection or session is established, similar to making sure someone is listening on the other end of a phone call before you start talking. TCP uses a three-step process called a three-way handshake to establish a TCP connection. This process is described in detail below. Only after TCP establishes this connection does it transmit the actual data, such as an HTTP request for a Web page.

- *sequencing and checksums*—In the analogy of a phone call, you might ask the other person if he can hear you clearly and repeat a sentence as necessary. In the same vein, TCP sends a character string called a checksum; TCP on the destination host then generates a similar string. If the two checksums fail to match, the destination host asks the source to retransmit the data. In addition, because messages don't always arrive in the same order they were created, TCP attaches a chronological sequence number to each segment so the destination host can, if necessary, reorder segments as they arrive.

Protocols at other layers of the OSI model can also require checksums. In Chapter 7, you'll learn more about how similar checks are made at other layers.

- *flow control*—You might need to slow down your talking over the phone if the other person needs a slower pace in order to hear every word and understand your message. Similarly, **flow control** is the process of gauging the appropriate rate of transmission based on how quickly the recipient can accept data. For example, suppose a server indicates its buffer can handle up to 4000 bytes at a time. Also suppose the client has already issued 1000 bytes, 250 of which have been received and acknowledged by the server. That means that the server is still buffering 750 bytes. Therefore, the client can only issue 3250 additional bytes before it receives acknowledgment from the server for the 750 bytes.

TCP manages the three-way handshake, checksums, sequencing, and flow control by posting data to fields in the TCP header at the beginning of a TCP segment.

Fields in a TCP Segment Figure 3-3 lists the fields or items included in a TCP segment. All the fields except the last one, the data field, are contained in the TCP header. Keep in mind that this data field is the entire message sent from the layer above the Transport layer:

$$\text{TCP segment} = \text{TCP header} + \text{data from higher layer}$$

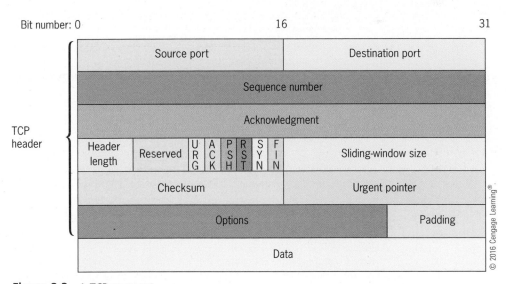

Figure 3-3 A TCP segment

Fields belonging to a TCP segment are defined in Table 3-1. The data field in the bottom row of the table does not actually belong to the TCP header. Next, when the TCP segment is sent down to the Network layer (Layer 3), the segment becomes the data portion of the IP message. This data is then encapsulated in the IP packet.

Headers are constructed in groups of 32 bits, called words. Each word consists of 4 bytes, also called blocks, of 8 bits each. This explains why diagrams of headers, such as the one in Figure 3-3, are always depicted in 32-bit groups.

Table 3-1   Fields in a TCP segment

Field	Length	Function
Source port	16 bits	Indicates the port number at the source node. Recall that a port number is the part of an address that identifies an application on a host. The port number allows an application to be available for incoming or outgoing data.
Destination port	16 bits	Indicates the port number at the destination node.
Sequence number	32 bits	Identifies the data segment's position in the stream of data segments already sent.
Acknowledgment number (ACK)	32 bits	Confirms receipt of the data via a return message to the sender.
TCP header length	4 bits	Indicates the length of the TCP header in bytes. The header can be a minimum of 20 bytes to a maximum of 60 bytes in 20-byte increments. Also called the Data offset field because it's the offset from the beginning of the segment until the start of the data carried by the segment.
Reserved	6 bits	Indicates a field reserved for later use.
Flags	6 bits	Identifies a collection of six 1-bit fields or flags that signal special conditions about other fields in the header. The following flags are available to the sender: • URG—If set to *1*, the Urgent pointer field later in the segment contains information for the receiver. (If set to *0*, the receiver will ignore the Urgent pointer field.) • ACK—If set to *1*, the Acknowledgment field earlier in the segment contains information for the receiver. (If set to *0*, the receiver will ignore the Acknowledgment field.) • PSH—If set to *1*, it indicates that data should be sent to an application without buffering. • RST—If set to *1*, the sender is requesting that the connection be reset. • SYN—If set to *1*, the sender is requesting a synchronization of the sequence numbers between the two nodes. This code indicates that no payload is included in the segment, and the acknowledgment number should be increased by 1 in response. • FIN—If set to *1*, the segment is the last in a sequence and the connection should be closed.
Sliding-window size (or window)	16 bits	Indicates how many bytes the sender can issue to a receiver while acknowledgment for this segment is outstanding. This field performs flow control, preventing the receiver's buffer from being deluged with bytes.
Checksum	16 bits	Allows the receiving node to determine whether the TCP segment became corrupted during transmission.
Urgent pointer	16 bits	Indicates a location in the data field where urgent data resides.
Options	0–32 bits	Specifies special options, such as the maximum segment size a network can handle.
Padding	Variable	Contains filler information to ensure that the size of the TCP header is a multiple of 32 bits.
Data	Variable	Contains data originally sent by the source host. The data field is not part of the header—it is encapsulated by the header. The size of the data field depends on how much data needs to be transmitted, the constraints on the TCP segment size imposed by the network type, and the limitation that the segment must fit within an IP packet at the next layer.

Now let's see how the fields in the TCP header are used to perform the three-way handshake that establishes a TCP session.

TCP Three-Way Handshake The TCP three-way handshake is performed before TCP transmits the actual data, such as an HTTP request for a Web page. Figure 3-4 shows the three transmissions in the handshake. The following list summarizes the three transmissions sent before data is transmitted:

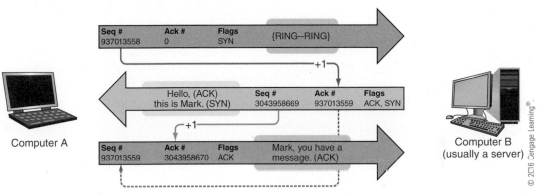

Figure 3-4 The three-way handshake process establishes a TCP session

1. *request for a connection (SYN)*—Computer A issues a message to computer B with its SYN bit set, indicating the desire to communicate and synchronize sequence numbers. It's as if computer A is calling computer B to see if there will be a response. In its message, it sends a random number that will be used to synchronize the communication. In Figure 3-4, for example, this number is 937013558. The ACK bit is usually set to 0.

2. *response to the request (SYN/ACK)*—After computer B receives this message, it responds with a segment whose ACK and SYN flags are both set, essentially saying, "Yes, I'm here and I'm listening." In computer B's transmission, the ACK field contains a number that equals the sequence number computer A originally sent, plus 1. As Figure 3-4 illustrates, computer B sends the number 937013559. In this manner, computer B signals to computer A that it has received the request for communication and further, it expects computer A to respond with the sequence number 937013559. In its SYN field, computer B sends its own random number (in Figure 3-4, this number is 3043958669), which computer A will insert in the next message to acknowledge that it received computer B's transmission.

3. *connection established (ACK)*—Computer A issues a segment whose sequence number is 937013559 (because this is what computer B indicated it expects to receive). In the same segment, computer A also communicates a sequence number via its Acknowledgment field. This number equals the sequence number that computer B sent, plus 1. The connection has been established, and computer A will then begin data transmission.

The Initial Sequence Number (ISN) of the first SYN message in the three-way handshake appears to be random, but in reality, it is calculated by a specific, clock-based algorithm, which varies by operating system. The existence of these algorithms and their predictability is actually a security loophole that hackers can use to undermine a host's availability for other, legitimate connections.

Up until this point, no payload has been included in any of the three initial messages, and the sequence numbers have increased by exactly 1 in each acknowledgment. After these three transmissions, the payload or data is sent. This can be done in a single message for a small amount of data, such as a Web page request, or fragmented over several messages, such as the data for the Web page itself.

At this point, the sequence numbers will each be increased by the number of bits included in each received segment, as confirmation that the correct length of message was received. In the example shown in Figure 3-4, computer A will send the next message, which will include the payload (such as an HTTP request) from a higher layer. Suppose that computer A's Web page request message, the fourth message in this session, is 725 bits long. Computer B will receive this message, count the bits, and add 725 to the sequence number (937013559) of the received message. This new number, 937014284, becomes the acknowledgment number for the return message (which would be the fifth message in the session).

With each successive message, each computer will determine the length in bits of the message it just received, add that number to the message's sequence number, and that new number becomes the acknowledgment number of the outgoing message.

The two hosts continue communicating in this manner until computer A issues a segment whose FIN flag is set, indicating the end of the transmission.

Network+
1.9
5.2
5.9

Applying Concepts

Examine a TCP Header

In one of the Chapter 2 projects, you looked at a TCP segment from an actual Wireshark capture (see Figure 2-40). However, you might not have understood what all of the data meant. Now that you know the function of each TCP segment field, you can interpret its contents. Figure 3-5 shows a sample TCP segment.

Transmission Control Protocol, Src Port: http (80), Dst Port: 1958 (1958), Seq: 3043958669, Ack: 937013559, Len: 0
 Source port : http (80)
 Destination port: 1958 (1958)
 Sequence number: 3043958669
 Acknowledgment number: 937013559
 Header length: 24 bytes
⊟Flags:_ 0xx0012 (SYN, ACK)
  0... .... = Congestion Window Reduced (CWR): Not set
  .0.. .... = ECN-Echo: Not set
  ..0. .... = Urgent: Not set
  ...1 .... = Acknowledgment: Set
  .... 0... = Push: Not set
  .... .0.. = Reset: Not set
  .... ..1. = Syn: Set
  ....0 = Fin: not set
 window size: 5840
 Checksum: 0x206a (correct)
⊟Options: (4bytes)
  Maximum segment size: 1460 bytes

Figure 3-5 TCP segment data

Source: The Wireshark Foundation

Suppose the segment in Figure 3-5 was sent from computer B to computer A. Table 3-2 interprets the rows shown in Figure 3-5, beginning with the second row, which is labeled "Source port."

Table 3-2   Translation of TCP field data

Field name	TCP header data
Source port	The segment was issued from computer B's port 80, the port assigned to HTTP by default.
Destination port	The segment was addressed to port 1958 on computer A.
Sequence number	The segment is identified by sequence number 3043958669.
Acknowledgment number	By simply containing a value other than zero, this field performs its duty of letting a host know that its last communication was received. The next segment that computer B expects to receive from computer A will have the sequence number of 937013559.
Header length	The TCP header is 24 bytes long—4 bytes larger than its minimum size—which means that some of the available options were specified or the padding space was used.
Flags: Congestion Window Reduced (CWR) and ECN-Echo	These optional flags can be used to help TCP react to and reduce traffic congestion. They are only available when TCP is establishing a connection. However, in this segment, they are not set.
Flags: Acknowledgment and SYN	Of all the possible flags in the Figure 3-5 segment, only the ACK and SYN flags are set. This means that computer B is acknowledging the last segment it received from computer A and also negotiating a synchronization scheme for sequencing.
Window size	The window size is 5840, meaning that computer B can accept 5840 more bytes of data from computer A even while this segment remains unacknowledged.
Checksum	This field indicates the valid outcome of the error-checking algorithm used to verify the segment's header. In this case, the checksum is 0x206a. When computer A receives this segment, it will perform the same algorithm, and if the result matches, it will know the TCP header arrived without damage.
Maximum segment size	This segment uses its option field to specify a maximum TCP segment size of 1460 bytes.

© 2016 Cengage Learning®

NOTE   Note that a computer doesn't "see" the TCP segment as it's organized and formatted in Figure 3-5. This figure was obtained by using a data analyzer program, in this case Wireshark, which translates each message into a user-friendly form. From the destination computer's standpoint, the TCP segment arrives as a series of bits. TCP relies on the protocol standards to know how to interpret each bit in the segment based on its location and value.

TCP is not the only core protocol at the Transport layer. A similar but less-complex protocol, UDP, is discussed next.

UDP (User Datagram Protocol)

Network+
1.9
5.2
5.9

7 APPLICATION
6 PRESENTATION
5 SESSION
4 TRANSPORT
3 NETWORK
2 DATA LINK
1 PHYSICAL

UDP (User Datagram Protocol) provides no error checking or sequencing. This would be like talking on a radio show where you can send out your signal whether anyone is listening or not.

UDP's lack of sophistication makes it more efficient than TCP. It can be useful in situations in which a great volume of data must be transferred quickly, such as live audio or video transmissions over the Internet. In these cases, TCP—with its acknowledgments, checksums, and flow-control mechanisms—would only add more overhead to the transmission. UDP is also more efficient for carrying messages that fit within one data packet.

In contrast to a TCP header's 10 fields, the UDP header contains only four fields: Source port, Destination port, Length, and Checksum. Use of the Checksum field in UDP is optional in IPv4, but required for IPv6 transmissions. Figure 3-6 depicts a UDP datagram. Contrast its header with the much larger TCP segment header shown in Figure 3-3.

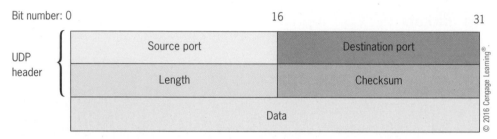

Figure 3-6   A UDP datagram

Now that you understand the functions of and differences between TCP and UDP, you are ready to learn more about IP (Internet Protocol).

IP (Internet Protocol)

IP (Internet Protocol) belongs to the Network layer of the OSI model. It specifies how and where data should be delivered, including the data's source and destination addresses. IP is the protocol that enables TCP/IP to internetwork—that is, to traverse more than one LAN segment and more than one type of network through a router.

As you know, at the Network layer of the OSI model, data is packaged into packets. The IP packet acts as an envelope for data and contains information necessary for routers to transfer data between different LAN segments.

IP is an unreliable, connectionless protocol. The term *unreliable* does not mean that IP can't be used reliably. Instead, it means that IP does not guarantee delivery of data and no connection is established before data is transmitted. IP depends on TCP to ensure that data packets are delivered to the right addresses.

What's the difference between a packet and a datagram? You may see both terms used interchangeably when talking about Layer 3 messages. The term *datagram* generally means a message that stands alone; that is, delivery is not guaranteed and no prior transmission was required before sending it. Because these characteristics apply to messages sent by Layer 4 UDP as well as Layer 3 IP, the term *datagram* is sometimes used at both layers, as in a *UDP datagram* and an *IP datagram*.

In this book, to avoid confusion, we use the terms *TCP segment* and *UDP datagram* for Layer 4 messages. When referring to messages at the Network layer, we stick with *packet*.

As discussed in Chapter 2, two versions of the IP protocol are used on networks today. IPv4, which was introduced to the public in 1981, is still the standard on most networks. IPv6 was released in 1998 and offers better security, better prioritization provisions, more automatic IP address configurations, and additional IP addresses. Most new applications, servers, clients, and network devices support IPv6. However, due to the cost of upgrading infrastructure, many organizations have hesitated to upgrade from IPv4.

As a network support technician, you need to know how to support both versions of IP. Let's first see how IPv4 packets are constructed and then you'll learn about IPv6 packets.

IPv4 Packets Figure 3-7 depicts an IPv4 packet. Its fields are explained in Table 3-3. Note that the data field in the bottom row of the table does not belong to the IPv4 header.

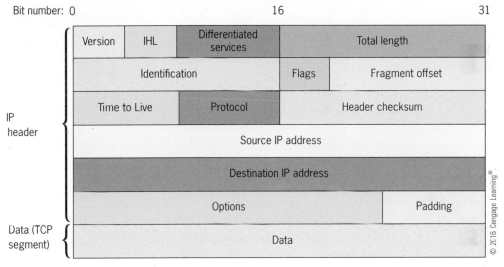

Figure 3-7   An IPv4 packet

Table 3-3   Fields in an IPv4 packet

Field	Length	Function
Version	4 bits	Identifies the version number of the protocol—for example, IPv4 or IPv6. The receiving workstation looks at this field first to determine whether it can read the incoming data. If it cannot, it will reject the packet.
Internet header length (IHL)	4 bits	Indicates the length of the TCP header in bytes. The header can be a minimum of 20 bytes to a maximum of 60 bytes, in groups of 20-byte increments. Also called the Data offset field because it's the offset from the beginning of the packet until the start of the data.
Differentiated services (DiffServ)	8 bits	Informs routers the level of precedence they should apply when processing the incoming packet. Differentiated services allows up to 64 values and a wide range of priority-handling options.

Table 3-3 Fields in an IPv4 packet (*continued*)

Field	Length	Function
Total length	16 bits	Identifies the total length of the IP packet, including the header and data, in bytes. An IP packet, including its header and data, cannot exceed 65,535 bytes.
Identification	16 bits	Identifies the message to which a packet belongs and enables the receiving host to reassemble fragmented messages. This field and the following two fields, Flags and Fragment offset, assist in reassembly of fragmented packets.
Flags	3 bits	Indicates whether a message is fragmented and, if it is fragmented, whether this packet is the last in the fragment.The first bit is reserved for future use. When the second bit is set, it prevents the packet from being fragmented. A value of 1 in the third bit indicates more fragments are on the way.
Fragment offset	13 bits	Identifies where the packet fragment belongs in the incoming set of fragments.
Time to Live (TTL)	8 bits	Indicates the maximum duration that the packet can remain on the network before it is discarded. Although this field was originally meant to represent units of time, on modern networks it represents the number of times a packet can still be forwarded by a router, or the maximum number of router hops it has remaining. The TTL for packets varies and can be configured; it is usually set at 32 or 64. Each time a packet passes through a router, its TTL is reduced by 1. When a router receives a packet with a TTL equal to 0, it discards that packet and sends an ICMP TTL expired message back to the source host.
Protocol	8 bits	Identifies the type of protocol that will receive the packet (for example, TCP, UDP, or ICMP).
Header checksum	16 bits	Allows the receiving host to calculate whether the IP header has been corrupted during transmission. If the checksum accompanying the message does not match the calculated checksum when the packet is received, the packet is presumed to be corrupt and is discarded.
Source IP address	32 bits	Identifies the full IP address of the source host.
Destination IP address	32 bits	Indicates the full IP address of the destination host.
Options	Variable	May contain optional routing and timing information.
Padding	Variable	Contains filler bits to ensure that the header is a multiple of 32 bits.
Data	Variable	Includes the data originally sent by the source host, plus the TCP or UDP header in the Transport layer. The data field is not part of the header—it is said to be encapsulated by the header.

The first bit of the Flags field played a role in a 2003 April Fool's Day joke, as the so-called "evil bit." That day, a new regulation was circulated on the Internet explaining that this bit must be set to 0 unless the packet originates from a hacker. In other words, hackers were "required" to set this bit in order to alert firewalls of their impending attacks. Of course, hackers aren't usually very concerned with rules, so no one spent much time configuring their firewalls to filter for messages with this bit set. In reality, the bit is reserved for later use.

Applying Concepts

Examine a Sample IPv4 Packet

Let's examine the IPv4 header shown in Figure 3-8. The fields are explained in Table 3-4, beginning with the Version field.

```
⊟Internet Protocol, Src Addr: 140.147.249.7 (140.147.249.7), Dst Addr: 10.11.11.51 (10.11.11.51)
    Version: 4
    Header length: 20 bytes
  ⊞Differentiated Services Field: 0x00 (DSCP 0x00: Default; ECN 0x00)
    Total Length: 44
    Identification: 0x0000 (0)
  ⊟Flags: 0x04
      .1.. = Don't fragment: Set
      ..0. = More fragments: Not set
    Fragment offset: 0
    Time to live: 64
    Protocol: TCP (0x06)
    Header checksum: 0x9ff3 (correct)
    Source: 140.147.249.7 (140.147.249.7)
    Destination: 10.11.11.51 (10.11.11.51)
```

Figure 3-8   IPv4 packet header

Source: The Wireshark Foundation

Table 3-4   **Explanation of IPv4 header fields listed in Figure 3-8**

Field name	IPv4 header data
Version	The transmission relies on version 4 of the Internet Protocol.
Header length	The packet has a header length of 20 bytes. Because this is the minimum size for an IP header, you can deduce that the packet contains no options or padding.
Differentiated Services Field	No options for priority handling are set, which is not unusual in routine data exchanges such as requesting a Web page.
Total Length	The total length of the packet is 44 bytes. This makes sense when you consider that its header is 20 bytes and the TCP segment that it encapsulates is 24 bytes. Considering that the maximum size of an IP packet is 65,535 bytes, this is a very small packet.
Identification	This field uniquely identifies the packet. This packet, the first one issued from computer B to computer A in the TCP connection exchange, is identified in hexadecimal notation as 0x0000 or simply 0.
Flag: Don't fragment and Fragment offset	The Don't fragment option is set with a value of 1, so you know that this packet is not fragmented. And because it's not fragmented, the Fragment offset field does not apply and is set to 0.
Time to live	This packet's TTL is set to 64. That means that if the packet were to keep traversing networks, it would be allowed 64 more hops before it was discarded.
Protocol	This field indicates that a TCP segment is encapsulated within the packet. TCP is always indicated by the hexadecimal string of 0x06.
Header checksum	This field provides the correct header checksum answer, which is used by the recipient of this packet to determine whether the header was damaged in transit.
Source and Destination	These last two fields show the logical addresses for the packet's source and destination, respectively.

IPv6 Packets Due to the added information it carries, IPv6 uses a different packet format than IPv4. The fields in an IPv6 packet header are shown in Figure 3-9 and described in Table 3-5. In the table, the data field in the bottom row does not belong to the IPv6 header.

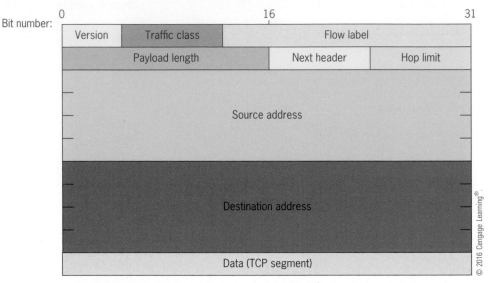

Figure 3-9   An IPv6 packet

Table 3-5   Fields in an IPv6 packet

Field	Length	Function
Version	4 bits	Indicates which IP version the packet uses.
Traffic class	8 bits	Identifies the packet's priority. It is similar to, but not the same as, the DiffServ field in IPv4 packets.
Flow label	20 bits	Indicates which flow, or sequence of packets from one source to one or multiple destinations, the packet belongs to. Routers interpret flow information to ensure that packets belonging to the same transmission arrive together. Flow information may also help with traffic prioritization.
Payload length	16 bits	Indicates the size of the payload, or data, carried by the packet. Unlike the Total length field in IPv4 packets, the Payload length in IPv6 packets does not refer to the size of the whole packet.
Next header	8 bits	Identifies the type of header that immediately follows the IP packet header, usually TCP or UDP.
Hop limit	8 bits	Indicates the number of times that the packet can be forwarded by routers on the network, similar to the TTL field in IPv4 packets. When the hop limit reaches 0, the packet is discarded.
Source address	128 bits	Identifies the full IP address of the transmitting host.
Destination address	128 bits	Identifies the full IP address of the receiving host.
Data	Variable	Includes the data originally sent by the source host, plus the TCP or UDP header in the Transport layer. The data field is not part of the IPv6 header—it is encapsulated by the header.

If you compare the fields and functions listed in Table 3-5 with those listed for the IPv4 packet in Table 3-3, you'll notice some similarities and some differences. For example, both packets begin with a 4-bit Version field. Other fields, such as the TTL in IPv4 and the hop limit in IPv6, are similar, but slightly different. One striking difference between the two versions is that IPv6 packets accommodate the much longer IPv6 addresses.

Applying Concepts

Examine a Sample IPv6 Header

Figure 3-10 shows the contents of an actual IPv6 packet header, and Table 3-6 breaks down what it all means. This packet formed part of a message issued by ping.

```
⊟ Internet Protocol Version 6, Src: 2001:470:1f10:1a6::2 (2001:470:1f10:1a6::2), Dst: 2001:470:1f10:1a6::1 (2001:470:1f10:1a6::1)
  ⊞ 0110 .... = Version: 6
  ⊞ .... 0000 0000 .... .... .... .... .... = Traffic class: 0x00000000
    .... .... .... 0000 0000 0000 0000 0000 = Flowlabel: 0x00000000
    Payload length: 64
    Next header: ICMPv6 (0x3a)
    Hop limit: 64
    Source: 2001:470:1f10:1a6::2 (2001:470:1f10:1a6::2)
    Destination: 2001:470:1f10:1a6::1 (2001:470:1f10:1a6::1)
```

Figure 3-10   IPv6 packet header

Source: The Wireshark Foundation

Table 3-6   **Explanation of IPv6 header fields listed in Figure 3-10**

Field name	IPv6 header data
Version	Version 6 of the Internet Protocol is used, expressed in binary format as 0110.
Traffic class and Flowlabel	Both of these fields are set to 0x00000000, which means neither field has a specified value. Routers receiving a packet that lacks Traffic class or Flow label information will not prioritize the packet or make any guarantees that it will reach its destination at the same time as any other packets. For many types of traffic, this is perfectly acceptable.
Payload length	This packet carries 64 bits of data. Considering that IPv6 packets can carry payloads as large as 64 KB, this is a very small packet.
Next header	The data in this packet's payload belongs to an ICMP transmission. ICMP is used by ping and is described later in this section.
Hop limit	This packet can be forwarded by routers up to 64 times before it is discarded.
Source and Destination	The IP address for the packet's source is 2001:470:1f10:1a6::2 and the IP address for the packet's destination is 2001:470:1f10:1a6::1.

You're now ready to apply the differences between IPv4 and IPv6 transmissions to other TCP/IP protocols. For example, the ICMP protocol described next works on both IPv4 and IPv6 networks, but the IGMP and ARP protocols are used only on IPv4 networks. Let's see how these three protocols work.

ICMP (Internet Control Message Protocol)

Whereas IP helps direct data to its correct destination, ICMP (Internet Control Message Protocol) is a Network layer core protocol that reports on the success or failure of data delivery. It can indicate when part of a network is congested, when data fails to reach its destination, and when data has been discarded because the allotted Time to Live has expired. ICMP announces these transmission failures to the sender, but does not correct errors it detects—those functions are left to higher-layer protocols, such as TCP. However, ICMP's announcements provide critical information for troubleshooting network problems.

IPv6 relies on ICMPv6 (Internet Control Message Protocol for use with IPv6) to perform the functions that ICMPv4, IGMP, and ARP perform in IPv4. In other words, ICMPv6 on IPv6 networks performs the functions of IGMP and ARP on IPv4 networks to detect and report data transmission errors, discover other nodes on a network, and manage multicasting.

IGMP (Internet Group Management Protocol) on IPv4 Networks

On IPv4 networks, IGMP (Internet Group Management Protocol or Internet Group Multicast Protocol) operates at the Network layer of the OSI model to manage multicasting. Unlike a broadcast transmission, a multicast transmission does not necessarily issue transmissions to every node on a segment. Multicasting can, for example, be used for teleconferencing or videoconferencing over the Internet. Routers use IGMP to determine which nodes belong to a certain multicast group and to transmit data to all nodes in that group. Network nodes use IGMP to join or leave multicast groups at any time.

ARP (Address Resolution Protocol) on IPv4 Networks

ARP (Address Resolution Protocol) works in conjunction with IPv4 to discover the MAC (physical) address of a host or node on the local network and to maintain a database that maps IP addresses to MAC addresses on the local network. ARP is a Layer 2 protocol that uses IP in Layer 3, and operates only within its local network bound by routers.

ARP relies on broadcasting, which transmits simultaneously to all nodes on a particular network segment. For example, if one node needs to know the MAC address of another node on the same network, the first node issues a broadcast message to the network, using ARP, that essentially says, "Will the computer with the IP address 1.2.3.4 please send me its MAC address?" The node that has the IP address 1.2.3.4 then transmits a reply that contains the physical address of the destination host.

The database of IP-to-MAC address mappings is called an **ARP table** (also called an **ARP cache**) and is kept on a computer's hard drive. Each OS can use its own format for the ARP table. A sample ARP table is shown in Figure 3-11.

```
IP Address          Hardware Address    Type

123.45.67.80        60:23:A6:F1:C4:D2   Static
123.45.67.89        20:00:3D:21:E0:11   Dynamic
123.45.67.73        A0:BB:77:C2:25:FA   Dynamic
```

Figure 3-11 Sample ARP table

Source: Mircrosoft LLC

An ARP table can contain two types of entries: dynamic and static. **Dynamic ARP table entries** are created when a client makes an ARP request that could not be satisfied by data already in the ARP table. Static ARP table entries are those that someone has entered manually using the ARP utility. This ARP utility, accessed via the `arp` command from a Windows command prompt or a UNIX or Linux shell prompt, provides a way of obtaining information from and manipulating a device's ARP table.

To view a Windows workstation's ARP table, go to the command line and enter the command: `arp –a`. Figure 3-12 shows sample results of this command run on a home network. The first line contains the interface IP address, which is the local computer's address—that is, the address of the computer that issued the command. The columns below it contain the addresses of other nodes on the network, along with their physical addresses (MAC addresses) and record types.

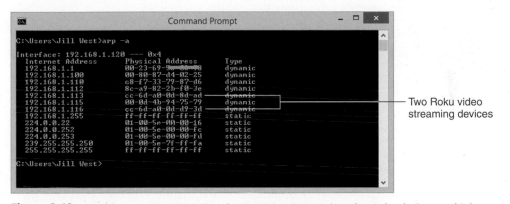

Two Roku video streaming devices

Figure 3-12 IP addresses 192.168.1.113 and 192.168.1.116 are assigned to Roku devices on this home network

Source: Mircrosoft LLC

Recall that the first half of a MAC address can be used to identify the manufacturer of that NIC, which may help you in identifying a NIC among other NICs. Several Web sites provide online MAC address lookup tables to access databases correlating manufacturers with their respective OUIs. (Recall from Chapter 2 that an OUI is the unique number in the first half of a network interface's physical address assigned by the IEEE that identifies the NIC's manufacturer.) Notice that Figure 3-12 lists two Roku devices, which are used to stream video from the Internet to a television. Each device has an OUI of CC-6D-A0, which are the first six hex characters in the physical addresses.

NOTE Recall from Chapter 1 that a LAN is defined as a group of computers and other devices that can directly address each other. Technically, a LAN can also be defined as a broadcast domain, which means the group of nodes that a broadcast reaches (for example, the group that an ARP broadcast can reach). Routers don't forward broadcast messages, thus creating a boundary for a LAN.

Network+
1.9
5.2

Applying Concepts

Identify a NIC Manufacturer

When collecting network data on Wireshark using the default settings, some of the OUIs are already resolved. In Figure 3-13, you can see where Wireshark has identified the manufacturer of a laptop NIC on this network.

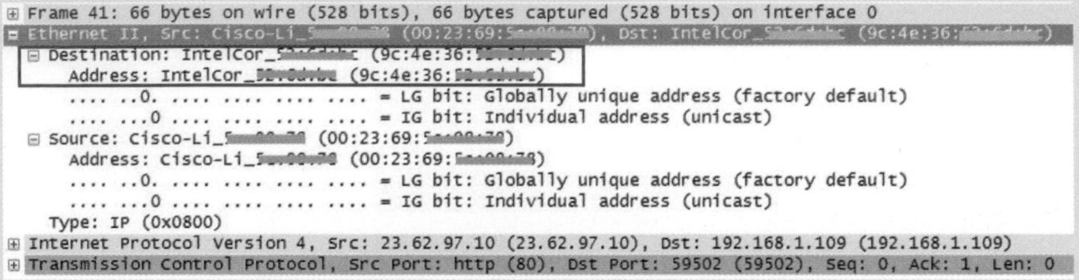

```
⊞ Frame 41: 66 bytes on wire (528 bits), 66 bytes captured (528 bits) on interface 0
⊟ Ethernet II, Src: Cisco-Li_5        (00:23:69:5       ), Dst: IntelCor_         (9c:4e:36:         )
  ⊟ Destination: IntelCor_         (9c:4e:36:         )
      Address: IntelCor_         (9c:4e:36:         )
      .... ..0. .... .... .... .... = LG bit: Globally unique address (factory default)
      .... ...0 .... .... .... .... = IG bit: Individual address (unicast)
  ⊟ Source: Cisco-Li_5        (00:23:69:5       )
      Address: Cisco-Li_5        (00:23:69:5       )
      .... ..0. .... .... .... .... = LG bit: Globally unique address (factory default)
      .... ...0 .... .... .... .... = IG bit: Individual address (unicast)
    Type: IP (0x0800)
⊞ Internet Protocol Version 4, Src: 23.62.97.10 (23.62.97.10), Dst: 192.168.1.109 (192.168.1.109)
⊞ Transmission Control Protocol, Src Port: http (80), Dst Port: 59502 (59502), Seq: 0, Ack: 1, Len: 0
```

Figure 3-13   Wireshark capture shows that the destination node's NIC is made by Intel

Source: The Wireshark Foundation

If you're working with physical addresses provided by a command output, however, or if you need a little more information than what is provided by a Wireshark capture, you can use an online MAC address lookup table, such as Wireshark's OUI Lookup Tool.

1. Do a Google search for *Wireshark oui lookup*. The *wireshark.org* Web site will probably be the first search result. Click on it to go to the OUI Lookup Tool Web site.

   Notice in Figure 3-13 that the MAC address of the device is referenced. The first three bytes of this address, 9c:4e:36, make up the OUI of the device's manufacturer. We can type the numbers into Wireshark's Lookup Tool or copy and paste them to the Web site search box.

2. Open Wireshark and run a scan for a few seconds then stop the capture. Click on any message that includes a Source or Destination MAC address on the Ethernet II line of output in the middle pane, as shown in Figure 3-13.

3. To copy and paste, select the field for this address in the Wireshark output, click **Edit** at the top of the page, point to **Copy**, then click **Value**.

4. Paste the address into the box on Wireshark's Web site. You'll need to delete the last three bytes so that only the first three bytes are still in the field, then click **Find**.

You can perform the same lookup using output from a command prompt:

5. Open a Command Prompt window and enter `ipconfig /all` to identify the NIC's physical address.

6. Enter the first three bytes of the physical address into the Wireshark Lookup Tool. Who is the manufacturer of your NIC?

Routers and How They Work

Network+
1.1
1.9
4.2

7 APPLICATION
6 PRESENTATION
5 SESSION
4 TRANSPORT
3 NETWORK
2 DATA LINK
1 PHYSICAL

Returning to the Layer 3 discussions of how packets traverse networks, you're ready to learn about routers. A router joins two or more networks and passes packets from one network to another. Routers are responsible for determining the next network to which a packet should be forwarded on its way to its destination. A typical router has an internal processor, an operating system, memory, input and output jacks for different types of network connectors (depending on the network type), and, usually, a management console interface. Three examples of routers are shown in Figure 3-14, with the most complex on the left and the simplest on the right. High-powered, multiprotocol routers may have several slot bays to accommodate multiple network interfaces. At the other end of the scale are simple, inexpensive routers often used in small offices and homes, and require little configuration.

Courtesy of Juniper Networks, Inc (left and center images). Courtesy of NETGEAR (right image)

Figure 3-14   Routers

A router's strength lies in its intelligence. Although any one router can be specialized for a variety of tasks, all routers can do the following:

- Connect dissimilar networks, such as a LAN and a WAN, which use different types of routing protocols.

- Interpret Layer 3 and often Layer 4 addressing and other information (such as quality of service indicators).

- Determine the best path for data to follow from point A to point B. The **best path** is the most efficient route to the message's destination calculated by the router, based upon the information the router has available to it.

- Reroute traffic if the path of first choice is down but another path is available.

In addition to performing these basic functions, routers may perform any of the following optional functions:

- Filter broadcast transmissions to alleviate network congestion.

- Prevent certain types of traffic from getting to a network, enabling customized segregation and security.

- Support simultaneous local and remote connectivity.
- Provide high network fault tolerance through redundant components such as power supplies or network interfaces.
- Monitor network traffic and report statistics.
- Diagnose internal or other connectivity problems and trigger alarms.

Routers are often categorized according to the scope of the network they serve. The various categories are described in the following list and diagrammed in Figure 3-15:

- **Interior routers** direct data between networks within the same autonomous system. An **autonomous system (AS)** is a group of networks, often on the same domain, that are operated by the same organization. For example, Cengage, the company that published this book, might have several LANs that all fall under the *cengage.com* domain, with each LAN connected to the others by interior routers.
- **Border routers** (or **gateway routers**) connect an autonomous system with an outside network. For example, the router that connects a business with its ISP is a border router.
- **Exterior routers** direct data between autonomous systems. Routers that operate on the Internet backbone are considered exterior routers. An exterior router can also be a border or gateway router if it stands between an autonomous system and an outside network.

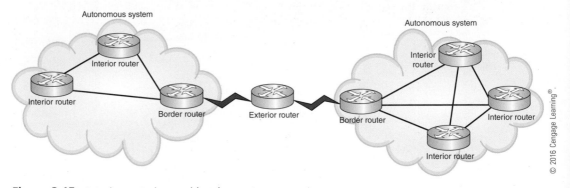

Figure 3-15 Interior, exterior, and border routers

On small office or home LANs, routers are simple to install: Plug in the network cable from the cable modem connected to your ISP on one port and connect your computer(s) to your LAN through another port or by a wireless connection. Turn on the router and computer, and use a Web-based utility program on the router to set it up.

However, high-powered, multiprotocol routers can be a challenge to install on sizable networks. Typically, an engineer must be very familiar with routing technology to figure out how to place and configure a router to best advantage. If you plan to specialize in network design or management, you should research router types and their capabilities further.

Multilayer Switches

A **Layer 3 switch** is a switch that is capable of interpreting Layer 3 data and works much like a router: It supports the same routing protocols and makes routing decisions. Layer 3 switches were designed to work on large LANs, similar to interior routers, except they're faster and less expensive. The primary difference is the way the hardware is built, but, in fact, it's often hard to distinguish between a Layer 3 switch and a router. In some cases, the difference comes down to what the manufacturer has decided to call the device in order to improve sales.

Layer 4 switches also exist and are capable of interpreting Layer 4 data. They operate anywhere between Layer 4 and Layer 7 and are also known as content switches or application switches. Among other things, the ability to interpret higher-layer data enables switches to perform advanced filtering, keep statistics, and provide security functions. The features of Layer 3 and Layer 4 switches vary widely depending on the manufacturer and price and can cost three times more than Layer 2 switches. This variability is exacerbated by the fact that key players in the networking trade have not agreed on standards for these switches. They are typically used as part of a network's backbone and are not appropriate on a LAN. In general, however, Layer 4, Layer 3, and Layer 2 switches are all optimized for fast Layer 2 data handling.

As you learn about routers, keep in mind that Layer 3 switches can work the same way.

Routing Tables

A routing table is a database that maintains information about where hosts are located and the most efficient way to reach them. A router relies on its routing table to identify which router is the next hop to reach a particular destination host. The routing table contains IP addresses and network masks that identify a network that a host or another router belongs to.

For example, in Figure 3-16, suppose a workstation in LAN A wants to print to the printer in LAN B. Here is how the routing tables would be used in this transmission:

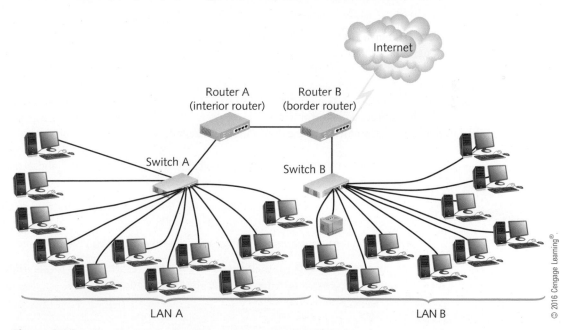

Figure 3-16   The placement of routers on an autonomous system

1. The workstation issues a print command to a network printer. IP on the workstation recognizes that the IP address of the printer is on a different LAN and forwards the transmission through switch A to its gateway, router A.

2. Router A examines the destination IP address in the message and consults its routing table to find out to which network and router to send the message. Before it forwards the message, however, router A decreases the number of hops tallied in the TTL field of the packet header. It then sends the message to router B.

3. Router B decreases the packet's hop count by 1, reads the packet's destination IP address, searches its routing tables, and determines the packet is destined for LAN B. It sends the packet through switch B on LAN B.

4. Based on the destination MAC address in the message, switch B delivers the transmission to the printer, which picks up the message, and begins printing.

Static or Dynamic Routing

Routers may employ one of two methods for directing data on the network: static or dynamic routing. Static routing is a technique in which a network administrator configures a routing table to direct messages along specific paths between networks. Static routes are appropriate in certain situations, such as the static route between a small business and its ISP. However, static routes used to traverse several networks don't account for occasional network congestion, failed connections, or device moves, and they require human intervention.

Dynamic routing, on the other hand, automatically calculates the best path between two networks and accumulates this information in the routing table. If congestion or failures affect the network, a router using dynamic routing can detect the problems and reroute messages through a different path. By default, when a router is added to a network, dynamic routing ensures that the new router's routing tables are updated.

Most networks primarily use dynamic routing, but may include some static routing to indicate, for example, a gateway of last resort, which is the router that accepts all unroutable messages from other routers. When a router cannot determine a path to a message's destination, the router sends the message along a default route, usually to another router. This next router will also attempt to determine a path for the message, but is also programmed with a default route if a path cannot be determined. The routers will continue resorting to default routes until the hop limit is depleted or until a path can be determined and the destination is reached, whichever comes first.

What's the difference between a default gateway, a default route, and a gateway of last resort?

- Messages are sent to a *default gateway*—a router or Layer 3 switch—when their destination is not on the host's local network.

- A *default route* is a backup route when no other route can be determined.

The default route points to the *gateway of last resort*, which is the router assigned to receive unroutable messages from other routers.

The route Utility

The `route command` allows you to view a host's routing table. On a Linux or UNIX system, such as OS X (the operating system on Apple computers), you can view the routing table by entering `route` at the command prompt. On a Windows-based system, use the command `route print` instead. On a Cisco-brand router or another brand that uses Cisco command conventions, use the command `show ip route`.

The CompTIA Network+ exam expects you to know about the most common routing protocols: RIPv2, OSPF, IS-IS, and BGP.

The most common routing protocols are summarized in Table 3-8 and are described in more detail in the following sections. Additional routing protocols exist, but their discussions exceed the scope of this book.

Table 3-8   **Summary of common routing protocols**

Routing protocol	Type	Router location	Algorithm used
RIP (Routing Information Protocol)	IGP	Interior	Distance-vector
RIPv2 (Routing Information Protocol version 2)	IGP	Interior	Distance-vector
OSPF (Open Shortest Path First)	IGP	Interior or border	Link-state
IS-IS (Intermediate System to Intermediate System)	IGP	Interior	Link-state
BGP (Border Gateway Protocol)*	EGP	Exterior or border	Advanced distance-vector or path vector

© 2016 Cengage Learning®

*CompTIA classifies BGP as a "hybrid routing protocol."

Interior and Exterior Gateway Routing Protocols

As you examine Table 3-8, you can see that a routing protocol is classified as IGP or EGP. Here's an explanation of the two types, which are diagrammed in Figure 3-18:

- IGPs (interior gateway protocols) are routing protocols used by interior routers and border routers within autonomous systems. IGPs are often grouped according to the algorithms they use to calculate best paths:

  - Distance-vector routing protocols calculate the best path to a destination on the basis of the distance to that destination. Some distance-vector routing protocols factor only the number of hops to the destination, whereas others take into account route latency and other network traffic characteristics. Distance-vector routing protocols periodically exchange their route information with neighboring routers. However, routers relying on this type of routing protocol must accept the data they receive from their neighbors and cannot independently assess network conditions two or more hops away. RIP and RIPv2 are distance-vector routing protocols.

  - Link-state routing protocols enable routers to communicate beyond neighboring routers, after which each router can independently map the network and determine the best path between itself and a message's destination node. These protocols tend to adapt more quickly to changes in the network, but can also be more complex to configure and troubleshoot. OSPF and IS-IS are link-state routing protocols.

- EGP (exterior gateway protocols) are routing protocols used by border routers and exterior routers to distribute data outside of autonomous systems. The one EGP protocol we discuss in this chapter, which is the only EGP currently in use, is BGP.

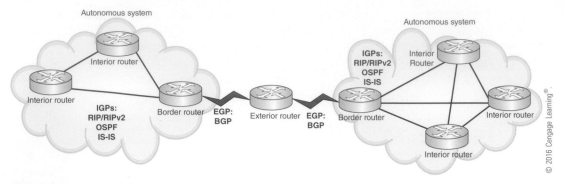

Figure 3-18   BGP is the only routing protocol that communicates across the Internet

An older routing protocol named Exterior Gateway Protocol is now obsolete. However, the term *exterior gateway protocol* is now the generic term to refer to routing protocols that route information between autonomous systems.

Although each of these routing protocols has its own methods of calculating best routes, the information they collect can still be shared between routers using different routing protocols. This is accomplished by a complex, manual process called route redistribution, in which route information is adapted to another routing protocol's specifications. Let's look at the details of these routing protocols, beginning with RIP and RIPv2, which are both outdated but still in use on many networks because of their simplicity and compatibility with older routers.

Network+
1.9

Legacy Networking

RIP and RIPv2

RIP (Routing Information Protocol), a distance-vector routing protocol, is the oldest routing protocol. RIP only factors in the number of hops between nodes when determining the best path from one point to another. It does not consider network congestion or link speed, for example.

Routers using RIP broadcast their routing tables every 30 seconds to other routers, regardless of whether the tables have changed. This broadcasting creates excessive network traffic, especially if a large number of routes exist. If the routing tables change, it may take several minutes before the new information propagates to routers at the far reaches of the network; thus, the convergence time for RIP is poor. However, one advantage to RIP is its stability. For example, RIP prevents routing loops from continuing indefinitely by limiting the number of hops a message can take between its source and its destination to 15. If the number of hops in a path exceeds 15, the network destination is considered unreachable. Thus, RIP does not work well in very large network environments in which data may have to travel through more than 15 routers to reach their destination (for example, on a metro network). Also, compared with other routing protocols, RIP is slower and less secure.

Developers have improved RIP since its release in 1988 and informally renamed the original RIP as RIPv1 (Routing Information Protocol version 1). The latest version, RIPv2 (Routing Information Protocol version 2), generates less broadcast traffic and functions more securely than RIPv1. Still, RIPv2 cannot exceed 15 hops, and it is also considered an outdated routing protocol.

OSPF OSPF (Open Shortest Path First) is an IGP and a link-state routing protocol used on interior or border routers. It was introduced as an improvement to RIP and can coexist with RIP (or RIPv2) on a network. Unlike RIP, OSPF imposes no hop limits on a transmission path. Also, OSPF uses a more complex algorithm for determining best paths than what RIP uses. Under optimal network conditions, the best path is the most direct path between two points. If excessive traffic levels or an outage preclude data from following the most direct path, a router may determine that the most efficient path actually goes through additional routers. Each router running OSPF maintains a database of the other routers' links. If OSPF learns of the failure of a given link, the router can rapidly compute an alternate path. This calculation demands more memory and CPU power than RIP would, but it keeps network bandwidth to a minimum and provides a very fast convergence time, often invisible to users. The algorithms used by link-state protocols and their faster convergence time also prevent routing loops. OSPF is supported by all modern routers. Therefore, it is commonly used on autonomous systems that rely on a mix of routers from different manufacturers.

IS-IS Another IGP, which is also a link-state routing protocol, is IS-IS (Intermediate System to Intermediate System). IS-IS uses a best-path algorithm similar to OSPF's and was originally codified by ISO, which referred to routers as "intermediate systems," thus the protocol's name. Unlike OSPF, however, IS-IS is designed for use on interior routers only. Also, IS-IS is not handcuffed to IPv4 like OSPF is, so it's easy to adapt to IPv6. Service providers generally prefer to use IS-IS in their own networks because it's generally more scalable than OSPF, but OSPF is still more common.

BGP The only current EGP is BGP (Border Gateway Protocol), which has been dubbed the "protocol of the Internet." Whereas OSPF and IS-IS scouting parties only scout out their home territory, a BGP scouting party can go cross-country. BGP can span multiple autonomous systems and is used by border and exterior routers on the Internet.

BGP is a path-vector routing protocol that communicates via BGP-specific messages that travel between routers over TCP sessions. Using BGP, routers can determine best paths based on many different factors. In addition, network administrators can configure BGP to follow policies that might, for example, avoid a certain router or instruct a group of routers to prefer one particular route over other available routes. BGP is the most complex of the routing protocols mentioned in this chapter. If you maintain networks for an ISP or large telecommunications company, you will need to understand BGP.

BGP considers many factors to determine best paths, and is more complex than other distance-vector routing protocols. In fact, its adaptability has earned it the official classification of advanced distance-vector routing protocol. You might also sometimes see BGP classified as a path-vector protocol because it maintains dynamic path information beyond the device's neighboring routers. However, because of its complexity and the number of factors it can consider when calculating best paths, the CompTIA Network+ exam may classify BGP as a hybrid routing protocol, implying that it exhibits characteristics of both distance-vector and link-state routing protocols.

BGP helps speed up routing by grouping networks according to their IP routing prefix and common network administrator, such as an ISP. Each of these autonomous systems can be identified by a globally unique autonomous system number (ASN). ASNs work similarly to

IP addresses that identify individual nodes on a network. Like IP addresses, ASNs have been expanded to accommodate increasing numbers of networks. Each ASN now consists of 32 bits instead of 16 bits, and they are assigned by IANA.

The 16-bit numbers, like port numbers, can range from 0 to 65535. The 32-bit numbers go up to 4,294,967,295. The first and last numbers in each range are reserved. ASNs in the range of 64,512 to 65,534 and in the range of 4,200,000,000 to 4,294,967,294 are available for private use. Network administrators can use these private ASNs within their own network, but private ASNs, like private IP addresses, cannot be used on the open Internet. Also like port numbers, ASNs are usually written as integers. The 32-bit numbers may be written in two blocks of up to 16 bits each with a period between them, such as 1.10.

NETWORK+ EXAM TIP

Table 3-8 provides an overview of the routing protocols covered in this chapter. For the CompTIA Network+ exam, it's important to know which routing protocols function within an autonomous system, and which of these protocols communicate between these systems. You'll also want to know the classification of protocols, especially distance-vector versus link-state.

Troubleshooting Router Issues

Network+
4.2
4.6
5.9

As with any type of communication, many potential points of failure exist in the TCP/IP transmission process, and the number of points increases with the size of the network and the distance of the transmission. Fortunately, TCP/IP comes with a complete set of utilities that can help you track down most TCP/IP-related problems without using expensive software or hardware to analyze network traffic. You should be familiar with the purposes of the following tools and their parameters, not only because the CompTIA Network+ certification exam covers them, but also because you will regularly need these tools in your work with TCP/IP networks.

Network+
4.2
5.9

Troubleshooting Tools

You've already learned about four very important TCP/IP utilities—ping, ipconfig, ifconfig, and nslookup. The following sections present additional TCP/IP commands that can help you discover information about your node and network.

netstat The netstat utility displays TCP/IP statistics and details about TCP/IP components and connections on a host. Information that can be obtained from the netstat command includes the port on which a particular TCP/IP service is running, regardless of whether a remote node is logged on to a host; which network connections are currently established for a client; how many messages have been handled by a network interface since it was activated; and how many data errors have occurred on a particular network interface. As you can imagine, with so much information available, the netstat utility makes a powerful diagnostic tool.

For example, suppose you are a network administrator in charge of maintaining file, print, and Web servers for an organization. You discover that your Web server, which has multiple processors, sufficient hard disk space, and multiple NICs, is suddenly taking twice as long to respond to HTTP requests. Of course, you would want to check the server's memory resources as well as its Web server software to determine that nothing is wrong with either of those. In addition, you can use the netstat utility to determine the characteristics of the traffic going into and out of each NIC. You may discover that one network card is consistently handling

80 percent of the traffic, even though you had configured the server to share traffic equally between the two. This fact may lead you to run hardware diagnostics on the NIC, and perhaps discover that its onboard processor has failed, making it much slower than the other NIC. The `netstat` command provides a quick way to view traffic statistics, without having to run a more complex traffic analysis program, such as Wireshark.

Like other TCP/IP commands, `netstat` can be used with a number of different parameters. Table 3-9 shows some of these options.

Table 3-9 `netstat` command options

`netstat` command	Description
`netstat`	Displays a list of all active TCP/IP connections on the local machine, including the Transport layer protocol used (usually just TCP), messages sent and received, IP address, and state of those connections.
`netstat -n`	Lists current connections, including IP addresses and port numbers.
`netstat -f`	Lists current connections, including IP addresses, port numbers, and FQDNs.
`netstat -a`	Lists all current TCP connections and all listening TCP and UDP ports.
`netstat -p tcp`	Lists current connections, including IP addresses, port numbers, and FQDNs, for the specified protocol (TCP or UDP).
`netstat -e`	Displays statistics about messages sent over a network interface, including errors and discards.
`netstat -s`	Displays statistics about each message transmitted by a host, separated according to protocol type (IP, TCP, UDP, or ICMP).
`netstat -r`	Displays routing table information.
`netstat -o`	Lists the processor identifier (PID) for each process using a connection and information about the connection.
`netstat -b`	Lists the name of each process using a connection and information about the connection. Requires an elevated command prompt.

© 2016 Cengage Learning®.

Command parameters can be combined into a single command. For example, entering the command `netstat -an` will display the IP addresses and port numbers of active TCP connections and listening TCP and UDP ports.

Network+
4.2 **Applying Concepts**

Identify a Process Hogging Network Resources

Suppose you notice a sudden decrease in network performance and suspect malware is hogging network resources. Follow these steps to identify a process, which can be a legitimate process or malware that is affecting network performance:

1. Every process is assigned a process identifier (PID). To display the PID associated with each network connection, open an elevated command prompt and enter the command `netstat -o`.

2. You can identify the names of the processes for each PID by looking in Task Manager (press CTRL+ALT+DEL and then click **Task Manager**.) On the Processes tab, if the PID column is not showing, right-click a column heading and check **PID**. (You may have to click the More details option at the bottom of the window first.)

3. Alternatively, you can have netstat resolve process names with the `netstat -b` command, though it will take longer for the utility to run. If you don't recognize the name, do a quick Google search to learn about it.

4. You might need to forcefully stop an out-of-control process. To stop a process that refuses to stop by normal means (such as when using the Windows Services console), you can use the `taskkill` command with the `/f` parameter and the process's PID to forcefully kill the process. For example, if the PID is 2212, enter the command:

```
taskkill /f /pid:2212
```

nbtstat NetBIOS is a Windows protocol that was once an alternative to TCP/IP for networking. Windows still supports NetBIOS for backward compatibility with legacy applications that rely on NetBIOS, and on UNIX and Linux systems, you can implement NetBIOS through the Samba suite of programs. NetBIOS requires each workstation that uses it to have a NetBIOS name, and NetBIOS has its own name resolution service. NetBIOS alone is not routable. However, when encapsulated in another protocol such as IP, it can be routed. In that case, as you may recall from Chapter 2, it is called NBT (NetBIOS over TCP/IP). For networks that require NetBIOS to support older applications, the nbtstat (NetBIOS over TCP/IP Statistics) utility can provide information about NetBIOS statistics and resolve NetBIOS names to their IP addresses. In other words, if you know the NetBIOS name of a workstation, you can use `nbtstat` to determine its IP address.

If a network administrator needs the NetBIOS name of a system running Windows, she uses the `nbtstat -A` command with the IP address to obtain the NetBIOS name and MAC address of the NIC. In Figure 3-19, the `nbtstat -A 192.168.1.3` command yields the device's NetBIOS name *SLANE-LAPTOP* and the MAC address C0-CB-38-25-A8-1B.

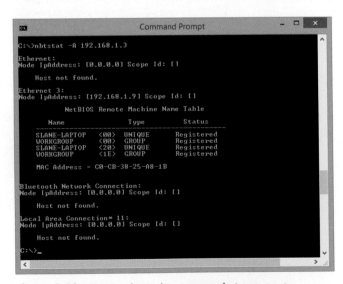

Figure 3-19 Output from the command `nbtstat -A`

Source: Mircrosoft LLC

Table 3-10 covers several parameters available for the `nbtstat` command. Notice that they are case sensitive: The `-a` parameter has a different meaning than the `-A` parameter.

Table 3-10   `nbtstat` **command options**

`nbtstat` **command**	**Description**
`nbtstat -a StudentPC`	Displays a machine's name table given its NetBIOS name; the name of the machine must be supplied after the `-a` parameter.
`nbtstat -A 192.168.1.114`	Displays a machine's name table given its IP address; the IP address of the machine must be supplied after the `-A` parameter.
`nbtstat -n`	Displays the lmhosts file, which is the NetBIOS name table, and is similar to the hosts file.
`nbtstat -r`	Purges and rebuilds the NetBIOS name cache on the local computer using entries in the lmhosts file.
`nbtstat -RR`	Releases and renews the NetBIOS names kept by the WINS server. WINS (Windows Internet Name Service) resolves NetBIOS names to IP addresses and is similar to the DNS name resolution service.
`nbtstat -s`	Displays a list of all the current NetBIOS sessions for a machine.

© 2016 Cengage Learning®

tracert or traceroute The Windows tracert utility uses ICMP echo requests to trace the path from one networked node to another, identifying all intermediate hops between the two nodes. Linux, UNIX, and OS X systems take a slightly different approach with their traceroute utility by sending UDP messages to a random port on the destination node, but the concept is still the same. Suppose, for example, you work in technical support for a large company and one afternoon you receive calls from several employees complaining about slow Internet connections. With only that knowledge, you can't say whether the problem lies with your company's LAN (for example, a backbone switch or router), DNS server, WAN connection, or your service provider's incoming signal. In this situation, the traceroute or tracert utility can help you assess where network performance has deteriorated.

Both traceroute and tracert utilities employ a trial-and-error approach to discover the nodes at each hop from the source to the destination. Traceroute targets a random, unused port on the destination node, and listens for an ICMP "Port Unreachable" message in response from the destination node. The tracert utility simply listens for an ICMP echo reply from the destination. However, both utilities limit the life span of these repeated trial messages, called probes, thereby triggering routers along the route to return specific information about the route being traversed. In fact, three probes are sent with each iteration so that averages can be calculated from the three responses at each step. Study Figure 3-20 to see how a trace works with `traceroute`.

1. The first three datagrams transmitted have their TTL set to 1. Because the TTL determines how many more network hops a datagram can make, datagrams with a TTL of 1 expire as they hit the first router. When they expire, a message is returned to the source—in this case, the node that began the trace.

2. Using the return messages, the trace now knows the identity of the first router. After it learns about the first router in the path, it transmits a series of datagrams with a TTL of 2 to determine the identity of the second router.

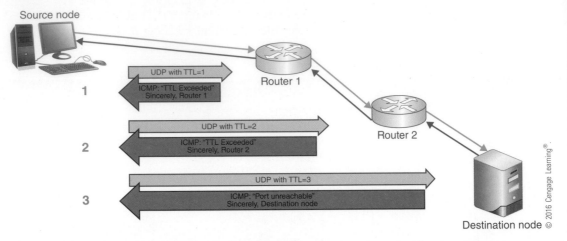

Figure 3-20 The traceroute utility uses error messages from routers to map nodes on a route

3. The process continues for the next router in the path, and then the fourth, fifth, and so on, until the destination node is reached. The trace also returns the amount of time it took for the datagrams to reach each router in the path.

This process is identical for `tracert` in Windows except for two modifications. First, the probes sent from the source are ICMP echo request messages. (Each message is still limited by the specific TTL restrictions.) Second, the final reply from the destination node is an ICMP echo reply rather than an ICMP port unreachable error message.

Network+
4.2

Applying Concepts

Trace the Route to *Google.com*

You can perform a trace using an IP address or a host name. On a UNIX or Linux system, the command syntax would be:

traceroute 8.8.8.8 or **traceroute google.com**

Because tracert is installed by default on Windows, you'll use a Windows machine for this exercise instead:

1. On a Windows system, use `tracert` to perform a trace on one of Google's public DNS servers with the command **tracert 8.8.8.8**. How many hops were traced? What is the IP address of the final hop?

2. Use `tracert` to perform a trace on Google's Web server with the command **tracert google.com**. How many hops were traced this time? What is the IP address of the final hop? Why is this IP address different than the IP address of the final hop in the previous step?

The `traceroute` or `tracert` command has several available parameters. For example, on a Windows-based system, `tracert -4` forces the utility to use only IPv4 transmission. Table 3-11 describes some of the popular `traceroute` parameters. These parameters work similarly with `tracert`, though `tracert` may require different letters for the same parameters.

Table 3-11   `traceroute` and `tracert` command options

`traceroute` **command**	**Description**

`traceroute -n google.com`
or
`tracert -d google.com`
	Instructs the command to not resolve IP addresses to host names.

`traceroute -m 12 google.com`
or
`tracert -h 12 google.com`
	Specifies the maximum number of hops the messages should take when attempting to reach a host. This parameter must be followed by a specific number of hops; if you do not use this option to specify a maximum number of hops, the command defaults to 30.

`traceroute -w 2 google.com`
or
`tracert -w 2000 google.com`
	Identifies a timeout period for responses; this parameter must be followed by a variable to indicate the number of seconds in Linux or milliseconds in Windows that the utility should wait for a response. The default time is usually between 3 and 5 seconds for Linux and 4000 milliseconds (4 seconds) for Windows.

`traceroute -f 3 google.com`	Sets the first TTL value and must be followed by a variable to indicate the number of hops for the first probe. The default value is 1, which begins the trace at the first router on the route. Beginning at later hops in the route can help narrow down the location of a network problem. Tracert does not have a corresponding parameter for this function.

`traceroute -6 google.com`
or
`tracert -6 google.com`
	Forces the command to use IPv6 packets instead of IPv4. The other parameters can be added to these IPv6 commands and function essentially the same as they do in IPv4.

Note that a trace test might stop before reaching the destination. This usually happens for one of three reasons. One, the device the trace is attempting to reach is down. Two, it's too busy to process lower-priority messages such as UDP or ICMP. Or three, it does not accept the UDP or ICMP transmissions being sent because a firewall blocks these types of messages, especially if it receives several in a short period of time. If you are trying to trace a route to a host situated behind a firewall, your efforts might be thwarted. (Because `ping` uses ICMP transmissions, the same limitations exist for that utility.)

NOTE

UNIX and Linux systems can be configured to use ICMP `traceroute` messages instead of UDP by adding the following parameters to the command: `traceroute -I -n google.com`. The `-I` parameter instructs traceroute to use ICMP echo requests instead of UDP datagrams. The `-n` parameter prevents `traceroute` from attempting to resolve host names for every node encountered.

There is a third type of `traceroute` available on UNIX and Linux systems: TCP. Sometimes TCP messages will get through a firewall where ICMP and UDP are restricted from access. Use the `-T` parameter to produce TCP messages during the trace.

One possible work-around for firewall-imposed limitations on multiple UDP or ICMP probes in a short period of time is to add more of a delay between the probe repetitions. This can be done with the `-z` parameter followed by the number of seconds (up to 10) for the minimum wait time between probes. This option, like many others, is only available for `traceroute`, not `tracert`.

Many Linux distributions, like Ubuntu, do not include the traceroute utility by default. You will have to install traceroute to use it on those systems. You may find in its place a simpler utility called tracepath. The `tracepath` command does not provide as many options as `traceroute`. However, it is based on the same principles, and might be sufficient to save you the time of installing the traceroute package.

A trace cannot detect router configuration problems or predict variations of routes over a period of time. Therefore, a trace is best used on a network with which you are already familiar. The traceroute or tracert utility can help you diagnose network congestion or network failures. You can then use your judgment and experience to compare the actual test results with what you anticipate the results should be.

pathping The Windows utility **pathping** combines elements of both ping and tracert to provide deeper information about network issues along a route. It sends multiple pings to each hop along a route, then compiles the information into a single report. To see a sample of the type of information `pathping` provides, try the following command:

`pathping google.com`

When a command like `pathping` takes a while to run, you might want to stop it before it's completed. To stop a command while it's running, press CTRL+C.

One of the primary disadvantages of `pathping` is the amount of time it takes to run. You can shorten running time by limiting the number of queries per hop with the –q parameter. By default, `pathping` sends 100 pings per hop. To reduce that number to 4, you could modify the previous command as follows:

`pathping –q 4 google.com`

Like the other command-line utilities we've studied, `pathping` can be used with any of several parameters. Table 3-12 gives some examples.

Table 3-12   `pathping` command options

`pathping` command	Description
`pathping –n google.com`	Instructs the command to not resolve IP addresses to host names.
`pathping –h 12 google.com`	Specifies the maximum number of hops the messages should take when attempting to reach a host (the default is 30); this parameter must be followed by a specific number of hops.
`pathping –p 2000 google.com`	Identifies the wait time between pings; this parameter must be followed by a variable to indicate the number of milliseconds to wait. The default time is 4000 milliseconds (4 seconds).
`pathping –q 4 google.com`	Limits the number of queries per hop; must be followed by a variable to indicate the number of queries allowed.

Linux offers its own version of the pathping utility, called mtr, which is short for "my traceroute." Even though it's named after traceroute, it actually functions more like pathping, by combining traits of both ping and traceroute. Like tracepath, mtr may be installed by default on several Linux distributions. Ubuntu, for example, includes a non-GUI "tiny" version of mtr, called "mtr-tiny," by default. If it's not available on your current system or if you want to upgrade to the full version, do a Google search for the command needed to install mtr on your distribution because the installation command varies by distribution.

Solving Common Routing Problems

You can use the tools presented in this chapter to troubleshoot and solve several common problems on your network. Table 3-13 gives a brief summary of all of the command-line utilities we've covered so far and how they can help you. Using the table as a reference, let's next see which utilities might be helpful when facing some common routing problems.

Table 3-13   Command-line utilities

Command	Common uses
ping	Verifies connectivity between two nodes on a network
ipconfig or ifconfig	Provides information about TCP/IP network connections and the ability to manage some of those settings
nslookup	Queries DNS servers and provides the ability to manage the settings for accessing those servers
netstat	Displays TCP/IP statistics and details about TCP/IP components and connections on a host
nbtstat	Provides information about NetBIOS statistics and resolves NetBIOS names to their IP addresses
traceroute or tracert	Traces the path from one networked node to another, identifying all intermediate hops between the two nodes
arp	Provides a way of obtaining information from and manipulating a device's ARP table
pathping (mtr on Linux/UNIX/OS X)	Sends multiple pings to each hop along a route, then compiles the information into a single report

© 2016 Cengage Learning®.

Interface Errors   Interface errors occur when a logical (not physical) connection between a node and a network is malfunctioning. They can be prompted by any number of problems, including interface misconfiguration. Something as simple as having the wrong port assigned to a service can prevent the service from doing its job. Sometimes the problem may be hiding deep inside a network device or table, in which case the network administrator will probably have to solve the problem. But a network technician can get started on the problem by keeping in mind these two important guidelines:

1. The ping command is a great place to start with an interface error. Use ping to narrow down where the trouble is located.

2. The `netstat` command can give you a list of interfaces on a device, and then can be used to troubleshoot network interface errors. Make sure that running services are listening to the correct network ports. Watch for signs of malicious software listening for connections on your network, and notice what active connections are reported as well. Take special note of the status of each interface reported, and be sure to interpret and understand any flags in the output.

Hardware Failure When a router, switch, NIC, or other hardware goes down, your job as a network technician includes identifying the location of the hardware failure. Even on smaller networks, it can be a challenge to determine exactly which device is causing problems. Though you could manually check each device on your network for errors, you might be able to shorten your list with a little detective work first. Here's how:

1. Use `tracert` or `traceroute` (depending your network) to track down malfunctioning routers and other devices on larger networks. Because ICMP messages are considered low priority, be sure to run the command multiple times and compare the results before drawing any conclusions.

2. Keep in mind that routers are designed to route traffic to other destinations. You might get more accurate `tracert` or `traceroute` feedback on a questionable router if you target a node on the other side of that router rather than aiming for the router itself.

Discovering Neighbor Devices Routers learn about all of the devices on their networks via a process called **neighbor discovery**. This process can go awry when changes are made to the network, or when a problem is developing but is only producing sporadic symptoms.

On IPv4 networks, the process now called *neighbor discovery* is managed by ARP with help from ICMP. The `arp` command can be used on IPv4 devices to diagnose and repair problems with ARP tables. If you notice inconsistent connectivity issues related to certain addresses, you may need to flush the ARP table on any device experiencing the problem. This forces the device to repopulate the ARP table in order to correct any errors.

IPv6 devices use Neighbor Discovery Protocol (NDP) to automatically detect neighboring devices, and to automatically adjust when neighboring nodes fail or are removed from the network. NDP eliminates the need for ARP and some ICMP functions in IPv6 networks, and is much more resistant to hacking attempts than ARP.

Path MTU Black Hole Recall that an MTU is the maximum transmission size, in bytes, that routers in a message's path will allow. For Ethernet, the MTU is 1500 bytes, a value that is generally considered the Internet standard. However, other Layer 2 technologies might allow higher MTUs, or require lower MTUs.

Some special-purpose networks use a proprietary version of Ethernet that allows for a jumbo frame, in which the MTU can be as high as 9198 bytes, depending on the type of Ethernet architecture used.

When a router receives a message that is too large for the next segment's MTU, the router is supposed to respond with an ICMP error message to the sender. Sometimes, though, these error messages are not returned correctly. This can result in an MTU black hole along the path, where messages are being lost for no apparent reason.

If you suspect an MTU black hole is causing messages to not get through to their destinations, you can use the `ping` command to determine the largest size message that can successfully traverse a path to its destination by adjusting the buffer size of the ICMP echo message. Using too large of a buffer will prevent the messages from returning in response to your ping. Start with a smaller buffer and work your way up to determine the largest MTU that the route can handle. The `ping` parameters needed in Windows are −f (do not fragment the IP packet) and −l (packet or buffer size is specified following the lowercase L). For example, to ping the given IP address with a buffer size of 1024, enter this command on a Windows machine:

```
ping -f -l 1024 92.13.200.5
```

Missing IP Routes Certain routes must be statically routed. This is true for the gateway of last resort, or routes to networks connected directly to the local network. But sometimes this information becomes corrupted, outdated, or is simply lost from the routing table, resulting in missing IP routes. This is particularly a problem when the default route is the one affected.

To begin troubleshooting the device's static routes and determine which routes have been compromised, use the `netstat -r` command to display the routing table's contents. Be sure to check that IP addresses are configured correctly for all interfaces. You might also need to troubleshoot the routing protocol settings being used on the network's routers. Also confirm that none of the affected routers are in passive-interface mode because you want these routers to communicate routing table information with neighboring nodes.

Chapter Summary

TCP/IP Core Protocols

- TCP (Transmission Control Protocol) is an OSI Transport layer, connection-oriented protocol that requires a connection to be established between communicating nodes before it will transmit data. TCP provides reliability through checksum, flow control, and sequencing information.

- UDP (User Datagram Protocol), like TCP, is a Transport layer protocol. UDP is a connectionless service and offers no delivery guarantees. But UDP is more efficient than TCP and useful in applications that require fast data transmission, such as videoconferencing.

- IP (Internet Protocol) belongs to the Network layer of the OSI model and provides information about how and where data should be delivered.

- ARP (Address Resolution Protocol) belongs to the Data Link layer of the OSI model. It obtains the MAC (physical) address of a host, or node, and then creates a local database that maps the IP (logical) address to the host's MAC (physical) address.

- ICMP (Internet Control Message Protocol) is a Network layer core protocol that reports on the success or failure of data delivery, although it does not correct the errors that it detects. On IPv6 networks, ICMPv6 detects and reports data transmission errors, discovers other nodes on a network, and manages multicasting.

Routers and How They Work

■ A router is a multiport device that can connect dissimilar LANs and WANs running at different transmission speeds, using a variety of protocols. Routers interpret logical addresses and determine the best path between nodes. They operate at the Network layer (Layer 3) or higher of the OSI model.

■ Static routing is a technique in which a network administrator programs a router to use specific paths between nodes. Dynamic routing automatically calculates the best path between two nodes and accumulates this information in a routing table. If congestion or failures affect the network, a router using dynamic routing can detect the problems and reroute data through a different path. Most modern networks use dynamic routing.

■ To determine the best path, routers communicate with each other through routing protocols, including RIP, RIPv2, OSPF, IS-IS, and BGP. Different routing protocols use different algorithms and routing metrics to choose the best path.

■ Routing metrics may factor in the number of hops between nodes, throughput, delay, MTU, cost, load, and reliability.

■ RIP (Routing Information Protocol), a distance-vector routing protocol, is the slowest and least secure routing protocol and limits transmissions to 15 hops. RIPv2 makes up for some of the original RIP's overhead and security limitations, but its forwarding ability is limited to 15 hops. RIP belongs to the IGP (interior gateway protocol) category of protocols that can forward data only within an autonomous LAN.

■ OSPF (Open Shortest Path First) is a link-state routing protocol used on interior or border routers. It was introduced as an improvement to RIP and can coexist with RIP (or RIPv2) on a network. Unlike RIP, OSPF imposes no hop limits on a transmission path. Also, OSPF uses a more complex algorithm for determining best paths than RIP uses.

■ IS-IS uses virtually the same methods as OSPF to calculate best paths, is less common, and is limited to interior routers.

■ BGP (Border Gateway Protocol), designed primarily for routing over Internet backbones, uses the most complex best-path calculation of all the commonly used routing protocols. It's considered an exterior routing protocol.

Troubleshooting Router Issues

■ The netstat utility displays TCP/IP statistics and the state of current TCP/IP components and connections. It also displays ports, which can signal whether services are using the correct ports.

■ The nbtstat utility provides information about NetBIOS names and their addresses. If you know the NetBIOS name of a workstation, you can use `nbtstat` to determine the workstation's IP address.

■ The traceroute utility, known as tracert on Windows-based systems, uses ICMP to trace the path from one networked node to another, identifying all intermediate hops between the two nodes. This utility is useful for determining router or subnet connectivity problems.

- The `route` command allows you to view a host's routing table and add, delete, or modify preferred routes.

Key Terms

For definitions of key terms, see the Glossary near the end of the book.

AD (administrative distance)

ARP cache

ARP table

AS (autonomous system)

ASN (autonomous system number)

best path

BGP (Border Gateway Protocol)

border router

broadcast domain

checksum

connectivity device

convergence time

default route

distance-vector routing protocol

dynamic ARP table entry

dynamic routing

EGP (exterior gateway protocol)

exterior router

flow

flow control

gateway of last resort

gateway router

hop

hop limit

hybrid routing protocol

IGMP (Internet Group Management Protocol or Internet Group Multicast Protocol)

IGP (interior gateway protocol)

interface error

interior router

internetwork

IS-IS (Intermediate System to Intermediate System)

ISN (Initial Sequence Number)

jumbo frame

latency

Layer 3 switch

Layer 4 switch

link-state routing protocol

looking glass site

MAC address lookup table

MTU (maximum transmission unit)

MTU black hole

nbtstat (NetBIOS over TCP/IP Statistics)

neighbor discovery

netstat

OSPF (Open Shortest Path First)

pathping

probe

RIP (Routing Information Protocol)

RIPv2 (Routing Information Protocol version 2)

`route` command

route redistribution

routing cost

routing loop

routing metric

routing protocol

routing table

sequence number

static ARP table entry

static routing

three-way handshake

traceroute

tracert

TTL (Time to Live)

Review Questions

1. Which protocol's header would a Layer 4 device read and process?

    a. IP

    b. TCP

    c. ARP

    d. HTTP

2. What number does a host use to identify the application involved in a transmission?

    a. IP address

    b. MAC address

    c. Port number

    d. Sequence number

3. What field in a TCP segment is used to determine if an arriving data unit exactly matches the data unit sent by the source?

    a. Source port

    b. Acknowledgment number

    c. Data

    d. Checksum

4. At which OSI layer does IP operate?

    a. Application layer

    b. Transport layer

    c. Network layer

    d. Data Link layer

5. Which OSI layer is responsible for directing data from one LAN to another?

    a. Transport layer

    b. Network layer

    c. Data Link layer

    d. Physical layer

6. What kind of route is created when a network administrator configures a router to use a specific path between nodes?

    a. Trace route

    b. Static route

    c. Default route

    d. Best path

7. When a router can't determine a path to a message's destination, where does it send the message?

    a. Default gateway

    b. Default route

    c. Gateway of last resort

    d. Routing table

8. A routing protocol's reliability and priority are rated by what measurement?

    a. Routing table

    b. MTU

    c. Latency

    d. AD

9. Which routing protocol does an exterior router use to collect data to build its routing tables?

    a. RIPv2

    b. BGP

    c. OSPF

    d. IS-IS

10. When messages to a remote Web server are being lost for no apparent reason and you suspect the problem might be a path MTU black hole, which TCP/IP utility can you use to diagnose the problem?

    a. netstat

    b. traceroute

    c. nbtstat

    d. ping

11. What three characteristics distinguish TCP from UDP?

12. What process is used to establish a TCP connection?

13. Which two protocols are essential to IPv4 networks, but whose functions are performed by ICMPv6 on IPv6 networks?

14. What is the difference between dynamic ARP table entries and static ARP table entries?

15. What four functions do all routers perform?

16. What database does a router consult before determining the most efficient path for delivering a message?

17. Manually modifying a routing table can cause messages to get stuck hopping between a limited number of routers. What is this problem called?

18. Give three examples of routing metrics used by routers to determine the best of various available routing paths.

19. What kind of Web site allows you to remotely collect network routing information back to your actual location?

20. List three interior gateway protocols (IGPs).

Hands-On Projects

Project 3-1: Repair a Duplicate IP Address

ARP can be a valuable troubleshooting tool for discovering the identity of a machine whose IP address you know, or for identifying the problem of two machines assigned the same IP address. Let's see what happens when two devices on the network have the same IP address. First you change the IP address of a local Windows 7 or Windows 8.1 machine to match an IP address of another device—in other words, you "break" the computer. Then you see how the arp command helps you diagnose the problem.

1. Open a Command Prompt window and enter the command **arp –a**. Your device's IP address is listed as the Interface address at the top of the list. Write down this IP address and the address of another device on the network.

2. Open the Network and Sharing Center, click **Change adapter settings**, right-click the active network connection, and click **Properties**. If necessary, enter an administrator password in the UAC box and click **Yes**.

3. Select Internet Protocol Version 4 (TCP/IPv4) and click **Properties**. Set the IP address to match the other device's IP address that you wrote down in Step 1. The system automatically assigns the Subnet mask, as shown in Figure 3-21. Click **OK**.

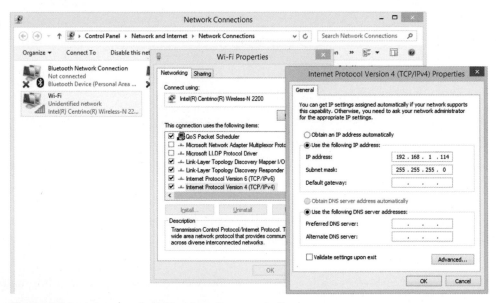

Figure 3-21   Subnet mask field assigned automatically

Source: Mircrosoft LLC

4. Back at the command prompt, enter **ipconfig /all**.

5. Find the appropriate network connection and identify your computer's current IPv4 address. Has your computer identified the duplicate IP address problem yet? Your

computer may also have autoconfigured another IP address. If so, what address did your computer resort to?

6. In the window on the left side of Figure 3-22, you can see a warning that the IP address is a duplicate. The system also shows a preferred IPv4 address of 169.254.181.132, which is an APIPA address. How can you tell this is an APIPA address?

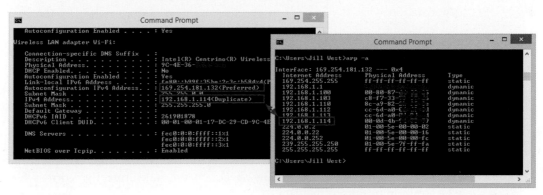

Figure 3-22   The computer automatically configured an APIPA address

Source: Mircrosoft LLC

7. To confirm the duplication of IP addresses, enter the command **arp –a**.

You can see on the right side of Figure 3-22 that the local computer's IPv4 address matches another IP address in the ARP table, and again you see the APIPA address assigned to the local interface. The solution to this problem is to set a different static IP address through the Network and Sharing Center, or to configure the NIC to use DHCP to request a unique IP address.

8. Open the Internet Protocol Version 4 (TCP/IPv4) Properties dialog box again and select the option **Obtain an IP address automatically**, then click **OK**. Close the Wi-Fi Properties dialog box, the Network Connections window, and the Network and Sharing Center window.

9. Run the **ipconfig** command or the **arp –a** command to confirm that a unique IP address has been assigned, then close the command window.

Project 3-2: Redirect Command Output to a Text File

Sometimes when you're using a command, such as the `pathping` command, the sheer amount of output can be daunting to work with. There's no way to search through the output for specific information, and you can only expand the Command Prompt window so far. One solution to this problem is to redirect the command output to a text file where you can search the text, copy and paste text, and save the output for future reference.

1. To accomplish this feat, you'll need to add a redirection operator to the command whose output you want to export to a text file. Try this simple command:

```
ipconfig > ipconfigtest.txt
```

In this case, you have run the `ipconfig` command and redirected the output to a text file named ipconfigtest.txt. By default, the file is saved to the current default folder, for example, C:\Users\JillWest.

2. To specify the location of the file when you create it, you can add the path to the file in the command line. For example, to save the file to the desktop of JillWest, use the following command:

```
ipconfig > C:\Users\JillWest\Desktop\ipconfigtest.txt
```

3. If you already have a file on the desktop by that name, the file will be overwritten with the new data. So what if you want to append data to an existing file? Use the >> operator. (Substitute the correct file path to your desktop.)

```
ipconfig >> C:\Users\JillWest\Desktop\ipconfigtest.txt
```

Now the new output will appear at the end of the existing file, and all of the data is preserved within this single file. This option is useful when collecting data from repeated tests or from multiple computers, where you want all of the data to converge into a single file for future analysis.

4. Where do command parameters fit when redirecting output? Show the IP address and port number of all TCP and UDP connections on the computer using the netstat command. In the following command, substitute the correct file path to your desktop to output the data to a new file:

```
netstat -an > C:\Users\JillWest\Desktop\connections.txt
```

Notice that any parameters you want to use should be inserted after the command itself and before the redirection operator. Also note that, if you wanted to, you could include a space in the filename by putting quotation marks around the entire filename *and* location:

```
ping 8.8.8.8 > "C:\Users\JillWest\Desktop\find google.txt"
```

What do you do if you've already run a command, and there is data in the output that you desperately want to save? You may realize already that you can't perform a normal copy-and-paste operation in the Command Prompt window. However, there is a way to copy the output on the screen and paste it into another program.

5. To see how this works, run the command **ipconfig /all**. The new output populates your Command Prompt window.

6. Scroll up to the portion of data reported by ipconfig so that all of the data you want to keep is visible in the Command Prompt window.

7. Right-click anywhere in the Command Prompt window and click **Mark**.

8. Press and hold the mouse button, drag the mouse to highlight all the text you want to copy, and then press Enter. The text is copied into the Clipboard.

9. Go to any text editor program and paste the selected text into your document.

Project 3-3: Create a Routing Table Entry in Windows

HANDS-ON PROJECTS

The routing table can be viewed and modified using the route command at an elevated command prompt.

1. In this chapter, you used both route print and netstat -r to view the routing table. Because you'll need the route command to modify the routing table, use the **route print** command to view the routing table.

The list of interfaces on your computer should look familiar—you saw these when you ran `ipconfig` in Chapter 2. Several of the IPv4 routes on your routing table should look familiar as well. 127.0.0.1 is your loopback address, and the surrounding 127.x.y.z routes refer to reserved addresses in that domain. In Figure 3-23, you can see that this computer's IP address is 192.168.1.108. You can also see surrounding reserved addresses for that private domain. 224.0.0.0 is reserved for multicasting, and 255.255.255.255 for certain broadcast messages.

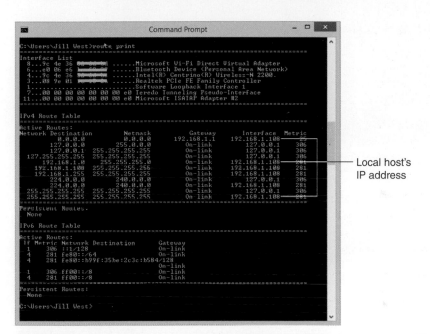

Figure 3-23   Several of the active routes on this computer involve its own IP address

Source: Mircrosoft LLC

In the IPv6 section, ::1/128 is the loopback address. FE80::/64 is the link local address, and the other FE80 address is the IPv6 address assigned to this computer. FF00::/8 is the multicast address.

2. Now add an entry to the routing table that will reroute messages destined for the private network 172.16.50.0/24 to another internal IP address, 192.168.10.8. Enter the following command:

   `route add 172.16.50.0 mask 255.255.255.0 192.168.10.8`

   Now all messages generated by this routing table's local host and addressed to an IP address in the network 172.16.50.0/24 will instead be routed to the host at 192.168.10.8. You can see in Figure 3-24 where this new entry has been inserted.

   Windows resets its routing table during reboot, so you can add the –p parameter after the word `route` if you want the route to persist beyond reboot. (See Figure 3-25.)

3. You can now delete the route you just added with the following command:

   `route delete 172.16.50.0`

Figure 3-24   The static route has been successfully added

Source: Mircrosoft LLC

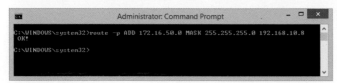

Figure 3-25   The **-p** parameter will ensure this route persists through reboot

Source: Mircrosoft LLC

Project 3-4: Practice Solving Path MTU Black Hole Problems

What is the largest MTU that can be used to reach the *course.com* host from your computer without creating an MTU black hole?

1. To find out, ping *course.com* using an IP packet size of 1024.

2. Keep increasing the packet size until the packet does not return. Do not allow the packet to be fragmented.

3. What is the first `ping` command you used?

4. What is the maximum MTU that got through?

5. What error message appears when an MTU error occurs?

Case Projects

Case Project 3-1: Set Up Ubuntu Server in a VM

In Chapter 2, Case Project 2-1, you created a virtual network using Oracle VirtualBox or Windows 8 Client Hyper-V. In this case study, you create a third VM in your virtual network and install Ubuntu Server in the VM. You also learn how to use some Linux commands. In the next chapter, you'll install an FTP server in Ubuntu Server and make FTP services available to other computers in your network.

Using the same computer that you used in Case Projects 1-1 and 1-2 (which should have Oracle VirtualBox or Client Hyper-V installed), follow these steps:

1. Go to **ubuntu.org** and download the Ubuntu Server OS to your hard drive. The file that downloads is an ISO file.

2. Open the Oracle VM VirtualBox Manager or Hyper-V Manager. Following the directions in the Chapter 1 Case Projects, create a new VM named VM40. Mount the ISO file that contains the Ubuntu Server download to a virtual DVD in your VM.

> Ubuntu Server is only available as a 64-bit OS. To install a 64-bit guest OS in a VM, the host OS must also be 64-bit.

3. Start up the VM and install Ubuntu Server, accepting all default settings. Be sure to write down your Ubuntu host name, Ubuntu username, and password. When given the option, decline to install any extra software bundled with the OS.

4. After you restart the VM, Ubuntu Server launches, which does not have a GUI interface. You should see the shell command interface, as shown in Figure 3-26.

Figure 3-26   Ubuntu Server is installed in a VM in Windows 8.1 Client Hyper-V

Source: Mircrosoft LLC and Canonical Ltd.

5. The shell shows the shell prompt, which usually includes your username and current directory followed by a $. First, enter your username and press **Enter**. Then enter your password and press **Enter**. You're now logged on to your Ubuntu Server.

6. Practice using Ubuntu Server by trying out the commands in Table 3-14. As you do so, you'll examine the directory structure, create a new directory, and put a blank file in it.

Table 3-14   Practice using Linux commands

	Command	Description
1	dir	Lists files and directories in the current directory. In Linux, a directory is treated more like a file than a Windows directory.
2	pwd	Displays the full path to the current directory. When you first log in to a system, that directory is /home/*username*.
3	mkdir mydir	Creates a directory named mydir. The directory is created in the current directory. You must have permission to edit the current directory.
4	cd mydir	Goes to the directory you just created in the /home/*username* directory.
5	touch myfile	Creates a blank file named myfile in the current directory.
6	ls	Similar to dir, lists current directory contents.
7	cd ..	Moves up one level in the directory tree.
8	cd /etc	Changes directory to the /etc directory, where text files are kept for configuring installed programs.
9	ls	Examines the contents of the /etc directory.
10	cd/home	Changes directory to the /home directory.
11	ping 127.0.0.1	Pings the loopback address. Pinging continues until you stop it by using CTRL+C.
12	CTRL+C	Breaks out of a command or process; use it to recover after entering a wrong command or to stop a command that requires you manually halt the output.
13	ifconfig	Displays TCP/IP configuration data.
14	man ifconfig	Displays the page from the Linux Manual about the ifconfig command.
15	df	Displays the amount of free space on your hard drive.
16	exit	Logs out; the login shell prompt appears, where you can log on again. Enter your username and password to log on again.
17	sudo poweroff	Shuts down the VM. You'll need to enter your password and then the system shuts down.

CASE PROJECTS

Case Project 3-2: Decode a TCP Segment in a Wireshark Capture

In this chapter, you walked through a TCP segment to interpret the data included in its header. In this project, you use Wireshark to capture your own HTTP messages, examine the TCP headers, and practice interpreting the data you'll find there.

1. Open Wireshark and snap the window to one side of your screen. Open a browser and snap that window to the other side of your screen so you can see both windows.

In Windows, you can quickly snap a window to one side of your screen by holding down the Win key on your keyboard, pressing either the left or right arrow key, then releasing both keys. Alternately, you can drag a window to one side of your screen until it snaps into position.

2. Start the Wireshark capture. In the browser, navigate to *google.com*. Once the page loads, stop the Wireshark capture. You'll have fewer messages to sort through if you can do this entire process fairly quickly.

3. Now apply a filter to expose the messages involved with your Web site request. Somewhere in your capture, a DNS message will show the original request to resolve the name *google.com* to its IP address. A series of TCP messages will then show the three-way handshake, along with the rest of the data transmission. Because your transmission has to do with requesting a Web page, you need to filter to port 80. Apply the following filter to your capture:

dns or tcp.port eq 80

4. This filter helps reduce the number of messages to the ones you actually want to see. But you'll still probably have to scroll through your results to find exactly the right DNS message that started this process. You'll see DNS in the Protocol field, and something to the effect of "Standard query" and "www.google.com" in the Info field, as shown in Figure 3-27.

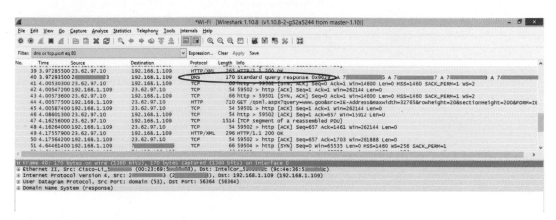

Figure 3-27   This DNS message is a request to resolve the domain name *www.google.com*

Source: The Wireshark Foundation

5. Once you've located this message, click on it and examine the details of the message in the second pane. Answer the following questions:

   a. What is the OUI of the source's NIC?

   b. Which IP version was used?

   c. If the message used IPv4, what was the TTL? If IPv6, what was the hop limit?

   d. Did the message use TCP or UDP?

   e. What is the source port? The destination port?

6. Now check your filter results for the first [SYN] message after this DNS request. Open the TCP segment header in the second pane, and answer the following questions:

If you can't find the TCP stream for this Web page request, your system may have used port 443 instead of port 80. Port 443 is assigned to HTTPS, which is a secure version of HTTP. Run your filter again using port 443 instead of port 80.

a. What is the sequence number?

b. Which flags are set in the TCP segment?

If you're using the default settings in Wireshark, you probably found a sequence number of 1. That's because Wireshark shows relative numbers instead of the actual, random numbers used in the segments themselves. Relative numbers are easier for humans to keep up with, but they provide no security in that they're very predictable. Random numbers, on the other hand, are more difficult to fake.

7. To find the actual, random sequence number assigned to this segment, click on the sequence number field in the second pane, then find the corresponding value now highlighted in the third pane. The actual value is presented in hexadecimal format.

8. Switch the output to show the actual, random numbers (in decimal form) in your capture by clicking on the **Edit** menu, then click **Preferences**, expand the Protocols list, click **TCP**, and uncheck **Relative sequence numbers**. Then click **OK**. Look back at the relative numbers shown in Figure 3-27, and compare the data in that figure to the random numbers shown in Figure 3-28.

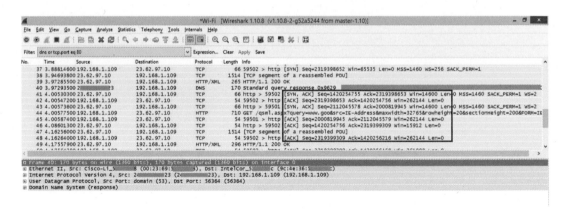

Figure 3-28 The captured messages now show the actual, random numbers used in the Seq and Ack fields

Source: The Wireshark Foundation

9. Apply another filter layer to show only the messages for this TCP conversation. Right-click the [SYN] message and click **Follow TCP Stream**. Close the Follow TCP Stream dialog box that opens, as you will be examining data in the actual capture.

10. Immediately after that initial [SYN] message, locate the [SYN, ACK] message and answer the following questions:

    a. What is the source IP address? The destination IP address?

    b. What is the sequence number? The acknowledgment number?

    c. Which flags are set in the TCP segment?

11. Locate the third message in this three-way handshake, the [ACK] message, and answer the following questions:

    a. What is the source IP address? The destination IP address?

    b. What is the sequence number? The acknowledgment number?

    c. Which flags are set in the TCP segment?

12. The three-way handshake establishes the session, but the conversation continues as the Web server begins to respond to your browser's request for the Web page. At some point later in the conversation, locate an HTTP/XML message that contains the actual data for Google's search page. Recall that there are several layers of headers encapsulating this payload, so you'll need to look at the deepest layer in the message to find the Web page's data. Locate the correct message, and answer the following questions:

    a. List the types of headers included in this message, in order.

    b. What is the source IP address? The destination IP address?

    c. Which flags are set in the TCP segment?

## chapter 4

Structured Cabling and Networking Elements

After reading this chapter and completing the exercises, you will be able to:

- Identify the best practices for managing network and cabling equipment in commercial buildings and work areas

- Explain issues related to managing power and the environment in which networking equipment operates

- Describe characteristics of NIC and Ethernet interfaces

- Troubleshoot network devices and create a network map to be used for network troubleshooting

On the Job

Over the years, our need for localized services or "remote" backups has steadily increased. Part of the solution has been to convert several of our larger wiring closets into small server rooms to host the additional equipment. We place climate monitors in these locations to help monitor temperature and humidity conditions. These monitors report climate conditions via SNMP to our network monitoring system. The network monitoring system then sends notifications to IT staff members if the temperature moves out of a threshold range.

One summer, we placed one of these temperature monitors in a closet where servers had recently been added, and things were good. A few months later, as the temperature cooled outside, we started getting alarms about temperature spikes. The spikes were small at first, but increased as the temperature outside dropped. That was kind of odd.

A little investigation revealed that although the server room had air conditioning, the room's temperature was not managed independently of the nearby offices. As autumn weather cooled the offices in the building, the staff would turn on the heat, warming themselves and, unfortunately, the servers. A tweak of the air conditioning layout quickly resolved this issue and things were once again good.

Robert Wilson
Information Systems Director, McCallie School

So far in this book, you've learned about the OSI model, how computers find each other on a network, and how data gets transported over a network. In this chapter, you explore the basic elements required to build a network. Just as an architect must decide where to place walls and doors, where to install electrical and plumbing systems, and how to manage traffic patterns through rooms to make a building more livable, a network architect must consider many factors regarding hardware and software when designing a network.

This chapter details the hardware used in network architecture: devices, location of those devices, environmental and equipment limitations, and other hardware considerations. You'll see how Ethernet enables the flow of data across the physical network, and how to find the problems that can develop when any piece of this puzzle fails to do its part. These basics are crucial to understanding network design, troubleshooting, and management.

In future chapters, you will dig deeper into the various layers of network components, including the details of cabling and wireless networking.

Network Equipment in Commercial Buildings

Network+
1.5
1.11
4.4
4.6
5.7

If you were to tour hundreds of data centers and equipment rooms at established enterprises—that is, organizations or businesses, especially on a large scale—you would see similar equipment and cabling arrangements. That's because organizations tend to follow a single cabling standard formulated by **TIA (Telecommunications Industry Association)**, and its former parent company **EIA (Electronic Industries Alliance)**. This standard, known as the TIA/EIA-568 Commercial Building Wiring Standard, or **structured cabling**, describes uniform, enterprise-wide cabling systems, regardless of who manufactures or sells the various parts used in the system.

The structured cabling standard describes the best way to install networking media to maximize performance and minimize upkeep. The principles of structured cabling apply no matter what type of media, transmission technology, or networking speeds are involved. It begins at the demarc and ends at a user's workstation. Recall from Chapter 1 that the demarc is the device at the point where a telecommunications service provider's network ends and the organization's network begins, as shown in Figure 4-1. Structured cabling is based on a hierarchical design and assumes a network is based on the star topology.

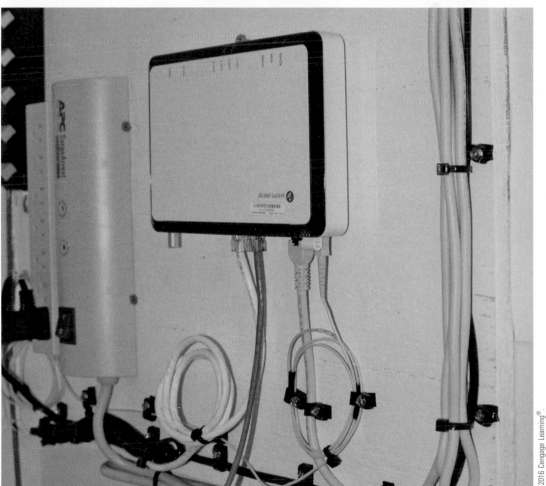

Figure 4-1 Demarc for Internet service to a campus network

TIA and EIA are commonly referred to collectively with the acronym TIA/EIA. Occasionally, including on the CompTIA Network+ exam, you may see the acronyms reversed, as follows: EIA/TIA.

EIA was actually dissolved in 2011. Oversight of the relevant standards was assigned to ECA, the Electronic Components, Assemblies, Equipment & Supplies Association. The standards brand name EIA, however, will continue to be used.

Components of Structured Cabling

Figure 4-2 illustrates from a bird's-eye view the components of structured cabling in an example of an enterprise environment. Figure 4-3 gives a glimpse of structured cabling in a cross-section of a single building. The following list gives detailed descriptions of the components referenced in these figures:

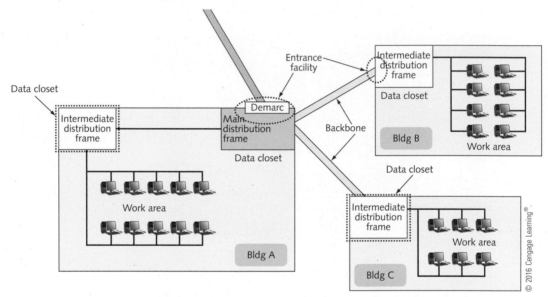

Figure 4-2 TIA/EIA structured cabling in a campus network with three buildings

- *entrance facility*—The location where an incoming network interface enters a building and connects with the building's backbone cabling. This interface might connect the building's network with a campuswide network, or might designate where the telecommunications service provider (whether it is a local phone company, Internet service provider, or long-distance carrier) accepts responsibility for the external connection. The entrance facility includes the demarc if one exists, as well as any entry through a wall to access the demarc if necessary, and may also include space surrounding this point to encircle any of the service provider's equipment, such as cabling and protective boxes.

- *MDF (main distribution frame)*—Also known as the main cross connect, the first point of interconnection between an organization's LAN or WAN and a service provider's facility. An MDF contains the demarc (or an extension from the demarc, if the demarc itself is located outside the building) and other connectivity devices (such as switches and routers) and media (such as fiber-optic cable, which is capable of the greatest throughput). Often,

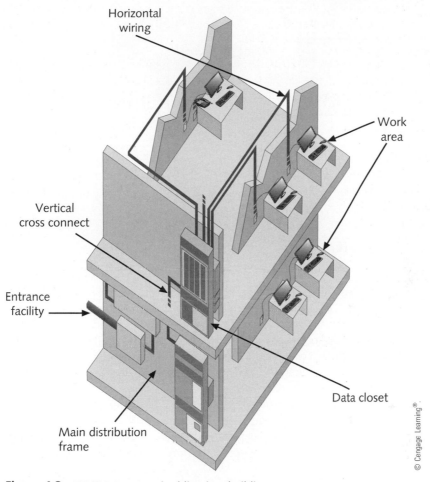

Figure 4-3   TIA/EIA structured cabling in a building

it also houses an organization's main servers. In an enterprise-wide network, equipment held by an MDF connects to equipment housed by another building's IDF, discussed next. The room where the MDF is located is called the data closet, or sometimes equipment room or data room. Because data closets are usually small, enclosed spaces, good cooling and ventilation systems are crucial for maintaining a constant temperature.

• *IDF (intermediate distribution frame)*—A junction point between the MDF and end-user equipment. The TIA/EIA standard specifies at least one IDF per floor, although large organizations may have several data closets per floor to better manage the data feed from the main data facilities.

• *horizontal wiring*—Wiring that connects workstations to the closest data closet. The maximum allowable distance for horizontal wiring is 100 m. This span includes 90 m to connect a data jack on the wall to the data closet plus a maximum of 10 m to connect a workstation to the data jack on the wall. Figure 4-4 depicts a horizontal wiring configuration.

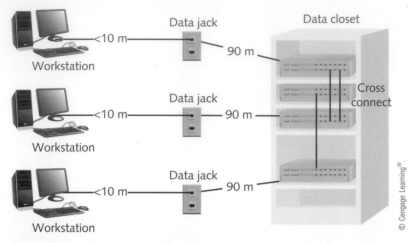

Figure 4-4 Horizontal wiring

TIA/EIA recognizes three possible cabling types for horizontal wiring: UTP, STP, or fiber-optic cable. UTP (unshielded twisted pair) cable is a type of copper-based cable that consists of one or more insulated twisted-wire pairs encased in a plastic sheath. Figure 4-5 shows four grades of UTP cables used with Ethernet. The second cable in the figure is terminated with an RJ-45 connector. STP (shielded twisted pair) cable is a type of copper-based cable containing twisted-wire pairs that are not only individually insulated, but also surrounded by a shielding made of a metallic substance such as foil. Fiber-optic cable is a form of cable that contains one or several glass or plastic fibers in its core and comes in two types: single-mode fiber (SMF) or multimode fiber (MMF). Copper-based cable transmits data via electric signals, and fiber-optic cable transmits data via pulsing light sent from a laser or light-emitting diode (LED). In Chapter 5, you'll learn more about these cables.

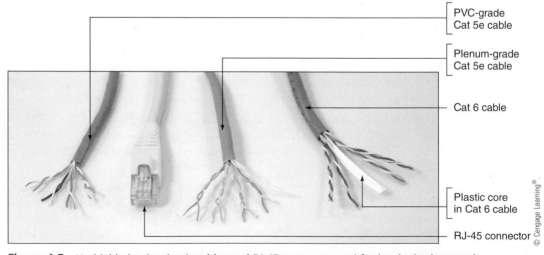

Figure 4-5 Unshielded twisted-pair cables and RJ-45 connector used for local wired networks

- *backbone wiring*—The cables or wireless links that provide interconnection between entrance facilities and MDFs, and between MDFs and IDFs. One component of the backbone is the **vertical cross connect**, which runs between a building's floors. For example, it might connect an MDF and IDF or two IDFs within a building. On modern networks, backbones are usually composed of fiber-optic or UTP cable.

- *work area*—An area that encompasses all patch cables and horizontal wiring necessary to connect the NICs in workstations, printers, and other network devices to the data closet. A **patch cable** is a relatively short (usually between 3 and 25 feet) length of cabling with connectors at both ends. The TIA/EIA standard calls for each wall jack to contain at least one voice and one data outlet, as pictured in Figure 4-6. Realistically, you will encounter a variety of wall jacks. For example, in a student computer lab lacking phones, a wall jack with a combination of voice and data outlets is unnecessary.

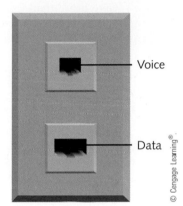

Figure 4-6   A standard TIA/EIA outlet

Figure 4-7 illustrates a cable installation using UTP from the data closet to the work area.

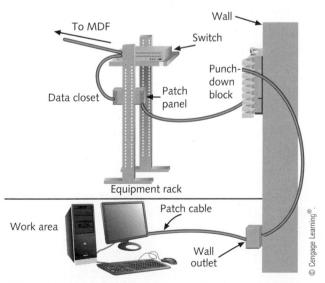

Figure 4-7   A typical UTP cabling installation

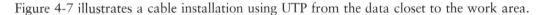

The following sections provide some practical information that you can apply when working with physical networking media. Let's begin by looking at standards for cable management in a building or enterprise.

Cable Management

Network+
1.5
4.4
4.6
5.7

Many network problems can be traced to poor cable installation techniques. The good news is that if you follow both the manufacturers' installation guidelines and the TIA/EIA standards, you are almost guaranteed success. The art of proper cabling could fill an entire book. If you plan to specialize in cable installation, design, or maintenance, you should invest in a reference dedicated to this topic. As a network professional, you will likely occasionally add new cables to a data closet, repair defective cable ends, or install a data outlet. Following are some cable installation tips that will help prevent Physical layer failures:

- *termination*—When terminating twisted-pair cabling, don't leave more than 1 inch of exposed (stripped) cable before a twisted-pair termination. Doing so would increase the possibility for transmission interference between wires, a phenomenon called **cross-talk**. You'll learn how to terminate cable in Chapter 5.

- *bend radius*—Each type of cable has a prescribed **bend radius**, which is the radius of the maximum arc into which you can loop a cable without impairing data transmission. Generally, a twisted-pair cable's bend radius is equal to or greater than four times the diameter of the cable. Be careful not to exceed it.

- *verify continuity*—Use a cable tester to verify that each segment of cabling you install transmits data reliably. This practice will prevent you from later having to track down errors in multiple, long stretches of cable. Chapter 5, which covers network cabling in detail, explains the tools and methods needed to test cable continuity.

- *cinch cables loosely*—Avoid cinching cables so tightly with cable ties that you squeeze their outer covering, a practice that leads to difficult-to-diagnose data errors.

- *protect cables*—Avoid laying cable across the floor where it might sustain damage from rolling chairs or foot traffic. If you must take this tack, cover the cable with a cable protector or cord cover.

- *avoid EMI*—Install cable at least 3 feet away from fluorescent lights or other sources of **EMI (electromagnetic interference)**, which is a type of interference that may be caused by motors, power lines, televisions, copiers, fluorescent lights, or other sources of electrical activity. This will reduce the possibility of noise (interference) that can affect your network's signals.

- *plenum cabling*—If you run cable in the plenum, the area above the ceiling tile or below the subflooring, make sure the cable sheath is plenum-rated, and consult with local electric installation codes to be certain you are installing it correctly. A plenum-rated cable is coated with a flame-resistant jacket that produces less smoke than regular cable coated with **PVC (polyvinyl chloride)**. In the event of a fire, smoke produced by plenum cabling is less toxic than that produced by PVC cabling. Refer back to Figure 4-5 to see a PVC cable compared with a plenum-rated cable.

- *grounding*—Pay attention to grounding requirements and follow them religiously.

- *slack in cable runs*—Measure first, and always leave some slack in cable runs. Stringing cable too tightly risks connectivity and data transmission problems.

- *cable trays*—Use cable management devices such as cable trays, braided sleeving, and furniture grommets, but don't overfill them. Cable trays are usually metal trays built into equipment racks, office desks, or even along the ceiling to help collect cables into a single track.

- *patch panels*—Use patch panels to organize and connect lines. Recall from Chapter 1 that a patch panel is a rack-mounted panel of data receptors. It does nothing to the data transmitted on a line other than pass the data along through the connection. But patch panels do help keep lines organized as they run from walls to racks to network devices, and they make it easy to switch out patch cables of variable lengths when devices are moved or changed.

- *company standards and stock*—Besides adhering to structured cabling hierarchies and standards, you or your network manager should specify standards for the types of cable used by your organization and maintain a list of approved cabling vendors. Keep a supply room stocked with spare parts so that you can easily and quickly replace defective parts.

- *documentation*—Follow these guidelines to manage documentation at your cabling plant:

  ○ Keep your cable plant documentation in a centrally accessible location. Make sure it includes locations, installation dates, lengths, and grades of installed cable.

  ○ Label every data jack or port, patch panel or punch-down block, and connector or circuit. You'll learn more about labeling later in this chapter.

  ○ Use color-coded cables for different purposes and record the color schemes in your documentation. Cables can be purchased in a variety of sheath colors, as shown in Figure 4-8. For example, you might want to use pink for patch cables, green for horizontal wiring, purple for DMZ lines, and gray for vertical (backbone) wiring.

Figure 4-8 Different colors of cables can indicate the general purpose of each cable

© 2016 Cengage Learning®

  ○ Be certain to update your documentation as you make changes to the network. The more you document, the easier it will be to move or add cable segments in the future.

Legacy Networking

Punch-Down Blocks

The precursor to the patch panel is the punch-down block, which is a panel of voice or data receptors into which twisted-pair wire is inserted, or punched down using a punch down tool, to complete a circuit. The type of punch-down block used on data networks is known as the 110 block. 110 blocks are more suitable for data connections than the older 66 block, which was used primarily for telephone connections. (The numerals 66 and 110 refer to the model numbers of the earliest blocks.) 110 blocks are still available in several different capacities. If you do come across 110 blocks in the field, be careful not to untwist twisted-pair cables more than one-half inch before inserting them into the punch-down block. Figure 4-9 shows a patch panel and Figure 4-10 shows a punch-down block.

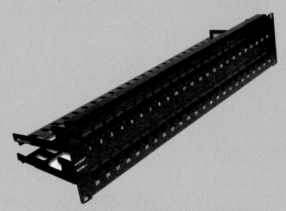

Figure 4-9   Patch panel. Courtesy of Siemon

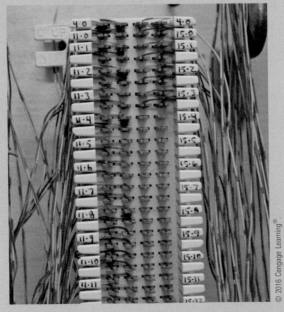

Figure 4-10   Punch-down block

Network+
5.7
Device Management

Keeping track of all your network devices is just as important as cable management. Maintaining up-to-date records about your network devices will reduce your workload and make troubleshooting easier and more efficient. Adequate record keeping also saves money by preventing unnecessary purchases. The secret to keeping track of devices is naming them systematically, and then labeling them with those names. A good naming convention can serve double duty by including essential information about the device.

Labeling and Naming Conventions A word to the wise network technician: Learn to view good labeling as a beautiful thing! For the meticulous technician, labeling can become an art form. Here are some tips to get started:

- As discussed earlier, you can use color-coded cables for different general purposes. However, don't rely on the cable colors alone; use cable tags to identify each cable's specific purpose, as shown in Figure 4-11.

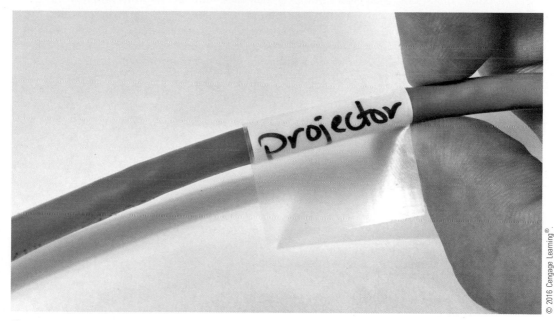

© 2016 Cengage Learning®

Figure 4-11 Cable label with a wrap-around, protective cover

- In addition to labeling cables, also label the ports and jacks that cables connect to. Place the labels directly on patch panels, switches, routers, wall plates, and computers, and be sure that labels are used to identify systems, circuits, and connections.

- A portable label maker is indispensable for creating labels. Choose labels that are durable and that are designed to stick to plastic and metal, not paper. Keep your label maker handy in your toolbox as you work. Whenever you find a device, wall jack, or port not labeled and you are able to identify its purpose, take the time to label it correctly. Others in your organization will soon see you as the "label champion."

- Where labels won't fit on the device itself, draw a simple diagram of each device that indicates how each port is used and what connection is made through that port, such as the example in Figure 4-12.

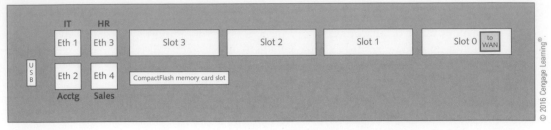

Figure 4-12   Simple port diagram of a Cisco router with red labels identifying how five ports are used

Use names that are as descriptive as possible (without giving away too much information to potential hackers). Pay attention to any established naming convention already in use by your employer. For example, using existing acronyms for the various departments in your corporation will make this information more recognizable for employees. Think big-picture-down-to-details when designing device name fields, such as starting with the building name, then floor, then closet number, then rack number. If your company has national locations or international locations, certain names may need to include codes for continent, country, state, city, and so on. Think in terms of "top-down" or "outside-in" and be consistent. Be sure to only include fields that are absolutely essential in identifying the device. Don't overcomplicate the name with useless or redundant information.

Network+ 5.7 **Applying Concepts**

Examine a Naming Convention

A good naming convention will save you a lot of time that would otherwise be lost looking up device names. Consider the following device names:

```
002-09-03-01-03
```

```
phx-09-nw-01-rtr3
```

The first name is simply a string of numbers, which many people would have a hard time recognizing as meaningful information. A numeric system like that would force new employees to spend too much of their precious time looking up device names.

In the second name, which is designed to be easier to interpret on the fly, the numbers have been replaced with abbreviated names, locations, and other identifying information. The first field tells you that the device is located in Phoenix, which is abbreviated as phx. For most people, identifying devices by such an easily recognized abbreviation is easier than using numbers, which have to be memorized. The second field (09) refers to the floor number, so using a number is unavoidable. The third field (nw) refers to the data closet's location within the building (the northwest corner) rather than the data closet's number, which would also be onerous to memorize. The fourth field contains the rack number (01), and the final field (rtr3) identifies the type of device (a router) and the number of the router (3).

When designing a naming convention, be sure to include enough digits in each field to allow for future expansion. A two-digit field is much more limited than a three- or four-digit field. One digit will work fine for numbering the racks in a small data closet, which can't possibly hold 10 racks. But if you're numbering employees or workstations, your company may quickly outgrow a two-digit workstation field.

Not every company needs long device names; and small devices, such as the ports on a switch, won't have enough space for long names. For example, when labeling ports on a patch panel or switch in a data closet, a connection type (vertical versus horizontal, storage versus workstation, etc.) plus a room number may be sufficient. For jacks on a wall, consider names such as the employee's job title, desk location, or something similar. Avoid using employee names because many of those will change over the lifetime of the device. Ultimately, the name of the game is *consistency*.

Rack Systems

Rack systems provide mounting hardware for network equipment to optimize the use of square footage in equipment rooms and ensure adequate spacing, access, and ventilation for these devices. Equipment racks come in a standard 19-inch frame, meaning that the front is 19 inches wide. You might also come across a 23-inch rack. The measurement includes the entire width of the rack, from outside surface to outside surface, so you can accurately predict exactly how many racks will fit side by side in a given space. Generally, you'll see open frame **two-post rack** and **four-post rack** varieties, though six-post racks are also available. You can see examples of the two-post and four-post racks in Figure 4-13. The side posts provide bracketing for attaching devices, such as routers, servers, switches, patch panels, audio-visual equipment, or telephony equipment. This equipment often comes with attached brackets, called **rack ears**, for securing the device to the posts, as shown in Figure 4-14. Post holes can be round or square, threaded or nonthreaded. Square-hole racks are the most recent attachment innovation, allowing for bolt-free mounting.

Racks may be wall- or ceiling-mounted, or freestanding on the floor. They can also be open-framed, which provides greater accessibility, or enclosed, which provides greater protection. Other features may include power strips, rack fans for cooling, cable trays, or drawers. Racks are measured in **rack units (RU or U)** with the industry standard being 42U tall—about 6 feet. You may also see **half-racks**, which are only 18U–22U tall. However, rack *depths* can vary considerably between manufacturers.

Figure 4-13 Two-post and four-post racks

Rack ear

Figure 4-14 Attach network equipment to rack systems by inserting bolts through rack ears

Rack units are especially important when planning how much rack space you need and where equipment will go within the rack. Hole pairs on the posts are grouped by rack unit with space between these regions that allows for air circulation. Rack equipment is rated by the number of U required for that device on the rack. For example, most rack-mountable computers are 1U–4U high, whereas a server may only require 1U. Racks may also include server rails or slides to make service access easier so that technicians can slide servers out of the rack without completely removing them. The server rails are mounted directly to the rack, but the equipment may also be bolted to the rack after installation for added safety.

 When selecting devices to replace existing ones or to expand your network, consider choosing devices that support newer technologies that you are not yet implementing so you don't hinder future expansion by equipment limitations. Also, plan for expanding your network. For example, if your organization is rapidly enlarging, consider replacing your backbone with fiber and leave plenty of space in your data closets for more racks.

Hardware should be installed as close to the front of the rack as possible to allow for proper airflow in the back. Minimizing cable clutter can also help prevent airflow blockages. In a typical rack system, airflow through the chassis is typically designed to move from front to back. Rack-monitoring systems should be installed to sound an alarm if the rack's overall temperature rises too much, if air quality (moisture or smoke) falls below acceptable levels, or if airflow is restricted. Because rack security is also a concern, these monitoring systems can alert technicians when a door is left open, or use motion sensors to detect the presence of an intruder. In data rooms containing multiple rows of racks, a hot aisle/cold aisle layout, as shown in Figure 4-15, pulls cool air from vents in the floor or from nearby, low-lying wall

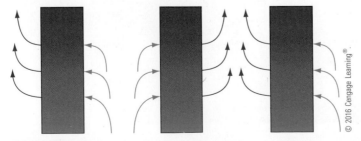

Figure 4-15 Hot aisle/cold aisle rack layout

vents into the rows of racks. The hot air aisles are used to direct the heated air away from the racks into exhaust vents for cooling.

It's impractical to install separate consoles for every device on a rack. Typically, racks have a KVM (keyboard, video, and mouse) switch, which connects to a single console to provide a central control portal for all devices on the rack.

Network+
1.11
NAS (Network Attached Storage)

4

The term **fault tolerance** refers to techniques that allow data storage or other operations to continue in the event of a failure or fault of one of its components, for example, storing redundant data on multiple storage devices in the event one device fails. One important form of fault tolerance in a network is NAS (network attached storage), which is a specialized storage device or group of storage devices that provides centralized fault-tolerant data storage for a network. You can think of NAS as a unique type of server dedicated to data sharing. The advantage to using NAS over a typical file server is that a NAS device contains its own file system that is optimized for saving and serving files (as opposed to also managing printing, authenticating logon IDs, and so on). Because of this optimization, NAS reads and writes from its disk significantly faster than other types of servers.

Another advantage to using NAS is that it can be easily expanded without interrupting service. You can physically install a new hard drive without shutting down the system. The NAS device recognizes the added storage and immediately adds it to its pool of available reading and writing space.

A NAS device cannot communicate directly with clients on the network. Clients on the LAN go through a file server, which communicates with the NAS device on the LAN. Figure 4-16 depicts how a NAS device logically connects to a LAN.

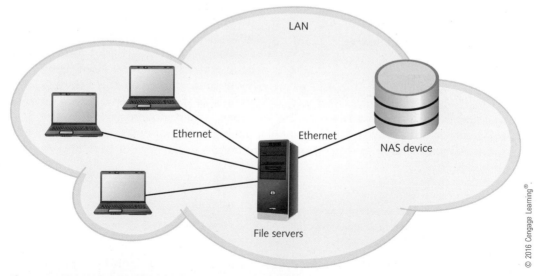

Figure 4-16   Network attached storage (NAS) on a LAN

© 2016 Cengage Learning®

NAS is appropriate for enterprises that require not only fault tolerance, but also fast access for their data. For example, an ISP might use NAS to host its customers' Web pages. Because NAS devices can store and retrieve data for any type of client (providing the client can run TCP/IP), NAS is also appropriate for organizations that use a mix of different operating systems on their desktops.

SANs (Storage Area Networks)

Large enterprises that require even faster access to data and larger amounts of storage might prefer storage area networks (SANs) over NAS. Whereas a NAS device requires a file server to interact with other devices on the network, a SAN (storage area network) is a distinct network of storage devices that communicate directly with each other and with other networks.

In a typical SAN, multiple storage devices are connected to multiple, identical servers. This type of architecture is similar to the mesh topology, which is the most fault-tolerant type of topology possible. If one storage device within a SAN suffers a fault, data is automatically retrieved from elsewhere in the SAN. If one server in a SAN suffers a fault, another server steps in to perform its functions.

SANs are not only extremely fault tolerant, they are also extremely fast. SANs use one of two types of Transport layer protocols:

- Fibre Channel (FC) is a Transport layer protocol used on fiber-optic media instead of TCP or UDP. Fibre Channel connects devices within the SAN and also connects the SAN to other networks. It is capable of over 5 Gbps throughput. By using Fibre Channel, rather than the Ethernet connections used on the LAN, the SAN is not limited to the speed of the client-server network for which it provides data storage. Figure 4-17 shows a SAN using Fibre Channel to connect to a traditional Ethernet network. The disadvantages of Fibre Channel are that it is expensive and requires extensive training for IT personnel to support it.

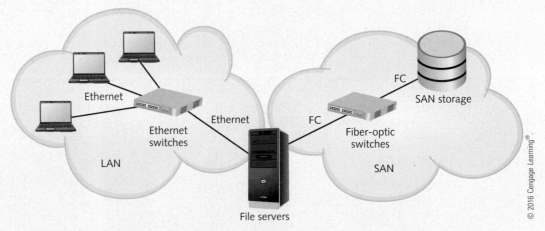

Figure 4-17 A storage area network (SAN) using Fibre Channel (FC) connected to a LAN

- iSCSI (Internet SCSI), pronounced "i-scuzzy," is a Transport layer protocol that runs on top of TCP to allow fast transmissions over LANs, WANs, and the Internet. It can work on a twisted-pair Ethernet network with ordinary Ethernet NICs. iSCSI is an evolution of SCSI (Small Computer System Interface), which is a fast transmission standard used by internal hard drives and operating systems in file servers.

The advantages of iSCSI over Fibre Channel are that it is not as expensive, can run on the already established Ethernet LAN by installing iSCSI software (called an iSCSI initiator) on network clients and servers, and does not require as much special training for IT personnel. Some network administrators configure iSCSI to use jumbo frames on the Ethernet LAN. You can see in Figure 4-18 that iSCSI architecture is very similar to FC. The primary difference is that Ethernet equipment and interfaces can be used throughout the network.

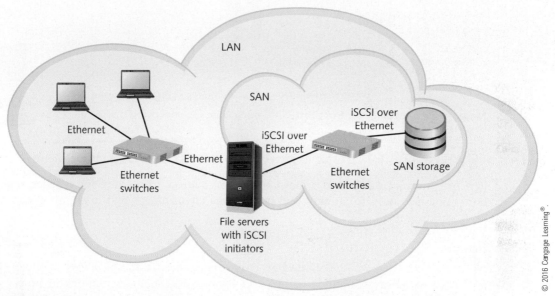

Figure 4-18   A storage area network (SAN) using iSCSI on a LAN where the file servers run iSCSI initiators and the client computers do not

Instead of requiring a separate network infrastructure, Fibre Channel is now available as FCoE (FC over Ethernet). This improvement provides yet another systemic option for accessing SAN services. FCoE offers the best of both worlds, with the higher speeds of FC, and the convenience and cost-efficiency of using existing network equipment, as shown in Figure 4-19.

A SAN can be installed in a location separate from the LAN it serves. For example, remote SANs can be kept in an ISP's data center, which can provide greater security and fault tolerance and also allows an organization to outsource the management of its SAN.

SANs are highly scalable and have a very high fault tolerance, massive storage capabilities, and fast data access. SANs are best suited to environments with huge quantities of data that must always be quickly available.

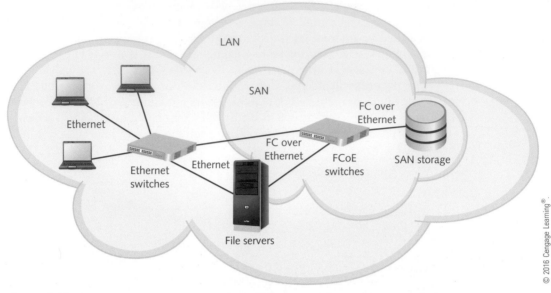

© 2016 Cengage Learning®

Figure 4-19   A storage area network (SAN) using Fibre Channel over Ethernet (FCoE) on a LAN

Managing Power Sources and the Environment

Part of managing a network is managing power sources to account for outages and fluctuations. You also need to monitor and manage the environment that might affect sensitive network equipment.

Power Management

No matter where you live, you have probably experienced a complete loss of power (a **blackout**) or a temporary dimming of lights (a **brownout**). Such fluctuations in power are frequently caused by forces of nature, such as hurricanes, tornadoes, or ice storms. They might also occur when a utility company performs maintenance or construction tasks. Power surges, even small ones, can cause serious damage to sensitive computer equipment and can be one of the most frustrating sources of network problems.

Before you learn how to manage power sources so as to avoid these problems, first arm yourself with an understanding of the nature of an electric circuit and some electrical components that manage electricity.

Applying Concepts

AC and DC Power and Converters

An **electric circuit** provides a medium for the transfer of electrical power over a closed loop. If the loop is broken in any way, the circuit won't conduct electricity. In a circuit, **direct current (DC)** flows at a steady rate in only one direction. By contrast, **alternating current (AC)** continually switches direction on the circuit.

A flashlight, for example, uses DC. The batteries in a flashlight have positive and negative poles, and the current always flows at a steady rate in the same direction between those poles, as shown on the left side of Figure 4-20. AC, however, travels in compression waves, similar to the coils of a Slinky®, alternating direction on the power line back and forth between the source and destination. Just as waves can travel across a huge body of water, power moving in an AC wave pattern can travel efficiently for long distances, as illustrated on the right side of Figure 4-20. Because AC power can be conducted at very high voltages, the source of the current can be far away from the point of use, where it is transformed to lower voltages. Consider the power running a typical laptop computer. AC power comes from the power station through the wall outlet to the laptop's power supply, which converts it to DC before the laptop can use it.

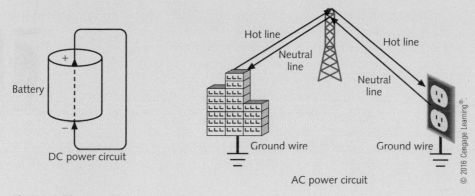

Figure 4-20   DC circuit and AC circuit

 **NOTE**   For AC power to travel from the electric company to your house, three wires are required. The hot wire carries electricity from the power station to your house. The neutral wire carries unused power from your house back to the power station. A third wire, the ground wire, is used to channel the electric charge in case of a short. These three wires are illustrated in Figure 4-20.

Power converters change the form of electrical energy in some way. The four types of converters you need to be aware of are:

- An **inverter** converts DC to AC. A generator might contain an inverter. The better inverters will also condition the power, which helps protect sensitive electronic equipment from power fluctuations.

- A **rectifier** converts AC to DC. All computers require the constant flow of electricity that DC power provides. The power supply in a laptop or desktop computer contains a rectifier to convert AC to DC.

- A **transformer** changes the voltage of AC, such as when the power over the main line from the electric company is transformed before being delivered to your house.

- A **voltage regulator** maintains a constant voltage level for either AC or DC power.

You're now ready to investigate the types of power fluctuations, or flaws, that network administrators should prepare for. Then you'll learn about alternate power sources, such as a UPS (uninterruptible power supply) or an electrical generator that can compensate for power loss.

Power Flaws   Whatever the cause, power loss or less-than-optimal power cannot be tolerated by networks. The following list describes power flaws that can damage your equipment:

- *surge*—A momentary increase in voltage due to lightning strikes, solar flares, or electrical problems. Surges might last only a few thousandths of a second, but can degrade a computer's power supply. Surges are common. You can guard against surges by making sure every computer device is plugged into a surge protector, which redirects excess voltage away from the device to a ground, thereby protecting the device from harm. Without surge protectors, systems would be subjected to multiple surges each year.

- *noise*—Fluctuation in voltage levels caused by other devices on the network or EMI. Some noise is unavoidable on an electrical circuit, but excessive noise can cause a power supply to malfunction, immediately corrupting program or data files and gradually damaging motherboards and other computer circuits. If you've ever turned on fluorescent lights or a microwave oven and noticed the lights dim, you have probably introduced noise into the electrical system. Power that is free from noise is called *clean* power. To make sure power is clean, a circuit must pass through an electrical filter.

- *brownout*—A momentary decrease in voltage; also known as a sag. An overtaxed electrical system can cause brownouts, which you might recognize in your home as a dimming of the lights. Such voltage decreases can cause computers or applications to fail and potentially corrupt data.

- *blackout*—A complete power loss. A blackout could cause significant damage to your network. For example, if a server loses power while files are open and processes are running, its NOS might be damaged so extensively that the server cannot restart and the NOS must be reinstalled from scratch. A backup power source, however, can provide power long enough for the server to shut down properly and avoid harm.

UPS (Uninterruptible Power Supply)   A UPS (uninterruptible power supply) is a battery-operated power source directly attached to one or more devices and to a power supply, such as a wall outlet, that prevents undesired fluctuations of the wall outlet's AC power from harming the device or interrupting its services. A power supply issue may be long in developing, with on-again, off-again symptoms for some time before the power issue finally solidifies and reveals itself. A good UPS in each data closet will help prevent these kinds of problems from affecting the entire network at once. Each critical workstation should also be equipped with a UPS, which also helps to protect the computers themselves.

UPSs are classified into two general categories: standby and online. A standby UPS, also called a standby power supply (SPS), provides continuous voltage to a device by switching virtually instantaneously to the battery when it detects a loss of power from the wall outlet. Upon restoration of the power, the standby UPS switches the device back to AC power. The problem with standby UPSs is that, in the brief amount of time that it takes the UPS to discover that power from the wall outlet has faltered, a device may have already detected the power loss and shut down or restarted. Technically, a standby UPS doesn't provide continuous power; for this reason, it is sometimes called an offline UPS. Nevertheless, standby UPSs may prove adequate even for critical network devices, such as servers, routers, and gateways. They cost significantly less than online UPSs.

An **online UPS** uses the AC power from the wall outlet to continuously charge its battery, while providing power to a network device through its battery. In other words, a server connected to an online UPS always relies on the UPS battery for its electricity. Because the server never needs to switch from the wall outlet's power to the UPS's power, there is no risk of momentarily losing service. Also, because the UPS always provides the power, it can handle noise, surges, and sags before the power reaches the attached device. As you can imagine, online UPSs are more expensive than standby UPSs. Figure 4-21 shows some online UPSs.

© 2016 Cengage Learning®

Figure 4-21   Online UPSs installed on a rack

UPSs vary widely in the type of power aberrations they can rectify, the length of time they can provide power, and the number of devices they can support. Of course, they also vary widely in price. UPSs intended for home and small office use are designed merely to keep your workstation running long enough for you to properly shut it down in case of a blackout. Other UPSs perform sophisticated operations such as line filtering or conditioning, power supply monitoring, and error notification. To decide which UPS is right for your network, consider a number of factors:

- *amount of power needed*—The more power required by your device, the more powerful the UPS must be. Electrical power is measured in volt-amperes, also called *volt-amps*. A **volt-ampere (VA)** is the product of the voltage and current (measured in amps) of the electricity on a line. To determine approximately how many VAs your device requires, you can use the following conversion: 1.4 volt-amps = 1 watt (W). A desktop computer, for example, may use a 200 W power supply, and, therefore, require a UPS capable of at least 280 VA to keep the CPU running in case of a blackout. A medium-sized server with a monitor and external tape drive might use 402 W, thus requiring a UPS capable of providing at least 562 VA power.

Determining your power needs can be a challenge. You must account for your existing equipment and consider how you might upgrade the supported device(s) over the next several years. Consider consulting with your equipment manufacturer to obtain recommendations on power needs.

- *period of time to keep a device running*—The longer you anticipate needing a UPS to power your device, the more powerful your UPS must be. For example, a medium-sized server that relies on a 574 VA UPS to remain functional for 20 minutes needs an 1100 VA UPS to remain functional for 90 minutes. To determine how long your device might require power from a UPS, research the length of typical power outages in your area.

- *line conditioning*—A UPS should offer surge suppression to protect against surges, and line conditioning (a type of filtering) to guard against line noise. A UPS that provides line conditioning includes special noise filters that remove line noise. The manufacturer's technical specifications should indicate the amount of filtration required for each UPS. Noise suppression is expressed in decibel levels (dB) at a specific frequency (KHz or MHz). The higher the decibel level, the greater the protection.

- *cost*—Prices for good UPSs vary widely, depending on the unit's size and extra features. A relatively small UPS that can power one server for 5 to 10 minutes might cost between $100 and $300. A large UPS that can power a sophisticated router for three hours might cost up to $5000. Still larger UPSs, which can power an entire data center for several hours, can cost hundreds of thousands of dollars. On a critical system, you should not try to cut costs by buying an off-brand, potentially unreliable, or weak UPS.

As with other large purchases, research several UPS manufacturers and their products before selecting a UPS. Make sure the manufacturer provides a warranty and lets you test the UPS with your equipment. Testing UPSs with your equipment is an important part of the decision-making process. Popular UPS manufacturers are APC, Emerson, Falcon, and Tripp Lite.

After installing a new UPS, follow the manufacturer's instructions for performing initial tests to verify the UPS's proper functioning. Make it a practice to retest the UPS monthly or quarterly to be sure it will perform as expected in case of a sag or blackout.

Generators   A generator serves as a backup power source, providing power redundancy in the event of a total blackout. Generators can be powered by diesel, liquid propane gas, natural gas, or steam. Standard generators provide power that is relatively free from noise and are used in environments that demand consistently reliable service, such as an ISP's or telecommunications carrier's data center. In fact, in those environments, they are typically combined with large UPSs to ensure that clean power is always available. In the event of a power failure, the UPS supplies electricity until the generator starts and reaches its full capacity, typically no more than three minutes. If your organization relies on a generator for backup power, be certain to check fuel levels and quality regularly.

Figure 4-22 illustrates the power infrastructure of a network (such as a data center's) that uses both a generator and dual UPSs. Because a generator produces DC power, it must contain an inverter component to convert the power to AC before the power can be released to the existing AC infrastructure that distributes power in a data center.

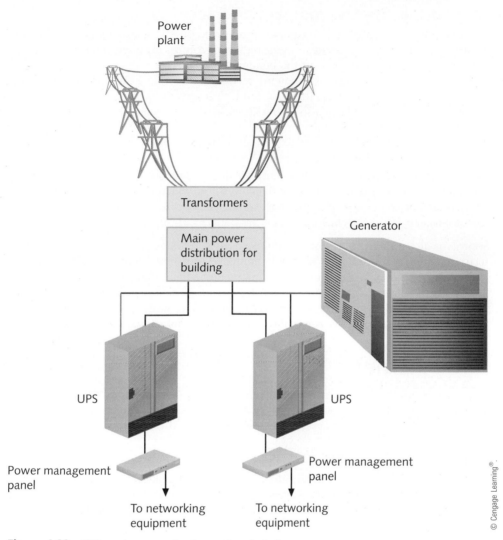

Figure 4-22   UPSs and a generator in a network design

Before choosing a generator, first calculate your organization's crucial electrical demands to determine the generator's optimal size. Also estimate how long the generator may be required to power your building. Depending on the amount of power draw, a high-capacity generator can supply power for several days. Gas or diesel generators can cost between $10,000 and $3,000,000 (for the largest industrial types). For a company such as an ISP that stands to lose up to $1,000,000 per minute if its data facilities fail completely, a multi-million-dollar investment to ensure available power is a wise choice. Smaller businesses, however, might choose the more economical solution of renting an electrical generator. To find out more about options for renting or purchasing generators in your area, contact your local electrical utility.

Monitoring the Environment and Security

Due to the sensitive nature of the equipment mounted on racks, environmental and security monitoring are both critical preventive measures. Data rooms are often serviced by HVAC systems that are separate from the rest of the building. Specialized products are available that monitor the critical factors of a data closet's environment. For example, ITWatchDogs offers several environmental monitoring products that can alert technicians to unacceptable temperature, humidity, or airflow conditions, and can also send text or email alerts when a secure door is left open, when the power supply is compromised, or even when light and sound conditions are unacceptable. These alarms can be programmed to escalate as the severity of the situation increases, such as alerting higher-level staff if the problem is not resolved. Increasing humidity, for example, is caused by rising levels of water in the air, which can damage sensitive electronic equipment. Of even greater concern is the source of that moisture, which could pose a safety hazard if, say, water is leaking into the room. The monitoring system will likely also record the information so technicians can review recent data to look for patterns of fluctuations.

Security is also a huge priority with data rooms and rack equipment. Every data room should be secured behind a locked door with only limited IT personnel having copies of the keys. Never leave the room unlocked, even for a few moments. Many companies place security cameras to monitor any data room entrance—or at least to monitor any access point leading to the area where the data room is located—to serve as a deterrent to tampering, and to provide critical information should a break-in ever occur. Physical security is discussed more extensively in Chapter 12.

NICs and Ethernet

Each workstation, server, printer, connectivity device, or other node device on a network uses a NIC to access the network. For local networks, a NIC uses Ethernet standards for communication. This part of the chapter discusses NICs and Ethernet.

Characteristics of NICs

The NIC (network interface card, also called network adapter or network card) contains a transceiver that transmits and receives data signals over the network media. As you learned in Chapter 1, NICs belong to both the Physical layer and Data Link layer of the OSI model because they issue data signals (either to a wire or into the air) and assemble or disassemble data frames. They interpret physical addressing information to ensure data is delivered to its proper destination, and they perform the routines that determine which node has the right to transmit data over a network at any given instant.

Many NICs can also perform prioritization, network management, buffering, and traffic-filtering functions. NICs do not, however, analyze information added by the protocols in Layers 3 through 7 of the OSI model. For example, they cannot determine whether the frames they transmit and receive use IP packets or a different Layer 3 protocol. Nor can they determine whether the Presentation layer has encrypted the data in those packets.

As you design or troubleshoot a network, you will need to know the characteristics of the NICs used by its clients, servers, and connectivity devices. For example, when you order a switch, you'll have to specify the network interfaces that match your network's speed and cabling connectors. NICs come in a variety of types depending on the following:

- Connection type (for example, Ethernet or Wi-Fi)

- Maximum network transmission speed (for example, 100 Mbps versus 1 Gbps)

- Connector interfaces (for example, RJ-45 versus SC)

- Number of connector interfaces, or ports

- Manufacturer (popular NIC manufacturers include Adaptec, D-Link, IBM, Intel, Kingston, Linksys, Netgear, SMC, and Western Digital, to name just a few)

- Support for enhanced features, such as PoE+, buffering, or traffic management

- Method of interfacing with the computer's motherboard and interface standard; a NIC interfaces with the computer's motherboard by one of these three methods:

a. *integrated into the motherboard*—An integrated NIC is by far the most common arrangement, and in fact it would be difficult to buy a new computer without one. When integrated, the motherboard provides a network port along with several other ports on the rear of a desktop computer case or laptop, and the NIC is called an onboard NIC. Figure 4-23 shows a workstation's motherboard with two onboard NICs.

Two LAN ports

Courtesy of EVGA USA

Figure 4-23   Motherboard with two onboard NICs

b. *installed in an expansion slot on the motherboard*—PCI (Peripheral Component Interconnect) slots are slowly becoming obsolete, but can often still be found on new computers. Today's computers primarily offer the newer and faster PCIe (PCI Express) slots. Figure 4-24 shows a NIC that can be installed in a PCIe slot.

Courtesy of Intel Corporation

Figure 4-24   PCIe expansion board NIC

c. *installed as a peripheral device*—NICs can be plugged into USB slots or Thunderbolt slots on desktops and laptops. (**Thunderbolt** is Apple's proprietary competitor to the USB port and can be used to connect several types of external peripheral devices to Mac computers.) A wireless USB NIC is shown in Figure 4-25.

Figure 4-25   A USB NIC

Most new clients, servers, and connectivity devices will arrive with their NICs preinstalled and functional. However, you might need to make modifications. For example, you might want to upgrade the NIC in a client workstation to one that can handle faster transmission speeds, or you might want to add NICs to your server. In that case, you need to know how to install NICs properly. You'll get a chance to practice this process in the projects at the end of this chapter. Here are a few general tips:

- *install hardware and software*—Installing a NIC is a two-step process: You first install the hardware, and then install the software that the OS uses to communicate with the NIC, which is known as the **device driver** (sometimes called, simply, the **driver**). Operating systems like Windows come with a multitude of built-in device drivers and may already have the one that you need. But if the correct driver is not included or you want to use extra features not available with the default OS drivers, you can manually install the manufacturer's drivers that came bundled on CD with the NIC or those you download from the manufacturer's Web site.

- *install a peripheral NIC*—First insert the device into the appropriate port. Make sure that the device is firmly inserted. If you can wiggle it, you need to realign it or push it in farther. The OS is likely to autodetect the device and automatically install its drivers. If you want to manually install other manufacturer drivers, follow the directions from the manufacturer to perform the installation. Sometimes you install the drivers before plugging in the NIC and sometimes you install the drivers after the NIC is physically installed.

- *install an expansion card NIC*—Install the expansion card and then install the drivers or use the OS default drivers. Step-by-step instructions are given in the Hands-On Projects at the end of this chapter.

- *install multiple NICs*—On servers and other high-powered computers, you may need to install multiple NICs. For the hardware installation, you can simply repeat the installation process for the first NIC, choosing a different slot. The OS installs drivers for each NIC and you can manually install your own drivers instead. For UNIX or Linux installations, the first NIC the operating system detects is called, by default, eth0, which says this is the first Ethernet interface. If a second NIC is present, it is called eth1. Because they provide the network interface, eth0 and eth1 are simply called, in UNIX and Linux terminology, interfaces.

Simplex, Half-Duplex, and Duplex

You can change the settings on a NIC to comply with a network's transmission settings. You've already learned about transmission speeds. Another characteristic of data transmission is the direction in which signals travel over the media and the number of signals that can traverse the media at any given time. These methods of transmission are:

- *full-duplex, also called duplex*—Signals are free to travel in both directions over a medium simultaneously. As an analogy, talking on the telephone is a full-duplex transmission because both parties in the conversation can speak at the same time. All modern NICs for wired connections support full-duplex transmissions.

- *half-duplex*—Signals may travel in both directions over a medium but in only one direction at a time. For example, an apartment building's intercom system may be half-duplex if only one person can speak at a time.

- *simplex*—Signals may travel in only one direction, and is sometimes called one-way, or unidirectional, communication. Broadcast radio and garage door openers are examples of simplex transmissions.

Many network devices, including NICs, allow you to specify whether the device should use half- or full-duplex communication. Modern NICs use full-duplex by default. If you configure a computer's NIC to use half-duplex while the device on the other end of the connection is using full-duplex, that connection will be unnecessarily slow.

In Windows, use Device Manager to configure a NIC, including speed and duplex settings. For example, notice in Figure 4-26 that you can choose Half Duplex, Full Duplex, or Auto

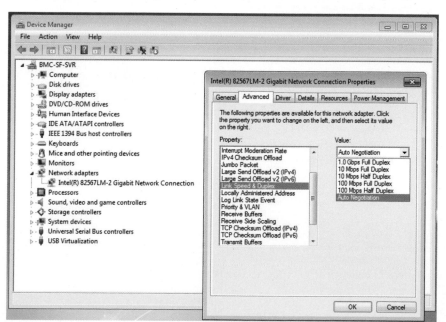

Figure 4-26 A network adapter's Link Speed and Duplex configuration can be changed

Source: Microsoft LLC

Negotiation, which allows the NIC to select the best link speed and duplex that is also supported by a neighboring device. However, if you specify a particular speed and duplex that's not supported by the neighboring device, the result is a speed and duplex mismatch and, therefore, failed transmissions.

Using UNIX or Linux, the ethtool utility allows you to view and change NIC settings. For example, to display the properties of a computer's first network interface, type `ethtool eth0` at a Linux command prompt and press Enter. In the example shown in Figure 4-27, the line *Supports auto-negotiation: Yes* indicates that the network interface is configured to automatically sense, or autonegotiate, the speed at which it should transmit and receive data on the network. Ethtool may be bundled with a Linux distribution, but might not be installed by default. In some Linux distributions, it might need to be downloaded before it's installed. To list all the options you can use with the command, type `man ethtool` and press Enter. The Linux manual pages for ethtool will display.

```
Settings for eth0:
        Supported ports: [ TP ]
        Supported link modes:   10baseT/Half 10baseT/Full
                                100baseT/Half 100baseT/Full
                                1000baseT/Full
        Supported pause frame use: No
        Supports auto-negotiation: Yes
        Advertised link modes:  10baseT/Half 10baseT/Full
                                100baseT/Half 100baseT/Full
                                1000baseT/Full
        Advertised pause frame use: No
        Advertised auto-negotiation: Yes
        Speed: 100Mb/s
        Duplex: Full
        Port: Twisted Pair
        PHYAD: 2
        Transceiver: internal
        Auto-negotiation: on
        MDI-X: off
        Supports Wake-on: pumbg
        Wake-on: g
        Current message level: 0x00000001 (1)
                               drv
        Link detected: yes
```

Figure 4-27   Linux network interface properties shown by the `ethtool` command

Source: The Linux Foundation

Ethernet Frames

Ethernet is a Layer 2 standard that is flexible, capable of running on a variety of network media, and offers excellent throughput at a reasonable cost. Because of its many advantages, Ethernet is, by far, the most popular network technology used on modern LANs. **Ethernet II** is the current Ethernet standard and was developed by DEC, Intel, and Xerox (abbreviated as DIX) before IEEE began to standardize Ethernet.

Figure 4-28 depicts an Ethernet II frame, and the details of the Ethernet II frame fields are listed in Table 4-1.

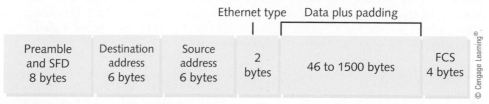

Figure 4-28 Ethernet II frame

Table 4-1 Fields of an Ethernet II Frame

Field name		Length	Description
Preamble and SFD		8 bytes	Signals to the receiving node that bytes following this preamble are the actual frame. *Not included when calculating a frame's total size.
Header	Destination address	6 bytes	Provides the MAC address of the recipient of the data frame.
	Source address	6 bytes	Provides the MAC address of the network node that originally sent the data.
	Type field	2 bytes	Specifies the upper-layer protocol carried in the frame. For example, an IP packet has 0x0800 in the Type field.
Data		46 bytes to 1500 bytes	If the data is not at least 46 bytes, padding is added to make a minimum of 46 bytes.
Trailer FCS (frame check sequence)		4 bytes	The FCS trailer ensures that the data at the destination exactly matches the data issued from the source using the CRC (cyclic redundancy check) algorithm.

Together, the FCS and the header make up the 18-byte "frame" for the data. The data portion of an Ethernet frame may contain from 46 to 1500 bytes of information (and recall that the MTU of 1500 bytes is the Network layer packet). Therefore, we can calculate the minimum and maximum frame sizes:

- 18-byte frame + 46-bytes minimum data size = 64 bytes minimum frame size
- 18-byte frame + 1500-bytes maximum data size = 1518 bytes maximum frame size

Ethernet frames on a virtual LAN (VLAN) can have an extra 4-byte field between the Source address field and the Type field, which is used to manage VLAN traffic. If this field exists, the maximum frame size is 1522 bytes.

Because of the overhead present in each frame and the time it takes for the NIC to manage a frame, the use of larger frame sizes on a network generally results in faster throughput. Although you cannot control actual frame sizes used (only the range of acceptable frame sizes), you can help improve network performance by properly managing frames. For example, network administrators should strive to minimize the number of broadcast frames on their networks because broadcast frames tend to be very small and, therefore, inefficient. Also, recall from Chapter 3 that some special-purpose networks use a proprietary version of Ethernet that allows for a jumbo frame, in which the MTU can be as high as 9198 bytes, depending on the type of Ethernet architecture used.

Legacy Networking

CSMA/CD and Hubs

When IEEE released the first Ethernet standard in 1980, it was officially called IEEE 802.3 CSMA/CD, and was unofficially called Ethernet. A CSMA/CD frame used a slightly different layout than the Ethernet II frame layout used on today's networks. The earlier frame was called an 802.3 frame, and the current Ethernet II frame was called a DIX frame. CSMA/CD networks often used a hub at the Physical layer of the OSI model.

A hub is an inefficient and outdated networking device that has been replaced by switches. A hub accepted signals from a transmitting node and repeated those signals to all other connected nodes in a broadcast fashion. On Ethernet networks, hubs once served as the central connection point for a star topology. Also, hubs only supported half-duplex transmission.

All nodes connected to the hub competed for access to the network. The media access control (MAC) method used by the nodes for arbitration on the network is CSMA/CD (Carrier Sense Multiple Access with Collision Detection). Take a minute to think about the full name *Carrier Sense Multiple Access with Collision Detection.* The term *Carrier Sense* refers to an Ethernet NIC listening and waiting until no other nodes are transmitting data. The term *Multiple Access* refers to several nodes accessing the same network media. *Collision Detection* refers to what happens when two nodes attempt a transmission at the same time.

When the transmissions of two nodes would interfere with each other, a collision happened. After a collision, each node waited a random amount of time and then resent the transmission. A collision domain is the portion of a network in which collisions could occur. Hubs connecting multiple computers in a star-bus topology resulted in massive collisions.

On today's Ethernet networks, switches, which support full-duplex transmissions, have now replaced hubs. In addition, traffic is greatly reduced with switches because, when a switch receives a transmission from a node, the switch sends it only to the destination node or nodes rather than broadcasting to all nodes connected to the switch.

Structured cabling guidelines provide detailed recommendations on the maximum distances cable segments can run between nodes. You'll learn more about this topic in Chapter 5. For now, it's interesting to note that these maximum cable lengths are partly determined by CSMA/CD. If a cable is too long, the entire message can be transmitted before a collision can be detected. In this case, the node does not know to resend the corrupted transmission.

To ensure that any collisions are detected, frames are made large enough to fill the entire cable during transmission. It might seem odd to think about a transmission "filling a cable," but think about water going through a water hose. You can turn on the spigot and run the water for a very short time. The water runs through the hose to the other end but the hose isn't filled all at the same time. Only if you leave the water running long enough, will water start coming out the other end while it's still entering the hose at the spigot. With a long enough transmission, a similar thing happens on a cable—the beginning of the message starts arriving at its destination before the end of the message has been completely transmitted.

The CompTIA Network+ exam expects you to be able to contrast a broadcast domain and a collision domain, and you're now ready to do that. Both types of domains are defined by the group of nodes that transmissions can reach. Recall from Chapter 3 that transmissions in a broadcast domain reach all nodes on a LAN, but are not forwarded by routers. Therefore, routers define the borders of a broadcast domain, which is, by definition, a LAN.

In contrast, transmissions in a collision domain reach only those nodes directly connected to a hub. Therefore, the hub defines the borders of its collision domain. Figure 4-29 illustrates the difference between broadcast domains and a collision domain.

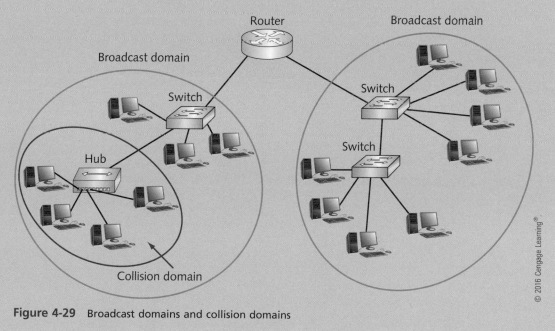

Figure 4-29 Broadcast domains and collision domains

Troubleshooting Network Devices

Let's look at some approaches to troubleshooting NIC problems. Then you'll apply what you've learned so far to a troubleshooting situation. Finally, you'll learn about the many benefits of having a well-documented network map when troubleshooting network problems.

Applying Concepts

Troubleshoot NIC Problems

It's helpful to start at the bottom OSI layer to troubleshoot network problems. For example, you can use these three methods to determine if the NIC is functioning properly:

- *Look at the NIC itself*—Most NICs have LEDs that indicate whether they are communicating with the network (see Figure 4-30). The precise location, type, and meaning of LED indicators vary from one manufacturer to another. The only way to know for certain what your NIC's LEDs are trying to tell you is to read the documentation. In general, a steady or blinking green LED indicates that the NIC is functional and has a connection to the network. Sometimes this light is labeled LNK. Blinking yellow or orange LEDs may indicate that the NIC is transmitting or receiving data. The transmit and receive LEDs on some ports are labeled TX and RX, respectively. If they exist, red LEDs may indicate a problem with the NIC or its ability to connect to the network.

© Cengage Learning®.

Figure 4-30   Status indicator lights for the embedded network port

- *Test the NIC or cable with a loopback plug*—A loopback plug (also called a loopback adapter) plugs into a port, such as an RJ-45 port, and crosses the transmit line with the receive line to test the port or cable for connectivity. See Figure 4-31. If a NIC fails a physical component test, it needs to be replaced.
- *Update device drivers*—In Windows, use Device Manager to update the device drivers. Device Manager also reports any errors that Windows finds with the device. In Linux, use the ethtool utility.

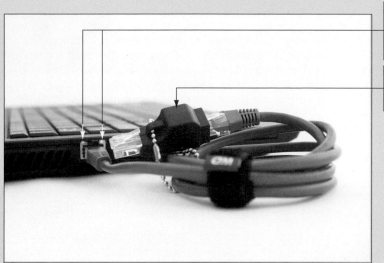

Network activity and connection LED lights indicate cable and port are good

Loopback plug is testing cable and Ethernet port

© Cengage Learning®

Figure 4-31   A loopback plug verifies the cable and network port are good

- *Use the configuration utility provided by the NIC's manufacturer*—NIC configuration utilities allow you to test the NIC's physical components and connectivity. Most of the tests can be performed without additional hardware. However, to perform the entire group of diagnostic tests in the NIC's utility software, you must have a loopback plug.

- *Check the TCP/IP configuration for the NIC's interface and access to the network*—As explained in Chapter 3, ping the loopback address—127.0.0.1 on a computer running IPv4 or ::1 on a computer running IPv6. If pinging the loopback address fails, the TCP/IP settings are probably configured incorrectly. You can also ping nodes on the LAN and hosts on the Web to check network connectivity. On a Windows computer, use `ipconfig /all` to view information about your interfaces. On a Linux or UNIX computer, the `ifconfig -a` command will do the same.

Network+
1.12
4.6
4.7

Applying Concepts

Scenario: Stingy IP Camera

7 APPLICATION
6 PRESENTATION
5 SESSION
4 TRANSPORT
3 NETWORK
2 DATA LINK
1 PHYSICAL

Suppose you arrive at work one morning to find a new service ticket waiting in your inbox. The day before, two new surveillance IP cameras were installed outside a data closet in a newly renovated office building. These IP cameras transmit their feed over the network to the Security Department. Security is receiving the feed from one camera with no problem. However, they're not getting anything from the other camera. As far as the security system is concerned, the camera doesn't exist.

After confirming the lack of data feed in the monitoring program, you ping the camera but get no response. Knowing the camera is new, your next stop is the camera itself. Knowing that rebooting a device often solves problems, your first move is to pull out the ladder, climb up to the camera, and hit the power button to reboot it. You've brought along your laptop and, while the camera is rebooting, you connect to the LAN in that building to check the feed again. From this vantage point, the camera is working fine. The feed is coming through clearly now. Thinking you've solved the problem, you return to your desk and notify security that the camera is fixed. Unfortunately, they disagree. When you pull up the security program again, the camera feed isn't there. You know it was working a few minutes ago back at the camera. So why isn't it visible in the security program?

As you do a little more exploration, here are some of the things you find:

- The feed from the other camera installed at the same time on the same LAN is still coming through fine.
- All the other nodes you've tested on that LAN are fully functional and responding to `ping`.
- There are no errors reported on the LAN that hosts the security program.

Why is the camera's transmission not making it to the security program? Below are several possible resolutions. Select the best one and explain your reasoning:

a. The Ethernet cable from the camera to the network is malfunctioning and should be replaced.

b. The security program doesn't recognize the authenticity of the camera's data, so a static route should be configured from the camera to Security's LAN.

c. The switch for the cameras' LAN is inadequate for the amount of traffic on the LAN now that the new cameras have been added. The switch should be replaced with a more powerful device.

d. The camera's NIC is malfunctioning and should be replaced.

e. The camera's default gateway is misconfigured or unreachable and should be corrected.

f. The Ethernet cable leading from the camera to the network is placed too closely to some nearby fluorescent lights, which is causing interference in the transmission. The cable should be relocated farther away from the lights.

g. Power fluctuations in that building's data closet are causing intermittent problems with the devices on that LAN. The UPS servicing that closet should be replaced.

Building and Maintaining Network Documentation

Having up-to-date and detailed documentation of your network is essential to good troubleshooting. Chapter 1 discussed the importance of knowledge bases and how to document problem resolutions in a call tracking system. Recall that a knowledge base is a collection of accumulated insights and solutions to the problems encountered on a network. Another critically useful form of documentation is **network diagrams**, which are graphical representations of a network's devices and connections. These diagrams may show physical layout, logical topology, IP address reserves, names of major network devices, and types of transmission media. A network diagram can be created as a product of **network mapping**, which is the process of discovering and identifying the devices on a network. Network mapping is a fascinating field of study in its own right, and its relevance and importance will only increase as the complexity of today's networks increases. Every network technician can benefit from understanding some general concepts related to network mapping.

The way you gather, format, and store your network documentation can vary, but to adequately manage your network, you should at least record the following:

- *network diagrams*—A visual diagram or map of networked devices can be drawn based on logical or physical connectivity. A picture is worth a thousand words and glancing at an accurate network diagram can quickly help you identify a point of failure when troubleshooting.

- *physical topology*—Which types of LAN and WAN topologies does your network use: bus, star, ring, hybrid, mesh, or a combination of these? Which type and grade of cabling does your network use? What types of cables are used and where are they located?

- *access method*—Does your network use Ethernet, Wi-Fi (802.11), WiMAX (802.16), cellular, satellite, or a mix of transmission methods? What transmission speed(s) does it provide? Which switching method is used?

- *protocols*—Which protocols are used by servers, nodes, and connectivity devices?

- *devices*—How many of the following devices are connected to your network: switches, routers, gateways, firewalls, access points, servers, UPSs, printers, backup devices, and clients? Where are they located? Are they physical or virtual? If physical, what are their model numbers and vendors?

- *operating systems*—Which network and desktop operating systems are on the network? Which versions of these operating systems are used by each device? Which type and version of operating systems are used by connectivity devices such as routers?

- *applications*—Which applications are used by clients and servers? Where do you store the applications? From where do they run?

- *configurations*—What versions of operating systems and applications does each workstation, server, and connectivity device run? How are these programs configured? How is hardware configured? The collection, storage, and assessment of such information belongs to a category of network management known as **configuration management**. Ideally, you would rely on configuration management software to gather and store the information in a database, where those who need it can easily access and analyze the data.

If you have not already collected and centrally stored the answers to the questions just listed, it could take the efforts of several people and several weeks to compile them, depending on the size and complexity of your network. This evaluation would entail visits to data closets, an examination of servers and desktops, a review of receipts for software and hardware purchases, and, potentially, the use of a protocol analyzer or network management software package. Still, all this effort would save you work in the future. After you have compiled the information, organize it into a database that can be easily updated and searched. That way, staff can access the information in a timely manner and keep it current.

A diagram or map of your networked devices can be sketched on the back of a napkin, or you could draw it on your computer using a graphics program. However, many people use software designed for mapping networks, such as Dia, Edraw, Gliffy, Microsoft Visio, or Network Notepad. Such applications come with icons that represent different types of devices and connections. Cisco Systems long ago set the standard for the symbols used in network diagrams to represent routers, switches, firewalls, and other devices. These symbols are widely accepted and understood in the networking field. Figure 4-32 shows a simplified network diagram that uses standard icons based on Cisco's iconography, with each device labeled. Notice that a router is represented by a hockey-puck shape with two arrows pointing inward and two arrows pointing outward. A wireless router looks the same, but has two antennas attached. A workgroup switch is represented by a small rectangular box, which also contains four arrows pointing in opposite directions.

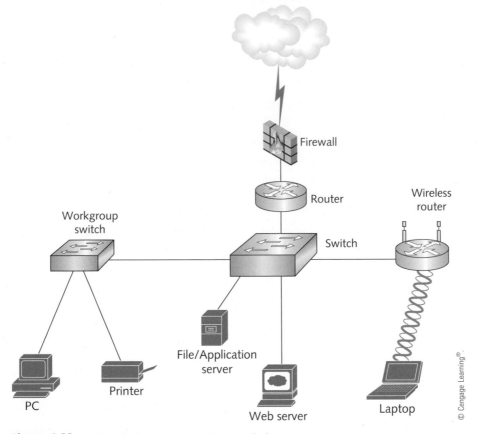

Figure 4-32 Network diagram using Cisco symbols

Network+
1.12
2.3

Applying Concepts

Install and Use Zenmap

7	APPLICATION
6	PRESENTATION
5	SESSION
4	TRANSPORT
3	NETWORK
2	DATA LINK
1	PHYSICAL

Several programs are available to assist in detecting, identifying, and monitoring the devices on your network. One of the simpler and most popular tools is Nmap. Nmap was originally designed for Linux as a command-line only utility, but has since been expanded for compatibility on several other OSs and is now available in GUI form. In this activity, you will download the GUI version of Nmap for Windows, which is called Zenmap.

1. Go to **nmap.org** and look for the Zenmap GUI download. At the time of this writing, the download was called the "Latest release self-installer" with the file named **nmap-6.47-setup.exe**. Download and install the Zenmap GUI version of Nmap. Use default settings throughout the installation process.

2. After you've installed it, open Zenmap from your desktop. Start with a quick scan of your local computer. In the Target field, enter **localhost**, and in the Profile field, select **Quick scan**. Click **Scan**.

The scan will show a list of ports on your computer and the services assigned to them, as you can see in Figure 4-33. Next try a scan of your local network and see how the output changes. This time you will target all IP addresses in the same range as your computer's IP address. The easiest way to do this is to first determine your computer's IP address.

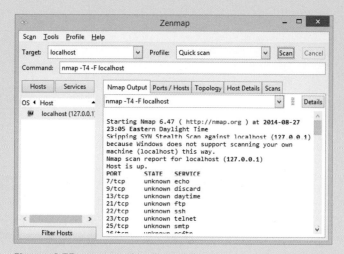

Figure 4-33   Zenmap localhost scan output

Source: Zenmap

3. Open a Command Prompt window and enter the command `ipconfig`. Find the IPv4 address and write it down if necessary.

4. Go back to Zenmap. In the Target field, type your local computer's IPv4 address. However, so that you can scan a range of IP addresses, replace the final block of digits in your IPv4 address with **1-254**. For example, if your IPv4 address is 192.168.1.106, you would enter **192.168.1.1-254** in the Target field.

5. Click **Scan**.

6. This time the output shows information about other hosts on your network as well as the information you've already seen for your own computer. Scroll through the output and answer the following questions:

   a. How many IP addresses were scanned? How many hosts are up?

   b. Compared with the information you saw earlier about your own computer, what different information is revealed about the other hosts? What explanation does Zenmap provide for why this is so?

   c. Find a host with open ports reported and list the ports and their services in your answer. What other information is provided about that host?

Most network diagrams provide broad snapshots of a network's physical or logical topology. This type of view is useful for planning where to insert a new switch or determining how a particular router, gateway, and firewall interact. However, if you're a technician who needs to find a fault in a client's wired connection to the LAN, a broad overview might be too general. Instead, you need a wiring schematic. A wiring schematic is a graphical representation of a network's wired infrastructure. In its most detailed form, it shows every wire necessary to interconnect network devices. Some less-detailed wiring schematics might use a single line to represent the group of wires necessary to connect several clients to a switch. Figure 4-34 provides an example of a detailed wiring schematic for a small office network connection that relies on cable broadband service to access the Internet.

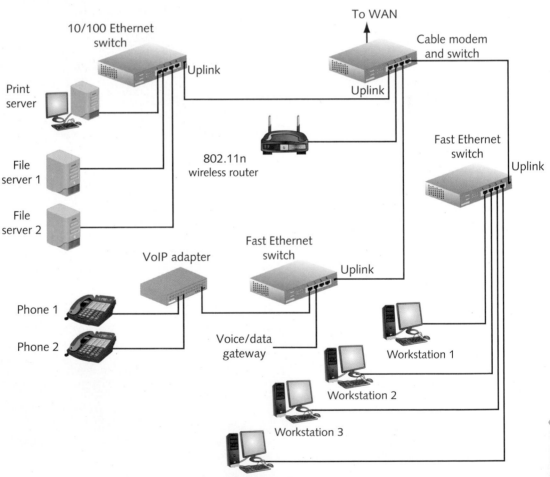

Figure 4-34 Wiring schematic

Chapter Summary

Network Equipment in Commercial Buildings

- TIA/EIA created a joint cabling standard known as structured cabling that provides guidelines for uniform, enterprise-wide cabling systems, regardless of vendor.

- Physical layer failures can be caused by a range of issues, including poor termination, excessive bend radius, damaged cables, and EMI.

- 110 blocks are suitable for data connections, whereas the older 66 blocks were designed primarily for telephone connections.

- When developing a naming convention for network devices, use names that are as descriptive as possible. But be sure to only include fields that are absolutely essential to identifying the device.

- Rack systems provide mounting hardware for network equipment to optimize the use of square footage in equipment rooms and ensure adequate spacing, access, and ventilation for these devices.

- NAS (network attached storage), which is a device optimized for saving and serving files, provides centralized fault-tolerant data storage for a network.

- SAN (storage area network) is a distinct network of multiple storage devices that collectively provide faster access to data and larger amounts of storage than a NAS can do. Two Transport layer protocols used by SANs are Fibre Channel and iSCSI.

- Fibre Channel connects devices within a SAN and also connects the SAN to other networks.

- iSCSI runs on top of TCP on an already established Ethernet LAN and may use jumbo frames for transmissions.

Managing Power Sources and the Environment

- A UPS is a battery-operated power source directly attached to one or more devices and to a power supply, such as a wall outlet, that prevents undesired fluctuations of the wall outlet's AC power from harming the device or interrupting its services.

- Standard generators do not provide surge protection, but they can provide a backup power source, which is called power redundancy.

- Electrical equipment cannot use raw power directly from a generator unless it also contains an inverter component.

- Due to the sensitive nature of the equipment mounted on racks, environmental and security monitoring are critical preventive measures.

NICs and Ethernet

- NICs interpret physical addressing information to ensure data is delivered to its proper destination. NICs may also perform prioritization, network management, buffering, and traffic-filtering functions.

- On a Linux workstation, a popular utility called ethtool allows you to view and change NIC settings. In Windows, use Device Manager for the same purpose.

- Ethernet is a Layer 2 standard that is a flexible technology, capable of running on a variety of network media, and offering excellent throughput at a reasonable cost.

- An Ethernet II frame can range in size from 64 to 1522 total bytes. In addition, proprietary Ethernet standards might use jumbo frames.

Troubleshooting Network Devices

- To troubleshoot NIC problems, use a loopback plug, Device Manager in Windows or ethtool in Linux or UNIX, NIC diagnostics software, and command-line utilities.

- Network maps may show physical layout, logical topology, IP address reserves, names of major network devices, and types of transmission media.

- Several programs are available to assist in detecting, identifying, and monitoring the devices on your network. One of the simpler and most popular tools is Nmap.

Key Terms

For definitions of key terms, see the Glossary near the end of the book.

110 block
66 block
airflow
alternating current (AC)
bend radius
blackout
brownout
cable tray
collision
collision domain
configuration management
CRC (cyclic redundancy check)
cross-talk
CSMA/CD (Carrier Sense Multiple Access with Collision Detection)
device driver
direct current (DC)
driver
duplex
EIA (Electronic Industries Alliance)
electric circuit
EMI (electromagnetic interference)
entrance facility
Ethernet II

ethtool
fault tolerance
FCS (frame check sequence)
fiber-optic cable
Fibre Channel (FC)
four-post rack
full-duplex
half-duplex
half-rack
horizontal wiring
hub
IDF (intermediate distribution frame)
inverter
iSCSI (Internet SCSI)
KVM (keyboard, video, and mouse) switch
loopback adapter
loopback plug
main cross connect
MDF (main distribution frame)
media access control (MAC)
NAS (network attached storage)
network diagram
network mapping

Nmap
offline UPS
online UPS
patch cable
power converter
power redundancy
preamble
punch down tool
PVC (polyvinyl chloride)
rack system
rack unit (RU or U)
rectifier
sag
SAN (storage area network)
server rail
simplex
speed and duplex mismatch
standby power supply (SPS)
standby UPS
STP (shielded twisted pair)
structured cabling
surge
surge protector
Thunderbolt

TIA (Telecommunications Industry Association)

transformer

two-post rack

UPS (uninterruptible power supply)

UTP (unshielded twisted pair)

vertical cross connect

voltage regulator

volt-ampere (VA)

wiring schematic

Review Questions

1. Which of the following cabling types is *not* recognized by the TIA/EIA for horizontal wiring?

   a. UTP

   b. STP

   c. Coaxial

   d. Fiber-optic

2. What kind of networking device on today's racks does nothing to the data transmitted on a line other than pass it along through the connection?

   a. Patch panel

   b. Punch-down block

   c. 110 block

   d. Hub

3. In which layer(s) of the OSI model do NICs operate?

   a. Layers 5, 6, and 7

   b. Layers 1 and 2

   c. Layer 4

   d. Layers 2 and 3

4. What are the two primary standard widths for rack systems?

   a. 3 feet and 6 feet

   b. 18U and 42U

   c. 19 inches and 23 inches

   d. 1U and 4U

5. What device provides a central control portal for all devices on a rack?

   a. Server rails

   b. Rack ears

   c. Rack-monitoring system

   d. KVM switch

6. What device protects computer equipment from a momentary increase in voltage due to lightning strikes, solar flares, or electrical problems?

    a. NAS

    b. Surge protector

    c. Generator

    d. Power converter

7. Providing a backup power source is called _____.

    a. power conversion

    b. power redundancy

    c. power inversion

    d. line conditioning

8. What generator component converts DC power from the generator to AC power that the electrical infrastructure in a data center can use?

    a. Inverter

    b. Rectifier

    c. Transformer

    d. Voltage regulator

9. Which type of Ethernet frames do today's networks use?

    a. Jumbo frame

    b. Ethernet II frame

    c. 802.3 frame

    d. CSMA/CD frame

10. What is the very beginning of an Ethernet frame called?

    a. Header

    b. Data

    c. Preamble

    d. Trailer

11. Why is it important to use a structured cabling standard when installing and managing cabling systems?

12. What is the first point of interconnection between an organization's LAN or WAN and a service provider's facility, and what components are generally included at this location?

13. Why is it important to use plenum-rated cabling in the area above the ceiling tile?

14. What are the three methods by which a NIC can interface with a computer's motherboard?

15. What does a loopback plug do?

16. What is the unit of measurement that defines the space available in a rack? How tall are standard racks?

17. What are the two general categories of UPSs?

18. What are some elements that are typically included in network diagrams?

19. What is the GUI version of Nmap for Windows?

20. What is a wiring schematic?

Hands-On Projects

Project 4-1: Install and Configure NIC Hardware

It's always advisable to start by reading the manufacturer's documentation that accompanies the NIC hardware. The following steps generally apply to any kind of expansion card NIC installation in a desktop computer, but your experience may vary.

To install an expansion card NIC:

1. Make sure that your toolkit includes a Phillips-head screwdriver, a ground strap, and a ground mat to protect the internal components from electrostatic discharge. Also, make sure that you have ample space in which to work, whether on the floor, a desk, or a table.

2. Turn off the computer's power switch, and then unplug the computer. In addition to endangering you, opening a PC while it's turned on can damage the PC's internal circuitry. Also unplug attached peripherals and the network cable, if necessary.

3. Attach the ground strap to your wrist and make sure that it's connected to the ground mat underneath the computer.

4. Open the computer's case. Desktop computer cases are attached in several different ways. They might use four or six screws to attach the housing to the back panel, or they might not use any screws and slide off instead. Remove all necessary screws and then remove the computer's case.

5. Select a slot on the computer's motherboard where you will insert the NIC. Make sure that the slot matches the type of expansion card you have. Remove the metal slot cover for that slot from the back of the PC. Some slot covers are attached with a single screw; after removing the screw, you can lift out the slot cover. Other slot covers are merely metal parts with perforated edges that you can punch or twist out with your hands.

6. Insert the NIC by lining up its slot connector with the slot and pressing it firmly into the slot. Don't be afraid to press down hard, but make sure the expansion card is properly aligned with the slot when you do so. If you have correctly inserted the NIC, it should not wiggle near its base. A loose NIC causes connectivity problems. Figure 4-35 shows a close-up of a NIC firmly seated in its slot.

7. The metal bracket at the end of the NIC should now be positioned where the metal slot cover was located before you removed the slot cover. Attach the bracket with a screw to the back of the computer cover to secure the NIC in place.

8. Make sure that you have not loosened any cables or cards inside the PC or left any screws or debris inside the computer.

Figure 4-35   An expansion card NIC properly inserted in a PCI expansion slot

9. Replace the cover on the computer and reinsert the screws that you removed in Step 4, if applicable. Also reinsert any cables you removed.

10. Plug in the computer and turn it on. Proceed to configure the NIC's software, as discussed in the next project.

Project 4-2: Install and Configure NIC Software

In this project, you learn how to install drivers for a NIC and update the drivers. As with any device installation, always use the device drivers specifically designed for the operating system and the model of NIC you are installing. Drivers come bundled with the NIC and you can also download them from the NIC manufacturer's Web site. Follow these steps to configure NIC software on a Windows 7 or Windows 8.1 system:

1. Install the NIC as described in Project 4-1, and then restart the computer. Log on to the computer with an account that has administrator privileges.

2. Windows automatically detects the new hardware and installs the NIC drivers. To verify Windows recognized the NIC with no errors, open Control Panel, open the System window, and then, from within the System window, open Device Manager.

3. The Device Manager window displays a list of installed devices. Expand the Network adapters group and double-click the NIC. On the General tab, Windows should report the device is working properly.

4. The Driver tab shows details about the currently installed NIC drivers (see Figure 4-36). To update the drivers, click **Update Driver**.

5. In the dialog boxes that follow, you can browse your computer and point to the driver software you have on disc or downloaded from the Web. Alternately, you can have

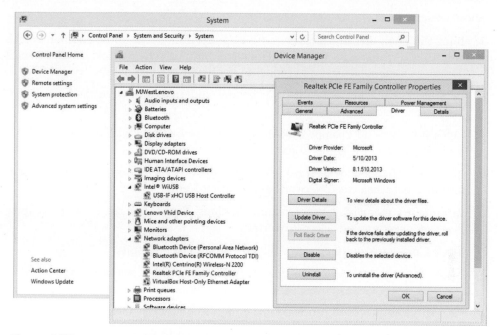

Figure 4-36 Network adapter properties dialog box with Driver tab selected

Source: Microsoft LLC

Windows search the Internet for the latest drivers. If Windows recognizes the NIC manufacturer, it will search the manufacturer's Web site. Follow directions on screen to install the drivers.

6. After installing a NIC, you might need to modify its transmission characteristics—for example, whether it uses full-duplexing, whether it can detect a network's speed, or even its MAC address. For Windows, you can find these settings on the Advanced tab of the NIC's properties dialog box in Device Manager.

7. After you have installed and configured the drivers and settings as you want them, test network connectivity by opening a Web browser and navigating to a Web site. If problems arise, follow the steps given earlier in the chapter for troubleshooting NIC problems. If you suspect newly installed drivers is the problem, you can roll back the drivers to the previous version. To do so, use the Roll Back Driver button on the Driver tab of the NIC's properties dialog box.

Project 4-3: Set Up Advanced IP Scanner and Wake-on-LAN

Many times, a technician needs to be able to identify and control machines on a network. Modern motherboards often have a Wake-on-LAN feature, which enables a technician to control that machine without having to be at the machine. This increases efficiency of managing machines and decreases time needed to complete support activities.

Follow these steps to set up the Wake-on-LAN:

1. Boot the computer and access its BIOS setup utility. For most computers, this means you'll need to press F1 or F2 while it's still booting. Do a quick search online for your computer's manufacturer and model to confirm the BIOS access key for your machine.

2. In BIOS, locate the Wake-on-LAN feature and enable it. Save the setting change and reboot the machine.

3. Open a Command Prompt window and use `ipconfig /all` to determine the computer's IP address. Close the Command Prompt window.

4. Next, you'll enable Wake-on-LAN in Windows. Open Control Panel, select **Network and Internet**, then click **Network and Sharing Center**.

5. In the left pane, click **Change adapter settings**. Right-click the network adapter for the wired connection and select **Properties**.

6. Click **Configure** and then select the **Power Management** tab.

7. Make sure that the **Allow the computer to turn off this device to save power** option is selected. This enables Power Management in Windows.

8. Check **Allow this device to wake the computer** and click **OK**.

Go to a different workstation and install the Advanced IP Scanner utility. Follow these steps:

1. Using your Web browser, go to **advanced-ip-scanner.com** and download and install the software utility Advanced IP Scanner.

2. Open Advanced IP Scanner. Once it loads, click the **Scan** button to scan your network. As the scanning progresses, the lower pane shows network devices and machines that the utility discovers. See Figure 4-37.

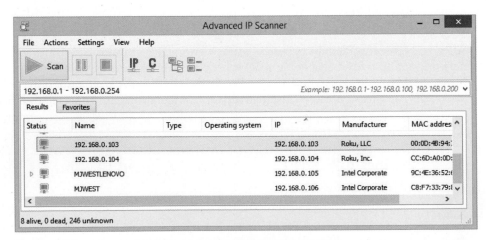

Figure 4-37   Advanced IP Scanner detects devices on a network

Source: Famatech

3. In the Status column, select one of the machines listed and expand it to view the contents. You can access shared folders and devices by double-clicking items listed under a machine.

4. Select the machine that has the IP address with the Wake-on-LAN feature enabled that you configured earlier.

5. At the top of the Advanced IP Scanner window, click **Actions** and then, in the Actions menu, click **Shut down**. If needed, provide a username and password for the remote machine. Did the machine **shut down?**

6. In the Actions menu, click **Wake-On-LAN** to send Wake-on-LAN packets. Did the machine boot up?

When using the scan feature of Advanced IP Scanner, what information does it tell you about the network?

Project 4-4: Ethernet Jumbo Frames

In Chapter 3, you learned about MTUs and used `ping` to determine the largest MTU for a route over the Internet. Earlier in this chapter, you saw the elements of an Ethernet frame that determine its size. The larger the Ethernet frame, the more efficient network communications can become because of the overhead included with many smaller frames. In some cases, especially where file transfer is a high priority on the network such as on a SAN, configuring network devices to handle larger, jumbo frames can benefit the throughput of the network.

Not all NICs support jumbo frames, and these large packet sizes can cause problems with dropped messages if portions of the network are not configured to handle them. But in contained network situations such as a SAN or a virtual network, jumbo frames may be the best choice. In this project, you configure your computer's NIC to implement jumbo frames.

You could use the `netsh` command to change the Ethernet frame size. In the previous project, you used the network adapter's properties dialog box to make changes, so you use that approach here as well, but this time with Windows 8.1.

1. In Windows 8.1, right-click the **Start** button and click **Device Manager**. Expand the Network adapters list, then locate and double-click the Ethernet adapter (look for "PCIe" in the name).

2. Click the **Advanced** tab. Under Property, look for the **Jumbo Frame** option and click it. (If this option is not listed, then your NIC does not support jumbo frames.) The default value on the right is Disabled. Change this to **9KB MTU**, as shown in Figure 4-38, and click **OK**.

3. Open a Web browser and navigate to a couple of different Web sites. Challenge the Internet connection by streaming a video on YouTube.

4. You can leave this setting as it is if it doesn't cause any problems. Try to notice whether the performance of your network for various tasks is affected positively or negatively. If required by your instructor or if you encounter problems, you can go back and disable jumbo frames on your network adapter.

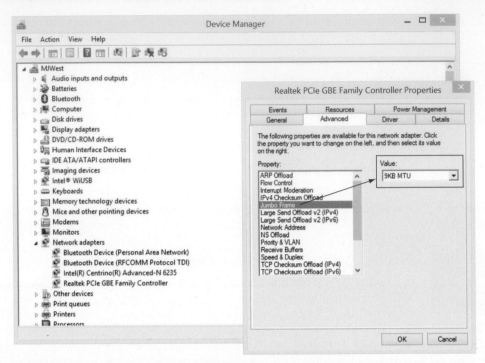

Figure 4-38   Jumbo frames are enabled on this NIC for a maximum MTU of 9 KB

Source: Microsoft LLC

Case Projects

Case Project 4-1: Set Up an FTP Server in Ubuntu Server

In Chapter 3, in Case Project 3-1, you installed Ubuntu Server in a VM and learned to use some Linux commands in Ubuntu. In this case project, you set up an FTP server in Ubuntu. Follow these steps:

1. Using the same VM you created in Case Project 3-1, log on to Ubuntu Server with your username and password.

2. To install a program, you need to have the security privileges of a superuser. In Linux, a superuser is named *root*. You can apply root privileges to any command by preceding the command with the `sudo` command. To use root privileges to install the FTP program named vsftpd, enter this command:

```
sudo apt-get install vsftpd
```

3. Respond to the prompts and then wait for the package to install.

4. Now you need to configure the FTP program by editing the vsftpd.conf text file stored in the /etc directory. But before you edit the file, go to the /etc directory and make a backup copy of the file just in case you need it later:

```
cd /etc
sudo cp vsftpd.conf vsftpd.backup
```

5. Ubuntu has several text editors; we'll use the vim editor. Let's first install the editor:

   sudo apt-get install vim

6. Now let's edit the FTP configuration file:

   sudo vim vsftpd.conf

   Here are a few tips on using the vim editor. You can find out more about it by doing a Google search:

   - Use the arrow keys to move over the file.
   - To edit the file, type **i** to enter Insert mode. INSERT appears at the bottom of your VM screen.
   - To leave Insert mode, press **Escape**.
   - To save your changes, type **:w**.
   - To exit without saving your changes, type **:q**.
   - To save your changes and exit, type **:wq**.

7. Using vim, find and, if necessary, change three lines in the config file to create the settings listed. Part of the file, including the three lines, is shown in Figure 4-39.

anonymous_enable=NO	Disable anonymous logins.
local_enable=YES	Remove the # to uncomment the line and allow local users to log in.
write_enable=YES	Remove the # to uncomment the line and allow users to write to a directory.

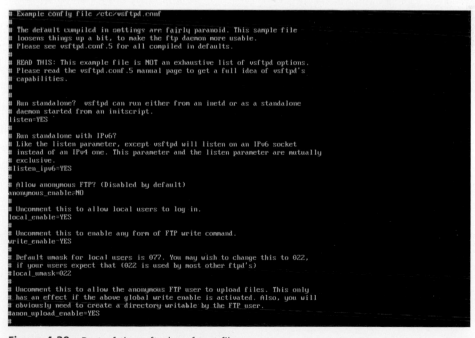

Figure 4-39 Part of the vsftpd.conf text file

Source: vsftpd, vim editor, Ubuntu Server

8. Exit the vim editor, saving your changes. Restart the FTP service using this command: `sudo restart vsftpd`

9. To test your FTP server using the local machine, enter `ftp 127.0.0.1`. Then enter your username and password. Next use the `dir` command to see a list of directories and files. You should see the mydir directory that you created in your /home/*username* directory when doing Case Project 3-1. Type `bye` to disconnect from the FTP server.

10. To find out the IP address of the server, type `ifconfig`.

11. Go to another computer on your local network or in your virtual network and use the same commands in Step 9 to connect to your FTP server, this time using the IP address of your server rather than the loopback address.

   If you want to transfer files with FTP commands, use the `get` and `put` commands.

CASE PROJECTS

Case Project 4-2: Download and Use Spiceworks

Earlier in this chapter, you downloaded and used Zenmap, the Nmap GUI, to collect data about the devices on your network. You also used Advanced IP Scanner to scan the network in an earlier project. A very popular program for monitoring network devices is Spiceworks. You might be familiar with Spiceworks for its help desk features, but it also includes some powerful network mapping and monitoring functionality. In this project, you download and install Spiceworks, scan your network, and view a network map.

1. To begin, go to the Spiceworks Web site at **spiceworks.com**. Download and install Spiceworks. Accept the default port 80. Decline Nmap and WinPCap because you already installed those programs when you installed Zenmap, which typically includes more recent versions of those programs than Spiceworks does. Accept all other defaults during the installation process.

2. Create a free Spiceworks account, and be sure to record your account information in a safe place. (You can decline the special offers and survey options if you'd like.)

3. First you need to discover network devices, so click the **Discover My Devices** button.

   Spiceworks automatically configures the IP search range, as shown in Figure 4-40. In this example, Spiceworks was also able to resolve a few device names already. If you wanted to search a different IP address range than the one automatically selected by Spiceworks, that option is available in the drop-down menu on the right. For now, you can stick with the default range.

4. Click **Enter Credentials**.

5. Type your user credentials and click **Start Scan**. Depending on the type of credentials you used, your device scan may have been more or less successful, but that's fine for the level of work you'll be doing in this project. You don't need to fix the errors at this time. Take a couple of minutes to explore the results of your scan and answer the following questions:

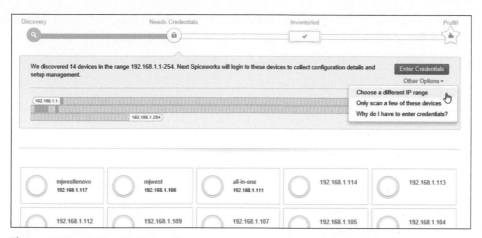

Figure 4-40   Automatic IP search range

Source: Spiceworks

    a.   How many devices were successfully inventoried? How many errors were reported?

    b.   Click on the Inventoried section in the left pane. Which devices were successfully added to the inventory?

    c.   Click on one of the Errors sections in the left pane. What additional percentage of your network could be inventoried if you fixed those errors?

You can skip the remainder of the scan process and see what kinds of results you can see already.

6. Click **Overview** at the top of the left pane, then click the **Skip this step** button to choose not to address the errors at this time. Finally, click the **Finished** button to complete the scan process.

On the Scan Overview page, notice the Scan Range Breakdown chart at the bottom of the page, which highlights the portion of the IP address range that is in use. (See Figure 4-41.)

Figure 4-41   Scan Range Breakdown chart

Source: Spiceworks

Spiceworks provides several options for monitoring the devices on your network. Spend a few minutes exploring what you can discover about the inventoried devices, and perhaps even try to fix a few of the errors. When you're ready, use the following steps to build a graphical network map:

7. On the menu bar at the top of the window, point to **Inventory**, then click **Network Map**. In the Select a Network Map dialog box, under Default Maps, click **All Devices**.

   After the map is created, answer the following questions:

   a. How many devices appear on the Network Map?

   b. What is the IP address of your network's default gateway? How did you identify this device on your map?

## chapter 5

Network Cabling

After reading this chapter and completing the exercises, you will be able to:

- Explain basic data transmission concepts, including signaling, data modulation, multiplexing, bandwidth, baseband, and broadband

- Describe the physical characteristics and Ethernet standards of coaxial cable, STP, UTP, and fiber-optic media

- Compare the benefits and limitations of different networking media

- Explore the connectors, converters, and couplers for each cabling type

- Examine common cable problems and differentiate between various tools for troubleshooting those problems

On the Job

I was asked to consult on a network problem concerning slow speeds and dead network jacks. The business was located in a building that was configured for two rental spaces with a single entrance. After entering the front door, I encountered a door to one set of offices on the right and the same on the left. Straight ahead was a door to the mechanical rooms.

When I removed the wall plates, I found that the installer had untwisted the pairs by at least one inch on all of the jacks. On some of the nonfunctional wall jacks, the pairs were untwisted three inches or more and stuffed haphazardly into the wall box.

The next mystery was the single 12-port switch, which didn't make sense because I was now able to achieve link on 19 wall sockets. This meant that it was time to start removing ceiling tiles and following wires. Fortunately, all of the wires came together in a bundle that exited into the ceiling above the entryway. From there, most of the bundle turned and went toward the mechanical room, where the fiber-modem and 12-port switch were located. Unfortunately, a few of the wires went toward the other rental space. The other set of offices was not currently rented, and so was not accessible without contacting the landlord. The landlord was hesitant to give access to the other space. He insisted that the problem could not have anything to do with the wiring in that part of the building because his nephew, who was an electrician, had done all of the network cabling in the building. Instead, the landlord insisted that the tenants must have messed up the wall jacks on their side.

After tracing cable after cable above the suspended ceiling, I finally found another network switch hiding on top of one of the ceiling tiles. All of the cable terminations had around two inches of the pairs untwisted to make it easier to install the RJ-45 terminals.

I reconnected all the wall jacks and replaced all of the terminals on the cables at the hidden switch. All of the client's wall jacks were now able to achieve link and connect, transferring at 100 Mbps full-duplex.

Todd Fisher Wallin
Operations Coordinator, Driftless Community Radio

Just as highways and streets provide the foundation for automobile travel, networking media provides the physical foundation for data transmission. Networking media is the physical or atmospheric paths that signals follow. The first networks used thick coaxial cables. Today's local area networks use twisted copper wire cabling, whereas long-distance connections between LANs typically use fiber-optic cable. In addition, both local and long-distance connections often use wireless transmissions. Wireless networking is covered in Chapter 6. Because networks are always evolving to meet the demand for greater speed, versatility, and reliability, networking media technologies change rapidly.

Understanding the characteristics of various networking media is critical to designing and troubleshooting networks. You also need to know how data is transmitted over the media. This chapter discusses the details of data transmission and physical networking media. You'll learn what it takes to make data transmission dependable and how to correct some common transmission problems.

Transmission Basics

The transmission techniques in use on today's networks are complex and varied. In the following sections, you will learn about some fundamental characteristics that define today's data transmission.

Analog Signaling

On a network, information can be transmitted via one of two signaling methods: analog or digital. **Analog signals**, such as electromagnetic waves in the air or in copper wire, vary infinitely and continuously and appear as a wavy line when graphed over time, as shown in Figure 5-1.

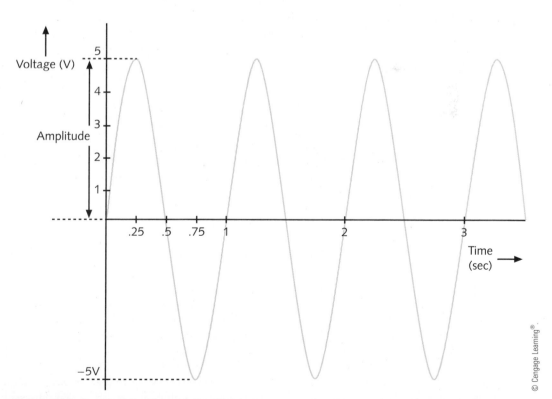

Figure 5-1 An example of an analog signal

An analog signal, like other waveforms, is characterized by four fundamental properties: amplitude, frequency, wavelength, and phase. These properties are described in the following list:

- *amplitude*—A measure of a signal's strength at any given point in time. On a wave graph, the amplitude is the height of the wave at any point in time. For example, in Figure 5-1, the following is true:
  - At .25 seconds, the amplitude is 5 volts.
  - At .5 seconds, the amplitude is 0 volts.
  - At .75 seconds, the amplitude is −5 volts.

- *frequency*—The number of times that a wave's amplitude cycles from its starting point, through its highest amplitude and its lowest amplitude, and back to its starting point over a fixed period of time. Frequency is expressed in cycles per second, or hertz (Hz), named after German physicist Heinrich Hertz, who experimented with electromagnetic waves in the late nineteenth century. For example, in Figure 5-1:
  - The wave cycles to its highest then lowest amplitude and returns to its starting point in 1 second.
  - Therefore, the frequency is 1 cycle per second, or 1 Hz; this is an extremely low frequency.

- *wavelength*—The distance between corresponding points on a wave's cycle (for example, between one peak and the next) expressed in meters or feet. For electromagnetic waves, a wave's wavelength is inversely proportional to its frequency. In other words, the higher the frequency, the shorter the wavelength. For example:
  - A radio wave with a frequency of 1,000,000 cycles per second (1 MHz) has a wavelength of 300 meters.
  - A wave with a frequency of 2,000,000 Hz (2 MHz) has a wavelength of 150 meters.

- *phase*—The progress of a wave over time in relationship to a fixed point. Suppose two separate waves have identical amplitudes and frequencies. If one wave starts at its lowest amplitude at the same time the second wave starts at its highest amplitude, these waves will have different phases. More precisely, they will be 180 degrees out of phase (using the standard assignment of 360 degrees to one complete wave). Had the second wave also started at its lowest amplitude, the two waves would be in phase. For example, in Figure 5-2, two waves have identical amplitudes and frequencies and their phases are 90 degrees apart.

NOTE   Frequencies used to convey speech over telephone wires fall in the 300 to 3300 Hz range. Humans can hear frequencies between 20 and 20,000 Hz. An FM radio station may use a frequency between 850,000 Hz (or 850 kHz) and 108,000,000 Hz (or 108 MHz) to transmit its signal through the air. You will learn more about radio frequencies used in networking later in this chapter.

One drawback to analog signals is that they have infinite variations, which are susceptible to transmission flaws such as noise, or any type of interference that may degrade a signal. If you have tried to listen to AM radio on a stormy night, you have probably heard the crackle and

Degrees

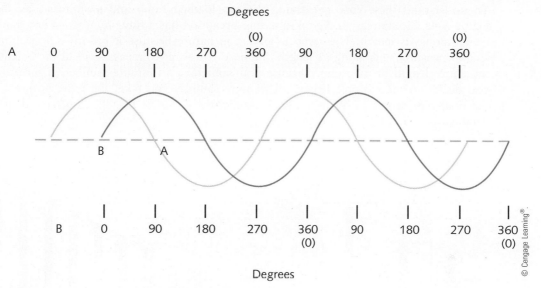

Figure 5-2   Waves with a 90-degree phase difference

static of noise affecting the signal. One way to compensate for these flaws is to digitize the analog signal.

Network+
5.2

Digital Signaling

Digital signals are composed of pulses of precise, positive voltages and zero voltages. There's nothing infinite or continuous about a digital signal because it is inherently either on or off. A pulse of positive voltage represents a 1. A pulse of zero voltage (in other words, the lack of any voltage) represents a 0. The use of 1s and 0s to represent information is characteristic of a binary system. Every pulse in the digital signal is a binary digit, or bit. Contrast the analog signals pictured in Figures 5-1 and 5-2 to a digital signal, as shown in Figure 5-3. Whereas the waves in Figures 5-1 and 5-2 have infinite heights, the signal in Figure 5-3 has only two heights, 0 and 1.

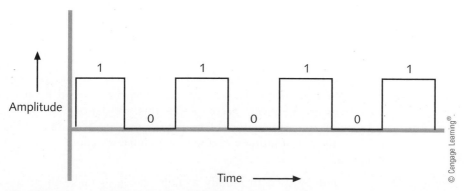

Figure 5-3   An example of a digital signal

To understand these concepts, think about a loading ramp and a staircase, as shown in Figure 5-4. The staircase is digital in nature because it has a finite number of height measurements along its length. The ramp is analog in nature because it has an infinite number of height measurements along its length. Suppose you want to measure all of the heights along the entire length of the ramp. Because you can't take an infinite number of measurements, you decide to take sample heights. The more samples you take, the more accurate will be the final representation of the ramp. In taking these sample heights, you have digitized the heights of the ramp.

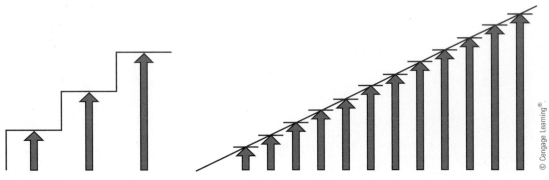

Figure 5-4   It's impossible to measure every height along a ramp

© Cengage Learning®

An analog signal, such as the sound of the human voice or music, has an infinite number of tones and subtle inflections. When digitizing sound, the higher the sampling rate, the more accurate the representation of the analog signals. For example, the sampling rate for digitized voice, such as that used by iPhone's Siri, is much lower than the sampling rate used for music albums.

Data Modulation

Computers are digital through and through. Every calculation and processing of data is done using bits (1s and 0s). For example, when you play music on your computer, the music is digitized and stored as bits. It's only converted to analog sound by the audio component in your computer just before output to your speakers.

However, in many cases the types of connections used in your network are capable of handling only analog signals. For example, telephone lines are designed to carry analog signals. If you connect to your ISP's network via DSL (digital subscriber line) through a telephone line, the data signals issued by your computer must be converted into analog form before they get to the phone line. Later, they must be converted back into digital form when they arrive at the ISP's access server. A modem accomplishes this translation. The word modem reflects this device's function as a *modulator/dem*odulator—that is, it modulates digital signals into analog signals at the transmitting end, then demodulates analog signals into digital signals at the receiving end.

Data modulation is a technology used to modify analog signals to make them suitable for carrying data over a communication path. In modulation, a simple wave, called a carrier wave, is combined with another analog signal, known as the information or data wave, to produce a unique signal that gets transmitted from one node to another. The carrier wave has preset properties (including frequency, amplitude, and phase). Its purpose is to help convey information; in other words, it's only a messenger. When the information wave is added, it modifies one property of the carrier wave (for example, the frequency, amplitude, or phase). The result is a new, blended signal that contains properties of both the carrier wave and added data. When the signal reaches its destination, the receiver separates the data from the carrier wave. The data is sent on its way to the computer once again as 0s and 1s.

Modulation can be used to make a signal conform to a specific pathway, as in the case of **FM (frequency modulation)** radio, in which the data must travel along a particular frequency. In frequency modulation, the frequency of the carrier signal is modified by the application of the data signal. In **AM (amplitude modulation)**, the amplitude of the carrier signal is modified by the application of the data signal. Modulation may also be used to issue multiple signals to the same communications channel and prevent the signals from interfering with one another. Figure 5-5 depicts an unaltered carrier wave, a data wave, and the combined wave as modified through frequency modulation. Later in this book, you will learn about networking technologies, such as DSL, that require modulation.

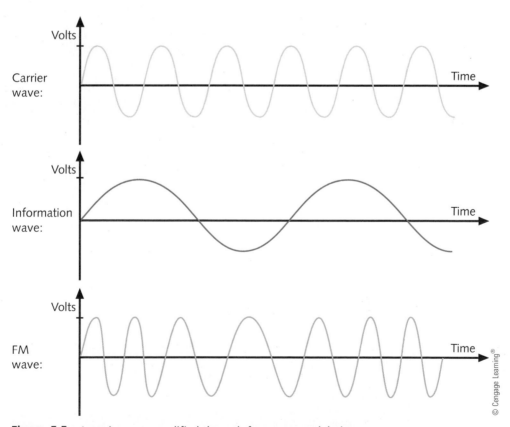

Figure 5-5   A carrier wave modified through frequency modulation

Baseband and Broadband

The term baseband refers to transmissions that are carried on a single channel, with no other transmission sharing the media. Ethernet is an example of a baseband technology. The term broadband refers to technologies in which multiple transmissions share a single media. Cable TV and cable Internet share the same coaxial cable and are therefore examples of broadband. Other broadband technologies include regular telephone signals sharing copper wire with DSL Internet service and mobile broadband in which voice and data share a wireless cellular network. Broadband transmissions sharing the same media rely on multiplexing to manage the multiple signals.

Multiplexing

A form of transmission that allows multiple signals to travel simultaneously over one medium is known as multiplexing. Networks rely on multiplexing to increase the amount of data that can be transmitted in a given timespan over a given bandwidth. To carry multiple signals, the medium's channel is logically separated into multiple smaller channels, or subchannels. Many different types of multiplexing are available, and the type used in any given situation depends on what the media, transmission, and reception equipment can handle. For each type of multiplexing, a device that can combine many signals on a channel, a multiplexer (mux), is required at the transmitting end of the channel. At the receiving end, a demultiplexer (demux) separates the combined signals.

Different types of multiplexing manipulate the signals in different ways to enable this multitasking on network media. Some common types of multiplexing are discussed next.

TDM (Time Division Multiplexing) TDM (time division multiplexing) divides a channel into multiple intervals of time, or time slots. It then assigns a separate time slot to every node on the network and, in that time slot, carries data from that node. For example, if five stations are connected to a network over one wire, five different time slots are established in the communications channel. Workstation A may be assigned time slot 1, workstation B time slot 2, workstation C time slot 3, and so on. Time slots are reserved for their designated nodes regardless of whether the node has data to transmit. If a node does not have data to send, nothing is sent during its time slot. This arrangement can be inefficient if some nodes on the network rarely send data. Figure 5-6 shows a simple TDM model.

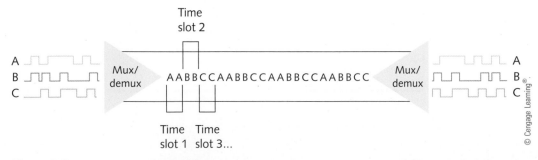

Figure 5-6   Time division multiplexing

Statistical Multiplexing

Statistical Multiplexing Statistical multiplexing is similar to TDM, but rather than assigning a separate slot to each node in succession, the transmitter assigns slots to nodes according to priority and need. This method is more efficient than TDM because in statistical multiplexing time slots are unlikely to remain empty. To begin with, in statistical multiplexing, as in TDM, each node is assigned one time slot. However, if a node doesn't use its time slot, statistical multiplexing devices recognize that and assign its slot to another node that needs to send data. The contention for slots may be arbitrated according to use or priority or even more sophisticated factors, depending on the network. Most importantly, statistical multiplexing maximizes available bandwidth on a network. Figure 5-7 depicts a simple statistical multiplexing system.

Figure 5-7 Statistical multiplexing

FDM (Frequency Division Multiplexing)

FDM (Frequency Division Multiplexing) FDM (frequency division multiplexing) assigns a unique frequency band to each communications subchannel. Signals are modulated with different carrier frequencies, then multiplexed to simultaneously travel over a single channel. The first use of FDM was in the early twentieth century when telephone companies discovered they could send multiple voice signals over a single cable. That meant that, rather than stringing separate lines for each residence (and adding to the urban tangle of wires), they could send as many as 24 multiplexed signals over a single neighborhood line. Each signal was then demultiplexed before being brought into a home.

Telephone companies still multiplex signals on the phone line that enters your residence. Voice communications use the frequency band of 300–3400 Hz (because this matches approximately the range of human hearing), for a total bandwidth of 3100 Hz. Telephone companies implement FDM to subdivide and send signals in the bandwidth above 3400 Hz, for example, to provide DSL services as an ISP providing Internet access. Because the frequencies can't be heard, you don't notice the data transmission occurring while you talk on the telephone. Figure 5-8 provides a simplified view of FDM, in which waves representing three different frequencies are carried simultaneously by one channel.

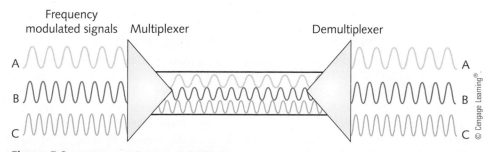

Figure 5-8 Frequency division multiplexing

WDM (Wavelength Division Multiplexing)

WDM (wavelength division multi-plexing) is a technology used with fiber-optic cable, which enables one fiber-optic connection to carry multiple light signals simultaneously. Using WDM, a single fiber can transmit as many as 20 million telephone conversations at one time. WDM can work over any type of fiber-optic cable.

WDM divides a beam of light into up to 40 different wavelengths or colors, with each serving as a carrier wave capable of transmitting data signals up to 10 Gpbs. The beam is then multiplexed and sent by a laser over a strand of fiber within the fiber-optic cable. The demultiplexer at the receiving end acts like a prism to separate the combined signals into the original wavelengths or colors. If the signal risks losing strength between the multiplexer and demultiplexer, an amplifier might be used to boost it. Figure 5-9 illustrates WDM transmission.

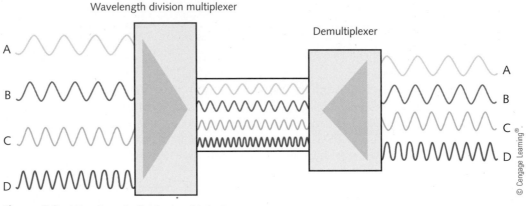

Figure 5-9   Wavelength division multiplexing

DWDM (Dense Wavelength Division Multiplexing)

Most modern fiber-optic networks use a type of WDM called DWDM (dense wavelength division multiplexing). In DWDM, a single fiber in a fiber-optic cable can carry between 80 and 160 channels. It achieves this increased capacity because it uses more wavelengths for signaling. In other words, there is less separation between the usable carrier waves in DWDM than there is in the original form of WDM. Because of its extraordinary capacity, DWDM is typically used on high-bandwidth or long-distance WAN links, such as the connection between a large ISP and its (even larger) network service provider.

CWDM (Coarse Wavelength Division Multiplexing)

Another type of WDM is CWDM (coarse wavelength division multiplexing), which is defined by wavelength instead of frequency. CWDM was developed after DWDM in an effort to lower the cost of the transceiver equipment needed. With CWDM, channels are spaced more widely apart across the entire frequency band to allow for the use of cheaper transceiver equipment. CWDM typically uses 8 or fewer channels per fiber, though some manufacturers may use up to 16 channels. The effective distance of CWDM is more limited because the signal is not amplified.

Throughput and Bandwidth

Two transmission characteristics often discussed and analyzed by networking professionals is throughput and bandwidth. **Throughput**, also called payload rate or effective data rate, is the measure of how much data is actually transmitted during a given period of time. Bandwidth is similar to but slightly different than throughput. Bandwidth is the theoretical potential for data to transmit during a given period of time. As an analogy, the bandwidth of a three-lane freeway is the theoretical potential for bumper-to-bumper traffic to get through at the maximum speed limit, but in practice that never happens. Throughput measures the actual traffic that gets through under given conditions.

Throughput and bandwidth are commonly expressed as bits transmitted per second, called **bit rate**, such as 1000 bits per second or 1 Kbps (1 kilobit per second). Table 5-1 summarizes the terminology and abbreviations used when discussing different throughput and bandwidth amounts.

Table 5-1   **Throughput and bandwidth measures**

Quantity	Prefix	Abbreviation
1 bit per second	n/a	1 bps = 1 bit per second
1000 bits per second	kilo	1 Kbps = 1 kilobit per second
1,000,000 bits per second	mega	1 Mbps = 1 megabit per second
1,000,000,000 bits per second	giga	1 Gbps = 1 gigabit per second
1,000,000,000,000 bits per second	tera	1 Tbps = 1 terabit per second

© Cengage Learning®

As an example, a low-cost residential broadband Internet connection might be rated for a maximum bandwidth of 3 Mbps, but actual throughput is usually lower. This explains why providers often advertise "up to 3 Mbps." A fast LAN that achieves a throughput or payload rate of 1 Gbps might require a bandwidth transmission rate of 1.25 Gbps because of the overhead in Ethernet frames. Applications that require significant throughput include video-conferencing and telephone signaling. By contrast, instant messaging and email, for example, require much less throughput.

NOTE Be careful not to confuse bits and bytes when discussing throughput. Although data storage quantities are typically expressed in multiples of bytes, data transmission quantities (in other words, throughput) are more commonly expressed in multiples of bits per second. When representing different data quantities, a small *b* represents bits, whereas a capital *B* represents bytes. To put this into context, a modem may transmit data at 56.6 Kbps (kilobits per second); a data file may be 56 KB (kilobytes) in size.

Another difference between data storage and data throughput measures is that in data storage the prefix *kilo* means 2 to the 10th power, or 1024, not 1000.

For analog transmissions, throughput and bandwidth can also be measured by the number of symbols transmitted per second, and this measurement is called the **baud rate (Bd)**, modulation rate, or symbol rate. A symbol is a voltage, frequency, pulse, or phase change in the analog transmission. Few consumers or technicians concern themselves with baud rate and are more interested in the bit rate measurements of throughput.

NOTE Baud rate is named after the French engineer Emile Baudot, who invented a 5-bit teletype code in 1870 (patented in 1874) called the Baudot code. The Baudot code was used by teleprinters and was eventually replaced by ASCII, a character encoding system consisting of 128 characters. The original ASCII was a 7-bit system, so each character's code was 7 bits long. ASCII was later incorporated as a subset of UTF-8, an 8-bit system, which is the most common character encoding system used today.

Now that you understand several concepts of data transmission, you're ready to learn about different types of transmission media. Let's begin with a little bare-bones details about an outdated media, coaxial cable.

NETWORK+ EXAM TIP

The CompTIA Network+ exam expects you to know the characteristics and limitations of each type of media, how to install and design a network with each type, how to troubleshoot networking media problems, and how to provide for future network growth with each option.

Network+
1.5
5.4
Legacy Networking
Coaxial Cable

Coaxial cable, called "coax" for short, was the foundation for Ethernet networks in the 1980s and remained a popular transmission medium for many years. You'll most likely never see a coaxial cable network, as coax has been replaced by twisted-pair cable and fiber; however, a form of coax is still used for cable Internet and cable TV.

Coaxial cable has a central metal core (often copper) surrounded by an insulator, a braided metal shielding, called braiding or shield, and an outer cover, called the sheath or jacket (see Figure 5-10). The core can have a solid metal wire or several thin strands of metal wire and carries the electromagnetic signal. The shielding protects the signal against noise and is a ground for the signal. The plastic insulator can be PVC (polyvinyl chloride) or Teflon and protects the core from the metal shielding because if the two made contact, the wire would short-circuit. The sheath protects the cable from physical damage and may be PVC or a more expensive fire-resistant plastic.

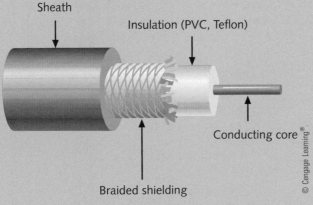

Figure 5-10 Coaxial cable

Coaxial cabling comes in hundreds of specifications, which are all assigned an RG specification number. (RG stands for *radio guide*, which is appropriate because coaxial cabling can be used by radio frequencies in broadband transmission.) The RG ratings measure the materials used for shielding and conducting cores, which in turn influence their transmission characteristics, such as impedance (or the resistance that contributes to controlling the signal, as expressed in ohms), attenuation, and throughput.

Each type of coax is suited to a different purpose. When discussing the size of the conducting core in a coaxial cable, we refer to its American Wire Gauge (AWG) size. The larger the AWG size, the smaller the diameter of the core wire. Table 5-2 is a list of coaxial cable specifications used historically with data networks.

Table 5-2   **Coaxial cable specifications**

Type	Impedance	Core	Uses
RG-6	75 ohms	18 AWG conducting core, usually made of solid copper	Used to deliver broadband cable Internet service and cable TV, particularly over long distances. Cable Internet service entering your home is RG-6.
RG-8	50 ohms	10 AWG core	Currently outdated; used by the earliest Ethernet networks, and was called Thicknet.
RG-58	50 ohms	24 AWG core	Used in the 1980s and 1990s, and was called Thinnet because it is thinner than Thicknet cables. More flexible and easier to handle and install than Thicknet. Its core is typically made of several thin strands of copper.
RG-59	75 ohms	20 or 22 AWG core, usually made of braided copper	Still used for relatively short connections, for example, when distributing video signals from a central receiver to multiple monitors within a building. RG-59 is less expensive than the more common RG-6, but suffers from greater attenuation.

© Cengage Learning®

NETWORK+ EXAM TIP

The CompTIA Network+ exam expects you to know about RG-6 and RG-59 cables, F-connector, BNC connector, BNC coupler, and 10Base2. Note that BNC connectors and couplers and the 10Base2 standard are all legacy technology.

The two coaxial cable types commonly used in networks today, RG-6 and RG-59, can terminate with one of two connector types:

- F-connectors attach to coaxial cable so that the pin in the center of the connector is the conducting core of the cable. Therefore, F-connectors require that the cable contain a solid metal core. After being attached to the cable by crimping or compression, connectors are threaded and screwed together like a nut-and-bolt assembly. A male F-connector, or plug, attached to coax is shown in Figure 5-11. A corresponding female F-connector, or jack, would be coupled with the male connector. F-connectors are most often used with RG-6 cables.

Courtesy of MCM Electronics, Inc.

Figure 5-11 F-connector

- **BNC** stands for *Bayonet Neill-Concelman*, a term that refers to both an older style of connection and its two inventors. (Sometimes the term *British Naval Connector* is also used.) A **BNC connector** is crimped, compressed, or twisted onto a coaxial cable. It connects to another BNC connector via a turn-and-lock mechanism—this is the bayonet coupling referenced in its name. Unlike an F-connector, a male BNC connector provides its own conducting pin. BNC connectors are used with RG-59 coaxial cables, and less commonly, with RG-6. Figure 5-12 shows a BNC connector that is not attached to a cable. In addition, you can use a **BNC coupler** to connect two coaxial cables. Today, F-connectors are much more common.

© Igor Smichkov/Shutterstock.com.

Figure 5-12 BNC connector

When sourcing connectors for coaxial cable, you need to specify the type of cable you are using. For instance, when working with RG-6 coax, choose an F-connector made specifically for RG-6 cables. That way, you'll be certain that the connectors and cable share the same impedance rating. If impedance ratings don't match, data errors will result and transmission performance will suffer.

Like later generations of Ethernet cabling, a variety of coax cables were named for the standards that defined their functionality. One example is the legacy 10Base2, dubbed cheapernet, Thinnet, or thinwire, because it used RG-58 cabling that was thinner than the earlier RG-8 cabling. In the 1980s, 10Base2 was the most commonly available 10-Mbps Ethernet cable.

Next, you will learn about a medium you are more likely to find on modern LANs, twisted-pair cable.

Twisted-Pair Cable

Twisted-pair cable consists of color-coded pairs of insulated copper wires, each with a diameter of 0.4 to 0.8 mm (approximately the diameter of a straight pin). Every two wires are twisted around each other to form pairs, and all the pairs are encased in a plastic sheath, as shown in Figure 5-13. The number of pairs in a cable varies, depending on the cable type.

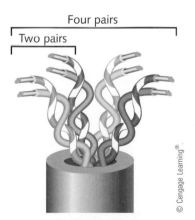

Figure 5-13   Twisted-pair cable

The more twists per foot in a pair of wires, the more resistant the pair will be to cross-talk or noise. Higher-quality, more-expensive twisted-pair cable contains more twists per foot. The number of twists per meter or foot is known as the twist ratio. Because twisting the wire pairs more tightly requires more cable, however, a high twist ratio can result in greater attenuation. For optimal performance, cable manufacturers must strike a balance between minimizing cross-talk and reducing attenuation.

Because twisted pair is used in such a wide variety of environments and for a variety of purposes, it comes in hundreds of different designs. These designs vary in their twist ratio, the number of wire pairs they contain, the grade of copper used, the type of shielding (if any), and the materials used for shielding, among other things. A twisted-pair cable may contain from 1 to 4200 wire pairs. Modern networks typically use cables that contain four wire pairs, in which one pair is dedicated to sending data and another pair is dedicated to receiving data.

In 1991, the TIA/EIA organizations finalized their specifications for twisted-pair wiring in a standard called "TIA/EIA 568." Since then, this body has continually revised the international standards for new and modified transmission media. The standards now cover cabling media, design, and installation specifications. The TIA/EIA 568 standard divides twisted-pair wiring into several categories. The types of twisted-pair wiring you will hear about most often are Cat (category) 3, 5, 5e, 6, and 6a, and Cat 7. All of the category cables fall under the TIA/EIA 568 standard. Modern LANs use Cat 5e or higher wiring.

Twisted-pair cable is relatively inexpensive, flexible, and easy to install, and it can span a significant distance before requiring a repeater, which is a device that retransmits a digital signal in its original form. Twisted-pair cable easily accommodates several different topologies, although it is most often implemented in star or star-hybrid topologies. All twisted-pair cable falls into one of two categories: STP (shielded twisted pair) or UTP (unshielded twisted pair).

STP (Shielded Twisted Pair)

Network+
1.5

Recall from Chapter 4 that STP (shielded twisted pair) cable consists of twisted-pair wires that are not only individually insulated, but also surrounded by a shielding made of a metallic substance such as foil. Some STP cables use a braided copper shielding. The shielding acts as a barrier to external electromagnetic forces, thus preventing them from affecting the signals traveling over the wire inside the shielding. It also contains the electrical energy of the signals inside. The shielding must be grounded to enhance its protective effects and prevent reflection issues. The effectiveness of STP's shield depends on the level and type of environmental noise, the thickness and material used for the shield, the grounding mechanism, and the symmetry and consistency of the shielding. Figure 5-14 depicts an STP cable.

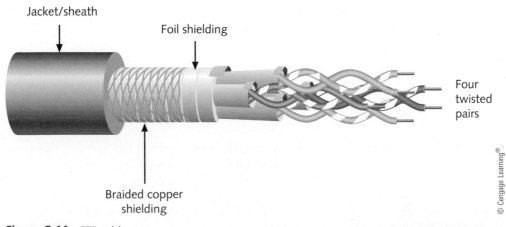

Jacket/sheath

Foil shielding

Four twisted pairs

Braided copper shielding

© Cengage Learning®

Figure 5-14   STP cable

UTP (Unshielded Twisted Pair)

UTP cabling consists of one or more insulated wire pairs encased in a plastic sheath. As its name implies, UTP does not contain additional shielding for the twisted pairs. As a result, UTP is both less expensive and less resistant to noise than STP, and is more popular than STP, primarily because of its lower cost. Figure 5-15 depicts three types of UTP cable: PVC-grade Cat 5e, plenum-grade Cat 5e, Cat 6 with its plastic core, and a UTP cable with the RJ-45 connector attached.

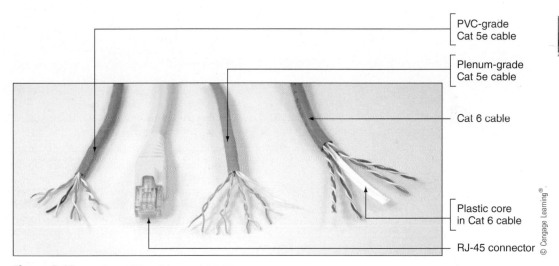

Figure 5-15   Various UTP cables and RJ-45 connector

Earlier, you learned that the TIA/EIA consortium designated standards for twisted-pair wiring. To manage network cabling, you need to be familiar with the standards for use on modern networks, particularly Cat 5e or higher, as described in Table 5-3. Note that Cat 5e or higher is required to support Gigabit Ethernet, which can transmit data at 1 Gbps or higher. Cat 6 and above, however, are certified for multigigabit transmissions. (Cat 4 cabling exists, too, but it is rarely used.)

Table 5-3   **UTP cabling standards**

Standard	Maximum supported throughput	Bandwidth/ signal rate	Description
Cat 3 (Category 3)	10 Mbps	Up to 16 MHz	Used for 10-Mbps Ethernet or 4-Mbps Token Ring networks. Rarely found on any modern network.
Cat 5 (Category 5)	100 Mbps	100 MHz	Required minimum standard for Fast Ethernet, also known as 100-BaseT Ethernet that runs at 100 Mbps.

Table 5-3 UTP cabling standards (*continued*)

Standard		Maximum supported throughput	Bandwidth/ signal rate	Description
Gigabit Ethernet	Cat 5e (Enhanced Category 5)	1000 Mbps (1 Gbps)	350 MHz	A higher-grade version of Cat 5 wiring that contains high-quality copper, offers a high twist ratio, and uses advanced methods for reducing cross-talk.
	Cat 6* (Category 6)	10 Gbps	250 MHz	Includes a plastic core to prevent cross-talk between twisted pairs in the cable, as shown in Figure 5-15. Cat 6 can also have foil insulation that covers the bundle of wire pairs and a fire-resistant plastic sheath.
	Cat 6a* (Augmented Category 6)	10 Gbps	500 MHz	Reduces attenuation and cross-talk and allows for potentially exceeding traditional network segment length limits. Can reliably transmit data at multigigabit per second rates. Cat 6a cabling is backward compatible with Cat 5, Cat 5e, and Cat 6 cabling, which means that it can replace lower-level cabling without requiring connector or equipment changes.
	Cat 7* (Category 7) Not included in TIA/ EIA standards	10 Gbps	600 MHz	Contains multiple wire pairs, each surrounded by its own shielding, then packaged in additional shielding beneath the sheath. Cat 7 requires different connectors than other versions of UTP because its twisted pairs must be more isolated from each other to ward off cross-talk. Because of its added shielding, Cat 7 cabling is also larger and less flexible than other versions of UTP cable. Cat 7 is less common than Cat 5, Cat 6, or Cat 6a on modern networks.
	Cat 7a* (Augmented Category 7) Not included in TIA/ EIA standards	40–100 Gbps	1000 MHz	ISO standards for Cat 7a cabling are still being drafted and simulations conducted.

© Cengage Learning®

*Technically, because Cat 6 and Cat 7 contain wires that are individually shielded, they are not unshielded twisted pair. Instead, they are more similar to shielded twisted pair.

NOTE

It can be difficult to tell the difference between four-pair Cat 3 cables and four-pair Cat 5 or Cat 5e cables. However, some visual clues can help. On Cat 5 cable, the jacket is usually stamped with the manufacturer's name and cable type, including the Cat 5 specification. A cable whose jacket has no markings is more likely to be Cat 3. Also, pairs in Cat 5 cables have a significantly higher twist ratio than pairs in Cat 3 cables. Although Cat 3 pairs might be twisted as few as three times per foot, Cat 5 pairs are twisted at least 12 times per foot. Other clues, such as the date of installation (old cable is more likely to be Cat 3), looseness of the jacket (Cat 3's jacket is typically looser than Cat 5's), and the extent to which pairs are untwisted before a termination (Cat 5 can tolerate only a small amount of untwisting) are also helpful, though less definitive.

Because Cat 6 cables have the plastic core, they are thicker and less flexible than Cat 5.

UTP cabling may be used with any one of several IEEE Physical layer networking standards that specify throughput maximums of 10, 100, 1000, and even 10,000 Mbps. These standards are described in detail later in this chapter.

Comparing STP and UTP

STP and UTP share several characteristics. The following list highlights their similarities and differences:

- *throughput*—STP and UTP can both transmit data at 10 Mbps, 100 Mbps, 1 Gbps, and 10 Gbps, depending on the grade of cabling and the transmission method in use.

- *cost*—STP and UTP vary in cost, depending on the grade of copper used, the category rating, and any enhancements. Typically, STP is more expensive than UTP because it contains more materials and it has a lower demand. It also requires grounding, which can lead to more expensive installation. High-grade UTP can be expensive, too, however. For example, Cat 6a costs more per foot than Cat 5 cabling.

- *connector*—STP and UTP use RJ-45 (registered jack 45) modular connectors and data jacks, which look similar to analog telephone connectors and jacks. However, telephone connections follow the RJ-11 (registered jack 11) standard. Figure 5-16 shows a close-up of an RJ-45 connector for a cable containing four wire pairs. For comparison, this figure also shows a traditional RJ-11 phone line connector. All types of Ethernet that rely on twisted-pair cabling use RJ-45 connectors.

© Cengage Learning®

Figure 5-16   RJ-45 and RJ-11 connectors

A third type of RJ connector might show up on the CompTIA Network+ exam: RJ-48C. As with all RJ jacks, the number (in this case, *48*) refers to the standard that defines the pinout for the jack. Adding a letter at the end indicates the wiring or mounting method used; in this case, the *C* indicates this jack is flush with the surface. On the job, you could also see RJ-48S (a single-line jack) or RJ-48X (a complex multiline jack). The RJ-48C connector is typically used with T-1 or ISDN lines. Both T-1 and ISDN are WAN technologies and are covered in Chapter 11.

- *noise immunity*—Because of its shielding, STP is more noise resistant than UTP. On the other hand, signals transmitted over UTP may be subject to filtering and balancing techniques to offset the effects of noise.

- *size and scalability*—The maximum segment length for both STP and UTP is 100 m, or 328 feet, on Ethernet networks that support data rates from 1 Mbps to 10 Gbps. These accommodate a maximum of 1024 nodes. However, attaching so many nodes to a segment is very impractical, as it would slow traffic and make management nearly impossible.

Ethernet Standards for Twisted-Pair Cabling

Table 5-4 lists the various Ethernet standards that can be used with twisted-pair cabling. So long as the proper category of twisted-pair cabling is used, a network can support a variety of Ethernet standards, which makes it possible to progressively upgrade a network, one device or NIC at a time. Most local area networks today use devices and NICs that can support 10Base-T, 100Base-T (Fast Ethernet), and 1000Base-T (Gigabit Ethernet) standards. When they first connect, devices and computers autonegotiate for the fastest standard.

In Ethernet technology, the most common theoretical maximum data transfer rates are 10 Mbps, 100 Mbps, 1 Gbps, and 10 Gbps. Actual data transfer rates on a network will vary, just as you might average 22 miles per gallon (mpg) driving your car to work and back, even though the manufacturer rates the car's gas mileage at 28 mpg.

Table 5-4 Ethernet standards used with twisted-pair cabling

Standard	Maximum transmission speed (Mbps)	Maximum distance per segment (m)	Physical media	Pairs of wires used for transmission
10Base-T Regular Ethernet	10	100	Cat 3 or better UTP	2 pair
100Base-T Fast Ethernet	100	100	Cat 5 or better UTP	2 pair
1000Base-T Gigabit Ethernet	1000	100	Cat 5 or better UTP (Cat 5e is preferred)	4 pair
1000Base-TX Gigabit Ethernet	1000	100	Cat 6	2 pair*
10GBase-T 10-Gigabit Ethernet	10,000	100	Cat 6a or Cat 7 (Cat 7 is preferred)	

© Cengage Learning®

*1000Base-TX achieves the same 1000-Mbps speed as 1000Base-T and still uses only two pairs of wires for transmission; however, it does require the better Cat 6 cabling to do so.

Memorize every detail in Table 5-4. You'll need them to pass the exam.

The latest Ethernet standard is 10GBase-T, which achieves dramatic transmission rates with twisted-pair cabling, comparable to fiber-optic cabling, and is less expensive than fiber-optic. Still, as with other twisted-pair Ethernet standards, the maximum segment length for 10GBase-T is 100 meters. This limitation means that 10GBase-T is not appropriate for long-distance WANs, but could easily allow the use of converged services, such as video and voice, at every desktop in a LAN.

Cable Pinouts

Network+
1.5
5.4

Proper cable termination is a basic requirement for two nodes on a network to communicate. Poor terminations, as you read in the On the Job story at the beginning of the chapter, can lead to loss or noise—and consequently, errors—in a signal. Closely following termination standards, then, is critical. TIA/EIA has specified two different methods of inserting twisted-pair wires into RJ-45 plugs: TIA/EIA 568A and TIA/EIA 568B. Functionally, there is no difference between these two standards. You only have to be certain that you use the same standard on every RJ-45 plug and jack on your network, so that data is transmitted and received correctly. Figure 5-17 depicts pin numbers and assignments (called pinouts) for the TIA/EIA 568A standard when used on an Ethernet network. Figure 5-18 depicts pin numbers and assignments for the TIA/EIA 568B standard.

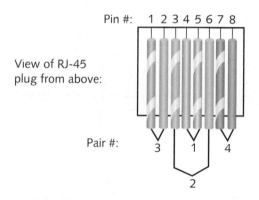

Pin #	Color	Pair #	Function
1	White with green stripe	3	Transmit +
2	Green	3	Transmit -
3	White with orange stripe	2	Receive +
4	Blue	1	Unused
5	White with blue stripe	1	Unused
6	Orange	2	Receive -
7	White with brown stripe	4	Unused
8	Brown	4	Unused

© Cengage Learning®

Figure 5-17 TIA/EIA 568A standard terminations

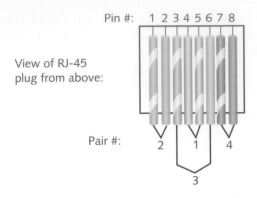

Pin #:   1 2 3 4 5 6 7 8

View of RJ-45
plug from above:

Pair #:   2   1   4

3

Pin #	Color	Pair #	Function
1	White with orange stripe	2	Transmit +
2	Orange	2	Transmit -
3	White with green stripe	3	Receive +
4	Blue	1	Unused
5	White with blue stripe	1	Unused
6	Green	3	Receive -
7	White with brown stripe	4	Unused
8	Brown	4	Unused

© Cengage Learning®

Figure 5-18   TIA/EIA 568B standard terminations

Although networking professionals commonly refer to wires in Figures 5-17 and 5-18 as *transmit* and *receive*, their original *T* and *R* designations stand for *Tip* and *Ring*, terms that come from early telephone technology but are irrelevant today.

If you terminate the RJ-45 plugs at both ends of a patch cable identically, following one of the TIA/EIA 568 standards, you will create a straight-through cable. A **straight-through cable**, also called a patch cable, is so named because it allows signals to pass "straight through" from one end to the other and is the most common type of cable.

Network+
1.5
5.4
Legacy Networking
Crossover Cable

Older networking devices could transmit on only one wire and receive only on another. A straight-through cable was always used to connect two unlike devices—for example, to connect a PC transmitting on the one wire that a switch received on, or a switch transmitting on the one wire that a router received on. See Figure 5-19. When you needed to connect two like devices (for example, a switch to a switch), a problem occurred because the two switches were both transmitting on the same wire and listening to receive on the other wire. The solution was to use a crossover cable. A **crossover cable** has the transmit and receive wires reversed and is used to connect a PC to a PC, a switch to a switch, or a PC to a router.

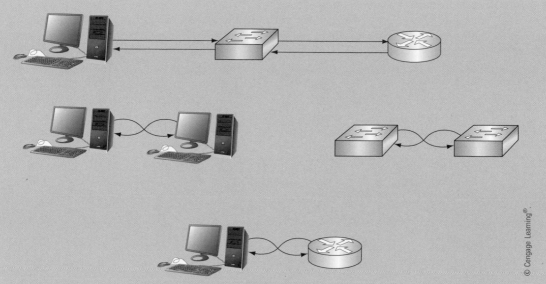

Figure 5-19 Straight-through cables connect unlike devices and crossover cables connect like devices. A crossover cable can also connect a computer to a router.

Modern devices have an autosense function that enables them to detect the way wires are terminated in a plug and then adapt their transmit and receive signaling accordingly. This means crossover cables are now largely obsolete, except when they are needed to support older devices.

In a crossover cable, the transmit and receive wires are reversed, as shown in Figure 5-20. The diagram on the left in Figure 5-20 has pairs 2 and 3 reversed (orange and green) and will work with 10- or 100-Mbps Ethernet because these types of Ethernet transmit on two pairs. The diagram on the right in Figure 5-20 has pairs 1, 2, 3, and 4 (blue, orange, green, and brown) reversed and will work with Gigabit Ethernet because Gigabit Ethernet transmits on four pairs.

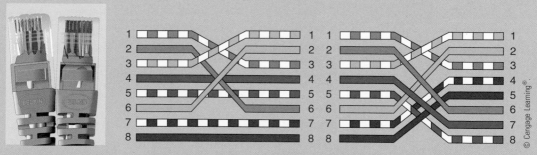

Figure 5-20 Two crossed pairs in a crossover cable are compatible with 10Base-T or 100Base-T Ethernet; four crossed pairs in a crossover cable are compatible with Gigabit Ethernet

The CompTIA Network+ exam expects you to know what a crossover cable is and how it can be used.

Rollover Cable Whereas a crossover cable reverses the transmit and receive wire pairs, a rollover cable reverses all of the wires without regard to how they are paired. With a rollover cable, it's as if the cable terminations are a mirror image of each other, as shown in Figure 5-21. Rollover cables, also called Yost cables or Cisco console cables, can be used to connect a computer to the console port of a router. Routers have two different kinds of ports: Ethernet ports and the console port. Ethernet ports allow for network communications and are the type of port used to create LANs through the router. A router's console port is used to communicate with the router itself, such as when making programming changes to the device. Straight-through and crossover cables are designed to transmit data between devices, but a rollover cable creates an interface with the device itself.

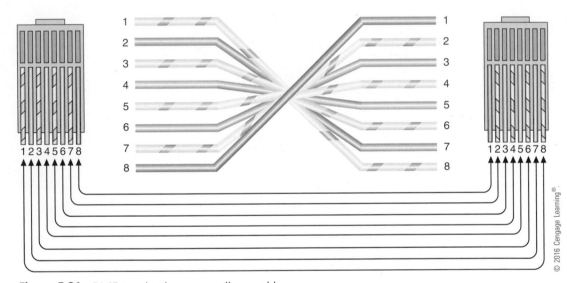

© 2016 Cengage Learning®.

Figure 5-21   RJ-45 terminations on a rollover cable

Network+
1.5

Applying Concepts

Terminate Twisted-Pair Cable

It's likely that at some point you will have to replace an RJ-45 connector on an existing cable. This section describes how to terminate twisted-pair cable. The tools you'll need to terminate a twisted-pair cable with an RJ-45 connector are a wire cutter, wire stripper, and crimping tool, which are pictured in Figures 5-22, 5-23, and 5-24, respectively. Alternatively, you can use a single device that contains all three of these tools. A wire stripper is designed to pull the protective covering off the inside wires without damaging the wires themselves. A crimping tool, also called a cable crimper, causes the internal RJ-45 pins to pierce the insulation of the wire, thus creating contact between the two conductors.

Figure 5-22   Wire cutter

Figure 5-23   Wire stripper

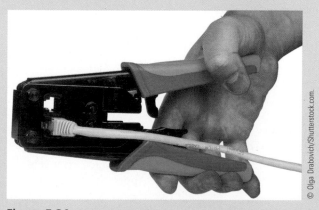

Figure 5-24   Crimping tool

5

Following are the steps to create a straight-through patch cable using Cat 5e twisted-pair cable. To create a crossover cable or rollover cable, you would simply reorder the wires in Step 4 to match Figure 5-20 or Figure 5-21, respectively. The process of fixing wires inside the connector is called crimping, and it is a skill that requires practice—so don't be discouraged if the first cable you create doesn't reliably transmit and receive data. You'll get to practice making cables in the projects at the end of this chapter.

To create a straight-through patch cable using Cat 5e twisted-pair cable:

1. Using the wire cutter, make a clean cut at both ends of the twisted-pair cable. Cut the cable the length you want the final cable to be plus a few extra inches.

2. Using the wire stripper, remove the sheath off of one end of the twisted-pair cable, beginning at approximately 1 inch from the end. Be careful to neither damage nor remove the insulation that's on the twisted pairs inside.

3. In addition to the four wire pairs, inside the sheath you'll find a string. This string, known as a strip string, is included to make it possible to cut through the outer sheath if a wire stripper is not available. (You use a pocketknife or scissors to start the cut, then pull the string through the cut to expose the inner wires.) Cut the string, then separate the four wire pairs in the full 1 inch of exposed cabling. Carefully unwind each pair and straighten each wire.

4. To make a straight-through cable, align all eight wires on a flat surface, one next to the other, ordered according to their colors and positions listed in Figure 5-18. It might be helpful first to groom—or pull steadily across the length of—the unwound section of each wire to straighten it out and help it stay in place.

5. Measure 1/2" from the end of the wires, and cleanly cut the wires at this length. Keeping the wires in line and in order, gently slide them into their positions in the RJ-45 plug. The plug should be positioned with the flat side facing toward you and the pin side facing away from you so the appropriate wires enter the correct slots for the wiring standard, and the sheath should extend into the plug about 3/8".

6. After the wires are fully inserted, place the RJ-45 plug in the crimping tool and press firmly to crimp the wires into place. Be careful not to rotate your hand or the wire as you do this, otherwise only some of the wires will be properly terminated.

7. Remove the RJ-45 connector from the crimping tool. Examine the end and see whether each wire appears to be in contact with the pin. It may be difficult to tell simply by looking at the connector. The real test is whether your cable will successfully transmit and receive signals.

8. Repeat Steps 2 through 7 for the other end of the cable. After completing Step 7 for the other end, you will have created a straight-through patch cable.

Even after you feel confident making your own cables, it's a good idea to verify that they can transmit and receive data at the necessary rates using a cable tester. Cable testing is discussed later in this chapter.

Copper Connectors and Couplers

Every networking medium requires a specific kind of connector, which connects a cable to a network device. You'll find a list of network connectors in Appendix C. Connectors are specific to a particular media type, but you can integrate two media types by using media converters. A media converter is hardware that enables networks or segments running on different media to interconnect and exchange signals. For example, suppose an Ethernet segment leading from your company's data center uses fiber-optic cable to connect to a workgroup switch that only accepts twisted-pair (copper) cable. In that case, you could use a media converter to interconnect the switch with the fiber-optic cable. The media converter completes the physical connection and also converts the electrical signals from the copper cable to light wave signals that can traverse the fiber-optic cable, and vice versa. Such a media converter is shown in Figure 5-25. Other types of converters include fiber-optic to coaxial cable and fiber-optic single mode to fiber-optic multimode.

Figure 5-25 Copper wire-to-fiber media converter

Another, simpler kind of connector is a coupler, which passes data through a homogenous connection without any modification. A UTP coupler, for example, can connect two UTP cables. This is helpful if you need to lengthen a cable without installing a new, longer cable.

> The terms *wire* and *cable* are used synonymously in some situations. Strictly speaking, however, *wire* is a subset of *cabling* because the *cabling* category may also include fiber-optic cable, which is almost never called *wire*. The exact meaning of the term *wire* depends on context. For example, if you said, in a somewhat casual way, "We had 6 gigs of data go over the wire last night," you would be referring to whatever transmission media helped carry the data—whether fiber, radio waves, coax, or UTP.

PoE (Power over Ethernet)

In 2003, IEEE released its 802.3af standard, which specifies a method for supplying electrical power over twisted-pair Ethernet connections, also known as PoE (Power over Ethernet). Although the standard is relatively new, the concept is not. In fact, your home telephone receives power from the telephone company over the lines that enter your residence. This power is necessary for dial tone and ringing. On an Ethernet network, carrying power over signaling connections can be useful for nodes that are far from traditional power receptacles or need a constant, reliable power source. The amount of power provided is relatively small—15.4 watts for standard PoE devices and 25.5 watts for the newer PoE+ devices, defined by the 802.3at standard. But that's enough to power a wireless access point at an outdoor theater, a telephone that receives digitized voice signals, a security camera mounted high on a wall, an Internet gaming station in the center of a mall, or a critical router at the core of a network's backbone.

The PoE standard specifies two types of devices: PSE and PD. PSE (power sourcing equipment) refers to the device that supplies the power; usually this device depends on backup power sources (in other words, not the electrical grid maintained by utilities). PDs (powered devices) are those that receive the power from the PSE. PoE requires Cat 5 or better copper cable. In the cable, electric current may run over an unused pair of wires or over the pair of wires used for data transmission in a 10Base-T, 100Base-TX, 1000Base-T, or 10GBase-T network. The standard allows for both approaches; however, on a single network, the choice of current-carrying pairs should be consistent between all PSE and PDs.

A switch or router that is expected to provide power over Ethernet must support the technology. This is the case with the switch shown in Figure 5-26. Also the end node must be capable of receiving PoE. The IEEE standard requires that a PSE device first determine whether a node is PoE-capable before attempting to supply it with power. That means that PoE is compatible with current 802.3 installations.

Figure 5-26   PoE-capable switch

On networks that demand PoE but don't have PoE-capable equipment, you can add PoE adapters, like the ones shown in Figure 5-27. One type of adapter connects to a switch or router to allow it to supply power. The other adapter attaches to a client, such as an outdoor camera, to receive power over the Ethernet connection.

Figure 5-27   PoE adapters

Legacy Networking

Serial Cables and Connectors

Occasionally, you might encounter a router, switch, or server with an older console port, called a serial port. Serial ports and serial cables (which are sometimes called RS-232 ports and cables) follow the TIA/EIA standards known as RS-232 (Recommended Standard 232). Different connector types comply with this standard, including RJ-45 connectors, DB-9 connectors, and DB-25 connectors. You are already familiar with RJ-45 connectors (also called plugs). Figures 5-28 and 5-29 illustrate male DB-9 and DB-25 connectors, respectively. Notice that the arrangement of the pins on both connectors resembles a sideways letter D. Also notice that a DB-9 connector contains 9 contact points and a DB-25 connector contains 25, each with two rows of pins.

Figure 5-28   DB-9 connector

Figure 5-29   DB-25 connector

The fact that a serial cable terminates in an RJ-45 connector does not mean it will work if plugged into a device's RJ-45 Ethernet port! When using a serial cable with an RJ-45 connector, be certain to plug it into the appropriate serial interface.

We've discussed several copper cable connectors in this section. You can see a list of all of the ones you'll need to know for the CompTIA Network+ exam, along with images to help you identify them visually, in Appendix C.

Now that you have learned about transmission media that use copper wires to conduct signals, you are ready to learn how signals are transmitted over glass fibers.

Fiber-Optic Cable

Fiber-optic cable, or simply *fiber*, contains one or several glass or plastic fibers at its center, or core. Data is transmitted through the central fibers via pulsing light sent from a laser (in the case of 1- and 10-gigabit technologies) or an LED (light-emitting diode), which is a cool-burning, long-lasting technology that creates light by the release of photons as electrons move through a semiconductor material. Surrounding the fibers is a layer of glass or plastic called cladding. The cladding has a different density from the glass or plastic in the strands. It reflects light back to the core in patterns that vary depending on the transmission mode. This reflection allows the fiber to bend around corners without diminishing the integrity of the light-based signal (although bend radius limitations do apply). Outside the cladding, a plastic buffer protects the cladding and core. Because the buffer is opaque, it also absorbs any light that might escape. To prevent the cable from stretching, and to protect the inner core further, strands of Kevlar (a polymeric fiber) surround the plastic buffer. Finally, a plastic sheath covers the strands of Kevlar. Figure 5-30 shows a fiber-optic cable with multiple, insulated fibers.

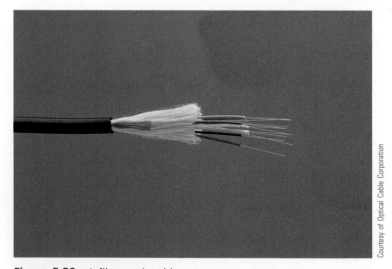

Figure 5-30 A fiber-optic cable

Like twisted-pair and coaxial cabling, fiber-optic cabling comes in a number of different varieties, depending on its intended use and the manufacturer. For example, fiber-optic cables used to connect the facilities of large telephone and data carriers may contain as many as 1000 fibers and be heavily sheathed to prevent damage from extreme environmental conditions. At the other end of the spectrum, fiber-optic patch cables for use on LANs may contain only two strands of fiber and be pliable enough to wrap around your hand. Because each strand of glass in a fiber-optic cable transmits in one direction only—in simplex fashion—two strands are needed for full-duplex communication. One solution is to use a zipcord cable, in which two strands are combined side by side in conjoined jackets, as depicted in Figure 5-31. You'll find zipcords where fiber-optic cable spans relatively short distances, such as connecting a server and switch. A zipcord may come with one of many types of connectors on its ends, as described later in this section.

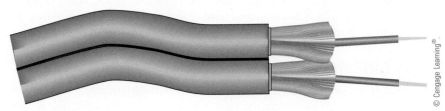

© Cengage Learning®

Figure 5-31   Zipcord fiber-optic patch cable

Fiber-optic cable provides the following benefits over copper cabling:

- Extremely high throughput
- Very high resistance to noise
- Excellent security
- Ability to carry signals for much longer distances before requiring repeaters
- Industry standard for high-speed networking

The most significant drawback to the use of fiber is that covering a certain distance with fiber-optic cable is more expensive than using twisted-pair cable. Also, fiber-optic cable requires special equipment to splice, which means that quickly repairing a fiber-optic cable in the field (given little time or resources) can be difficult. Fiber's characteristics are summarized in the following list:

- *throughput*—Fiber has proved reliable in transmitting data at rates that can reach 100 gigabits (or 100,000 megabits) per second per channel. Fiber's amazing throughput is partly due to the physics of light traveling through glass. Unlike electrical pulses traveling over copper, the light experiences virtually no resistance. Therefore, light-based signals can be transmitted at faster rates and with fewer errors than electrical pulses. In fact, a pure glass strand can accept up to 1 billion laser light pulses per second. Its high throughput capability makes it suitable for network backbones and for serving applications that generate a great deal of traffic, such as video or audio conferencing.

- *cost*—Fiber-optic cable is the most expensive transmission medium. Because of its cost, most organizations find it impractical to run fiber to every desktop. Not only is the cable itself more expensive than copper cabling, but fiber-optic transmitters and connectivity equipment can cost as much as five times more than those designed for UTP networks. In addition, hiring skilled fiber cable installers costs more than hiring twisted-pair cable installers.

- *noise immunity*—Because fiber does not conduct electrical current to transmit signals, it is unaffected by EMI. Its impressive noise resistance is one reason why fiber can span such long distances.

- *size and scalability*—Depending on the type of fiber-optic cable used, segment lengths vary from 150 to 40,000 meters. This limit is due primarily to optical loss, or the degradation of the light signal after it travels a certain distance away from its source (just as the light of a flashlight dims after a certain number of feet). Optical loss accrues over long distances and grows with every connection point in the fiber network. Dust or oil in a connection (for example, from people handling the fiber while splicing it) can further exacerbate optical loss. Some types of fiber-optic cable can carry signals 40 miles, while others are suited for distances under a mile. The distance a cable can carry light depends partly on the light's wavelength. It also depends on whether the cable is single mode or multimode.

SMF (Single Mode Fiber)

SMF (single mode fiber) consists of a narrow core of 8 to 10 microns in diameter. Laser-generated light travels a single path over the core, reflecting very little. Because it reflects little, the light does not disperse as the signal travels along the fiber. This continuity allows single mode fiber to accommodate the highest bandwidths and longest distances (without requiring repeaters) of all network transmission media. Figure 5-32 depicts a simplified version of how signals travel over single mode fiber.

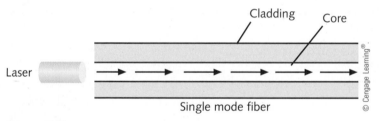

Figure 5-32   Transmission over single mode fiber-optic cable

Looking back at Figure 5-30, the clear strands you see protruding from each line are not the actual cores—these are the visible cladding around each core. The core itself, especially in SMF, is microscopic in width.

The Internet backbone depends on single mode fiber. However, because of its relatively high cost, single mode fiber is rarely used for shorter connections, such as those between a server and switch.

MMF (Multimode Fiber)

MMF (multimode fiber) contains a core with a larger diameter than single mode fiber, usually 50 or 62.5 microns, over which many pulses of light generated by a laser or LED travel at different angles. Signals traveling over multimode fiber experience greater attenuation than those traversing single mode fiber. Therefore, multimode fiber is not suited to distances longer than a few miles. On the other hand, multimode fiber is less expensive to install. It is often found on cables that connect a router to a switch or a server on the backbone of a network. In cases where fiber connects desktop workstations to the network, multimode fiber is preferred because of its lower cost. Figure 5-33 depicts a simplified view of how signals travel over multimode fiber.

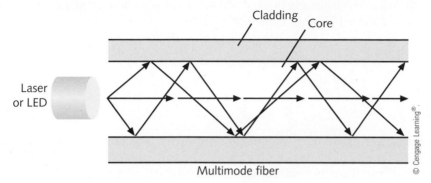

Figure 5-33   Transmission over multimode fiber-optic cable

 ## Fiber Connectors and Couplers

Just as fiber cables are classified by SMF or MMF, fiber-cable connectors are also grouped along these lines. Recall that media converters, for example, are used to connect Ethernet segments of different types. You must, however, select the correct media converter for the type of fiber being connected, whether it's SMF to copper or MMF to copper.

MMF connectors can be classified by the number of fibers, and SMF connectors are classified by the size and shape of the ferrule. The **ferrule** is the extended tip of a connector that makes contact with the receptacle in the jack or other connector, as you can see in Figure 5-34.

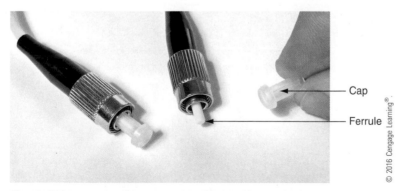

Figure 5-34   A cap protects the ferrule when the connector is not in use

SMF connectors are designed to reduce **back reflection**, which is the return of the light signal back into the fiber that is transmitting the signal. Back reflection is measured as optical loss in dB (decibels). Shapes and polishes used by SMF ferrules to reduce back reflection include:

- *Physical Contact (PC)*—This early generation of ferrule is curved, which allows the two fibers to meet, creating a **Physical Contact (PC)** connection.

- *Ultra Polished Connector (UPC)*—Extensive polishing of the tips creates an **Ultra Polished Connector (UPC)**, which increases efficiency through the connection.

- *Angle Polished Connector (APC)*—The latest advancement in ferrule technology uses the principles of reflection to its advantage. The **Angle Polished Connector (APC)** still uses a polished curved surface, but the end faces are placed at an angle to each other. The industry standard for this angle is 8°.

UPC adapters and connectors are typically blue and APC adapters and connectors are typically green.

You can see the three types of ferrule shapes in Figure 5-35. The red arrows indicate the back reflection for each connection. Notice how the APC connection reflects any signal loss in a different direction than the source of the signal. Back reflection worsens in the first two connections over time, but the APC connection is not as sensitive to degradation from repeatedly disconnecting and reconnecting the cables.

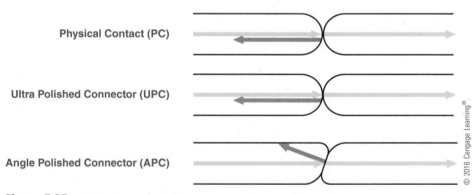

Figure 5-35   Three types of mechanical connections in fiber-optic connectors

Table 5-5 summarizes the fiber connectors you'll need to know for the CompTIA Network+ exam. SMF connectors are typically available with a 1.25-mm ferrule or a 2.5-mm ferrule, though other sizes can be found. The most common 1.25-mm ferrule connector is the **LC** (local connector). Three 2.5-mm ferrules are the **SC** (subscriber connector or standard connector), **ST** (straight tip), and **FC** (ferrule connector or fiber channel), although the FC connector is much less common than the others. The most common type of MMF connector is the **MT-RJ** (Mechanical Transfer-Registered Jack).

Existing fiber networks might use ST or SC connectors. However, LC and MT-RJ connectors are used on the very latest fiber-optic technology. LC and MT-RJ connectors are preferable to ST and SC connectors because of their smaller size, which allows for a higher density of connections at each termination point. The MT-RJ connector is unique because it contains two strands of fiber in a single ferrule. With two strands in each ferrule, a single MT-RJ

Table 5-5 **Characteristics of Fiber Connectors**

Photo	Connector	Polish	Ferrule characteristics	Full-duplex?
	LC	PC, UPC, APC	1.25 mm	Yes
	ST	PC, UPC	2.5 mm	No
	FC	PC, UPC, APC	2.5 mm	Yes
	SC	PC, UPC, APC	2.5 mm	Can be
	MT-RJ	N/A	2 fibers	Yes

Figures A, B, D and E courtesy of SENKO Advanced Components Inc.

connector provides for full-duplex signaling. SC and LC connectors are also available in full-duplex mode.

Just as with copper cables, fiber couplers can be used to connect like terminations, such as when you need to join two shorter cables to make a longer one. Fiber couplers can also combine signals from multiple lines into a single line. There are some restrictions on the capability of these couplers, however. A coupler can join signals of different wavelengths without significant signal loss, but not of identical wavelengths. Wavelengths that are too similar to each other will interfere with one another.

Applying Concepts

Terminating Fiber-Optic Cable

Fiber cables can be identified by the types of connectors on each end, such as FC-FC or FC-SC. It's helpful to be able to replace a fiber connector with a different connector, and the Comp-TIA Network+ exam expects you to be familiar with this process.

NETWORK+ EXAM TIP

If you don't have the equipment to practice terminating fiber-optic cable, prepare for the CompTIA Network+ exam by watching a few videos on the Web demonstrating this process.

In this project, you install an ST or LC connector. Make sure you have the following tools:

- Fiber cleaver (Figure 5-36 shows a simple cleaver from a kit on the left, and a high-precision cleaver on the right)

© 2016 Cengage Learning®.

Courtesy of OptiLink, a unit of Dalton Utilities

Figure 5-36   Two types of fiber cleaver

- Fiber stripper (such as the one shown in Figure 5-37)
- Miscellaneous: scissors (sometimes called **snips**) and alcohol wipes

You'll also, of course, need a fiber-optic cable (MMF is easiest to work with) and an unused, field-installable ST or LC connector, which might come with a **boot** (a plastic cover to protect the fiber strands where they enter the connector).

1. Use the scissors to score the covering on the fiber cable, then pull off that part of the covering to expose the fiber strands inside. Bend the Kevlar strands out of the way, and spread the fiber strands apart so one strand is easy to get to. Thread the strand into the boot before doing anything else to the fiber strand. You might damage the fiber strand's tip if you try to put the boot on it later in the process.

Figure 5-37 Fiber stripper

2. Determine the correct opening on the fiber stripper—you need a slot that will cut into the outer layers without cutting all the way through the cable. Then score and remove the jacket, buffer, and cladding on a single fiber strand. Be sure to remove small pieces at a time to minimize the chance of damage to the fiber inside. Wipe the exposed strand clean with an alcohol wipe.

3. On the fiber cleaver, slide the stripped fiber to the measurement recommended by the connector's manufacturer. The edge of the insulation on the fiber strand should line up to the proper measurement on the cleaver. Press the cleaver down gently and firmly. Be sure to collect the shard immediately if your cleaver does not include a collection bin. (The specific instructions for your fiber cleaver may vary. Please consult the user's manual or check with your instructor.)

NOTE To properly dispose of the leftover fiber strands, take a piece of tape, stick the strands to the tape, and fold the tape over so the fiber is completely enclosed. You can then dispose of the tape with the fiber strands inside.

4. Gently slide the fiber strand into the lead-in tube on the connector. The lead-in tube is a tubelike opening that guides the strand to the right location within the connector. Be sure to push it all the way in, but don't force it. You can press into it at an angle so the fiber strand bends a little, which puts about the right amount of pressure on it to seat the fiber at the proper depth.

5. Slide the boot up and over the end of the connector to stabilize and secure the fiber strand to the connector.

Network+
1.5
4.4
4.5
Fiber-Optic Converters and Modular Interfaces

As long as networks contain both copper and fiber media, some kind of conversion must take place. Converters are needed to connect the fiber- and copper-based parts of a network and are also needed to connect networks using multimode fiber with networks using single mode fiber. A bidirectional converter accepts the signal from one part of the network, then retransmits or regenerates the signal and sends it on to the next part of the network. This process of retransmitting a signal is known as regeneration. Figure 5-38 shows a converter that connects single mode and multimode portions of a network. Refer to Figure 5-25 to see a converter that connects multimode fiber with an Ethernet network using UTP. Figure 5-39 shows a fiber to coax converter.

Courtesy of Omnitron Systems Technology

Figure 5-38   Single mode to multimode converter

Courtesy of Omnitron Systems Technology

Figure 5-39   Fiber to coax converter

As you learned in Chapter 1, it makes sense to purchase workstations or servers with onboard NICs already installed because most of these have limited network-media compatibility needs; however, it might be more practical to customize network interfaces on a large network's connectivity devices. For example, suppose you were creating a network for a new, fast-growing business. At first, the business might need only two fiber-optic connections for its backbone and 24 RJ-45 Gigabit Ethernet connections for its clients and servers. In the future, however, the business might plan to bring fiber-optic connectivity to every desktop.

Rather than ordering a switch that contains exactly this number and type of onboard interfaces, you could order a switch that allows you to change and upgrade its interfaces at any time. The switch would contain sockets that allow one of many types of modular interfaces to be plugged in. Such interfaces are easily inserted into the sockets to connect with its motherboard, also called a backplane. A hardware component that can be changed in this manner, without disrupting operations, is known as hot-swappable. Using hot-swappable interfaces means you don't have to purchase a new switch, open the chassis of the existing switch (causing network downtime and risking hardware damage), or even turn off the switch to upgrade the network. Modular interfaces can also be found on some expansion board NICs and media converters.

GBIC (Gigabit interface converter), pronounced *jee-bick*, is a standard type of modular interface designed in the 1990s for Gigabit Ethernet connections. GBICs may contain RJ-45 or fiber-optic cable ports (such as LC, SC, or ST). Figure 5-40 shows a GBIC that can be used on a 1000Base-T network.

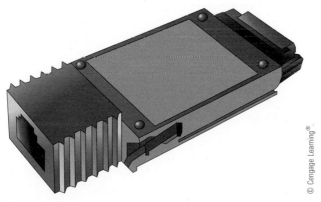

© Cengage Learning®

Figure 5-40   GBIC (Gigabit interface converter) with an RJ-45 port

A newer modular interface has made the GBIC largely obsolete. SFP (small form-factor pluggable) transceivers provide the same function as a GBIC, but allow more ports per inch—in other words, they are more compact. For this reason, they are also sometimes known as mini GBICs or SFP GBICs. Two types of transceivers can send and receive data at rates of up to 10 Gbps: XFP, which came first, and SFP+, which was developed later and is the same module size as SFP. Figure 5-41 shows an SFP with ports for fiber-optic cable connectors, one for transmitting and another for receiving data.

Installing a GBIC or SFP is simply a matter of sliding the transceiver into a socket on the back of the connectivity device. Most SFPs come with a tab or latch system that you can use

Figure 5-41 SFP (small form-factor pluggable) transceiver for use with fiber connections

to lock them into place. They are also keyed so that they will slide into the socket only when they are aligned properly. The switch or router need not be powered down when you add or remove transceivers. However, do not attach cables before inserting a transceiver, and always remove the cables before removing a transceiver. As an example, Figure 5-42 illustrates how a fiber-optic SFP is installed in a switch.

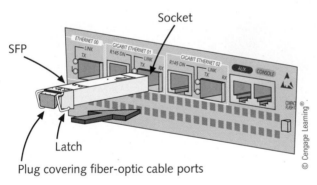

Figure 5-42 Installing an SFP in a switch

Some SFPs contain management interfaces separate from the switch's configuration utility. For example, the 10-Gbps SFP+ on a router could have its own IP address. A network administrator could use the Telnet utility to connect to the SFP and configure its ports to use a particular speed or routing protocol without accessing the router's operating system.

A helpful tool when testing an SFP's functionality or checking for a mismatch is a loopback adapter. Recall from Chapter 4 that a loopback adapter can create a closed loop to trick a device into thinking it's connected to a network. A loopback adapter can do much the same thing with an SFP, and a fiber-optic loopback adapter is specifically needed for use on a fiber network. Figure 5-43 shows a fiber-optic loopback adapter with two LC fiber-cable connectors.

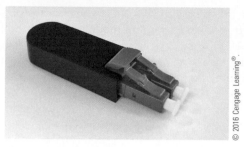

Figure 5-43   Fiber-optic loopback adapter

Ethernet Standards for Fiber-Optic Cable

Long before IEEE developed a 10GBase-T standard for twisted-pair cable, it had established standards for achieving high data rates over fiber-optic cable. In fact, fiber optic is the best medium for delivering high throughput. Table 5-6 lists the various Ethernet standards established by IEEE for fiber-optic cabling. Notice in the table that Fast Ethernet has one standard for fiber optic, Gigabit Ethernet has two standards, and 10-Gigabit Ethernet has six standards that use fiber-optic cables.

Table 5-6   Ethernet standards using fiber-optic cable

Standard	Maximum transmission speed (Mbps)	Maximum distance per segment (m)	Physical media
100Base-FX Fast Ethernet	100	412 for half-duplex 2000 for full-duplex	MMF
1000Base-LX Gigabit Ethernet	1000	550 for MMG 5000 for SMF	MMF or SMF
1000Base-SX Gigabit Ethernet	1000	Up to 550, depending on modal bandwidth and fiber core diameter	MMF
10GBase-SR and 10GBase-SW 10-Gigabit Ethernet	10,000	Up to 300, depending on modal bandwidth and fiber core diameter	MMF
10GBase-LR and 10GBase-LW 10-Gigabit Ethernet	10,000	10,000	SMF
10GBase-ER and 10GBase-EW 10-Gigabit Ethernet	10,000	40,000	SMF

Here are some important details about the Fast Ethernet and Gigabit Ethernet standards:

- **100Base-FX** is the fiber version of Fast Ethernet, uses baseband transmission, is largely outdated, and requires at least two strands of multimode fiber.
- **1000Base-LX** is the more common fiber version of Gigabit Ethernet and uses long wavelengths (hence the *L* in its name *LX*) of 1300 nanometers. (A nanometer equals 0.000000001 meters, or about the width of six carbon atoms in a row.) It can use single mode or multimode fiber. Because of long segments, it's used for long backbones connecting buildings in a MAN or for connecting an ISP with its telecommunications carrier.

- **1000Base-SX** is also a form of Gigabit Ethernet, and uses short wavelengths of 850 nanometers (hence the *S* in its name *SX*). It relies only on multimode fiber-optic cable. This makes it less expensive to install than 1000Base-LX. The maximum segment length for 1000Base-SX depends on two things: the diameter of the fiber and the modal bandwidth used to transmit signals. **Modal bandwidth** is a measure of the highest frequency of signal a multimode fiber can support over a specific distance and is measured in MHz-km. It is related to the distortion that occurs when multiple pulses of light, although issued at the same time, arrive at the end of a fiber at slightly different times. The higher the modal bandwidth, the longer a multimode fiber can carry a signal reliably.

When used with fibers whose diameters are 50 microns each, and with the highest possible modal bandwidth, the maximum segment length on a 1000Base-SX network is 550 meters. When used with fibers whose diameters are 62.5 microns each, and with the highest possible modal bandwidth, the maximum segment length is 275 meters. Only one repeater may be used between segments. Therefore, 1000Base-SX is best suited for shorter network runs than 1000Base-LX—for example, connecting a data center with a data closet in an office building.

In 2002, IEEE published its **802.3ae** standard for fiber-optic Ethernet networks transmitting data at 10 Gbps. **NSPs (network service providers)** that sell direct access to the Internet backbone and ISPs both use 10-Gigabit Ethernet where traffic is aggregated and customers demand faster data transfer. The 10-Gigabit Ethernet fiber-optic standards differ significantly in the wavelength of light each uses to issue signals and, as a result, their maximum allowable segment length differs also. Here's the list of six 10-Gigabit Ethernet fiber-optic standards:

- **10GBase-SR** and **10GBase-SW** have the shortest segment lengths. 10GBase-SR is designed to work with LANs, and 10GBase-SW is designed to work with WAN links that use a highly reliable fiber-optic ring topology called SONET. (The *W* in 10GBase-SW stands for WAN.) You'll learn more about SONET in Chapter 11.

   10GBase-SR and 10GBase-SW rely on multimode fiber and transmit signals with wavelengths of 850 nanometers. As with the 1-Gigabit Ethernet standards, the maximum segment length on a 10GBase-SR or 10GBase-SW network depends on the diameter of the fibers used. It also depends on the modal bandwidth used. For example, if 50-micron fiber is used with the maximum possible modal bandwidth, the maximum segment length is 300 meters. If 62.5-micron fiber is used with the maximum possible modal bandwidth, a 10GBase-SR or 10GBase-SW segment can be 66 meters long. Either way, this 10-Gigabit Ethernet technology is best suited for connections within a data center or building, as its distance is the most limited.

- **10GBase-LR** and **10GBase-LW** carry signals with wavelengths of 1310 nanometers through single mode fiber. Their maximum segment length is 10,000 meters.

   10GBase-LW (the *W* stands for WAN) uses an encoding method that allows it to work over SONET WAN links. 10GBase-LR and 10GBase-LW technology is suited to WAN or MAN implementations.

- **10GBase-ER** and **10GBase-EW** have the longest segment lengths (40,000 meters or nearly 25 miles), rely on single mode fiber, through which they transmit signals with wavelengths of 1550 nanometers, and are best suited for use on WANs. 10GBase-EW is compatible with SONET.

Even faster Ethernet networks are on the way. IEEE has recently ratified standards for 40- and 100-Gigabit Ethernet.

Troubleshooting Cable Problems

Symptoms of cabling problems can be as elusive as occasional lost packets or as obvious as a break in network connectivity. In this section, you learn about common cabling problems, then you learn how different tools can help isolate problems with network cables.

Transmission Flaws

Both analog and digital signals are susceptible to degradation between the time they are issued by a transmitter and the time they are received. One of the most common transmission flaws affecting data signals is noise.

Noise Noise can degrade or distort a signal. A common source of noise is EMI. Motors, power lines, televisions, copiers, fluorescent lights, microwave ovens, manufacturing machinery, and other sources of electrical activity (including a severe thunderstorm) can cause EMI. One type of EMI is RFI (radio frequency interference), or electromagnetic interference caused by radio waves. (Often, you'll see EMI referred to as EMI/RFI.) Strong broadcast signals from radio or TV antennas can generate RFI. When EMI noise affects analog signals, this distortion can result in the incorrect transmission of data, just as if static prevented you from hearing a radio station broadcast. However, this type of noise affects digital signals much less. Because digital signals do not depend on subtle amplitude or frequency differences to communicate information, they are more apt to be readable despite distortions caused by EMI noise.

Another form of noise that hinders data transmission is cross-talk. Cross-talk occurs when a signal traveling on one wire or cable infringes on the signal traveling over an adjacent wire or cable, as shown in Figure 5-44. The resulting noise, or cross-talk, is equal to a portion of the second line's signal. If you've ever been on the phone and heard the conversation on your second line in the background, you have heard the effects of cross-talk.

Cross-talk can happen, for instance, when wires from different twisted pairs in twisted-pair cable are improperly yoked together, creating a split pair, rather than wiring twisted pairs

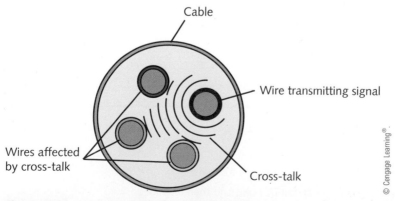

Figure 5-44 Cross-talk between wires in a cable

together according to the appropriate pinout. Standard pinouts are designed with the avoidance of cross-talk in mind.

In data networks, cross-talk can be extreme enough to prevent the accurate delivery of data. Three common types are:

- *alien cross-talk*—Cross-talk that occurs between two cables
- *near end cross-talk (NEXT)*—Cross-talk that occurs between wire pairs near the source of a signal
- *far end cross-talk (FEXT)*—Cross-talk measured at the far end of the cable from the signal source

One potential cause of NEXT is an improper termination—for example, one in which wire insulation has been damaged, where wire pairs have been untwisted too far, or where straight-through or crossover standards have been mismatched. This last problem can happen when the transmission (Tx) and receive (Rx) wires are crossed, which on the CompTIA Network+ exam, is called a Tx/Rx reverse.

In every signal, a certain amount of noise is unavoidable. However, engineers have devised a number of ways to limit the potential for noise to degrade a signal. One way is simply to ensure that the strength of the signal exceeds the strength of the noise. Proper cable design and installation are also critical for protecting against noise effects. Note that all forms of noise are measured in decibels (dB).

Attenuation Another transmission flaw is attenuation, or the loss of a signal's strength as it travels away from its source. Just as your voice becomes fainter as it travels farther, so do signals fade with distance. To compensate for attenuation, both analog and digital signals are boosted en route. Here are the two ways analog and digital signals are boosted:

- *amplifier*—Analog signals pass through an amplifier, an electronic device that increases the voltage, or strength, of the signals. Unfortunately, the boost can also boost the noise that has accumulated in the signal, which causes the analog signal to worsen progressively. After multiple amplifications, an analog signal may become difficult to decipher. Figure 5-45 shows an analog signal distorted by noise and then amplified once.

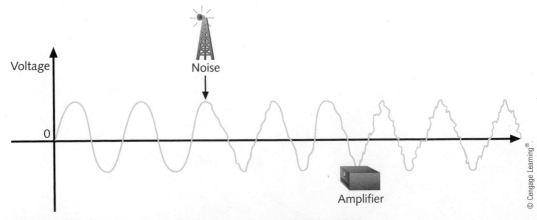

Figure 5-45 An analog signal distorted by noise and then amplified

- *repeater*—Recall that a repeater is a device that regenerates a digital signal in its original form, without the noise it might have previously accumulated. Figure 5-46 shows a digital signal distorted by noise and then regenerated by a repeater. A switch on an Ethernet network works as a multiport repeater as the bits transmitted "start over" at each port on the switch.

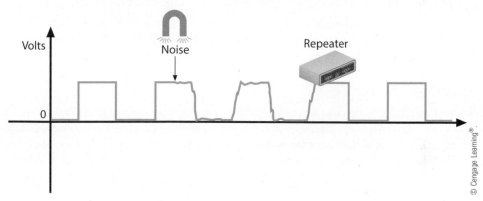

Figure 5-46   A digital signal distorted by noise and then repeated

Latency   Although electrons travel rapidly, they still have to travel, and a brief delay takes place between the instant data leaves the source and when it arrives at its destination. Recall from Chapter 3 that this delay is called latency.

The length of the cable involved affects latency, as does the existence of any intervening connectivity device, such as a router. Different devices affect latency to different degrees. For example, modems, which must modulate both incoming and outgoing signals, increase a connection's latency far more than switches, which simply repeat a signal. The most common way to measure latency on data networks is by calculating a packet's **RTT (round trip time)**, or the length of time it takes for a packet to go from sender to receiver, then back from receiver to sender. RTT is usually measured in milliseconds.

Latency causes problems only when a receiving node is expecting some type of communication, such as the rest of a data stream it has begun to accept. If that node does not receive the rest of the data stream within a given time period, it assumes that no more data is coming. This assumption may cause transmission errors on a network. When you connect multiple network segments and thereby increase the distance between sender and receiver, you increase the network's latency. To constrain latency and avoid its associated errors, each type of cabling is rated for a maximum number of connected network segments, and each transmission method is assigned a maximum segment length.

Common Fiber Cable Problems   Working with fiber cable presents a set of troubleshooting challenges that don't arise when you are working with copper cables. Problems that are unique to fiber cable include:

- *fiber type mismatch*—This term is misleading because a fiber type mismatch is actually more of a fiber core mismatch. Connecting an SMF cable to an MMF cable will prevent the transmission from traversing the connection successfully, though some of the signal can get through. However, even same-mode cables can be mismatched, if the cores have different widths. A cable with a 50-micron core, for example, should not be connected to a cable with a 62.5-micron core, even though they're both MMF.

- *wavelength mismatch*—SMF, MMF, and POF (Plastic Optical Fiber) each use different wavelengths for transmissions. A wavelength mismatch occurs when transmissions are optimized for one type of cable but sent over a different type of cable.

- *dirty connectors*—If fiber connectors get dirty or just a little dusty, signal loss and other errors can start to cause problems. Always keep protectors on fiber connectors and dust covers over fiber jacks.

Troubleshooting Tools

Network+
1.5
4.2
4.4
4.5

You need to know which tools are designed to analyze and isolate problems related to a particular type of network media. Several tools are available, ranging from simple continuity testers that indicate whether a cable is faulty, to sophisticated cable performance testers that graphically depict a cable's attenuation and cross-talk characteristics over the length of the cable. Knowing the specific tool to use for a particular troubleshooting situation can help you quickly zero in on the problem and solution.

The following sections describe a variety of network troubleshooting tools, their functions, and their relative costs.

Tone Generator and Tone Locator Ideally, you and your networking colleagues would label each port and wire termination in a data closet so that problems and changes can be easily managed. However, because of personnel changes and time constraints, a data closet might be disorganized and poorly documented. If this is the case where you work, you might need a tone generator and a tone locator to determine where one pair of wires, possibly out of hundreds, terminates.

A **tone generator** (or **toner**) is a small, electronic device that issues a signal on a wire pair. A **tone locator** (or **probe**) is a device that emits a tone when it detects electrical activity on a wire pair. They are sold together as a set, often called a **toner and probe kit** or just **toner probe** (see Figure 5-47).

By placing the tone generator at one end of a wire and attaching a tone locator to the other end, you can verify the location of the wire's termination. Figure 5-48 depicts the use of a tone generator and a tone locator. Of course, you must work by trial and error, guessing which termination corresponds to the wire over which you've generated a signal until the tone locator indicates the correct choice.

Tone generators and tone locators cannot be used to determine any characteristics about a cable, such as whether it's defective or whether its length exceeds IEEE standards for a certain type of network. They are only used to determine where a wire pair terminates.

A tone generator should never be used on a wire that's connected to a device's port or network adapter. Because a tone generator transmits electricity over the wire, it could damage the device or network adapter.

Connectors to
connect to cable
or wire

Toner

Probe

© Cengage Learning®

Figure 5-47   A toner and probe kit by Fluke Corporation

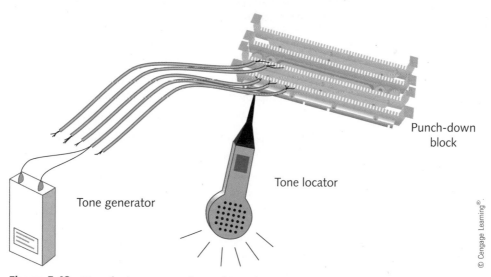

Punch-down
block

Tone locator

Tone generator

© Cengage Learning®

Figure 5-48   Use of a tone generator and tone locator

Multimeter   A **multimeter** is a simple instrument that can measure many characteristics of an electric circuit, including its resistance, voltage, and impedance (see Figure 5-49). Although you could use separate instruments for measuring impedance, resistance (opposition to electrical current), and voltage on a wire, it is more convenient to have one instrument that accomplishes all of these functions.

Courtesy of Fluke Networks

Figure 5-49 A multimeter

Impedance is the telltale factor for ascertaining where faults in a cable lie. A certain amount of impedance is required for a signal to be properly transmitted and interpreted. However, very high or low levels of impedance can signify a damaged wire, incorrect pairing, or a termination point. In other words, changes in impedance can indicate where current is stopped or inhibited.

As a network professional, you might use a multimeter to do the following:

- Measure voltage to verify that a cable is properly conducting electricity—that is, whether its signal can travel unimpeded from one node on the network to another.

- Check for the presence of noise on a wire (by detecting extraneous voltage).

- Verify that the amount of resistance presented by terminators on coaxial cable networks is appropriate, or whether terminators are actually present and functional.

- Test for short or open circuits in the wire (by detecting unexpected resistance or loss of voltage). A short circuit is an unwanted connection, such as when exposed wires touch each other. An open circuit is one where needed connections are missing, such as when a wire breaks.

Cable Continuity Testers In troubleshooting a Physical layer problem, you may find the cause of a problem by simply testing whether your cable is carrying a signal to its destination. Tools used to test the continuity of the cable may be called cable checkers, continuity testers, or cable testers. The term cable tester, however, is a general term that also includes more sophisticated tools that can measure cable performance, as discussed in the following section.

A continuity tester (see Figure 5-50) is battery operated and has two parts. The base unit connects to one end of the cable and generates voltage, and the remote unit connects to the other end of the cable and detects the voltage. Most cable checkers provide a series of lights that signal pass/fail. An open circuit, where the transmission does not get through, will give

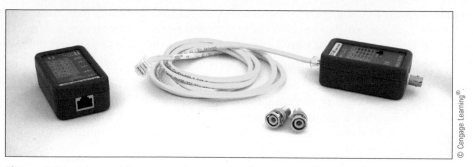

© Cengage Learning®

Figure 5-50 Use a cable tester pair to determine the type of cable and/or if the cable is good

a fail result. Some also indicate a cable pass/fail with an audible tone. A pass/fail test provides a simple indicator of whether a component can perform its stated function.

In addition to checking cable continuity, some continuity testers will verify that the wires in a UTP or STP cable are paired correctly following TIA/EIA 568 standards and that they are not shorted, exposed, or crossed. Make sure that the cable checker you purchase can test the type of network you use—for example, 100Base-TX or 1000Base-T Ethernet.

Continuity testers for fiber-optic cables issue light pulses on the fiber and determine whether they reached the other end of the fiber. Some continuity testers offer the ability to test both copper and fiber-optic cable.

Whether you make your own cables or purchase cabling from a reputable vendor, test the cable to ensure that it meets your network's required standards. Just because a cable is labeled "Cat 6a," for example, does not necessarily mean that it will live up to that standard. Testing cabling before installing it could save many hours of troubleshooting after the network is in place.

Do not use a continuity tester on a live network cable. Disconnect the cable from the network, and then test its continuity.

For convenience, most continuity testers are portable and lightweight, and typically use one 9-volt battery. A continuity tester can cost between $30 and $300 and can save many hours of work. Popular manufacturers of these cable testing devices include Belkin, Fluke, and Paladin.

Line Testers and Cable Certifiers Suppose you hire a cabling company to install all the network cabling in a new building and require that the company certify the entire cabling structure for VoIP and Gigabit Ethernet. To certify the cabling structure as specified by TIA's strict certification standards, the cabling company must measure and warrant the performance of the entire cabling system, including the cabling itself, as well as couplers, patch panels, and other connecting devices. In addition, the company must check for alien cross-talk and provide a wire map of the entire structure. Certification typically happens in two phases as the installation is nearing completion: First, every cable segment in the structure is measured independently of other segments, meaning that measurements are taken from each end of that specific cable segment. Second, the longest cable segment and shortest cable segment are measured as test samples, as they are considered the most probable points of failure for certain issues.

Whereas continuity testers can determine whether a single cable is carrying current, more sophisticated equipment is needed to measure the overall performance of a cabling structure. A device used for this sophisticated testing is called a cable performance tester, line tester, certifier, or network tester. It allows you to perform the same continuity and fault tests as a continuity tester, but can also be used to:

- Measure the distance to a connectivity device, termination point, or cable fault
- Measure attenuation along a cable
- Measure near end cross-talk between wires as well as alien cross-talk
- Measure termination resistance and impedance
- Issue pass/fail ratings for Cat 3, Cat 5, Cat 5e, Cat 6, Cat 6a, or Cat 7 standards
- Store and print cable testing results or directly save data to a computer database
- Graphically depict a cable's attenuation and cross-talk characteristics over the length of the cable

A sophisticated performance tester will include a TDR (time domain reflectometer). A TDR issues a signal on a cable and then measures the way the signal bounces back (or reflects) to the TDR. Bad connectors, crimps, bends, short circuits, cable mismatches, bad wiring, or other defects modify the signal's amplitude before it returns to the TDR, thus changing the way it reflects. The TDR then accepts and analyzes the return signal, and based on its condition and the amount of time the signal took to return, determines cable imperfections. In the case of a coaxial cable network, a TDR can indicate whether terminators are properly installed and functional. A TDR can also indicate the distance between nodes and segments.

In addition to performance testers for coaxial and twisted-pair connections, you can also find performance testers for fiber-optic connections. Such performance testers use OTDRs (optical time domain reflectometers). Rather than issue an electrical signal over the cable as twisted-pair cable testers do, an OTDR transmits light-based signals of different wavelengths over the fiber. Based on the type of return light signal, the OTDR can accurately measure the length of the fiber; determine the location of faulty splices, breaks, bad or mismatched connectors, or bends; and measure attenuation over the cable.

Because of their sophistication, performance testers for both copper and fiber-optic cables cost significantly more than continuity testers. A high-end unit could cost up to $30,000, and a low-end unit could sell for just under $4000. On the left side of Figure 5-51, you can see an example of a high-end cable performance tester that is capable of measuring the characteristics of both copper and fiber-optic cables.

OPM (Optical Power Meter) An optical power meter (OPM), also called a laser power meter or a light meter, measures the amount of light power transmitted on a fiber-optic line. The device must be calibrated precisely following highly accurate optical power standards set by the NIST (National Institute of Standards and Technology), which is a nonregulatory agency of the U.S. Department of Commerce. Field-use conditions further degrade the accuracy. The surrounding room temperature, the connection type, and the skill of the technician conducting the test all affect the final test results.

A simple light meter is pictured on the right side of Figure 5-51. Much fancier and more accurate meters are available at much higher price points.

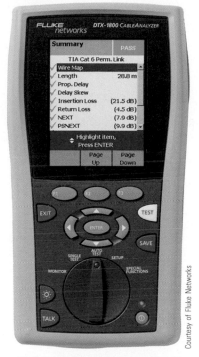

Figure 5-51 On the left, the DTX-1800 device by Fluke Networks is a high-end cable performance tester designed to certify structured cabling. The optical power meter on the right is a more budget-friendly device that measures light power transmitted on a fiber-optic line.

Chapter Summary

Transmission Basics

- Computers generate and interpret digital signals as electrical current where voltage is finitely measured as on or off and interpreted as binary data. In analog data signals, voltage varies infinitely and continuously, and can be characterized by amplitude, frequency, wavelength, and phase.

- A channel is a distinct communication path between nodes and may be separated either logically or physically. Multiple channels on a line enable full-duplex transmission, which is simultaneous, two-way communication.

- A baseband transmission is the only transmission on the media, whereas in broadband, multiple transmissions share a single media.

- Broadband transmissions, which allow multiple signals to travel simultaneously over one medium, require a technique known as multiplexing. The medium's channel is logically separated into multiple smaller channels, called subchannels, with each subchannel carrying a separate signal.

- Different types of multiplexing manipulate the signals in different ways. The various types include TDM (time division multiplexing), statistical multiplexing, FDM (frequency division multiplexing), WDM (wavelength division multiplexing), DWDM (dense wavelength division multiplexing), and CWDM (coarse wavelength division multiplexing).

- Throughput is the measure of how much data is transmitted during a given time period, not regarding overhead. It is typically measured as bit rate, although analog transmissions are sometimes measured as baud rate.

Coaxial Cable

- Coaxial cable was the foundation for Ethernet networks in the 1980s and remained a popular transmission medium for many years. It's still used today for cable Internet and cable TV.

- The two coaxial cable types still in use today, RG-6 and RG-59, can terminate with one of two connector types: F-connectors or BNC connectors.

Twisted-Pair Cable

- Twisted-pair cable consists of color-coded pairs of insulated copper wires. Every two wires are twisted around each other to form pairs, and all the pairs are encased in a plastic sheath.

- STP cable consists of twisted-pair wires that are not only individually insulated, but also surrounded by a shielding made of a metallic substance such as foil. The shielding acts as a barrier to external electromagnetic forces, thus preventing them from affecting the signals traveling over the wire inside the shielding.

- UTP does not contain additional shielding for the twisted pairs. As a result, UTP is both less expensive and less resistant to noise than STP.

- So long as the proper category of twisted-pair cabling is used, a network can support a variety of Ethernet standards, which makes it possible to progressively upgrade a network, one device or NIC at a time.

- TIA/EIA has specified two different methods of inserting twisted-pair wires into RJ-45 plugs: TIA/EIA 568A and TIA/EIA 568B. Functionally, there is no difference between the standards. You only have to be certain that you use the same standard on every RJ-45 plug and jack on your network, so that data is transmitted and received correctly.

- A rollover cable uses a reverse image of the pinout on the other end of a cable, and can be used to connect a computer to the console port of a router in order to communicate with the router itself (rather than transport data *through* the router).

- A media converter enables networks or segments running in different media to interconnect and exchange signals. A simpler kind of connector, a coupler, passes data through a homogenous connection without any modification.

- PoE provides electrical power over twisted-pair Ethernet connections to devices, such as a wireless access point mounted in a public place, that don't have their own power source. PoE+ carries more wattage than PoE.

Fiber-Optic Cable

- Fiber-optic cable contains one or several glass or plastic fibers at its core. Surrounding the fibers is a layer of glass or plastic called cladding, which reflects light back to the core in patterns that vary depending on the transmission node. Outside the cladding, a plastic buffer protects the cladding and core. Strands of Kevlar surround the plastic buffer, and, finally, a plastic sheath covers the strands of Kevlar.

- SMF accommodates the highest bandwidths and longest distances of all network transmission media because the laser-generated light travels a single path over the narrow core, reflecting very little.

- MMF contains a core with a larger diameter, over which many pulses of light can travel at different angles.

- Fiber cable connectors are classified by the size and shape of the ferrule and, for MMF, the number of fibers incorporated into the cable.

- Converters can connect the fiber- and copper-based portions of a network, and are also needed in order to connect networks using MMF with networks using SMF.

- Fiber-optic cabling is the best medium for delivering high throughput. Eight different fiber-optic standards developed by IEEE support Gigabit Ethernet or better.

Troubleshooting Cable Problems

- A common source of noise, which can degrade or distort a signal, is EMI, which are waves that emanate from electrical devices or cables carrying electricity. One type of EMI is RFI, or electromagnetic interference caused by radio waves.

- Cross-talk occurs when a signal traveling on one wire or cable infringes on the signal traveling over an adjacent wire or cable. Cross-talk can happen when wires from different twisted pairs in twisted-pair cable are improperly yoked together, creating a split pair, rather than wiring twisted pairs together according to the appropriate pinout.

- Attenuation is the loss of a signal's strength as it travels away from its source. To compensate for attenuation, both analog and digital signals can be boosted en route.

- Latency is the delay between the instant data leaves the source and when it arrives at its destination. The length of the cable involved affects latency, as does the existence of any intervening connectivity device, such as a router.

- A tone generator is a small, electronic device that issues a signal on a wire pair. A tone locator is a device that emits a tone when it detects electrical activity on a wire pair. They are sold together as a set, often called a toner and probe kit.

- A multimeter is a simple instrument that can measure many characteristics of an electric circuit, including its resistance, voltage, and impedance.

- Tools used to test the continuity of a cable may be called cable checkers, continuity testers, or cable testers. In addition to checking cable continuity, some continuity testers will verify that the wires in a UTP or STP cable are paired correctly following TIA/EIA 568 standards, and that they are not shorted, exposed, or crossed.

- The difference between continuity testers and performance testers lies in their sophistication and price. A performance tester, also called a certifier or line tester, allows you to perform the same continuity and fault tests as a continuity tester, and is also used for many additional tasks required to certify a cabling structure.

- A light meter measures the amount of light power transmitted on a fiber-optic line. This device must be calibrated precisely.

Key Terms

For definitions of key terms, see the Glossary near the end of the book.

1000Base-LX	baud rate (Bd)	crossover cable
1000Base-SX	bit rate	cross-talk
1000Base-T	BNC	CWDM (coarse wavelength division multiplexing)
1000Base-TX	BNC connector	
100Base-FX	BNC coupler	DB-25 connector
100Base-T	boot	DB-9 connector
10Base2	braiding	demultiplexer (demux)
10Base-T	broadband	digital signal
10GBase-ER	cable checker	DWDM (dense wavelength division multiplexing)
10GBase-EW	cable crimper	
10GBase-LR	cable performance tester	Ethernet port
10GBase-LW	cable tester	far end cross-talk (FEXT)
10GBase-SR	Cat (category)	Fast Ethernet
10GBase-SW	Cat 3 (Category 3)	FC (ferrule connector or fiber channel)
10GBase-T	Cat 5 (Category 5)	
10-Gigabit Ethernet	Cat 5e (Enhanced Category 5)	F-connector
802.3ae	Cat 6 (Category 6)	FDM (frequency division multiplexing)
802.3af	Cat 6a (Augmented Category 6)	
802.3at	Cat 7 (Category 7)	ferrule
alien cross-talk	Cat 7a (Augmented Category 7)	fiber coupler
AM (amplitude modulation)	certifier	fiber type mismatch
American Wire Gauge (AWG)	Cisco console cable	FM (frequency modulation)
amplifier	cladding	frequency
amplitude	coaxial cable	GBIC (Gigabit interface converter)
analog signal	connector	Gigabit Ethernet
Angle Polished Connector (APC)	console port	hot-swappable
ASCII	continuity tester	impedance
attenuation	core	LC (local connector)
back reflection	coupler	LED (light-emitting diode)
backplane	crimping	light meter
baseband	crimping tool	line tester
		media converter

mini GBIC

MMF (multimode fiber)

modal bandwidth

modem

modulation

MT-RJ (Mechanical Transfer-Registered Jack)

multimeter

multiplexer (mux)

multiplexing

near end cross-talk (NEXT)

NIST (National Institute of Standards and Technology)

NSP (network service provider)

open circuit

optical loss

optical power meter (OPM)

OTDR (optical time domain reflectometer)

PD (powered device)

phase

Physical Contact (PC)

pinout

PoE (Power over Ethernet)

PoE+

probe

PSE (power sourcing equipment)

regeneration

repeater

RFI (radio frequency interference)

RG-58

RG-59

RG-6

RG-8

RJ-11 (registered jack 11)

RJ-45 (registered jack 45)

RJ-48C

rollover cable

RS-232 (Recommended Standard 232)

RTT (round trip time)

SC (subscriber connector or standard connector)

SFP (small form-factor pluggable) transceiver

SFP GBIC

SFP+

sheath

shield

short circuit

SMF (single mode fiber)

snips

split pair

ST (straight tip)

statistical multiplexing

straight-through cable

subchannel

TDM (time division multiplexing)

TDR (time domain reflectometer)

Thicknet

Thinnet

throughput

tone generator

tone locator

toner

toner and probe kit

toner probe

twist ratio

twisted pair

Tx/Rx reverse

Ultra Polished Connector (UPC)

UTF-8

UTP coupler

wavelength

wavelength mismatch

WDM (wavelength division multiplexing)

wire stripper

XFP

Yost cable

zipcord cable

5

Review Questions

1. When an Ethernet NIC has been configured by the OS to use half-duplex, the transmit pair of the twisted-pair cable uses _____ transmissions, the receive pair in the cable uses _____ transmissions, and the twisted-pair cable uses _____ transmissions.

   a. Simplex, half-duplex, half-duplex

   b. Half-duplex, simplex, simplex

   c. Simplex, simplex, half-duplex

   d. Simplex, half-duplex, simplex

2. Which of the following is *not* an example of a broadband transmission?

    a. Cable TV

    b. Telephone signal

    c. Mobile voice

    d. Ethernet

3. Which kind of multiplexing assigns slots to nodes according to priority and need?

    a. WDM (wavelength division multiplexing)

    b. Statistical multiplexing

    c. TDM (time division multiplexing)

    d. CWDM (coarse wavelength division multiplexing)

4. Which type of transmission is measured by baud rate?

    a. Analog

    b. Digital

    c. Baseband

    d. Broadband

5. What kind of cable uses BNC connectors? F-connectors? Which connector is likely to be used by cable TV?

    a. Coaxial cable, coaxial cable, F-connector

    b. Coaxial cable, UTP, BNC connector

    c. STP, UTP, F-connector

    d. SMF, MMF, BNC connector

6. Which categories of twisted-pair cable can support Gigabit Ethernet?

    a. Cat 5 and lower

    b. Cat 5 and higher

    c. Cat 5e and higher

    d. Cat 6 and lower

7. What is the earliest twisted-pair cabling standard that meets the minimum requirements for 10GBase-T transmissions?

    a. Cat 5

    b. Cat 5e

    c. Cat 6

    d. Cat 6a

8. Which type of cross-talk occurs between wire pairs near the source of a signal?

    a. Alien cross-talk

    b. Tx/Rx reverse

    c. FEXT

    d. NEXT

9. What device can boost an analog signal? A digital signal?

    a. Toner probe, multimeter

    b. Repeater, certifier

    c. Amplifier, repeater

    d. TDR, multimeter

10. Which part of a toner and probe kit emits a tone when it detects electrical activity on a wire pair?

    a. Probe

    b. Tone generator

    c. Toner probe

    d. Toner

11. What are the four fundamental properties of an analog signal?

12. What does a modem do?

13. What is twist ratio and why is it important?

14. What fiber is used in fiber-optic cabling to protect the inner core and prevent the cable from stretching?

15. What characteristic of optical transmissions is primarily responsible for the distance limitations of fiber-optic cabling?

16. Why is SMF more efficient over long distances than MMF?

17. Why do APC ferrules create less back reflection than do UPC ferrules?

18. What does a fiber cleaver do?

19. How is latency measured and in what unit?

20. What is the difference between short circuits and open circuits?

Hands-On Projects

Enter ←

HANDS-ON PROJECTS

Project 5-1: Create a Loopback Plug

In this chapter, you practiced terminating an Ethernet cable by attaching an RJ-45 jack. In Chapter 4, you learned that a loopback plug crosses the transmit line with the receive line to trick a device into thinking it's connected to a network. You can create your own loopback plug simply by altering the pinout on the connector and forcing the transmissions to loop back in on themselves. A loopback plug is helpful for determining if a NIC on a workstation or a port on a switch is working or not.

To make your own loopback plug, you'll need a 6-inch length of UTP cabling (Cat 5 or Cat 5e), an unused RJ-45 plug (and boot if it's included with the plug), wire cutters, and a cable crimper.

1. Cut to loosen the cable's covering, then slide the covering off the cable and flatten out the wire pairs. Do not untwist the wire pairs. Select one wire pair (one solid and one striped) and lay the other pairs aside because you won't need them.

2. Untwist the wires on each end an inch or less and straighten out the tips. If needed, give each wire a clean cut to make sure the two wires on each end are even with each other.

3. Insert one end of the twisted pair into the RJ-45 plug, making sure the solid color wire goes into slot 1, and the striped wire goes into slot 2. Be sure to push the wires all the way into the slots.

4. Loop the wire pair around and insert the other end into the plug. The solid color wire goes into slot 3, and the striped wire goes into slot 6. (Slots 4, 5, 7, and 8 are not needed unless you'll be testing VoIP equipment.)

5. Push the wires all the way in, and use the crimpers to secure the wires in the plug. If a boot came with the plug, you can insert it over the wire loop and push it all the way through to cover the wire/plug connection, as shown in Figure 5-52.

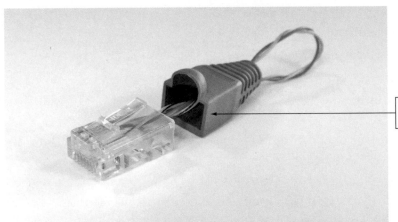

Push boot over connector after crimping wires

© 2016 Cengage Learning®

Figure 5-52   Adding the boot to the loopback plug is optional

6. Insert the loopback plug into a switch's port that is known to be working correctly. If the port's link indicator lights up (this may take a minute), you've successfully created a loopback plug.

NOTE

If you want to include the other two pins in the adapter so you can test VoIP and similar equipment, you'll need to use a second twisted pair from your original cable. Before crimping, insert one end of the second pair into the plug. Press the solid color wire into slot 4 and the striped wire into slot 5. Loop the wire around and press the solid color wire into slot 7 and the striped wire into slot 8. Crimp, and you're done.

Enter ↵

HANDS-ON PROJECTS

Project 5-2: Create a Loopback Jack

A loopback plug can be used to test a port on a switch or a workstation's NIC. A loopback jack, however, can be used to test a cable or to identify which port a cable is connected to. This is especially helpful when the cable is already run through the wall or is tangled up with other cables.

Creating a loopback plug is pretty straightforward, but wiring a loopback jack is even easier. For this project, you'll need a 2-inch length of UTP cabling (Cat 5 or Cat 5e), an unused

RJ-45 data/phone jack (these are very inexpensive and easily found at many home improvement stores), and a punch down tool.

1. Cut to loosen the cable's covering, slide the covering off the cable, select one wire pair, and untwist it completely. Lay the other pairs aside because you won't need them.

2. Turn the jack so the slots are easily accessible. Take a single wire and press one end into the slot next to the "A--green/white" icon. Press the other end into the slot with the "A--orange/white" icon.

There is some variation in how RJ-45 jacks are designed. If these generic directions don't match the jack you're using, check the documentation that came with the jack.

NOTE

3. Take the other, single wire, and press one end into the slot next to the "A--orange" icon, and press the other end into the slot next to the "A--green" icon. In some cases, depending on the actual jack you use, the two wires will create an "X" shape through the center of the jack between the slots, as shown in Figure 5-53. With other jacks, the wires may cross over each other on one side only.

Figure 5-53 With this jack, the wires simply cross in the middle

4. Use the punch down tool to punch the wires all the way into their respective slots. The punch down tool will also clip the excess length off the wires. Make sure to orient the punch down tool so the cutting side will slice the outside length of the wire and not the inside length. If a cover came with the jack, place it over the wires.

5. To test your loopback jack, plug a patch cable you know to be good into a switch port that you know works, then plug the jack onto the other end of the cable. Wait up to a minute to give the link sufficient time to be established. If the port's link indicator lights up, you've successfully created a loopback jack.

For storage, you can plug your loopback plug into your loopback jack (see Figure 5-54), giving you a handy two-in-one tool for your toolkit.

© 2016 Cengage Learning®.

Figure 5-54 Attach the plug and jack together to protect their connections when storing them

Project 5-3: Latency Around the World

HANDS-ON PROJECTS

In this chapter, you learned that latency is the delay caused by the time it takes messages to travel over network media from one place to another. This concept is easy to see in the real world, where it takes longer, for example, to travel across the country than it does to go to the grocery store. Even though network messages travel much faster than a car or even a jet plane, it still takes time for them to get from one place to another.

In the following steps you will experiment to see how distance affects a message's RTT (round trip time).

1. Open a command prompt and run `tracert` on a Web site whose servers are located on a different continent from you, across one ocean. If you're located in the Midwest or Eastern United States, for example, you can run the command **tracert www.london.edu** (London Business School). If you are on the West Coast, however, you might get more useful results for this step by targeting a server across the Pacific Ocean, such as **tracert www.tiu.ac.jp** (Tokyo International University).

NOTE

For an Ubuntu or other Linux installation, you can use `traceroute` rather than `tracert` for this project. But you first must install the traceroute utility. On Ubuntu, use this command:
sudo apt-get install traceroute

2. Examine the output and find at what point in the route messages started jumping across the ocean. By what percentage does the RTT increase after the jump compared with before it? You can see an example in Figure 5-55.

   To calculate the percentage for this jump, you would select a time from just after the jump (126, for example) and divide it by a time from just before the jump (such as 45), then multiply by 100 percent: 126 / 45 × 100 = 280. In this case, the sample data would yield a 280 percent increase. It takes nearly three times as long for a message to go round trip across the Atlantic from the United States to Manchester, England (the location of this first European router) as it does for a message to travel round trip between two servers that are both located on the U.S. East Coast (this local computer and the last U.S. router in the route).

3. Choose a Web site whose servers are on a continent even farther away from you. For example, you could trace the route to the University of Delhi in India at the address du.ac.in. How many hops did it take until the route crossed an ocean? What other anomalies do you notice about this global route?

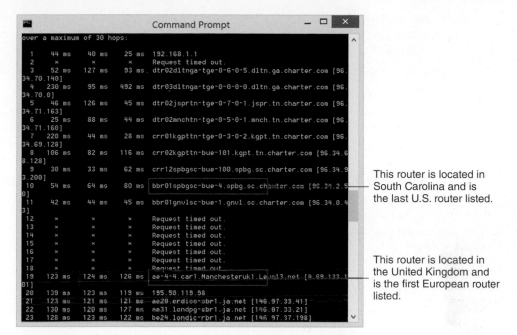

This router is located in South Carolina and is the last U.S. router listed.

This router is located in the United Kingdom and is the first European router listed.

Figure 5-55 The latency time increases significantly as the messages start to cross the ocean

Source: Microsoft LLC

4. Choose one more Web site as close to directly across the globe from you as possible. U.S. locations may want to use the University of Western Australia at uwa.edu.au. How many hops are in the route? Did the route go east or west around the world from your location? How can you tell?

5. Scott Base in Antarctica runs several webcams from various research locations. Run a trace to the Scott Base Web site at antarcticanz.govt.nz. Is this Web server located in Antarctica? How can you tell?

6. Think about other locations around the world that might be reached through an interesting route. Find a Web site hosted in that location and trace the route to it. Which Web site did you target? Where is it located?

7. Try the ping command on several of these same IP addresses. Did it work? Why do you think this is the case?

Project 5-4: Investigate a Speed and Duplex Mismatch Error

Using a Windows workstation, follow these steps to create a speed and duplex mismatch error and examine the results:

1. Open the Network Connections window (for Windows 8.1, right-click Start and click Network Connections) and double-click the wired local area connection icon. In the status box, note the current speed of the connection (for example, 1.0 Gbps).

2. Open Device Manager (for Windows 8.1, right-click Start and click Device Manager) and then open the properties box of the wired network adapter. On the Advanced tab,

if the NIC is configured correctly, you should see the Speed & Duplex set to Auto Negotiation. Change the link speed to a value other than the one you observed in Step 1. Change the duplex to half-duplex. Save your changes.

3. Note the new connection speed or error message reported in the status box you opened in Step 1.

4. Open your browser and attempt to surf the Web. If the speed and duplex are slower than the negotiated speed and duplex, the connection should work, though slower. If the speed and duplex are higher than the negotiated speed and duplex, the connection will not work.

5. Go back to Step 2 and return the network adapter properties to Auto Negotiation. Save your changes and close all windows.

Case Projects

CASE PROJECTS

Case Project 5-1: Manage Log Files in Ubuntu Server

Working with Linux operating systems, compared to working with Windows, is like driving a stick shift rather than an automatic. As you've already learned, to configure an installed program in Ubuntu, a distribution of Linux, you edit a text file. For example, in Case Project 4-1, you edited the /etc/vsftpd.conf text file when configuring the FTP program you installed in Ubuntu.

Ubuntu creates various logs to track just about any event, and these logs are stored as text files. By default, most are stored in the /var/log directory. The FTP program maintains its own activity log in a text file that, by default, is /var/log/vsftpd.log. (You can change the default path and filename by editing the /etc/vsftpd.conf file.) This log file is essential to a technician who needs to monitor which users have logged on to the FTP server, when and from where they logged on, and what files they uploaded or downloaded. You can also monitor failed logons, which can tip you off to someone or a robot trying to hack into your system.

Using the installation of Ubuntu Server you created in Case Project 3-1 in a VM, follow along to learn how to manage log files in Ubuntu:

1. Start Ubuntu Server and log on with your username and password.

2. Enter the commands shown in Table 5-7.

Table 5-7 Commands for Case Project 5-1, Step 2

Command	Explanation
cd /var/log	Go to the directory that contains log files.
ls -l	List all files and subdirectories and details about the item. Look for log files that have gotten excessively large. If a technician doesn't monitor and control log files, they may get large enough to take up all available hard drive space and bring a system down.

Table 5-7 **Commands for Case Project 5-1, Step 2** (*continued*)

Command	Explanation
`ls –l vsftpd.log`	List details about vsftpd.log. Notice the file is owned by root. Also notice the file size. If it is 0, look for another log file named vsftpd.log.1 that has a nonzero file size. Ubuntu might use rotating filenames in this manner so that one log file doesn't get too large. You might find several vsftpd.log.* files.
`ls –l vsftpd.log*`	List all vsftpd.log files—for example, vsftpd.log and vsftpd.log.1. In the next three commands, if the vsftpd.log file is empty, use one that has contents.
`sudo less vsftpd.log`	Use the `less` command to view and page through the contents of the file. You must use the `sudo` command to access the file because it is owned by root.
`sudo grep "LOGIN" vsftpd.log`	Use the `grep` command to narrow down a search in a text file for a particular string of text. You must use the `sudo` command to access the file because it is owned by root. The `grep` command is particularly useful for large text files when you're searching for a particular username, event, or command.
`sudo grep –i "LOGIN" vsftpd.log`	Ignore case when searching. For example, the `"LOGIN"` string gives the same results as `"login"`.

3. You might be interested in learning about other log files in the /var/log directory. Search the help.ubuntu.com Web site or do a general Google search on three logs files you find in the directory and write a one-sentence description of the type of information kept in the file and why a technician might find this information helpful.

CASE PROJECTS

Case Project 5-2: LAN Testing

A variety of software and Web-based tools are available to help you establish baseline measurements—and later, detect fluctuations and problems—in the efficiency of your network and Internet connections. This project walks you through two different tests you can do on your school's lab network or at home on your own LAN.

TotuSoft's LAN Speed Test is a small, free program you can download from totusoft.com. Because the program runs from your own Windows computer, it can be used to test connections on your LAN rather than being subject to speed limitations resulting from your connection to the Internet. It's a very simple program that only needs access to a shared folder on the local area network. The Public Users folder on another workstation meets this requirement. Figure 5-56 shows the result of a sample test, which was run over a wireless connection.

1. To test the speed of your LAN, download the software *LAN Speed Test (Lite) (Free version)*, and run the .exe file. The program will automatically detect your own computer's IP address.

Figure 5-56   Another workstation's Public Users folder

Source: TotuSoft

2. Find a shared folder on another workstation or on a server (on the same LAN as your computer), select it as the target folder, accept the default settings, and run the test.

3. How do your test results compare with the various Ethernet standards discussed in the chapter? Is this what you expected, based on the network media supporting this connection?

4. If your test results differ from the standards you were expecting, how do you explain these results?

TamoSoft offers a free Throughput Test that works on both wired and wireless LAN connections.

5. Look for the Throughput Test in the Download Area of tamos.com, then download and install it on two computers on the same LAN. One computer will act as the client and one as the server.

6. To install the software, navigate to the folder containing the download and click the **setup.exe** file.

7. The program probably will not create a shortcut on your desktop, so you'll need to open the Program Files (x86) folder in Windows Explorer (File Explorer in Windows 8.1) and double-click the appropriate executable for each computer. For example, the server computer will use the *TTServer.exe* file.

8. On the computer acting as the server, leave the default settings. Nothing more is needed on this end of the connection because the server will listen for the client before doing anything else.

9. On the computer acting as the client, enter the server's IP address, then click **Connect**. Figure 5-57 shows the client and server consoles side by side.

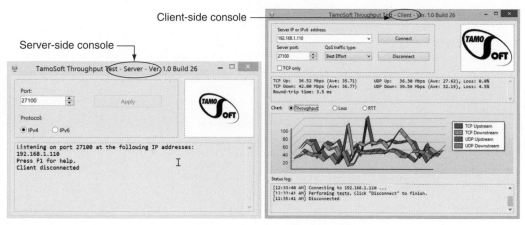

Figure 5-57   Server and client consoles for Throughput Test. The client side is showing results after the test was run.

Source: TamoSoft

10. Let the test run for a while, then click **Disconnect**. Examine the results, and answer the following questions.

a. On the Throughput chart, what was the highest reading obtained, and what kind of traffic was it?

b. On the Loss chart, were there any significant loss results, and what kind of traffic was involved? What theories do you have about why this might be? Where would you look next to resolve this problem?

c. On the RTT (round trip time) chart, were there any spikes? Do you notice any correlation between the timing of the spikes on this chart and the timing of problem indicators on the other two charts?

## chapter 6

Wireless Networking

After reading this chapter and completing the exercises, you will be able to:

- Explain how nodes exchange wireless signals
- Identify potential obstacles to successful wireless transmission and their repercussions, such as interference and reflection
- Understand WLAN (wireless LAN) architecture
- Specify the characteristics of popular WLAN transmission methods, including 802.11 a/b/g/n/ac
- Install and configure wireless access points and their clients
- Explore wireless security concerns
- Evaluate common problems experienced with wireless networks

On the Job

I've installed wireless network equipment for the past 15 years. Our company builds and repairs computers and installs wireless networks and surveillance systems in office buildings, warehouses, and homes. We work with both directional wireless and open-space, broadcast wireless.

When installing a wireless AP, we're always careful to take note of any device specifications, such as the AP's range, and we have to consider what obstacles are in the device's line of sight. We evaluate any walls, ceilings, and other obstacles that come in between the source of the wireless signal and the various locations of receiving devices, such as printers, computers, and cell phones.

One installation comes to mind that really baffled us. It was an older home here in Dalton, Georgia, and was built around the early 1900's.

The house wasn't huge, and we installed an AP in the kitchen area. We initially tested the signal in the kitchen and, as expected, received 4 bars of signal strength. Next we walked into the living room, which was just on the other side of the wall from the kitchen. In the living room, however, we barely received 1 bar.

We put in a higher wattage output AP and upon repeating the test, we still just received 1 bar in the living room. As part of our investigation, we went into the attic and discovered that this wall between the kitchen and the living room was built of plaster instead of sheetrock. Further investigation revealed that underneath the plaster was a layer of chicken wire. A little research revealed that in the old days, some walls incorporated chicken wire in the internal structure to hold the plaster against the wall. This wall was like a fortress, blocking our wireless signal.

We installed a second AP in another room to solve the problem. The moral to this story is, when installing wireless, beware of what an impact a single wall can have, especially in older homes.

Scott Merritt, Service Mgr.
Dalton Computer Services, Inc.

Air provides an intangible means of transporting data over networks. For decades, radio and TV stations have transmitted analog signals through the air. Such analog signals are also capable of carrying data. This chapter first looks at how wireless transmissions work, regardless of the type of wireless technology used. These wireless characteristics apply to satellite, Bluetooth, Wi-Fi, cellular, WiMAX, and other wireless signals. Some of these wireless signals, such as satellite and cellular, can traverse long distances. However, this chapter focuses on wireless signals used for local networks. Later, Chapter 11 will cover cellular (such as LTE), WiMAX, and other wireless WAN technologies in more detail.

Characteristics of Wireless Transmissions

In previous chapters, you learned about signals that travel over a physical medium, such as a copper or fiber-optic cable. Networks that transmit signals through the air via radio frequency (RF) waves are known as wireless networks or WLANs (wireless local area networks). Wireless transmission media is now common in business and home networks and necessary in some specialized network environments. Wired and wireless signals share many similarities, including use of the same Layer 3 and higher protocols, for example. However, the nature of the atmosphere makes wireless transmission vastly different from wired transmission. Let's look at what wireless signals are, then we'll see how they're transmitted.

The Wireless Spectrum

All wireless signals are carried through the air by electromagnetic waves. The wireless spectrum is a continuum of the electromagnetic waves used for data and voice communication. On the spectrum, waves are arranged according to their frequencies, from lowest to highest. The wireless spectrum (as defined by the FCC, which controls its use) spans frequencies between 9 KHz and 300 GHz. Each type of wireless service can be associated with one area of the wireless spectrum. AM broadcasting, for example, sits near the low-frequency end of the wireless communications spectrum, using frequencies between 535 KHz and 1605 KHz. Infrared waves belong to a wide band of frequencies at the high-frequency end of the spectrum, between 300 GHz and 300,000 GHz. Most wireless networks, such as Wi-Fi networks, use frequencies around 2.4 GHz or 5 GHz. Figure 6-1 shows the wireless spectrum and roughly identifies the range of frequencies associated with major wireless services.

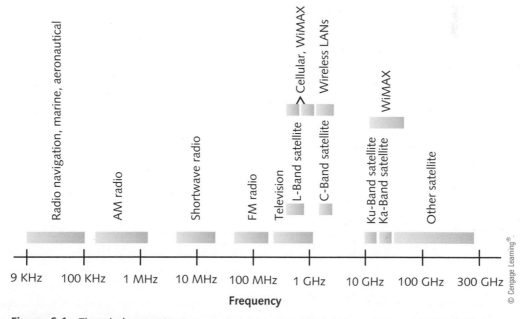

Figure 6-1   The wireless spectrum

In the United States, the collection of frequencies available for communication—also known as *the airwaves*—is considered a natural resource available for public use. The FCC grants organizations in different locations exclusive rights to use each frequency. It also determines what frequency ranges can be used for what purposes. Of course, signals propagating through the air do not necessarily remain within one nation. Therefore, it is important for countries across the world to agree on wireless communications standards. The ITU (International Telecommunication Union) is a United Nations agency that sets standards for international telecommunications such as wireless services, including frequency allocation, signaling, and protocols used by wireless devices; wireless transmission and reception equipment; satellite orbits; and so on. If governments and companies did not adhere to ITU standards, chances are that a wireless device could not be used outside the country in which it was manufactured.

The air provides no fixed path for signals to follow, so signals travel without guidance. Contrast this to guided media, such as UTP or fiber-optic cable, which do provide a fixed signal path. The lack of a fixed path requires wireless signals to be transmitted, received, controlled, and corrected differently than wired signals.

Just as with wired signals, wireless signals originate from electrical current traveling along a conductor. The electrical signal travels from the transmitter to an antenna, which then emits the signal, as a series of electromagnetic waves, to the atmosphere. The signal propagates through the air until it reaches its destination. At the destination, another antenna accepts the signal, and a receiver converts it back to current. Figure 6-2 illustrates this process.

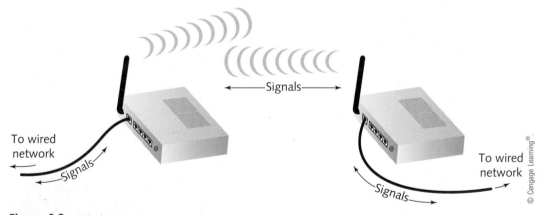

Figure 6-2   Wireless transmission and reception

Notice that antennas are used for both the transmission and reception of wireless signals. As you would expect, to exchange information, two antennas must be tuned to the same frequency. In communications terminology, this means they share the same channel.

Antennas

Each type of wireless service requires an antenna specifically designed for that service. The service's specifications determine the antenna's power output, frequency, and radiation pattern. An antenna's radiation pattern describes the relative strength over a three-dimensional area of all the electromagnetic energy the antenna sends or receives.

A unidirectional antenna, also called a directional antenna, issues wireless signals along a single direction. This type of antenna is used when the source needs to communicate with one destination, as in a point-to-point link, or in a specific area. A satellite downlink (for example, the kind used to receive digital TV signals) uses directional antennas. In contrast, an omnidirectional antenna issues and receives wireless signals with equal strength and clarity in all directions. This type of antenna is used when many different receivers must be able to pick up the signal, or when the receiver's location is highly mobile. TV and radio stations use omnidirectional antennas, as do most towers that transmit cellular signals.

The geographical area that an antenna or wireless system can reach is known as its range. Receivers must be within the range to receive accurate signals consistently. Even within an antenna's range, however, signals may be hampered by obstacles and rendered unintelligible.

Signal Propagation

Ideally, a wireless signal would travel directly in a straight line from its transmitter to its intended receiver. This type of propagation, known as LOS (line of sight), maximizes distance for the amount of energy used and results in reception of the clearest possible signal. However, because the atmosphere is an unguided medium and the path between a transmitter and a receiver is not always clear, wireless signals do not usually follow a straight line.

The only forms of wireless transmission media that require a clear line of sight are satellite, infrared, and some WiMAX transmissions. Keep in mind, however, that some signals might be blocked in what appears to your eyes to be a clear line-of-sight. For example, many energy-efficient windows are covered with a film that filters out certain layers of sunlight. Even though you can see through the window, a satellite signal, such as an XM radio satellite signal, might not be able to get through. Other signal types benefit from a clearer LOS, but are not as sensitive to LOS issues.

When an obstacle stands in a signal's way, the signal may pass through the object or be absorbed by the object, or it may be subject to any of the following phenomena: reflection, diffraction, or scattering. The object's geometry governs which of these three phenomena occurs:

- Reflection (also known as bounce) in wireless signaling is no different from reflection of other electromagnetic waves, such as light. The wave encounters an obstacle and reflects—or bounces back—toward its source. A wireless signal will bounce off objects whose dimensions are large compared with the signal's average wavelength. In the context of a wireless LAN, which may use signals with wavelengths between 1 and 10 meters, such objects include walls, floors, ceilings, and the Earth. In addition, signals reflect more readily off conductive materials, such as metal, than off insulators, such as concrete.

- In diffraction, a wireless signal splits into secondary waves when it encounters an obstruction. The secondary waves continue to propagate in the direction in which they were split. If you could see wireless signals being diffracted, they would appear to be bending around the obstacle. Objects with sharp edges—including the corners of walls and desks—cause diffraction.

- Scattering is the diffusion, or the reflection in multiple different directions, of a signal. Scattering occurs when a wireless signal encounters an object that has small dimensions compared with the signal's wavelength. Scattering is also related to the roughness of the surface a wireless signal encounters. The rougher the surface, the more likely a signal is to scatter when it hits that surface. In an office building, objects such as chairs, books, and computers cause scattering of wireless LAN signals. For signals traveling outdoors, rain, mist, hail, and snow may all cause scattering.

Because of reflection, diffraction, and scattering, wireless signals follow a number of different paths to their destination. Such signals are known as multipath signals. Figure 6-3 illustrates multipath signals caused by these three phenomena.

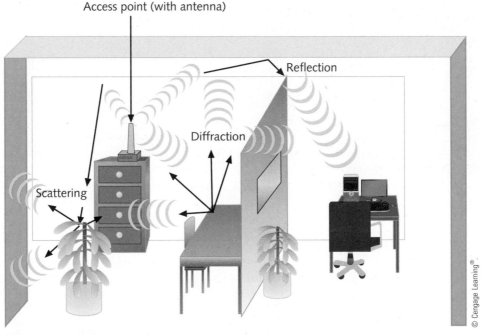

Figure 6-3   Multipath signal propagation

© Cengage Learning®

The multipath nature of wireless signals is both a blessing and a curse. On one hand, because signals bounce off obstacles, they have a better chance of reaching their destination. In environments such as an office building, wireless services depend on signals bouncing off walls, ceilings, floors, and furniture until they arrive at their destination. Imagine how inconvenient and inefficient it would be, for example, to make sure you were standing within clear view of a transmitter to receive a text message.

The downside to multipath signaling is that, because of their various paths, multipath signals travel different distances between their transmitter and a receiver. Thus, multiple instances of the same signal can arrive at a receiver at different times. This may cause signals to be misinterpreted, resulting in data errors. Error-correction algorithms will detect the errors and the sender will have to retransmit the signal. The more errors that occur, the slower the throughput. Environments such as manufacturing plants, which contain myriad reflective surfaces, experience greater throughput degradation than relatively open spaces, such as homes.

Network+
1.12
2.7
4.2
4.3

Signal Degradation

No matter what paths wireless signals take, they are bound to run into obstacles. When they do, the original signal issued by the transmitter will experience **fading**, or a variation in signal strength as a result of some of the electromagnetic energy being scattered, reflected, or diffracted after being issued by the transmitter. Multipath signaling is a significant cause of fading. Because of fading, the strength of the signal that reaches the receiver is lower than the transmitted signal's strength. This makes sense because as more waves are reflected, diffracted, or scattered by obstacles, fewer are likely to reach their destination on time and without errors. Excessive fading can cause dropped calls or slow data transmission. This affects the quality of the user's experience, which is quantified as goodput. **Goodput** is the throughput experienced at the application level, such as the quality of a video feed or the speed of a Web page loading in the browser, and can also be measured on a wired connection. Some Web sites, called **speed test sites**, can measure your upload and download speeds, respectively, to give you an idea of how your connection's throughput is affecting your goodput. You'll use a speed test site in a project at the end of this chapter.

As with wired signals, wireless signals also experience attenuation. After a signal is transmitted, the farther it moves away from the transmission antenna, the more it weakens. Similar to wired transmission, wireless signals can be amplified by increasing the power of the transmission or extended by repeating the signal from a closer broadcast point called a **range extender**, such as the one designed for a home network shown in Figure 6-4.

However, attenuation is not the most severe flaw affecting wireless signals. Wireless signals are also susceptible to noise. As you learned in Chapter 5, noise is also known as EMI (electromagnetic interference), or, in the context of wireless communications, interference. Interference is a significant problem for wireless communications because the atmosphere is saturated with electromagnetic waves. For example, wireless LANs may be affected by cellular phones, hands-free headsets, microwaves, machinery, or overhead lights.

Interference can distort and weaken a wireless signal in the same way that noise distorts and weakens a wired signal. However, because wireless signals cannot depend on a conduit or shielding to protect them from extraneous EMI, they are more vulnerable to noise. The proportion of noise to the strength of a signal is called the **signal-to-noise ratio** (SNR or S/N). The extent of interference that a wireless signal experiences depends partly on the density of signals within a geographical area. Signals traveling through areas in which many wireless communications systems are in use—for example, the center of a metropolitan area—are the most apt to suffer interference.

© 2016 Cengage Learning®

Figure 6-4   Wi-Fi range extender

Network+
2.2
2.7
4.3
Frequency Ranges

You've learned some characteristics of wireless transmissions in general, regardless of the type of transmission. From this point forward, we'll focus on wireless transmissions on a local area network. For many years, wireless networks relied on frequencies in the range of 2.4 GHz to 2.4835 GHz, more commonly known as the 2.4-GHz band, to send and receive signals. This band offers 11 communications channels that are unlicensed in the United States, and up to 14 channels that might be available in other countries. An unlicensed frequency is one for which the FCC does not require users to register their service and reserve it for their sole use. Because the 2.4-GHz band also carries cordless telephone and other types of signals, it is highly susceptible to interference. For example, on your home wireless network, your tablet computer might lose connectivity when your cordless telephone rings. One way to guard against this type of interference is to make sure your access point and cordless telephone use different channels within the 2.4-GHz band.

Wireless LANs may instead use the 5-GHz band, which comprises four frequency bands: 5.1 GHz, 5.3 GHz, 5.4 GHz, and 5.8 GHz. Figure 6-5 shows a comparison of the channels provided by both the 2.4-GHz band and the 5-GHz band. The 5-GHz band consists of 24 unlicensed bands, each 20-MHz wide. Because the 5-GHz band is also used by weather and military radar communications in the United States, WLAN equipment using this range of frequencies must be able to monitor and detect radar signals and, if one is detected, switch to a different channel automatically.

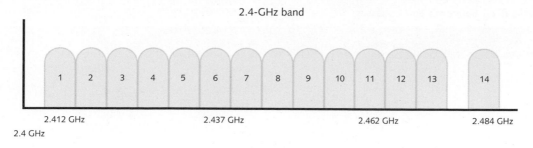

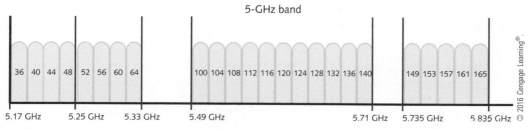

Figure 6-5 Channels on the 2.4-GHz and 5-GHz bands

Wireless PAN

Before you dig into a more extensive discussion of Wi-Fi, first take a look at a special subset of wireless transmissions used in accessory devices. A miniversion of a network is a PAN (personal area network), and the purely wireless version is a WPAN (wireless PAN). PANs rarely exceed a few meters in geographical width, and usually only contain a few personal devices, such as a PC, cell phone, USB printer, and perhaps a Bluetooth headset or even an infrared, wireless mouse. Three of the most common wireless technologies used to connect PAN devices are Bluetooth, infrared (IR), and near-field communication (NFC).

Bluetooth Bluetooth is named after a medieval king of Denmark named Harald Bluetooth, who fought to merge several Danish tribes under a single government. Like its namesake, Bluetooth technology unites separate entities. To be precise, it unites mobile devices, PCs, and accessories under a single communications standard. Bluetooth operates in the radio band of 2.4 GHz to 2.485 GHz and hops between frequencies within that band (up to 1600 hops/sec), called frequency hopping, to help reduce interference. Most Bluetooth devices require close proximity to form a connection, with the exact distance requirements depending on the class of Bluetooth device. Class 1 devices provide the greatest flexibility, with their ability to maintain a reliable connection up to 100 meters apart. Table 6-1 describes the three classes along with their power output. Bluetooth power output is measured in mW (milliwatts), which is one thousandth of a watt. (Compare this with a 60-watt light bulb, and you'll get an idea of how tiny this amount of power is.)

These days, most new computers come with an integrated Bluetooth adapter, and a plethora of Bluetooth electronic accessories are available, from wearable technology like headsets and watches to highly responsive gaming equipment or high-throughput media players. Manufacturers of Bluetooth devices must obtain approval from the Bluetooth Special Interest Group (SIG) before selling a new Bluetooth device, which must meet high

Table 6-1 Bluetooth power classes

Class	Maximum power output	Typical range	Purpose
1	100 mW	Up to 100 m	Used for industrial purposes
2	2.5 mW	Up to 10 m	Used for mobile devices
3	1 mW	Up to 1 m	Rarely used

© 2016 Cengage Learning®

standards defined by SIG. The various protocols integrated into Bluetooth span all layers of the OSI model, from the Physical layer up through the Application layer, depending on the device.

Before you can connect two Bluetooth devices, they must be paired, as shown in Figure 6-6. This pairing process entails turning on the Bluetooth antenna for each device (if it is not turned on by default), making the devices discoverable, and entering a PIN if required. Bluetooth interfaces are susceptible to a range of security risks, especially undesired Bluetooth connections such as bluejacking, in which a connection is used to send unsolicited data, and bluesnarfing, in which a connection is used to download data without permission. Wireless security concerns are discussed later in this chapter.

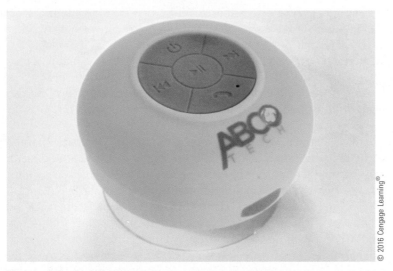

© 2016 Cengage Learning®

Figure 6-6 The flashing red light indicates this Bluetooth device is in discoverable mode for pairing with a smartphone or MP3 player

NFC (Near-Field Communication) If you've ever shared your virtual business card or a photo with a friend by tapping your smartphones together, you've used NFC. NFC (near-field communication) is a form of radio communication that transfers data wirelessly over very short distances (usually 10 cm or less). A tiny antenna embedded in the device sends its radio signal at a frequency of 13.56 MHz. The signal can also be transmitted one way by an **NFC tag**, or **smart tag**, such as when employees need to access a secure area of a building. Other uses of NFC tags include ticketing, cashless payment, shopping loyalty or membership programs, identification, data sharing, and PC logon capabilities.

NFC tags, such as the ones shown in Figure 6-7, require no power source other than the receiving device's power field. The NFC tag collects power from the smartphone or other device by magnetic induction, which is a form of wireless power transmission. Once power is introduced to the NFC tag by the receiving device's proximity, the tag transmits its data, up to 32 KB depending upon the tag's type. The four tag types are listed in Table 6-2.

Figure 6-7   These programmable NFC tags have sticky backs for attaching to a flat surface like a wall, desk, or car dashboard

Table 6-2   **Four types of NFC tags**

Tag type	Storage	Speed	Configuration
Type 1	96 bytes–2 Kb	106 Kbps	User-configured for read/write or read-only
Type 2	48 bytes–2 Kb	106 Kbps	
Type 3	Up to 1 Mb	212 Kbps	Manufacturer-configured for read/write or read-only
Type 4	Up to 32 Kb	106 Kbps–424 Kbps	

NFC tags are very inexpensive and can be purchased blank, ready to be loaded and integrated into posters, stickers, business cards, prescription bottles, or equipment labels. They can be programmed to transmit stored data, launch apps, direct a browser to a Web page, or change device settings. This makes them useful even for casual, personal use, such as changing your phone's settings when you pass through your front door at home or when you get into your car.

Now that you understand some characteristics of wireless transmission, you are ready to learn about the way most wireless LANs are structured. Later, you'll learn about their access methods and how to install wireless connectivity devices.

Legacy Networking
Infrared (IR)

Infrared (IR) is an outdated wireless technology that has been mostly replaced by Bluetooth to connect personal devices. IR requires an unobstructed line of sight between the transmitter and receiver. Today, the most common use of infrared is by remote controls. Figure 6-8 shows a remote control that can be used with multimedia applications installed on a notebook computer. The remote communicates with the notebook by way of an IR transceiver connected to a USB port. To use the remote, the device drivers that came bundled with the device are installed and then the IR transceiver is connected to the USB port.

Figure 6-8   This remote control is an infrared device that uses an IR transceiver connected to a notebook by way of a USB port.

Infrared standards are defined by the Infrared Data Association (IrDA). Its Web site is *irda.org*.

Wi-Fi WLAN (Wireless LAN) Architecture

1.1
1.7
1.12
2.7
3.2
4.3
5.2
5.3
Because they are not bound by cabling paths between nodes and connectivity devices, wireless networks are not laid out using the same topologies as wired networks. They have their own, different layouts, as described in the following list:

* *ad hoc*—Smaller wireless networks, in which a small number of nodes closely positioned need to exchange data, can be arranged in an ad hoc fashion.

In an **ad hoc WLAN**, wireless nodes, or **stations**, transmit directly to each other via wireless NICs without an intervening connectivity device, as shown in Figure 6-9.

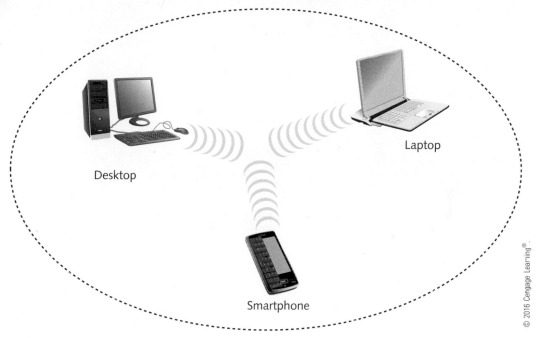

Figure 6-9 An ad hoc WLAN

- *infrastructure*—Nearly all wireless networks use an infrastructure WLAN topology, which depends on an intervening connectivity device called a wireless access point, as shown in Figure 6-10. A wireless access point (WAP)—also known simply as an access point (AP) or a base station—is a device that accepts wireless signals from multiple nodes and retransmits them to the rest of the network. Access points for use on small office or home networks often include routing functions. As such, they may also be called wireless routers or wireless gateways. To cover its intended range, an access point must have sufficient power and be strategically placed so that stations can communicate with it.

- *mesh*—It's common for a WLAN to include several access points. When these APs work as peer devices on the same network, they form a mesh WLAN, also called a wireless mesh network (WMN). A wireless mesh topology is illustrated in Figure 6-11 where you can see that AP devices cooperate to provide more fault-tolerant network access to clients.

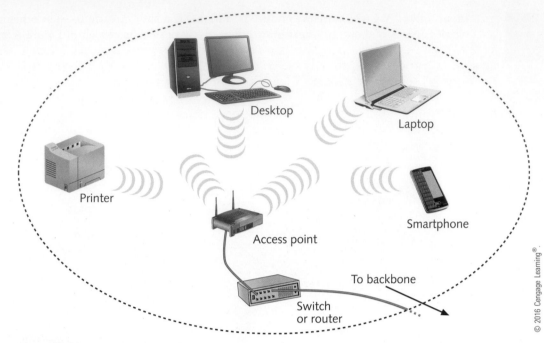

Figure 6-10 An infrastructure WLAN

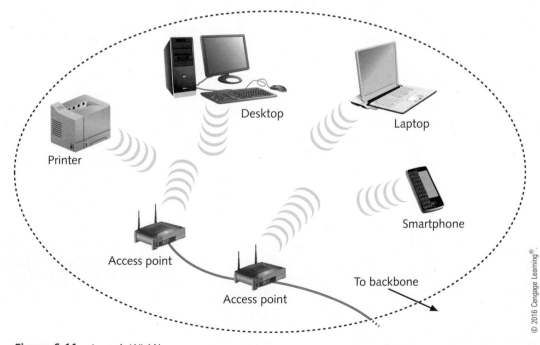

Figure 6-11 A mesh WLAN

Mobile networking allows wireless nodes to roam from one location to another within a certain range of their access point, depending on the wireless access method, the equipment manufacturer, and the office environment. As with other wireless technologies, WLAN signals are subject to interference and obstruction that cause multipath signaling. Therefore, a building with many thick, concrete walls or with metal studs, for example, will limit the effective range of a WLAN more severely than an open area divided into cubicles. In most WLAN scenarios, stations must remain within 300 feet of an access point to maintain optimal transmission speeds.

In addition to connecting multiple nodes within a LAN, wireless technology can be used to connect two different parts of a LAN or two separate LANs. Such connections typically use a fixed link with directional antennas between two access points, as shown in Figure 6-12.

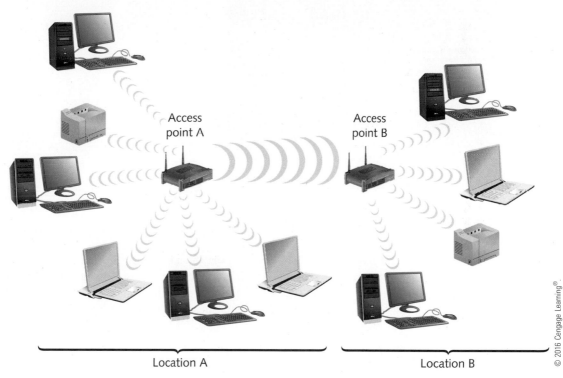

Figure 6-12 Wireless LAN interconnection

Because point-to-point links only have to transmit in one direction, they can apply more energy to signal propagation through a unidirectional antenna, such as the one in Figure 6-13. This allows them to achieve a greater transmission distance than mobile wireless links can offer. For example, access points connecting two WLANs could be up to 1000 feet apart.

© 2016 Cengage Learning®

Figure 6-13   An outdoor unidirectional antenna

WLANs work at OSI Layers 1 and 2. They support the same TCP/IP higher-layer OSI protocols and operating systems (for example, UNIX, Linux, or Windows) as wired LANs. This
compatibility ensures that wireless and wired transmission methods can be integrated on the
same network. The following section describes the most popular OSI Physical and Data Link
layer standards used by WLANs.

802.11 WLAN Standards

The most popular wireless standards used on contemporary LANs are those developed by
IEEE's 802.11 committee. IEEE released its first wireless network standard in 1997. Since
then, its WLAN standards committee, also known as the 802.11 committee, has published several distinct standards related to wireless networking. Each IEEE wireless network access standard is named after the 802.11 task group (or subcommittee) that
developed it. The IEEE 802.11 task groups that have generated notable wireless standards
are 802.11b, 802.11a, 802.11g, 802.11n, and 802.11ac. Collectively, these 802.11 standards and their amendments, extensions, and corrections are known as Wi-Fi, for *wireless*

fidelity. Although some of their Physical layer services vary, all of these standards use half-duplex signaling. In other words, a wireless station using one of the 802.11 techniques can either transmit or receive, but cannot do both simultaneously (unless the station has more than one transceiver installed).

Some wireless access points can simulate full-duplex signaling by using multiple frequencies. But the transmission for each antenna is still only half-duplex.

The 802.11 standards vary at the Physical layer. In addition, 802.11n and later standards modify the way frames are used at the MAC sublayer. The following list describes those differences. Table 6-3 summarizes the technical details of the 802.11 standards.

- *802.11b*—In 1999, the IEEE released its 802.11b standard, which separates the 2.4-GHz band into 22-MHz channels. Among all the 802.11 standards, 802.11b was the first to take hold. It is also the least expensive of all the 802.11 WLAN technologies. However, most network administrators have replaced 802.11b with a faster standard, such as 802.11n.

- *802.11a*—Although the 802.11a task group began its standards work before the 802.11b group, 802.11a was released *after* 802.11b. The higher throughput of 802.11a, as compared with 802.11b, is attributable to its use of higher frequencies, its unique method of modulating data, and more available bandwidth. Perhaps most significant is that the 5-GHz band is not as congested as the 2.4-GHz band. Thus, 802.11a signals are less likely to suffer interference from microwave ovens, cordless phones, motors, and other (incompatible) wireless LAN signals. However, higher-frequency signals require more power to transmit, and they travel shorter distances than lower-frequency signals. As a result, 802.11a networks require a greater density of access points between the wired LAN and wireless clients to cover the same distance that 802.11b networks cover. The additional access points, as well as the nature of 802.11a equipment, make this standard more expensive than either 802.11b or 802.11g. For this and other reasons, 802.11a is rarely preferred.

- *802.11g*—IEEE's 802.11g WLAN standard is designed to be just as affordable as 802.11b while increasing its maximum theoretical throughput with different data modulation techniques. In addition to its higher throughput, 802.11g benefits from being compatible with 802.11b networks. This was a significant advantage at the time when network administrators were upgrading their wireless access points to the 802.11g technology while still needing to offer wireless access compatible with their older computers.

- *802.11n*—In 2009, IEEE ratified the 802.11n standard. However, it was in development for years before that, and as early as mid-2007, manufacturers were selling 802.11n-compatible transceivers in their networking equipment. The primary goal of IEEE's 802.11n committee was to create a wireless standard that provided much higher effective throughput than the other 802.11 standards. By all accounts, they succeeded. 802.11n boasts a maximum throughput of 600 Mbps, making it a realistic platform for telephone and video signals. IEEE also specified that the 802.11n standard must be backward compatible with the 802.11a, b, and g standards. This is possible because 802.11n uses both the 2.4-GHz and the 5.0-GHz frequency bands.

- *802.11ac*—Officially approved in early 2014, 802.11ac operates on the 5-GHz band and exceeds benchmarks set by earlier standards by increasing its useful bandwidth and amplitude. 802.11ac is the first Wi-Fi standard to approach Gigabit Ethernet capabilities, providing better support for more wireless clients at a time. In fact, 802.11ac access points function more like a switch than a hub in that they can handle multiple transmissions at one time over the same frequency spectrum. This new standard is being deployed in three waves, with Wave 1 devices already available.

The actual geographic range of any wireless technology depends on several factors, including the power of the antenna, physical barriers or obstacles between sending and receiving nodes, and interference in the environment. Therefore, although a technology is rated for a certain average geographic range, it may actually transmit signals in a shorter or longer range at various times under various conditions.

A more relevant measure of an AP's performance in a particular environment is how well it saturates its range with a strong, fast signal. This is one of the primary advantages of 802.11ac over 802.11n: The newer standard's geographic range does a better job of providing faster transmissions throughout its geographic range. So, for example, at 75 m, the signal from an 802.11ac AP will be much faster than the signal from an 802.11n AP under the same conditions.

To qualify for CompTIA Network+ certification, you need to understand the differences between the 802.11 wireless standards. Be sure to memorize the WLAN standards shown in Table 6-3.

How Wi-Fi Works

Regardless of the standard followed, all 802.11 networks share many features and innovations in common. All 802.11 networks follow the same access method, for example, as described in the following section. In addition, some newer innovations give the later standards a significant performance edge over earlier standards.

Access Method In Chapter 2, you learned that the MAC sublayer of the Data Link layer is responsible for appending physical addresses to a data frame and for governing multiple nodes' access to a single medium. As with 802.3 (Ethernet), the 802.11 MAC services append 48-bit physical addresses to a frame to identify its source and destination. The use of the same physical addressing scheme allows 802.11 networks to be easily combined with other IEEE 802 networks, including Ethernet networks. However, because

Table 6-3   Technical details for 802.11 wireless standards

Standard		Frequency band	Max. theoretical throughput	Effective throughput	Geographic range
802.11b		2.4 GHz	11 Mbps	5 Mbps	100 m
802.11a		5 GHz	54 Mbps	11–18 Mbps	20 m
802.11g		2.4 GHz	54 Mbps	20–25 Mbps	100 m
802.11n		2.4 GHz or 5 GHz	65–600 Mbps	65–500 Mbps	400 m (if MIMO is used)
802.11ac	Wave 1 (3 data streams)	5 GHz	1.3 Gbps	Documented as high as 561 Mbps per client	Exact range is unknown at the time this book was printed, but throughput is improved throughout range
	Wave 2 (4 data streams)	5 GHz	3.47 Gbps	(Unknown at time of printing)	
	Wave 3 (8 data streams)	5 GHz	6.93 Gbps	(Unknown at time of printing)	

wireless devices are not designed to transmit and receive simultaneously, and, therefore, cannot prevent collisions, 802.11 networks use a different access method than Ethernet networks.

802.11 standards specify the use of CSMA/CA (Carrier Sense Multiple Access with Collision Avoidance) to access a shared medium. Using CSMA/CA, a station on an 802.11 network checks for existing wireless transmissions before it begins to send data. If the source node detects no transmission activity on the network, it waits a brief, random amount of time, and then sends its transmission. If the source does detect activity, it waits a brief period of time before checking the channel again. The destination node receives the transmission and, after verifying its accuracy, issues an acknowledgment (ACK) packet to the source. If the source receives this acknowledgment, it assumes the transmission was properly completed. However, interference or other transmissions on the network could impede this exchange. If, after transmitting a message, the source node fails to receive acknowledgment from the destination node, it assumes its transmission did not arrive properly, and it begins the CSMA/CA process anew.

Compared with CSMA/CD (Carrier Sense Multiple Access with Collision Detection), CSMA/CA minimizes the potential for collisions, but cannot detect the occurrence of a collision and so cannot take steps to recover from the collisions that occur. The use of ACK packets to verify every transmission means that 802.11 networks require more overhead than 802.3 networks. Therefore, a wireless network with a theoretical maximum throughput of 10 Mbps will, in fact, transmit less data per second than a wired Ethernet network with the same theoretical maximum throughput. In reality, most wireless networks tend to achieve between one-third and one-half of their theoretical maximum throughput. For example, 802.11g is rated for a maximum of 54 Mbps, but most 802.11g networks achieve between 20 and 25 Mbps. As described later in this chapter, however, the 802.11n and 802.11ac standards include several techniques for reducing overhead and making the technologies' actual throughput more closely match their theoretical throughput.

Nodes that are physically located far apart from each other on a wireless network present a particular challenge in that they are too far apart to collaborate in preventing collisions. This is called the hidden node problem, where a node is not visible to other nodes on the other side of the coverage area. One way to ensure that packets are not inhibited by other transmissions is to reserve the medium for one station's use. In 802.11, this can be accomplished through the optional RTS/CTS (Request to Send/Clear to Send) protocol. RTS/CTS enables a source node to issue an RTS signal to an access point requesting the exclusive opportunity to transmit. If the access point agrees by responding with a CTS signal, the access point temporarily suspends communication with all stations in its range and waits for the source node to complete its transmission. RTS/CTS is not routinely used by wireless stations, but for transmissions involving large packets (those more subject to damage by interference), RTS/CTS can prove more efficient. On the other hand, using RTS/CTS further decreases the overall efficiency of the 802.11 network. Figure 6-14 illustrates the CSMA/CA process.

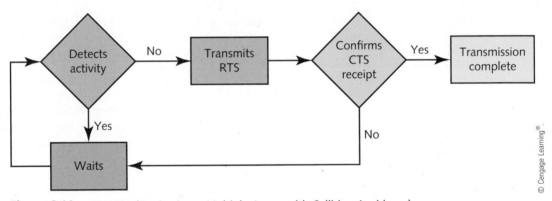

Figure 6-14   CSMA/CA (Carrier Sense Multiple Access with Collision Avoidance)

© Cengage Learning®

Association Suppose you have just purchased a new laptop with a wireless NIC that supports one of the 802.11 wireless standards. When you bring your laptop to a local Internet café and turn it on, your laptop soon prompts you to log on to the café's wireless network to gain access to the Internet through this hot spot. This seemingly simple process, known as association, involves a number of packet exchanges between the café's access point and your computer. Association is another function of the MAC sublayer described in the 802.11 standard.

As long as a station is on and has its wireless protocols running, it periodically surveys its surroundings for evidence of an access point, a task known as scanning. A station can use either active scanning or passive scanning. In active scanning, the computer transmits a special frame, known as a probe, on all available channels within its frequency range. When an access point finds the probe frame, it issues a probe response. This response contains all the information a computer needs to associate with the access point, including a status code and station ID number for that computer. After receiving the probe response, a computer can agree to associate with that access point. The final decision to associate with an access point, at least for the first time, usually requires the consent of the user. Once association is complete, the two nodes begin communicating over the frequency channel specified by the access point.

In passive scanning, a wireless-enabled computer listens on all channels within its frequency range for a special signal, known as a beacon frame, issued from an access point. The beacon frame contains information that a wireless node requires to associate itself with the access point. For example, the frame indicates the network's transmission rate and the SSID (service set identifier), a unique character string used to identify an access point. After detecting a beacon frame, the computer can choose to associate with that access point. The two nodes agree on a frequency channel and begin communicating.

When setting up a WLAN, most network administrators use the access point's configuration utility to assign a unique SSID, rather than the default SSID provided by the manufacturer. The default SSID often contains the name of the manufacturer and perhaps even the model number of the access point, which can give hackers a head start on cracking into the network. Changing the SSID contributes to better security and easier network management, though there are a couple of points to keep in mind. On the one hand, it's important to disguise the nature of the network identified by the SSID to avoid giving hackers more information than necessary. For example, it's probably not a good idea to name the Accounting Department's access point "Acctg." However, you can minimize confusion for employees by using easily recognized—though uncommon—SSIDs. The point of using an uncommon SSID is to increase security on client devices as they travel to other areas, so they don't inadvertently attempt to connect to networks with the same name.

In IEEE terminology, a group of stations that share an access point are said to be part of one BSS (basic service set). The identifier for this group of stations is known as a BSSID (basic service set identifier). Some WLANs are large enough to require multiple access points. A group of access points connected to the same LAN are known collectively as an ESS (extended service set). BSSs that belong to the same ESS share a special identifier, called an ESSID (extended service set identifier). In practice, many networking professionals don't distinguish between the terms *SSID* and *ESSID*. They simply configure every access point in a group or LAN with the same SSID.

Within an ESS, a client can associate with any one of many access points that use the same ESSID. That allows users to roam about an office without losing wireless network service. In fact, roaming is the term applied to a station moving from one BSS to another without losing connectivity.

Figure 6-15 illustrates a network with only one BSS; Figure 6-16 shows a network encompassing multiple BSSs that form an ESS.

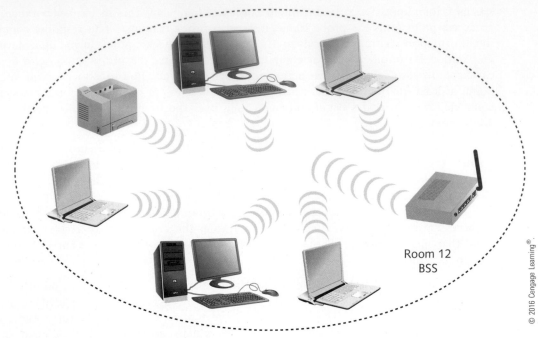

Figure 6-15 A network with a single BSS

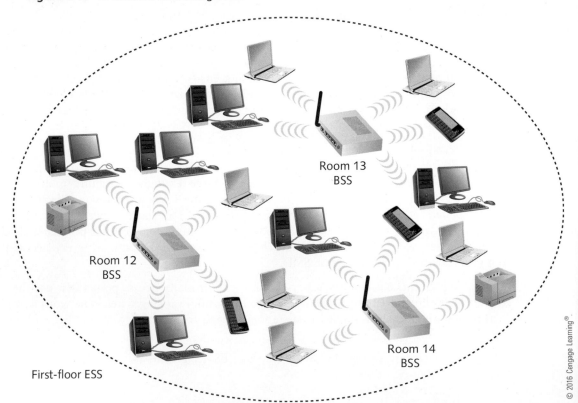

Figure 6-16 A network with multiple BSSs forming an ESS

Clients running Windows 7 or 8.1 or modern versions of Linux or OS X will first attempt to associate with a known access point. For example, suppose the SSID for your access point at home is "SpaceInvader." When you visit a café on the other side of the city, your laptop will recognize that the "SpaceInvader" SSID doesn't exist in that location. Instead, your laptop's operating system will detect the presence of other access points in the area. If the café has an access point, for example, it will offer you the option of associating with that access point.

Suppose the café is in a busy metropolitan area where every business on the block has its own access point. In that case, the operating system (or the NetworkManager program, if you are running Linux) will present you with a list of all access points within range. Further, your client software will prioritize the access point with the strongest signal and the lowest error rate compared with others.

Note that a station does not necessarily prioritize the *closest* access point. For example, suppose another user brings his own access point to the café and his access point has a signal that is twice as strong as the café's access point. In that case, even if the new access point is farther away, your laptop will recognize the other user's access point as the best option. When you are presented with this option, however, you would be wise to not confirm the association. If a client is configured to indiscriminately connect with the access point whose signal is strongest, that client is susceptible to being compromised by a powerful rogue access point. If your system associates with this unauthorized access point, the person controlling that access point could steal your data or gain access to another network that trusts your system. Rogue access points can exist inadvertently, too, as when a user brings his own access point to work or uses software to turn his workstation into an access point.

On a network with several authorized access points in an ESS, however, a station must be able to associate with any access point while maintaining network connectivity. Suppose that when you begin work in the morning at your desk, your laptop associates with an access point located down the hall. Later, you need to give a presentation in the company's main conference room on another floor of your building. Without your intervention, your laptop will choose a different access point as you travel to the conference room (perhaps more than one, depending on the size of your company's building and network).

Connecting to a different access point requires reassociation. Reassociation occurs when a mobile user moves out of one access point's range and into the range of another, as described in the previous example. It might also happen if the initial access point is experiencing a high rate of errors. On a network with multiple access points, network managers can take advantage of the stations' scanning feature to automatically balance transmission loads between those access points.

IEEE 802.11 Frames You have learned about some types of overhead required to manage access to the 802.11 wireless networks—for example, ACKs, probes, and beacons. For each function, the 802.11 standard specifies a frame type at the MAC sublayer. These multiple frame types are divided into three groups—management, control, and data:

- *management frames*—Involved in association and reassociation; examples of this type of frame include probe and beacon frames. (Details of management frames are beyond the scope of this book.)

- *control frames*—Related to medium access and data delivery; examples of this type of frame include ACK and RTS/CTS frames. (Details of control frames are beyond the scope of this book.)

- *data frames*—Responsible for carrying data between stations. An 802.11 data frame is illustrated in Figure 6-17. Compare the 802.11 data frame with the Ethernet data frame also shown in Figure 6-17. As you can see in the figure, the 802.11 data frame carries significant overhead—that is, it includes a large quantity of fields in addition to the data field.

802.11 data frame:

802.3 (Ethernet) frame:

MAC header

Figure 6-17   Basic 802.11 data frame compared with an 802.3 Ethernet frame

The 802.11 data frame's fields are summarized in Table 6-4.

Notice that the 802.11 data frame contains four address fields; by contrast, the 802.3 (Ethernet) frame has only two. The transmitter and receiver addresses refer to the access point or another intermediary device (if used) on the wireless network.

Another unique characteristic of the 802.11 data frame is its Sequence Control field. This field is used to indicate how a large packet is fragmented—that is, how it is subdivided into smaller packets for more reliable delivery. Recall that on wired TCP/IP networks, error checking occurs at the Transport layer of the OSI model and packet fragmentation, if necessary, occurs at the Network layer. However, in 802.11 networks, error checking and packet fragmentation are handled at the MAC sublayer of the Data Link layer. By

Table 6-4   Fields in an 802.11 data frame*

Field	Length	Function
Frame control	2 bytes	Holds information about the protocol in use, the type of frame being transmitted, whether the frame is part of a larger, fragmented packet, whether the frame is one that was reissued after an unverified delivery attempt, what type of security the frame uses, and so on.
Duration	2 bytes	Indicates how long the field's transmission will take so other stations know when the channel will be available again.
Address 1	6 bytes	Source address.
Address 2	6 bytes	Transmitter address.
Address 3	6 bytes	Receiver address.
Sequence control	2 bytes	Indicates how a large packet is fragmented.
Address 4	6 bytes	Destination address.
Data	0–2312 bytes	Includes the data originally sent by the source host, plus headers from higher layers. The Data field is not part of the frame header or trailer—it is said to be encapsulated by the frame.
Frame check sequence	6 bytes	Uses a cyclical code to check for errors in the transmission.

*All the fields before the Data field belong to the frame header, and the field following the Data field is the frame trailer.

© 2016 Cengage Learning®

handling fragmentation at a lower layer, 802.11 makes its transmission—which is less efficient and more error-prone—transparent to higher layers. This means 802.11 nodes are more easily integrated with 802.3 networks and prevent the 802.11 segments of an integrated network from slowing down the 802.3 segments.

Wireless Innovations   Beginning with 802.11n, several innovations have been implemented that contribute to making later 802.11 standards much faster and much more reliable:

- *MIMO (multiple input-multiple output)*—In this innovation, which was first available in 802.11n, multiple antennas on an access point may issue a signal to one or more receivers. There are some multiantenna 802.11g APs available, but these antennas take turns processing the data stream. 802.11n APs, however, simultaneously process data through both antennas, multiplying the amount of data that can be handled at any given time. As you learned earlier, wireless signals propagate in a multipath fashion. Therefore, multiple signals cannot be expected to arrive at the same receiver in concert. To account for this in MIMO, the phases of these signals are adjusted when they reach a receiving station, and the strengths of the multiple signals are summed. To properly adjust phases, MIMO requires stations to update access points with information about their location. In addition to increasing the network's throughput, MIMO can increase an access point's range. Figure 6-18 shows an 802.11n access point with three antennas.

- *MU-MIMO (multiuser MIMO)*—Related to MIMO, MU-MIMO is an even newer technology that allows multiple antennas to service multiple clients simultaneously. This feature will reduce congestion and thereby contribute to faster data transmission. MU-MIMO will become available with Wave 2 802.11ac products.

© Olesky Mark/Shutterstock.com.

Figure 6-18   802.11n access point with three antennas

- *channel bonding*—In 802.11n, two adjacent 20-MHz channels can be combined, or bonded, to make a 40-MHz channel, as shown in Figure 6-19. In fact, bonding two 20-MHz channels more than doubles the bandwidth available in a single 20-MHz channel. That's because the small amount of bandwidth normally reserved as buffers against interference at the top and bottom of the 20-MHz channels can be assigned to carry data instead. Because the 5-GHz band contains more channels and is less crowded (at least, for now), it's better suited to channel bonding than the 2.4-GHz band, which is another factor contributing to 802.11ac's improved performance over 802.11n. The newer 802.11ac standard takes channel bonding to another level by supporting 20-, 40-, and 80-MHz channels, with optional use of 160-MHz channels.

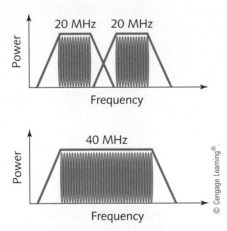

© Cengage Learning®.

Figure 6-19   Channel bonding

- *frame aggregation*—Beginning with 802.11n, networks can use one of two techniques for combining multiple data frames into one larger frame: Aggregated Mac Service Data Unit (A-MSDU) or Aggregated Mac Protocol Data Unit (A-MPDU). Both approaches combine multiple frames to reduce overhead. 802.11ac actually uses A-MPDU for all transmissions by default. To understand how frame aggregation works, suppose three small data frames are combined into one larger frame. Each larger frame will have only one copy of the same addressing information that would appear in the smaller frames. Proportionally, the data field takes up more of the aggregated frame's space. In addition, replacing four small frames with one large frame means an access point and station will have to exchange one-quarter the number of statements to negotiate media access and error control. Maximum frame sizes for both 802.11n and 802.11ac are shown in Table 6-5. Compare these numbers to the maximum 802.11a, b, and g frame size of 4,095 bytes. The potential disadvantage to using larger frames is the increased probability of errors when transmitting larger blocks of data. Figure 6-20 illustrates the lowered overhead accomplished by both A-MSDU and A-MPDU. The advantage of A-MSDU over A-MPDU is that more of the frame's information is combined with other frames transmitted at the same time. The advantage of A-MPDU, however, is that each frame added to the mix retains some of its error checking data, resulting in greater reliability.

Table 6-5 **Maximum frame sizes using frame aggregation**

Wi-Fi standard	A-MSDU	A-MPDU
802.11n	7935 bytes	65,535 bytes
802.11ac	11,454 bytes	4,692,480 bytes

© 2016 Cengage Learning®.

Figure 6-20 A-MSDU and A-MPDU aggregated frames

Note that not all of the techniques listed here are used in every 802.11n or 802.11ac implementation. Further, reaching maximum throughput depends on the number and type of these strategies used. It also depends on whether the network uses the 2.4-GHz (for 802.11n) or the 5-GHz band. Considering these factors, an 802.11n network's actual throughputs vary between 65 Mbps and 500 Mbps, while an 802.11ac Wave 1 network's actual throughputs have been documented, at the time of this writing, as high as 561 Mbps *per client* (with total throughput expected to be somewhere near its theoretical throughput of 1.3 Gbps).

As mentioned earlier, 802.11n and 802.11ac are compatible with all three earlier versions of the 802.11 standard. However, in mixed environments, some of the new standards' techniques for improving throughput will not be possible. To ensure the fastest data rates on your 802.11n LAN, it's optimal to use only 802.11n-compatible devices. However, 802.11ac can be implemented more gradually, with both 802.11n and 802.11ac devices in operation at the same time.

The CompTIA Network+ exam covers two additional, unofficial connection types: 802.11a-ht and 802.11g-ht. Along with the advent of 802.11n, the demand for more efficient wireless networks sparked the development of improvements by some manufacturers to 802.11a (5 GHz) and 802.11g (2.4 GHz) devices. The ht extension stands for *high throughput*, and is accomplished by a variety of adaptations. For example, a DIDO (distributed-input distributed-output) system coordinates transmissions from multiple clients through multiple access points. Basically, the APs talk to each other and work together to get information to and from the client more quickly than either AP working alone could do. Another adaptation is Super G, which increases throughput via several improvements, including channel bonding. Any time you see –ht appended to the standard, you're effectively getting speeds comparable to 802.11n.

Implementing a WLAN

Now that you understand how wireless signals are exchanged, what can hinder them, and which Physical and Data Link layer standards they may follow, you are ready to put these ideas into practice. This section first describes how to design small WLANs, the types you might use at home or in a small office. Then it walks you through installing and configuring access points and clients.

Determining the Design

You have learned that WLANs may be arranged as ad hoc or infrastructure networks. You also know that infrastructure WLANs are far more common. This section assumes your WLAN follows the infrastructure model, and as such, will include access points.

A home or small office network might call for only one access point. In this case, the access point, often combined with switching and routing functions, connects wireless clients to the LAN and acts as their gateway to the Internet. Note that the access point functions independently from the Internet access technology. In other words, configuring your home or small office WLAN follows the same principles no matter whether you connect to the Internet using broadband cable or DSL.

Figure 6-21 illustrates the typical arrangement of a home or small office WLAN. Notice that the access point (or wireless router) is connected to the cable or DSL modem using an RJ-45 cable. The cable is inserted into the access point's WAN port, which is set apart from the other data ports and might be labeled "Internet" or remain unlabeled. The additional ports on the access point allow for wired access to the router, which contains switch hardware inside the device to manage these ports. An access point that does not include routing or switching functions would lack these extra ports and act much like a wireless hub.

Placement of an access point on a WLAN must take into account the typical distances between the access point and its clients. If your small office spans three floors, for instance, and clients are evenly distributed among the floors, you might choose to situate the access point on the second floor. Consider the type and number of obstacles between the access

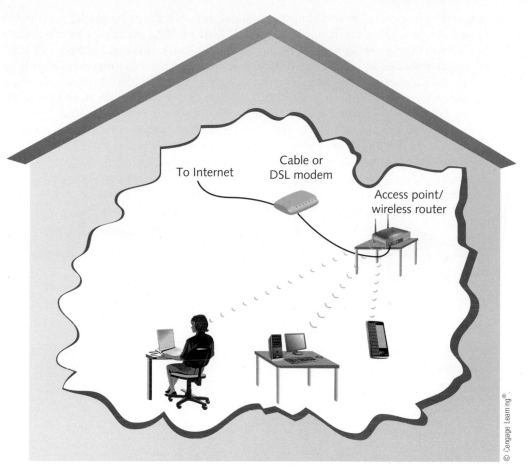

Figure 6-21   Home or small office WLAN arrangement

point and clients, and the distance restrictions for the 802.11 standard your access point is using. For example, if your three-story building is constructed like a bunker with massive concrete floors, you might consider installing a separate access point on each floor. If a building or office space is long and narrow, you might need two access points—one at each end of the building. For best signal coverage, place the access point in a high spot, such as on a shelf or rack or in a drop ceiling. Also, make sure it's not close to potential sources of interference, including cordless phones and microwave ovens.

Larger WLANs warrant a more systematic approach to access point placement. Before placing access points in every data room, it's wise to conduct a site survey. A **site survey** assesses client requirements, facility characteristics, and coverage areas to determine an access point arrangement that will ensure reliable wireless connectivity within a given area.

For example, suppose you are the network manager for a large organization whose wireless clients are distributed over six floors of a building. On two floors, your organization takes up 2000 square feet of office space, but on the other four floors, your offices are limited to only 200 square feet. In addition, clients move between floors regularly, but the lobby-level floor has less wireless traffic than the others. Other building occupants are also running wireless networks. As part of a site survey, you should study building blueprints to help identify potential obstacles and clarify the distances your network needs to span on each floor as well as the anticipated wireless demand from devices that tend to occupy each floor during the course of business. Also consider whether Wi-Fi access points will be used as wireless bridges to create remote wired access to the network, as shown in Figure 6-22. The throughput demands of a wireless bridge can be significantly higher than typical Wi-Fi clients. The site survey will indicate whether certain floors require multiple access points. Visually inspecting the floors will also help determine coverage areas and best access point locations. Measuring the signal coverage and strength from other WLANs will inform your decision about the optimal strength and frequency for your wireless signals.

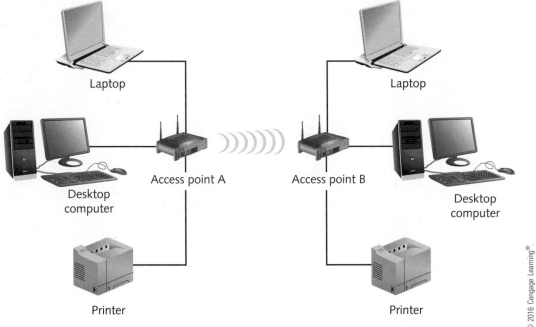

Figure 6-22 A wireless bridge provides remote wired access

© 2016 Cengage Learning®

A site survey also includes testing proposed access point locations. In testing, a "dummy" access point is carried from location to location while a wireless client connects to it and measures its range and throughput. (Some companies sell software specially designed to conduct such testing.) Most important is testing wireless access from the farthest corners of your space. Also, testing will reveal unforeseen obstacles, such as EMI issued from lights or heavy machinery. And don't forget to consider the materials used in objects that aren't always present in the environment, such as stocked inventory in a warehouse.

The site survey can be completed more efficiently with the use of wireless survey tools such as site survey software. Fluke Networks offers AirMagnet, for example, or inSSIDer by MetaGeek is another option. After the initial setup, these programs can continue to be used to monitor WLAN performance and possible interference or intrusion by other wire-less signals in the area. Many of these programs, for example, offer a **heat map** feature that maps Wi-Fi signals and other noise in your location. This is an effective way to iden-tify rogue access points that pose a security threat to the devices for which you're respon-sible. An accurate heat map can also pinpoint gaps in Wi-Fi coverage, called **dead zones**, throughout the building to ensure that employee productivity isn't adversely affected by dropped Wi-Fi connections or unnecessarily slow connections.

After a site survey has identified and verified the optimal quantity and location of access points, you are ready to install them. Recall that to ensure seamless connectivity from one coverage area to another, all access points must belong to the same ESS and share an ESSID. Configuring access points, including assigning ESSIDs, is described in the next section.

Figure 6-23 shows an example of an enterprise-wide WLAN.

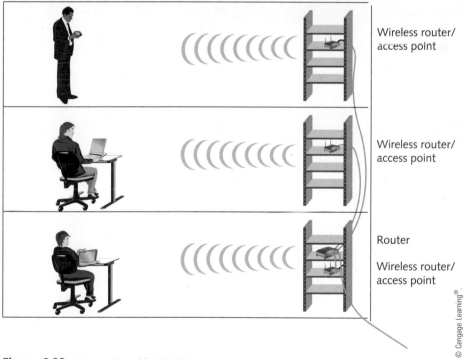

Figure 6-23   Enterprise-wide WLAN

When designing an enterprise-wide WLAN, you must consider how the wireless portions of the LAN will integrate with the wired portions. Access points connect the two. But an access point may perform other functions as well. It may provide security features by, for example, including and excluding certain clients. It may participate in VLANs (virtual local area networks), allowing mobile clients to move from one access point's range to another while belonging to the same virtual LAN. Every wireless client's MAC address can be associated with an access point and each access point can be associated with a port on a switch. When these ports are grouped together in a VLAN, it doesn't matter which access point a client associates with. Because the client stays in the same grouping, it can continue to communicate with the network as if it had remained in one spot. You'll learn more about VLANs in Chapter 10.

Configuring Wireless Connectivity Devices

You have learned that access points provide wireless connectivity for mobile clients on an infra-structure WLAN. Access points vary in which wireless standards they support, antenna strength, and optional features, such as support for voice signals or the latest security measures. You can find a small access point or wireless router suitable for home or small-office use for less than $50. More sophisticated or specialized access points—for example, those designed for rugged outdoor use, as on city streets or at train platforms—cost much more. However, as wireless networking has become commonplace, sophistication in even the least expensive devices has increased.

Each access point comes with an installation program on CD-ROM or DVD, or is available for download from the Internet, that guides you through the setup process. The process for installing such devices is similar no matter the manufacturer or model. The variables you will set during installation include:

- Administrator password
- SSID
- Whether or not DHCP is used; note that most network administrators do not configure their wireless access point as a DHCP server and, in fact, doing so when another DHCP server is already designated will cause addressing problems on the network
- Whether or not the SSID is broadcast
- Security options such as which type, and for each type, what credentials are necessary to associate with the access point

In the Hands-On Projects at the end of this chapter, you will have the chance to install and configure a popular wireless router/access point.

If something goes awry during your wireless router configuration, you can force all of the variables you changed to be reset. Wireless routers feature a reset button on their back panel. To reset the wireless router, first unplug it. Then, using the end of a paper clip, depress the reset button while you plug it in. Continue holding down the button for at least 30 seconds (this time period varies among manufacturers; check your wireless router's documentation for the duration yours requires). At the end of this period, the wireless router's values will be reset to the manufacturer's defaults.

After successfully configuring your access point/wireless router, you are ready to introduce it to the network. In the case of a small office or home WLAN, this means using a patch cable to connect the device's WAN port and your cable or DSL modem's LAN port. Afterward, clients should be able to associate with the access point and gain Internet access. The following section describes how to configure clients to connect to your WLAN.

Configuring Wireless Clients

Wireless access configuration varies from one type of client to another. A gaming or media device will require a slightly different process than a laptop or tablet. The specific steps vary by device type and manufacturer. In general, as long as an access point is broadcasting its

SSID, clients in its vicinity will detect it and offer the user the option to associate with it. If the access point uses encryption, you will need to know the type of encryption and provide the right credentials to associate with it successfully. Later in the chapter, you'll have the chance to change some of the settings on a wireless client.

In an enterprise environment, configuring clients for wireless access to the network can entail a much more involved process called on-boarding. Users or network technicians might need to install a specific program or app onto a user's device, whether the device is a cell phone, laptop, or tablet, in order to give that device trusted access to certain portions of the network. Access to email services, file-sharing services, and certain network administrative features may all be controlled by the device's permission levels enabled by on-boarding that device.

The reverse process of on-boarding, which is called off-boarding, involves removing the programs that gave the device special permissions on the network. For security purposes, network administrators need the ability to do this remotely, in case a device is lost or stolen. For this reason, the programs installed during on-boarding include the ability to perform a remote wipe on a device, which means to clear a device of all important information, permissions, and programs without having physical access to the device. A remote wipe feature may even allow you to completely disable the device and make it unusable for any network access at all.

Network+
2.3
2.7
Applying Concepts
Explore a Linux Wireless Interface

As with Windows operating systems, most Linux and UNIX clients provide a graphical interface for configuring their wireless interfaces. Because each version differs somewhat from the others, describing the steps required for each graphical interface is beyond the scope of this book. However, iwconfig, a command-line utility for viewing and setting wireless interface parameters is common to nearly all versions of Linux and UNIX. Following is a basic primer for using the iwconfig command:

1. Before using iwconfig, make sure your wireless NIC is installed and that your Linux or UNIX workstation is within range of a working access point. You must also be logged in as root or a user with root-equivalent privileges. (The root user on UNIX or Linux systems is comparable to an administrative user on Windows systems.)

2. Open a terminal session (i.e., Command Prompt window), type `iwconfig` at the prompt and press **Enter**. The iwconfig output should look similar to that shown in Figure 6-24. Notice that in this example, "eth0" represents an interface that is not wireless (that is, a wired NIC), while "eth1" represents the wireless interface. The "lo" portion of the output indicates the loopback interface. On your computer, the wireless NIC might have a different designation. Also notice that iwconfig reveals characteristics of your access point's signal, including its frequency, power, and signal and noise levels.

3. For more detailed information, type `man iwconfig` and press **Enter**.

Using the iwconfig command, you can modify the SSID of the access point you choose to associate with, as well as many other variables. Some examples are detailed below. The syntax of the following examples assumes your workstation has labeled your wireless NIC "eth1":

- `iwconfig eth1 essid CLASS_1`—Instructs the wireless interface to associate with an access point whose SSID (or ESSID, as shown in this command) is CLASS_1.

```
% iwconfig

lo        no wireless extensions.


eth0      no wireless extensions.


eth1      IEEE 802.11abgn  ESSID:"CLASS_1"

          Mode:Managed  Frequency:2.412 GHz  Access Point: 00:0F:66:8E:19:89

          Bit Rate:54 Mb/s   Tx-Power:14 dBm

          Retry long limit:7  RTS thr:off   Fragment thr:off

          Power Management:on

          Link Quality=60/70  Signal level=-50 dBm

          Rx invalid nwid:0  Rx invalid crypt:0  Rx invalid frag:0

          Tx excessive retries:0  Invalid misc:747   Missed beacon:0
```

© Cengage Learning®

Figure 6-24 Output from `iwconfig` command

- `iwconfig eth1 mode Managed`—Instructs the wireless interface to operate in infrastructure mode (as opposed to ad hoc mode).

- `iwconfig eth1 channel auto`—Instructs the wireless interface to automatically select the best channel for wireless data exchange.

- `iwconfig eth1 freq 2.422G`—Instructs the wireless interface to communicate on the 2.422-GHz frequency.

- `iwconfig eth1 key 6e225e3931`—Instructs the wireless interface to use the hexadecimal number 6e225e3931 as its key for secure authentication with the access point. (6e225e3931 is only an example; on your network, you will choose your own key.)

In this and the previous section, you have learned how to configure wireless clients and access points. The following section summarizes some key points about securing a wireless network.

802.11 Wireless Network Security

As you have learned, most organizations use one of the 802.11 protocol standards on their WLANs. By default, the 802.11 standard does not offer any security. The client only needs to know the access point's SSID, which many access points broadcast. Network administrators may prevent their access points from broadcasting the SSIDs, making them harder to detect. However, this does not provide true security.

One solution is to authenticate devices before giving them access to the network. **Authentication** is the process of comparing and matching a client's credentials with the credentials in a client database to enable the client to log on to the network. The authentication process can be somewhat strengthened by using **MAC filtering**, or **MAC address filtering**, which prevents the AP from authenticating any device whose MAC address is not listed by the network administrator. (MAC address filtering can also be instituted on a switch instead of an AP.) It can be time consuming, however, to maintain a current list of all approved MAC addresses, and MAC addresses can be impersonated.

Another layer of security is provided by encrypting the data. **Encryption** is the use of an algorithm to scramble data into a format that can be read only by reversing the algorithm—that is by decrypting the data. The purpose of encryption is to keep information private. Many forms of encryption exist, with some being more secure than others. You'll learn more about the processes of authentication and encryption more thoroughly in Chapter 7. Here you'll explore the techniques for securing wireless networks with authentication and encryption.

Network+ 3.3 **Legacy Networking**

WEP (Wired Equivalent Privacy)

For some measure of security, 802.11 allows for optional encryption using the **WEP (Wired Equivalent Privacy)** standard. When configuring WEP, you establish a character string required to associate with the access point, also known as the **network key**. When the client detects the presence of the access point, the user is prompted to provide a network key before the client can gain access to a network via the access point. The network key can be saved as part of the client's wireless connection's properties. WEP uses keys both to authenticate network clients and to encrypt data in transit.

The first implementation of WEP allowed for 64-bit network keys, and current versions of WEP allow for more secure, 128-bit or even 256-bit network keys. Still, WEP's use of the shared key for authenticating all users and for exchanging data makes it more susceptible to discovery than a dynamically generated, random, or single-use key. An exploit in which a hacker uses a program to determine a WEP key is known as a **WEP attack**, or **WEP cracking**. Even 128-bit network keys can be cracked in a matter of minutes. Moreover, because WEP operates in the Physical and Data Link layers of the OSI model, it does not offer end-to-end data transmission security. WEP was replaced with a quick-fix improvement called WPA, which was later improved yet again with WPA2. Both of these standards are discussed next.

Network+ 3.3 ## WPA/WPA2 (Wi-Fi Protected Access)

A significant disadvantage to WEP is that it uses the same network key for all clients and the key is static, which means it won't change without intervention. Due to this inherent insecurity, a replacement security technology was developed, called **WPA (Wi-Fi Protected Access** or **Wireless Protected Access)**, which dynamically assigns every transmission its own key. The encryption protocol used in WPA was replaced by a stronger encryption protocol for the updated version, called **WPA2**, which can be enabled on most consumer-grade APs. WPA2 includes support for the previously released WPA protocol. The most secure Wi-Fi communication is made possible by combining a RADIUS server with WPA or WPA2, known as WPA-Enterprise or WPA2-Enterprise, respectively. You'll learn about RADIUS servers, and encryption protocols used in WPA and WPA2, in Chapter 7.

Network+
3.3
3.6
4.3

Applying Concepts

Check a Router's Compatibility for New Firmware

Now that you understand more about what keeps a wireless network secure, you're ready to explore some of the options that can be enabled on APs. Many establishments—and home-owners, for that matter—create a separate guest network through their Wi-Fi router/access point. This is a smart security precaution, as it gives guests access to Internet service through an open network without opening the doors to the entire LAN on that router. Parents, also, may want to give their children use of an SSID with more limited network access in order to enforce household rules with children who have their own computers or smartphones.

If you do provide a guest network, either at home or at a business, be sure to set up a captive portal page. This is the first page a new client sees in the browser when connecting to the guest network, and usually requires the user to agree to a set of terms and conditions before gaining further access to the guest network.

Users should be informed that they are connected to a network that does not provide user authentication or data encryption, and that data is not secure when transmitted over this connection. Remind users to be careful about what data they provide, even over email, while using the guest network. Also (for your own protection) remind them not to engage in any illegal activity through this network connection, as that activity could be traced back to your IP address.

Some wireless routers are designed for this arrangement and require no special firmware to enable a second (or more) SSID. If necessary, however, you can install DD-WRT on a router to add desired features. DD-WRT is open source, Linux-based firmware that can be installed on routers or access points to expand their capabilities. The functionality available through the firmware is dependent upon the extent of its compatibility with the device on which you install it. In this activity, you check a router's information against the Router Database on the DD-WRT Web site to see which version of the firmware the router can support. Then you check the Database Report to see which of the firmware's features are compatible with your router. This project does *not* include installing the firmware, as the process tends to be very specific to the hardware and other variables, and requires more advanced understanding of installation challenges and troubleshooting skills.

To do this project, you need a SOHO router, such as Linksys, Asus, or Netgear, manufactured for any 802.11 standard through N.

1. Examine the device itself and locate the router's model number. Write this number down for easy reference.

2. Go to DD-WRT's Web site at **dd-wrt.com** and navigate to the **Router Database**. Enter your router's model number to search the database. Note: If at some point you decide to attempt downloading and installing DD-WRT, it is especially important to ensure you're obtaining the download from a reputable source, such as the one mentioned here. Many rogue versions exist that could cause a great deal of damage to your system and data.

3. Some routers require a license to use DD-WRT, in which case you'd have to purchase a license for your router. Some routers are not supported at all, while some are "works in progress." Most routers, however, are supported. If yours is, click the correct router in the list to see which variations are available for your router. Which variations did the database report for your router?

4. Different variations provide different features and require different levels of expertise to administer. Explore the additional information provided in the DD-WRT Wiki links in the *Additional information* section. What are some known issues reported for your router? Are there any warnings listed on the *Build variations* page? (Note: If your router's listing does not provide this kind of information, do a search for a Linksys WRT320N and answer the remaining questions for this router.)

5. Continue browsing through the Build Features table, which you accessed in the previous step through the DD-WRT Wiki link for *Build variations*. Which variations are supported by your router *and* provide each of the following features, respectively? (Hint: You'll need to cross-reference this table back to the database report for your router to make sure you're only listing variations that are compatible with your router. This table may contain variations that were not listed for your router.) As you go, provide a brief description of what functions or options each feature can provide.

    a. Access restrictions

    b. Chillispot

    c. Kaid, Xlink Kai, or some other form of Kaid

    d. OpenVPN

    e. Repeater

    f. Samba/CIFS client

    g. Wake On LAN

    h. Wiviz

Installing the DD-WRT firmware to your router is done through a process called flashing, and is beyond the scope of this book. If you're using an old router that you can afford to risk bricking (which means to ruin the device to the point where it is no longer functional, effectively turning it into a brick), you might want to try it. But be sure to do your research first! The DD-WRT Wiki is chock-full of helpful articles to walk you through the process with your specific router. Once installed, even the most basic DD-WRT variation can provide helpful features such as repeater functionality (greatly expanding the reach of your Wi-Fi network) and access restrictions (increasing the control you have over who can do what on your network).

Security Threats to Wireless Networks

Network+
3.2
3.3
4.3

Wireless transmissions are particularly susceptible to eavesdropping. You already learned about bluejacking and bluesnarfing with Bluetooth connections. Several additional security threats to wireless networks are discussed in the following list:

- *war driving*—A hacker searches for unprotected wireless networks by driving around with a laptop configured to receive and capture wireless data transmissions. (The term is derived from the term *war dialing*, which is a similar tactic involving old, dial-up modems.) War driving is surprisingly effective for obtaining private information. Years ago, the hacker community publicized the vulnerabilities of a well-known store chain, which were discovered while war driving. The retailer used wireless cash registers to help customers make purchases when the regular, wired cash registers were busy. However, the wireless cash registers transmitted purchase information, including credit card numbers and customer names, to network access points in cleartext. By chance, a person in the parking lot who was running a protocol analyzer program on his laptop obtained several credit card numbers in a very short time. The person alerted the retailer to the security risk (rather than exploiting the information he gathered). Needless to say, after the retailer discovered its error, it abandoned the use of wireless cash registers until after a thorough evaluation of its data security.

- *war chalking*—Once hackers discover vulnerable access points, they make this information public by drawing symbols with chalk on the sidewalk or wall within range of an access point. The symbols, patterned after marks that hobos devised to indicate hospitable places for food or rest, indicate the access point's SSID and whether it's secured.

- *evil twin*—A rogue access point can be configured with a legitimate-sounding SSID to pose as an authorized access point. As a network technician, check regularly for evil twins or other rogue access points within your network's geographical area. Especially be on the lookout for access points that show a stronger signal than your corporate AP because Windows lists access points by signal strength and users are accustomed to selecting the access point at the top of the list.

- *WPA attacks*—These attacks, also called WPA cracking, involve an interception of the network keys communicated between stations and access points.

- *WPS attack*—WPS (Wi-Fi Protected Setup) is a user-friendly—but not very secure—security setting available on some consumer-grade APs. Part of the security involves requiring a PIN (personal identification number) in order to access the AP's settings or to associate a new device with the network. The problem is that the PIN can be easily cracked through a brute force attack, which means simply trying numerous possible character combinations to find the correct combination. This gives the attacker access to the network's WPA2 key. The PIN feature in WPS should be disabled if possible.

Network+
3.2
3.3
4.3

Applying Concepts
Examine Wireless Security Settings

Now that you understand some of the security options available for a wireless network connection, you can explore how to check the current settings on your AP and change them if necessary.

Using a Windows 7 or 8.1 computer that is connected to a local network via Wi-Fi, do the following steps:

1. Right-click the Wi-Fi connection icon in the taskbar and click **Open Network and Sharing Center**.

2. Under *View your active networks*, click the Wi-Fi connection, then click **Wireless Properties**.

3. In the Wireless Network Properties dialog box, look for the following information on both the Connection and the Security tabs. You may need to click additional buttons within this dialog box (such as a *Configure* button) to dig for additional details.

   a. What are the network's Name and SSID?

   b. What is the connection's band setting?

   c. What are the network's Security and Encryption types?

6

Troubleshooting Wireless LANs

Network+
2.1
2.7
4.2
4.3
4.6
5.3

In Chapter 5, you learned about several tools used to test copper and fiber-optic cables in Ethernet networks. Cable continuity and performance testers, of course, will tell you nothing about the wireless connections, stations, or access points on a network. For that, you need tools that contain wireless NICs and run wireless protocols. As you learned earlier in the chapter, you can start learning about a wireless environment by viewing the wireless network connection properties on your workstation. However, viewing the status of the wireless connection on your workstation tells you only a little about your wireless environment—and this information only applies to one workstation. To get the full picture of your wireless environment, you need to use more advanced wireless network tools, as described in the following section.

Network+
2.1
4.2
4.3

Wireless Network Tools

Many programs exist that can scan for wireless signals over a certain geographical range and discover all the access points and wireless stations transmitting in the area. This is useful for determining whether an access point is functioning properly, whether it is positioned correctly so that all the stations it serves are within its range, and whether stations and access points are communicating over the proper channels within a frequency band. Here are two types of software you should have in your toolkit:

- *wireless analyzer (also called Wi-Fi analyzer)*—Software that can evaluate Wi-Fi network availability as well as help optimize Wi-Fi signal settings or help identify Wi-Fi security threats. Identifying the wireless channels being used nearby helps you optimize the wireless channel utilization in your vicinity.

- *spectrum analyzer*—A software tool that can assess the quality of the wireless signal. Spectrum analysis is useful, for example, to ascertain where interference is greatest.

Software that can perform wireless network assessment is often available for free and may be provided by the access point's manufacturer. Following is a list of specific capabilities common to wireless network testing tools:

- Identify transmitting access points and stations and the channels over which they are communicating
- Measure signal strength from and determine the range of an access point
- Indicate the effects of attenuation, signal loss, and noise
- Interpret signal strength information to rate potential access point locations
- Ensure proper association and reassociation when moving between access points
- Capture and interpret traffic exchanged between wireless access points and stations
- Measure throughput and assess data transmission errors
- Analyze the characteristics of each channel within a frequency band to indicate the clearest channels

---

Network+
2.1
4.2
4.3

Applying Concepts

Wireless Analyzer on Your Smartphone

You can turn your smartphone into a Wi-Fi analyzer by installing a free or inexpensive app through your phone's app store. These days, these apps are easy to find, easy to use, and provide useful information without much hassle. In this project, you install a Wi-Fi analyzer app on your phone and try it out on your home or school Wi-Fi network. These instructions are specific to an Android smartphone installing the Wifi Analyzer app, but you can adjust the steps to work for other smartphones and different apps.

1. On an Android smartphone, go to the Play Store and search for the app **Wifi Analyzer**. The app used in this specific example was created by farproc, but you can choose a different app if you want to.

2. Install the app and open it. You can look at the Online Help page at this time, or you can wait until later.

3. At the time of this writing, the app is programmed to automatically start scanning for Wi-Fi signals. It provides a live feed of signal strength and channel coverage for the wireless networks in its reach. You can see in Figure 6-25 that three networks were available at the time of the reading, two of which were using overlapping channels. The local network provided the strongest signal.

Wireless networks provide the best performance when the channels being used don't overlap with those used by nearby networks. For this reason, it's best to program the network for channels at the beginning, center, and end of the channel bandwidth. For example, recall that 2.4-GHz-band devices offer up to 14 channels, although most only offer 11 channels, especially in the United States. In the U.S., then, neighboring Wi-Fi networks typically use channels 1, 6, and 11 in order to minimize overlap. (When all 14 channels are available, such as in many parts of Europe, the channel spread might still be 1-6-11, to maximize compatibility with devices from other areas of the world, or it might instead be 1-5-9-13 to maximize use of the available bandwidth.) If your wireless network is programmed for the same channel as your neighbor's wireless network, you'll get better performance if you change your network's channel to part of the channel range not currently in use in your vicinity.

4. What channel is your network programmed to?

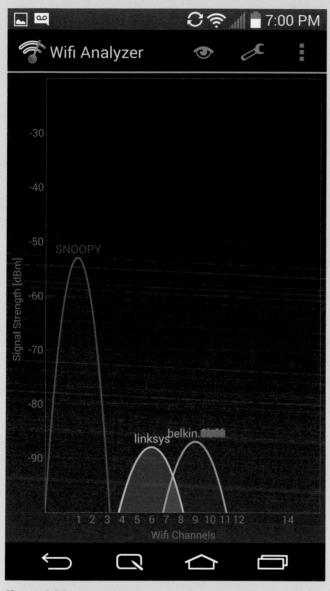

Figure 6-25   This Wifi Analyzer app detected three wireless networks

Source: Wifi Analyzer app for Android

5. The Wifi Analyzer app provides some interesting features, including a signal meter, as shown on the left side of Figure 6-26, and a list of other hosts on the smartphone's LAN, as shown on the right side of Figure 6-26. Notice in the list of LAN neighbors that device MAC addresses and manufacturers are also listed. Take a few minutes to explore your wireless analyzer app's features. What features and information did you find? What changes might you want to make to your Wi-Fi network's settings to increase its performance or security?

Figure 6-26 Readings from the Wifi Analyzer app

Source: Wifi Analyzer app for Android

Avoiding Pitfalls

You might have had the frustrating experience of not being able to log on to a network, even though you were sure you'd typed in your username and password correctly. Maybe it turned out that your Caps Lock key was on, changing your case-sensitive password. Or maybe you were trying to log on to the wrong server. On every type of network, many variables must be accurately set on clients, servers, and connectivity devices in order for communication to succeed. Wireless networks add a few more variables. As a reminder, following are some wireless configuration pitfalls to avoid:

- *SSID mismatch*—Your wireless client must specify the same SSID as the access point it's attempting to associate with. As you have learned, you may instruct clients to search for any available access point (or clients might be configured to do this by default). However, if the access point does not broadcast its SSID, or if your workstation is not configured to look for access points, you will have to enter the SSID during client configuration. Also, bear in mind that SSIDs are case sensitive. That is, *CLASS_1* does not equal *Class_l*. An SSID mismatch will result in failed association.

- *incorrect encryption*—Your wireless client must be configured to (a) use the same type of encryption as your access point, and (b) use a key or passphrase that matches the access point's. If either of these is incorrect, your client cannot authenticate with the access point.

- *incorrect or overlapping channels or frequencies*—You have learned that the access point establishes the channel and frequency over which it will communicate with clients. Clients, then, automatically sense the correct channel and frequency. However, if you have instructed your client to use only a channel or frequency different from the one your access point uses, association will fail to occur. Similarly, using channels or frequencies that are too close to each other on the frequency spectrum can interfere with each other's transmissions.

- *mismatched standards (802.11 b/a/g/n/ac)*—If your access point is set to communicate only via 802.11g, even if the documentation says it supports 802.11b and 802.11g, clients must also follow the 802.11g standard. Clients may also be able to detect and match the correct type of 802.11 standard. However, if they are configured to follow only one standard, they will never find an access point broadcasting via a different standard.

- *incorrect antenna placement*—On a network, many factors can cause data errors and a resulting decrease in performance. Be sure to check the recommended geographic range for your AP, and keep clients well within that distance. If a client is too far from an AP, communication might occur, but data errors become more probable. Also remember to place your antenna in a high spot for best signal reception.

- *interference*—If intermittent and difficult-to-diagnose wireless communication errors occur, interference might be the culprit. Check for sources of EMI, such as fluorescent lights, heavy machinery, cordless phones, and microwaves in the data transmission path.

- *simultaneous wired and wireless connections*—A workstation's NIC is designed to transmit either via a wired or a wireless connection, but not both at the same time. When troubleshooting connection issues, consider whether the computer is making conflicting attempts to communicate with the network through both types of connections. You can resolve the issue by disabling the Wi-Fi adapter or by unplugging the Ethernet cable.

- *problems with firmware updates*—Updates to a NIC or access point's firmware can help patch vulnerabilities and increase functionality. The flip side of this issue, however, is that updates should be tested before being rolled out system-wide.

- *unoptimized access point power levels*—Each access point's power level, or the strength of the signal the access point emits, should be optimized for the geographic area covered by that access point. Power levels that are too low will result in dropped signals as clients roam to the peripheral areas of the AP's range. However, maxed out power levels will result in too much overlap between AP coverage areas, causing clients from other coverage areas to attempt to connect with APs that are farther away but transmitting the stronger signal. Begin with a 50% power setting, and make incremental changes as needed to optimize the amount of overlap between APs. Also keep in mind that even if a client can receive a signal from a high-powered AP installed on the other end of the building, the return signal from the client might not be reliably strong enough to reach the AP, which is called a near-far effect.

- *inappropriate antenna type*—You might think that omnidirectional antennas would nearly always be the best choice when setting up Wi-Fi coverage. The idea is to place the AP in the center of its coverage area, then send the signal out in all directions. However, in many situations, installing unidirectional antennas instead will enhance a signal's availability, directing the signal right where you need it while not wasting a signal in areas where you don't. For example, suppose a company installs an omnidirectional antenna near a factory's 30-foot-high ceiling. Because the antenna's signal is broadcast in all directions from its location, distributing its signal strength in a spherical shape, the best possible signal would only be available to workers who could walk on the ceiling—obviously, that's not a viable situation. To be useful, the signal needs to be directed down to the floor. A unidirectional antenna, in this case, can be positioned and pointed to create a dome-shaped coverage that spreads out as it nears the plant floor, as shown in Figure 6-27.

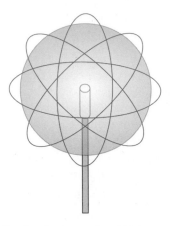
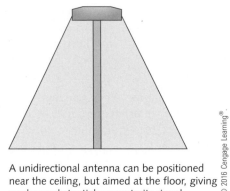

An omnidirectional antenna placed high near a ceiling broadcasts a signal in all directions, but the signal is mostly inaccessible to workers on the floor

A unidirectional antenna can be positioned near the ceiling, but aimed at the floor, giving workers substantial access to its signal

© 2016 Cengage Learning®

Figure 6-27 A unidirectional antenna provides more useful signal coverage in this situation

- *client saturation*—APs vary in the number of device connections they can handle at any given time. A SOHO network's AP might take 10–15 devices before becoming overwhelmed, whereas a high-powered, commercial AP can handle a much larger client load without exceeding its bandwidth saturation limitations. The 802.11ac standard also provides this advantage, in that this newest standard expands available bandwidth while also managing that bandwidth more efficiently to support more clients. Keep in mind, when shopping for a new AP, that the actual, effective capacity in the real world will be significantly less than the AP's advertised capacity.

Network+
2.7
4.3
4.6
5.3

Applying Concepts

Scenario: Snail-Speed Wi-Fi

Your company recently rented new office space across town to make room for expansion in the Accounting Department, and part of your responsibility with the new acquisition was to install three new 802.11n APs. You completed the job just before the weekend, at the same time as the 19 accounting employees finished setting up their file cabinets and reception area furniture. Some of your fellow IT technicians completed workstation setup that same day; most of the workstations are connected to the network via wireless due to restrictions imposed by your company's contract with the property owner. Today, Monday, the accounting personnel reported for work at the new building.

At first, the new location's network seems to be working fine. The local network is communicating well with the home office's network, and everyone has access to all of the files they need on the file servers. As everyone gets settled in for the day and starts their Monday duties, however, the network slows to a snail's pace. It's not long before you start to get complaints about emails being delayed, files not being accessible, and print jobs to network printers getting lost. You make a beeline across town to figure out what's wrong.

During the course of your investigation, you find that all of the hosts on the local network are accessible, although you find it odd that even though your ping tests are usually successful, sometimes they aren't. You know the APs are all new devices, and you double-check their configurations to try to determine a common source for all the problems you've noted. Here's a summary of the results you've gathered:

- All three APs are active and communicating successfully with your laptop.

- All three APs are configured with identical SSIDs and other settings.

- For good measure, you also walk around the office space with your wireless analyzer to confirm that there are no significant dead zones or interference.

Why are wireless transmissions being lost in transit? Below are several possible resolutions. Select the best one and explain your reasoning:

a. One of the APs is faulty and not processing transmissions. It should be removed and replaced.

b. The NICs in the employees' workstations were damaged during the move. Probably several just need to be reseated while some might need to be replaced.

c. The APs should not have the same SSID. Rename each AP so their SSIDs don't match.

d. Three APs are insufficient for the wireless load of the Accounting Department. More APs should be added.

e. The APs are all part of the same LAN and should be separated into separate LANs.

f. The workstation computers are programmed to search for and connect with the wrong SSID, or the network keys are entered wrong. Every workstation's wireless interface settings should be checked.

g. The APs are all programmed to use the same channel. They should be programmed for different channels.

Chapter Summary

Characteristics of Wireless Transmissions

- Most wireless networks, such as Wi-Fi networks, use frequencies around 2.4 GHz or 5 GHz.

- An antenna's radiation pattern describes the relative strength over a three-dimensional area of all the electromagnetic energy the antenna sends or receives.

■ When an obstacle stands in a signal's way, the signal may pass through the object or be absorbed by the object, or it may be subject to any of the following phenomena: reflection, diffraction, or scattering.

■ The extent of interference that a wireless signal experiences depends partly on the density of signals within a geographical area.

■ The 2.4-GHz band offers 11 communications channels that are unlicensed in the United States. The 5-GHz band consists of 24 unlicensed bands, each 20-MHz wide.

■ Personal area networks (PANs) rarely exceed a few meters in geographical width, and usually only contain a few personal devices.

■ Bluetooth technology unites mobile devices with PCs under a single communications standard. Bluetooth operates in the radio band of 2.4 GHz to 2.485 GHz.

■ NFC (near-field communication) is a form of radio communication that transfers data wirelessly over very short distances.

■ Today, the most common use of infrared (IR) is for remote controls. IR requires an unobstructed LOS between the transmitter and the receiver.

Wi-Fi WLAN (Wireless LAN) Architecture

■ Wireless networks might use an ad hoc, infrastructure, or mesh topology. Wireless nodes can roam from one location to another within a certain range of their access point, depending on the wireless access method, the equipment manufacturer, and the office environment.

■ The IEEE 802.11 task groups that have generated notable wireless standards are 802.11b, 802.11a, 802.11g, 802.11n, and 802.11ac. Collectively, these 802.11 standards and their amendments, extensions, and corrections are known as Wi-Fi, for wireless fidelity.

■ Compared with CSMA/CD, CSMA/CA minimizes the potential for collisions, but cannot detect the occurrence of a collision and so cannot take steps to recover from the collisions that occur.

■ As long as a station is on and has its wireless protocols running, it periodically surveys its surroundings for evidence of an access point, a task known as scanning.

■ For each function of an overhead type required to manage access to 802.11 wireless networks, the 802.11 standard specifies a frame type at the MAC sublayer: control, management, and data.

■ Several innovations were implemented with later 802.11 standards that make them much faster and much more reliable, such as MIMO, MU-MIMO, channel bonding, and frame aggregation. Not all of these techniques are used in every 802.11n or 802.11ac network implementation, however.

Implementing a WLAN

■ Placement of an access point on a WLAN must take into account the typical distances between the access point and its clients.

■ Each access point comes with an installation program on CD-ROM or DVD, or is available for download from the Internet, that guides a user through the setup process. This process is similar no matter the manufacturer or model.

- If an access point is broadcasting its SSID, clients in its vicinity will detect it and offer the user the option to associate with it. If the access point uses encryption, the user will need to provide the right credentials to associate with it successfully.

- iwconfig is a command-line function for viewing and setting wireless interface parameters. It is common to nearly all versions of Linux and UNIX.

802.11 Wireless Network Security

- By default, the 802.11 standard does not offer any security. One solution is to authenticate devices before giving them access to the network. Another layer of security is provided by encrypting the data.

- When configuring WEP, you establish a character string required to associate with the access point, also known as the network key.

- WEP was replaced by WPA, which dynamically assigns every transmission its own key. The encryption protocol used in WPA was replaced by a stronger encryption protocol for the updated version, WPA2.

- Many establishments—and homeowners, for that matter—create a separate guest network through their Wi-Fi router/access point.

- Wireless networks are particularly susceptible to eavesdropping and must defend against threats that are different from a wired network's vulnerabilities.

Troubleshooting Wireless LANs

- Many programs exist that can scan for wireless signals over a certain geographical range and discover all the access points and wireless stations transmitting in the area.

- Wireless networks provide the best performance when the channels being used don't overlap with those used by nearby networks.

- On every type of network, many variables must be accurately set on clients, servers, and connectivity devices in order for communication to succeed. Wireless networks add a few more variables.

Key Terms

For definitions of key terms, see the Glossary near the end of the book.

2.4-GHz band	active scanning	brute force attack
5-GHz band	ad hoc WLAN	BSS (basic service set)
802.11a	association	BSSID (basic service set identifier)
802.11ac	authentication	captive portal page
802.11a-ht	base station	channel bonding
802.11b	beacon frame	CSMA/CA (Carrier Sense Multiple Access with Collision Avoidance)
802.11g	bluejacking	
802.11g-ht	bluesnarfing	data frame
802.11n	Bluetooth	DD-WRT
access point (AP)	bounce	dead zone

diffraction

directional antenna

encryption

ESS (extended service set)

ESSID (extended service set identifier)

evil twin

fading

frame aggregation

frequency hopping

goodput

guest network

heat map

hidden node problem

hot spot

infrared (IR)

infrastructure WLAN

ITU (International Telecommunication Union)

iwconfig

LOS (line of sight)

MAC address filtering

MAC filtering

mesh WLAN

MIMO (multiple input-multiple output)

multipath

MU-MIMO (multiuser MIMO)

near-far effect

network key

NFC (near-field communication)

NFC tag

off-boarding

omnidirectional antenna

on-boarding

paired

passive scanning

probe

radiation pattern

range

range extender

reassociation

reflection

remote wipe

roaming

rogue access point

RTS/CTS (Request to Send/Clear to Send)

scanning

scattering

signal-to-noise ratio (SNR or S/N)

site survey

smart tag

spectrum analyzer

speed test site

SSID (service set identifier)

station

unidirectional antenna

war chalking

war driving

WEP (Wired Equivalent Privacy)

WEP attack

WEP cracking

Wi-Fi

Wi-Fi analyzer

wireless

wireless access point (WAP)

wireless analyzer

wireless bridge

wireless gateway

wireless mesh network (WMN)

wireless router

wireless spectrum

WLAN (wireless local area network)

WPA (Wi-Fi Protected Access or Wireless Protected Access)

WPA attack

WPA cracking

WPA2

WPA2-Enterprise

WPA-Enterprise

WPAN (wireless PAN)

WPS (Wi-Fi Protected Setup)

WPS attack

Review Questions

1. What is the lowest layer of the OSI model at which wired and wireless transmissions share the same protocols?

    a. Layer 4

    b. Layer 3

    c. Layer 2

    d. Layer 1

2. Which one of the following wireless transmission types does NOT require a clear LOS to function?

    a. Satellite

    b. Infrared

    c. Wi-Fi

    d. WiMAX

3. Which Bluetooth class has the highest power output?

    a. Class 1

    b. Class 2

    c. Class 3

    d. NFC

4. A hacker takes advantage of a Bluetooth connection to send a virus to a user's phone. What kind of security breach has occurred?

    a. Data breach

    b. Bluejacking

    c. War driving

    d. Bluesnarfing

5. A user swipes her smartphone across a tag on a poster to obtain showtimes for a movie she wants to see later that evening. What wireless technology transmitted the data?

    a. Bluetooth

    b. WiMAX

    c. NFC

    d. Infrared

6. A student has completed his part of a group research paper, and needs to share it with a classmate. He sees the classmate as they're crossing the parking lot between classes. Which WLAN architecture could they use to transfer the file from one laptop to the other?

    a. Ad hoc

    b. Mesh

    c. Star

    d. Infrastructure

7. Which 802.11 standard can be used in both the 2.4-GHz and the 5-GHz bands?

    a. 802.11g

    b. 802.11n

    c. 802.11b

    d. 802.11a

8. Which Carrier Sense technology is used on wireless networks to reduce collisions?

   a. CSMA/CD

   b. 802.3

   c. 802.11

   d. CSMA/CA

9. You've just completed a survey of the wireless signals traversing the airspace in your employer's vicinity, and you've found an unauthorized AP with a very strong signal near the middle of the 100-acre campus. What kind of threat do you need to report to your boss?

   a. Rogue access point

   b. War driving

   c. Bluesnarfing

   d. Hidden node

10. You just settled in for some study time at the local coffee shop, and you pause long enough to connect your computer to the Wi-Fi so you can listen to some music while you study. As you're about to sign in, you realize you clicked on an SSID called "Free Coffee and Internet." What kind of security trap did you almost fall for?

    a. Guest network

    b. Bluejacking

    c. Evil twin

    d. Brute force attack

11. To exchange information, two antennas must be tuned to the same _____.

12. Which kind of antenna is used in a point-to-point link?

13. When a wireless signal encounters a large obstacle, what happens to the signal?

14. Signals traveling through areas in which many wireless communications systems are in use will exhibit a lower _____ because of the high proportion of noise.

15. Which frequency band offers 24 unlicensed communications channels in the United States?

16. Why do wireless networks experience such a great reduction in actual throughput compared with their respective theoretical throughputs?

17. 802.11ac provides an advantage over 802.11n by incorporating increased channel bonding capabilities. What size channels does 802.11ac support?

18. What feature of a site survey maps the Wi-Fi signals and other noise in your location?

19. An employee has lost his company-provided phone during a business trip. What process ensures that he can now perform a remote wipe?

20. You're setting up a home network for your neighbor, who is a music teacher. She has students visiting her home regularly for lessons and wants to provide Internet access for their parents while they're waiting on the children. However, she's concerned about keeping her own data private. What wireless feature can you set up on her AP to meet her requests?

Hands-On Projects

Project 6-1: Configure a Wireless Router

In this project, you set up and configure a wireless access point/router. Configuration steps on various SOHO wireless connectivity devices differ, but they involve a similar process and require you to modify the same variables.

This project assumes that the router is brand new or that it has been reset so any previous configuration has been erased. (To reset the router manually, use the end of a paper clip or pen to press and hold the reset button on the back of the router for 10 seconds.) In addition, this project assumes you are working on a Windows 7 or 8.1 workstation logged on as a user with administrative privileges. The computer must have a wireless NIC (a USB wireless NIC can be installed if the computer does not have an onboard wireless NIC). Also, the project requires the installation CD that ships with the router.

1. From the installation CD, run the setup program on one of your computers on the network (it doesn't matter which one). Follow the instructions on the setup screen or in the accompanying user's manual to use network cables to physically connect the computer to the router, plug in the router, and turn it on either before or after you run the setup CD. A computer can connect directly to a network (Ethernet) port on the router (see Figure 6-28), or you can connect through a switch to the router.

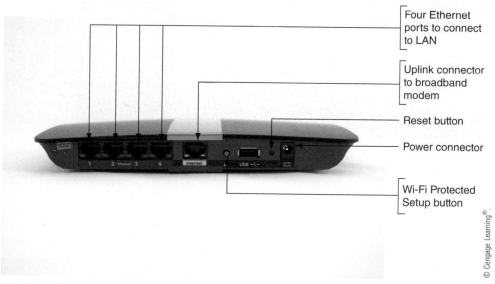

Four Ethernet ports to connect to LAN

Uplink connector to broadband modem

Reset button

Power connector

Wi-Fi Protected Setup button

© Cengage Learning®

Figure 6-28 Connectors and ports on the back of a Cisco home or small office router

2. Connect to the router any other computers on the network that require a wired connection.

3. Firmware on the router (which can be flashed for updates) contains a configuration program that you can access using a Web browser from anywhere on the network. In your browser address box, enter the IP address of the router (for many routers, that address is 192.168.1.1) and press **Enter**. What is the name and IP address for your router?

4. You'll probably be required to sign in to the router firmware utility using a default password. After you sign in, reset the password so that others cannot change your router setup. Write down your new router password and store it in a safe place.

5. The main Setup window appears, as shown in Figure 6-29. For most situations, the default settings on this and other screens should work without any changes. The setup program will take you through the process of configuring the router. After you've configured the router, you might have to turn your cable or DSL modem off and then turn it back on so that it correctly syncs up with the router. What basic steps did the setup program have you follow to configure the router?

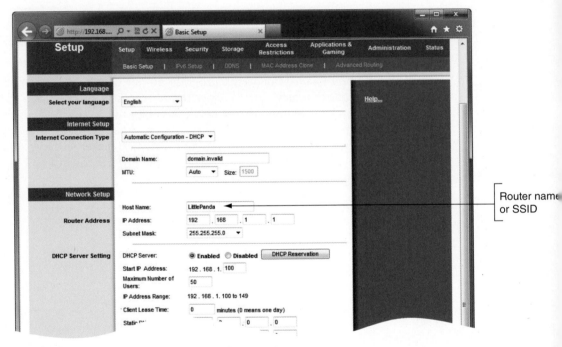

Figure 6-29 Basic Setup screen used to configure a Cisco router

Source: Cisco Systems, Inc.

6. Spend some time examining the various features of your router. What is the public IP address of the router on the ISP network? Why is it necessary for the router to have two IP addresses?

Project 6-2: Modify Router Settings for Wireless Connections

HANDS-ON PROJECTS

Now that you have installed your new wireless access point/router, you modify its configuration through the administrator interface. This project picks up where Project 6-1 left off and requires the same Windows 7 or 8.1 computer connected to one of the router's data ports with a Cat 5 or better patch cable.

1. Log on to your router's administrative interface with the same IP address and password you used in Project 6-1.

2. Access the wireless settings page. Review the settings that appear on this page, including the SSID you assigned in Project 6-1. Which 802.11 standards will this router use to communicate with wireless clients? Which channel is selected by default? Why do you think this channel was selected, and how do you think you can change it? Is the SSID set to broadcast or not? What would happen if you disabled the broadcast? Would clients still be able to communicate with it?

3. Which network mode is your router set to use? Under what circumstances might you want to limit the standards this router supports?

4. Disconnect the patch cable between your computer and the router.

5. Click the **Network** icon in your taskbar. Windows displays a list of wireless networks that are broadcasting availability. List all the networks that are available.

6. Select the name of your wireless network. If you are comfortable with automatically connecting to this network in the future, check **Connect automatically** and then click **Connect**. If you are attempting to connect to a secured network, Windows will prompt you for the security key.

7. After connecting, open a browser and navigate to **speedtest.net** or a similar speed test Web site. Run a speed test to determine your connection's download and upload speeds, respectively. What are your test results?

Project 6-3: Optimize Wireless Security on an AP

Properly securing a wireless access point is not the kind of chore that most home users think to do. Some IT students have actually created businesses securing home networks for their neighbors, friends, and family. In this project, you see which AP settings you should check to increase a home wireless network's security. These steps are specific to a Linksys router, but can easily be adapted for other consumer-grade AP brands.

1. On your (or a friend's) home network, sign in to the router's configuration console. If no factory settings have been changed yet, you can use the default access credentials provided by the manufacturer.

2. As you make changes, be sure to write down access information for the network owner. Give them instructions on where to keep this information safe, such as locked up in a safe or stored at a separate location.

3. On the Wireless tab, change the wireless configuration to Manual. Change the Network Name (SSID) to a name that is unique and completely unrelated to the brand or type of router being used or to the names of the residents.

4. Whether the SSID is broadcast or not is a personal preference. It's more convenient to broadcast the SSID and does not seriously affect the network's security. You can leave the default setting at Enabled or change to Disabled. Click **Save Settings**.

5. Check the Security Mode on the Wireless Security tab. If the **WPA Auto** option is available, this will provide the highest security level while still accommodating older devices.

If it's not available, select WPA2. Encryption type should be AES unless older devices are in use, in which case you'll have to resort to the *TKIP or AES* setting. These protocols are discussed in Chapter 7.

6. Change the Passphrase to a nondictionary code that includes both letters and numbers, and at least 10 digits. The more digits, the more secure the passphrase. A long passphrase is more secure than a completely random passphrase, so consider using a line from a favorite song with a couple of numbers thrown in. Click **Save Settings**.

7. On the Administration tab, set the Router Password to a phrase that, again, includes both letters and numbers, the longer the better. Also disable Remote Management. Click **Save Settings**.

8. Go to each device that is used regularly on the network and force each device to "forget" the network so the previous settings will be removed from each device. Reconnect each device to the network with the new settings.

Project 6-4: Research Tomato Router Firmware

In the chapter, you learned about the open source firmware DD-WRT. Another alternative router firmware is Tomato. Spend some time researching Tomato and answer the following questions:

1. What is the latest version of Tomato?

2. What features does Tomato provide?

3. List 10 routers that are known to be compatible with Tomato.

4. Explain the process for flashing Tomato to a router.

Case Projects

Case Project 6-1: Configure TCP/IP in Ubuntu Server

In this project, you learn to configure TCP/IP in Ubuntu Server. Ubuntu stores TCP/IP configuration settings in the /etc/network/interfaces text file. These settings are persistent, which means they are used each time a NIC reconnects to the network. To use autoconfiguration and dynamic IP addressing for eth0, the first NIC interface, you should see these two lines in the interfaces file:

```
auto eth0
iface eth0 inet dhcp
```

To use autoconfiguration and static IP addressing for eth0, here are sample entries you might find in the interfaces file:

```
auto eth0
iface eth0 inet static
    address 10.0.0.10
    netmask 255.255.255.0
```

```
gateway 10.0.0.1
dns-nameservers 10.0.0.200 10.0.0.210
```

You can temporarily change TCP/IP settings by using the `ifconfig`, `route`, `nameserver`, and other commands and by editing the /etc/resolv.conf text file. Using the VM you created in Chapter 3, Case Project 3-1, that has Ubuntu Server installed, follow the steps in the table to examine TCP/IP settings and temporarily change these settings.

1. Start the VM and log on to Ubuntu Server.

2. To view the current TCP/IP settings for the network adapter, use this command:

   `ifconfig eth0`

3. Write down the IP address, MTU, network mask, and MAC address for eth0.

4. To go to the /etc directory, use this command:

   `cd /etc`

5. Ubuntu temporarily stores the IP addresses of name servers in the /etc/resolv.conf file. Use the following `cat` command to view the contents of this file:

   `cat resolv.conf`

6. Write down the IP addresses of the current DNS name server(s).

7. To go to the /etc/network directory, use this command:

   `cd network`

8. Use the following `cat` command to view the contents of the /etc/network/interfaces file:

   `cat interfaces`

9. Use the `route` command to view the IP address of your current default gateway:

   `route -n`

10. Recall that 8.8.8.8 is the IP address of one of Google's public DNS servers. Use `ping` to verify you have Internet connectivity (to stop the ping, press CTRL+C):

    `ping 8.8.8.8`

11. Now let's make some temporary changes to the TCP/IP configuration. Change your IP address to 10.0.0.100 and your network mask to 255.255.255.0, using the following command:

    `sudo ifconfig eth0 10.0.0.100 netmask 255.255.255.0`

12. Most likely you no longer have Internet connectivity. To verify that is the case, use this command:

    `ping 8.8.8.8`

13. Use the following `ifdown` command to release the current TCP/IP settings for eth0:

    `sudo ifdown eth0`

14. Use the following `ifup` command to renew the network interface using the persistent TCP/IP settings for eth0:

    `sudo ifup eth0`

15. Verify Internet connectivity is restored:

    ```
    ping 8.8.8.8
    ```

16. Verify DNS works:

    ```
    ping google.com
    ```

17. Power down your Ubuntu Server VM:

    ```
    sudo poweroff
    ```

CASE PROJECTS

Case Project 6-2: Establish a Wireless Network Baseline

One of the first pieces of information you'll want to have handy when trouble-shooting wireless issues is a baseline with which to compare current conditions at the time of the problem. Free software like NetStress can help you gather this kind of information while your network is working well.

You'll need two Windows 7 or 8.1 computers on the same LAN to complete this project. Both computers need to be connected wirelessly to the LAN. You'll also need an Ethernet patch cable to create a wired connection for one computer.

1. Go to **nutsaboutnets.com** and look for the free NetStress download. Download and install the NetStress program on two different computers that are connected to the same LAN. One computer will function as the transmitter computer, and the other will function as the receiver.

2. Open the NetStress program on both computers. In the Select Network Interface (local host) box, click on your wireless interface and click **OK**. If you get any Windows Security Alerts, click **Allow access** to allow access through your firewall.

3. On the Transmitter computer, click the blinking **Remote Receiver IP** button at the top of the window. In the Select Remote Receiver window, type the IP address of the Receiver computer into the white IP address field and click **OK**.

4. In the menu bar, click **Start**.

5. Allow the test to run for a couple of minutes, then click **Stop** in the menu bar.

6. Using Snipping Tool, which is included as part of Windows, take a screenshot of the results of your test on the Receiver computer. Be sure to get results for both the Time-course (Total) tab and the Timecourse (TCP) tab. Remember to save your screenshots in a place where you can find them easily in a few minutes.

7. Connect one of the computers to the router/AP with an Ethernet cable and rerun the test for a couple of minutes again. Take a screenshot of these results as well, then answer the following questions:

    a. What were your results when both computers were using wireless interfaces?

    b. What were your results when one computer was using a wired interface?

    c. How can you explain the differences?

## chapter 7

Cloud Computing and Remote Access

After reading this chapter and completing the exercises, you will be able to:

- Identify the features and benefits of cloud computing

- Explain methods for remotely connecting to a network

- Discuss VPNs (virtual private networks) and the protocols they rely on

- Understand methods of encryption, such as IPsec, SSL/TLS, SFTP, and SSH, that can secure data in storage and in transit

- Describe how user authentication protocols such as RADIUS, TACACS+, EAP, and Kerberos function

- Recognize symptoms of connectivity and security problems commonly encountered with remote connections

On the Job

My company provided a full networking kit so I could work from my home office through a virtual private network (a virtual connection between a client and a remote network). Everything worked well for over a year, until a newly hired coworker came to my location for on-the-job training.

I had wired my laptop and printer to two of the four available switched ports on my home router, which also offered wireless access. The coworker's laptop had built-in wireless, so we turned it on, tested it (perfect!), and both went to work. The problems began almost immediately.

The first problem we noticed was that our previously smooth-running applications began to pause for random lengths of time, and then resume. As we became busier, the pauses became freezes and timeouts. Work became impossible. The training session switched to network troubleshooting.

Whenever a previously functioning network becomes unreliable, even from apparently trivial changes like adding a new host, my initial troubleshooting approach is to return to the previous configuration. I switched off the new laptop's wireless radio (the transmitter and receiver portion of the NIC), and everything returned to normal. With the radio on, the intermittent problems returned.

I quickly ruled out obvious potential conflicts, such as a duplicate IP address. I switched the second laptop to a wired connection. No improvement. The router's error log showed no errors.

My suspicions now turned to the VPN. With a single VPN session, or no VPN sessions, simultaneous access to random sites on the Internet worked perfectly. The second VPN session triggered the problems. I contacted the IT Department head, who agreed we had encountered a router limitation. Namely, its NAT (Network Address Translation) capabilities were not sophisticated enough to maintain the proper status and state of two simultaneous VPN sessions.

Any VPN-capable router can support a single worker in a home office. A second (or subsequent) VPN session can only be reliably established if the router has been designed to support it. We solved the problem by replacing the router with a model from a different manufacturer.

David Butcher
Client Services Director

The IT industry innovates quickly, and has excelled at developing less-expensive, more-efficient long-distance solutions for a world on the go. Whether you're bringing the world's services into the corporate office, or making enterprise resources readily available to telecommuters and remote offices, the issues of security and reliability for these connections stand at the forefront.

In this chapter, you will learn about the growing fields of cloud computing and remote access, IT innovations that touch nearly every industry. You'll also investigate the protocols, standards, and techniques for securing data in transit and for authenticating that clients are who they say they are.

Cloud Computing

On network diagrams, the Internet is frequently depicted as a cloud. More recently, the cloud concept in networking has taken on new meanings, thanks in large part to the marketing efforts of network service providers. Cloud computing, also called Web services, refers to the flexible provision of data storage, applications, or services to multiple clients over a network. You might already be familiar with cloud storage services such as Dropbox, OneDrive, and Google Drive. The term includes a broad range of offerings, from hosting Web sites and database servers, or delivering specialized applications, to providing virtual servers for collaboration or software development. However, all cloud computing offers the following:

- *on-demand service available to the user at any time*—Services, applications, and storage in a cloud are available to users at any time, upon the user's request. For example, if you subscribe to Google's Gmail or Google Docs services, you can log on and access your mail and documents whenever you choose.

- *elastic services and storage*—Services and storage capacity can be quickly and dynamically—sometimes even automatically—scaled up or down. In other words, they are elastic. The elasticity of cloud computing means that storage space can be reduced, and that applications and clients can be added or removed, upon demand. For example, if your database server on the cloud needs additional hard disk space, you can upgrade your subscription to expand it yourself, without your having to alert the service provider. To make things even more convenient, a cloud-based server can be configured to require no intervention in this situation. The amount of space you can add and the flexibility with which it can be added depend on your agreement with the service provider.

- *support for multiple platforms*—Clients of all types, including smartphones, laptops, desktops, thin clients, and tablet computers, can access services, applications, and storage in a cloud, no matter what operating system they run or where they are located, as long as they have a network connection.

- *resource pooling and consolidation*—In the cloud, as on host computers that contain multiple virtual machines, resources such as disk space, applications, and services are consolidated. That means a single cloud computing provider can host hundreds of Web sites for hundreds of different customers on just a few servers. This is an example of a multi-tenant model, in which multiple customers share storage locations or services without knowing it. In another example of resource pooling, a single backup program might ensure that the Web sites are backed up several times a day.

- *metered service*—Everything offered by a cloud computing provider, including applications, desktops, storage, and other services, is measured. A provider might limit or charge by the amount of bandwidth, processing power, storage space, or client connections available to customers.

An organization that develops software might choose to keep its test platform on virtual servers in the cloud, rather than on servers in its computer room. Suppose it employs dozens of developers on one project, and these developers, half of them working from home, are located in six different countries. By contracting with a cloud services organization to host its servers, the software company can ensure continuous, easy access for its developers, no matter where they are or what type of computer they use. Developers can load any kind of software on the servers and test it from afar. If more hard disk space is needed, it can be dynamically allocated, which means the disk space set aside for the software can be increased automatically as the need arises and then freed up again for other developers. In addition, the cloud services provider can make sure the development servers are secure and regularly backed up. In this case, cloud computing removes from the company's IT personnel the burden of managing the servers. Figure 7-1 illustrates this type of cloud computing.

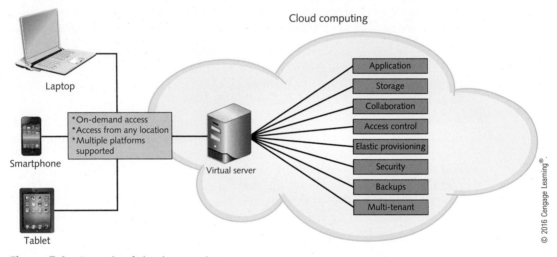

Figure 7-1   Example of cloud computing

© 2016 Cengage Learning®

The characteristics of cloud computing resemble those associated with virtualization, which you'll explore in more depth in Chapter 10. In fact, most cloud service providers use virtualization software to supply multiple platforms to multiple users. For example, industry leaders Rackspace (in its Private, Public, or Managed Cloud products) and Amazon (in its Elastic Compute Cloud, or EC2, service) use Xen virtualization software by Citrix to create virtual environments for their customers.

Cloud Computing Categories

Cloud computing service models are categorized by the types of services they provide. NIST has developed a standard definition for each category, which varies by the division of labor implemented. For example, as shown in Figure 7-2, an organization is traditionally responsible for their entire network, top to bottom. In this arrangement, the organization has its own network infrastructure devices, manages its own network services and data storage, and purchases licenses for its own applications. The other three cloud computing service models illustrated in Figure 7-2 incrementally increase the amount of management responsibilities outsourced to cloud computing vendors. The following list describes these service models:

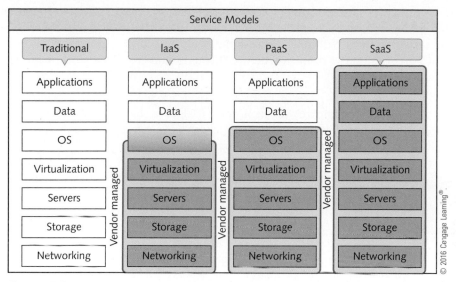

Figure 7-2 At each progressive level, the vendor takes over more computing responsibility for the organization

- *IaaS (Infrastructure as a Service)*—Hardware services are provided virtually, including network infrastructure devices such as virtual servers. IaaS can even provide hosted virtual desktops (HVD), which are desktop operating environments hosted virtually on a different physical computer from the one the user interacts with. These devices rely on the network infrastructure at the vendor's site, but customers are responsible for their own application installations, data management and backup, and possibly operating systems. For example, customers might use the vendor's servers to store data, host Web sites, and provide email, DNS, or DHCP services, but could provide their own NOS licenses and productivity software, such as customer tracking, sales management, and an office suite.

- *PaaS (Platform as a Service)*—Developers often require access to multiple platforms during the development process. A platform in this context includes the operating system, the runtime libraries or modules the OS provides to applications, and the hardware on which the OS runs. Rather than purchasing and maintaining a separate device for each platform, another option is to subscribe to PaaS services. Developers can build and test their applications within these virtual, online environments, which are tailored to the specific needs of the project. At times, other platforms might also need to be integrated into an existing network infrastructure to provide specific functions, such as managing a database. Alternatively, an organization's entire network might be built on platform services provided by a vendor. Any platform managed by a vendor resides on the vendor's hardware and relies on their uptime and accessibility to meet performance parameters. However, the customers are responsible for their own applications and data.

- *SaaS (Software as a Service)*—Applications are provided through an online user interface and are compatible with a multitude of devices and operating systems. Online email services, such as Gmail and Yahoo!, are good examples of SaaS. Google offers an entire suite of virtual software applications through Google Drive and their other embedded products. Except for the interface itself (the device and whatever browser software is required to access the Web site), the vendor provides every level of support from network infrastructure through data storage and application implementation.

- *XaaS (Anything as a Service or Everything as a Service)*—In this broader model, the "X" represents an unknown, just as it does in algebra. Here, the cloud can provide any combination of functions depending on a client's exact needs, including, for example, monitoring, storage, applications, and virtual desktops.

Another SaaS implementation that doesn't quite fit the official definition of SaaS is rentable software, or software by subscription. Many companies are moving toward this subscription model, such as Adobe and Microsoft. When you buy an annual subscription to Office 365, for example, you must still install the software on your own computer, which means you must provide your own hardware, including a functioning OS. However, the downloadable software is available in formats that are compatible with multiple OSs, and the license provides for installation on multiple devices. This particular SaaS does include built-in data storage, if desired by the user, by connecting the licensed account with OneDrive, a virtual data storage service.

Deployment Models

Cloud services may be managed and delivered by any of a variety of deployment models, depending on who manages the cloud and who has access to it. The main deployment models you are likely to encounter are:

- *public cloud*—Service provided over public transmission lines, such as the Internet. Most of the examples discussed in this part of the chapter take place in public clouds.

- *private cloud*—Service established on an organization's own servers in its own data center, or established virtually for a single organization's private use. If hosted internally, this arrangement allows an organization to use existing hardware and connectivity, potentially saving money. If hosted virtually, the organization benefits from the usual advantages of virtual services, such as scalability and accessibility.

- *community cloud*—Service shared between multiple organizations, but not available publicly. Organizations with common interests, such as regulatory requirements, performance requirements, or data access might share resources in this way. For example, a medical database might be made accessible to all hospitals in a geographic area. In that case, the community cloud could be hosted internally by one or more of the organizations involved, or hosted by a third-party provider.

- *hybrid cloud*—A combination of the other service models into a single deployment, or a collection of services connected within the cloud. In the real world, the hybrid cloud infrastructure is a common result of transitory solutions. (In IT, *solution* refers to a product, service, or combination of products and services, and often includes extra features such as ongoing customer service.) An example of a hybrid cloud by design might arise when a company stores data in a private cloud, but uses a public cloud email service.

Cloud computing provides an increasing array of customization and service options, but one of the primary concerns when using cloud computing is the security and reliability of access to those services. Through the rest of the chapter, you'll learn how remote access works and what processes and protocols are in place to keep remote communications secure.

Remote Access

As a remote user, you can connect to a network via remote access, a service that allows a client to connect with and log on to a server, LAN, or WAN in a different geographical location. After connecting, a remote client can access files, applications, and other shared resources, such as printers, like any other client on the server, LAN, or WAN. To communicate via remote access, the client and host need a transmission path plus the appropriate software to complete the connection and exchange data.

Several types of remote access methods exist:

- Point-to-point remote access over a dedicated (usually leased) line, such as DSL or T-1 access to an ISP.

- A virtual private network (VPN), which is a virtual connection between a client and a remote network, two remote networks, or two remote hosts over the Internet or other types of networks, to remotely provide network resources.

- Remote terminal emulation, also called remote virtual computing, which allows a remote client to take over and command a host computer. Examples of terminal emulation software are Telnet, SSH, Remote Desktop, and Virtual Network Computing (VNC).

Regardless of the hardware used or the security implemented, all types of remote access techniques connecting to a network require some type of remote access server (RAS) to accept a remote connection and grant it privileges to the network's resources. Also, software must be installed on both the remote client and the remote access server to negotiate and maintain the connection.

There are two types of remote access servers:

- *dedicated devices*—Devices such as Cisco's AS5800 access servers run software that, in conjunction with their operating system, performs authentication for clients. An ISP might use a dedicated device to authenticate client computers or home routers to access the ISP resources and the Internet. See Figure 7-3.

- *software running on a server*—The remote access service might run under a network operating system to allow remote logon to a corporate network. For example, DirectAccess is a service embedded in Windows Server 2008 R2, 2012, and 2012 R2 that can automatically authenticate remote users and computers to the Windows domain and its corporate network resources. See Figure 7-4. Windows 7 and Windows 8.1 running on the remote client computer support DirectAccess.

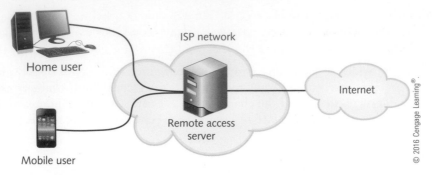

Figure 7-3 An ISP uses a remote access server to authenticate subscribers to its services, including access to the Internet

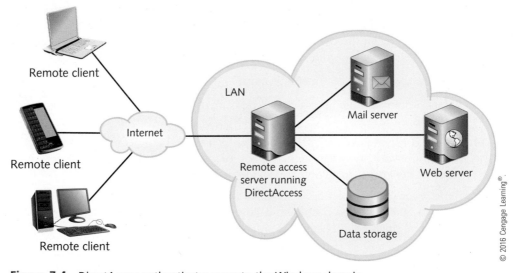

Figure 7-4 DirectAccess authenticates users to the Windows domain

Network+ 1.2

Legacy Networking

RAS (Remote Access Service) in Windows

The CompTIA Network+ exam expects you to know about the legacy software, RAS (Remote Access Service), which was used for dial-up connections made by client computers running Windows 95, 98, NT, and 2000 to connect to a remote network. The remote access server receiving the dial-up connection to the network ran Windows NT or Windows 2000. Beginning with Windows 2000, RAS was replaced by Routing and Remote Access Service (RRAS), which is discussed later in the chapter.

Note that *RAS* can refer to Microsoft's proprietary *Remote Access Service*, or it can refer to the more generic term *remote access server*.

Point-to-Point Remote Access Protocols

To establish sessions between them and exchange data, remote access servers and clients require special protocols. Three you need to be aware of are SLIP, PPP, and PPPoE.

SLIP (Serial Line Internet Protocol) and PPP (Point-to-Point Protocol) are Data Link layer protocols that were originally designed to connect WAN endpoints in a direct connection, such as when a client computer connects to a server at an ISP using a dial-up or DSL connection and modem. Because they directly connect two computers, they are sometimes called point-to-point or end-to-end protocols.

SLIP is an earlier protocol that does not support encryption, can carry only IP packets, and works strictly on serial connections such as dial-up or DSL. SLIP has been replaced by PPP as the preferred communications protocol for remote access communications.

PPP headers and trailers used to create a PPP frame to encapsulate Network layer packets total only 8 or 10 bytes, the difference depending on the size of the FCS field (recall from Chapter 4 that the FCS field ensures the data is received intact). Here's what PPP can do:

- As a connection protocol, PPP can negotiate and establish a connection between the two computers.

- PPP can use an authentication protocol, such as PAP or CHAP (discussed later in the chapter) to authenticate a client to the remote system.

- PPP can support several types of Network layer protocols that might use the connection.

- PPP can encrypt the transmissions, although PPP encryption is considered weak by today's standards.

NETWORK+ EXAM TIP

When PPP is used over an Ethernet network (no matter what the connection type), it is known as PPPoE (PPP over Ethernet). PPPoE, for example, might be used to connect a computer to a modem by way of an Ethernet network adapter and patch cable.

When implementing a VPN, PPP is sometimes used as the Data Link layer protocol. In this next section, you'll learn about VPNs and how they work.

VPNs (Virtual Private Networks)

VPNs are virtual networks that are logically defined for secure communication over public transmission systems. For example, a national insurance provider could use VPNs on the Internet to serve its agent offices across the country with secure access to its databases at the national headquarters. By relying on the public transmission networks already in place, VPNs reduce the expense of having to lease private point-to-point connections between each office and the national headquarters.

To ensure a VPN can carry all types of data in a private manner over any kind of connection, special VPN protocols encapsulate higher-layer protocols in a process known as tunneling. Recall in Chapter 2 you learned that IPv6 hosts can tunnel through an IPv4 network and vice versa. The same process is used by VPN protocols to create a virtual connection, or **tunnel**, between two VPN endpoints.

Based on the kinds of endpoints they connect, VPNs can be classified according to two models:

- *site-to-site VPN*—Tunnels connect multiple sites on a WAN, as shown in Figure 7-5. At each site, a **VPN gateway** on the edge of the LAN establishes the secure connection. Each gateway is a router or remote access server with VPN software installed and encrypts and encapsulates data to exchange over the tunnel. Meanwhile, clients, servers, and other hosts on the protected LANs communicate through the VPN gateways as if they were on the same, private network and do not have to run special VPN software.

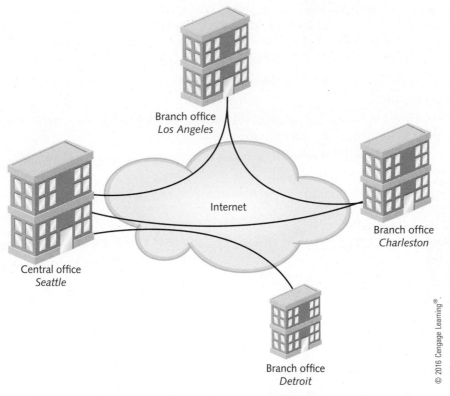

Figure 7-5   A VPN gateway connects each site to one or more other sites

- *client-to-site VPN*, *also called host-to-site VPN or remote-access VPN*—Remote clients, servers, and other hosts establish tunnels with a private network using a VPN gateway at the edge of the LAN, as shown in Figure 7-6. Each remote client on a client-to-site VPN must run VPN software to connect to a VPN gateway and a tunnel is created between them to encrypt and encapsulate data. This is the type of VPN typically associated with remote access. As with site-to-site VPNs, clients and hosts on the protected LAN communicate with the remote clients by way of the VPN gateway and are not required to run VPN software.

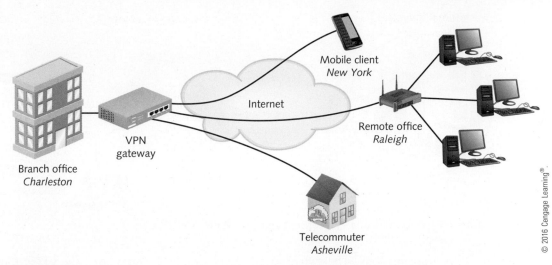

Figure 7-6 A client connects to the LAN through the VPN gateway

The CompTIA Network+ exam covers one more VPN model, the host-to-host VPN. In this scenario, two computers create a VPN tunnel directly between them. Both computers must have the appropriate software installed, and they don't serve as a gateway to other hosts on their respective networks.

The software or hardware required to establish VPNs is usually inexpensive, and in some cases is included in the OS or hardware. Here are some examples:

- *software embedded in the OS*—RRAS (Routing and Remote Access Service) is Microsoft's remote access server software and VPN solution, first available with the Windows Server 2003 NOS, and in desktops, first available with Windows XP. RRAS can implement a VPN and enables a computer to accept multiple remote client connections over any type of transmission path. The software manages data encryption and can route incoming packets to destinations on the local network. Beginning with Windows Server 2008 R2 and Windows 7 (Enterprise or Ultimate), RRAS now works in conjunction with DirectAccess to enable always-on remote connections while also allowing VPN connections to the network.

- *third-party solutions*—Third-party software companies also provide VPN programs that work with Windows, UNIX, Linux, and Macintosh OS X Server network operating systems. For example, OpenVPN is open source and so is available on a variety of platforms. OpenVPN requires more effort to set up than software embedded in the OS, but it is extremely adaptable and generally more secure than other options.

- *implemented by routers or firewalls*—Many routers and firewalls have embedded VPN solutions. This is the most common implementation of VPNs on UNIX-based networks, as opposed to the server-based VPNs that Windows networks so often use.

For large organizations where more than a few simultaneous VPN connections must be maintained, a specialized device known as a VPN concentrator, such as the Cisco VPN Concentrator 3030, can be used as the VPN server, as shown in Figure 7-7. A VPN concentrator authenticates VPN clients, establishes tunnels for VPN connections, and manages encryption

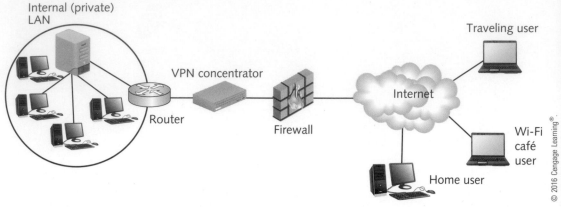

Figure 7-7 Placement of a VPN concentrator on a WAN

for VPN transmissions. The two primary encryption techniques used by VPNs today are IPsec and SSL. Most VPN concentrators support either standard. Because the VPN concentrator performs encryption, it is also known as an encryption device.

An enterprise-wide VPN can include elements of both the client-to-site and site-to-site models. The beauty of VPNs is that they can be tailored to a customer's distance, user, and bandwidth needs, so, of course, every one is unique. However, all share the characteristics of privacy achieved over public transmission facilities using encapsulation. In addition, encryption can be used to increase the security of the transmissions.

VPN Tunneling Protocols

To understand how a VPN tunnel works, imagine a truck containing such valuable and private cargo that it must remain totally untouched while in transit over public roads. The truck is completely wrapped in shrink-wrap, piggybacked on the bed of another truck, and carried over the public road system to its destination. At its destination, the shrink-wrap is removed and the precious cargo is unloaded. Similarly, with VPN tunneling protocols, complete frames are encrypted, encapsulated, and transported inside normal IP packets and Data Link layer frames. In other words, a frame travels across the network as the payload inside another frame.

Most VPN tunneling protocols operate at the Data Link layer to encapsulate the VPN frame into a Network layer packet, no matter what Network layer protocol is used. PPP is normally the Data Link layer protocol used by the tunneling protocol for the VPN frame (see Figure 7-8).

Two VPN tunneling protocols discussed next are PPTP and L2TP.

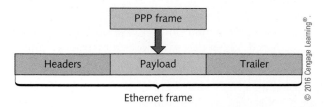

Figure 7-8 The VPN frame is encapsulated inside the Network layer packet

Legacy Networking
PPTP (Point-to-Point Tunneling Protocol)

PPTP (Point-to-Point Tunneling Protocol) is a Layer 2 protocol developed by Microsoft that encapsulates PPP data frames so that the frame can traverse the Internet masked as an IP transmission. It uses TCP segments at the Transport layer. PPTP supports the encryption, authentication, and access services provided by RRAS. Users can either directly contact an RRAS access server that's part of the VPN, or they can access their ISP's remote access server first, then connect to a VPN.

The CompTIA Network+ exam might also refer to the Point-to-Point Tunneling Protocol with the acronym PTP (Point to Point). In general usage, you'll more likely see PTP refer to the point-to-point network topology (such as the point-to-point remote access discussed earlier in this chapter), or to Precision Time Protocol, a protocol that syncs clocks on a network.

GRE (Generic Routing Encapsulation) After PPTP establishes the VPN tunnel, GRE (Generic Routing Encapsulation), developed by Cisco, is used to transmit PPP data frames through the tunnel. GRE encapsulates PPP frames to make them take on the temporary identity of IP packets at Layer 3. To the WAN, messages look like inconsequential IP traffic—the private information is masked inside a new layer of IP headers. But the points at each end of the tunnel only see the original protocols that were safely wrapped inside the GRE frame. Encapsulating alone does not provide security, though, so GRE is used in conjunction with IPsec, an encryption protocol, to increase the security of the transmissions. Figure 7-9 shows the general form of a GRE packet as implemented by Microsoft.

Data Link header	IP header	GRE header	PPP header	PPP payload	Data Link trailer

© 2016 Cengage Learning®.

Figure 7-9 The GRE protocol encapsulates a PPP frame, which in turn is encapsulated in an IP packet

Windows, UNIX, Linux, and Mac OS clients are all capable of connecting to a VPN using PPTP. PPTP is easy to install, and is available at no extra cost with Microsoft networking services. However, it is no longer considered secure, and Microsoft now recommends using L2TP (discussed next) in combination with IPsec (an encryption protocol), or SSTP instead.

SSTP (Secure Socket Tunneling Protocol) is a proprietary Microsoft protocol, first available with Windows Vista, though it is also available for Linux and some other operating systems (but not Apple products).

L2TP (Layer 2 Tunneling Protocol) L2TP (Layer 2 Tunneling Protocol) is a VPN tunneling protocol based on technology developed by Cisco and standardized by the IETF (Internet Engineering Task Force), which is an organization of volunteers who help develop Internet standards. L2TP encapsulates PPP data in a similar manner to PPTP, but differs in a few key ways. Unlike PPTP, L2TP is a standard accepted and used by multiple vendors, so it can connect a VPN that uses a mix of equipment types—for example, a Juniper router, a Cisco router, and a NETGEAR router. Also, L2TP can connect two routers, a router and a remote access server, or a client and a remote access server.

Terminal Emulation or Remote Virtual Computing

Remote virtual computing, also called terminal emulation, allows a user on one computer, called the client, to control another computer, called the host or server, across a network connection. Examples of command-line software that can provide remote virtual computing include Telnet and SSH, and some GUI-based software examples are Remote Desktop for Windows, join.me, VNC, and TeamViewer. A host may allow clients a variety of privileges, from merely viewing the screen to running programs and modifying data files on the host's hard disk. For example, a traveling salesperson can use her laptop to "remote in" to her desktop computer at corporate headquarters so she can remotely update a workbook stored on her desktop computer using Excel installed on her desktop. After connecting, if the remote user has sufficient privileges, she can send keystrokes and mouse clicks to the host and receive screen output in return. In other words, to the remote user, it appears as if she is working on the LAN- or WAN-connected host.

Network+
1.2   **Applying Concepts**

Use Remote Virtual Computing Software

Several vendors provide a variety of inexpensive or free remote virtual computing services. In this project, you will install join.me on a host computer, and share the host's desktop with a client computer.

1. On the host computer, open a Web browser and navigate to **join.me**. Click **start meeting** to begin the download. Access the Downloads folder and double click the **join.me** executable file. If you get a security warning requesting permission to run the application, click **Run**. The application will download and will automatically initiate a sharing session. If you see a features advertisement, close the ad box.

2. Look for the mini toolbar at the top of your screen and locate the nine-digit number. On the client computer, open a Web browser and navigate to **join.me**. Type the nine-digit number in the *join meeting* field and press **Enter** on your keyboard to access the meeting.

3. Take a few minutes to explore the features available on the client computer's portal. How can you open a chat? How can you request control of the mouse?

4. Now explore the features available on the host computer's portal. How can you share mouse control? What special features are only available with a Pro subscription?

5. To end the meeting, click **Meeting tools** on the host computer and click **Exit this meeting**. Close the Web browsers on both computers.

Encryption Techniques, Protocols, and Utilities

Network+
1.2
1.3
1.12
3.2
3.3
5.9
5.10

Cloud computing and remote access both require encryption techniques to protect data in transit. In addition, encryption can also protect stored data. Encryption is the use of a mathematical code, called a cipher, to scramble data into a format that can be read only by reversing the cipher—that is, by deciphering, or decrypting, the data. The purpose of encryption is to keep information private. Many forms of encryption exist, with some being more secure than others. Even as new forms of encryption are developed, new ways of cracking their codes emerge, too.

Encryption is the last means of defense against data theft. In other words, if an intruder has bypassed all other methods of access, including physical security (for instance, he has broken into the data center) and network design security (for instance, he has defied a firewall's packet-filtering techniques or removed encapsulated frames from VPN transmissions), data may still be safe if it is encrypted. To protect data, encryption provides the following assurances:

- *confidentiality*—Data can only be viewed by its intended recipient or at its intended destination.

- *integrity*—Data was not modified after the sender transmitted it and before the receiver picked it up.

- *availability*—Data is available and accessible to the intended recipient when needed, meaning the sender is accountable for successful delivery of the data.

Together, these three tenets form the standard security model called the CIA (confidentiality, integrity, and availability) triad. Other security principles above and beyond the fundamental CIA triad include the following, among others:

- *utility* (similar to availability)—Data arrives in a format that is useful to the receiver.

- *authenticity* (similar to integrity)—Data received is the data that was issued by the stated sender and not forged.

- *non-repudiation* (similar to confidentiality and authenticity)—Provides proof of delivery (protects the sender) and proof of the sender's identity (protects the receiver).

NOTE

Even if data is encrypted in transit, at some point data is accessed, stored, or otherwise manipulated in its unencrypted form, and this is when vulnerability is greatest. Security experts call this endpoint security vulnerability because data is exposed in its unencrypted form at an endpoint of use, such as when a password is entered on a user's smartphone. For example, suppose a user has taken all precautions to create a long, complex password for his online bank account. The bank's Web site stores his account access information in an encrypted, hash-protected database. However, if the user then writes his password on a sticky note and hides it under his keyboard on his desk, his highly secured bank account is still extremely vulnerable to thieves.

The following sections describe data encryption techniques used to protect data stored on or traveling across networks.

Key Encryption

The most popular kind of encryption encodes the original data's bits using a key, or a random string of characters—sometimes several times in different sequences—to generate a unique data block. The key is created according to a specific algorithm, which is a set of rules that tell a computer how to accomplish a particular task. The scrambled data block is known as ciphertext. The longer the key, the less easily the ciphertext can be decrypted by an unauthorized system. For example, a 128-bit key allows for 2^{128} possible character combinations, whereas a 16-bit key only allows for 2^{16} possible character combinations. Hackers may attempt to crack, or discover, a key by using a brute force attack. Recall from Chapter 6 that a brute force attack simply means trying numerous possible character combinations to find the correct combination. Typically, a hacker runs a program to carry out the attack. Through a brute force attack, a hacker could discover a 16-bit key quickly and without using sophisticated computers, but would have difficulty discovering a 128-bit key. 128-bit keys are considered the minimum standard for security today, although this is expected to be insufficient within a few years.

Adding 1 bit to an encryption key makes it twice (2^1 times) as hard to crack. For example, a 129-bit key would be twice as hard to crack as a 128-bit key. Similarly, a 130-bit key would be four (2^2) times harder to crack as a 128-bit key.

Private Key Encryption Key encryption can be separated into two categories: private key and public key encryption. In private key encryption, data is encrypted using a single key that only the sender and the receiver know. Private key encryption is also known as symmetric encryption because the same key is used during both the encryption and decryption of the data.

Suppose Leon wants to send a secret message to Mia via private encryption, as shown in Figure 7-10. Assume he has chosen a private key. Follow the steps below as they correlate to the blue, circled numbers in the figure:

1. Leon must share his private key with Mia.

2. Leon runs a program that encrypts his message with his private key.

3. Leon sends Mia the encrypted message.

4. After Mia receives Leon's encrypted message, she runs a program that uses Leon's private key to decrypt the message. The result is that Mia can read the original message Leon wrote.

Public Key Encryption A potential problem with private key encryption is that the sender must somehow share his key with the recipient. For example, Leon could call Mia and tell her his key, or he could send it to her in an email message. But neither of these methods is very secure. To overcome this vulnerability, a method of associating publicly available keys with private keys was developed. This method is called public key encryption.

In public key encryption, data is encrypted using two keys: One is a key known only to a user (that is, a private key), and the other is a public key associated with the user. A user's public key can be obtained the old-fashioned way—by asking that user—or it can be

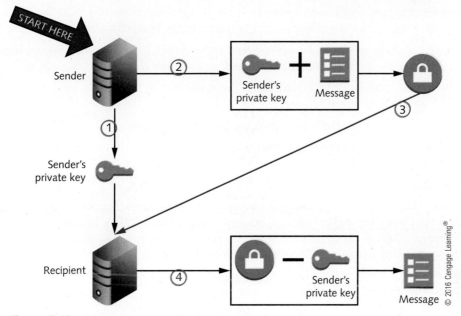

Figure 7-10 Private key encryption begins with the sender

obtained from a third-party source, such as a public key server. A **public key server** is a publicly accessible host (such as a server on the Internet) that freely provides a list of users' public keys, much as a telephone book provides a list of peoples' phone numbers. Figure 7-11 illustrates the process of public key encryption.

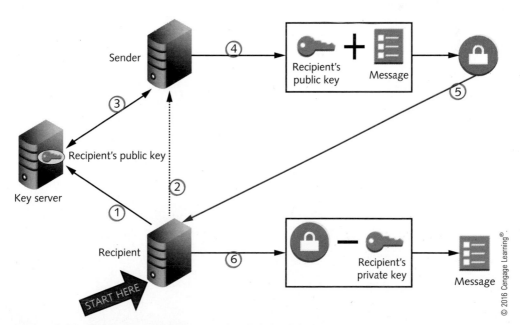

Figure 7-11 Public key encryption begins with the recipient

For example, suppose that Leon wants to use public key encryption to send Mia a message via the Internet. Follow the steps below as they correlate to the blue, circled numbers in the figure:

1. Mia has already established a private key and a public key. She stores her public key on a key server on the Internet, and keeps her private key to herself.

2. Before Leon can send Mia a message, he must know her public key. Mia tells Leon where he can find her public key.

3. Leon retrieves Mia's public key from the public key server.

4. Leon writes Mia a message and then uses his encryption software to scramble his message with Mia's public key.

5. Leon sends his encrypted message to Mia over the Internet.

6. When Mia receives the message, her software recognizes that the message has been encrypted with her public key. In other words, the public key has an association with the private key. A message that has been encrypted with Mia's public key can only be decrypted with her private key. The program then prompts Mia for her private key to decrypt the message.

To respond to Leon in a publicly encrypted message, Mia must obtain Leon's public key. Then, the steps illustrated in Figure 7-11 are repeated, with Mia and Leon's roles reversed.

The combination of a public key and a private key is known as a **key pair**. In the private key encryption example discussed previously, Mia has a key pair, but only she knows her private key, whereas the public key is available to people, like Leon, who want to send her encrypted messages. Because public key encryption requires the use of two different keys, one to encrypt and the other to decrypt, it is also known as **asymmetric encryption**.

With the abundance of private and public keys, not to mention the number of places where each may be kept, users need easier key management. One answer to this problem is to use digital certificates. A person or a business, called the user, can request a **digital certificate**, which is a small file containing verified identification information about the user and the user's public key. The digital certificate is issued and maintained by an organization called a **certificate authority (CA)**. The CA attaches its own digital signature to the digital certificate to validate the certificate. The use of certificate authorities to associate public keys with certain users is known as **PKI (Public-key Infrastructure)**.

The process of requesting and receiving a digital certificate is shown in Figure 7-12 and described below:

1. The user sends a digital certificate request to the CA with the user's identification information, and both a public and private key. The CA might offer to generate these keys for the user, but many users prefer to create their own.

2. The CA verifies the user's identification information.

3. The CA builds the digital certificate file, which contains the user's identification information, the user's public key, and the CA's information and digital signature. Then the CA issues the digital certificate to the user.

4. The user installs the digital certificate on a Web server, for example, or in email client software.

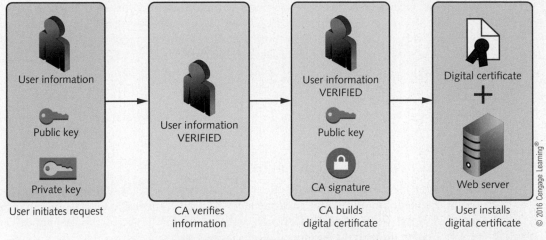

Figure 7-12   It's important to obtain digital certificates only from trusted CAs

Digital certificates are primarily used to certify and secure Web sites where financial and other sensitive information is exchanged, but they're also used for other types of Web sites and for email clients, domain controllers, and smart cards. For digital certificates to do their job, customers, visitors, and other users must have a way to verify the legitimacy of the digital certificate, as shown in Figure 7-13 and described below:

1. The visitor's browser checks the CA's information and digital signature in the digital certificate against its list of trusted CAs and their digital signatures.

2. If that checks out, the browser generates a random, symmetric key and encrypts it using the public key of the Web server.

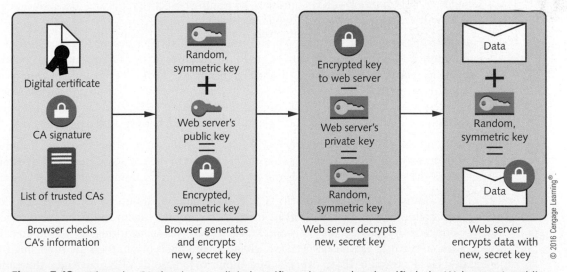

Figure 7-13   When the CA that issues a digital certificate is trusted and verified, the Web server's public key can be trusted

3. The browser then sends the encrypted, symmetric key to the Web server where the Web server decrypts the symmetric key using its private key. This new key is symmetric, meaning that it will be used for both encrypting and decrypting messages. It's also secret because it was encrypted before being transmitted.

4. The Web server and browser both then go on to use that symmetric key for the remainder of the session.

The following sections detail specific techniques of encrypting data as it is transmitted over a network.

IPsec (Internet Protocol Security)

IPsec (Internet Protocol Security) is an encryption protocol that defines the rules for encryption, authentication, and key management for TCP/IP transmissions. It is an enhancement to IPv4 and is native to IPv6. IPsec works at the Network layer of the OSI model and adds security information to the header of all IP packets and transforms the data packets.

IPsec creates secure connections in five steps, as follows:

1. *IPsec initiation*—Noteworthy traffic, as defined by a security policy, triggers the initiation of the IPsec encryption process.

2. *key management*—The term key management refers to the way in which two nodes agree on common parameters for the keys they will use. This phase primarily includes two services:

   ○ *IKE (Internet Key Exchange)*—Negotiates the exchange of keys, including authentication of the keys

   ○ *ISAKMP (Internet Security Association and Key Management Protocol)*—Works within the IKE process to establish policies for managing the keys

3. *security negotiations*—IKE continues to establish security parameters and associations that will serve to protect data while in transit.

4. *data transfer*—After parameters and encryption techniques are agreed on, a secure channel is created, which can be used for secure transmissions until the channel is broken. Data is encrypted and then transmitted. Either AH (authentication header) encryption or ESP (Encapsulating Security Payload) encryption may be used. Both types of encryption provide authentication of the IP packet's data payload through public key techniques. In addition, ESP encrypts the entire IP packet for added security.

5. *termination*—IPsec requires regular reestablishment of a connection to minimize the opportunity for interference. The connection can be renegotiated and reestablished before the current session times out in order to maintain communication.

IPsec can be used with any type of TCP/IP transmission. In transport mode, for example, IPsec can connect two hosts. However, it most commonly runs in tunnel mode on routers or other connectivity devices in the context of VPNs. When working as a VPN encryption technique, IPsec first establishes a secure channel with encryption, then the tunneling protocol (usually L2TP, though IPsec can be used alone to create a VPN) provides the tunnel for encapsulation.

SSL (Secure Sockets Layer) and TLS (Transport Layer Security)

SSL (Secure Sockets Layer) and TLS (Transport Layer Security) are both methods of encrypting TCP/IP transmissions—including Web pages and data entered into Web forms—en route between the client and server using public key encryption technology. The two protocols can work side by side and are widely known as SSL/TLS or TLS/SSL. All browsers today (for example, Google Chrome, Firefox, and Internet Explorer) support SSL/TLS to create secure transmissions of HTTP sessions.

SSL was originally developed by Netscape and operates in the Application layer. Since that time, the IETF has standardized SSL in the similar TLS protocol. TLS operates in the Transport layer and uses slightly different encryption algorithms than SSL, but otherwise is essentially the updated version of SSL. When you see one or the other referred to, it's likely that both TLS and SSL are enabled because they are usually implemented together, giving the client multiple options depending on the server's capabilities (because many servers are not yet TLS-compatible).

As you recall from Chapter 1, HTTP uses TCP port 80, whereas HTTPS (HTTP Secure) uses SSL/TLS encryption and TCP port 443, rather than port 80. Each time a client and server establish an SSL/TLS connection, they establish a unique SSL session, or an association between the client and server that is defined by an agreement on a specific set of encryption techniques. An SSL session allows the client and server to continue to exchange data securely as long as the client is still connected to the server. An SSL session is created by the SSL handshake protocol, one of several protocols within SSL, and perhaps the most significant. As its name implies, the handshake protocol allows the client and server to introduce themselves to each other and establishes terms for how they will securely exchange data.

This handshake conversation is similar to the TCP three-way handshake discussed in earlier chapters. Given the scenario of a browser accessing a secure Web site, the SSL/TLS handshake works as follows:

1. The browser, representing the client computer in this scenario, sends a client_hello message to the Web server, which contains information about what level of security the browser is capable of accepting and what type of encryption the browser can decipher. The client_hello message also establishes a randomly generated number that uniquely identifies the client and another number that identifies the SSL session.

2. The server responds with a server_hello message that confirms the information it received from the browser and agrees to certain terms of encryption based on the options supplied by the browser. Depending on the Web server's preferred encryption method, the server may choose to issue to the browser a public key or a digital certificate.

3. If the server requests a certificate from the browser, the browser sends it. Any data the browser sends to the server is encrypted using the server's public key. Session keys used only for this one session are also established.

After the browser and server have agreed on the terms of encryption, the secure channel is in place and they begin exchanging data.

A variant of TLS is TTLS (Tunneled Transport Layer Security), which provides authentication like SSL/TLS, but does not require a certificate for each user. Instead, TTLS authenticates the server end of the connection by certificate, and users are authenticated by password only or some other legacy method. The password is transmitted through the tunnel established on the credentials of the server's certificate. TTLS was developed for the purpose of supporting legacy authentication mechanisms, and works in tandem with EAP, discussed later in this chapter.

Transmissions over secure connections, such as when using HTTPS Web sites, might be intercepted but cannot be read. For example, suppose you are using unsecured Wi-Fi at a coffee shop and log on to Facebook from your laptop browser. Without SSL, TLS, and TTLS protecting your logon information, anyone lounging nearby can hack in to, read, and steal your unencrypted wireless transmissions.

Some online activities, however, such as online banking, should never be performed on unsecure Wi-Fi hot spots. Despite the security provided by these encryption techniques, other steps of the process can break down. One example might include browsing an insecure portion of a Web site (HTTP) for part of the browsing session, which provides a brief opportunity for your browser to be hijacked by a hacker and sent to what looks like the official logon page, but really is not.

Applying Concepts

Internet Explorer Security

You can change the settings in Internet Explorer to make sure you're using the latest version of SSL in addition to TLS options.

1. Open Internet Explorer and click the **Tools** icon. Click **Internet options**.

2. On the Advanced tab, scroll down to the Security section. Which SSL/TLS options are currently enabled?

3. If necessary, select **Use SSL 3.0**, **Use TLS 1.0**, **Use TLS 1.1**, and **Use TLS 1.2**. (In some browsers, SSL 2.0 is not compatible with TLS.) If you're using an unsecured wireless network like at a coffee shop or a restaurant, also select **Warn if changing between secure and not secure mode** so you'll be notified when interacting with an unsecured Web site. Click **OK**.

Note that some browsers will prevent navigation to unsecured Web sites when the warning option is checked as instructed above. This is a good thing if you're using a questionable network. But if you have trouble navigating to unsecured sites, you'll need to go back and uncheck this option in Internet options.

When visiting secure Web sites, it's important to notice if you have a secure connection with a trusted Web site before entering personal information on that site. Internet Explorer, for example, shows a padlock icon when the site's certificate has been identified and confirmed.

4. In Internet Explorer, navigate to **paypal.com**. What is the exact address shown in the address box after the page loads in the browser?

5. Use the mouse pointer to point to the padlock icon. What CA verified the legitimacy of the Web site?

6. Click the padlock icon. What additional information is provided about the Web site?

SSL VPN

Recall that a VPN provides encapsulation whereas an encryption protocol provides encryption. To maximize security, a VPN uses IPsec or SSL/TLS for encryption. For example, OpenVPN and SSTP use TLS for encryption, whereas PPTP and L2TP use IPsec for encryption. When encryption is used with a VPN, the encryption protocol (IPsec or TLS) creates a secure channel and uses it to encrypt VPN frames. Although PPP can also encrypt transmissions, recall it's no longer considered a secure encryption technique and should not be used. PPP encryption happens inside the VPN frame, whereas IPsec and TLS happen outside the VPN frame.

To understand the distinction between a VPN and encryption, remember the analogy of a shrink-wrapped truck piggybacked on another truck. In the analogy, the VPN is the piggyback encapsulation (a frame inside another frame), and the encryption is the shrink-wrap (all or part of the inside frame is encrypted and cannot be read).

With these concepts in mind, you're ready to understand what an SSL VPN is. An SSL VPN is a VPN that is configured to support SSL transmissions to and from services running on its protected network. An SSL VPN is typically created and supported by software running on a VPN concentrator such as the Cisco 3030 VPN Concentrator.

Suppose, for example, a radiologist is awakened in the middle of the night and asked to read an MRI graphics report for an emergency patient. She sits down at her home computer to log on to the SSL VPN to the hospital network and patient database, where she can access the report, as follows:

1. The client initiates a connection to the VPN concentrator. SSL encryption is used to establish a secure channel for the connection. The encryption to be used for all transmissions is SSL. During the initial handshake, the authentication protocol (for example, RADIUS, discussed later in this chapter) is also agreed upon.

2. The physician enters logon credentials to the corporate domain. Her username and password are encrypted using RADIUS, the entire IP packet is encrypted using SSL, and the transmission is sent to the VPN concentrator.

3. The VPN concentrator is configured to send the logon credentials to a corporate database, such as Active Directory, for authentication. After Active Directory authenticates, the VPN concentrator completes establishing the VPN connection.

4. The radiologist is now able to use the VPN to access the hospital database. The database server is programmed to use a Web-based interface to present the MRI graphics in HTTP to a requesting browser. The interface is configured to encrypt the HTTP data using SSL, producing an HTTPS transmission, which is managed by the VPN concentrator.

5. After the radiologist finishes reading the MRI report and calls the emergency physician to let him know the problem is not serious, she decides to take a moment to check her hospital email inbox. The SSL VPN also encrypts email so it, too, is secured. Protocols used, for example, might be SMTPS or POP3S, which both rely on SSL for encryption.

6. When she's finished, the radiologist logs off the hospital network, which closes the VPN session, and she goes back to bed.

An SSL VPN is accessed by the user almost exclusively through a Web browser, though some configurations can be accessed through special client software. For less-secure SSL VPNs, no additional software is required. For the best-secured VPNs, a user must install a personal digital certificate on her client computer along with SSL VPN software, which is called an SSL VPN client. For most configurations, the VPN client is issued an IP address by the VPN concentrator when a connection is first made, and this IP address is used for the duration of the virtual network connection. The IP address is available to technicians on the corporate network, which makes it easier to troubleshoot a failed VPN.

SSH (Secure Shell)

In Chapter 1 you learned about Telnet, a terminal emulation utility that provides remote connections to hosts. For example, if you were a network administrator working at one of your company's satellite offices and had to modify the configuration on a router at the home office, you could use Telnet to access the router and run commands to modify its configuration. However, Telnet provides little security for establishing a connection (poor authentication) and no security for transmitting data (no encryption).

SSH (Secure Shell) is a collection of protocols that does both. With SSH, you can securely log on to a host, execute commands on that host, and copy files to or from that host. SSH encrypts data exchanged throughout the session. It guards against a number of security threats, including unauthorized access to a host, IP spoofing, interception of data in transit (even if it must be transferred via intermediate hosts), and DNS spoofing, in which a hacker forges name server records to falsify his host's identity. Depending on the version, SSH may use DES, Triple DES, RSA, Kerberos, or other, less-common encryption algorithms or techniques.

SSH was developed by SSH Communications Security, and use of their SSH implementation requires paying for a license. However, open source versions of the protocol suite, such as OpenSSH, are available for most computer platforms. To form a secure connection, SSH must be running on both the client and server. Like Telnet, the SSH client is a utility that can be run at the shell prompt on a UNIX or Linux system or at the command prompt on a Windows-based system. Other versions of the program come with a graphical interface. The SSH suite of protocols is included with all modern UNIX and Linux distributions and with Mac OS X Server and Mac OS X client operating systems. For Windows-based computers, you need to download a freeware SSH client, such as PuTTY.

SSH allows for password authentication or authentication using public and private keys. For authentication using keys, you must first generate a public key and a private key on your client workstation by running the `ssh keygen` command (or by choosing the correct menu options in a graphical SSH program). The keys are saved in two different, encrypted files on your hard disk. Next, you must transfer the public key to an authorization file on the host to which you want to connect. When you connect to the host via SSH, the client and host exchange public keys, and if both can be authenticated, the connection is completed.

SSH listens at port 22, and is highly configurable. For example, you can choose among several types of encryption methods and it can also be configured to perform port forwarding, which means it can redirect traffic that would normally use an insecure port (such as FTP) to an SSH-secured port. This allows you to use SSH for more than simply logging on to a host and manipulating files. With port forwarding, you could, for example, exchange HTTP traffic with a Web server via a secured SSH connection. You learn to use SSH in Ubuntu in Case Project 7-1 at the end of this chapter.

SFTP (Secure File Transfer Protocol)

Recall that FTP is a utility that can transfer files to and from a host computer running the FTP server software. You learned to use FTP in Windows in Hands-On Project 2-4 in Chapter 2 and you learned how to set up an FTP server in Linux in Case Study 4-1 in Chapter 4. SFTP (Secure File Transfer Protocol) is a secure version of FTP, which uses SSH for encryption, and is sometimes called FTP over SSH or SSH FTP. Recall from Chapter 2 that FTP listens at port 21. SFTP can be configured to listen on any port, although it normally uses SSH's port 22.

Applying Concepts

Configure Port Forwarding

Recall from Chapter 1 that the Windows Remote Desktop application uses RDP to provide a secure, encrypted connection that allows technicians to remotely control a computer. To allow this connection to be created, the router must be configured to forward RDP traffic (port 3389) to the correct computer. In this project, you will learn how to set up port forwarding for RDP on a SOHO router. At the end of the chapter, you will configure a pair of computers for an RDP connection.

1. On the host computer (the computer to receive the connection), configure a static IP address. You learned how to do this as part of Hands-On Project 3-1. Write down the static IP address.

2. Open a Web browser, navigate to your router's administration Web site, and log on.

3. Look for a port forwarding or port range forwarding option on the router's admin interface. For the Linksys router in Figure 7-14, for example, this feature is accessed under the Applications & Gaming tab.

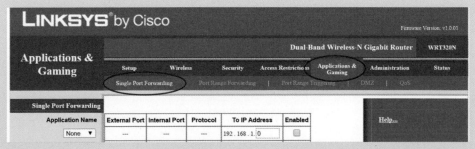

Figure 7-14 This Linksys router's port forwarding feature is configured on the Applications & Gaming tab

Source: Cisco Systems, Inc.

4. RDP uses port 3389. Type **Remote Desktop** for the application name, and **3389** for both the external and internal ports. For Protocol, select **Both**. In the *To IP Address* column, type the IP address of the host computer, then check **Enabled**.

5. Click **Save Settings** and close the browser.

As a general rule, do not leave port forwarding enabled unless you're using it. You will need this port forwarding configuration enabled for a project at the end of this chapter, but, if you are concerned about security, disable it for now, then enable it again later.

Server applications such as Remote Desktop listen for network activity from clients. If you want these server applications to be available at all times, you can set your network adapter properties to Wake on LAN (WoL). You enabled WoL as part of Hands-On Project 4-3. WoL causes the host computer to turn on from a powered-off state when a specific type of network activity happens. When a computer is powered off or asleep, the network adapter retains power and listens for network activity. When it receives a specific type of network activity, it wakes up or powers up the computer.

System administrators might use utilities to remotely wake a computer to perform routine maintenance. In a project at the end of this chapter, you will configure a computer to enable WoL.

Hashes: MD5 and SHA

Technically, hashing is not the same thing as encryption, though it's often listed as a type of encryption and does, in a similar manner, transform data from one format to another. Encrypted data can be decrypted, but hashed data cannot, and is mostly used to ensure data integrity—that is, to verify the data has not been altered in transit, which is similar to the purpose of a checksum. Hashes can play a critical role in a good encryption protocol, however. Hashed data is data that has been transformed through a particular algorithm that generally reduces the amount of space needed for the data, and mathematically is nearly impossible to reverse. Stored data that has been hashed can only be retrieved by comparing it with known data, which receives the same hash function and then produces the same hash output. If the output does not match, this indicates the data has likely been altered.

The two best-known hash algorithms are discussed next.

Legacy Networking
MD5 (Message Digest 5) Hash

The first usable Message Digest (MD) hash algorithm, MD2, was developed in 1989 at MIT. The most recent version of this hash in common use is MD5 (Message Digest algorithm 5), which uses 128-bit hash values to replace actual data with values computed according to the hash algorithm. (MD6 does exist, but multiple vulnerabilities were discovered before it could be approved.) Inherent flaws in the MD5 design have compromised the security of this hash function. One of the primary weaknesses of MD5 hashes is a propensity for collisions, which occur when the input of two different data sets result in the same hash value. MD5 is still in widespread use. However, it's usually only enabled alongside the more secure SHA hash, which is described next.

SHA (Secure Hash Algorithm) Hashes The primary advantage of SHA over MD5 is its resistance to collisions, although the added security requires more time to perform the hashing process. The original version of SHA (Secure Hash Algorithm), later dubbed SHA-0, was developed by the NSA and used a 160-bit hash function. This version, structured similarly to MD5, was quickly replaced by the next, slightly modified version, SHA-1, due to an undisclosed flaw. SHA-1 has also since been retired in favor of the next two iterations of SHA, although many systems still rely on SHA-1.

SHA-2, also designed by the NSA, supports a variety of hash sizes, the most popular of which are SHA-256 (with a 256-bit hash) and SHA-512 (with a 512-bit hash). Note that the 2 in SHA-2 refers to the version number, whereas the larger numbers in SHA-256 and SHA-512 refer to the length of the hash functions.

The most recent iteration of SHA is SHA-3, developed by private designers for a public competition in 2012. SHA-3 is very different in design from SHA-2, even though it uses the same 256- and 512-bit hash lengths. SHA-2 and SHA-3 are often implemented together for increased security. It's also common for data to be hashed in multiple passes, along with encryption passes layered in to the process.

Authentication Protocols

You have learned that authentication, in this case, user authentication, is the process of verifying a user's credentials (typically a username and password) to grant the user access to secured resources on a system or network. Authentication protocols are the rules that computers follow to accomplish authentication. Several types of authentication protocols exist. They vary according to which encryption schemes they rely on and the steps they take to verify credentials. The following sections describe some common authentication protocols in more detail.

RADIUS and TACACS+

In environments that support many simultaneous connections and several user IDs and passwords, it makes sense to use a centralized service to manage access to resources. This section describes a category of protocols known as AAA (authentication, authorization, and accounting) that do the following:

- Authenticate a client's identity by prompting a user for a valid username and a valid password

- Authorize a user for certain privileges on a system or network
- Keep an account of the client's system or network usage

By far, the most popular AAA service is RADIUS (Remote Authentication Dial-In User Service). RADIUS was standardized by the IETF. It runs in the Application layer, is transported over UDP in the Transport layer, and provides centralized network authentication, authorization, and accounting for multiple users.

RADIUS can operate as a software application on a remote access server or on a computer dedicated to this type of authentication, called a RADIUS server. Because RADIUS servers are highly scalable, many ISPs use a RADIUS server as a central authentication point for wireless, mobile, and remote users. RADIUS services are often combined with other network services on a single machine. For example, an organization might combine a DHCP server with a RADIUS server to manage allocation of addresses and privileges assigned to each address on the network.

Figure 7-15 illustrates a RADIUS server used for remote access. RADIUS can run on UNIX, Linux, Windows, or Macintosh networks.

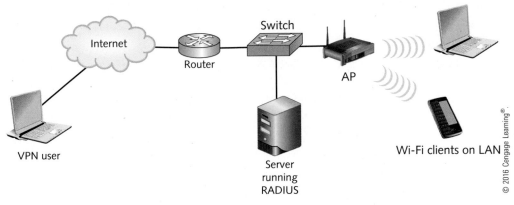

Figure 7-15 A RADIUS server on a network servicing a VPN client and Wi-Fi clients

Another AAA protocol, TACACS+ (Terminal Access Controller Access Control System Plus), offers network administrators the option of separating the access, authentication, and auditing capabilities. For instance, TACACS+ might provide access and accounting functions, but use another technique, such as Kerberos (discussed later in this chapter), to authenticate users. TACACS+ differs from RADIUS in that it:

- Relies on TCP, not UDP, at the Transport layer
- Was developed by Cisco Systems, Inc., for proprietary use (which means it only works on Cisco products)
- Is typically installed on a router or switch, rather than on a server
- Encrypts all information transmitted for AAA (RADIUS only encrypts the password)

Each of the protocols described in the following sections may play a role in the authentication step of AAA.

Legacy Networking

PAP (Password Authentication Protocol)

Earlier in this chapter, you were introduced to PPP (Point-to-Point Protocol), which belongs to the Data Link layer of the OSI model and provides the foundation for direct connections between remote clients and hosts. PPP alone, however, does not secure authentications to the network. For this, it requires an authentication protocol.

In fact, several types of authentication protocols can work over PPP. One is PAP (Password Authentication Protocol). After establishing a link with a server through PPP, a client uses PAP to send an authentication request that includes its credentials—usually a username and password. The server compares the credentials to those in its user database. If the credentials match, the server responds to the client with an acknowledgment of authentication and grants the client access to secured resources. If the credentials do not match, the server denies the request to authenticate. Figure 7-16 illustrates PAP's two-step authentication process.

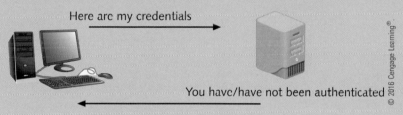

Figure 7-16 Two-step authentication used in PAP

Thus, PAP is a simple authentication protocol, but it is not considered secure. It sends the client's credentials in cleartext, without encryption, and this opens the way for eavesdroppers to capture a username and password. In addition, PAP does not protect against the possibility of a malicious intruder attempting to guess a user's password through a brute force attack. For these reasons, PAP is rarely used on modern networks. Instead, more sophisticated protocols, such as those described in the following sections, are preferred.

CHAP and MS-CHAP

CHAP (Challenge Handshake Authentication Protocol) is another authentication protocol that can operate over PPP. Unlike PAP, CHAP encrypts usernames and passwords for transmission. It also differs from PAP in that it requires three steps to complete the authentication process. Together, these steps use a three-way handshake. Figure 7-17 illustrates the three-way handshake used in CHAP. The steps of the process are described below as they correlate with the blue circles in the figure:

1. *challenge*—The server sends the client a randomly generated string of characters.

2. *response*—The client adds its password to the challenge and encrypts the new string of characters. It sends this new string of characters in a response to the server. Meanwhile, the server also concatenates the user's password with the challenge and encrypts the new character string, using the same encryption scheme the client used.

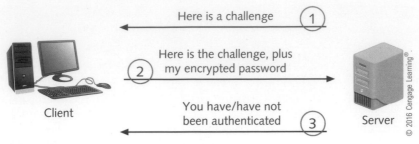

Figure 7-17 Three-way handshake used in CHAP

3. *accept/reject*—The server compares the encrypted string of characters it received from the client with the encrypted string of characters it has generated. If the two match, it authenticates the client. But if the two differ, it rejects the client's request for authentication.

The primary benefit of CHAP over PAP is that in CHAP, a password is never transmitted alone, and never as cleartext. This same type of security is offered in **MS-CHAP (Microsoft Challenge Handshake Authentication Protocol)**, a similar authentication protocol from Microsoft used with Windows-based computers. One potential flaw in CHAP and MS-CHAP authentication is that someone eavesdropping on the network could capture the string of characters that is encrypted with the password, decrypt that string, and obtain the client's password.

To address this, Microsoft released **MS-CHAPv2 (Microsoft Challenge Handshake Authentication Protocol, version 2)**, which uses stronger encryption, does not use the same encryption strings for transmission and reception, and requires mutual authentication. In **mutual authentication**, both computers verify the credentials of the other—for example, the client authenticates the server just as the server authenticates the client. This is more secure than requiring only one of the communicating computers to authenticate the other.

MS-CHAPv2 and its preceding authentication protocols (PAP, CHAP, and MS-CHAPv1) could all arguably be labeled as legacy technology due to the recent hacking successes against them. However, you'll still encounter MS-CHAPv2 in the course of business, especially with older VPN systems and in WPA2-Enterprise environments (recall from Chapter 6 that WPA2-Enterprise adds RADIUS to WPA2 authentication). An authentication protocol that is more secure than any of these protocols and is supported by multiple operating systems is EAP, discussed next.

EAP (Extensible Authentication Protocol)

EAP (Extensible Authentication Protocol) is another extension to the PPP protocol suite. It differs from the authentication protocols discussed previously in that it only provides the framework for authenticating clients and servers. It does not perform encryption or authentication on its own. Instead, it works with other encryption and authentication schemes to verify the credentials of clients and servers.

Like CHAP, EAP requires the authenticator (for example, the server) to initiate the authentication process by asking the connected computer (for example, the client) to verify itself. In EAP, the server usually sends more than one request. In its first request, it asks the client's identity and indicates what type of authentication to use. In subsequent requests, it asks the client for authentication information to prove the client's identity. The client responds to each of the server's requests in the required format. If the responses match what the server expects, the server authenticates the client.

One of EAP's advantages is its flexibility. It is supported by nearly all modern operating systems and can be used with any authentication method. For example, although the typical network authentication involves a user ID and password, EAP also works with biometrics methods, such as retina or hand-scanning. EAP is also adaptable to new technology. Several versions and adaptations of EAP exist, including PEAP, EAP-TLS, EAP-TTLS, EAP-FAST, and EAPoL.

In the case of wireless LANs, EAP is used with older encryption and authentication protocols to form a new, more secure method of connecting to networks from wireless stations. A distinct implementation of EAP, described next, forms the basis of one of the most secure wireless authentication techniques.

802.1X (EAPoL)

The 802.1X standard, codified by IEEE, specifies the use of one of many authentication methods, plus EAP, to grant access to and dynamically generate and update authentication keys for transmissions to a particular port. Although it's primarily used with wireless networks now, it was originally designed for wired LANs; thus, it's also known as EAPoL (EAP over LAN). 802.1X only defines a process for authentication. It does not specify the type of authentication or encryption protocols clients and servers must use. However, 802.1X is commonly used with RADIUS authentication. As you might expect, for nodes to communicate using 802.1X, they must agree on the same authentication method.

What distinguishes 802.1X from other authentication standards is the fact that it applies to communication with a particular port—for example, a physical switch port or a logically defined port on an access point. When a client wants to access the network, a port on the authenticator (such as a switch or access point) challenges the client to prove its identity. If the client is running the proper 802.1X software, the client will supply the authenticator with its credentials. The authenticator next passes on the client's credentials to an authentication server—for example, a RADIUS server—which in turn communicates with Active Directory to determine the user's domain privileges and to log the event. Only after the authentication server has verified a client's legitimacy will the switch or access point port be opened to the client's Layer 3 traffic. For this reason, 802.1X is sometimes also called port authentication, or port-based authentication.

After the port is opened, the client and network communicate using EAP and an agreed-upon encryption scheme. Figure 7-18 illustrates the process followed by 802.1X when used with a WLAN (wireless LAN). You'll learn more about wireless network security techniques next.

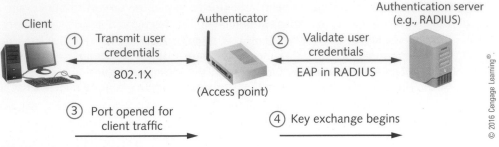

Figure 7-18   802.1X authentication process

TKIP (Temporal Key Integrity Protocol) and AES (Advanced Encryption Standard)

Recall from Chapter 6 that a significant disadvantage to WEP was that it used the same key for all clients and the key might never change. Due to this inherent insecurity, IEEE devised a new wireless security protocol, called 802.11i, which included the subset standard WPA (later replaced by WPA2). 802.11i uses 802.1X (EAPoL) to authenticate devices and dynamically assigns every transmission its own key. WPA relies on an encryption key generation and management scheme known as TKIP (Temporal Key Integrity Protocol), pronounced *tee-kip*. WPA2 later improved on the security of WPA with the implementation of AES (Advanced Encryption Standard), which provides faster and more secure encryption than TKIP for wireless transmissions.

In reality, TKIP was a quick fix, designed more as an integrity check for WEP transmissions than as a sophisticated encryption protocol. WPA's TKIP used the same encryption mechanism as WEP but with improved algorithms to wrap the older WEP transmissions in a more securely encrypted transmission. AES, on the other hand, uses a more sophisticated family of ciphers along with multiple stages of data transformation. WPA2 does continue to offer TKIP, though, to provide compatibility with older wireless devices.

As you can imagine, EAPoL makes logging on to a wireless network more complex than it is with WEP. In 802.11i, a wireless station first issues a request to the access point. The access point functions as a proxy between the remote access server and station until the station has successfully authenticated with a remote access server. Meanwhile, the access point prevents any direct exchange of data between the two. After obtaining data from an unknown station, the access point repackages the data and then transmits it to the remote access server. It also repackages data from the remote access server before issuing it to the station. Thus, 802.11i requires mutual authentication—the station authenticates with the remote access server, and also, the remote access server authenticates with the station.

After mutual authentication, the remote access server instructs the access point to allow traffic from the client into the network without first having to be repackaged. Next, the client and server agree on the encryption key they will use with the encryption scheme. Finally, they exchange data that has been encrypted through the mutually agreed-upon method. Beginning with WPA2, 802.11i specified mixing each packet in a data stream with a different key.

Kerberos

Kerberos is a cross-platform authentication protocol that uses key encryption to verify the identity of clients and to securely exchange information after a client logs on to a system. It is an example of a private key encryption service. Kerberos provides significant security advantages over simple NOS authentication. Whereas an NOS client-server logon process assumes that clients are who they say they are and only verifies a user's name against the password in the NOS database, Kerberos does not automatically trust clients. Instead, it requires clients to prove their identities through a third party. This is similar to what happens when you apply for a passport. The government does not simply believe that you are "Leah Torres," but instead requires you to present proof, such as your birth certificate. In addition to checking the validity of a client, Kerberos communications are encrypted and unlikely to be deciphered by any device on the network other than the client. Contrast this type of transmission to the normally unencrypted and vulnerable communication between an NOS and a client.

To understand specifically how a client uses Kerberos, you need to understand some of the terms used when discussing this protocol:

- *KDC (Key Distribution Center)*—The server that issues keys to clients during initial client authentication

- *AS (authentication service)*—The process that runs on a KDC to initially validate a client

- *ticket*—A temporary set of credentials that a client uses to prove that its identity has been validated (note that a ticket is not the same as a key, which is used to initially validate its identity)

- *principal*—A Kerberos client, or user

Now that you have learned the terms used by Kerberos, you can follow the process it requires for client-server communication. Bear in mind that the purpose of Kerberos is to connect a valid user with the *service* that user wants to access. To accomplish this, both the user and the service must register their keys with the authentication service.

Suppose the principal is Jamal Sayad and the service is called "inventory." Jamal first logs on to his network as usual. Next, he attempts to log on to the "inventory" service with his Kerberos principal name and password. The KDC confirms that Jamal Sayad is in its database and that he has provided the correct password. Then, the AS running on the KDC randomly generates two copies of a new key, called the session key. The AS issues one copy to Jamal's computer and the other copy to the inventory service. Further, it creates a ticket that allows Jamal to use the inventory service. This ticket contains the inventory service key and can only be decrypted using Jamal Sayad's key.

The AS sends the ticket to Jamal Sayad. Jamal's computer decrypts the session key with Jamal's personal key. It then creates a time stamp associated with his request, and encrypts this time stamp with the session key. The encrypted time stamp is known as the authenticator. This time stamp helps the service verify that the ticket is indeed associated with Jamal Sayad's request to use the inventory service.

Next, Jamal's computer sends his ticket and authenticator to the service. The service decrypts the ticket using its own key and decrypts the authenticator using its session key.

Finally, the service verifies that the principal requesting its use is truly Jamal Sayad as the KDC indicated.

The preceding events illustrate the original version of the Kerberos authentication process. The problem with the original version was that a user had to request a separate ticket each time he wanted to use a different service. To alleviate this inconvenience, Kerberos developers created the **TGS (Ticket-Granting Service)**, an application separate from the AS that also runs on the KDC.

Figure 7-19 shows how TGS works. So that the client does not need to request a new ticket from the TGS each time it wants to use a different service on the network, the TGS issues the client a **TGT (Ticket-Granting Ticket)**. After receiving the TGT, anytime the user wants to contact a service, he requests a ticket not from the AS, but from the TGS. Furthermore, the reply is encrypted not with the user's personal key, but with the session key that the AS provided for use with the TGS. Inside that reply is the new session key for use with the regular service. The rest of the exchange continues as described previously.

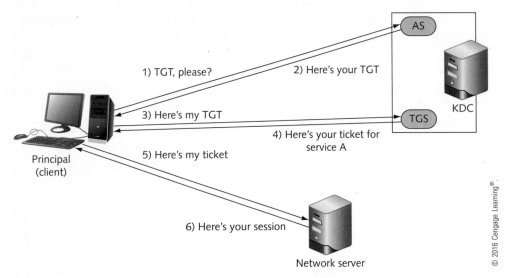

Figure 7-19   The Ticket-Granting Service holds a client's Ticket-Granting Ticket for repeated use

Kerberos, which is named after the three-headed dog in Greek mythology who guarded the gates of Hades, was designed at MIT (Massachusetts Institute of Technology). MIT still provides free copies of the Kerberos code. In addition, many software vendors have developed their own versions of Kerberos.

SSO (Single Sign-On)

Kerberos is an example of **single sign-on (SSO)**, a form of authentication in which a client signs on one time to access multiple systems or resources. The primary advantage of single sign-on is convenience. Users don't have to remember several passwords, and network administrators can limit the time they devote to password management. The biggest disadvantage to single sign-on authentication is that once the obstacle of authentication is cleared, the user has access to numerous resources. A hacker needs fewer credentials to gain access to potentially many files or connections.

For greater security, some systems require clients to supply two or more pieces of information to verify their identity. For example, in a two-factor authentication scenario, a user must provide something and know something. For example, he might have to provide a fingerprint scan as well as know and enter his password.

In general, an authentication process that requires two or more pieces of information is known as multifactor authentication (MFA). The three categories of authentication factors are:

- *knowledge*—something you know, such as a password
- *possession*—something you have, such as an ATM card
- *inherence*—something you are, such as your fingerprint

Multifactor authentication requires at least one authentication method from at least two different categories. For example, entry to a secure building might require a password, a fingerprint scan, plus a piece of information generated from a security token. A security token is a device or piece of software that stores or generates information, such as a series of numbers or letters, known only to its authorized user. One example of a hardware-based token is the popular SecurID key chain fob from RSA Security, as shown in Figure 7-20. The SecurID device generates a password that changes every 60 seconds. When logging on, a user provides the number that currently appears on the SecurID fob. Before he is allowed access to secured resources, his network checks with RSA Security's service to verify that the number is correct. Google Authenticator, Google's number generator service, provides free, software-based security tokens.

Figure 7-20 SecurID fob

Troubleshooting Cloud Computing and Remote Access

Network+
1.2
1.4
3.3
3.6
4.6
4.7 Security presents one of the biggest concerns when accessing, storing, and interacting with data and applications in the cloud. In this chapter, you've learned about several methods and protocols that assist in authenticating devices for remote access, whether through VPN tunnels or standard IP traffic through the cloud. Two primary areas of failure during the authentication process are due to misconfigurations on one end or the other, or problems with user passwords and device settings.

Network+
4.6

Passwords

Choosing a secure password is one of the easiest and least expensive ways to guard against unauthorized access. Unfortunately, too many people prefer to use an easy-to-remember password. If your password is obvious to you, however, it may also be easy for a hacker to figure out. The following guidelines for selecting passwords should be part of your organization's security policy. It is especially important for network administrators to choose difficult passwords, and also to keep passwords confidential and to change them frequently.

Tips for making and keeping passwords secure include the following:

- Always change system default passwords after installing new programs or equipment. For example, after installing a router, the default administrator's password on the router might be set by the manufacturer to be *password*.

- Do not use familiar information, such as your name, nickname, birth date, anniversary, pet's name, child's name, spouse's name, user ID, phone number, address, or any other words or numbers that others might associate with you.

- Do not use any word that might appear in a dictionary. Hackers can use programs that try a combination of your user ID and every word in a dictionary to gain access to the network. This is known as a **dictionary attack**, and it is typically the first technique a hacker uses when trying to guess a password (besides asking the user for her password).

- Make the password longer than eight characters—the longer, the better. Choose a combination of letters and numbers; add special characters, such as exclamation marks or hyphens, if allowed. Use a combination of uppercase and lowercase letters.

- Do not write down your password or share it with others. Never store passwords in a Web browser. Many browsers store these passwords in plaintext and can be easily hacked.

- Change your password at least every 60 days, or more frequently. If you are a network administrator, establish controls through the NOS to force users to change their passwords at least every 60 days.

- Do not reuse passwords after they have expired.

- Use different passwords for different applications. For example, choose separate passwords for your email program, online banking, VPN connection, and so on. That way, if someone learns one of your passwords, he won't necessarily be able to access all of your secured accounts.

- Make it easier to keep a secure record of long, random passwords by installing and using password management software. These programs can generate unique strings of random letters and numbers for each password, and store them securely in an encrypted database which is accessible from multiple devices through a single, master password. This way, users only need to remember one, well-formed password that is sufficiently long to help maximize security of their password database.

Password guidelines should be clearly communicated to everyone in your organization through your security policy. Although users might grumble about choosing a combination of letters and numbers and changing their passwords frequently, you can assure them that the company's financial and personnel data is safer as a result.

Misconfigurations

With all of the available options for authentication, encryption, and automatic sign-in (where credentials are stored in the device for automated use), configuring a device for a remote connection can sometimes be a hassle. Start with the simplest, default settings if you don't have specific instructions otherwise for the appropriate settings. Use feedback from error messages as a breadcrumb trail to determine which settings need to be changed. Common issues to look out for include the following:

- Mistyped username or password
- Incompatible encryption or authentication settings
- Improperly activated or inactivated user account
- Incorrectly assigned port
- Improperly configured firewall
- Network connection failure
- Failed handshake

NOTE Because secure connections require an established session in order to function, a failed handshake can result in end-to-end connectivity issues. End-to-end connectivity means that two endpoints can communicate with each other through an established session that is not dependent upon intermediate devices directing each hop for each transmission, such as when establishing a TLS session. Failed authentication and incompatible encryption methods can both prevent the end-to-end connectivity required for a secure connection.

Also be sure to check configurations on the server handling AAA services, such as TACACS+ or RADIUS protocols. For example, make sure the server's security certificate has not expired and is installed correctly. Also make sure the server's date and time are correct. User roles must be properly defined, and user accounts properly activated. Most servers maintain ongoing logs; check the logs for issues about configuration or individual client access.

When it comes to clients connecting to servers running TACACS+ or RADIUS, remember your other network connection troubleshooting tools, such as `ping` and `tracert`, which can help you narrow down the location of a connection problem.

Applying Concepts

Protocol Synopsis

Each of the protocols covered in this chapter plays an important role in securing transmissions between remote locations. It's important to have the big picture in mind regarding how these protocols interact with each other in various parts of the system when troubleshooting connectivity and security issues.

In this project, you synthesize the major characteristics of each protocol into a single refer-ence table. You can create Table 7-1 below in a word-processing program or a spreadsheet program. Then refer to the information given in this chapter to fill in the missing pieces.

Table 7-1   Notable encryption and authentication methods

Security method	Type	Primary use(s)	Notes
PPP	Connection	Remote access	
GRE	Encapsulation		
L2TP	Tunneling	VPN	
IPsec			
SSL			
TLS			Secure transmission of HTTP sessions
SSL VPN			
SFTP	Encryption	File transfer	
SSH			
SHA	Hashing		
RADIUS			Central authentication point for wireless, mobile, and remote users
TACACS+	Authentication, Authorization, and Accounting (AAA)		
MS-CHAPv2	Authentication		
EAP			
802.1X	Authentication		
AES	Encryption	Wi-Fi	
Kerberos			Verify the identity of clients and to securely exchange information after a client logs on to a system

© 2016 Cengage Learning®

Chapter Summary

Cloud Computing

- Cloud computing refers to the flexible provision of data storage, applications, or services to multiple clients over a network.

- Cloud computing service models incrementally increase the amount of management responsibilities outsourced to cloud computing vendors.

- Cloud services may be managed and delivered by any of a variety of deployment models, depending on who manages the cloud and who has access to it.

Remote Access

■ After connecting to a remote network, a remote client can access files, applications, and other shared resources, such as printers, like any other client on the server, LAN, or WAN.

■ SLIP is an earlier Point-to-Point Protocol that does not support encryption, can carry only IP packets, and works strictly on serial connections. SLIP has been replaced by PPP, which can support several types of Network layer protocols and can provide weak encryption.

■ To ensure a VPN can carry all types of data in a private manner over any kind of connection, special VPN protocols encapsulate higher-layer protocols in a process known as tunneling.

■ A VPN tunneling protocol operates at the Data Link layer to encapsulate the VPN frame into a Network layer packet, no matter what Network layer protocol is used.

■ GRE encapsulates PPP frames to make them take on the temporary identity of IP packets at Layer 3. To the WAN, messages look like inconsequential IP traffic.

■ Unlike PPTP, L2TP is a standard accepted and used by multiple vendors, so it can connect a VPN that uses a mix of equipment types.

■ Remote virtual computing, also called terminal emulation, allows a user on one computer, called the client, to control another computer, called the host or server, across a network connection.

Encryption Techniques, Protocols, and Utilities

■ Encryption is the use of a mathematical code, called a cipher, to scramble data into a format that can be read only by reversing the cipher—that is, by deciphering, or decrypting, the data.

■ The most popular kind of encryption encodes the original data's bits using a key—sometimes several times in different sequences—to generate a unique data block.

■ Private key encryption is also known as symmetric encryption because the same key is used during both the encryption and decryption of the data.

■ In public key encryption, a user's public key can be obtained from a third-party source, such as a public key server. But the encrypted message can only be decrypted with the user's private key.

■ IPsec is an encryption protocol that works at the Network layer and adds security information to the header of all IP packets to transform them into data packets.

■ SSL and TLS are both methods of encrypting TCP/IP transmissions en route between the client and server using public key encryption technology. The two protocols work together and are widely known as SSL/TLS.

■ When encryption is used with a VPN, the encryption protocol creates a secure channel and uses it to encrypt VPN frames.

■ SFTP is a secure version of FTP, which uses SSH for encryption, and is sometimes called FTP over SSH or SSH FTP.

■ With SSH, you can securely log on to a host, execute commands on that host, and copy files to or from that host. SSH encrypts data exchanged throughout the session.

- Encrypted data can be decrypted, but hashed data cannot, and is mostly used for authentication and integrity—to verify the data has not been altered in transit, similar to the purpose of a checksum.

- SHA-2, designed by the NSA, supports a variety of hash sizes, the most popular of which are SHA-256 and SHA-512.

Authentication Protocols

- Authentication protocols vary according to which encryption schemes they rely on and the steps they take to verify credentials.

- RADIUS can operate as a software application on a remote access server or on a computer dedicated to this type of authentication, called a RADIUS server.

- MS-CHAPv2 uses stronger encryption than earlier encryption protocols, does not use the same encryption strings for transmission and reception, and requires mutual authentication.

- EAP only provides the framework for authenticating clients and servers. It does not perform encryption or authentication on its own. Instead, it works with other encryption and authentication schemes to verify the credentials of clients and servers.

- The 802.1X standard specifies the use of one of many authentication methods, plus EAP, to grant access to and dynamically generate and update authentication keys for transmissions to a particular port.

- AES uses a more sophisticated family of ciphers than TKIP does, and transforms the data in multiple stages.

- Kerberos is a cross-platform authentication protocol that uses key encryption to verify the identity of clients and to securely exchange information after a client logs on to a system.

- For greater security, some systems require clients to supply two or more pieces of information to verify their identity.

Troubleshooting Cloud Computing and Remote Access

- Choosing a secure password is one of the easiest and least expensive ways to guard against unauthorized access. Unfortunately, too many people prefer to use an easy-to-remember password.

- When troubleshooting problems with remote connections, be sure to check configurations on the server handling AAA services, such as TACACS+ or RADIUS.

Key Terms

For definitions of key terms, see the Glossary near the end of the book.

802.11i	AH (authentication header)	authenticator
802.1X	algorithm	certificate authority (CA)
AAA (authentication, authorization, and accounting)	AS (authentication service)	challenge
	asymmetric encryption	CHAP (Challenge Handshake Authentication Protocol)
AES (Advanced Encryption Standard)	authentication protocols	

CIA (confidentiality, integrity, and availability) triad

cipher

ciphertext

client_hello

client-to-site VPN

cloud computing

collision

community cloud

dictionary attack

digital certificate

DirectAccess

DNS spoofing

EAP (Extensible Authentication Protocol)

EAPoL (EAP over LAN)

elastic

encryption device

endpoint security vulnerability

end-to-end connectivity

ESP (Encapsulating Security Payload) encryption

GRE (Generic Routing Encapsulation)

handshake protocol

hashed data

hosted virtual desktop (HVD)

host-to-host VPN

host-to-site VPN

hybrid cloud

IaaS (Infrastructure as a Service)

IETF (Internet Engineering Task Force)

IKE (Internet Key Exchange)

IPsec (Internet Protocol Security)

ISAKMP (Internet Security Association and Key Management Protocol)

KDC (Key Distribution Center)

Kerberos

key

key management

key pair

L2TP (Layer 2 Tunneling Protocol)

MD5 (Message Digest algorithm 5)

MS-CHAP (Microsoft Challenge Handshake Authentication Protocol)

MS-CHAPv2 (Microsoft Challenge Handshake Authentication Protocol, version 2)

multifactor authentication (MFA)

multi-tenant

mutual authentication

OpenSSH

OpenVPN

PaaS (Platform as a Service)

PAP (Password Authentication Protocol)

PKI (Public-key Infrastructure)

platform

port authentication

port forwarding

port-based authentication

PPP (Point-to-Point Protocol)

PPPoE (PPP over Ethernet)

PPTP (Point-to-Point Tunneling Protocol)

principal

private cloud

private key encryption

PTP (Point to Point)

public cloud

public key encryption

public key server

RADIUS (Remote Authentication Dial-In User Service)

RADIUS server

RAS (Remote Access Service)

remote access

remote access server (RAS)

remote-access VPN

RRAS (Routing and Remote Access Service)

SaaS (Software as a Service)

secure channel

security token

server_hello

session key

SHA (Secure Hash Algorithm)

SHA-1

SHA-2

SHA-256

SHA-3

SHA-512

single sign-on (SSO)

site-to-site VPN

SLIP (Serial Line Internet Protocol)

SSL session

SSL VPN

SSTP (Secure Socket Tunneling Protocol)

subscription model

symmetric encryption

TACACS+ (Terminal Access Controller Access Control System Plus)

TGS (Ticket-Granting Service)

TGT (Ticket-Granting Ticket)

ticket

TKIP (Temporal Key Integrity Protocol)

TTLS (Tunneled Transport Layer Security)

tunnel

two-factor authentication

virtual private network (VPN)

VPN concentrator

VPN gateway

Web services

XaaS (Anything as a Service or Everything as a Service)

Xen

Review Questions

1. Which cloud computing service model gives software developers access to multiple operating systems for testing?

   a. IaaS

   b. PaaS

   c. SaaS

   d. XaaS

2. What service in Windows Server 2012 R2 authenticates remote users and computers to the Windows domain and its corporate network resources?

   a. Active Directory

   b. Group Policy

   c. DirectAccess

   d. RAS (Remote Access Service)

3. Which remote access protocol is used over an Ethernet network?

   a. PPPoE

   b. RAS

   c. PPP

   d. SLIP

4. Which encryption protocol does GRE use to increase the security of its transmissions?

   a. SSL

   b. SFTP

   c. IPsec

   d. SSH

5. Which tunneling protocol is accepted and used by multiple vendors?

   a. SSL VPN

   b. L2TP

   c. SSL

   d. SSH

6. A hacker runs a program that tries numerous character combinations until it stumbles on the correct combination and cracks the key. What offensive strategy is this program using?

   a. Brute force attack

   b. Zero-day exploit

   c. CIA triad

   d. Endpoint security vulnerability

7. What is the minimum acceptable key size for today's security standards?

   a. 8 bytes

   b. 128 bits

   c. 256 bits

   d. 512 bits

8. In public key encryption, which key is used to decrypt the message?

   a. Session key

   b. Private key

   c. Public key

   d. Network key

9. What feature must be configured on a router to redirect traffic from an insecure port to a secure one?

   a. AAA (authentication, authorization, and accounting)

   b. Mutual authentication

   c. TGS (Ticket-Granting Service)

   d. Port forwarding

10. Which of the following is NOT one of the three AAA services provided by RADIUS and TACACS+?

   a. Authentication

   b. Authorization

   c. Access control

   d. Accounting

11. Organizations with common interests, such as regulatory requirements, performance requirements, or data access, might share resources in a _____ .

12. All types of remote access techniques require some type of _____ , which accepts a remote connection and grants privileges to the network's resources.

13. Which Transport layer protocol does PPTP use? Which Transport layer protocol does L2TP use?

14. What unique VPN connection characteristic is provided by the conjunction of RRAS and DirectAccess?

15. What are the two primary encryption techniques used by VPNs today?

16. When surfing online, you get some strange data on an apparently secure Web site, and you realize you need to check the legitimacy of the site. What kind of organization issues digital certificates?

17. Which two protocols are available to create secure transmissions for HTTP sessions?

18. _____ is used for confidentiality while _____ is used for integrity and authentication.

19. EAPoL is primarily used with what kind of transmission?

20. What kind of ticket is held by Kerberos' TGS?

Hands-On Projects

Project 7-1: Remote Desktop

The host or server computer is the computer that serves up Remote Desktop to client computers. To prepare your host computer, you need to configure the computer for static IP addressing and also configure the Remote Desktop service. The following steps are specific to a Windows 7 (Professional, Ultimate, or Enterprise) machine, but can be adapted to Windows 8.1:

1. Configure the computer for static IP addressing. Recall that you learned how to do this as part of Hands-On Project 3-1.

2. If your computer is behind a firewall, configure the router for port forwarding and allow incoming traffic on port 3389. Forward that traffic to the IP address of your desktop computer. Recall that you learned how to set up port forwarding earlier in this chapter. If you completed the port forwarding project at that time, you do not need to perform this step now. However, do make sure that the port forwarding configuration is enabled if you want to test Remote Desktop over the Internet.

3. To turn on the Remote Desktop service, open the System window and click **Remote settings** in the left pane. The System Properties box appears with the Remote tab selected. In the Remote Desktop area, check **Allow connections from computers running any version of Remote Desktop (less secure).**

4. Users who have administrative privileges are allowed to use Remote Desktop by default, but other users need to be added. If you need to add a user, click **Select Users** and follow the directions on-screen. Then close all windows.

5. Verify that Windows Firewall is set to allow Remote Desktop activity to this computer. To do that, open the **Network and Sharing Center** and click **Windows Firewall**. In the left pane, click **Allow a program or feature through Windows Firewall.**

6. The Allowed Programs window appears. Scroll down to Remote Desktop and adjust the settings as needed (see Figure 7-21). Click **OK** to apply any changes. You will learn more about Windows Firewall in Chapter 8.

You are now ready to test Remote Desktop using your local network. Try to use Remote Desktop from another computer somewhere on your local network. Note that any version of Windows 7 or Windows 8.1 can serve as a client computer (the computer viewing the host computer's desktop) for a Remote Desktop connection. The following steps are written specifically for Windows 7.

Verify you have Remote Desktop working on your local network before you move on to the next step of testing the Remote Desktop connection from the Internet on your own.

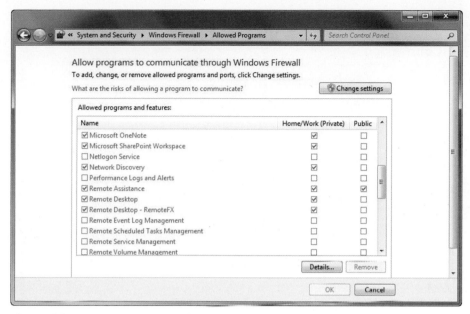

Figure 7-21 Allow Remote Desktop communication through Windows Firewall on your local computer

Source: Microsoft LLC

Follow these steps to use Remote Desktop on the client computer:

7. Click **Start,** enter **mstsc** in the search box, and press **Enter.** Alternately, you can click Start, All Programs, Accessories, and Remote Desktop Connection.

8. Enter the IP address or the host name of the computer to which you want to connect. If you decide to use a host name, begin the host name with two backslashes, as in *\\CompanyFileServer.*

9. If you plan to transfer files from one computer to the other, click **Options** and then click the **Local Resources** tab, as shown in the left side of Figure 7-22. Click **More.** The box on the right side of Figure 7-22 appears.

10. Check **Drives,** click **OK,** and then click **Connect** to make the connection. If a warning box appears, click **Connect** again. If another warning box appears, click **Yes.**

11. Log on using a username and password for the remote computer. If a warning box appears saying the remote computer might not be secure, click **Yes** to continue the connection.

12. The desktop of the remote computer appears in a window, as shown in Figure 7-23. When you click this window, you can work with the remote computer just as if you were sitting in front of it, except the response time will be slower. To move files back and forth between computers, use Windows Explorer on the remote computer. Files on your local computer and on the remote computer will appear in Windows Explorer on the remote computer in the Computer group. For example, in Figure 7-23, you can see drive C: on each computer labeled in the figure. To close the connection to the remote computer, log off the remote computer or close the desktop window.

Figure 7-22 Allow drives and other devices to be shared using the Remote Desktop Connection

Source: Microsoft LLC

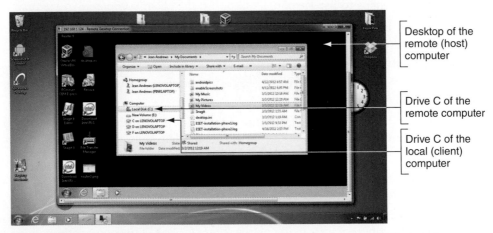

Figure 7-23 The desktop of the remote computer is available on your local computer

Source: Microsoft LLC

Even though Windows normally allows more than one user to be logged on at the same time, Remote Desktop does not. When a Remote Desktop session is opened, all local users on the remote computer are logged off.

Project 7-2: Remote Desktop Manager

In the previous project, you created a Remote Desktop connection between two computers. In the real world, you might need to manage several remote connections of several types, such as RDP, FTP, TeamViewer, VNC, VPN, etc. Remote Desktop Manager (RDM) by Devolutions, Inc., can corral all of these remote connections into a single interface.

Complete the following steps to set up Remote Desktop Manager on the computer that will manage the connections, called the client computer for the purposes of this project:

1. On the client computer, navigate to the Devolutions, Inc., Web site at **remotedesktopmanager .com** and click the **Download** link. Download and install the Free Edition of Remote Desktop Manager using the **Setup Installer** link. During installation, use the **Typical** profile option and accept all other default settings. View the **Readme** file and launch the application.

2. Create a free online account to register for Remote Desktop Manager Online (also free), activate your account when you receive the confirmation email, then complete registration for the software you just downloaded, and log on.

   RDM can manage many different types of remote sessions, including Citrix, FTP, PC Anywhere, TeamViewer, VPN, Telnet, SSH, and many others. For this project, you'll use Remote Assistance, which is available in all editions of Windows 7 and Windows 8.1, to create a session with another computer, the host computer. First you need to create an invitation file on the host computer, as follows:

3. On the host computer, open a Command Prompt window, type **msra.exe** and press **Enter**. Click **Invite someone you trust to help you,** then click **Save this invitation as a file.** Save the file where you can find it easily.

4. An invitation file is created, and a password is displayed in the Windows Remote Assistance window. Email the invitation file to yourself so that you can download the file to the client computer, the one with the RDM program installed.

   Now switch back to the client computer. Complete the following steps to create the Remote Assistance connection through RDM:

5. On the client computer, download the invitation file and save it where you can find it easily.

6. In RDM, in the center pane, click **Add Session.** Click **Remote Assistance** then click **OK.** Name the session **Remote Assist to lab computer** or something similar that makes sense to you, select **Expert (Opening an invitation),** then click **OK.**

7. Click **Open Session,** then click **Use an invitation file,** and open the invitation file on your computer. Enter the password from the host computer and click **OK.**

8. On the host computer, click **Yes** to accept the connection.

If you have trouble making the connection through RDM, try creating the Remote Assistance connection through Windows to make sure there are no configuration issues on either computer. Then attempt the connection through RDM again. You might need to check that Remote Assistance is enabled in Windows Firewall on both computers.

As you can see, RDM enabled you to create the Remote Assistance connection through the program's interface instead of needing to open Remote Assistance on the client computer. This might seem insignificant until you consider how this single interface can provide some consistency when working with multiple kinds of remote connections to multiple host and client devices.

9. Disconnect the computers by closing the Remote Assistance window on both computers.

10. In RDM on the client computer, click **Sessions** in the Navigation pane. This takes you back to the Actions menu where you can create a new session. Click **Add Session** and choose a different type of remote connection to create between the two computers. Build that entry and create that connection as well. You might need to download and install some software (such as TeamViewer) or make some configuration changes, depending upon which option you choose.

TeamViewer is an easy and free app to work with for creating remote connections. You've also learned how to create RDP connections. Alternatively, your instructor might want you to use a specific program, such as VNC or FTP.

Project 7-3: Password Management

Several good password management programs are available for free or at a low cost. In this project, you will research three of these programs, compare their strengths and weaknesses, and, optionally, install one of them.

1. Free versions are available of three popular password managers: KeePass, LastPass, and Dashlane. Choose two of these programs and a third of your own selection that interests you, then answer the following questions:

   a. Which platforms are supported?

   b. Which Web browsers are supported?

   c. From how many competitors can the program import passwords?

   d. What types of authentication are supported (e.g., master password, fingerprint, etc.)?

   e. What options are available for adding new passwords? For example, is this information collected automatically when the user creates a new account on a Web site?

   f. Where are the passwords stored? Are they synced across devices? How is the information protected, and what encryption options are available?

   g. What are some of the differences between the free edition of each program and the paid versions?

   h. What happens to the user's account if the user dies or is otherwise incapacitated?

2. *Optional:* Now that you know more about what a password manager can do and what its limitations are, select one of the programs you researched. Download and

install it on your computer(s), your smartphone, and/or your tablet. On how many devices did you install the software? What types of devices are they, and what are their respective OSs?

Project 7-4: Encrypt a Flash Drive

Beginning with Windows Vista, Microsoft included a feature called BitLocker that enables a user to encrypt the computer's hard drive as an added measure of security. Accessing data from an encrypted hard drive is no different from accessing data from an unencrypted hard drive, but if a thief were to steal the hard drive, the data would be more protected than it would be without BitLocker. With Windows 7, the BitLocker To Go feature allows a user to encrypt data on a flash drive in the same way.

To complete this project, you will need a computer running Windows 7 (Enterprise or Ultimate) or Windows 8.1 (Pro or Enterprise), which are the only Windows OSs that include BitLocker To Go. You will also need a USB flash drive, with or without existing data (although it's always wise to avoid experimenting with data you can't afford to lose).

1. Insert the flash drive into the computer. Open **Windows Explorer** (called File Explorer in Windows 8.1) and right-click the **Removable Disk** drive listed in the directory. Click **Turn on BitLocker**. BitLocker will begin initializing the drive, and will preserve any data already on the drive.

2. Check the **Use a password to unlock the drive** option, then enter your new password twice in the appropriate boxes. Click **Next**.

3. Where and how you store the recovery key depends upon whether you own the computer you're using or not, and if you have access to a printer:

   ○ Ideally, if you're using Windows 8.1 and you own the computer or you're signed in to your Microsoft account, you can choose the option to save the recovery key to your Microsoft account.

   ○ You can instead store the recovery key on your computer's hard drive if you own the computer. On a Windows 7 machine, click the **Save the recovery key to a file** option. On a Windows 8.1 machine, click **Save to a file**. Choose a location on your computer's hard drive. Another alternative might be to store the recovery key in an online file storage account, such as OneDrive, Google Drive, or Dropbox.

   ○ If you're using a school lab computer or a public computer and have access to a printer, click **Print the recovery key**.

   ○ *Windows 8.1 only*—You can choose whether to encrypt only the part of the flash drive that already contains data, or the entire drive. Future data will also be encrypted. Click **Encrypt used disk space only**. Click **Next**.

4. After saving the recovery key, click **Next**.

5. Click **Start encrypting** to begin the encryption process. This may take a while if the flash drive contains a lot of data.

6. When the encryption process is complete, click **Close**. Notice the altered drive icon in Windows Explorer (File Explorer for Windows 8.1).

7. Safely remove the flash drive from the computer using the **Safely Remove Hardware and Eject Media** option in your taskbar. Reinsert the flash drive and type your password to access the drive. If the computer you're using belongs to you, you might want to check the **Automatically unlock on this computer from now on** option so you don't have to enter the password every time you use this flash drive on this computer. (In Windows 8.1, you might have to click **More options** first, then click **Automatically unlock on this PC**.) This option stores the password on the computer in an encrypted file. Click **Unlock**. If you see an AutoPlay dialog box, click **Open folder to view files**.

Case Projects

CASE PROJECTS

Case Project 7-1: Use SSH in Ubuntu

In this project, you learn to use SSH in Ubuntu. Using the Ubuntu VMs you created in the case projects in Chapters 2 and 3, follow the steps to use SSH.

Using the VM that has Ubuntu Server installed, do the following:

1. Start the VM and log on.

2. SSH is included in Ubuntu Server but is not installed. Enter this command to install and start SSH: `sudo apt-get install ssh`

3. Enter the command `ifconfig` and write down the IP address of the Ubuntu Server VM.

Using the VM that has Ubuntu Desktop installed, do the following:

4. Start the VM and log on. Ubuntu Desktop launches.

5. Open a shell prompt. To do that, do one of the following:

   ○ Click the search icon in the upper-left corner of the screen and then click **Terminal** in the list that appears.

   ○ Click the search icon, type `gnome terminal` in the search box, and press **Enter**.

   ○ Press **CTRL+ALT+T**.

6. Using the shell prompt, enter the command `ifconfig` and note the IP address of the Ubuntu Desktop VM.

7. Enter the `ssh` command with the IP address of the Ubuntu Server VM. For example, if the server IP address is 192.168.1.147, enter this command:

   `ssh 192.168.1.147`

8. Enter your password on the server to log on to the server using SSH. You now have an SSH session established between the Ubuntu Desktop VM and the Ubuntu Server VM.

9. Enter the **dir** command. What directory is the server's current default directory?

10. Enter the **ifconfig** command. Which IP address is displayed in the command output, the Ubuntu Desktop VM or Ubuntu Server VM?

11. When you're finished using the SSH session, break the session using this command: **exit**

12. To shut down each VM, use this command in each VM: **sudo poweroff**

Case Project 7-2: Create a VPN Connection

For this project, you will set up a very simple VPN connection between two computers on a LAN. More complex, and therefore more secure, VPN software, such as OpenVPN, is a better solution for long-term use. However, the process for setting up this software is beyond the scope of this book. Also, if you were setting up a VPN connection over the Internet, you would have to configure your router for port forwarding on the VPN port, which for PPTP VPN as used in this project is 1723.

First you will set up the host, or server, for the VPN connection. Then you'll set up the client computer for the connection.

1. Windows 7 and 8 have PPTP VPN services embedded in the OS. Using a Windows 7 or Windows 8.1 computer, open the Network Connections window. (For Windows 8.1, right-click the **Start** button and click **Network Connections**. For Windows 7, open the **Network and Sharing Center** and click **Change adapter settings.**)

2. In the Network Connections window, press **ALT** on your keyboard. The menu bar appears. Click **File** and click **New Incoming Connection**. If necessary, enter an admin password in the UAC box and click **Yes**.

3. Check the user account that you want to allow VPN access to this computer. For best security, it should not be an administrator account, and it should have a very strong password. Click **Next**.

4. Check the **Through the Internet** option and click **Next**.

5. Make sure that **Internet Protocol Version 4 (TCP/IPv4)** is checked and click **Allow access**.

6. Write down the computer name, and then click **Close**.

7. Open a command prompt and use **ipconfig** to determine the computer's IP address. Write this information down as well.

8. Next, you need to open Windows Firewall to allow incoming traffic on TCP port 1723, which is the port PPTP uses. Open the **Network and Sharing Center** and click **Windows Firewall**.

9. In Windows Firewall, click **Advanced settings**. Click **Inbound Rules**.

10. In the right pane, click **New Rule**.

11. Click **Port,** and click **Next**. If necessary, select **TCP**.

12. In the Specific local ports box, type **1723**. Click **Next** three times.

13. In the Name box, enter a name for the firewall rule and click **Finish**. Close all windows.

    Next you will enable the client computer to initiate the VPN connection.

14. On a different Windows 7 or 8.1 computer, right-click the network icon in the icon tray. Click **Open Network and Sharing Center**. Then click **Set up a new connection or network**.

15. Click **Connect to a workplace,** then click **Next**.

16. Click **Use my Internet connection (VPN)**, type the IP address of the VPN host computer in the first field and the name of the computer in the second field. Click **Create**.

17. In the next dialog box, type the username that you authorized to use the VPN connection in the first field and the password in the second field. Click **Connect** or, in Windows 8.1, click **OK**. The connection is made.

## chapter 8

Network Risk Management

After reading this chapter and completing the exercises, you will be able to:

- Assess a network's security needs and vulnerabilities

- Describe security risks associated with people, hardware, software, and Internet access

- Discuss the elements of an effective security policy

- Apply appropriate security measures and devices when designing a network

- Prevent and respond to malware infections

On the Job

Security often involves synthesizing tidbits of information from many disparate sources in order to form an accurate picture of what has happened. My team once responded to a report that desktop computers at a biomedical corporation were crashing. Their hard drives had been erased, apparently, by a virus that circumvented the company's antivirus protections.

While examining an affected PC, we noticed that a few processes were still running—thanks to the fact that the operating system generally won't allow the deletion of files that are in use. Among these processes were several instances of svchost.exe. Closer examination revealed that one of these had the same name as the legitimate Windows executable, but was in fact an impostor: A saboteur was at work.

Using a disassembler, we determined that the Trojan checked a folder on a server every minute for the presence of a command file. It would then execute the contents of the command file. We built a program to monitor that directory and archive copies of any files that appeared; our program also recorded the user account that put the file there and the name of the system from which this was done.

The account had domain administrator privileges, and this led us to examine the domain's logon scripts, where we found the code that installed the Trojan on users' workstations. We wrote a second program to record the MAC address of the system when it registered its name with the DHCP server and inspect the ARP tables from the network's switches in order to find the physical port to which it was connected. Then, with a building wiring diagram, we were able to track the culprit to a specific cubicle.

Finding the source of this problem involved knowledge about network infrastructure, operating systems, administration techniques, programming, and reverse engineering. This is an extreme example, to be sure, but real-world security problems seldom confine themselves to a single technical area of specialization.

Peyton Engel
Technical Architect, CDW Corporation

In the early days of computing, when secured mainframes acted as central hosts and data repositories were accessed only by dumb terminals with limited rights, network security was all but unassailable. As networks have become more geographically distributed and heterogeneous, however, the risk of their misuse has also increased. Consider the largest, most heterogeneous network in existence: the Internet. Because it contains billions of points of entry, millions of servers, and billions of miles of transmission paths, it leads to millions of attacks on private networks every day. The threat of an outsider accessing an organization's network via the Internet, and then stealing or destroying data, is very real. In this chapter, you will learn about numerous threats to your network's data and infrastructure, how to manage those vulnerabilities, and, perhaps most important, how to convey the importance of network security to the rest of your organization through an effective security policy. If you choose to specialize in network security, consider attaining CompTIA's Security+ certification, which requires deeper knowledge of the topics covered in this chapter.

Security Assessment

Before spending time and money on network security, you should examine your network's security risks. As you learn about each risk facing your network, consider the effect that a loss or breach of data, programs, or access would have on your network. The more serious the potential consequences, the more attention you need to pay to the security of your network.

Different types of organizations have different levels of network security risk. For example, if you work for a large savings and loan institution that allows its clients to view their current loan status online, you must consider a number of risks associated with data and access. If someone obtained unauthorized access to your network, all of your customers' personal financial data could be vulnerable. On the other hand, if you work for a local car wash that uses its internal LAN only to track assets and sales, you may be less concerned if someone gains access to your network because the implications of unauthorized access or use of sensitive data, called a data breach, are less dire. When considering security risks, the fundamental questions are: "What is at risk?" and "What do I stand to lose if it is stolen, damaged, or eradicated?"

Every organization should assess its security risks by conducting a posture assessment, which is a thorough examination of each aspect of the network to determine how it might be compromised. Posture assessments should be performed at least annually and preferably quarterly. They should also be performed after making any significant changes to the network. For each threat listed in the following sections, your posture assessment should rate the severity of its potential effects, as well as its likelihood of happening. A threat's consequences may be severe, potentially resulting in a network outage or the dispersal of top-secret information, or it may be mild, potentially resulting in a lack of access for one user or the dispersal of a relatively insignificant piece of corporate data. The more devastating a threat's effects and the more likely it is to happen, the more rigorously your security measures should address it.

If your IT Department has sufficient skills and time for routine posture assessments, they can be performed in-house. A qualified consulting company can also assess the security of your network. If the company is accredited by an agency that sets network security standards, the assessment qualifies as a security audit.

Certain customers—for example, a military agency—might require your company to pass an accredited security audit before they'll do business with you. Regulators require some types of companies, such as accounting firms, to host periodic security audits. But even if an audit is optional, the advantage of having an objective third party analyze your network is that they might find risks that you overlooked because of your familiarity with your environment. Security audits might seem expensive, but if your network hosts confidential and critical data, they are well worth the cost.

8

In the next section, you will learn about security risks associated with people, hardware, software, and Internet access.

Security Risks

To understand how to manage network security, you first need to know how to recognize threats that your network could suffer. And to do that, you must be familiar with the terms coined by network security experts. A hacker, in the original sense of the word, is someone who masters the inner workings of computer hardware and software in an effort to better understand them. To be called a hacker used to be a compliment, reflecting extraordinary computer skills. Today, *hacker* is used more generally to describe individuals who gain unauthorized access to systems or networks with or without malicious intent. Hacking might also refer to finding a creative way around a problem, increasing functionality of a device or program, or otherwise manipulating resources beyond their original intent, and has even come to be used in reference to noncomputer related scenarios, such as *life hacking* or *guitar hacks*.

A weakness of a system, process, or architecture that could lead to compromised information or unauthorized access is known as a vulnerability. The act of taking advantage of a vulnerability is known as an exploit. For example, in Chapter 6 you learned about the possibility for unauthorized, or rogue, access points to make themselves available to wireless clients as an evil twin. Once unsuspecting clients associate with such access points, the hacker can steal data in transit or access information on the client's system. The evil twin masquerades as a valid access point, using the same SSID (service set identifier) and potentially other identical settings. This exploit takes advantage of a vulnerability inherent in wireless communications in which SSIDs are openly broadcast and Wi-Fi clients scan for connections.

A zero-day exploit, or zero-day attack, is one that takes advantage of a software vulnerability that hasn't yet become public, and is known only to the hacker who discovered it. Zero-day exploits are particularly dangerous because the vulnerability is exploited before the software developer has the opportunity to provide a solution for it. Most vulnerabilities, however, are well known. Throughout this chapter, you will learn about several kinds of exploits and how to prevent or counteract security threats.

As you read about each vulnerability, think about whether it applies to your network (and if so, how damaging it might be), how an exploit of the vulnerability could be prevented, and how it relates to other security threats. Keep in mind that malicious and determined intruders may use one technique, which then allows them to use a second technique, which then allows them to use a third technique, and so on. For example, a hacker might discover someone's username by watching her log on to the network; the hacker might then use a password-cracking program to access the network, where he might plant a program that generates an extraordinary volume of traffic that essentially disables the network's connectivity devices.

Risks Associated with People

End-user awareness and training can be a monumental task that requires regular attention and due diligence. Ultimately, it is the company's responsibility to ensure that its

characteristics match a permit statement, the packet moves on to the network. If the packet's characteristics match a deny statement, the packet is immediately discarded. If the packet's characteristics don't match the statement, the router moves down the list to the next statement in the ACL. If the packet does not match any criteria given in the statements in the ACL, the packet is dropped (as shown by the last "No" value in Figure 8-3). This last decision is called the implicit deny rule, which ensures that any traffic that the ACL does not explicitly permit is denied by default.

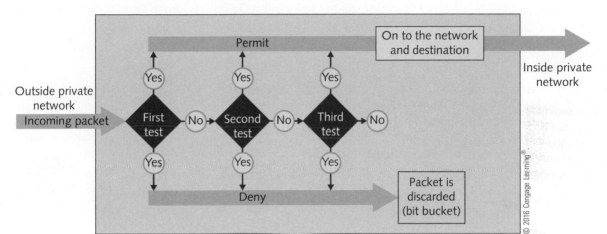

Figure 8-3   A router uses an ACL to deny or permit traffic to or from a network it protects

On most routers, each interface must be assigned a separate ACL, and different ACLs may be associated with inbound and outbound traffic. When ACLs are installed on routers, each ACL is assigned a number or name.

The `access-list` command is used to assign a statement to an already-installed ACL. The command must identify the ACL and include a permit or deny argument. Here are a few sample commands used to create statements in the ACL that controls incoming traffic to a router. The ACL is named `acl_2`:

- To permit ICMP traffic from any IP address or network to any IP address or network:

  `access-list acl_2 permit icmp any any`

- To deny ICMP traffic from any IP address or network to any IP address or network:

  `access-list acl_2 deny icmp any any`

- To permit TCP traffic from 2.2.2.2 host machine to 5.5.5.5 host machine:

  `access-list acl_2 permit tcp host 2.2.2.2 host 5.5.5.5`

- To permit TCP traffic to destination Web port 80 (eq www) from 2.2.2.2 host machine to 3.3.3.3 host machine:

  `access-list acl_2 permit tcp host 2.2.2.2 host 3.3.3.3 eq www`

Statements can also specify network segments (groups of IP addresses) by using a network address for the segment and a wildcard mask. A 0 in the wildcard mask says to match the IP address bits to the network address given, and 1 says you don't care what the IP address bits are. For example, a wildcard mask of 0.0.0.255 can be written as 00000000.00000000.00000000.11111111, which says the first three octets of an IP address must match the given network address, and the last octet can be any value. The following command permits TCP traffic to pass through for which the first three octets of an IP address must be 10.1.1, and the last octet can be any value:

```
access-list acl_2 permit tcp 10.1.1.0 0.0.0.255
```

In ACL statements, any is equivalent to using a wildcard mask of 0.0.0.0, which allows all IP addresses to pass through.

An access list is not automatically installed on a router. If you don't install an ACL, the router allows all traffic through. Once you create an ACL and assign it to an interface, you have explicitly permitted or denied certain types of traffic. Naturally, the more statements or tests a router must scan (in other words, the longer the ACL), the more time it takes a router to act, and, therefore, the slower the router's overall performance.

When troubleshooting problems with performance between two hosts or when some applications or ports can make the connection while others can't, consider the problem might be a misconfigured ACL. For example, suppose you can successfully ping a host, but Telnet and traceroute attempts are unsuccessful on the same host. You can use a process of elimination on the device's various ACLs to identify the misconfigured ACL and correct the problem.

Intrusion Detection and Prevention

An IDS (intrusion detection system) is a stand-alone device or software running on a workstation, server, or switch, which might be managed from another computer on the network (see the left side of Figure 8-4) and is used to monitor network traffic and create alerts when suspicious activity happens. Whereas a router's ACL or a firewall acts like a bouncer at a private club who checks everyone's ID and ensures that only club members enter through the door, an IDS is generally installed to provide security inside the network, similar to security personnel sitting in a private room monitoring closed-circuit cameras in the club and alerting other security personnel when they see suspicious activity.

An IDS sits off to the side of network traffic and is sent duplicates of packets traversing the network. One technique that an IDS may use to monitor traffic carried by a switch is port mirroring. In port mirroring, one port is configured to send a copy of all its traffic to a second port on the switch. The second port issues the copied traffic to a monitoring program. This monitoring program can be located on either the local network or at a remote location.

Two types of IDS implement... ...ed below, and the most thorough security employs both methods in order to de... ...re of threats and provide multiple levels of defense:

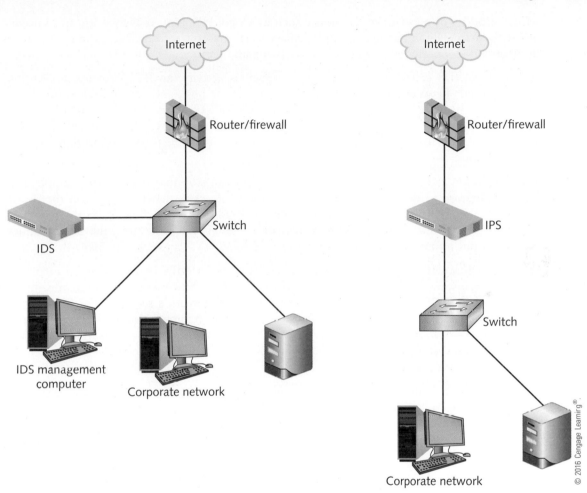

Figure 8-4   An IDS detects traffic, and an IPS can detect and also intercept traffic to protect a corporate network

- A **HIDS (host-based intrusion detection system)** runs on a single computer to alert about attacks to that one host. For example, a HIDS might detect an attempt to exploit an insecure application running on a server or repeated attempts to log on to the server.

- A **NIDS (network-based intrusion detection system)** protects a network and is usually situated at the edge of the network or in a network's protective perimeter, known as the DMZ, or demilitarized zone. Here, it can detect many types of suspicious traffic patterns, including those typical of denial-of-service or smurf attacks, for example.

One drawback to using an IDS is the number of false positives it can log. For instance, it might interpret multiple logon attempts of a legitimate user who's forgotten his password as a security threat. If the IDS is configured to alert the network manager each time such an event occurs, the network manager might be overwhelmed with such warnings and eventually ignore all the IDS's messages. Therefore, to be useful, IDS software must be thoughtfully customized. In addition, to continue to guard against new threats, IDS software must be updated and rules of detection reevaluated regularly.

Major vendors of networking hardware, such as Cisco, HP, Juniper Networks, and Lucent, sell IDS devices. Examples of popular open source IDS software, which can run on virtually any network-connected machine, include Tripwire and Snort.

Although an IDS can only detect and log suspicious activity, an **IPS (intrusion prevention system)** stands between the attacker and the network or host, and can prevent traffic from reaching the protected network or host (see the right side of Figure 8-4). If an IDS is similar to security personnel using closed-circuit cameras to monitor a private club, an IPS would be similar to security personnel walking around in the club available to escort unruly patrons to the exit door.

Because an IPS stands in-line with network traffic, it can stop that traffic. For example, if a hacker's attempt to flood the network with traffic is detected, the IPS can detect the threat and prevent that traffic, based on its originating IP address, from flowing to the network. Thereafter, the IPS will quarantine that malicious user. At the same time, the IPS continues to allow valid traffic to pass.

As with IDS, an IPS can protect entire networks through **NIPS (network-based intrusion prevention system)** or only certain hosts through **HIPS (host-based intrusion prevention system)**. Using NIPS and HIPS together increases the network's security. For example, a HIPS running on a file server might accept a hacker's attempt to log on if the hacker is posing as a legitimate client. With the proper NIPS, however, such a hacker would likely never get to the server. As with an IDS, an IPS must be carefully configured to avoid an abundance of false alarms.

Both an IDS and IPS can be placed inside a network or on the network perimeter. Notice in Figure 8-5, a NIPS is used to monitor traffic in the DMZ and another monitors traffic to one network segment. An IDS/IPS software running on the server or one of the clients within the internal LAN would be an example of HIDS/HIPS. In the figure, you can see HIPS software running on a server.

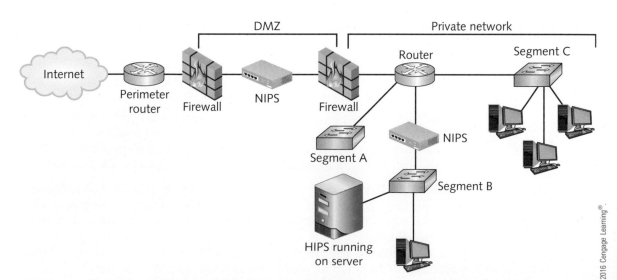

Figure 8-5   Placements of IPS devices and software on a network

Intrusion prevention systems were originally designed as a more comprehensive traffic analysis and protection tool than firewalls, which are discussed next. However, firewalls have evolved, and as a result, the differences between a firewall and an IPS have diminished.

Firewalls

As you learned in Chapter 2, a firewall is a specialized device, or a computer installed with specialized software, that selectively filters or blocks traffic between networks. Whereas IDS/IPS devices and software are installed inside a network to provide security by monitoring traffic on the inside, a firewall protects a network by denying entrance from its position at the edge of a network, similar to a bouncer checking IDs at the entrance to a private club.

A firewall typically involves a combination of hardware and software. The computer acting as a firewall may be placed internally, residing between two interconnected private networks or, more typically, it may be placed external to the private network, monitoring the connection between a private network and a public network (such as the Internet), as shown in Figure 8-6. This is an example of a network-based firewall, so named because it protects an entire network. Typically, traffic is routed to these firewalls before continuing on to various destinations, or alternatively the firewall might be installed in virtual wire mode, meaning the firewall is transparent to surrounding nodes as if it's just part of the wire. Figure 8-7 shows a firewall designed for use in a business with many users. Other types of firewalls, known as host-based firewalls, only protect the computer on which they are installed.

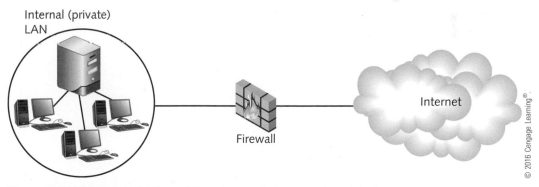

Figure 8-6 Placement of a firewall between a private network and the Internet

Figure 8-7 Firewall device

Source: NETGEAR

Many types of firewalls exist, and they can be implemented in many different ways. To understand secure network design and to qualify for CompTIA Network+ certification, you should recognize which functions firewalls can provide, where they can appear on a network, and how to determine what features you need in a firewall.

The simplest form of a firewall is a **packet-filtering firewall**, which is a router (or a computer installed with software that enables it to act as a router) that examines the header of every packet of data it receives (called **inbound traffic**) to determine whether that type of packet is authorized to continue to its destination. If a packet does not meet the filtering criteria, the firewall blocks the packet from continuing. However, if a packet does meet filtering criteria, the firewall allows that packet to pass through to the network connected to the firewall. This is a common feature of SOHO routers and in fact, nearly all routers can be configured to act as packet-filtering firewalls.

In addition to blocking traffic on its way *into* a LAN, packet-filtering firewalls can also block **outbound traffic**, which is traffic attempting to *exit* a LAN. One possible reason for blocking outbound traffic is to stop worms from spreading. For example, if you are running a Web server, which in most cases only needs to respond to incoming requests and does not need to initiate outgoing requests, you could configure a packet-filtering firewall to block certain types of outgoing transmissions initiated by the Web server. In this way, you help prevent spreading worms that are designed to attach themselves to Web servers and propagate themselves to other computers on the Internet.

Often, firewalls ship with a default configuration designed to block the most common types of security threats. In other words, the firewall may be preconfigured to accept or deny certain types of traffic. However, many network administrators choose to customize the firewall settings, for example, blocking additional ports or adding criteria for the type of traffic that may travel into or out of ports. Some common criteria by which a packet-filtering firewall might accept or deny traffic include the following:

- Source and destination IP addresses
- Source and destination ports (for example, ports that supply TCP/UDP connections, FTP, Telnet, ARP, ICMP, and so on)
- Flags set in the TCP header (for example, SYN or ACK)
- Transmissions that use the UDP or ICMP protocols
- A packet's status as the first packet in a new data stream or a subsequent packet
- A packet's status as inbound to or outbound from your private network

Based on these options, a network administrator could configure his firewall, for example, to prevent any IP address that does not begin with "196.57," the network ID of the addresses on his network, from accessing the network's router and servers. Furthermore, he could disable—or block—certain well-known ports, such as the NetBIOS ports (137, 138, and 139), through the router's configuration. Blocking ports prevents *any* user from connecting to and completing a transmission through those ports. This technique is useful to further guard against unauthorized access to the network. In other words, even if a hacker could spoof an IP address that began with *196.57*, he could not access the NetBIOS ports (which are notoriously insecure) on the firewall. Ports can be blocked not only on firewalls, but also on routers, servers, or any device that uses ports. For example, if you established a Web server for testing but did not want anyone in your organization to connect to your Web pages through his or her browsers, you could block port 80 on that server.

For greater security, you can choose a firewall that performs more complex functions than simply filtering packets. Among the factors to consider when making your decision are the following:

- Does the firewall support encryption?
- Does the firewall support user authentication?
- Does the firewall allow you to manage it centrally and through a standard interface?
- How easily can you establish rules for access to and from the firewall?
- Does the firewall support filtering at the highest layers of the OSI model, not just at the Data Link and Transport layers? For example, content-filtering firewalls can block designated types of traffic based on application data contained within packets. A school might configure its firewall to prevent responses from a Web site with questionable content from reaching the client that requested the site.
- Does the firewall provide internal logging and auditing capabilities, such as IDS or IPS?
- Does the firewall protect the identity of your internal LAN's addresses from the outside world?
- Can the firewall monitor packets according to existing traffic streams? A stateful firewall is able to inspect each incoming packet to determine whether it belongs to a currently active connection (called a stateful inspection) and is, therefore, a legitimate packet. A stateless firewall manages each incoming packet as a stand-alone entity without regard to currently active connections. Stateless firewalls are faster than stateful firewalls, but are not as sophisticated.

In response to the increasing complexity of threats against computing resources, vendors of firewalls and their related products continue to improve and innovate. One such innovation is Unified Threat Management (UTM), which is a security strategy that combines multiple layers of security appliances and technologies into a single safety net. When IDS/IPS works in conjunction with firewalls and other security measures, a UTM solution can provide a full spread of security services managed from a single point of control. One disadvantage to this arrangement is that the "total" really is the sum of its parts. So if one layer of coverage in a UTM is low quality, overall protection is significantly compromised. UTM, due to its multiplicity of features, also requires a great deal of processing power. Because this is less of a challenge today than it was in the past, UTM is regaining ground as a leading security strategy, especially for small- to medium-sized businesses that benefit the most from all-in-one style packages.

Sometimes considered a subset of UTM, Next Generation Firewalls (NGFW) have built-in Application Control features and are application aware, meaning they can monitor and limit the traffic of specific applications, including the application's vendor and digital signature. In addition to Application Control, NGFWs typically include IDS and/or IPS functionality, as well as user awareness, which means the firewall's configuration adapts to the class of a specific user or user group. Newer NGFWs are also context aware, which means they adapt to various applications, users, and devices. This more granular control of configuration settings enables network administrators to fine-tune their security strategies to the specific needs of their companies.

A SOHO wireless router typically acts as a firewall and includes packet-filtering options. At the other end of the spectrum, devices made by Cisco for enterprise-wide security are known as security appliances and can perform several functions, such as encryption, load balancing, and IPS, in addition to packet filtering. Examples of software that enable a computer to act as a packet-filtering firewall include iptables (for Linux systems), ZoneAlarm, and Comodo Firewall. Some operating systems, including Windows 7 and Windows 8.1, include firewall software.

The most common cause of firewall failure is firewall misconfiguration. Configuring an enterprise-level firewall can take weeks to achieve the best results. As you consider the type of traffic, the configuration must not be so strict that it prevents authorized users from transmitting and receiving necessary data, yet not so lenient that you unnecessarily risk security breaches.

Further complicating the matter is that you might need to create exceptions to the rules. For example, suppose that your human resources manager is working from a conference center in Salt Lake City while recruiting new employees and needs to access the Denver server that stores payroll information. In this instance, the Denver network administrator might create an exception to allow transmissions from the human resources manager's workstation's IP address to reach that server. In the networking profession, creating an exception to the filtering rules is called "punching a hole" in the firewall.

Network+
1.1
2.4
3.2
3.5
3.6
4.7

Applying Concepts
Windows Firewall

Follow these steps to find out how to configure Windows Firewall on a Windows 7 machine (the steps are similar for Windows 8.1):

1. Open Windows Firewall from Control Panel, as shown in Figure 8-8.

2. To control firewall settings for each type of network location, click **Turn Windows Firewall on or off** in the left pane. The Windows Firewall Customize Settings window appears (see Figure 8-9). Notice in the figure that Windows Firewall is turned on for each network location.

3. To allow no exceptions through the firewall on a home or work (private) network or public network, check **Block all incoming connections, including those in the list of allowed programs**. After you have made your changes, click **OK**.

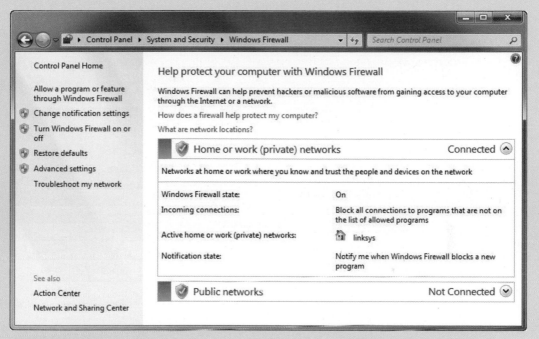

Figure 8-8   Windows Firewall shows the computer currently connected to a private network

Source: Microsoft LLC

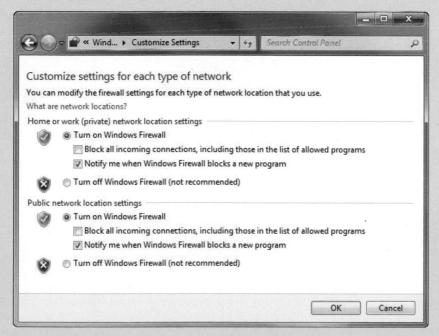

Figure 8-9   Customize settings for a private or public network

Source: Microsoft LLC

4. You can allow an exception to your firewall rules. To change the programs allowed through the firewall, in the left pane of the Windows Firewall window (shown earlier in Figure 8-8), click **Allow a program or feature through Windows Firewall**. The Allowed Programs window appears (see Figure 8-10).

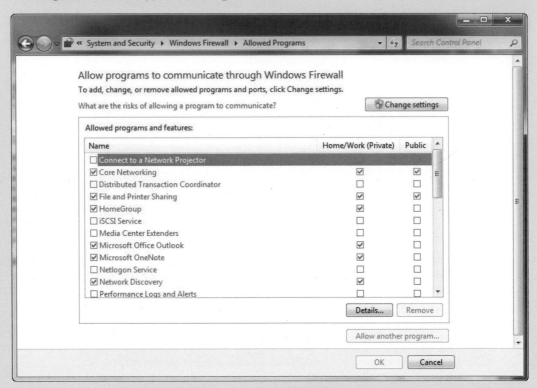

Figure 8-10   Allow programs to communicate through the firewall

Source: Microsoft LLC

5. Scroll down to find the program you want to allow to initiate a connection from a remote computer to this computer, and then, in the right side of the window, click the **Home/Work (Private)** check box and/or the **Public** check box to indicate which type of network location the program is allowed to use. If you don't see your program in the list, click **Allow another program**, near the bottom of the window, to see more programs or to add your own. (If the option is gray, click **Change settings** to enable it.) When you are finished making changes, click **OK** to return to the Windows Firewall window.

6. For even more control over firewall settings, in the Windows Firewall window, click **Advanced settings**. The Windows Firewall with Advanced Security window opens. In the left pane, select **Inbound Rules or Outbound Rules**. A list of programs appears. Right-click a program and select **Properties** from the shortcut menu. Using the Properties dialog box, you have full control of how exceptions work to get through the firewall, including which users, protocols, ports, and remote computers can use it (see Figure 8-11).

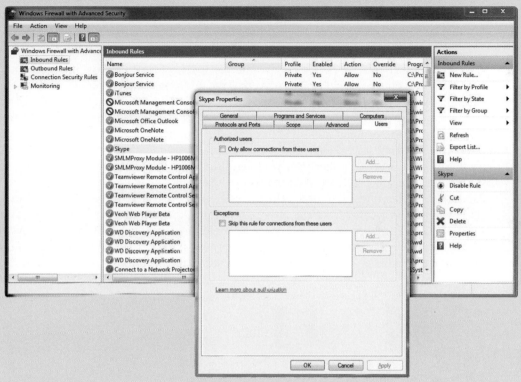

Figure 8-11   Use advanced settings to control exactly how a program can get through Windows Firewall
Source: Microsoft LLC

Because simple packet-filtering firewalls operate at the Network layer of the OSI model and examine only network addresses, they cannot distinguish between a user who is trying to breach the firewall and a user who is authorized to do so. For example, your organization might host a Web server, which necessitates accepting requests for port 80 on that server. In this case, a packet-filtering firewall, because it only examines the packet header, could not distinguish between a harmless Web browser and a hacker attempting to manipulate his way through the Web site to gain access to the network. For higher-layer security, a firewall that can analyze data at higher layers is required. The next section describes this kind of device.

Proxy Servers

One approach to enhancing the Network and Transport layer security provided by firewalls is to combine a packet-filtering firewall with a proxy service. A **proxy service** is a software application on a network host that acts as an intermediary between the external and internal networks, screening all incoming and outgoing traffic. The network host that runs the proxy service is known as a **proxy server** (or simply proxy). Proxy servers manage security at the Application layer of the OSI model. To understand how they work, think of the secure data on a server as the president of a country and the proxy server as the secretary of state. Rather than have the president risk his safety by leaving the country, the secretary of state travels abroad, speaks for the president, and gathers information on the president's behalf. In fact, foreign leaders may never actually meet the president. Instead, the secretary of state acts as his proxy. In a similar way, a proxy server represents a private network to another network (usually the Internet).

Although a proxy server appears to the outside world as an internal network server, in reality it is merely another filtering device for the internal LAN. One of its most important functions is preventing the outside world from discovering the addresses of the internal network. For example, suppose your LAN uses a proxy server, and you want to send an email message from your workstation to your mother via the Internet. Your message would first go to the proxy server (depending on the configuration of your network, you might or might not have to log on separately to the proxy server first). The proxy server would repackage the data frames that make up the message so that, rather than your workstation's IP address being the source, the proxy server inserts its own IP address as the source. Next, the proxy server passes your repackaged data to the packet-filtering firewall. The firewall verifies that the source IP address in your packets is valid (that it came from the proxy server) and then sends your message to the Internet. Examples of proxy server software include Squid (for use on UNIX or Linux systems) and Microsoft Forefront Threat Management Gateway (TMG) 2010, which includes firewall features as well. Figure 8-12 depicts how a proxy server might fit into a WAN design.

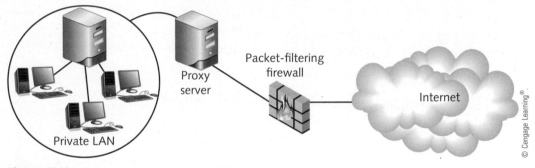

Figure 8-12   A proxy server used on a WAN

Microsoft has announced that it will be retiring Forefront TMG; however, the software is still considered to be a good option for providing proxy services on a network and will continue to be supported by Microsoft until early 2020.

You might have noticed that proxy services sound suspiciously similar to NAT, which you learned about in Chapter 2. However, there are some very significant differences. You've already learned that proxy servers can provide some filtering of content, which is possible because they function at the Application layer rather than at the lower, Network layer. Proxy servers can also improve performance for users accessing resources external to their network by caching files. For example, a proxy server situated between a LAN and an external Web server can be configured to save recently viewed Web pages. The next time a user on the LAN wants to view one of the saved Web pages, content is provided by the proxy server. This eliminates the time required to travel over a WAN and retrieve the content from the external Web server.

Whereas proxy servers access resources on the Internet for a client, a **reverse proxy** provides services to Internet clients from servers on its own network. In this case, the reverse proxy provides identity protection for the server rather than the client, as well as Application layer firewall protection. Reverse proxies are particularly useful when multiple Web servers are accessed through the same public IP address.

 Often, firewall and proxy server features are combined in one device. In other words, you might purchase a firewall and be able to configure it to block certain types of traffic from entering your network and also modify the addresses in the packets leaving your network.

 ## SIEM (Security Information and Event Management)

IDS, IPS, firewalls, and proxy servers all generate a great deal of data that is stored in logs and must be monitored and analyzed in order to be of particular use in real time. SIEM (Security Information and Event Management) systems can be configured to evaluate all of this data, looking for significant events that require attention from the IT staff according to predefined rules.

The capability required of the SIEM is determined by the amount of storage space needed for the amount of data generated, and by the number of events to be processed per second. Consider all of the devices, such as switches, routers, servers, and security systems that will feed data to the SIEM, and allow for future growth of this traffic as well.

The network administrator can fine-tune a SIEM's configuration rules for the specific needs of a particular network by defining which events should trigger which responses. The SIEM system can also be configured to monitor particular indicators of anticipated problems or issues. These rules should be reevaluated periodically. Also, network technicians should review the raw data on a regular basis to ensure that no glaring indicators are being missed by existing rules.

 ## Scanning Tools

Despite your best efforts to secure a network with router access lists, IDS/IPS, firewalls, and proxy servers, you might overlook a critical vulnerability. To ensure that your security efforts are thorough, it helps to think like a hacker. During a posture assessment, for example, you might use some of the same methods a hacker uses to identify cracks in your security architecture. Scanning tools provide hackers—and you—with a simple and reliable way to discover crucial information about your network, including, but not limited to, the following:

- Every available host
- Services, including applications and versions, running on every host
- Operating systems running on every host
- Open, closed, and filtered ports on every host
- Existence and type of firewalls
- Software configurations
- Unencrypted, sensitive data

For example, as you learned in Chapter 4, the popular scanning tool Nmap (Network Mapper) is designed to scan large networks quickly and provide information about a network and its hosts. Nmap began as a simple port-scanning tool, but developers later expanded its capabilities to include gathering information about hosts and their software. When running Nmap, you can choose what type of information to discover, thereby customizing your scan results.

Another tool, Nessus, from Tenable Security, performs even more sophisticated vulnerability scans than Nmap. Among other things, Nessus can identify unencrypted, sensitive data, such as credit card numbers, saved on your network's hosts. The program can be purchased to run on your network or to run on off-site servers continuously maintained and updated by the developer. Because of its comprehensive nature and its use for revealing security flaws that must be addressed, Nessus and utilities like it are known as penetration testing tools. Another popular penetration testing tool, metasploit, combines known scanning techniques and exploits to explore potentially new hybrids of exploits.

Used intentionally on your own network, scanning tools improve security by pointing out insecure ports, software and firmware that must be patched, permissions that should be restricted, and so on. They can also contribute valuable data to asset management and audit reports. Used by hackers—or, more likely, bots—these tools can lead to compromised security. In other words, each of these tools has legitimate uses as well as illegal uses. However, even if the scanning tools are used against you, you can learn from them. For example, a properly configured firewall will collect information about scanning attempts in its log. By reviewing the log, you will discover what kinds of exploits might be—or have been—attempted against your network. Another way to learn about hackers is to lure them to your network on purpose, as described next.

Honeypots and Honeynets

Staying a step ahead of hackers and constantly evolving exploits requires vigilance. Those who want to learn more about hacking techniques or nab a hacker in the act might create a honeypot, or a decoy system that is purposely vulnerable and filled with what appears to be sensitive (though false) content, such as financial data. To lure hackers, the system might be given an enticing name, such as one that indicates its role as a name server or a storage location for confidential data. Once hackers access the honeypot, a network administrator can use monitoring software and logs to track the intruder's moves. In this way, the network administrator might learn about new vulnerabilities that must be addressed on his real networked hosts.

To fool hackers and gain useful information, honeypots cannot appear too blatantly insecure, and tracking mechanisms must be hidden. In addition, a honeypot must be isolated from secure systems to prevent a savvy hacker from using it as an intermediate host for other attacks. In more elaborate setups, several honeypots might be connected to form a honeynet.

Decoy systems, also called lures, can provide unique information about hacking behavior. But in practice, security researchers or those merely curious about hacking trends are more likely than overworked network administrators to establish and monitor honeypots and honeynets.

Troubleshooting Malware Risks and Infections

Malware refers to any program or piece of code designed to intrude upon or harm a system or its resources. The term *malware* is derived from a combination of the words *malicious* and *software*. Included in this category are viruses, Trojan horses, worms, and bots, all of which are described in this section.

Strictly speaking, a **virus** is a program that replicates itself with the intent to infect more computers, either through network connections when it piggybacks on other files or through the exchange of external storage devices. Viruses are typically copied to a computer's storage device without the user's knowledge. A virus might damage files or systems, or it might simply annoy users by flashing messages or pictures on the screen, for example. In fact, some viruses cause no harm and can remain unnoticed on a system indefinitely.

Many other unwanted and potentially destructive programs are often called viruses, but technically do not meet the criteria used to define a virus. For example, a program that disguises itself as something useful but actually harms your system is called a **Trojan horse** (or simply, Trojan), after the famous wooden horse in which soldiers were hidden. Because Trojan horses do not replicate themselves, they are not considered viruses. An example of a Trojan horse is an executable file that someone sends you over the Internet, promising that the executable will install a great new game, when in fact it erases data on your hard disk or mails spam to all the users in your email program's address book.

In this section, you will learn about the different viruses and other malware that can infect your network, their methods of distribution, and, most important, protection against them. Malware can harm computers running any type of operating system—Macintosh, Windows, Linux, UNIX, or Android—at any time. As a network administrator, you must take measures to guard against them.

Network+
3.2
4.7

Malware Types and Characteristics

Malware can be classified into different categories based on where it resides on a computer and how it propagates itself. All malware belongs to one of the following categories:

- **Boot sector viruses** position their code in the boot sector of a computer's hard disk so that when the computer boots up, the virus runs in place of the computer's normal system files. Boot sector viruses are commonly spread from external storage devices to hard disks. Boot sector viruses vary in their destructiveness. Some merely display a screen advertising the virus's presence when you boot the infected computer. Others do not advertise themselves, but stealthily destroy system files or make it impossible for the file system to access at least some of the computer's files. Examples of boot sector viruses include Michelangelo and the Stoned virus, which was widespread in the early 1990s (in fact, it disabled U.S. military computers during the 1991 Persian Gulf War) and persists today in many variations. Until you disinfect a computer that harbors a boot sector virus, the virus propagates to every external disk to which that computer writes information. Removing a boot sector virus first requires rebooting the computer from an uninfected, write-protected disk with system files on it. Only after the computer is booted from a source other than the infected hard disk can you run software to remove the boot sector virus.

- **Macro viruses** take the form of a macro (such as the kind used in a word-processing or spreadsheet program), which can be executed as the user works with a program. For example, you might send a Microsoft Word document as an attachment to an email message. If that document contains a macro virus, when the recipient opens the document, the macro runs, and all future documents created or saved by that program are infected. Macro viruses were the first type of virus to infect data files rather than executable files. They are quick to emerge and spread because they are easy to write, and because users share data files more frequently than executable files.

- File-infector viruses attach themselves to executable files. When an infected executable file runs, the virus copies itself to memory. Later, the virus attaches itself to other executable files. Some file-infector viruses attach themselves to other programs even while their "host" executable runs a process in the background, such as a printer service or screen saver program. Because they stay in memory while you continue to work on your computer, these viruses can have devastating consequences, infecting numerous programs and requiring that you disinfect your computer, as well as reinstall virtually all software.

- Worms are programs that run independently and travel between computers and across networks. They may be transmitted by any type of file transfer, including email attachments. Worms do not alter other programs in the same way that viruses do, but they can carry viruses. Because they can transport and hide viruses, you should be concerned about picking up worms when you exchange files from the Internet, via email, or on flash drives.

- As mentioned earlier, a Trojan horse is a program that claims to do something useful but instead harms the computer or system. Trojan horses range from being nuisances to causing significant system destruction. The best way to guard against Trojan horses is to refrain from downloading an executable file whose origins you can't confirm. Suppose, for example, that you needed to download a new driver for a NIC on your network. Rather than going to a generic network support site on the Internet, you should download the file from the NIC manufacturer's Web site. Most important, never run an executable file that was sent to you over the Internet as an attachment to an email message whose sender or origins you cannot verify.

- Network viruses propagate themselves via network protocols, commands, messaging programs, and data links. Although all viruses can theoretically travel across network connections, network viruses are specially designed to take advantage of network vulnerabilities. For example, a network virus may attach itself to FTP transactions to and from your Web server. Another type of network virus may spread through Microsoft Outlook messages only.

- Another malware category defined by its propagation method is a bot. In networking, the term bot (short for robot) means a program that runs automatically, without requiring a person to start or stop it. One type of bot is a virus that propagates itself automatically between systems. It does not require an unsuspecting user to download and run an executable file or to boot from an infected disk, for example. Many bots spread through the IRC (Internet Relay Chat), a protocol that enables users running IRC client software to communicate instantly with other participants in a chat room on the Internet. Chat rooms require an IRC server, which accepts messages from an IRC client and either broadcasts the messages to all other chat room participants (in an open chat room) or sends the message to select users (in a restricted chat room). Malicious bots take advantage of IRC to transmit data, commands, or executable programs from one infected participant to others. After a bot has copied files on a client's hard disk, these files can be used to damage or destroy a computer's data or system files, issue objectionable content, and further propagate the malware. Bots are especially difficult to contain because of their fast, surreptitious, and distributed dissemination.

Certain characteristics can make malware harder to detect and eliminate. Some of these characteristics, which can be found in any type of malware, include the following:

- *encryption*—Some viruses, worms, and Trojan horses are encrypted to prevent detection. Most anti-malware software searches files for a recognizable string of characters that identify the virus. However, an encrypted virus, for example, might thwart the antivirus program's attempts to detect it.

- *stealth*—Some malware hides itself to prevent detection. For example, stealth viruses disguise themselves as legitimate programs or replace part of a legitimate program's code with their destructive code.

- *polymorphism*—Polymorphic viruses change their characteristics (such as the arrangement of their bytes, size, and internal instructions) every time they are transferred to a new system, making them harder to identify. Some polymorphic viruses use complicated algorithms and incorporate nonsensical commands to achieve their changes. Polymorphic viruses are considered the most sophisticated and potentially dangerous type of virus.

- *time dependence*—Some viruses, worms, and Trojan horses are programmed to activate on a particular date. This type of malware can remain dormant and harmless until its activation date arrives. Like any other malware, time-dependent malware can have destructive effects or might cause some innocuous event periodically. For example, viruses in the "Time" family cause a PC's speaker to beep approximately once per hour. Time-dependent malware can include logic bombs, or programs designed to start when certain conditions are met. (Logic bombs can also activate when other types of conditions, such as a specific change to a file, are met, and they are not always malicious.)

Malware can exhibit more than one of the preceding characteristics. The Natas virus, for example, combines polymorphism and stealth techniques to create a very destructive virus. Hundreds of new viruses, worms, Trojan horses, and bots are unleashed on the world's computers each month. Although it is impossible to keep abreast of every virus in circulation, you should at least know where you can find out more information about malware. An excellent resource for learning about new viruses, their characteristics, and ways to get rid of them is McAfee's Virus Information Library at *home.mcafee.com/virusinfo/*.

Anti-Malware Software

You might think that you can simply install a virus-scanning program on your network and move to the next issue. In fact, protection against harmful code involves more than just installing anti-malware software. It requires choosing the most appropriate anti-malware program for your environment, monitoring the network, continually updating the anti-malware program, and educating users.

Even if a user doesn't immediately notice malware on her system, the harmful software generally leaves evidence of itself, whether by changing the operation of the machine or by announcing its signature characteristics in the malware code. Although the latter can be detected only via anti-malware software, users can typically detect the operational changes without any special software. For example, you might suspect a virus on your system if any of the following symptoms arise:

- Unexplained increases in file sizes
- Significant, unexplained decline in system or network performance (for example, a program takes much longer than usual to start or to save a file)
- Unusual error messages with no apparent cause
- Significant, unexpected loss of system memory
- Periodic, unexpected rebooting
- Fluctuations in display quality

Often, however, you don't notice malware until it has already damaged your files.

Although malware programmers have become more sophisticated in disguising their software, anti-malware software programmers have kept pace with them. The anti-malware software you choose for your network should at least perform the following functions:

- Detect malware through **signature scanning**, a comparison of a file's content with known malware signatures (that is, the unique identifying characteristics in the code) in a signature database. This signature database must be frequently updated so that the software can detect new viruses as they emerge. Updates can be downloaded from the anti-malware software vendor's Web site. Alternatively, you can configure such updates to be copied from the Internet to your computer automatically, with or without your consent.
- Detect malware through **integrity checking**, a method of comparing current characteristics of files and disks against an archived version of these characteristics to discover any changes. The most common example of integrity checking involves using a checksum, though this tactic might not prove effective against malware with stealth capabilities.
- Detect malware by monitoring unexpected file changes or virus-like behaviors.
- Receive regular updates and modifications from a centralized network console. The vendor should provide free upgrades on a regular (at least monthly) basis, plus technical support.
- Consistently report only valid instances of malware, rather than reporting false alarms. Scanning techniques that attempt to identify malware by discovering "malware-like" behavior, also known as **heuristic scanning**, are the most fallible and most likely to emit false alarms.

Your implementation of anti-malware software depends on your computing environment's needs. For example, you might use a desktop security program on every computer on the network that prevents users from copying executable files to their hard disks or to network drives. In this case, it might be unnecessary to implement a program that continually scans each machine; in fact, this approach might be undesirable because the continual scanning adversely affects performance. On the other hand, if you are the network administrator for a student computer lab where potentially thousands of different users bring their own USB drives for use on the computers, you will want to scan the machines thoroughly at least once a day and perhaps more often.

When implementing anti-malware software on a network, one of your most important decisions is where to install the software. Some scenarios include:

- *host-based*—If you install anti-malware software on every desktop, you have addressed the most likely point of entry, but ignored the most important files that might be infected—those on the server. Host-based anti-malware also provides insufficient coverage when a significant portion of the network is virtualized, as you will learn in Chapter 10.

- *server-based*—If the anti-malware software resides on the server and checks every file and transaction, you will protect important files, but slow your network performance considerably.

- *network-based*—Securing the network's gateways, where the Internet connects with the interior network, can provide a formidable layer of defense against the primary source of intrusion—the Internet. However, this does nothing to prevent users from putting the network at risk with infected files on flash drives, laptops, or smartphones.

- *cloud-based*—Many anti-malware solutions already employ cloud-based resources within their programming. And cloud-based anti-malware provides the same kinds of benefits as other cloud-based solutions, such as scalability, cost efficiency, and shared resources. These cloud vendors are still working out bugs, and it can be a challenge to ensure that coverage soaks the entire network with no blind spots. Cloud solutions also increase the amount of Internet traffic in order to perform their duties.

To find a balance between sufficient protection and minimal impact on performance, you must examine your network's vulnerabilities and critical performance needs.

Anti-Malware Policies

Anti-malware software alone will not keep your network safe from malicious code. Because most malware can be prevented by applying a little technology and forethought, it's important that all network users understand how to prevent the spread of malware. An anti-malware policy provides rules for using anti-malware software, as well as policies for installing programs, sharing files, and using external storage such as flash drives. To be most effective, anti-malware policy should be authorized and supported by the organization's management. Suggestions for anti-malware policy guidelines include the following:

- Every computer in an organization should be equipped with malware detection and cleaning software that regularly scans for malware. This software should be centrally distributed and updated to stay current with newly released malware.

- Users should not be allowed to alter or disable the anti-malware software.

- Users should know what to do in case their anti-malware program detects malware. For example, you might recommend that the user stop working on his computer, and instead call the help desk to receive assistance in disinfecting the system.

- An anti-malware team should be appointed to focus on maintaining the anti-malware measures. This team would be responsible for choosing anti-malware software, keeping the software updated, educating users, and responding in case of a significant malware outbreak.

- Users should be prohibited from installing any unauthorized software on their systems. This edict might seem extreme, but in fact users downloading programs (especially games) from the Internet are a common source of malware. If your organization permits game playing, you might institute a policy in which every game must be first checked for malware and then installed on a user's system by a technician.

- Systemwide alerts should be issued to network users notifying them of a serious malware threat and advising them how to prevent infection, even if the malware hasn't been detected on your network yet.

When drafting an anti-malware policy, bear in mind that these measures are not meant to restrict users' freedom, but rather to protect the network from damage and downtime. Explain to users that the anti-malware policy protects their own data as well as critical system files. If possible, automate the anti-malware software installation and operation so that users barely notice its presence. Do not rely on users to run their anti-malware software each time they insert a USB drive or open an email attachment because they will quickly forget to do so.

Chapter Summary

Security Assessment

- Different types of organizations have different levels of network security risk. A posture assessment should be conducted at least annually if not quarterly, and should rate the severity of potential threats as well as the likelihood of their occurrence.

Security Risks

- A weakness of a system, process, or architecture that could lead to compromised information or unauthorized access is known as a vulnerability. The act of taking advantage of a vulnerability is known as an exploit.

- Human error accounts for so many security breaches because taking advantage of people is often an easy way to circumvent network security.

- Attacks at Layers 1, 2, and 3 of the OSI model require more technical sophistication than those that take advantage of human errors.

- Networked software is only as secure as you configure it to be.

- By keeping software current, staying abreast of emerging security threats, and designing your Internet access wisely, users can prevent most Internet-related security threats.

Effective Security Policies

- Effective security policies help minimize the risk of break-ins by communicating with and managing the users in an organization via a thoroughly planned security policy.

- A security policy must address an organization's specific risks. To understand your risks, you should conduct a posture assessment that identifies vulnerabilities and rates both the severity of each threat and its likelihood of occurring.

- Although compiling all of the information required for a good security policy might seem daunting, the process ensures that everyone understands the organization's stance on security and the reasons it is important.

Security in Network Design

- Preventing external security breaches from affecting your network is a matter of restricting access at every point where your LAN connects to the rest of the world.

- Network administrators should group users according to their security levels and assign additional rights that meet the needs of those groups.

- In addition to restricting users' access to files and directories on the server, a network administrator can constrain the ways in which users can access the server and its resources.

- A network access control (NAC) solution employs a set of rules, called network policies, which determine the level and type of access granted to a device when it joins a network.

- A router's main function is to examine packets and determine where to direct them based on their Network layer addressing information. Thanks to routers' ACLs, they can also decline to forward certain packets.

- A network administrator might use techniques to monitor and flag any unauthorized attempt to access an organization's secured network resources using an IDS. An IDS, though, can only detect and log suspicious activity. An IPS can react when alerted to such activity.

- A firewall typically involves a combination of hardware and software. The computer acting as a firewall may be placed internally, residing between two interconnected private networks or, more typically, it may be placed external to the private network, monitoring the connection between a private network and a public network.

- A proxy server represents a private network to another network. Proxy servers can provide some filtering of content, and can improve performance for users accessing resources external to their network by caching files.

- Scanning tools provide network administrators with a simple and reliable way to discover crucial information about their network.

- A honeypot is a decoy system used to attract hacking attacks in order to learn more about the techniques being used against a network.

Troubleshooting Malware Risks and Infections

- Malware can harm computers running any type of operating system at any time.

- Malware can be classified into different categories based on where it resides on a computer and how it propagates itself.

- Protecting a computer or a network from malware requires choosing the most appropriate anti-malware program for the specific environment, monitoring the network, continually updating the anti-malware program, and educating the users.

- Because most malware can be prevented by applying a little technology with a lot of forethought and caution, it's important that all network users understand how to prevent the spread of malware. An anti-malware policy provides rules for using anti-malware software, as well as policies for installing programs, sharing files, and using external storage.

Key Terms

For definitions of key terms, see the Glossary near the end of the book.

acceptable use policy (AUP)

access list

ACL (access control list)

agent

amplification attack

application aware

Application Control

ARP cache poisoning

backdoor

banner-grabbing attack

boot sector virus

bot

botnet

buffer overflow

consent to monitoring

content-filtering firewall

context aware

data breach

denial-of-service (DoS) attack

DHCP snooping

dissolvable agent

distributed DoS (DDoS) attack

distributed reflector DoS (DRDoS) attack

domain local group

dynamic ARP inspection (DAI)

emission security (EmSec)

encrypted virus

exploit

file-infector virus

flashing

friendly attack

FTP bounce

Group Policy (gpedit.msc)

hacker

hacking

hardening technique

heuristic scanning

HIDS (host-based intrusion detection system)

HIPS (host-based intrusion prevention system)

honeynet

honeypot

host-based firewall

IDS (intrusion detection system)

implicit deny

inbound traffic

integrity checking

IP spoofing

IPS (intrusion prevention system)

IRC (Internet Relay Chat)

jamming

logic bomb

lure

macro virus

malware

man-in-the-middle (MitM) attack

master zombie

metasploit

Nessus

network access control (NAC)

network policy

network segmentation

network virus

network-based firewall

Next Generation Firewall (NGFW)

NIDS (network-based intrusion detection system)

NIPS (network-based intrusion prevention system)

nonpersistent agent

outbound traffic

packet-filtering firewall

penetration testing

permanent DoS (PDoS) attack

persistent agent

phishing

physical attack

ping of death

polymorphic virus

port mirroring

port scanner

posture assessment

proxy server

proxy service

quarantine network

reflective attack

reflector

reverse proxy

RF (radio frequency) emanation

security audit

security policy (configuration)

security policy (document)

session hijacking attack

SIEM (Security Information and
Event Management)

signature scanning

slave zombie

smurf attack

social engineering

spoofing

stateful firewall

stateless firewall

stealth virus

TEMPEST

Trojan horse

Unified Threat Management
(UTM)

unintentional DoS attack

user awareness

virtual wire mode

virus

vulnerability

wildcard mask

worm

zero-day attack

zero-day exploit

zombie

zombie army

Review Questions

1. Your organization has just approved a special budget for a network security upgrade.
   What procedure should you conduct in order to make recommendations for the upgrade
   priorities?

   a. Data breach

   b. Security audit

   c. Exploitation

   d. Posture assessment

2. What wireless attack might a potential hacker execute with a specially configured
   transmitter?

   a. Jamming

   b. Vulnerability

   c. Evil twin

   d. Zero-day exploit

3. What kind of vulnerability is exploited by a ping of death?

   a. Zero-day exploit

   b. Buffer overflow

   c. Social engineering

   d. Backdoor

4. Which type of DoS attack orchestrates an attack using uninfected computers?

   a. DDoS (distributed DoS) attack

   b. Smurf attack

   c. DRDoS (distributed reflector DoS) attack

   d. PDoS (permanent DoS) attack

5. What software might be installed on a device in order to authenticate it to the network?

   a. Operating system

   b. Security policy

   c. NAC (network access control)

   d. Agent

6. What feature of Windows Server allows for agentless authentication?

   a. Active Directory

   b. ACL (access control list)

   c. IDS (intrusion detection system)

   d. Network-based firewall

7. What kind of firewall blocks traffic based on application data contained within the packets?

   a. Host-based firewall

   b. Content-filtering firewall

   c. Packet-filtering firewall

   d. Stateless firewall

8. What of the following features does *not* distinguish an NGFW from traditional firewalls?

   a. Application Control

   b. IDS and/or IPS

   c. User awareness

   d. UTM (Unified Threat Management)

9. At what layer of the OSI model do proxy servers operate?

   a. Layer 3

   b. Layer 2

   c. Layer 7

   d. Layer 4

10. What kind of virus runs in place of the computer's normal system files?

    a. Worms

    b. Macro viruses

    c. File-infector viruses

    d. Boot sector viruses

11. What unique characteristic of zero-day exploits make them so dangerous?

12. What characteristic of ARP makes it particularly vulnerable to being used in a DoS attack?

13. A neighbor hacks into your secured wireless network on a regular basis, but you didn't give him the password. What loophole was most likely left open?

14. Regarding managing security levels, why do network administrators create domain groups?

15. What kinds of issues might indicate a misconfigured ACL?

16. Any traffic that is not explicitly permitted in the ACL is _____ , which is called the _____ .

17. What's the difference between an IDS and an IPS?

18. What causes most firewall failures?

19. What are the two primary features that give proxy servers an advantage over NAT?

20. What distinguishes a virus from other types of malware?

Hands-On Projects

Project 8-1: Research Antivirus Software

For Windows machines, the built-in Windows Defender is considered to be a fairly decent solution for home users, but it does have inherent weaknesses. Several good antivirus solutions are available on the market today, some of which are OS agnostic (meaning they work for multiple operating systems) and some of which are customized to a specific OS. Many also have free versions. In this project, you research options for two different operating systems:

1. From the following list, select two operating systems for which you will research antivirus options: Windows, Linux, OS X, Android, Chrome OS, or UNIX.

2. Research and select three antivirus solutions for your chosen operating systems. Compare features, cost, reported effectiveness, and feedback from reviewers.

3. Create a table or spreadsheet comparing the pros and cons of each alternative. Which would you choose and why?

Project 8-2: Monitor Security Events in Windows 7

Repeated failures at logging on to a system might indicate someone is trying to guess a password and gain unauthorized access to a user account. Follow these steps to use Local Security Policy in Windows 7 (Professional, Ultimate, or Enterprise) to monitor failures when someone is attempting to log on to the system:

1. Log on as an administrator and create a new standard user account (**Start, Control Panel, User Accounts and Family Safety, Add or remove user accounts, Create a new account**) called **Newuser**. Create a password for this new user account.

NOTE   Although these steps are written for a Windows 7 machine, Windows 8.1 Pro and Enterprise editions also include a version of Local Security Policy called *secpol.msc*. The steps are somewhat different, so you'll have to adjust these steps as you go. To complete this first step on a Windows 8.1 machine, create the new account in PC Settings (Charms bar, Settings, Change PC settings, Accounts, Other accounts, Add an account). Click Sign in without a Microsoft account (not recommended) then click Local account. The new user account does not need an email address for the purposes of this project.

2. Using Control Panel, open **Administrative Tools**. Double-click **Local Security Policy**.

3. Expand the **Local Policies** group, and select **Audit Policy**. How many policies appear in the right pane for the Audit Policy group?

4. Double-click **Audit account logon events**. The Audit account logon events Properties dialog box opens.

5. Select the **Failure** check box, as shown in Figure 8-13, and then click **OK**. Do the same for **Audit logon events**.

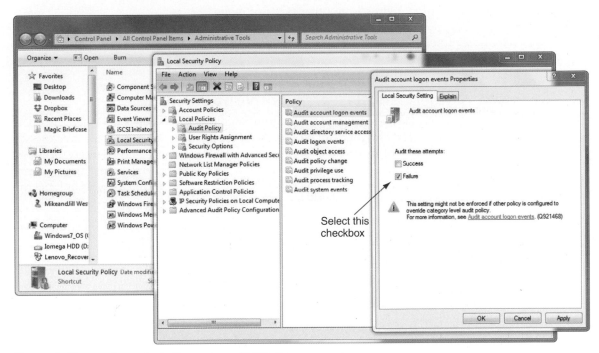

Figure 8-13   Local Security Policy set to audit failed logon events

Source: Microsoft LLC

6. Examine the other Audit Policy policies. Which one would you use to monitor when a password is changed? Close the Local Security Policy window.

7. To see the logged audit events, open **Event Viewer**. In the left pane, select **Windows Logs**, and then select **Security**. How many events are logged in this group of events? Does Event Viewer currently list any logon failures?

8. Log off and attempt to log on to the Newuser account using an incorrect password.

9. Now log back on using an administrator account.

10. Open Event Viewer and again select the **Security** logs, as shown in Figure 8-14. What is the date and time that Windows recorded for the failed logon attempt?

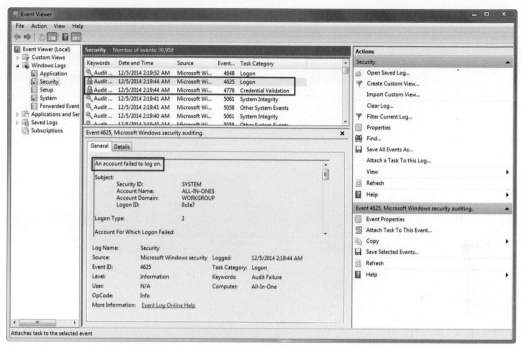

Figure 8-14 Event Viewer displays the failed logon event

Source: Microsoft LLC

11. Close all open windows.

Follow these steps to monitor changes to files and folders:

12. Open the Local Security Policy window and locate the Audit Policy policies, as you did earlier in this project. Double-click **Audit object access**. The Audit object access Properties dialog box appears. Click the **Explain** tab and answer the following questions:

a. What is a SACL (pronounced "sackel")?

b. Which dialog box do you use to set a SACL for a file system object?

13. On the Local Security Setting tab, select the **Success** and **Failure** check boxes, and then click **OK**. Close the Local Security Policy window.

14. Now let's set Windows to audit activity in the Public folder. To do so, open the Properties dialog box of the C:\Users\Public folder and click the **Security** tab.

15. Click **Advanced**, select the **Auditing** tab, and click **Continue**. You can now add users or groups that you want to monitor.

16. Click **Add**, click **Advanced**, click **Find Now**, select **Newuser,** and click **OK** to close the last Select User or Group dialog box.

17. Click **OK** to close the first Select User or Group dialog box.

18. Select the **Full control** check boxes in the Successful and Failed columns, and then click **OK** to close the Auditing Entry for Public dialog box.

19. Click **OK** to close the Advanced Security Settings for Public dialog box. If error boxes appear, click **Continue** to close each box.

20. Close all windows and log off the system.

21. Log on as Newuser and open the C:\Users\Public folder. While you're there, use Notepad to create a short text file and save it to this location. Write down the name of the file.

22. Log off as Newuser and log back on using your administrator account.

23. Open Event Viewer. In the left pane, select **Event Viewer (Local)**. In the Summary of Administrative Events section, double-click **Audit Success** to open that group of events.

24. Double-click the first event in the group named **Microsoft Windows security auditing**. Maximize the window so you can easily view information about each event.

25. Explore the recent events in this section until you find the events that are associated with Newuser's activity in the C:\Users\Public folder. Approximately how many events were created? List one event that is related to the creation of the new text file.

HANDS-ON PROJECTS

Project 8-3: Secure a Workstation

Securing a workstation is one of the most important tasks you will perform in the overall security strategy when setting up security for an organization or individual. A few simple tweaks to your computer's security policy will greatly improve its resistance to attack.

On a computer running Windows 7 Pro or higher edition, follow these steps to require that a user press CTRL+ALT+Del to log on:

1. Click **Start,** and in the Search box, type **netplwiz** and press **Enter.** Write down the usernames displayed in the User Accounts dialog box.

2. Select the **Advanced** tab and under Secure logon, check **Require users to press Ctrl+Alt+ Delete.**

3. Apply the changes and restart the computer to confirm the change.

Follow these steps to secure the computer using a screen saver and sleep mode:

4. Open Control Panel, select **System and Security,** and select **Require a password when the computer wakes** under Power Options.

5. Under Password protection on wakeup, make sure **Require a password (recommended)** is selected. If you need to change this setting, you might need to first click **Change settings that are currently unavailable.** Save your changes and close all windows.

6. Click **Start,** and in the Search box, type **Screen save** and press **Enter.** Select a screen saver to activate the screen saver function.

7. Check **On resume, display logon screen.** Apply your changes and close all windows.

Follow these steps to require that all users have a password:

8. Click **Start,** type `gpedit.msc` in the Search box, and then press **Enter.** The Local Group Policy Editor window opens.

9. Navigate to **Computer Configuration, Windows Settings, Security Settings, Account Policies, Password Policy.**

10. Change the Minimum password length policy to a value higher than zero. How many characters did you require?

Project 8-4: Perform a Penetration Test

In Chapter 4, you installed and used Zenmap, the GUI version of Nmap. In this project, you use Zenmap to do some light penetration testing on your own network.

It's illegal to perform penetration testing procedures on a network that you do not own or have specific permission to test. This project is best done on your own, home network. If you must use a network that you do not own, be sure to obtain explicit permission from the network owner, preferably in writing. If you complete this project in a school lab, be sure to follow your instructor's directions carefully.

1. Open Zenmap. In the Target field, select the IP address range for your network, such as 192.168.1.1-254. This instructs Zenmap to scan all of the devices on your LAN. Make sure that **Intense scan** is selected for the Profile field, then click **Scan**. The scan will take several minutes to complete.

2. Once the scan finishes, explore the results. Scroll through the data on the Nmap Output tab and look for any anomalies. What kind of information is provided for the hosts on your network? Notice in Figure 8-15 that the difficulty level for the TCP Sequence Prediction field, which is a measure of how easy it is to predict the initial TCP sequence number in a session, is rated at 256, which is a high rating. This loophole is generally secured in today's systems, as Zenmap indicates with the message "Good luck!" to refer to the fact that it would take a stroke of luck to crack this security measure.

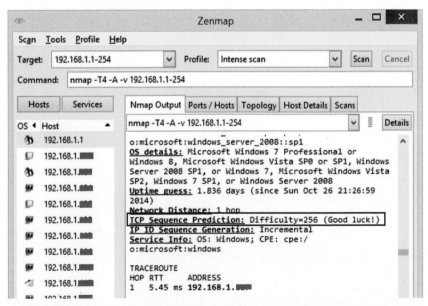

Figure 8-15 Zenmap indicates a high difficulty level for cracking the TCP Sequence Prediction algorithm on this computer

Source: Zenmap

3. Some ports are considered insecure, such as the RPC port 135 and NetBIOS's ports 137, 138, and 139. In Figure 8-16, two of these NetBIOS ports are open. What are the steps for closing these ports in Windows Firewall?

```
PORT       STATE  SERVICE       VERSION
135/tcp    open   msrpc         Microsoft Windows RPC
139/tcp    open   netbios-ssn
```

Figure 8-16   NetBIOS ports are notoriously insecure

Source: Zenmap

4. Click the **Topology** tab to see a network map. Figure 8-17 shows a SOHO network with over a dozen hosts, including the localhost. Each host's color indicates, generally, the number of open ports detected on the host. Yellow icons, for example, indicate between three and six open ports. A square icon would have indicated a router, switch, or wireless AP. The thicker, blue line to one of the hosts indicates a higher RTT. The dashed line indicates that no traceroute information is available for that host. The yellow padlock icon indicates the host has some filtered ports.

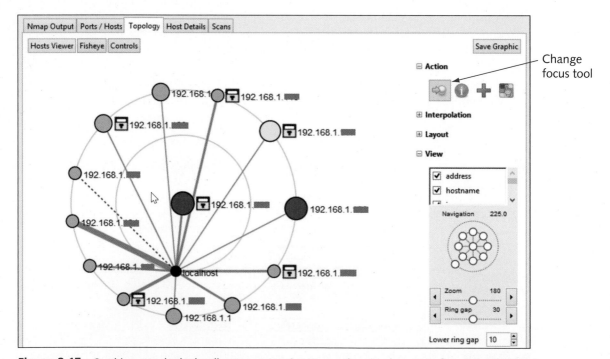

Figure 8-17   On this network, the localhost computer is no more than one hop away from any other host

Source: Zenmap

5. On your network map, click **Controls** to activate the Controls column, which is shown on the right side of Figure 8-15. Initially, the Change focus tool is selected. Click on a

host on the map and see what happens. Select the **Show information** tool, then click a host on the map to see additional information about the device. The zoom controls are located in the View section of the Controls column. Check the Zenmap GUI Users' Guide at nmap.org for additional information on how to interpret and manipulate the scan data.

Case Projects

Case Project 8-1: Research Kali Linux

Kali Linux is a unique distribution of Linux in that it is designed specifically for enhancing the security of a network. The operating system can be run from a flash drive or CD, and includes an impressive array of security tools. In this project, you research the features of Kali Linux, and, optionally, install the system on a flash drive:

1. Spend some time researching Kali Linux, and answer the following questions:

   a. Who created Kali Linux? What distribution was the predecessor to Kali Linux?

   b. What is the main purpose(s) of the Kali Linux distribution?

   c. What are the installation options for Kali Linux? For example, can you use a USB flash drive? Can you dual-boot Kali Linux next to other operating systems? Which ones?

Remember that hacking a network without the owner's express permission is illegal. If you decide to download and use Kali Linux, be sure to keep it inside your own network.

Case Project 8-2: Install and Play with Sandboxie

A sandbox provides an isolated space on your computer to run questionable software or multiple instances of the same software, or access Web sites that might present a threat to your computer's system. Web browsers themselves act as simple sandboxes, but you can create a safer environment with a dedicated sandbox program. Sandboxie is a popular sandbox program for Windows that is also free. In this project, you install Sandboxie and explore some of its features:

1. Using an administrator account on a Windows machine, go to sandboxie.com, then download and install the latest Sandboxie version. Accept all default settings, including software compatibility.

2. Read the Getting Started tutorial and follow the instructions for opening a sandboxed Web browser, downloading a file, and deleting the sandbox contents. (Hint: You can search for an image related to your favorite hobby and download a copy to your computer.)

3. Close the Sandboxie Control window. You saw during the tutorial how to open the sandboxed Web browser from the Sandboxed Web Browser icon on the desktop. This time, open a Web browser from the browser's own desktop icon. To do

this, right-click the icon and click **Run Sandboxed**. Make sure Default Box is selected, then click **OK**.

4. Use the mouse to point to the edge of the browser window. What visual cue notifies you that the browser is running in a sandbox?

5. Open a second window of the same browser, but this time open it normally—not in the Sandboxie sandbox.

6. Use the mouse to point to each of the browser icons in the taskbar at the bottom of your screen. What characters are different in the title of each preview window?

## chapter 9

Unified Communications and Network Performance Management

After reading this chapter and completing the exercises, you will be able to:

- Describe the basic concepts of network management

- Utilize system and event logs to evaluate, monitor, and manage network performance

- Explain how unified communications, including voice and video transmissions, affect network performance

- Explain three common quality of service techniques

- Troubleshoot network availability issues and evaluate network redundancy measures

On the Job

Intermittent errors (those that come and go) are among the most difficult to solve, and keeping careful logs of errors is often an essential troubleshooting technique. As an independent contractor for a large telecommunications company, I served on the third and final tier of a help desk that supported an application used by internal customers (company employees) over several wide area networks. The application functioned on more than 100 dedicated circuits that all terminated to feed a large database at corporate headquarters.

Transactions managed by the application were scanned for errors before they were posted to the database. Over time we were able to identify the source of most of these errors as bugs in the application. As we requested fixes from the application developer, we happily saw drastic reductions in the number of errors. However, a few intermittent errors proved to be most difficult to troubleshoot. After eliminating application bugs as the source of the problem, we began to suspect hardware. We carefully logged each error and searched for patterns of consistency: a particular circuit, client computer, branch office, type of transaction, currency, amount of transaction, time of day, and even day of the week. After weeks of logging and searching, we could not uncover a pattern and yet still intermittent errors persisted. Finally, it occurred to us to search for patterns of *no* errors. We went back through our logs and identified about 15 circuits that consistently yielded no errors since we had been keeping logs.

As we worked with the hardware teams, it came to light that these 15 or so circuits all had couplers installed and *none* of the other circuits used couplers. We all felt we had uncovered a significant clue, but still the problem wasn't solved. My team decided to request a network analyzer to monitor problematic circuits. Before we had the analyzer in place, the application developer was finally able to reproduce the problem in the lab by using progressively faster circuits. The application required a buffer on the receiving end, which held incoming data before it was processed by the application. Faster circuits produced a buffer overflow, resulting in corrupted transactions. The mystery was solved. The couplers had managed to slightly reduce performance of the circuits, which allowed the application buffer to keep up with these slightly slower circuits. After weeks of troubleshooting, the solution was a simple programmer fix: Increase the application buffer size.

Jean Andrews
Author and Independent Contractor

Because networks are a vital part of keeping an organization running, you must pay attention to measures that keep LANs and WANs safe and available. In this book, you have learned about building scalable, reliable networks as well as selecting the most appropriate hardware, topologies, and services to operate your network. You have also learned about security measures to guard network access and resources. In this chapter, you will learn how to optimize networks for today's high-bandwidth needs, and to protect your network's performance from faults and failures.

Fundamentals of Network Management

Network management is a general term that means different things to different networking professionals. At its broadest, **network management** refers to the assessment, monitoring, and maintenance of all aspects of a network. It can include controlling user access to network resources, checking for hardware faults, ensuring high QoS for critical applications, maintaining records of network assets and software configurations, and determining what time of day is best for upgrading a router.

The scope of network management techniques differs according to the network's size and importance. On some large networks, for example, administrators run network management applications that continually check devices and connections to make certain they respond within an expected performance threshold. If a device doesn't respond quickly enough or at all, the application automatically issues an alert that pages the network administrator responsible for that device. On a small network, however, comprehensive network management might not be economically feasible. Instead, such a network might run an inexpensive application that periodically tests devices and connections to determine only whether they are still functioning.

Several disciplines fall under the heading of network management, including topics discussed in previous chapters, such as posture assessments. All share the goals of enhancing efficiency and performance while preventing costly downtime or loss. Ideally, network management accomplishes this task by helping the administrator predict problems before they occur. For example, a trend in network usage could indicate when a switch will be overwhelmed with traffic. In response, the network administrator could increase the switch's processing capabilities or replace the switch before users begin experiencing slow or dropped connections. Before you can assess and make predictions about a network's health, however, you must first understand its logical and physical structure and how it functions under typical conditions.

Baseline Measurements

A **baseline** is a report of the network's current state of operation. Baseline measurements might include the utilization rate for your network backbone, number of users logged on per day or per hour, number of protocols that run on your network, statistics about errors (such as runts, jabbers, or giants, which are discussed later in this chapter), frequency with which networked applications are used, or information regarding which users take up the most bandwidth. The graph in Figure 9-1 shows a sample baseline for daily network traffic over a six-week period.

Baseline measurements allow you to compare future performance increases or decreases caused by network changes or events with past network performance. Obtaining baseline measurements is the only way to know for certain whether a pattern of usage has changed (and requires attention) or, later, whether a network upgrade made a difference. Each

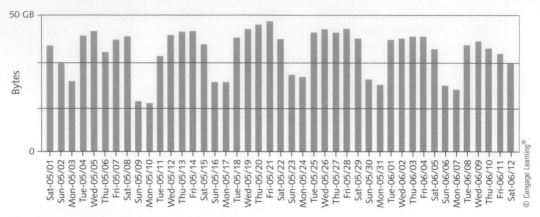

Figure 9-1   Baseline of daily network traffic

network requires its own approach. The elements you measure depend on which functions are most critical to your network and its users.

For instance, suppose that your network currently serves 500 users and that your backbone traffic exceeds 50 percent at 10:00 a.m. and 2:00 p.m. each business day. That pattern constitutes your baseline. Now suppose that your company decides to add 200 users who perform the same types of functions on the network. The added number of users equals 40 percent of the current number of users (200/500). Therefore, you can estimate that your backbone's capacity should increase by approximately 40 percent to maintain your current service levels.

The more data you gather while establishing your network's baseline, the more accurate your prediction will be. Network traffic patterns might be difficult to forecast because you cannot predict users' habits, effects of new technology, or changes in demand for resources over a given period of time. For instance, the preceding example assumed that all new users would share the same network usage habits as the current users. In fact, however, the new users may generate a great deal more, or a great deal less, network traffic.

How do you gather baseline data on your network? Several software applications can perform the baselining for you. These applications range from freeware available on the Internet to expensive, customizable hardware and software combination products. Before choosing a network-baselining tool, you should determine how you will use it. If you manage a small network that provides only one critical application to users, an inexpensive tool may suffice. If you work on a WAN with several critical links, however, you should investigate purchasing a more comprehensive package. The baseline measurement tool should also be capable of collecting the statistics needed. For example, only a sophisticated tool can measure traffic generated by each node on a network, filter traffic according to types of protocols and errors, and simultaneously measure statistics from several different network segments.

Policies, Procedures, and Regulations

Imagine you are the network administrator for a large enterprise network and that you supervise eight network technicians who are responsible for day-to-day installations, upgrades, and troubleshooting. Unless you and your technicians agree on policies for adding new users, for example, you might discover that some users have fewer access restrictions than they ought to have or that logon IDs don't follow a standard naming convention. The former could cause security vulnerabilities, and the latter could make future user management more challenging.

Following rules helps limit chaos, confusion, and possibly downtime for you and your users. In addition to internal policies, a network manager must consider state and federal regulations that might affect her responsibilities. In the United States, one such federal regulation is CALEA (Communications Assistance for Law Enforcement Act), which requires telecommunications carriers and equipment manufacturers to provide for surveillance capabilities. CALEA was passed by Congress in 1994 after pressure from the FBI, which worried that networks relying solely on digital communications would circumvent traditional wiretapping strategies. In other words, a phone call made using VoIP over a private WAN cannot be intercepted as easily as a phone call made via the PSTN. Therefore, if you work at an ISP, for example, your switches and routers must provide an interface for electronic eavesdropping and your staff must be ready to allow authorities access to those devices when presented with a warrant.

A second significant federal regulation in the United States is HIPAA (Health Insurance Portability and Accountability Act), which was passed by Congress in 1996. One aspect of this regulation addresses the security and privacy of medical records, including those stored or transmitted electronically. If you work at any organization that handles medical records, such as an insurance company, hospital, or transcription service, you must understand and follow federal standards for protecting the security and privacy of these records. HIPAA rules are very specific. They govern not only the way medical records are stored and transmitted, but also the policies for authorizing access and even the placement and orientation of workstations where such records might be viewed.

Some security standards, such as the PCI DSS (Payment Card Industry Data Security Standard), created by the PCI Security Standards Council to protect credit card data and transactions, require network segmentation as part of their security controls. Network segmentation separates the parts of a network that have access to sensitive information from parts that are more vulnerable to compromise. For example, a store's inventory-tracking system, which is used by vendors to manage inventory supplies, should be hosted on a different network segment than the store's payment processing server, where customer cardholder information is collected, stored, and processed. If the store maintains legacy equipment for processes such as human resources or business document creation, these legacy systems should be located on a different segment as well because older technology is more vulnerable to intrusion and compromise.

Many of the policies and procedures mentioned here are not laws, but best practices, aimed at preventing network problems before they occur. Next, you'll learn about techniques for detecting and managing network problems before they significantly impair access or performance.

Monitoring and Managing Network Traffic

After documenting every aspect of your network and following policies and best practices, you are ready to assess your network's status on an ongoing basis. This process includes both performance management (monitoring how well links and devices are keeping up with the demands placed on them) and fault management (the detection and signaling of device, link, or component faults).

SNMP Logs

To accomplish both fault and performance management, organizations often use enterprise-wide network management systems. Hundreds of such tools exist. All rely on a similar architecture, in which at least one network management console, which may be a server or workstation, depending on the size of the network, collects data from multiple networked devices at regular intervals, in a process called polling. This central collection point is called the **network management system**, or **NMS**.

In Chapter 8, you learned about agents that are used to authenticate a device to the network and might continue to monitor the device's compliance with policy rules. In the case of NMSs, each managed device runs a **network management agent**, which is a software routine that collects information about the device's operation and provides it to the NMS. So as not to affect the performance of a device while collecting information, agents do not demand significant processing resources.

A **managed device**, which is any network node monitored by the NMS, may contain several objects that can be managed, including components such as a processor, memory, hard disk, or NIC, or intangibles such as performance or utilization. For example, on a server, an agent can measure how many users are connected to the server or what percentage of the processor's resources are used at any given time. The list of objects and their descriptions that is managed by the NMS is kept in the **MIB (Management Information Base)**, which also contains data about an object's performance in a database format that can be mined and analyzed.

Agents communicate information about managed devices via any one of several Application layer protocols. On modern networks, most agents use SNMP (Simple Network Management Protocol). As you learned in Chapter 2, SNMP is part of the TCP/IP suite of protocols and typically runs over UDP on ports 161 and 162 (though it can be configured to run over TCP). Three versions of SNMP exist: SNMPv1, SNMPv2, and SNMPv3, as described below:

- *SNMPv1 (Simple Network Management Protocol version 1)*—This is the original version, released in 1988. Because of its limited features, it is rarely used on modern networks.

- *SNMPv2 (Simple Network Management Protocol version 2)*—This version improved on SNMPv1 with increased performance and slightly better security, among other features.

- *SNMPv3 (Simple Network Management Protocol version 3)*—This version is similar to SNMPv2, but adds authentication, validation, and encryption for messages exchanged between managed devices and the network management console.

SNMPv3 is the most secure version of the protocol. However, some administrators have hesitated to upgrade to SNMPv3 because it requires more complex configuration. Therefore, SNMPv2 is still widely used. Most, but not all, network management applications support multiple versions of SNMP.

Figure 9-2 illustrates the relationship between an NMS and managed devices on a network.

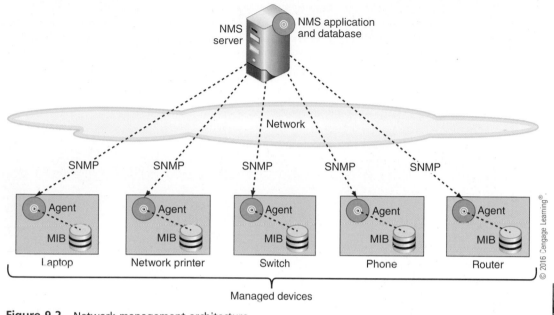

Figure 9-2 Network management architecture

An NMS retrieves data from a managed device by sending an **snmpget** command to the device's agent. The agent is then prompted to send an **SNMP response message** with the requested information. The NMS can issue an `snmpwalk` command to request a sequence of **snmpgetnext** requests to walk through sequential rows in the MIB data table.

Agents can also be programmed, using the `snmptrap` command, to detect certain abnormal conditions that prompt the generation of SNMP trap messages, where the agent sends the NMS unsolicited data once the specified conditions on the managed device are met. For example, on a Cisco server (which requires a space between the words in the command), you could use the command `snmp trap link-status` to instruct the SNMP agent to send an alert if or when an interface fails. The trap can later be disabled with the command `no snmp trap link-status`.

NETWORK+ EXAM TIP When using UDP, SNMP agents receive requests from the NMS on port 161. The NMS receives agent responses and traps on its port 162. SNMP messages can be secured with TLS, in which case agents receive requests on port 10161 and the NMS receives responses and traps on port 10162.

After data is collected, the network management application can present an administrator with several ways to view and analyze the data. For example, a very common way to analyze data is by a line graph. Alternatively, a popular way to view data is in the form of a map that shows fully functional links or devices in green, partially (or less than optimally) functioning links or devices in yellow, and failed links or devices in red. An example of the type of map generated by a network performance monitor is shown in Figure 9-3.

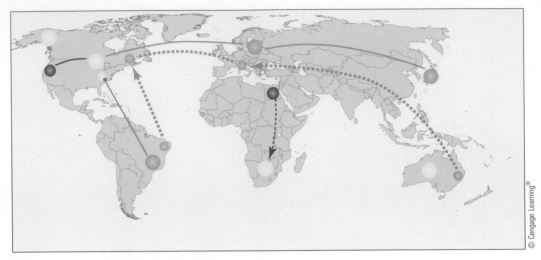

Figure 9-3   Map showing network status

Because of their flexibility, sophisticated network management applications are also challenging to configure and fine-tune. You have to be careful to collect only useful data and not an excessive amount of routine information. For example, on a network with dozens of routers, collecting SNMP-generated messages that essentially say "I'm still here" every five seconds would result in massive amounts of insignificant data. A glut of information makes it difficult to ascertain when a router in fact requires attention. Instead, when configuring a network management application to poll a router, you might choose to generate an SNMP-based message only when the router's processor is operating at 75 percent of its capacity, or to measure only the amount of traffic passing through a NIC every five minutes.

System and Event Logs

Virtually every condition recognized by an operating system can be recorded. Records of such activity are kept in a log. For example, each time your computer requests an IP address from the DHCP server and doesn't receive a response, this event can be recorded in a log. Likewise, a log entry can be added each time a firewall denies a host's attempt to connect to another host on the network that the firewall defends.

Different operating systems log different kinds of events by default. In addition, network administrators can customize logs by defining conditions under which new entries are created. For example, an engineer might want to know when the relative humidity in a data center exceeds 60 percent. If a device can monitor this information, the results can be written to a log.

On Windows-based computers, such a log is known as an event log and can be easily viewed with the Event Viewer application, as you will see in the following project.

Applying Concepts
Explore Event Viewer in Windows

In this project, you will use the Event Viewer application to explore the event log on a computer running Windows 7. Ideally, the computer will have been used for a while, so that the event log contains several entries. It need not be connected to a network. However, you must be logged on to the computer as a user with administrator privileges.

Beginning with Step 3 below, all of the steps can be completed on a Windows 8.1 computer instead. To open Event Viewer in Windows 8.1, right-click the **Start** button and click **Event Viewer**, then proceed beginning with Step 3.

NOTE

1. Click the **Start** button, and then click **Control Panel**. In the Control Panel window, click **System and Security**. Under Administrative Tools, click **View event logs**.

2. If a User Account Control window opens, requesting your permission to continue, click **Yes**.

3. The Event Viewer window opens, with three panes. The center pane lists a summary of administrative events. Notice that events are classified into several types, including *Critical, Error, Warning, Information, Audit Success* and, in some cases, *Audit Failure*. The number of events that have been logged in each category is listed to the right of the classification entry. How many Error events has your workstation logged in the last 24 hours? In the last seven days?

4. If your workstation has logged any errors in the past seven days, click the plus sign next to the event type *Error*. A list of error events appears. (If you do not have any entries in the Error category, click the plus sign next to the event type *Warning* instead.)

5. Notice that each event log entry is identified by an Event ID, its source, and the type of log on which it's recorded. (Event Viewer's default screen lists entries for all types of logs kept by the Windows operating system.) Scroll through the entries until you find one that was logged by the system—if possible, one that has occurred more than once in the past seven days. Double-click that entry to read more about it. The Summary page events pane appears in the center of the Event Viewer display.

6. Notice when these errors were recorded. In the General tab, read a detailed description of the error you chose to view. If you were a network manager, would you choose to be alerted whenever this error occurred on a workstation or server?

7. Now click **Windows Logs** in the left pane of the Event Viewer display to view the different types of logs maintained by the operating system. The Windows Logs listing appears in the center pane, as shown in Figure 9-4.

8. Which of the five logs has recorded the highest number of events? How large is that log file?

9. Suppose you want to limit the size of the system log. Right-click the **System** entry in the Windows Logs listing, and then click **Properties** in the shortcut menu that appears.

10. The Log Properties - System (Type: Administrative) dialog box opens. Next to the Maximum log size (KB) text box, enter **16000** to limit the log file size to 16 MB.

11. Click **OK** to save your change. If you receive a message that indicates that your current log's size exceeds the maximum limit you just entered, click **OK** to accept the recommended practice of enforcing the maximum after the log is cleared.

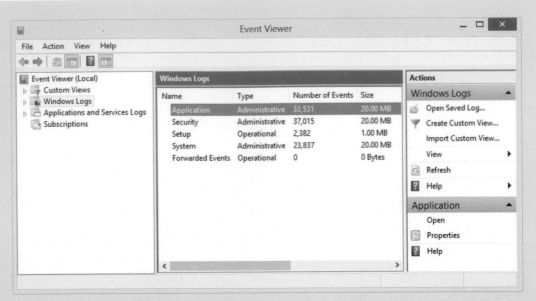

Figure 9-4 Windows Logs listing in Event Viewer

Source: Microsoft LLC

In Hands-On Project 9-1, you'll learn how to work with the data collected in Windows event logs.

Similar information is routinely recorded by computers running Linux or UNIX via the syslog utility. The **syslog** protocol is a standard for generating, storing, and processing messages about events on a system. It describes methods for detecting and reporting events and specifies the format and contents of messages. It also defines roles for each computer that participates in logging events:

- *generator*—The computer that is monitored by a syslog-compatible application and that issues event information

- *collector*—The computer that gathers event messages from generators

The syslog standard also establishes levels of severity for every logged event. For example, "0" indicates an emergency situation, whereas "7" points to specific information that might help in debugging a problem.

Computers running Linux and UNIX record syslog data in a **system log**. Table 9-1 shows the locations of system logs in some versions of Linux and UNIX.

Table 9-1 Linux and UNIX system log locations

Version type	System log location
Newer versions of Linux	/var/log/messages
Older versions of UNIX	/var/log/syslog
Solaris versions of UNIX	/var/adm/messages

© 2016 Cengage Learning®

To find out where various logs are kept on your UNIX or Linux system, view the /etc/syslog.conf file (on some systems, this is the /etc/rsyslog.conf file). The /etc/syslog.conf file is also where you can configure the types of events to log and what priority to assign each event.

Bear in mind that the syslog utility doesn't alert you to any problems, but it does keep a history of messages issued by the system. It's up to you to monitor the system log for errors or filter log data to monitor packet flow when troubleshooting a problem or checking for patterns that might indicate developing problems. Most UNIX and Linux desktop operating systems provide a GUI application for easily viewing and filtering the information in system logs. Other applications are available for sifting through syslog data and generating alerts. In Case Project 9-1 at the end of this chapter, you'll view and sort through data in a system log.

Using the information collected in event logs and system logs for fault management requires thoughtful data filtering and sorting. After all, you can't assume that all of the information in these logs points to a problem, even if it is marked with a warning. For example, you might have typed your password incorrectly while trying to log on to your computer, thus generating a log entry.

Network+
2.1
2.2
4.7
5.2

7 APPLICATION
6 PRESENTATION
5 SESSION
4 TRANSPORT
3 NETWORK
2 DATA LINK
1 PHYSICAL

Traffic Analysis

A network monitor is a tool that continually monitors network traffic. A similar tool, an interface monitor, can monitor traffic at a specific interface between a server or client and the network. If you find the distinction vague, think about the difference between monitoring the traffic that a single device encounters versus monitoring devices and traffic patterns throughout a particular network. For example, Spiceworks is a type of network monitoring software because it can be configured to monitor multiple devices on a network at one time, and Wireshark is a type of interface monitor (or protocol analyzer) because it monitors the interface between a single device and the network. By capturing data, they provide either a snapshot of network activity at one point in time or a historical record of network activity over a period of time.

Wireshark or other monitoring software running on a single computer connected to a switch doesn't see all the traffic on a network, but only the traffic the switch sends to it, which includes broadcast traffic and traffic specifically addressed to this computer (see the computer on the right in Figure 9-5). To track more of the network traffic, you can use one of these methods, illustrated in Figure 9-5:

9

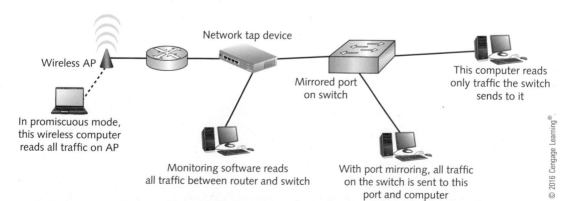

Wireless AP

Network tap device

This computer reads only traffic the switch sends to it

Mirrored port on switch

In promiscuous mode, this wireless computer reads all traffic on AP

Monitoring software reads all traffic between router and switch

With port mirroring, all traffic on the switch is sent to this port and computer

© 2016 Cengage Learning®

Figure 9-5   Methods to monitor network traffic

- Run the monitoring software on a router or on a computer connected to a hub or connected wirelessly to the network (see the computer on the left in Figure 9-5). Even so, the computer will still not "see" all traffic unless the network adapter supports promiscuous mode. In **promiscuous mode**, also called monitoring mode, a device driver directs the NIC to pass all frames to the operating system and on to the monitoring software, not just those broadcasted or intended for the host. If a NIC supports promiscuous mode, you must enable the feature. (For Windows, use the NIC's properties box.)

  For wireless adapters, you can use utility software to put the NIC in promiscuous mode. For example, Wireshark suggests Riverbed AirPcap, a wireless adapter that includes Windows device drivers that support monitoring mode.

- As discussed in Chapter 8, program a switch to use port mirroring, whereby all traffic sent to any port on the switch is also sent to the mirrored port, which can connect to a computer running monitoring software.

- Install a device, called a **network tap** or **packet sniffer**, in line with network traffic. The device usually has three ports: two ports to send and receive all traffic and a third port that mirrors the traffic, sending it to a computer running monitoring software in promiscuous mode.

Some NOSs come with network monitoring tools. In addition, you can purchase or download for free network monitoring tools developed by other software companies. Hundreds of such programs exist. After you have worked with one network monitoring tool, such as Spiceworks, you will find that other products work in much the same way. Most even use very similar graphical interfaces.

All network monitoring tools can perform at least the following functions:

- Set the NIC to run in promiscuous mode so that the NIC will pass all traffic it receives to the monitoring software
- Continuously monitor network traffic on a segment
- Capture network data transmitted on a segment
- Capture frames sent to or from a specific node
- Reproduce network conditions by transmitting a selected amount and type of data
- Generate statistics about network activity (for example, what percentage of the total frames transmitted on a segment are broadcast frames)

Some network monitoring tools can also perform the following functions:

- Discover all network nodes on a segment
- Establish a baseline, including performance, utilization rate, and so on
- Track utilization of network resources (such as bandwidth and storage) and device resources (such as CPU or memory usage) and present this information in the form of graphs, tables, or charts
- Store traffic data and generate reports
- Trigger alarms when traffic conditions meet preconfigured conditions (for example, if usage exceeds 50 percent of capacity)

- Identify usage anomalies, such as **top talkers** (hosts that send an inordinate amount of data) or **top listeners** (hosts that receive an inordinate amount of data)

How can capturing data help you solve networking problems? Imagine that traffic on a segment of the network you administer suddenly grinds to a halt one morning at about 8:00 a.m. You no sooner step in the door than everyone from the help desk calls to tell you how slowly the network is running. Nothing has changed on the network since last night, when it ran normally, so you can think of no obvious reasons for problems.

At the workstation where you have previously installed a network monitoring tool, you capture all data transmissions for approximately five minutes. You then sort the frames in the network monitoring software, arranging the nodes in order based on the volume of traffic each has generated. You might find that one workstation appears at the top of the list with an excessively high number of bad transmissions. Or, you might discover that a server has been compromised by a hacker and is generating a flood of data over the network. Or possibly your current sampling size doesn't yet reveal any problems, and you run a second, longer capture. By knowing the source of the problem, you know where to look for a resolution.

Before adopting a network monitor or protocol analyzer, you should be aware of some of the data errors that these tools can distinguish. The effective utilization of interface monitoring tools can help identify and prevent many types of complications, such as the following:

- *runts*—Packets that are smaller than the medium's minimum packet size. For instance, any Ethernet packet that is smaller than 64 bytes is considered a runt.

- *giants*—Packets that exceed the medium's maximum packet size. For example, an Ethernet packet larger than 1518 bytes (or 1522 bytes for VLAN packets) is considered a giant.

- *jabber*—A device that handles electrical signals improperly, usually affecting the rest of the network. A network analyzer will detect a jabber as a device that is always retransmitting, effectively bringing the network to a halt. A jabber usually results from a bad NIC. Occasionally, it can be caused by outside electrical interference.

- *ghosts*—Frames that are not actually data frames, but aberrations caused by a device misinterpreting stray voltage on the wire. Unlike true data frames, ghosts have an invalid pattern at the beginning of the frame pattern.

- *packet loss*—Packets lost due to an unknown protocol, unrecognized port, network noise, or some other anomaly. Lost packets never arrive at their destination.

- *discarded packets*—Packets that arrive at their destination, but are then deliberately discarded, or **dropped**, because issues such as buffer overflow, latency, bottlenecks, or other forms of network congestion delayed them beyond their usable time frame. A discarded packet is often referred to as a **discard**.

- *interface resets*—Repeated resets of the connection, resulting in lower-quality utilization; caused by an interface misconfiguration.

When it comes to monitoring network performance, data creation is the easy part. The challenge, as you'll see next, is to create—and then to efficiently analyze—useful and relevant data.

Network+
2.1
2.2
4.7
5.2
Applying Concepts

Adjust Spiceworks Monitors

When you suspect a particular problem on your network, it might help to adjust your monitoring software settings to look for and alert you to these specific problems. For example, you can change the settings for the monitors in your Spiceworks account. To complete this project, you must first complete Case Project 4-2, in Chapter 4. To adjust your Spiceworks monitors, complete the following steps:

1. Open your Spiceworks dashboard. One way to do this is to open a Web browser, navigate to *localhost/login*, and log on.

2. Open the Inventory menu in the toolbar at the top of the page, click **Settings**, and then click **Monitors & Alerts**. From this screen, you can adjust which conditions should generate an alert, and whether to send an email or create a ticket.

These instructions were accurate at the time of this writing. The exact steps might vary as Spiceworks updates their Web site.

As you can see in the preceding Spiceworks project, faults and conditions that exceed certain thresholds can trigger alarms in the NMS, which then alerts IT personnel. Depending on the software used, these alerts might be transmitted either by email or text message, also called SMS (Short Message Service), or they can automatically prompt support ticket generation. They can also be recorded by system and event logs.

Network+
1.1
2.2
2.4
Traffic Management

When a network must handle high volumes of network traffic, users benefit from a performance management and optimization technique known as traffic shaping. Traffic shaping, also called packet shaping, involves manipulating certain characteristics of packets, data streams, or connections to manage the type and amount of traffic traversing a network or interface at any moment. Its goals are to ensure timely delivery of the most important traffic while optimizing performance for all users.

Traffic shaping can involve delaying less-important traffic, increasing the priority of more-important traffic, limiting the volume of traffic flowing in or out of an interface during a specified time period, or limiting the momentary throughput rate for an interface. The last two techniques belong to a category of traffic shaping known as traffic policing. For example, an ISP might impose a maximum on the capacity it will grant a certain customer. That way, it ensures that the customer does not tie up more than a certain amount of the network's overall capacity. Traffic policing helps the service provider predict how much capacity it must purchase from its network provider. It also holds down costs because the ISP doesn't have to plan for every client using all the throughput he could at all times (an unlikely scenario). An ISP that imposes traffic policing might allow customers to choose their preferred maximum daily traffic volume or momentary throughput and pay commensurate fees.

A more sophisticated instance of traffic policing is dynamic and takes into account the network's traffic patterns. For example, the service provider might allow certain customers to exceed their maximums when few other customers are using the network.

Figure 9-6 illustrates how traffic volume might appear on an interface without limits compared with an interface subject to traffic policing.

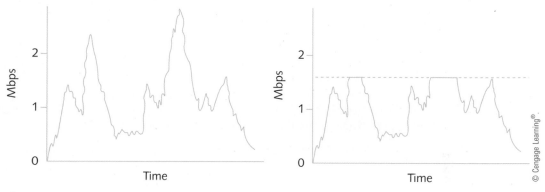

Figure 9-6 Traffic volume before and after applying limits

A controversial example of traffic shaping came to light in 2007. Comcast, one of the largest Internet service providers in the United States, was found to be clandestinely discriminating against certain types of traffic. For users uploading files to P2P (peer-to-peer) networks such as BitTorrent, Comcast was interjecting TCP segments with the RST (reset) field set. These segments were spoofed to appear as if they originated from the accepting site, and they cut the connection as the user attempted to upload files. Soon customers figured out the pattern and used monitoring software such as Wireshark to reveal the forged TCP RST segments. They complained to authorities that Comcast had violated their user agreement. The FCC investigated, upheld the customers' claims, and ordered Comcast to stop this practice. Comcast chose a different method of traffic shaping. It assigned a lower priority to data from customers who generate a high volume of traffic when the network is at risk of congestion.

Several types of traffic prioritization—that is, treating more-important traffic preferentially—exist. Software running on a router, multilayer switch, gateway, server, or even a client workstation can act as a **traffic shaper**, or **packet shaper**, by prioritizing traffic according to any of the following characteristics:

- Protocol
- IP address
- User group
- DiffServ (Differentiated Services) flag in an IP packet
- VLAN tag in a Data Link layer frame
- Service or application

Depending on the traffic prioritization software, different types of traffic might be assigned priority classes, such as *high*, *normal*, *low*, or *slow*; alternatively, it can be rated on a prioritization scale from 0 (lowest priority) to 7 (highest priority). For example, traffic generated by time-sensitive VoIP applications might be assigned high priority, while online gaming might be assigned low priority. Traffic prioritization is needed most when the network is busiest. It ensures that during peak usage times, the most important data gets through quickly, while less-important data waits. When network usage is low, however, prioritization might have no noticeable effects.

Caching

In addition to traffic shaping, a network or host might use caching to improve performance. Caching is the local storage of frequently needed files that would otherwise be obtained from an external source. By keeping files close to the requester, caching allows the user to access those files quickly. For example, an ISP is likely to use a technique called Web caching, where frequently requested Web pages are stored on a server at the ISP rather than having to retrieve the pages from the Web each time they are requested.

When a network is expected to simultaneously support voice, video, and data communications, performance is always a major concern. This discussion of network performance would not be complete without addressing these concerns in the following section.

Unified Communications Technologies

One of the greatest challenges to performance on today's networks is voice and video transmission. In Chapter 1, you learned that convergence is the use of one network to simultaneously carry voice, video, and data communications. For most of the twentieth century, voice and data signals traveled over separate networks. The PSTN (Public Switched Telephone Network), based on Alexander Graham Bell's circuit-switched model, carried telephone calls and fax transmissions. Switching determines how connections are created between nodes. On circuit-switched networks, a connection is established between two network nodes before they begin transmitting data. Bandwidth is dedicated to this connection and remains available until the users terminate communication between the two nodes. While the nodes remain connected, all data follows the same path initially selected by the switch.

As you can deduce, based on your knowledge of how IP packets are assembled and routed, circuit switching is much less common today. Instead, packet-switched networks break data into packets before they are transported. Packets can travel any path on the network to their destination because, as you learned in Chapter 3, each packet contains the destination address and sequencing information. Consequently, packets can attempt to find the fastest circuit available at any instant. When packets reach their destination node, the node reassembles them based on control information included in the packets. The greatest advantage to packet switching lies in the fact that it does not waste bandwidth by holding a connection open until a message reaches its destination, as circuit switching does. Ethernet networks and the Internet are the most common examples of packet-switched networks.

In the latter part of the twentieth century, the two types of networks began intersecting and this intersection has not always been seamless or efficient. In some cases, modems are required to convert digital data into analog signals and vice versa. Networks achieve more unified integration, however, by packetizing voice—that is, digitizing the voice or video signal and issuing it as a stream of packets over the network.

Over time, voice and video services over packet-switched networks have matured, and as a result more users rely on them. In Chapter 1, you learned that unified communications (sometimes called **unified messaging**) is a service that makes several forms of communication available from a single user interface. In unified communications, a user can, for example, access the Web; send and receive faxes, email messages, voice mail messages, instant messages, or telephone calls; and participate in videoconference calls—all from one computer.

 In discussions of unified communications, the use of multiple terms to refer to the same or similar technologies is common. This is partly a result of a market that developed rapidly while many different vendors marketed their own solutions and applied their preferred terminology. The terms used throughout this chapter are those most frequently cited by standards organizations such as IETF (Internet Engineering Task Force), which was introduced in Chapter 7, and the ITU (International Telecommunication Union), which was introduced in Chapter 6.

VoIP Applications and Interfaces

VoIP (Voice over IP), also known as **IP telephony**, is the use of any network (either public or private) to carry voice signals using TCP/IP protocols. VoIP is used in cloud-based PBX systems, called **unified voice services**. (**PBX** stands for **private branch exchange**, which is the term used to describe a telephone switch that connects and manages calls within a private organization.)

VoIP can be used on private and public networks. When VoIP relies on the Internet, it is often called **Internet telephony**. VoIP on private networks can be more easily controlled than on the Internet, which often translates into better sound quality than an Internet telephone call can provide. However, given the Internet's breadth and low cost, VoIP on the Internet is gaining popularity over the PSTN.

Significant reasons for implementing VoIP include the following:

- Lower costs for voice calls
- Readily incorporates new or enhanced features and applications
- Centralized voice and data network management

VoIP can run over any packet-switched network. Virtually any type of data connection can carry VoIP signals, including T-carriers, ISDN, DSL, broadband cable, satellite connections, Wi-Fi, WiMAX, HSPA+, LTE, and cellular telephone networks, all of which you'll learn more about in Chapter 11. Voice and data can be combined on a network using several different types of UC devices as clients. These clients and the UC server that hosts these clients, however, might be on the same network, or might access one another over the Internet. On any VoIP network, a mix of the following three types of clients is possible:

- *analog telephones*—If a VoIP caller uses a traditional telephone, signals issued by the telephone must be converted to digital form before being transmitted on a TCP/IP-based network. To accomplish this transition, an analog telephone must be connected to one of the following:

- ○ A VoIP adapter, called an ATA (analog telephone adapter).

- ○ A switch, router, or gateway capable of accepting analog voice signals, converting them into packets, then issuing the packets to a data network, and vice versa.

- ○ An analog-to-digital voice conversion device called a digital PBX or, more commonly, an IP-PBX. In general, an IP-PBX is a private switch that accepts and interprets both analog and digital voice signals. Thus, it can connect with both traditional PSTN lines and data networks.

- ○ An analog PBX, which then connects to a voice-data gateway. In this case, the gateway connects the traditional telephone circuits with a TCP/IP network (such as the Internet or a private WAN).

- *IP telephones*—Most new VoIP installations use IP telephones (or IP phones), which, unlike traditional phones, transmit and receive only digital signals. To communicate on the network, each IP phone, such as the one shown in Figure 9-7, must have a unique IP address. The IP phone looks like a traditional touch-tone phone, but connects to an RJ-45 wall jack, like a computer workstation. Its connection may then pass through a connectivity device, such as a switch or router, before reaching the IP-PBX. An IP-PBX may contain its own voice-data gateway, or it may connect to a separate voice-data gateway, which is then connected to the network backbone. Figure 9-8 illustrates different ways IP phones can connect with a data network.

Figure 9-7 An IP phone

Source: Grandstream Networks, Inc.

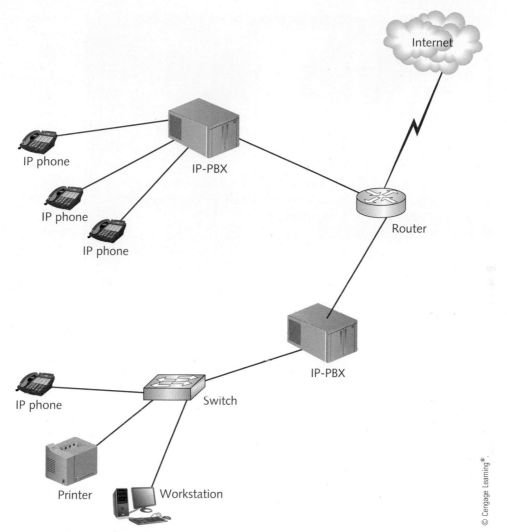

Figure 9-8   Accessing a VoIP network from IP phones

- *softphones*—A softphone is a computer programmed to act like an IP phone. Before it can be used as a softphone, a computer must have the following:
  - An IP telephony client, such as Skype or CounterPath
  - The ability to communicate with a digital telephone switch, such as that provided by the Skype or CounterPath services
  - A microphone and speakers, or a headset
  - For video calls, a web cam

The softphone client software provides features such as methods to enter a telephone number, call forwarding, caller's address book, speed dialing, conferencing, call logs, and ending a call. Figure 9-9 shows the interface for one softphone client.

Figure 9-9 Softphone interface

Source: CounterPath Corporation

Now that you understand the variety of ways VoIP services may be implemented, you are ready to learn about the different types of video services that packet-switched networks may carry.

Video over IP Applications and Interfaces

Videoconferencing, or video teleconferencing (VTC), which you first learned about in Chapter 1, allows multiple participants to communicate and collaborate in a real-time meeting (not prerecorded) through audiovisual means. VTC is often used to link students in multiple classrooms on satellite campuses to the instructor, who is located at the school's main campus. IPTV, videoconferencing, and streaming video belong to the range of services known as video over IP.

Cisco Systems, Inc., the largest supplier of networking hardware in the world, estimates that by 2018, about 79 percent of the traffic carried by the Internet will be video traffic, not including P2P file sharing. That's nearly one million minutes of video content transmitted every second. This extraordinary growth is thanks to the large quantity of video content from providers such as Netflix, YouTube, and Hulu, the increasing volume of devices accessing the Internet, including smartphones and tablet PCs, plus the decreasing cost of bandwidth and equipment. Given these networking trends, it's important to understand the types of video services that TCP/IP networks can carry and the hardware and software they rely on.

Streaming Video Streaming video refers to video signals that are compressed and delivered in a continuous stream. For example, when you watch a television episode on the Web, you are requesting a streaming video service. You don't have to download the entire episode before you begin to see and hear it. When streaming videos are supplied via the Web, they may be called Webcasts. Because most networks are TCP/IP-based, most streaming video belongs to the category of video over IP.

Among all video-over-IP applications, streaming video is perhaps the simplest. A user needs only to have a computer with sufficient processing and caching resources, plus the appropriate audiovisual hardware and software to view encoded video. On the transmission end, video can be delivered by any computer with sufficient capabilities to store and send the video. This might be a streaming server dedicated to the task, or any computer that performs video streaming among other tasks. Streaming video can traverse any type of TCP/IP network, though it often relies on the Internet.

Two popular ways of providing video streams are video-on-demand and live streaming:

- *video-on-demand (VoD)*—Makes videos available as stored files (saved in any one of a number of popular video formats) on a server. The viewer watches the video at his convenience and controls his viewing experience, for example, by pausing, rewinding, or fast-forwarding. When you watch a news report from your local TV channel's Web page, you are making use of VoD.

- *live streaming video*—Issues video feed directly from the source to the user as the camera captures it. For example, suppose you wanted to watch a political debate that's being broadcast by a TV network. You could access the network's Web site and watch the debate as it happens using live streaming video. One drawback to live streaming is that viewers must connect with the stream as it occurs, whereas they can use VoD at their convenience. Another potential drawback is that content cannot be fully edited before it's distributed. However, this issue can be addressed with time-shifted video, in which the broadcast is delayed by a few minutes to allow for editing processes and licensing concerns.

Figure 9-10 illustrates video-on-demand and live streaming video services.

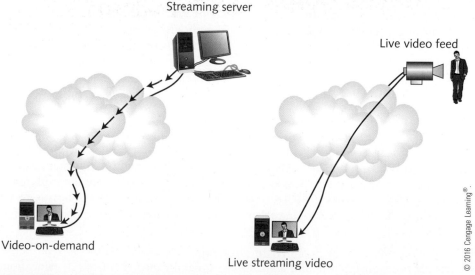

Streaming server

Live video feed

Video-on-demand

Live streaming video

© 2016 Cengage Learning®

Figure 9-10 Video-on-demand and live streaming video

Also consider the number of clients receiving each service. For example, an IT manager in one office might use his laptop and its built-in camera to capture and issue a video of himself explaining a technical topic to one of his employees in another office. This is an example of point-to-point video over IP, and is accomplished via a unicast transmission. Alternatively, he might issue the video stream to a whole group of employees in a point-to-multipoint manner, which can be accomplished through a multicast transmission.

You might recall the terms *unicast* and *multicast* from Chapter 2 and assume that point-to-multipoint streaming video is, by definition, multicast transmission. That's not necessarily the case. In IP multicasting, a source issues data to a defined group of IP addresses. However, many streaming video services—and nearly all of those issued over a public network, such as the Internet—are examples of unicast transmissions. In a unicast transmission, a single node issues a stream of data to one other node. In a VoIP call, for example, one IP phone addresses another in unicast fashion. If many Internet users watch CSPAN's streaming video on the Web simultaneously, the CSPAN source would issue encoded audiovisual signals to each viewer via separate unicast transmissions. In the example of an IT manager sharing a video discussion with his employees in another office, the transmission might be unicast or multicast, depending on how he configured it.

Streaming video services might also be classified according to the type of network they use, private or public. Watching YouTube videos or TV episodes on Hulu are obviously cases of streaming video issued over a public network, the Internet. Examples of streaming video on private networks include educational videos delivered over the private networks of schools, businesses, or other organizations. For example, a guest speaker's presentation at a college's main campus auditorium could be filmed and transmitted via live streaming to classrooms on the college's satellite campuses, all without ever leaving the college's private network.

Videoconferencing So far in this chapter, you have learned about unidirectional video-over-IP services—that is, video delivered to a user who only watches the content, but does not respond with her own. In most examples of videoconferencing, connections are full-duplex, and participants may send and receive audiovisual signals. This allows two or more people in different locations to see and hear each other in real time. As you can imagine, the cost savings and convenience of such a service make it especially attractive to organizations with offices, clients, or consultants scattered across the nation or the globe. Besides replacing face-to-face business meetings and allowing collaboration, uses for videoconferencing include the following:

- *Telemedicine, or the provision of medical services from a distance*—For example, a physician can view and listen to a patient in another location. Often, the patient is accompanied by a nurse or physician's assistant, who might administer tests and supply information about the patient's condition. For patients who live far from major medical facilities, this saves the cost, time, and potential health risks of having to travel long distances. NASA is developing telemedicine capabilities for diagnosing patients in space.

- *Tele-education, or the exchange of information between one or more participants for the purposes of training and education*—A significant benefit of tele-education is the capability for one or a few experts to share their knowledge with many students.

- *Judicial proceedings, in which judges, lawyers, and defendants can conduct arraignments, hearings, or even trials while in different locations*—This not only saves costs, but may minimize potential security risks of transporting prisoners.

- *Surveillance, or remotely monitoring events happening at one or more distant locations*— Unlike previously mentioned videoconferencing applications, surveillance is typically unidirectional. In other words, security personnel watch (and perhaps also listen) to live video feeds from multiple locations around a building or campus, but do not send audiovisual signals to those locations.

Hardware and software requirements for videoconferences include, at minimum, a means for each participant to generate, send, and receive audiovisual signals. This may be accomplished by workstations that have sufficient processing resources, plus cameras, microphones, and videoconferencing software to capture, encode, and transmit audiovisual signals. Instead of a workstation, viewers may use a video terminal or a video phone, a type of phone that includes a screen, such as the one shown in Figure 9-11. These devices can decode compressed video and interpret transport and signaling protocols necessary for conducting videoconference sessions.

Figure 9-11   Video phone

Source: Grandstream Networks, Inc.

When more than two people participate in a videoconference—for example, in a point-to-multipoint or multipoint-to-multipoint scenario—a video bridge is required. A video bridge manages multiple audiovisual sessions so that participants can see and hear each other. Video bridges may exist as a piece of hardware or as software, in the form of a conference server. An organization that only occasionally uses videoconferencing can lease Internet-accessible video bridging services for a predetermined period. Organizations, such as universities, that frequently rely on videoconferencing might maintain their own conference servers or supply each auditorium with its own video bridge.

To establish and manage videoconferencing sessions, video bridges depend on signaling protocols, which are described next.

Signaling Protocols

In VoIP and video-over-IP transmission, signaling is the exchange of information between the components of a network or system for the purposes of establishing, monitoring, or releasing connections as well as controlling system operations. Simply put, signaling protocols set up and manage sessions between clients. Among other things, signaling protocols can:

- Detect presence, or the availability of a user, through states set by the user (for example, *online*, *away*, *busy*, or *invisible*) or by predetermined conditions (such as the time of day or a user's location)

- Request a call or videoconference setup

- Locate clients on the network and determine the best routes for call or video transmissions

- Acknowledge a request for a call or videoconference setup and establish the connection

- Manage ringing, dial tone, call waiting, and in some cases, caller ID and other telephony features

- Detect and reestablish dropped call or video transmissions

- Properly terminate a call or videoconference

In the early days of VoIP, vendors developed their own, proprietary signaling protocols, which meant that if you wanted to use the Internet to call your neighbor, you and your neighbor had to use hardware or software from the same manufacturer. Now, however, most VoIP and video-over-IP clients and gateways use standardized signaling protocols. The following sections describe the most common of these.

On the circuit-switched portions of the PSTN, a set of standards established by the ITU, known as SS7 (Signaling System 7), typically handles call signaling. You should be familiar with this term, as it might appear in discussions of interconnecting the PSTN with networks running VoIP.

H.323 H.323 is an ITU standard that describes an architecture and a group of protocols for establishing and managing multimedia sessions on a packet-switched network. H.323 protocols may support voice or video-over-IP services. Before learning about H.323 protocols, it's helpful to understand the set of terms unique to H.323 that ITU has designated. Elements of VoIP and video-over-IP networks have special names in H.323 parlance. Following are five key elements identified by H.323:

- *H.323 terminal*—Any node that provides audio, visual, or data information to another node. An IP phone, video phone, or a server issuing streaming video could be considered an H.323 terminal.

- *H.323 gateway*—A device that provides translation between network devices running H.323 signaling protocols and devices running other types of signaling protocols (for example, SS7 on the PSTN).

- *H.323 gatekeeper*—The nerve center for networks that adhere to H.323. Gatekeepers authorize and authenticate terminals and gateways, manage bandwidth, and oversee call routing, accounting, and billing. Gatekeepers are optional on H.323 networks.

- *MCU (multipoint control unit)*—A computer that provides support for multiple H.323 terminals (for example, several workstations participating in a videoconference) and manages communication between them. In videoconferencing, a video bridge serves as an MCU.

- *H.323 zone*—A collection of H.323 terminals, H.323 gateways, and MCUs that are managed by a single H.323 gatekeeper. Figure 9-12 illustrates an H.323 zone comprising four terminals, one gateway, and one MCU.

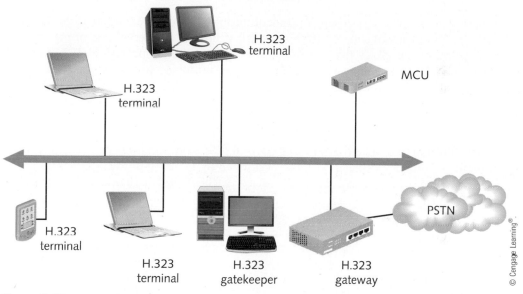

Figure 9-12 An H.323 zone

The H.225 and H.245 signaling protocols are also specified in the H.323 standard. Both protocols operate at the Session layer of the OSI model. However, each performs a different function. To begin, H.225 is the H.323 protocol that handles call or videoconference signaling.

For instance, when an IP phone user wants to make a call, the IP phone first creates a TCP connection with the H.323 gateway or, in a point-to-point connection, directly with the other terminal through the listening device's H.323 port 1720, and then requests a call setup (from the H.323 gateway) via H.225. The same IP phone would use the H.225 protocol to announce its presence on the network, to request the allocation of additional bandwidth, and to indicate when it wants to terminate a call.

H.245, on the other hand, ensures that the type of information—whether voice or video—issued to an H.323 terminal is formatted in a way that the H.323 terminal can interpret.

To perform this task, H.245 first sets up logical channels between the sending and receiving nodes. On a VoIP or video-over-IP network, these logical channels are identified as port numbers at each IP address. One logical channel is assigned to each transmission direction. Thus, for a call between two IP phones, H.245 would use two separate control channels. Note that these channels are distinct from the channels used for H.225 call signaling. They are also different from channels used to exchange the actual voice or video signals (for example, the words you speak during a conversation or the pictures transmitted in a videoconference).

In addition to the H.225 and H.245 signaling protocols, the H.323 standard also specifies interoperability with certain protocols at the Presentation layer, such as those responsible for coding and decoding signals, and at the Transport layer. Later in this chapter, you'll learn about the Transport layer protocols used with voice and video services.

ITU codified H.323 as an open protocol for multiservice signaling in 1996. Early versions of the H.323 protocol suffered from slow call setup, due to the volume of messages exchanged between nodes. Since that time, ITU has revised and improved H.323 standards several times, and H.323 remains a popular signaling protocol on large voice and video networks. After H.323 was released, however, another protocol for VoIP call signaling, SIP, emerged and attracted the attention of network administrators.

SIP (Session Initiation Protocol) SIP (Session Initiation Protocol) is a protocol that performs functions similar to those performed by H.323. SIP is an Application layer signaling and control protocol for multiservice, packet-based networks, and travels over either TCP or UDP, with the server listening on ports 5060 (unsecured) and 5061 (secured using TLS). The protocol's developers modeled it on HTTP, with the original intent of replacing HTTP for IP networks. For example, the text-based messages that clients exchange to initiate a VoIP call are formatted like an HTTP request and rely on URL-style addresses. Developers also aimed to reuse as many existing TCP/IP protocols as possible for managing sessions and providing enhanced services. Furthermore, they wanted SIP to be modular and specific. Among other things, SIP can:

- Determine the location of an endpoint, which in SIP terminology refers to any client, server, or gateway communicating on a network; this means SIP translates the endpoint's name into its current network address.

- Determine the availability of an endpoint; if SIP discovers that a client is not available, it returns a message indicating whether the client was already connected to a call or simply didn't respond.

- Establish a session between two endpoints and manage calls by adding (inviting), dropping, or transferring participants.

- Negotiate features of a call or videoconference when it's established; for example, agreeing on the type of encoding both endpoints will employ.

- Change features of a call or videoconference while it's connected; SIP's functions are more limited than those performed by the protocols in the H.323 group. For example, SIP does not supply some enhanced features, such as caller ID, that H.323 does. Instead, it depends on other protocols and services to supply them.

As with H.323, a SIP network uses the terms and follows the specific architecture mapped out in the standard. Components of a SIP network include the following:

- *user agent*—Any node that initiates or responds to SIP requests.

- *user agent client*—End-user devices, which may include workstations, tablet computers, smartphones, or IP phones. A user agent client initiates a SIP connection.

- *user agent server*—A server that responds to user agent clients' requests for session initiation and termination. Practically speaking, a device such as an IP phone can act as both a user agent client and a user agent server, thus allowing it to directly contact and establish sessions with other clients in a peer-to-peer fashion. As you have learned, however, peer-to-peer arrangements are undesirable because they become difficult to manage when more than a few users participate.

- *registrar server*—A server that maintains a database containing information about the locations (network addresses) of each user agent in its domain. When a user agent joins a SIP network, it transmits its location information to the SIP registrar server.

- *proxy server*—A server that accepts requests for location information from user agents, then queries the nearest registrar server on behalf of those user agents. If the recipient user agent is in the SIP proxy server's domain, then that server will also act as a go-between for calls established and terminated between the requesting user agent and the recipient user agent. If the recipient user agent is not in the SIP proxy server's domain, the proxy server will pass on session information to a SIP redirect server. Proxy servers are optional on a SIP network.

- *redirect server*—A server that accepts and responds to requests from user agents and SIP proxy servers for location information on recipients that belong to external domains. A redirect server does not get involved in establishing or maintaining sessions. Redirect servers are optional on SIP networks.

Figure 9-13 shows how the elements of a SIP system might be arranged on a network. In this example, user agents connect to proxy servers, which accept and forward addressing

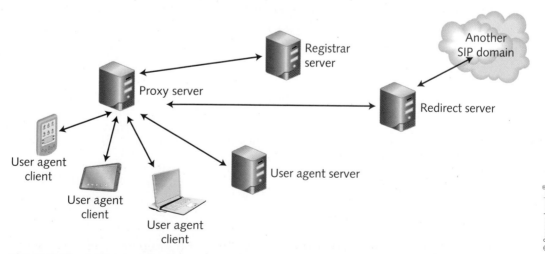

Figure 9-13   A SIP network

requests and also make use of redirect servers to learn about user agents on other domains. For purposes of illustration, the registrar server, proxy server, and redirect server are shown as separate computers in Figure 9-13. However, on a SIP network, all might be installed on a single computer.

Some VoIP vendors prefer SIP because of its simplicity, which makes SIP easier to maintain than H.323. And because it requires fewer instructions to control a call, SIP consumes fewer processing resources than H.323. In some cases, SIP is more flexible than H.323. For example, it is designed to work with many types of Transport layer protocols, not just one. One popular system based on SIP is Asterisk, an open source IP-PBX software package. Many carrier networks have replaced PSTN protocols with SIP, and companies that provide telephone equipment, such as 3Com, Avaya, Cisco, and Nortel, also supply SIP software with their hardware. However, SIP is limited to IP networks.

SIP and H.323 regulate call signaling and control for VoIP or video-over-IP clients and servers, but they do not account for communication between media gateways. This type of communication is governed by MGCP or Megaco, which are discussed next.

MGCP (Media Gateway Control Protocol) and Megaco (H.248)   You learned in Chapter 2 that a gateway is a device that a host uses to access another network. Gateways are integral to converged networks. A **media gateway**, or **UC gateway**, accepts PSTN lines, converts the analog signals into VoIP format, and translates between SS7, the PSTN signaling protocol suite, and VoIP signaling protocols, such as H.323 or SIP.

You have also learned that information transmissions (such as the speech carried by a VoIP network) use different channels from and may take different logical or physical paths than control signals. In fact, to expedite information handling, the use of separate physical paths is often preferable. The reason for this is that if media gateways are freed from having to process control signals, they can dedicate their resources (for example, ports and processors) to encoding, decoding, and translating data. As a result, they process information faster. And as you have learned, faster data processing on a converged network is particularly important, given quality and reliability concerns.

However, gateways still need to exchange and translate signaling and control information with each other so that voice and video packets are properly routed through the network. To do so, gateways rely on an intermediate device known as an **MGC (media gateway controller)**, or **call agent (CA)**. As its name implies, an MGC is a computer that manages multiple media gateways. This means that it facilitates the exchange of call signaling information between these gateways. It also manages and disseminates information about the paths that voice or video signals take between gateways. Because it is software that performs call-switching functions, an MGC is sometimes called a **Softswitch**.

For example, suppose a network has multiple media gateways, all of which accept thousands of connections from both the PSTN and from private TCP/IP WAN and LAN links. When a media gateway receives a call, rather than attempting to determine how to handle the call, the gateway simply contacts the media gateway controller with a message that essentially says, "I received a signal. You figure out what to do with it next." The media gateway controller then determines which of the network's media gateways should translate the information carried by the signal. It also figures out which physical media the call should be routed over, according to which signaling protocols the call must be managed by, and what devices the call should be directed to. After the media gateway controller has processed this information, it instructs the appropriate media gateways how to handle the call. The media gateways simply follow orders from the media gateway controller.

MGCs are especially advantageous on large VoIP networks—for example, at a telecommunications carrier's central office (CO). In such an environment, they make a group of media gateways appear to the outside world as one large gateway. This centralizes call control functions, which can simplify network management. Figure 9-14 illustrates this model. (Note that in this figure, as on most large networks, the media gateways supply access services.)

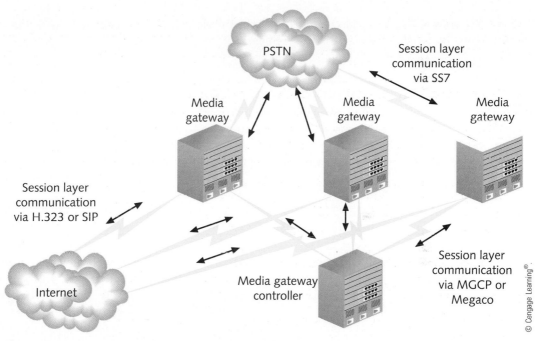

Figure 9-14 Use of an MGC (media gateway controller)

MGCs communicate with media gateways according to one of several protocols. The older protocol is MGCP (Media Gateway Control Protocol). MGCP is commonly used on multi-service networks that support a number of media gateways. It can operate in conjunction with H.323 or SIP call signaling and control protocols. MGCP operates over UDP with gateways listening to the MGC on port 2427 and MGCs listening on port 2727.

A newer gateway control protocol, **Megaco**, performs the same functions as MGCP, but using different commands and processes along with an increased feature set. Like MGCP, Megaco can operate with H.323 or SIP. Many network engineers consider Megaco superior to MGCP because it supports a broader range of network technologies, including ATM. Megaco was developed by cooperative efforts of the ITU and IETF, and the ITU has codified the Megaco protocol in its **H.248** standard.

Bear in mind that this chapter describes only some of the signaling protocols used on converged networks. In fact, some softphones, VoIP servers, and video-conferencing software packages (for example, Skype) use proprietary protocols, which means that these devices or applications will only work with other devices or applications that use the same proprietary protocols.

Now that you are familiar with the most popular session control protocols used on converged networks, you are ready to learn about the transport protocols that work in tandem with those session control protocols.

Transport Protocols

The protocols you just learned about only communicate information about a voice or video *session*. A different set of protocols use TCP and UDP at the Transport layer to actually deliver the voice or video payload—for example, the bits of encoded voice that together make up words spoken into an IP phone.

Recall that on a TCP/IP network, the UDP and TCP protocols operate at the Transport layer of the OSI model. TCP is connection-oriented and, therefore, provides some measure of delivery guarantees. UDP, on the other hand, is connectionless, and does not pay attention to the order in which messages arrive or how quickly they arrive. Despite this lack of accountability, UDP is preferred over TCP for real-time services, such as telephone conversations and videoconferences where data is transferred as it is created, because it requires less overhead and, as a result, can transport messages more quickly. However some commercial multimedia sites, such as YouTube, have developed methods of using TCP transmissions for video streaming. One reason for this is that many networks block UDP streams, but allow TCP streams. Under certain conditions, the disadvantages of TCP's overhead are minimized when balanced with the fuller functionality that it offers.

RTP (Real-time Transport Protocol) One protocol that helps voice and video networks overcome UDP's shortcomings is the RTP (Real-time Transport Protocol or Real-time Protocol), as you learned in Chapter 1. RTP operates at the Application layer of the OSI model (despite its name) and relies on UDP at the Transport layer. It applies sequence numbers to indicate the order in which messages should be assembled at their destination. Sequence numbers also help to indicate whether messages were lost during transmission. In addition, RTP assigns each message a time stamp that corresponds to when the data in the message was sampled from the voice or video stream. This time stamp helps the receiving node to compensate for network delay and to synchronize the signals it receives.

RTP alone does not, however, provide any mechanisms to detect whether or not it's successful. For that, it relies on a companion protocol, RTCP.

RTCP (Real-time Transport Control Protocol) RTCP (Real-time Transport Control Protocol, or RTP Control Protocol) provides feedback on the quality of a call or videoconference to its participants. Whereas RTP functions on an even port number, usually 5004, RTCP is carried on the next higher (and therefore) odd number, usually 5005. RTCP messages are transmitted periodically to all session endpoints, and the protocol allows for several types of messages. For example, each sender issues information about its transmissions' NTP (Network Time Protocol) time stamps, RTP time stamps, number of messages, and number of bytes. Recipients of RTP data use RTCP to issue information about the number and percentage of messages lost and delay suffered between the sender and receiver. RTCP also maintains identifying information for RTP sources.

The value of RTCP lies in what clients and their applications do with the information that RTCP supplies. For example, if a call participant's software uses RTCP to report that an excessive number of messages are being delayed during transmission, the sender's software can adjust the rate at which it issues RTP messages.

RTCP is not mandatory on networks that use RTP. In fact, on large networks running high-bandwidth services, RTCP might not be able to supply useful feedback in a timely manner. For that reason, some network administrators prefer not to use it.

It's important to realize that although RTP and RTCP can provide information about message order, loss, and delay, they cannot do anything to correct transmission flaws. Attempts to correct these flaws, and thus improve the quality of a voice or video signal, are handled by QoS protocols, which are discussed next.

QoS (Quality of Service) Assurance

Despite all the advantages to using VoIP and video over IP, it is more difficult to transmit these types of signals over a packet-switched network than it is to transmit data signals. First, more so than data transmissions, voice and video can easily be distorted by a connection's inconsistent quality of service, or QoS. When you talk with your friend, you need to hear his syllables in the order in which he uttered them, and preferably, without delay. When you watch a movie over the Web, you want to see the scenes sequentially and without interruption. In general, to prevent delays, disorder, and distortion, a voice or video connection requires more dedicated bandwidth than a data connection. In addition, it requires the use of techniques that ensure high QoS. A network that has been optimized for media transmissions is called a medianet.

QoS is a measure of how well a network service matches its expected performance. From the point of view of a person using VoIP or video over IP, high QoS translates into an uninterrupted, accurate, and faithful reproduction of audio or visual input. Low, or poor, QoS is often cited as a key disadvantage to using VoIP or video over IP. But although early attempts at converged services sounded and looked dreadful, thanks to technology improvements, these services now achieve quality comparable to the PSTN (in the case of VoIP) and cable television (in the case of video over IP).

Network engineers have developed several techniques to overcome the QoS challenges inherent in delivering voice and video over IP. The following sections describe some of these techniques, all of which are standardized by IETF.

DiffServ (Differentiated Service)

DiffServ (Differentiated Service) is a simple technique that addresses QoS issues by prioritizing traffic. DiffServ modifies the actual IP packets that contain payload data, and also takes into account all types of network traffic, not just the time-sensitive services such as voice and video. That way, it can assign voice streams a high priority and at the same time assign unessential data streams (for example, an employee surfing the Internet on his lunch hour) a low priority. This technique offers more protection for the time-sensitive voice and video services.

To prioritize traffic, DiffServ places information in the DiffServ field in an IPv4 packet. The first 6 bits of this 8-bit field are called Differentiated Services Code Point (DSCP). (For a review of the fields in an IP packet, refer to Chapter 3.) In IPv6 packets, DiffServ uses a similar field known as the Traffic Class field. This information indicates to the network routers how the data stream should be forwarded. DiffServ defines two types of forwarding: EF (Expedited Forwarding) or AF (Assured Forwarding). In EF, a data stream is assigned a minimum departure rate from a given node. This technique circumvents delays that slow normal data from reaching its destination on time and in sequence. In AF, different levels of router resources can be assigned to data streams. AF prioritizes data handling, but provides no guarantee that on a busy network messages will arrive on time and in sequence. This description of DiffServ's prioritization mechanisms is oversimplified, but a deeper discussion is beyond the scope of this book.

Because of its simplicity and relatively low overhead, DiffServ is well suited to large, heavily trafficked networks.

MPLS (Multiprotocol Label Switching)

Earlier in this chapter, you learned about circuit switching and packet switching. Another type of switching, MPLS (multiprotocol label switching), was introduced by the Internet Engineering Task Force (IETF) in 1999. As its name implies, MPLS enables multiple types of Layer 3 protocols to travel over any one of several connection-oriented Layer 2 protocols. MPLS supports IP and all the other Layer 3 and higher protocols used on TCP/IP networks. MPLS can operate over Ethernet frames, but is more often used with other Layer 2 protocols, like those designed for WANs. For this reason, MPLS is almost exclusively used within service provider networks instead of on private networks. One of its benefits is the ability to use packet-switched technologies over traditionally circuit-switched networks. MPLS can also create end-to-end paths that act like circuit-switched connections, such as VPNs.

In MPLS, the first router that receives a message in a data stream adds one or more labels to the Layer 3 packet. (Collectively, the MPLS labels are sometimes called a shim because of their placement between Layer 3 and Layer 2 information. Also, MPLS is sometimes said to belong to "Layer 2.5.") Then, the network's Layer 2 protocol header is added, as shown in Figure 9-15.

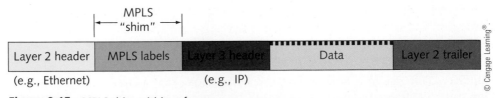

Figure 9-15 MPLS shim within a frame

MPLS labels include information about where the router should forward the message next and, sometimes, prioritization information. Each router in the data stream's path revises the label to indicate the data's next hop. In this manner, routers on a network can take into consideration network congestion, QoS indicators assigned to the messages, plus other criteria. Network engineers have significant control in setting these paths. Consequently, MPLS offers potentially faster transmission than traditionally packet-switched or circuit-switched networks. Because it can add prioritization information, MPLS can also offer better QoS. These advantages make MPLS especially well suited to WANs.

CoS (Class of Service)

CoS, or Class of Service, is often used synonymously with QoS, but there is an important technical distinction. The term QoS refers to techniques that are performed at various OSI layers via several different subprotocols. By contrast, the term CoS (Class of Service) refers only to techniques performed at Layer 2, on Ethernet frames. CoS is most often used to more efficiently route Ethernet traffic between VLANs, which you'll learn more about in Chapter 10. Frames that have been tagged (addressed to a specific VLAN) contain a 3-bit field in the frame header called the Priority Code Point, or PCP. CoS works by setting these bits to one of eight levels ranging from 0 to 7, which indicates to the switch the level of priority the message should be given if the port is receiving more traffic than it can forward at any one time. Waiting messages are cached until the port can get to them, or discarded, depending on the class assignment for that frame.

A network's connectivity devices and clients must support the same set of protocols to achieve their QoS benefits. However, networks can—and often do—combine multiple QoS techniques.

Troubleshooting Network Integrity and Availability

In the world of networking, the term integrity refers to the assurance that a network's programs, data, services, devices, and connections have not been altered without authorization. To ensure a network's integrity, you must protect it from anything that might render it unusable. Closely related to the concept of integrity is availability. The term availability refers to how consistently and reliably a file or system can be accessed by authorized personnel. For example, a server that allows staff to log on and use its programs and data 99.99 percent of the time is considered highly available, whereas one that is functional only 99.9 percent of the time is less available. In fact, the number of 9s in a system's availability rating is sometimes referred to colloquially as "four 9s" (99.99 percent) or "three 9s" (99.9 percent) availability. You might hear someone use the term in a statement such as, "We're a four 9s shop."

Another way to consider availability is by measuring a system or network's uptime, which is the duration or percentage of time it functions normally between failures. As shown in Table 9-2, a system that experiences 99.999 percent uptime is *unavailable*, on average, only 5 minutes and 15 seconds per year.

On a computer running Linux or UNIX, you can view the length of time your system has been running by typing uptime at the command prompt and pressing Enter. Microsoft offers

Table 9-2   Availability and downtime equivalents

Availability	Downtime per day	Downtime per month	Downtime per year
99%	14 minutes, 23 seconds	7 hours, 18 minutes, 17 seconds	87 hours, 39 minutes, 29 seconds
99.9%	1 minute, 26 seconds	43 minutes, 49 seconds	8 hours, 45 minutes, 56 seconds
99.99%	8 seconds	4 minutes, 22 seconds	52 minutes, 35 seconds
99.999%	.4 seconds	26 seconds	5 minutes, 15 seconds

© 2016 Cengage Learning®

an uptime.exe utility that allows you to do the same from a computer running a Windows operating system.

Applying Concepts

Windows Task Manager

Windows 7 and 8.1 both provide uptime data, along with a great deal of additional performance information, in Task Manager. Complete the following steps to view this information on a Windows 7 or Windows 8.1 computer:

1. Press **Ctrl+Alt+Del** and click **Task Manager**.

2. On the Performance tab, examine the CPU and Memory utilization statistics. What is the current uptime?

3. Click **Open Resource Monitor** (in Windows 8.1) or **Resource Monitor** (in Windows 7) to view additional performance data and its graphs. Be sure to take a look at the Listening Ports pane on the Network tab. You'll need to know where to find this information for a Hands-On Project and a Case Project at the end of this chapter.

General Guidelines

A number of phenomena can compromise both integrity and availability, including security breaches, natural disasters, malicious intruders, power flaws, and human error. Every network administrator should consider these possibilities when designing a sound network. You can readily imagine the importance of integrity and availability of data in a hospital, for example, in which the network stores patient records and also provides quick medical reference material, video displays for surgical cameras, and control of critical care monitors.

Although you can't predict every type of vulnerability, you can take measures to guard against most damaging events. Later in this chapter, you will learn about specific approaches to data protection. Following are some general guidelines for keeping your network highly available:

- *Allow only network administrators to create or modify NOS and application system files*—Pay attention to the permissions assigned to regular users (including the groups "users" or "everyone" and the username "guest"). Bear in mind that, in most cases, the worst consequence of applying overly stringent file restrictions is an inconvenience to users. In contrast, the worst consequence of applying overly lenient file restrictions could be a failed network.

- *Monitor the network for unauthorized access or changes*—You can install programs that routinely check whether and when the files you've specified have changed. Such monitoring programs are typically inexpensive and easy to customize. Some enable the system to text or email you when a system file changes.

- *Record authorized system changes in a change management system*—You'll learn about the importance of change management in Chapter 12. Routine changes should also be documented in a change management system. Recording system changes enables you and your colleagues to understand what's happening to your network and protect it from harm. For example, suppose that the remote access service on a Linux server has stopped accepting connections. Before taking troubleshooting steps that might create more problems and further reduce the availability of the system, you could review the change management log. It might indicate that a colleague recently installed an update to the Linux NOS. With this information in hand, you could focus on the update as a likely source of the problem.

- *Install redundant components*—The term **redundancy** refers to an implementation in which more than one component is installed and ready to use for storing, processing, or transporting data. Redundancy is intended to eliminate single points of failure. To maintain high availability, you should ensure that critical network elements, such as your connection to the Internet or your file server's hard disk, are redundant. Some types of redundancy—for example, redundant sources of electrical power for a building—require large investments, so your organization should weigh the risks of losing connectivity or data against the cost of adding duplicate components.

- *Perform regular health checks on the network*—Prevention is the best weapon against network downtime. By establishing a baseline and regular network monitoring, you can anticipate problems before they affect availability or integrity. For example, if your network monitor alerts you to rapidly rising utilization on a critical network segment, you can analyze the network to discover where the problem lies and perhaps fix it before it takes down the segment.

- *Check system performance, error logs, and the system log book regularly*—By keeping track of system errors and trends in performance, you have a better chance of correcting problems before they cause a hard disk failure and potentially damage your system files. By default, all NOSs keep error logs. On a Linux server, for example, a file called "messages" located in the /var/log directory collects error messages from system services, such as DNS, and other programs also save log files in the /var/log directory. It's important that you know where these error logs reside on your server and understand how to interpret them.

- *Keep backups, system images, and emergency repair disks current and available*—If your file system or critical boot files become corrupted by a system crash, you can use backups or system images to recover the system. Otherwise, you might need to reinstall the software before you can start the system. If you ever face the situation of recovering from a system loss or disaster, you must recover in the quickest manner possible. For this effort, you need a backup strategy tailored to your environment.

- *Implement and enforce security and disaster recovery policies*—Everyone in your organization should know what he is allowed to do on the network. For example, if you decide that it's too risky for employees to download games off the Internet because of the potential for virus infection, you should inform them of a ban on downloading games. You might enforce this policy by restricting users' ability to create or change executable files that are copied to the workstation during the downloading of games. Making such decisions and communicating them to staff should be part of your IT policy. Likewise, key personnel in your organization should be familiar with your disaster recovery plan, which should detail your strategy for restoring network functionality in case of an unexpected failure. Although such policies take time to develop and might be difficult to enforce, they can directly affect your network's availability and integrity.

These measures are merely first steps to ensuring network integrity and availability, but they are essential.

Fault Tolerance

Network+
1.1
2.4
2.6
3.1
4.6

Another key factor in maintaining the availability and integrity of data is **fault tolerance**, or the capacity for a system to continue performing despite an unexpected hardware or software malfunction. The key to fault tolerance in network design is supplying multiple paths that data can use to travel from any one point to another. Therefore, if one connection or component fails, data can be rerouted over an alternate path. The following sections describe examples of fault tolerance in network design.

To better understand the issues related to fault tolerance, it helps to know the difference between failures and faults as they apply to networks. In broad terms, a **failure** is a deviation from a specified level of system performance for a given period of time. In other words, a failure occurs when something doesn't work as promised or as planned. For example, if your car breaks down on the highway, you can consider the breakdown to be a failure. A **fault**, on the other hand, involves the malfunction of one component of a system. A fault can result in a failure. For example, the fault that caused your car to break down might be a leaking water pump. The goal of fault-tolerant systems is to prevent faults from progressing to failures.

Fault tolerance can be realized in varying degrees; the optimal level of fault tolerance for a system depends on how critical its services and files are to productivity. At the highest level of fault tolerance, a system remains unaffected by even the most drastic problem, such as a regional power outage. In this case, a backup power source, such as an electrical generator, is necessary to ensure fault tolerance. However, less dramatic faults, such as a malfunctioning NIC on a router, can still cause network outages, and you should guard against them.

The following sections describe network aspects that must be monitored and managed to ensure fault tolerance.

Devices and Interfaces Redundancy in your network offers the advantage of reducing the risk of lost functionality, and potentially lost profits, from a network fault. As you might guess, however, the main disadvantage of redundancy is its cost. Redundancy is like a homeowner's insurance policy: You might never need to use it, but if you don't get it, the cost when you do need it can be much higher than your premiums. Redundant ISP services, for example, can be fairly costly. Compared to the cost to a business of not having Internet access if a trunk line is severed, however, the additional WAN interface might make sense. As a general rule, you should invest in connection redundancies where they are absolutely necessary.

Even when dedicated links and VPN connections remain sound, a faulty device or interface in the data path can affect service for a user, a whole segment, or the whole network. To understand how to increase the fault tolerance of a connection from end to end, consider a typical T-1 link to the Internet. Figure 9-16 provides a representation of this arrangement.

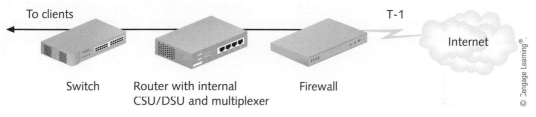

Figure 9-16   Single T-1 connectivity

Notice the many single points of failure in the arrangement depicted in Figure 9-16. In addition to the T-1 link failing—for example, if a backhoe accidentally cut a cable during road construction—any of the critical nodes in the following list could suffer a fault or failure and impair connectivity or performance: firewall, router, CSU/DSU, multiplexer, switch.

Figure 9-17 illustrates a network design that ensures full redundancy for all the components linking two locations via a T-1.

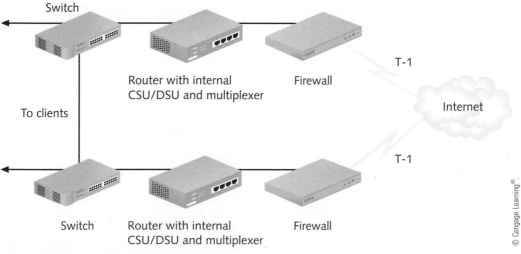

Figure 9-17   Fully redundant T-1 connectivity

To achieve the utmost fault tolerance, each critical device requires redundant NICs, SFPs, power supplies, cooling fans, and processors, all of which should, ideally, be able to immediately assume the duties of an identical component, a capability known as **automatic failover**. If one NIC in a router fails, for example, automatic failover ensures that the router's other NIC can automatically handle the first NIC's responsibilities.

In cases when it's impractical to have failover capable components, you can provide some level of fault tolerance by using hot-swappable parts. Recall from Chapter 5 that the term *hot-swappable* refers to identical components that can be changed (or swapped) while a machine is still running (hot). A hot-swappable SFP or hard disk, for example, is known as a **hot spare**, or a duplicate component already installed in a device that can assume the original component's functions in case that component fails. In contrast, **cold spare** refers to a duplicate component that is not installed, but can be installed in case of a failure. Replacing a component with a cold spare requires an interruption of service. When you purchase switches or routers to support critical links, look for those that contain failover capable or hot-swappable components. As with other redundancy provisions, these features add to the cost of your device.

Using redundant NICs allows devices, servers, or other nodes to participate in link aggregation. **Link aggregation**, also known as **port bonding**, is the seamless combination of multiple network interfaces or ports to act as one logical interface. In one type of link aggregation, **NIC teaming**, two or more NICs work in tandem to handle traffic to and from a single node. This allows for increased total throughput and automatic failover between the two NICs. It also allows for **load balancing** (or **content switching**), which is a distribution of traffic over multiple components or links to optimize performance and fault tolerance. For multiple NICs or ports to use link aggregation, they must be properly configured in each device's operating system.

NIC teaming accomplished with a single switch, as shown in Figure 9-18, is called **Switch Dependent Mode**. Note that this mode requires an **intelligent switch** with configuration capabilities to handle the traffic appropriately. One variety of this mode implements the **Link Aggregation Control Protocol (LACP)**, currently defined by IEEE's 802.1AX standard, to dynamically coordinate communications between the two hosts. If the network does not support LACP, another option is to configure **static teaming**, in which both the switch and the host are configured to handle the division of labor between the redundant links according to particular rules without the ability to compensate for errors.

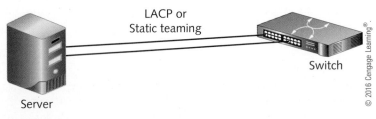

Figure 9-18 Switch Dependent Mode

Alternatively, NICs could be teamed to multiple switches using **Switch Independent Mode**, which can be used with nonintelligent switches. See Figure 9-19.

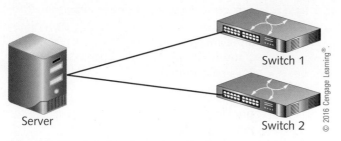

Figure 9-19   Switch Independent Mode

Another configuration option is to determine whether or not both connections should carry traffic by default. In active-active mode, both connections are active as a matter of course. If one fails, the other maintains the connection. In active-passive mode, however, only one connection is used at a time, with the other being a passive connection that is only activated if the first connection fails.

NIC teaming misconfigurations can be caused by overlapped teaming modes or overlapped teaming solutions (such as when using the embedded Windows NIC teaming tool alongside a third-party solution), and can cause unstable, problematic communications on the network. Another common problem encountered with NIC teaming when implemented in Switch Independent Mode is the duplication of multicast or broadcast messages over the teamed connections. Because the switches in this scenario are not aware of the link aggregation, the switches forward these multicast and broadcast messages to all ports, regardless of which ports are bonded to other ports. Switches configured for Switch Dependent Mode, however, are aware of the NIC teams and can adjust accordingly.

Naming and Addressing Services Naming or addressing services, such as DNS and DHCP, are critical to the functionality of a network because when they fail, nearly all traffic comes to a halt. The physical hardware on which these services run are also critical assets. Therefore, it's important to understand techniques for keeping these devices and their services available.

Most organizations rely on more than one DNS server to make sure that requests to resolve host names and IP addresses are always satisfied. At the very least, organizations specify a primary name server and a secondary name server. Primary name servers, which are queried first when a name resolution that is not already cached is requested, are also known as master name servers. Secondary name servers, which can take the place of primary name servers, are also known as slave name servers.

Network administrators who work on large enterprise networks are likely to add more than one slave name server to the DNS architecture. However, a thoughtful administrator will install only as many name servers as needed. Because the slave name servers regularly poll the master name servers to ensure that their DNS zone information is current, running too many slave name servers may add unnecessary traffic and slow performance. As shown in Figure 9-20, networks can also contain DNS caching servers, which save DNS information locally but do not provide resolution for new requests. If a client can resolve a name locally, it can access the host more quickly and reduce the burden on the master name server.

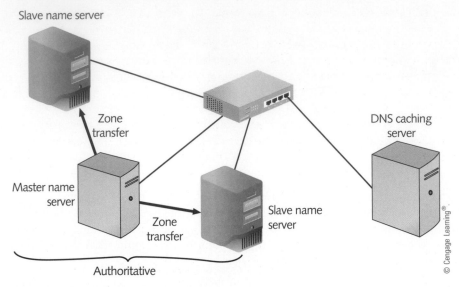

Figure 9-20 Redundant name servers

In addition to maintaining redundant name servers, DNS can point to redundant locations for each host name. For example, the master and slave name servers with the authority to resolve the same *cengage.com* host name could all have the same list of different IP addresses in multiple A records associated with this host. The portion of the zone file responsible for resolving the *cengage.com* location might look like the one shown in Figure 9-21. When a client requests the address for *cengage.com*, the response could be one of several IP addresses, all of which point to identical *cengage.com* Web servers. After pointing a client to one IP address in the list, DNS will point the next client that requests resolution for *cengage.com* to the next IP address in the list, and so on. This scheme is known as **round-robin DNS**. Round-robin DNS enables load balancing between the servers and increases fault tolerance. Notice that the sample DNS records in Figure 9-21 show a relatively low TTL of 800 seconds (a little over 13 minutes). Limiting the duration of a DNS record cache helps to keep each of the IP addresses that are associated with the host in rotation.

#Host name	TTL	Type		IP address
cengage.com	800	IN	A	192.168.7.1
cengage.com	800	IN	A	192.168.7.2
cengage.com	800	IN	A	192.169.7.3
cengage.com	800	IN	A	192.168.7.4

Figure 9-21 Redundant entries in a DNS zone file

More sophisticated load balancing for all types of servers can be achieved by using a **load balancer**, a device dedicated to this task. A load balancer distributes traffic intelligently among multiple computers. Whereas round-robin DNS simply doles out IP addresses sequentially with every new request, a load balancer can determine which among a pool of servers is experiencing the most traffic before forwarding the request to a server with lower utilization. Naming and addressing availability can be increased further by using **CARP (Common Address Redundancy Protocol)**, which allows a pool of computers or interfaces to share one or more IP addresses. This pool is known as a group of redundancy. In CARP, one computer, acting as the master of the group, receives requests for an IP address, then parcels out the requests to one of several computers in a group. Figure 9-22 illustrates how CARP and round-robin DNS, used together, can provide two layers of fault tolerance for naming and addressing services. CARP is often used with firewalls or routers that have multiple interfaces to ensure automatic failover in case one of the interfaces suffers a fault.

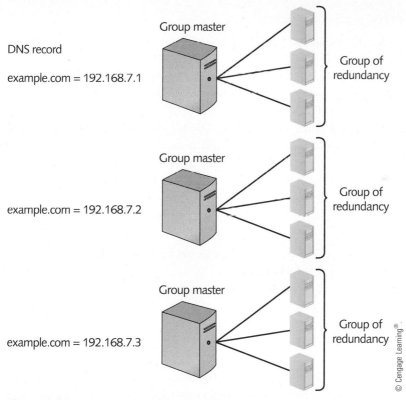

Figure 9-22   Round-robin DNS with CARP

Data Backup

You have probably heard or even spoken the axiom, "If you can't do without it, back it up!" A **backup** is a copy of data or program files created for archiving or safekeeping. Maintaining good backups is essential for providing fault tolerance and reliability.

When identifying the types of data to back up, remember to include configuration files for devices such as routers, switches, access points, gateways, and firewalls.

When designing and configuring your backup system, keep these points in mind:

- Use only proven and reliable backup software and hardware. For your backup system, now is not the time to experiment with the latest and greatest technology.

- Verify that backup hardware and software are compatible with your existing network hardware and software.

- Make sure your backup software uses data error-checking techniques.

- Verify that your backup storage media or system provides sufficient capacity, with plenty of room to spare and can also accommodate your network's growth.

- Be aware of how your backup process affects the system, normal network functioning, and your users' computing habits.

- As you make purchasing decisions, make sure you know how much the backup methods and media cost relative to the amount of data they can store.

- Be aware of the degree of manual intervention required to manage the backups, such as exchanging backup media on a regular basis or backing up operating systems on servers that run around the clock.

- Make wise choices for storage media, considering advantages and disadvantages of media types. For example, optical media (DVDs and Blu-ray) require more human intervention to exchange disks than exchanging tapes in tape drives or exchanging removable hard drives.

- When storing data to hard drives, recognize that the drives can be installed on computers on the local network, on a WAN, or in NAS devices, or even on a sophisticated SAN.

- Keep your backups secure, including keeping backup media off-site in the event of a major disaster such as fire or flooding.

- Consider **cloud backups**, where third-party vendors manage the backup hardware and software somewhere on the Internet. In general, cloud backups are more expensive and reliable than other methods. Because cloud backups are not stored at your local facility, you have the added advantage that backups are protected in case the entire facility is destroyed.

- Decide what to back up. Besides the obvious folders used to hold user and application data, you might also want to back up user profile folders and folders that hold configuration files for your applications, services, routers, switches, access points, gateways, and firewalls.

- Plan what type of backup will be done. **Full backups** back up everything every time a backup is done. An **incremental backup** backs up only data that has changed since the last backup. **Differential backups** back up data that has changed since the last full backup. (The OS knows which files to back up for incremental and differential backups because it maintains an **archive bit** in the attributes for each file.)

- Plan when backups will be done. In general, you want to back up data after about four hours of actual data entry. Depending on user habits, this might mean you back up daily or weekly, although Windows 8.1 performs incremental backups hourly. Most organizations perform daily backups, which happen in the middle of the night when there's less network activity.

- Develop a backup schedule. For example, you might perform a full backup every Thursday night and an incremental backup daily. You might take backup media off-site every Friday and overwrite backups (or destroy or rotate your backup media) every six months. You also must establish policies for who is responsible for the backups, what backup logs are kept, and what details are required in these logs.

- The final step in designing a backup system is to establish a regular schedule of verification. From time to time, depending on how often your data changes and how critical the information is, you should attempt to recover some critical files from your backup media. Many network administrators attest that the darkest hour of their career was when they were asked to retrieve critical files from a backup, and found that no backup data existed because their backup system never worked in the first place!

Chapter Summary

Fundamentals of Network Management

- Several disciplines fall under the heading of network management, but all share the goals of enhancing efficiency and performance while preventing costly downtime or loss.

- Baseline measurements allow you to compare future performance increases or decreases caused by network changes or events with past network performance. Obtaining baseline measurements is the only way to know for certain whether a pattern of usage has changed.

- In addition to internal policies, a network manager must consider state and federal regulations.

Monitoring and Managing Network Traffic

- The list of objects and their descriptions that is managed by the NMS is kept in the MIB (Management Information Base), which also contains data about an object's performance in a database format that can be mined and analyzed.

- The syslog protocol is a standard for generating, storing, and processing messages about events on a system.

- The effective utilization of interface system and event logs can help identify and prevent many types of complications.

- Traffic shaping, also called packet shaping, involves manipulating certain characteristics of packets, data streams, or connections to manage the type and amount of traffic traversing a network or interface at any moment.

- Caching is the local storage of frequently needed files that would otherwise be obtained from an external source.

Unified Communications Technologies

- The greatest advantage to packet switching lies in the fact that it does not waste bandwidth by holding a connection open until a message reaches its destination, as circuit switching does. Ethernet networks and the Internet are the most common examples of packet-switched networks.

- One difference between IP phones and softphones is that a softphone's versatile connectivity makes it an optimal VoIP solution for traveling employees and telecommuters.

- Cisco estimates that by 2018, about 79 percent of the traffic carried by the Internet will be video traffic. That's nearly one million minutes of video content transmitted every second.

- In a unicast transmission, a single node issues a stream of data to one other node. A multicast transmission is directed at several points at once.

- A video bridge manages multiple audiovisual sessions so that participants can see and hear each other. Video bridges may exist as a piece of hardware or as software.

- Signaling protocols set up and manage sessions between clients.

- On a VoIP or video-over-IP network, logical channels are identified as port numbers at each IP address. One logical channel is assigned to each transmission direction. These channels are distinct from the channels used for H.225 call signaling. They are also different from channels used to exchange the actual voice or video signals.

- SIP is an Application layer signaling and control protocol for multiservice, packet-based networks, and travels over either TCP or UDP. The protocol's developers modeled it on HTTP.

- MGCP and Megaco are commonly used on multiservice networks that support a number of media gateways. Either one can operate in conjunction with H.323 or SIP call signaling and control protocols.

- UDP is preferred over TCP for real-time services, such as telephone conversations and videoconferences where data is transferred as it is created, because it requires less overhead and, as a result, can transport messages more quickly.

- RTP alone does not provide any mechanisms to detect whether or not it's successful. For that, it relies on a companion protocol, RTCP.

- Recipients of RTP data use RTCP to issue information about the number and percentage of messages lost and delay suffered between the sender and receiver. RTCP also maintains identifying information for RTP sources.

QoS (Quality of Service) Assurance

- QoS is a measure of how well a network service matches its expected performance. From the point of view of a person using VoIP or video over IP, high QoS translates into an uninterrupted, accurate, and faithful reproduction of audio or visual input.

- To prioritize traffic, DiffServ places information in the DiffServ field, also called Differentiated Services Code Point (DSCP), in an IPv4 packet. In IPv6 packets, DiffServ uses a similar field known as the Traffic Class field.

- MPLS can operate over Ethernet frames, but it is more often used with other Layer 2 protocols. In fact, one of its benefits is the ability to use packet-switched technologies over traditionally circuit-switched networks. MPLS can also create end-to-end paths that act like circuit-switched connections.

- A tagged frame contains a 3-bit field in the frame header called the Priority Code Point, or PCP. CoS works by setting these bits to one of eight levels ranging from 0 to 7, which indicates to the switch what level of priority that message should be given if the port is receiving more traffic than it can forward at any one time.

Troubleshooting Network Integrity and Availability

- One way to consider availability is by measuring a system or network's uptime, which is the duration or percentage of time it functions normally between failures.

- Redundancy is intended to eliminate single points of failure. To maintain high availability, ensure that critical network elements are redundant.

- At the highest level of fault tolerance, a system remains unaffected by even the most drastic problem, such as a regional power outage. However, less-dramatic faults, such as a malfunctioning NIC on a router, can still cause network outages.

- Link aggregation is the seamless combination of multiple network interfaces or ports to act as one logical interface. It allows for load balancing, or a distribution of traffic over multiple components or links to optimize performance and fault tolerance.

- Most organizations rely on more than one DNS server to make sure that requests to resolve host names and IP addresses are always satisfied.

- After selecting the appropriate tool for performing your servers' data backups, you need to devise a backup strategy for performing reliable backups that provide maximum data protection.

9

Key Terms

For definitions of key terms, see the Glossary near the end of the book.

active-active mode

active-passive mode

AF (Assured Forwarding)

archive bit

ATA (analog telephone adapter)

automatic failover

availability

backup

baseline

caching

CALEA (Communications Assistance for Law Enforcement Act)

call agent (CA)

CARP (Common Address Redundancy Protocol)

circuit-switched

cloud backup

cold spare

collector

content switching

CoS (Class of Service)

differential backup

Differentiated Services Code Point (DSCP)

DiffServ (Differentiated Service)

digital PBX

discard

drop

EF (Expedited Forwarding)

endpoint

event log

Event Viewer

failure

fault

fault management

fault tolerance

full backup

generator

ghost

giant

H.225

H.245

H.248

H.323 gatekeeper

H.323 gateway

H.323 terminal

H.323 zone

highly available

HIPAA (Health Insurance Portability and Accountability Act)

hot spare

incremental backup

integrity

intelligent switch

interface monitor

Internet telephony

IP phone

IP telephone

IP telephony

IP-PBX

jabber

link aggregation

Link Aggregation Control Protocol (LACP)

live streaming video

load balancer

load balancing

managed device

master name server

MCU (multipoint control unit)

media gateway

medianet

Megaco

MGC (media gateway controller)

MIB (Management Information Base)

MPLS (multiprotocol label switching)

network management

network management agent

network management system (NMS)

network monitor

network tap

NIC teaming

packet loss

packet shaper

packet shaping

packet sniffer

packet-switched

PBX (private branch exchange)

PCI DSS (Payment Card Industry Data Security Standard)

performance management

polling

port bonding

presence

primary name server

Priority Code Point (PCP)

promiscuous mode

proxy server

PSTN (Public Switched Telephone Network)

real-time services

redirect server

redundancy

registrar server

round-robin DNS

RTCP (Real-time Transport Control Protocol, or RTP Control Protocol)

runt

secondary name server

signaling

slave name server

SMS (Short Message Service)

SNMP response message

snmpget

snmpgetnext

snmptrap

SNMPv1 (Simple Network Management Protocol version 1)

SNMPv2 (Simple Network Management Protocol version 2)

SNMPv3 (Simple Network Management Protocol version 3)

snmpwalk

softphone

Softswitch

SS7 (Signaling System 7)

static teaming

streaming video

Switch Dependent Mode

Switch Independent Mode

switching

syslog

system log

tagged

time-shifted video

top listener

top talker

traffic policing

traffic shaper

traffic shaping

UC gateway

unified messaging

unified voice services

uptime

user agent

user agent client

user agent server

video bridge

video over IP

video phone

videoconferencing

video-on-demand (VoD)

Web caching

Webcast

Review Questions

1. What federal organization sets strict standards to protect the privacy of patient records?

   a. CALEA

   b. HIPAA

   c. PCI DSS

   d. IETF

2. What command retrieves the next record in an SNMP log?

   a. `snmpget`

   b. `snmpwalk`

   c. `snmpgetnext`

   d. `snmptrap`

3. What port do SNMP agents listen on?

   a. Port 161

   b. Port 21

   c. Port 162

   d. Port 10162

4. What utility in Linux provides standards for generating, storing, and processing messages about events on a system?

   a. Event Viewer

   b. event log

   c. ls

   d. syslog

5. One of your coworkers downloaded several, very large video files for a special project she's working on for a new client. When you run your network monitor later this afternoon, what list will your coworker's computer likely show up on?

   a. Top talkers

   b. Top listeners

   c. Event Viewer

   d. Discarded packets

6. Your roommate has been hogging the bandwidth on your router lately. What technique can you use to limit the amount of bandwidth his computer can utilize at any one time?

   a. Interface reset

   b. Packet shaping

   c. Caching

   d. Traffic policing

7. What kind of phone is a Skype app?

    a. Analog phone

    b. IP phone

    c. Softphone

    d. Video phone

8. You're trying to choose a signaling protocol for your company's network because you're about to upgrade to a VoIP system. You need to keep it simple because this is a small company with a simple network. Which protocol should you choose?

    a. H.323

    b. SIP

    c. MGCP

    d. Megaco

9. RTP and RTCP operate at which layer of the OSI model?

    a. Application layer

    b. Transport layer

    c. Network layer

    d. Data Link layer

10. Which QoS technique operates at the OSI layer "2.5"?

    a. RTP

    b. DiffServ

    c. MPLS

    d. CoS

11. When you arrive at work one morning, your Inbox is full of messages complaining of a network slowdown. You collect a capture from your network monitor. What can you compare it with in order to determine what has changed?

12. How can network segmentation protect cardholder data?

13. What file must be accessed in order to analyze SNMP logs?

14. What kinds of alerts can you program your NMS to send to the IT personnel when it detects specific conditions?

15. What is the difference between circuit switching and packet switching?

16. What are three advantages to using VoIP instead of traditional PSTN phone service?

17. You need to see the physical switch at one of your company's remote locations to see if you can spot any visible reason why a link keeps failing. However, the remote office is three hours' drive away, and you're pretty sure this will be a simple fix if you can just see it. What kind of video service can you use, with the help of an employee at the remote office, to see the switch from your desk?

18. What are the two types of forwarding defined by DiffServ?

19. The _____ field in IPv4 packets and the _____ field in IPv6 packets are used to help prioritize traffic when managing QoS.

20. What protocol is used to accomplish port bonding on an intelligent switch?

Hands-On Projects

Project 9-1: Work with Data in Event Viewer

In this chapter, you learned how to access and view event log information through the Event Viewer application in Windows 7. In this project, you practice filtering the information contained in the log.

As in the "Applying Concepts: Explore Event Viewer in Windows" project, you need a computer running Windows 7. Ideally, it should be a computer that has been used for a while, so that the event log contains several entries. It need not be connected to a network. However, you must be logged on to the computer as a user with administrator privileges. Finally, you need to know your SMTP server information.

NOTE   All of these steps can also be followed in Windows 8.1 except for the final step of finishing the task creation. The emailed notifications feature in Event Viewer has been deprecated in Windows 8.1, meaning it's no longer an integrated feature. A work-around exists, but it requires the use of PowerShell, a command-line tool that is more powerful than the command prompt and is an integral component of Windows beginning with Windows 7 and Windows Server 2008 R2.

1. Open Event Viewer. In the left pane, click the **Custom Views** arrow and then click **Administrative Events**. A list of Administrative Events appears in the center pane of the Event Viewer window.

2. Suppose you want to find out whether your workstation has ever experienced trouble obtaining a DHCP-assigned IP address. In the Actions pane (the pane on the right), in the Administrative Events section, click **Find**. The Find dialog box opens.

3. In the Find what text box, type **dhcp**, and then click **Find Next**.

4. What is the first DHCP-related event you find? When did it occur? What was the source of this event? Read the description of the event in the General tab to learn more about it. Note: If the computer did not find a DHCP event, first make sure the topmost record is selected before beginning your search to ensure that all of the records are searched. If a DHCP event is still not found, search for a different kind of event such as *DNS* or *Service Control Manager*.

5. Click **Cancel** to close the Find dialog box. Keep the event listing that you found highlighted. (If the search found no DHCP-related errors, choose another event at random.)

6. Now suppose you want to be notified each time your workstation experiences this error. In the Actions pane, click **Attach Task To This Event**. The Create Basic Task Wizard dialog box opens.

9

7. In the Name text box, replace the default text with **DHCP_my_computer**, as shown in Figure 9-23, and then click **Next** to continue.

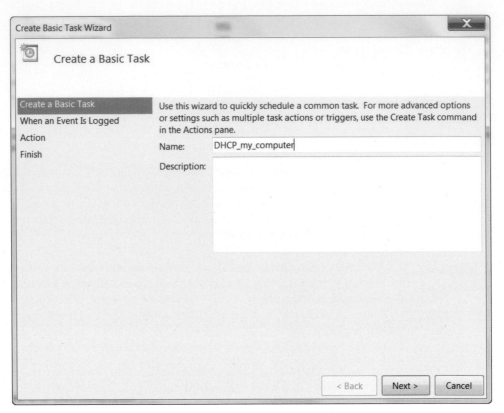

Figure 9-23 Create Basic Task Wizard in Windows Event Viewer

Source: Microsoft LLC.

8. You are prompted to confirm the Log, Source, and Event ID for this error. Click **Next** to continue. You are prompted to indicate the type of action the operating system should take when this error occurs. Select **Send an e-mail**, and then click **Next** to continue.

9. Now you are asked to provide information about the email you want the system to send. In the From box, type your email address; in the To box, type your email address again; in the Subject box, type **DHCP error**; in the Text box, type **My computer has experienced an error while attempting to obtain a DHCP-assigned IP address**. In the SMTP server text box, enter your SMTP server information. Click **Next** to continue.

10. A summary of your notification selections appears. Click **Finish** to create the task and add it to the actions your operating system will perform.

11. An Event Viewer dialog box opens, alerting you that the task has been created. Click **OK** to confirm. Close the Event Viewer application.

Project 9-2: SNMP Service in Windows 8.1

Windows contains an embedded SNMP service, but it's not enabled by default. In this project, you turn the SNMP service on, configure the service to start collecting SNMP messages, and enable the SNMP Trap service. The following instructions are written for either Windows 7 or Windows 8.1.

1. Open the Control Panel. Click **Programs**, then click **Turn Windows features on or off**. After a pause, the Turn Windows features on or off dialog box opens.

2. Scroll down and click the plus sign (+) next to "Simple Network Management Protocol (SNMP)." Click the **Simple Network Management Protocol (SNMP)** check box to select it, click the **WMI SNMP Provider** check box to select it, and then click **OK**. When Windows completes its changes, click **Close**.

3. To open the SNMP service from the Control Panel window, return to the Control Panel home screen, click **System and Security** and then click **Administrative Tools**. (You might need to scroll down to see Administrative Tools.)

4. In the Administrative Tools window, double-click the **Services** icon, and then, in the Services window, scroll down and double-click **SNMP Service**.

5. In the SNMP Service Properties (Local Computer) window, click the **Security** tab, verify that the **Send authentication trap** check box is selected, and then click **Add** under Accepted community names.

6. Leave the Community rights as READ ONLY, type **public** in the Community Name box, and then click **Add**.

7. Close the SNMP Service Properties (Local Computer) window, then double-click **SNMP Trap**. Near the bottom of the SNMP Trap Properties (Local Computer) window, click **Start**.

8. Open Task Manager and use the Resource Monitor to determine which ports the SNMP and SNMP Trap services are listening on, and which protocols (TCP or UDP) the services are using. What information did you find?

9. Return to the Services window, right-click on **SNMP Service**, click **Stop**, and repeat for the SNMP Trap service.

Project 9-3: OpManager by ManageEngine

The free version of ManageEngine's OpManager provides tools for monitoring activity and performance on a small network (fewer than 10 devices). In this project, you install and use the free version of OpManager on a Windows computer. This project is best done over a few days, so the software can collect longer-term data for analysis.

1. Go to the Web site at **manageengine.com**, click **Network**, and click **Network Monitoring Software**. Locate the free edition download link. At the time of this writing, you could click **Editions**, then scroll down and click **Free Edition**.

2. You do *not* have to complete the Register for Free Technical Support form. Click the **Download** button, then install the program.

3. Accept all default settings, except be sure to select the Free Edition option instead of the 30-day Trial Version. At the end of the installation process, open OpManager in the Web browser of your choice.

4. Create an account as a first-time user. OpManager automatically assigns the username *admin* and enters a password.

5. After signing in and before changing any other settings in your account, use the mouse to point to the **admin** username at the top of the dashboard, and then click **Change Password**. The default current password is *admin*. Type a new password and click **OK**.

6. On the menu in the left pane, under Discovery, click **Add Network**. Type in the starting and ending IP addresses for the address range on your LAN. Be sure the NetMask (another word for *subnet*) is correct, then click **Discover**.

7. Wait for the discovery process to complete. How many devices were discovered by OpManager? What information does it give about them?

8. If you have more than 10 devices on your network, you might be prompted to delete some of the devices from the account in order to conform to your license restrictions. To decide which devices to delete, you can enter `arp -a` at a command prompt to get a current listing of the devices on your network along with their MAC addresses. If you're having a hard time identifying which IP address belongs to which device, recall that you can perform an OUI lookup on Wireshark's Web site.

9. To interact with another device on the network, click **Inventory**, and then click **All Devices**. Double-click any device on the list. What is the IP address of the device you clicked? What is the DNS name of the device, if available?

10. Examine the device details, looking for any indications of a problem with the device. Click the **Ping** button in the top right of the page. What was the average round-trip time?

11. Click the **TraceRoute** button. How many hops were completed?

12. Notice that OpManager also provides the option to browse the other device or connect to it via Telnet or Remote Desktop. Spend a few minutes exploring the various options and features of OpManager. Notice there are several opportunities for plug-ins that you can use to expand the data available. If you find one that you're interested in, you can look into installing it as well.

13. Leave the software running and check back with it from time to time over the next few days. Check any errors that are reported. Notice any trends in network resource utilization or device availability.

Project 9-4: Research Backup Options for Home Networks

Home networks can be equipped with a solid backup system for a fairly low cost. Considering how much personal and sentimental data people keep on their home computers these days, and yet how poorly most of these systems are protected and maintained, having a good backup system in place can be well worth the expense. In this project, you research inexpensive backup options.

1. Backups can be kept on external hard drives, flash drives, disks, or in the cloud. Research these options at a high level first, listing pros and cons of each type of backup.

2. Select the type of backup that you feel is most secure and reasonable for your situation, then research at least three products that would provide that service. List pros and cons, cost, and features. Which product would you choose and why?

Case Projects

Case Project 9-1: Syslog

Earlier in this chapter, you viewed and manipulated log file entries on a computer running Windows. In this project, you do the same on a computer running the Linux operating system. Because Linux versions vary in the type of GUI application that allows you to open the system log, this exercise uses the command-line method instead.

For this exercise, you need a computer with a Linux operating system installed, such as the Ubuntu Desktop VM that you created in Chapter 2. It need not be connected to a network, but for best results, it should be a computer that has been used in the past and not a fresh install. You must be logged on to the Linux computer as a user with administrator privileges.

1. If you are not already at a command-line (or shell) prompt, open a terminal session now.

2. The syslog file contains information similar to that shown in Figure 9-24. The first step in viewing your Linux computer's system log is to find out where the file is located. Try each of these commands until you find the syslog file that contains information similar to that in Figure 9-24:
```
more /etc/syslog.conf
more /etc/rsyslog.conf
more /etc/rsyslog.d/50-default.conf
```

3. The first part of the syslog file appears. In this part of the file, you should see a list of log types and their locations, similar to the listing shown in Figure 9-24. (If you don't see the listing in this part of the file, press the **Enter** key until you do see it.)

```
auth,authpriv.*              /var/log/auth.log

*.*;auth,authpriv.none       -/var/log/syslog

#cron.*                      /var/log/cron.log

daemon.*                     -/var/log/daemon.log

kern.*                       -/var/log/kern.log

lpr.*                        -/var/log/lpr.log

mail.*                       -/var/log/mail.log

user.*                       -/var/log/user.log

uucp.*                       /var/log/uucp.log
```

Figure 9-24 Log files identified in `syslog.conf`

4. Write down the location and filename of the file that logs all events, as indicated by *.* in the first column. (For example, it might be /var/log/syslog or /var/adm/messages.)

5. Press the **Spacebar** enough times to view the entire log configuration file and return to the command prompt.

6. Now that you know the name and location of your system log, you can view its messages. At the command prompt, type **tail /var/log/syslog** if your log file is at /var/log/syslog; if your log file is at /var/adm/messages, type **tail /var/adm/messages**. Then press **Enter**.

7. The last 10 lines of your log file appear (assuming it is at least 10 lines long). What types of messages are recorded? When did the events occur?

8. Next you'll find out all the types of log files your computer saves. Type **cd /var/log** if your log file is in the /var/log directory, or type **cd /var/adm** if your log file is in the /var/adm directory. Then press **Enter**. You have changed your working directory to the same directory where log files are kept.

9. To view a listing of the directory's contents, type **ls -la** and press **Enter**. Notice the types of log files that appear in this directory.

10. Suppose you want to find every message in the system log file that pertains to DHCP addressing. At the command prompt, type **grep DHCP syslog** if your log file is named *syslog* or **grep DHCP messages** if your log file is named *messages*. Then press **Enter**. A list of messages containing the term *DHCP* appears. Consider how you might use grep and other UNIX commands in a script that would notify you each time a workstation on your network failed to obtain a DHCP-assigned IP address. (Note that this can be accomplished from most GUI system log interfaces, too.)

11. If your operating system is configured to start a new log file each day or each time the computer is restarted, your log file might be brief. Repeat Step 9 and, this time, look for other versions of the syslog or messages file in your working directory. For example, Ubuntu Linux will save older system messages in a file called syslog.0. If you find a larger, older log file, repeat Step 10 using this log file's name. How do the results differ?

12. Close the Linux terminal session window.

Case Project 9-2: Examine VoIP Traffic on the LAN

Today's app marketplace provides a plethora of options for phone calls over the Internet, two of the most popular being Skype (recently acquired by Microsoft) and Google Hangouts. In this project, you explore another program called Viber that is also available for multiple platforms and devices. Viber is primarily a voice calling app, as opposed to video (although video features are being added and improved). Skype, Google Hangouts, and Viber all provide free calls to other users of the same app, so using the same app that your friends do is vital to maximizing the app's usefulness. Although Skype enjoys a large market share in the United States, other apps, such as Viber, are more popular in other countries. For this reason, Viber can be especially useful in providing free phone calls via free Wi-Fi hot spots while traveling outside of the United States.

Viber attaches the user account to the user's mobile phone number, so the mobile app must be installed first:

1. On your smartphone (iPhone, Android, Windows Phone, or BlackBerry), find the Viber app in your application store and install it. Complete the registration process.

2. To install the desktop app on your computer (Windows, Mac, or Linux), go to **viber.com**, click **Get Viber**, and complete the installation process.

3. Connect with a friend or classmate through Viber so this person is listed in your contacts list.

Next, you use Wireshark to observe the traffic Viber creates on your network. This portion of the project will be easiest if you use a wired connection to somewhat limit the amount of traffic that Wireshark will detect.

4. Close all Web browsers and any other apps you can think of that might be creating Web traffic on your computer, except Viber.

5. Open Wireshark, and then click **Capture Options**. In the Wireshark: Capture Options window, select the interface to capture (preferably a wired connection instead of a wireless connection).

6. Uncheck **Use promiscuous mode on all interfaces** so that promiscuous mode is disabled for this capture, and then click **Start**.

7. Watch the capture for a minute or two and see if you notice any anomalies in the messages being captured. Are there large numbers of a particular type of message?

8. Watch the row numbers and when the capture hits a round number that is easy to remember (like 10,000), make a call to your contact in Viber. After about two rings, or after the person picks up, stop your capture in Wireshark.

9. Examine the capture from the point when you initiated the call. What change in the types of messages do you notice? Do any other anomalies stand out to you?

10. You should see large numbers of messages being exchanged between your computer and a public IP address. Perform an IP address lookup online using a Web site such as **who.is** or **whois.domaintools.com** to determine who owns the Web site. Google the name of that company and see if it is connected to the Viber app. You might want to do a search for both the name of the company and Viber's name together in order to determine if there is a connection.

11. If the company you found is not connected with Viber, look for another IP address in your capture that appears very frequently and try that one. Keep looking until you find the connection. What is the name of the company you found?

12. Open Task Manager and use the Resource Monitor to determine which port Viber is listening on and which protocol (TCP or UDP) the app is using. What information did you find?

## chapter 10

Network Segmentation and Virtualization

After reading this chapter and completing the exercises, you will be able to:

- Describe methods of network design unique to TCP/IP networks, including subnetting, CIDR, and supernetting

- Explain virtualization and identify characteristics of virtual network components

- Describe techniques for incorporating virtual components in VLANs

- Explain the advanced features of a switch and understand popular switching techniques, including VLAN management

- Identify methods of combining VM and VLAN technologies

On the Job

I recently provided the technical expertise to build a new FM radio station in rural Wisconsin. In addition to specifying and installing microphones, speakers, and sound boards, I also designed and created the station's network. Within the station's building, the network connects studios, office computers, and a Voice over IP (VoIP) telephone system. Beyond the building, the network sends the station's broadcast signal to its antenna.

When I set up the radio station network, I decided to separate different kinds of network traffic. To do this, I chose to create VLANs, rather than creating multiple physical networks, for several reasons, not the least of which is the cost of acquiring and maintaining multiple network switches. Managing multiple subnets on a single device has simplified deployment and long-term maintenance.

The VLANs are set up as follows:

- VLAN 101 (IP address subnet 10.10.1.0/24) is the transmitter network.
- VLAN 201 (IP address subnet 10.20.1.0/24) is the studio network.
- VLAN 301 (IP address subnet 10.30.1.0/24) is the office network.
- VLAN 401 (IP address subnet 10.40.1.0/24) is the telephone network.

Using VLANs allows the station to keep general Internet traffic off the latency-sensitive studio subnet. The systems on the studio subnet include the audio automation players and the analog-to-digital audio encoders. These computers receive and send digital audio over the network and demand timely delivery of packets. Further, these computers do not need to access Internet resources. We chose to isolate these systems from the others using VLANs (and access lists) to help guarantee the timely delivery of audio data.

Meanwhile, placing our VoIP telephones on a separate VLAN prevents studio audio traffic, as well as the general office and Internet traffic, from interfering with the telephone system traffic.

David Klann
WDRT 91.9FM

Network segmentation takes the divide-and-conquer approach to network management. When done well, it increases both performance and security on a network. In this chapter, you'll learn about two ways to logically segment a network, subnets and virtual LANs (or VLANS), which are both used when dividing a large LAN (broadcast domain) into multiple LANs. Fundamentally, a subnet is a group of IP addresses, and a VLAN is a group of ports on a switch. These two forms of network segmentation are used in conjunction with each other, but you'll learn about each of them separately first. Additionally, you'll learn about other virtual network components, such as switches, routers, and firewalls. The chapter begins with an explanation of the benefits of network segmentation and then discusses how subnet masks are used.

Segmentation and Subnetting

Before we get into how subnetting and VLANs work, let's step back and briefly look at why you might want to segment a network. When a network is segmented into multiple smaller networks, traffic on one network is separated from another network's traffic and each network is its own broadcast domain. A network administrator might separate traffic to accomplish the following:

- *Enhance security*—Broadcast domains are limited to each network so there's less possibility of hackers or malware reaching remote, protected networks in the enterprise domain.

- *Improve performance*—Segmenting limits broadcast traffic by decreasing the size of each broadcast domain. The more efficient use of bandwidth results in better overall network performance.

- *Simplify troubleshooting*—When troubleshooting, rather than examining the whole network for errors or bottlenecks, the network administrator can narrow down the problem area to a particular smaller network. For example, suppose a network is subdivided with separate smaller networks for accounting, human resources, and IT. One day there's trouble transmitting data only to a certain group of users—those on the accounting network. This fact gives the network administrator some significant insight into the nature of the problem.

How a Computer Uses a Subnet Mask

Let's review a little of what you learned in Chapter 2 regarding IP addresses and subnet masks. Recall that an IPv4 address has 32 bits and is divided into two parts: the network portion, which identifies the network, and the host portion, which identifies the host. The network portion is called the network ID. When a computer is ready to send a transmission to another host, it first compares the bits in its own network ID to the bits in the network ID of the destination host. If the bits match, the remote host is on the sending computer's own network, and it sends the transmission directly to that host. If the bits don't match, the destination host is on another network, and the computer sends the transmission to the default gateway on its network. The gateway is responsible for sending the transmission on its way.

You might sometimes find the term *network ID* used interchangeably with the terms network number or network prefix.

How does a computer know how many bits of its IP address is the network ID? The subnet mask gives that information. Recall that an IPv4 subnet mask is 32 bits. The number of 1s in the subnet mask determines the number of bits in the IP address that belong to the network ID. For example, suppose a computer has an IP address of 192.168.123.132 and its subnet mask is 255.255.255.0. To identify the bits that make up the network ID, first convert these numbers to binary, as follows:

- IP address 192.168.123.132 in binary: 11000000.10101000.01111011.10000100
- Subnet mask 255.255.255.0 in binary: 11111111.11111111.11111111.00000000

In this example, and in others in this chapter, a red font is used for the network ID portion of a subnet mask.

A subnet mask is always a series of 1s followed by a series of 0s. The 1s mark the network portion of an IP address and the 0s mark the host portion. Therefore, the network ID portion of the IP address is 24 bits, or the first three octets: 192.168.123. The host portion is the last octet: 132. (Using red for the network ID, we can write this IP address as 192.168.123.132.)

By convention, you see 0s used to complete the four octets when referring to the network ID and the host portion of an IP address, like this:

- Network ID: 192.168.123.0
- Host portion: 0.0.0.132

Now suppose this computer needs to communicate with a host at 192.168.30.140. Because the network IDs don't match (that is, 192.168.123 does not match 192.168.30), the computer knows the remote host is not on its own network and sends the transmission to its default gateway.

Network+ 1.8

Legacy Networking

Classful Addressing in IPv4

Recall from Chapter 2 that every IPv4 address can be associated with a network class—A, B, C, D, or E (though Class D and E addresses are reserved for special purposes). The simplest type of IPv4 addressing, which is known as classful addressing, uses only whole octets for the network ID and host portions. In our earlier example of 192.168.123.132, the network ID consists of three whole octets, and is, therefore, an example of classful addressing. Table 10-1 lists how the 32 bits are allocated with classful addressing for Classes A, B, and C.

Table 10-1   Classful addressing uses whole octets for the network ID

Class	Network portion in red n=network ID bit h=host address bit	Bits in network ID	Bits in host portion
A	nnnnnnnn.hhhhhhhh.hhhhhhhh.hhhhhhhh	8	24
B	nnnnnnnn.nnnnnnnn.hhhhhhhh.hhhhhhhh	16	16
C	nnnnnnnn.nnnnnnnn.nnnnnnnn.hhhhhhhh	24	8

© 2016 Cengage Learning®.

For example, the network ID for a Class A network might be 92.0.0.0, and the network ID for a Class B network might be 147.12.0.0. When using classful IPv4 addressing, a network ID always ends with the last octet equal to 0 (and may have additional, preceding octets equal to 0). Also, a workstation cannot be assigned the same address as the network ID, which explains why the last octet of a host's IP address is almost never 0.

Each network class is associated with a default subnet mask, as shown in Table 10-2. For example, by default, a Class A address's first octet (or 8 bits) represents network information. That means that if you work on a network whose hosts are configured with a subnet mask of 11111111 00000000 00000000 00000000, or 255.0.0.0, you know that the network is using Class A addresses.

Table 10-2 Default IPv4 subnet masks

Network class	Default subnet mask (binary)	Number of bits used for network information	Default subnet mask (dotted decimal)
A	11111111 00000000 00000000 00000000	8	255.0.0.0
B	11111111 11111111 00000000 00000000	16	255.255.0.0
C	11111111 11111111 11111111 00000000	24	255.255.255.0

© 2016 Cengage Learning®

CIDR (Classless Interdomain Routing)

Aside from our own convention of color-coding in red, as we did earlier, you can't tell by looking at the IP address alone how many of its bits are network bits and how many are host bits. You've seen instead how the subnet mask can help you determine this information. However, in 1993 the IETF devised CIDR (Classless Interdomain Routing and pronounced *cider*), which provides additional ways of arranging network and host information in an IP address, along with a new shorthand for denoting the distinction between network and host bits in an IP address. This shorthand method is known as CIDR notation (or slash notation).

CIDR notation takes the network ID or a host's IP address and follows it with a forward slash (/), followed by the number of bits that are used for the network ID. For example, this private IP address could be written as 192.168.89.127/24, where 24 represents the number of 1s in the subnet mask and the number of bits in the network ID. In CIDR terminology, the forward slash, plus the number of bits used for the network ID—for example, /24—is known as a CIDR block.

Now that you have the background information you need, you can turn your attention to subnetting.

Why Subnets?

Suppose a company's network has grown from 20 or 30 computers and other devices on one floor of a building to a few hundred computers on three floors. The network began as a single LAN with computers connected by several Layer 2 switches, then one switch connected to a router, and on to the ISP. See Figure 10-1. Because there is only a single LAN or broadcast domain, any host on the network can communicate directly with any other host, and the one router serves as the default gateway for the entire network. The entire LAN has one pool of IP addresses, for example, 192.168.89.0/24, with a subnet mask of 255.255.255.0. Using this IP address pool, any host can communicate with any other host on the LAN.

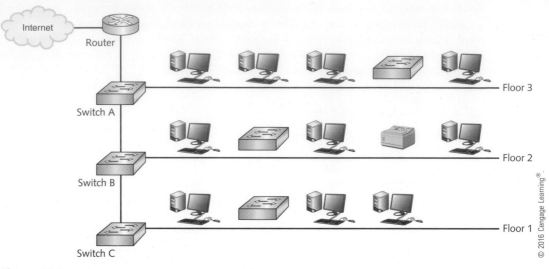

Figure 10-1 A single LAN with several switches and a router

Suppose you want to better manage network traffic by segmenting the network so that each floor contains one LAN, or broadcast domain. To accomplish this, you install routers on each floor, as illustrated in Figure 10-2. Next, you need to configure each router to ensure that it serves as the default gateway for its LAN and forwards traffic to the other two LANs as necessary. As you know, routers don't forward broadcast traffic. You can think of a router as a broadcast boundary, and fundamentally, routers are tools you use to divide and conquer network traffic.

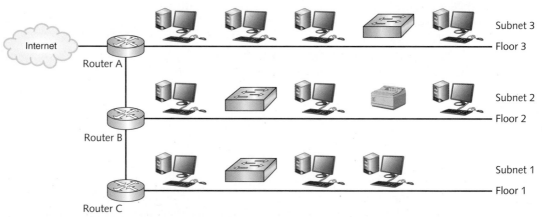

Figure 10-2 A separate subnet for each floor

Now that you have three separate LANs, one for each subnet, how do you divide the pool of IP addresses so that a computer on Subnet 1 knows to send a communication on Subnet 3 to its default gateway rather than unsuccessfully trying to communicate directly with the remote host? The solution is to divide your pool of IP addresses into three groups or subnets, one for each LAN or floor of the building, using a technique called subnetting, which you first learned about in Chapter 2. Networks are commonly subnetted according to geographic locations (for example, the floors of a building connected by a LAN, or the buildings connected by a WAN), departmental boundaries, or technology types.

Subnetting solves the fundamental problem with classful addressing, which is too many hosts in a classful network. For example, an entire Class B network can have up to 65,534 IP addresses and hosts all on the one network. Imagine the challenges involved in managing such a highly populated network, not to mention the poor performance that would result.

The next section describes how IPv4 addresses are grouped into subnets, how you can determine the range of usable host addresses on a subnet, and the subnet masks they use. Later in the chapter, you will learn how subnetting differs in IPv6.

Network+
1.8
Applying Concepts
Subnetting in IPv4

Subnetting alters the rules of classful IPv4 addressing. To create a subnet, you borrow bits that would represent host information in classful addressing and use those bits instead to represent network information. By doing so, you increase the number of bits available for the network ID, and you also reduce the number of bits available for identifying hosts. Consequently, you increase the number of networks and reduce the number of usable host addresses in each network or subnet. The more bits you borrow for network information, the more subnets you can have, and the fewer hosts each subnet can have.

For example, suppose you want to divide your local network, which has a network ID of 192.168.89.0 and a subnet mask of 255.255.255.0, into subnets. To keep things simple, start with just two subnets. Follow these steps:

1. *Borrow a bit*—Currently, the network ID is 24 bits. First convert it to binary:

   • Network ID 192.168.89.0 in binary: 11000000.10101000.01011001.00000000

   Borrow one bit from the host portion to give to the network ID, which will then have 25 bits (notice one more red bit):

   • 11000000.10101000.01011001.00000000

   How many subnets can you now have? That one red bit on the right can be a 0 or a 1, which gives you the possibility of two subnets.

2. *Determine the subnet mask*—Recall the subnet mask marks the bits in an IP address that belong to the network ID. Therefore, the subnet mask for both subnets is:

   • 11111111.11111111.11111111.10000000 or decimal 255.255.255.128

   To calculate that last octet, you had to convert binary 10000000 to decimal, which is 128. You can use a calculator to do the conversion or manually calculate it. (For a refresher on converting binary to decimal, see Appendix B.)

3. *Determine the network IDs*—Recall that in the network ID, the red bit on the right can be a 1 or 0. Therefore, the network ID for each subnet is:

- Subnet A: 11000000.10101000.01011001.00000000 or decimal 192.168.89.0
- Subnet B: 11000000.10101000.01011001.10000000 or decimal 192.168.89.128

In CIDR notation, the network ID for each subnet is:

- Subnet A: 192.168.89.0/25
- Subnet B: 192.168.89.128/25

4. *Determine the ranges of IP addresses*—Start with the range of IP addresses for subnet A. For host addresses, use the 7 bits in the last octet. (The first bit for this octet is always 0 and belongs to the network ID.) Start counting in binary and converting to decimal:

- 00000000 is not used because it's the network ID for this subnet
- 00000001 or decimal 1
- 00000010 or decimal 2
- 00000011 or decimal 3
- ...
- 01111110 or decimal 126
- 01111111 or decimal 127, which is used for broadcasting rather than a host address

Therefore, the range of IP addresses for subnet A is 192.168.89.1 through 192.168.89.126.

For subnet B, the first bit of the last octet is 1 and the range of host addresses is as follows:

- 10000000 is not used because it's the network ID for this subnet
- 10000001 in decimal: 129
- 10000010 in decimal: 130
- 10000011 in decimal: 131
- ...
- 11111110 in decimal: 254
- 11111111 in decimal: 255 is not used because it's used for broadcasting

Therefore, the range of IP addresses for subnet B is 192.168.89.129 through 192.168.89.254.

Now you're ready to move on to a more complicated example and see how the calculations are done using formulas and without so much binary involved. Suppose you want to divide your local network, which has a network ID of 192.168.89.0, into six subnets to correspond to your building's six floors. The following steps walk you through the process:

1. *Decide how many bits to borrow*—How many bits must you borrow from the host portion of the IP addresses in order to get six subnets? Use this formula to determine the number of bits:

$$2^n = Y$$

In this formula, *n* equals the number of bits that must be switched from the host address to the network ID, and *Y* equals the number of subnets that result.

Because you want six separate subnets (meaning that Y, in this case, is 6), the equation becomes $2^n = 6$.

Experiment with different values for *n* until you find a value large enough to give you at least the number of subnets you need. For example, you know that $2^2 = 4$; however, 4 is not high enough. Instead consider that $2^3 = 8$, which will give you enough subnets to meet your current needs and allow room for future growth. Now that *n* equals 3, you know that three bits in the host addresses of your Class C network must change to network ID bits. You also know that three bits in your subnet mask must change from 0 to 1.

2. *Determine the subnet mask*—As you know, the default subnet mask for a Class C network is 255.255.255.0, or 11111111 11111111 11111111 00000000. In this default subnet mask, the first 24 bits indicate the position of network information.

   Changing three of the default subnet mask's bits from host to network information gives you the subnet mask 11111111 11111111 11111111 11100000. In this modified subnet mask, the first 27 bits indicate the bits for the network ID. Note that for this Class C network whose network ID is 192.168.89.0, the slash notation would now be 192.168.89.0/27 because 27 bits of the subnets' addresses are used to provide network information.

   Converting from binary to the more familiar dotted decimal notation, this subnet mask becomes 255.255.255.224. When you configure the TCP/IP properties of clients on your network, you would specify this subnet mask.

 When examining the subnet mask for a network, if any octet is not 255 or 0, you know that this network is a subnet and classful addressing is not used. The unusual octet (224 in our example) is often called the *interesting octet*. Subtract the interesting octet value from 256 and you get what is called the magic number. In this example, the magic number is 256 − 224 = 32. This magic number can be used to calculate the network IDs in all the subnets of the larger network, which you'll see below.

3. *Calculate the network ID for each subnet*—The first three octets of the network ID for the Class C network 192.168.89.0 is the same for all eight possible subnets. The network IDs differ in the last octet. Use the magic number to calculate them as follows:

   - Subnet 1 Network ID: 192.168.89.0
   - Subnet 2 Network ID: 192.168.89.0 +32 yields 192.168.89.32
   - Subnet 3 Network ID: 192.168.89.32 +32 yields 192.168.89.64
   - Subnet 4 Network ID: 192.168.89.64 +32 yields 192.168.89.96
   - Subnet 5 Network ID: 192.168.89.96 +32 yields 192.168.89.128
   - Subnet 6 Network ID: 192.168.89.128 +32 yields 192.168.89.160
   - Subnet 7 Network ID: 192.168.89.160 +32 yields 192.168.89.192
   - Subnet 8 Network ID: 192.168.89.192 +32 yields 192.168.89.224

4. *Determine the IP address range for each subnet*—Recall that you have borrowed 3 bits from what used to be host information in the IP address. That leaves 5 bits instead of 8 available in the last octet of your Class C addresses to identify hosts. To calculate the number of possible hosts, use the formula:

$$2^h - 2 = Z$$

where *h* equals the number of bits remaining in the host portion, and *Z* equals the number of hosts available in each subnet. So $2^5 - 2$ yields 30 possible hosts per subnet.

Notice that this formula subtracts 2 from the total number of possible hosts. Recall that host addresses ending in all 0s (which equals 0 in decimal as well) or all 1s (which equals 255 in decimal) are not allowed because of addresses reserved for the network ID and broadcast transmissions. So, in this example, you can have a maximum of 8 (number of subnets) × 30 (number of hosts per subnet), or 240, unique host addresses on the entire larger network.

Once you know the network ID of the subnets, calculating the address range of hosts in a subnet is easy. For example, take subnet 5. The network ID is 192.168.89.128. Because you won't use the network ID for a host address, you start with the next value and keep going until you reach the broadcast address for the subnet, yielding for this particular subnet a total of 30 addresses. Therefore, the address range for subnet 5 is 192.168.89.129 through 192.168.89.158. (The last value 158 is 128 + 30.)

NOTE   If you're having trouble coming up with the broadcast address for a subnet, look at the network ID of the next subnet and drop back one address. For example, the network ID for subnet 6 is 192.168.89.160. One address below that address is 192.168.89.159, which is the broadcast address for subnet 5.

Table 10-3 lists the network ID, broadcast address, and the range of usable host addresses in between for each of the eight subnets in this sample Class C network. Together, the existing network ID plus the additional bits used for subnet information are sometimes called the extended network prefix.

Table 10-3   Subnet information for eight possible subnets in a sample IPv4 class C network

Subnet number	Network ID (extended network prefix)	Range of host addresses	Broadcast address
1	192.168.89.0 or 11000000 10101000 01011001 00000000	192.168.89.1-30	192.168.89.31 or 11000000 10101000 01011001 00011111
2	192.168.89.32 or 11000000 10101000 01011001 00100000	192.168.89.33-62	192.168.89.63 or 11000000 10101000 01011001 00111111
3	192.168.89.64 or 11000000 10101000 01011001 01000000	192.168.89.65-94	192.168.89.95 or 11000000 10101000 01011001 01011111
4	192.168.89.96 or 11000000 10101000 01011001 01100000	192.168.89.97-126	192.168.89.127 or 11000000 10101000 01011001 01111111

Table 10-3 **Subnet information for eight possible subnets in a sample IPv4 class C network** (*continued*)

Subnet number	Network ID (extended network prefix)	Range of host addresses	Broadcast address
5	192.168.89.128 or 11000000 10101000 01011001 10000000	192.168.89.129-158	192.168.89.159 or 11000000 10101000 01011001 10011111
6	192.168.89.160 or 11000000 10101000 01011001 10100000	192.168.89.161-190	192.168.89.191 or 11000000 10101000 01011001 10111111
7	192.168.89.192 or 11000000 10101000 01011001 11000000	192.168.89.193-222	192.168.89.223 or 11000000 10101000 01011001 11011111
8	192.168.89.224 or 11000000 10101000 01011001 11100000	192.168.89.225-254	192.168.89.255 or 11000000 10101000 01011001 11111111

© 2016 Cengage Learning®

NOTE

You can also calculate the magic number by raising 2 to the power of the number of bits in the host portion of the subnet mask. Use this formula:

2^h = magic number

In this example, the host portion has 5 bits. Therefore, the magic number is $2^5=32$. You can then use this number to determine the number of network IDs in subnets.

10

Subnet Mask Tables

Network+ 1.8

Class A, Class B, and Class C networks can all be subnetted. But because each class reserves a different number of bits for network information, each class has a different number of host information bits that can be used for subnet information. The number of hosts and subnets on your network will vary depending on your network class and the way you use subnetting. Several Web sites provide excellent tools that can help you calculate subnet information. One such site is *subnetmask.info*.

Table 10-4 illustrates the numbers of subnets and hosts that can be created by subnetting a Class B network. Notice the range of subnet masks that can be used instead of the default Class B subnet mask of 255.255.0.0. Also compare the listed numbers of hosts per subnet to the 65,534 hosts available on a Class B network that does not use subnetting.

Table 10-5 illustrates the numbers of subnets and hosts that can be created by subnetting a Class C network. Notice that a Class C network allows for fewer subnets than a Class B network. This is because Class C addresses have fewer host information bits that can be borrowed for network information. In addition, fewer bits are left over for host information, which leads to a lower number of hosts per subnet than the number available to Class B subnets.

Table 10-4 IPv4 Class B subnet masks

Subnet mask	CIDR notation	Number of subnets on network	Number of hosts per subnet
255.255.128.0 or 11111111 11111111 10000000 00000000	/17	2	32,766
255.255.192.0 or 11111111 11111111 11000000 00000000	/18	4	16,382
255.255.224.0 or 11111111 11111111 11100000 00000000	/19	8	8190
255.255.240.0 or 11111111 11111111 11110000 00000000	/20	16	4094
255.255.248.0 or 11111111 11111111 11111000 00000000	/21	32	2046
255.255.252.0 or 11111111 11111111 11111100 00000000	/22	64	1022
255.255.254.0 or 11111111 11111111 11111110 00000000	/23	128	510
255.255.255.0 or 11111111 11111111 11111111 00000000	/24	256	254
255.255.255.128 or 11111111 11111111 11111111 10000000	/25	512	126
255.255.255.192 or 11111111 11111111 11111111 11000000	/26	1024	62
255.255.255.224 or 11111111 11111111 11111111 11100000	/27	2048	30
255.255.255.240 or 11111111 11111111 11111111 11110000	/28	4096	14
255.255.255.248 or 11111111 11111111 11111111 11111000	/29	8192	6
255.255.255.252 or 11111111 11111111 11111111 11111100	/30	16,384	2

© 2016 Cengage Learning®

Table 10-5 IPv4 Class C subnet masks

Subnet mask	CIDR notation	Number of subnets on network	Number of hosts per subnet
255.255.255.128 or 11111111 11111111 11111111 10000000	/25	2	126
255.255.255.192 or 11111111 11111111 11111111 11000000	/26	4	62
255.255.255.224 or 11111111 11111111 11111111 11100000	/27	8	30
255.255.255.240 or 11111111 11111111 11111111 11110000	/28	16	14
255.255.255.248 or 11111111 11111111 11111111 11111000	/29	32	6
255.255.255.252 or 11111111 11111111 11111111 11111100	/30	64	2

© 2016 Cengage Learning®

Network+
1.3
1.8

Applying Concepts

Calculate Subnets

Now it's time to practice your subnetting skills. To get the most out of this exercise, don't look at the subnetting instructions and subnet mask tables shown earlier in the chapter, and do your own calculations. Suppose your organization uses the Class B network ID of 172.20.0.0 for its entire network and wants to create 15 subnets. Answer the following questions:

1. For the subnets, how many bits must be borrowed from the host address bits?

2. What is the subnet mask for these subnets, written in decimal?

3. What is the magic number you can use to calculate the network IDs?

4. What is the CIDR notation for the first subnet's network ID? For the second subnet's network ID? For the last subnet's network ID?

5. How many host addresses are possible in each subnet?

6. What is the range of host addresses for the first subnet? For the second subnet? For the last subnet?

Now that you've calculated the subnets for the scenario presented earlier in the chapter, how do you implement them? Figure 10-3 shows the subnets assigned to the three LANs you saw earlier in Figure 10-2. Also in Figure 10-3, you can see the IP address of the default gateway for each LAN, which is the IP address assigned to the router's interface on this LAN. Note that only three of the eight possible subnets listed earlier in Table 10-3 are used.

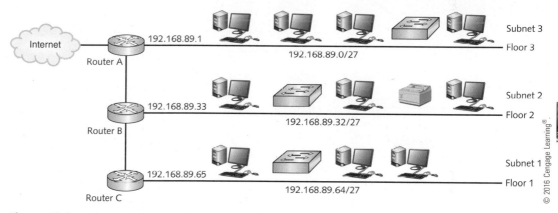

Figure 10-3   Subnets 1, 2, and 3 and their respective default gateways are defined

Figure 10-4 illustrates another situation in which an enterprise network is using the same Class C range of private addresses that begin with 192.168.89. The network administrator has subnetted this Class C network into six (of eight possible) smaller networks. As you know, routers connect different networks via their physical interfaces. In the case of subnetting, each subnet corresponds to a different network interface or port on the router.

The administrator must program each interface on the router with the network ID and subnet mask for its subnet. For dynamic IP addressing, the administrator programs each subnet's DHCP server with the network ID, subnet mask, range of IP addresses, and default gateway for the subnet. In an enterprise environment, the administrator might also need to configure on the DHCP server the DNS suffix for the domain, which identifies which domain a client belongs to when utilizing DNS services. If instead static IP addressing is used, Figure 10-5a shows a TCP/IPv4 properties dialog box of a workstation on the first subnet, and Figure 10-5b shows the static configuration for a workstation on the second subnet. As shown in the figure, best practice would assign the first IP address in the range of host addresses for the subnet to the router's interface on the subnet, which serves the subnet as its default gateway.

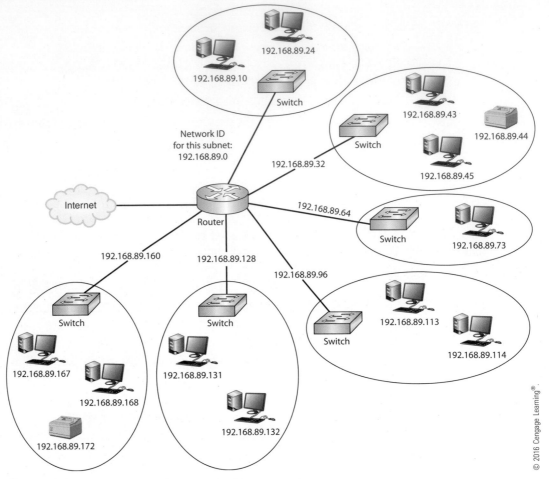

Figure 10-4 A router connecting several subnets

You have now learned how to subdivide an IPv4 network into smaller subnets. Next, you'll learn about combining networks into larger supernets.

Supernetting

With supernetting, also called classless routing or IP address aggregation, you can combine contiguous networks that all use the same CIDR block into one supernet. Supernetting is helpful for two reasons:

- It allows you to reduce the number of routing table entries by combining several entries, one for each network, into one entry that represents multiple networks. When used for this purpose, supernetting is called route aggregation or route summarization.

- It allows you to allow a company to create a single network made up of more than one Class C license. (This last reason is not as significant as the first and was needed because of a shortage of Class B licenses.)

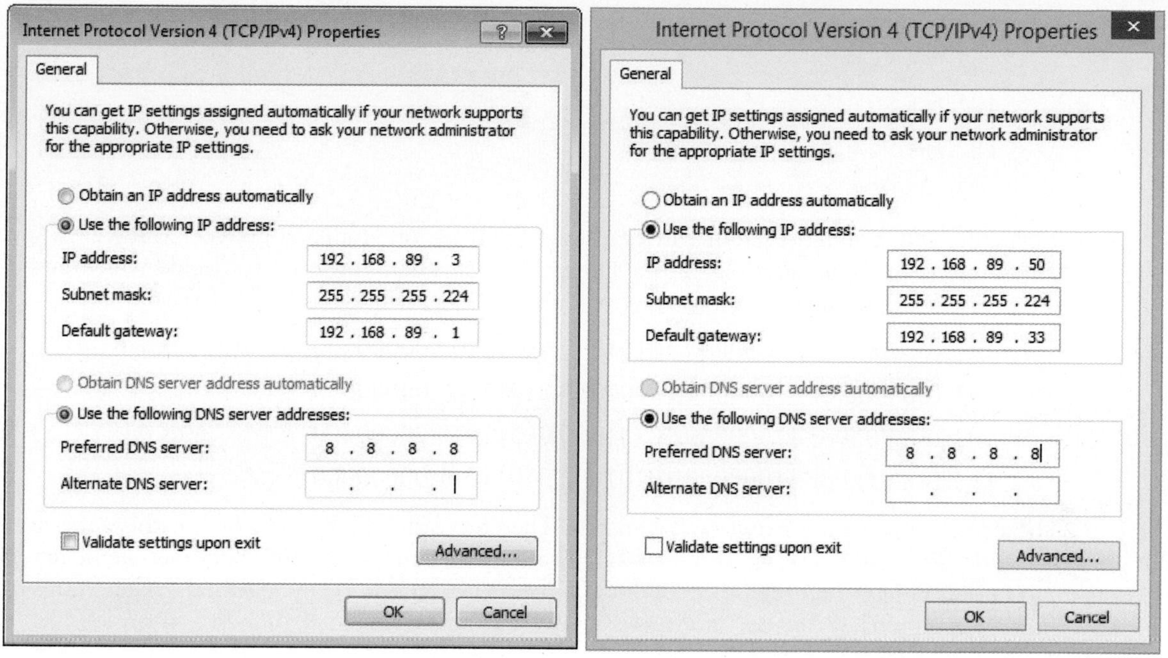

Figure 10-5   TCP/IP properties boxes for static IP address configuration for workstations on two subnets

Source: Microsoft LLC

The supernet is defined by a supernet mask, which moves the network prefix to the left, as opposed to a subnet mask, which moves the network prefix to the right. Figure 10-6 contrasts examples of a Class C supernet mask with a subnet mask.

Sample subnet mask:

Bit# 0	8	16	24
11111111	11111111	11111111	11100000

or

255.255.255.224

Sample supernet mask:

Bit# 0	8	16	24
11111111	11111111	11111100	00000000

or

255.255.252.0

Figure 10-6   Subnet mask and supernet mask for a Class C network

For example, suppose your organization has the following four networks:

> 192.168.88.0/24
>
> 192.168.89.0/24
>
> 192.168.90.0/24
>
> 192.168.91.0/24

Normally, you would need four entries in routing tables, one for each network. However, you can combine the four networks into a single supernet. First, you need to decide which bits in the network prefix they have in common. Convert the network IDs to binary, as follows:

> 192.168.88.0 or 11000000.10101000.01011000.00000000
>
> 192.168.89.0 or 11000000.10101000.01011001.00000000
>
> 192.168.90.0 or 11000000.10101000.01011010.00000000
>
> 192.168.91.0 or 11000000.10101000.01011011.00000000

The first 22 bits of the network IDs match. Therefore, the CIDR notation for this supernet's network ID would be 192.168.88.0/22. The supernet mask for this supernet in binary is 11111111.11111111.11111100.00000000, or 255.255.252.0 in decimal. The resulting supernet contains all the host addresses in the four networks.

Figure 10-7 shows how you can use the supernet. In an organization, router A is programmed to know about the one supernet, having only a single entry in its routing table. Router B has four entries in its routing table, and therefore is able to communicate with each network individually.

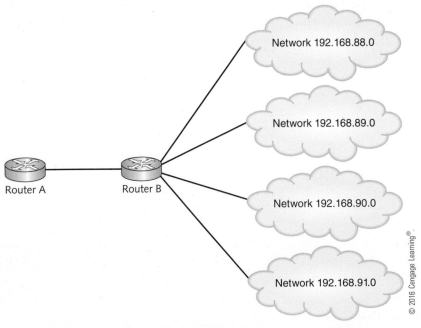

Figure 10-7 Supernetting reduces entries in router A's routing tables

Network+
1.8
1.9
Applying Concepts

Use the Logical ANDing Function to Calculate a Network ID

To calculate a host's network ID given its IPv4 address and subnet mask, you can follow a logical process of combining bits known as ANDing. In ANDing, a bit with a value of 1 combined, or anded, with another bit with a value of 1 results in a 1. A bit with a value of 0 anded with any other bit results in a 0. If you think of 1 as "true" and 0 as "false," the logic of ANDing makes sense.

ANDing a true statement to a true statement still results in a true statement. But ANDing a true statement to a false statement results in a false statement. ANDing logic is demonstrated in Table 10-6, which provides every possible combination of having a 1 or 0 bit in an IPv4 address or subnet mask.

Table 10-6 ANDing

IP address bit	1	1	0	0
Subnet mask bit	1	0	1	0
Resulting bit	1	0	0	0

© 2016 Cengage Learning®

A sample IPv4 host address, its default subnet mask, and its network ID are shown in Figure 10-8 in both binary and dotted decimal notation. Notice that the address's fourth octet could have been composed of any combination of 1s and 0s, and the network ID's fourth octet would still be all 0s.

	IP address:	11000000	00100010	01011001	01111111	192.34.89.127
and	Subnet mask:	11111111	11111111	11111111	00000000	255.255.255.0
Equals	Network ID:	11000000	00100010	01011001	00000000	192.34.89.0

Figure 10-8 Example of calculating a host's network ID

© 2016 Cengage Learning®.

Figure 10-8 shows how ANDing logic is applied to an IPv4 address plus a *default* subnet mask, but it works just the same way for networks that are subnetted and have different subnet masks.

Subnetting in IPv6

Recall that IPv6 addresses are composed of 128 bits, compared with IPv4's 32-bit addresses. That means 2^{128} addresses are available in IPv6, compared with IPv4's 2^{32} available addresses. Given so many addresses, an ISP can offer each of its customers an entire IPv6 subnet, or thousands of addresses, rather than a handful of IPv4 addresses that must be shared among all the company's nodes. That's only one example of how subnetting helps network administrators manage the enormous volume of IPv6 addresses.

Subnetting in IPv6 is simpler than subnetting in IPv4. One substantial difference is that unlike IPv4 addressing, IPv6 addressing does not use classes at all. There are no IPv6 equivalents to IPv4's Class A, Class B, or Class C networks. Every IPv6 address is classless.

Recall that a unicast address is an address assigned to a single interface on the network. Also recall that every unicast address can be represented in binary form, but is more commonly written as eight blocks of four hexadecimal characters separated by colons. For example,

2608:FE10:1:A:002:50FF:FE2B:E708 is a valid IPv6 address. In every unicast address, the last four blocks, which equate to the last 64 bits, identify the interface. (On many IPv6 networks, those 64 bits are based on the interface's EUI-64 MAC address.) The first four blocks or 64 bits normally identify the network and serve as the network prefix or routing prefix, as shown in Figure 10-9. In the IPv6 address 2608:FE10:1:A:002:50FF:FE2B:E708, the network prefix is 2608:FE10:1:A and the interface ID is 002:50FF:FE2B:E708.

Interfaces that share a network prefix belong to the same subnet. You may see network pre-

Figure 10-9   Network prefix and interface ID in an IPv6 address
© 2016 Cengage Learning®.

fixes represented as, for example, 2608:FE10:1:A::/64, where the number of bits that identify a subnet follow a slash. However, technically speaking, a subnet is most often represented by the leftmost 64 bits in an address, making the slash notation unnecessary for this purpose. Given 64 bits for network information and 64 bits for interface information, a single IPv6 subnet is capable of supplying 18,446,744,073,709,551,616 IPv6 addresses. Subnet masks are not used in IPv6 because the network prefix defines a subnet. Sometimes the slash notation is called the prefix mask. For example, the prefix mask might be 2608:FE10:1:A::/64.

Similar to supernetting, IPv6 enables network administrators to group interfaces that belong to the same route by specifying a route prefix. Because route prefixes vary in length, the slash notation is necessary when defining them. For example, the route prefix indicated by 2608:FE10::/32 includes all subnets whose prefixes begin with 2608:FE10 and, consequently, all interfaces whose IP addresses begin with 2608:FE10.

As shown in Figure 10-10, a regional Internet registry (RIR) might assign a regional ISP a block of addresses that share a 32-bit route prefix, such as 2608:FE10::/32. That regional ISP, in turn, might assign a local ISP a block of addresses that share the same 48-bit route prefix, such as 2608:FE10:1::/48. Finally, the local ISP could assign one of its large business customers a subnet—that is, a block of IPv6 addresses that share the same 64-bit network prefix, such as 2608:FE10:1:A::/64.

Now that you have learned how subnets are handled differently in IPv4 and IPv6 addressing, you are ready to explore virtualization options and another type of network segmentation: VLANs.

Virtualization

Virtualization is the emulation of all or part of a computer or network. It's a broad term that encompasses many possibilities. In the case of a single computer, virtualization can emulate the hardware, OS, and/or applications. In the case of a network, virtualization can emulate hardware, including cabling and network devices (for example, switches or routers), and software, including the NOS and network management systems. Beginning in Chapter 1, you've created and worked with a variety of virtual machines (VMs), whether virtual workstations or virtual servers, on one computer, which hosts the virtualization software that emulates

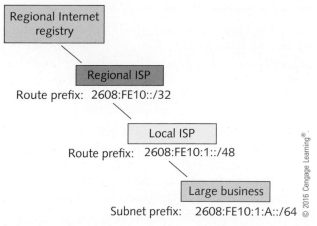

Figure 10-10 Hierarchy of IPv6 routes and subnets

virtual NICs and virtual switches. Together, all the VMs and virtual networking devices on a single computer share the same CPU, hard disk, memory, and physical network interfaces. Yet each VM can be configured to use a different operating system, and can emulate a different type of CPU, storage drive, or NIC than the physical computer it resides on.

Meanwhile, to users, a VM appears and acts no differently from a physical computer running the same software. For example, suppose you are the network administrator at an ISP and you establish separate virtual mail servers for five companies on one physical computer. When an employee at one company checks his email, he has no idea that he is accessing the same physical computer that an employee at another company uses to check her email.

In this type of virtualization, the physical computer is known as the **host** while each VM is known as a **guest**. The software that allows you to define VMs and manages resource allocation and sharing among them is known as a **virtual machine manager**, or, more commonly, a **hypervisor**. Figure 10-11 illustrates some of the elements of virtualization.

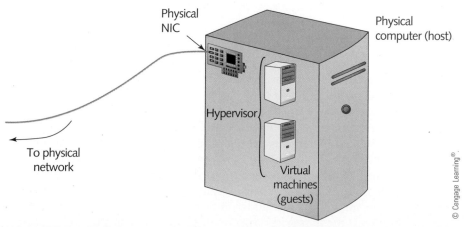

Figure 10-11 Elements of virtualization

Virtualization offers several advantages, including the following:

- *Efficient use of resources*—Physical clients or servers devoted to one function typically use only a fraction of their capacity. Without virtualization, a company might purchase six computers to run six different services—for example, mail server, DNS server, DHCP server, file server, remote access server, and database server. Each service might demand no more than 15 percent of its computer's processing power and memory. Using virtualization, however, a single, powerful computer can support all six services.

- *Cost and energy savings*—Organizations save money by purchasing fewer physical machines. They also save electricity because there are fewer computers drawing power and less demand for air conditioning in the computer room. Some institutions with thousands of users, such as Stanford University, are using virtualization as a way to conserve energy and are promoting it as part of campuswide sustainability efforts.

- *Fault and threat isolation*—In a virtual environment, the isolation of each guest system means that a problem with one guest does not affect the others. For example, an instructor might create multiple instances of an operating system and applications on a single computer that's shared by several classes. That allows each student to work on his own instance of the operating system environment. Any configuration errors or changes he makes on his guest machine will not affect other students. In another example, a network administrator who wants to try a beta version of an application might install that application on a guest machine rather than his host, in case the untested software causes problems. Furthermore, because a VM is granted limited access to hardware resources, security attacks on a guest may have little effect on a host or the physical network to which it's connected.

- *Simple backups, recovery, and replication*—Virtualization software enables network administrators to save snapshots, or images, of a guest machine. The images can later be used to re-create that machine on another host or on the same host. This feature allows for simple backups and quick recovery. It also makes it easy to create multiple, identical copies of one VM. Some virtualization programs even allow you to save snapshot files of VMs that can be imported into a competitor's virtualization program.

Not every type of client or server is a good candidate for virtualization, however. Potential disadvantages to creating multiple guests on a single host machine include the following:

- *Compromised performance*—When multiple virtual machines contend for finite physical resources, one virtual machine could monopolize those resources and impair the performance of other virtual machines on the same computer. In theory, careful management and resource allocation should prevent this. In practice, however, it is unwise to force a critical application—for example, a factory's real-time control systems or a hospital's emergency medical systems—to share resources and take that risk. Imagine a brewery that uses computers to measure and control tank levels, pressure, flow, and temperature of liquid ingredients during processing. These functions are vital for product quality and safety. In this example, where specialty software demands real-time, error-free performance, it makes sense to devote all of a computer's resources to this set of functions, rather than share that computer with the brewery's human resources database server, for example. In addition to multiple guest systems vying for limited physical resources, the hypervisor also requires some overhead.

- *Increased complexity*—Although virtualization reduces the number of physical machines to manage, it increases complexity and administrative burden in other ways. For instance, a network administrator who uses virtual servers and switches must thoroughly understand virtualization software. In addition, managing addressing and switching for multiple VMs is more complex than doing so for physical machines. (You will learn more about these techniques later in this chapter.) Finally, because VMs are so easy to set up, they may be created capriciously or as part of experimentation, and then forgotten. As a result, extra VMs may litter a server's hard disk, consume resources, and unnecessarily complicate network management. By contrast, abandoned physical servers might only take up rack space.

- *Increased licensing costs*—Because every instance of commercial software requires its own license, every VM that uses such software comes with added cost. In some cases, the added cost brings little return. For example, a software developer might want to create four instances of Windows 8.1 on a single computer to test new software using four testing procedures on four different OS installations. To comply with Microsoft's licensing restrictions, the developer will have to purchase four licenses for Windows 8.1. Depending on the developer's intentions, it might make more sense, instead, to share one installation of Windows 8.1 and separate the four testing procedures by using four different logon IDs.

- *Single point of failure*—If a host machine fails, all its guest machines will fail, too. For example, an organization that creates VMs for its mail server, DNS server, DHCP server, file server, remote access server, and database server on a single physical computer would lose all of those services if the computer went down. Wise network administrators implement measures such as clustering and automatic failover to prevent that from happening.

Most of the potential disadvantages in this list can be mitigated through thoughtful network design and virtualization control. You can choose from several virtualization programs to create and manage VMs. VMware makes the most widely implemented virtualization software today. The company provides several products, such as Fusion and Workstation, which are designed for managing virtual workstations on a single host, and others, such as vSphere and ESXi, are capable of managing hundreds of virtual servers across a WAN. Other virtualization products include Microsoft's Hyper-V, KVM (Kernel-based Virtual Machine), Oracle's VirtualBox, and Citrix's XenApp. All provide similar functionality, but differ in features, interfaces, and ease of use. You've used several of these products in the Case Projects throughout this book.

Virtual Network Components

It's possible to create a virtual network that consists of virtual machines and virtual networking devices on a single physical server. More practical and common, however, are networks that combine physical and virtual elements. In this section, you will learn how VMs connect to each other and to a physical network.

Virtual Machines and Network Adapters

You've already worked with VMs in projects throughout this book. This brief overview will help you understand better what other options you have when creating and working with VMs.

A VM's software and hardware characteristics are assigned when it is created in the virtualization program. As you have learned, these characteristics can differ completely from those of the host machine. You can select for the VM a guest operating system, amount of memory, hard disk size, processor type, and NIC type and speed, to name a few options. Figure 10-12 shows a screen from the VMware VM creation wizard that allows you to specify the amount of memory allocated to a VM.

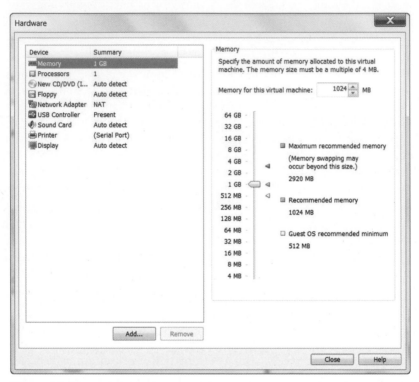

Figure 10-12 Specifying a VM's memory in VMware

Source: VMware

To connect to a network, a virtual machine requires a **virtual adapter**, or **vNIC (virtual network interface card)**. Just like a physical NIC, a vNIC operates at the Data Link layer and provides the computer with network access. Each VM can have several vNICs, no matter how many NICs the host machine has. The maximum number of vNICs on a VM depends on the limits imposed by the virtualization program. For example, VirtualBox allows up to eight vNICs per virtual machine. (By using the right software, you could configure this VM as a virtual router with eight ports connected to eight networks.)

Figure 10-13 shows a dialog box from the VMware wizard that allows you to customize properties of a virtual workstation's vNIC. One of many options you can configure for each NIC is its inbound and outbound transmission speeds. For example, you could select transmission speeds that simulate a T-1 or broadband cable connection.

Upon creation, each vNIC is automatically assigned a MAC address. Also, by default, every virtual machine's vNIC is connected to a port on a virtual switch, as described next.

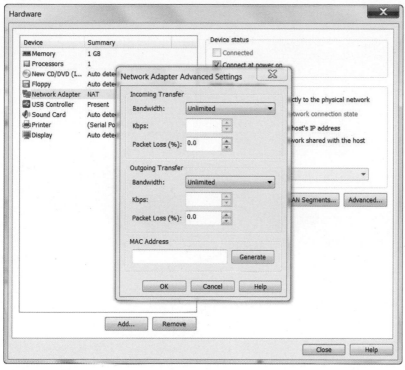

Figure 10-13 Customizing vNIC properties in VMware

Source: VMware

Virtual Switches and Bridges

As soon as the first virtual machine's vNIC is selected, the hypervisor creates a connection between that VM and the host. Depending on the virtualization software, this connection might be called a bridge or a switch. (Every port on a physical switch can be considered a bridge; thus, a switch is essentially a collection of bridges.) A **virtual switch** is a logically defined device that operates at the Data Link layer to pass frames between nodes. **Virtual bridges**, or ports on a virtual switch, connect vNICs with a network, whether virtual or physical. Thus, a virtual switch or bridge allows VMs to communicate with each other and with nodes on a physical LAN or WAN.

One host can support multiple virtual switches. The hypervisor controls the virtual switches and its ports, or bridges. Figure 10-14 illustrates a host machine with two physical NICs that supports several virtual machines and their vNICs. A virtual switch connects the vNICs to the network.

VMs can go through a virtual switch on the host computer to reach the physical network and can communicate with physical or virtual routers, other network devices, and other hosts on this or another network. For example, in Figure 10-15 a VM on Host A can communicate with a VM on Host B.

Virtual switches offer many possibilities for customizing and managing network traffic, as you will discover later in this chapter. First, however, it's necessary to understand the different ways in which virtual interfaces can appear on and communicate with a network.

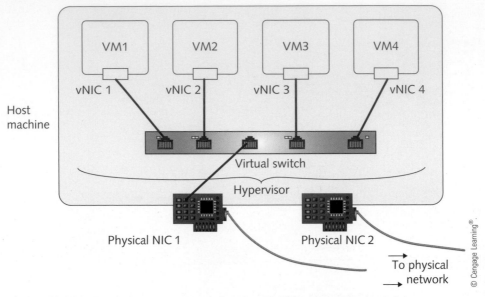

Figure 10-14   Virtual servers on a single host connected with a virtual switch

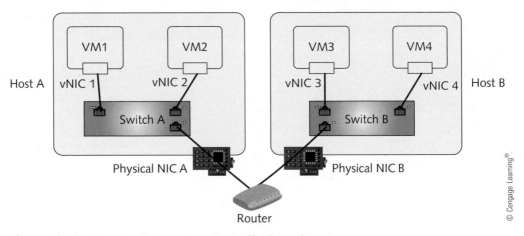

Figure 10-15   Virtual switches exchanging traffic through routers

 Network Connection Types

Earlier you learned that when creating a virtual network adapter on a VM, you choose its characteristics, such as speed. In addition, you are asked to identify what type of network connection, or networking mode, the vNIC will use. In the VMware or VirtualBox virtualization programs, you make this choice when you create or reconfigure a vNIC. In Hyper-V, you make the choice through the Virtual Network Manager. The most frequently used network connection types include bridged, NAT, and host-only, as described next.

Bridged Mode   In bridged mode, a vNIC accesses a physical network using the host machine's NIC, as shown in Figure 10-16. In other words, the virtual interface and the physical interface are bridged. If your host machine contains multiple physical adapters—for example, a wireless NIC and a wired NIC—you can choose which physical adapter to use as the bridge when you configure the virtual adapter.

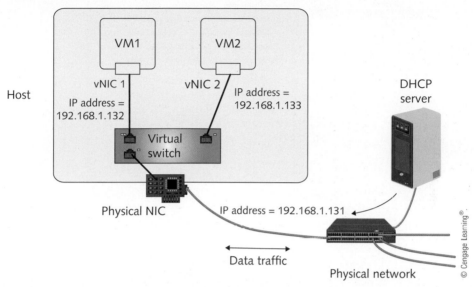

Figure 10-16   vNIC accessing a network in bridged mode

Although a bridged vNIC communicates through the host's adapter, it obtains its own IP address, default gateway, and subnet mask from a DHCP server on the physical LAN. For example, suppose your DHCP server is configured to assign addresses in the range of 192.168.1.129 through 192.168.1.254 to nodes on your LAN. The router might assign your host machine's physical NIC an IP address of 192.168.1.131. A guest on your host might obtain an IP address of 192.168.1.132. A second guest on that host might obtain an IP address of 192.168.1.133, and so on.

When connected using bridged mode, a VM appears to other nodes as just another client or server on the network. Other nodes communicate directly with the machine without realizing it is virtual.

In VMware and VirtualBox, you can choose the bridged connection type when you create or configure the virtual adapter. In KVM, you create a bridge between the VM and your physical NIC when you modify the vNIC's settings. In Hyper-V, you create a bridged connection type by assigning VMs to an external network switch. Figure 10-17 shows the Hardware dialog box that appears while creating a virtual machine in VMware with the Bridged network connection type selected.

VMs that must be available at a specific address, such as mail servers or Web servers, should be assigned bridged network connections. VMs that other nodes do not need to access directly can be configured to use the NAT networking mode.

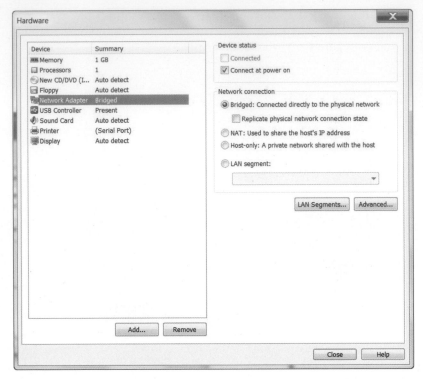

Figure 10-17   Selecting the Bridged option for a vNIC in VMware

Source: VMware

NAT Mode

In **NAT mode**, a vNIC relies on the host machine to act as a NAT device. In other words, the VM obtains IP addressing information from its host, rather than a server or router on the physical network. To accomplish this, the virtualization software acts as a DHCP server. A vNIC operating in NAT mode can still communicate with other nodes on the network and vice versa. However, other nodes communicate with the host machine's IP address to reach the VM; the VM itself is invisible to other nodes. Figure 10-18 illustrates a VM operating in NAT mode.

NAT is the default network connection type selected when you create a VM in VMware, VirtualBox, or KVM. In Hyper-V, the NAT connection type is created by assigning VMs to an internal network. Figure 10-19 shows the networking modes dialog box in VirtualBox, with the NAT option selected.

Once you have selected the NAT configuration type, you can configure the pool of IP addresses available to the VMs on a host. For example, suppose, as shown in Figure 10-18, your host machine has an IP address of 192.168.1.131. You might configure your host's DHCP service to assign IP addresses in the range of 10.1.1.129 through 10.1.1.254 to the VMs you create on that host. Because these addresses will never be evident beyond the host, you have flexibility in choosing their IP address range.

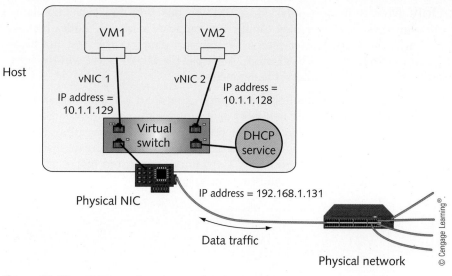

Figure 10-18 vNIC accessing a network in NAT mode

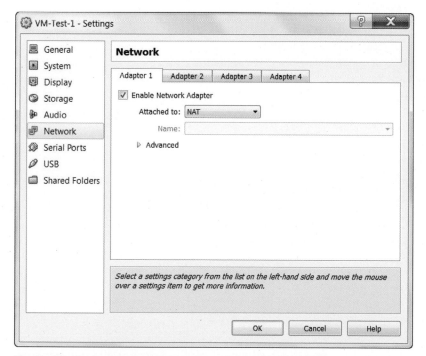

Figure 10-19 Selecting the NAT option for a vNIC in VirtualBox

Source: VirtualBox

The NAT network connection type is appropriate for VMs that do not need to be accessed at a known address by other network nodes. For example, virtual workstations that are mainly used to run stand-alone applications or serve as test beds to test applications or operating system installations are good candidates for NAT network connections.

Host-Only Mode In host-only mode, VMs on one host can exchange data with each other and with their host, but they cannot communicate with any nodes beyond the host. In other words, the vNICs never receive or transmit data via the host machine's physical NIC. In host-only mode, as in NAT mode, VMs use the DHCP service in the host's virtualization software to obtain IP address assignments.

Figure 10-20 illustrates how the host-only option creates an isolated virtual network. Host-only mode is appropriate for test networks or if you simply need to install a different operating system on your workstation to use a program that is incompatible with your host's operating system. For example, suppose a project requires you to create diagrams in Microsoft Visio and your workstation runs Red Hat Linux. You could install a Windows 7 VM solely for the purpose of installing and running Visio.

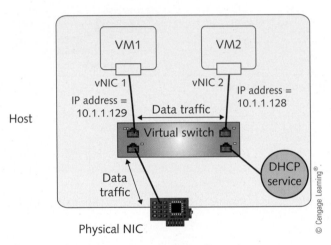

Figure 10-20 Host-only network configuration

Obviously, because host-only mode prevents VMs from exchanging data with a physical network, this choice cannot work for virtual servers that need to be accessed by clients across a LAN. Nor can it be used for virtual workstations that need to access LAN or WAN services, such as email or Web pages. Host-only networking is less commonly used than NAT or bridged mode networking.

You can choose host-only networking when you create or configure a VM in VMware or VirtualBox. In Hyper-V, the host-only connection type is created by assigning VMs to a private virtual network. In KVM, host-only is not a predefined option, but must be assigned to a vNIC via the command-line interface.

Virtualization software gives you the flexibility of creating several different networking types on one host machine. For example, on one host you could create a host-only, or private, network to test multiple versions of Linux. On the same host, you could create a group of Windows Server 2012 R2 servers that are connected to your physical LAN using the bridged connection type. Or, rather than specifying one of the four networking connection types described previously, you could also create a VM that contains a vNIC but is not connected to any nodes, whether virtual or physical. Preventing the VM from communicating with other nodes keeps it completely isolated. This might be desirable when testing unpredictable software or an image of untrusted origin.

Virtual Appliances and Virtual Network Services

Imagine you're a busy network administrator, and your company's IT director has asked you to provide a complete email and collaboration solution for everyone connected to the WAN. Traditionally, someone in your situation would research and obtain trial versions of the leading software, install the software on test machines, and evaluate each program over a period of weeks. You might struggle to get your hardware and operating system to work correctly with the software. Or you might wonder whether certain problems with the new software are related to the way you configured it. However, virtualization offers an alternative.

Instead of installing the program on a test server, you could install a virtual appliance, or an image that includes the appropriate operating system, software, hardware specifications, and application configuration necessary for the package to run properly. Virtual appliances may be virtual workstations, but more commonly they are virtual servers. Each virtual appliance varies in its features and complexity. Popular functions include firewall and other security measures, network management, email solutions, and remote access. Other virtual appliances are customized instances of operating systems designed to suit the needs of particular users.

All of these virtual devices, services, and appliances can be centrally managed by a network controller. For example, in the technical preview for the newest Windows Server (not yet named at the printing of this book), a new Network Controller role is provided for managing both physical and virtual network infrastructure.

More commonly, however, network controller is another word for a device's NIC or network adapter.

VRRP (Virtual Router Redundancy Protocol) and HSRP (Hot Standby Routing Protocol) Sometimes virtual services and devices are implemented for the purpose of redundancy. These virtual devices can provide backup services in the event a physical device or another virtual device fails. In Chapter 9, you learned about CARP and round-robin DNS. In the case of routers, VRRP (Virtual Router Redundancy Protocol), or Cisco's propriety version called HSRP (Hot Standby Routing Protocol), is used to assign a virtual IP address to a group of routers. The virtual IP address can be shared by the entire group. At first, messages routed to the virtual IP address are handled by the master router. If the master router fails, backup routers stand in line to take over responsibility of the virtual IP address. The routers involved in this scenario are all physical routers acting together as a single virtual router or as a group of virtual routers.

When using HSRP, the master router is called the active router, and the backup routers are called standby routers.

SDN (Software Defined Networking) Taking the idea of virtual appliances to the next level, imagine that you want to provide multiple network services, such as firewalls,

switches, and load balancers, as virtual services that are not directly tied to the physical devices on the network. **Software defined networking (SDN)** is the virtualization of network services in which a network controller manages these services instead of the services being directly managed by the hardware devices involved. The network controller also integrates all of the network's virtual and physical devices into one cohesive system. As you can see in Figure 10-21, the network controller is positioned between the virtual services and the physical devices. Protocols handle the process of making decisions (such as routing, blocking, and forwarding), which is called the **control plane**. The physical devices make actual contact with data transmissions as they traverse the network, which is called the **data plane**. One of the primary advantages to separating the control plane from the data plane is to provide network technicians with more centralized control of network settings and management—virtual devices can be managed from a central interface. SDN also creates the potential to implement more sophisticated network functions while using less-expensive devices. However, SDN is not "all or nothing"—you don't have to use all virtual services or no virtual services. These virtual services can be integrated into an existing network infrastructure alongside more traditional devices.

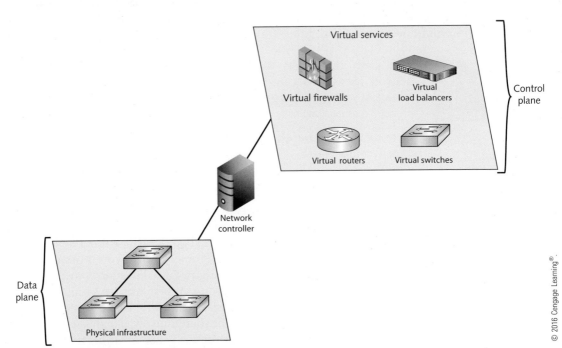

© 2016 Cengage Learning®

Figure 10-21   The virtual devices on the right are on the control plane; the physical devices on the left are on the data plane

The OpenFlow protocol is often used to implement this arrangement. **OpenFlow** provides a common language between the virtualized service applications and the network's physical devices, ensuring that the applications make decisions rather than the devices themselves.

Now that you are familiar with the elements that make up a virtual network, you are ready to learn techniques for managing them as part of an enterprise-wide network.

VLANs and Trunking

A subnet groups IP addresses so that routers can be introduced into a large network in order to segment it into smaller networks. By contrast, a **VLAN (virtual local area network)** groups ports on a switch so that some of the local traffic on the switch is forced to go through a router. The end goal of both subnetting and VLANs is the same: to allow routers to better manage network traffic using the divide-and-conquer mentality.

To create a VLAN, you need a programmable physical switch whose ports can be partitioned into groups. You can think of this as breaking a single switch into two or more switches so that a router can be inserted between them, thus creating two or more networks from the larger network. Because Layer 2 switches use MAC addresses for communication, and each port is assigned a MAC address, VLANs are considered a Layer 2 solution for segmenting a network. In effect, you divide the pool of MAC addresses (called the MAC address space) into two or more MAC address spaces, thus creating two or more broadcast domains from a single broadcast domain.

Figure 10-22 shows how a normal Layer 2 switch operates. This switch can manage all network traffic on the LAN unless a host on the network wants to communicate with a host on another network and then that traffic goes through the router.

Figure 10-22 A normal switch connecting a LAN to a router

© 2016 Cengage Learning®.

Figure 10-23 shows what happens when a programmable switch partitions its ports into two VLANs. Traffic within each VLAN still goes through the switch as normal, and traffic to hosts on other networks still goes through the router. However, traffic between hosts on VLAN 1 and VLAN 2 must now also go through the router. Earlier in the chapter, you saw how you can introduce new routers into a large network to segment the network and better manage traffic. By contrast, you can segment a large network into VLANs so that existing routers can better manage the traffic without purchasing new routers.

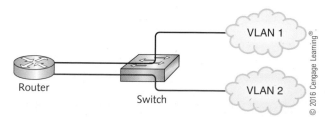

Figure 10-23 A programmable switch partitioned its ports into two groups, each belonging to a VLAN

802.1Q is the IEEE standard that specifies how VLAN information appears in frames and how switches interpret that information. In most situations, each VLAN is assigned its own subnet of IP addresses. This means that the subnet, working at Layer 3, includes the same group of hosts as the VLAN, working at Layer 2. Also, each VLAN and subnet normally is a broadcast domain. Although it is possible to do otherwise, network administrators find life much easier when they adhere to the following statement:

$$1 \text{ broadcast domain} = 1 \text{ VLAN} = 1 \text{ subnet}$$

A VLAN can include ports from more than one switch. For example, in Figure 10-24, VLAN 2 contains ports from switches A and B.

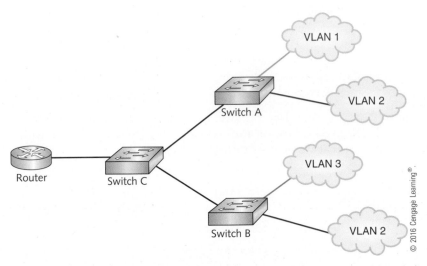

Figure 10-24 A single VLAN can be managed by multiple programmable switches

Recall the example given earlier in the chapter of a large network on three floors of a building, as shown in Figure 10-1. Rather than placing new routers on each floor of the building and making the network on each floor a subnet, you could use programmable switches, VLANs, and subnets to segment the network. For example, suppose you segment the network by department in the company rather than floors in the building, as shown in Figure 10-25. You can install programmable switches to replace switches A, B, and C and assign each host to a specific VLAN based on the ports on the switches the hosts connect to.

> **NOTE** Some types of broadcast traffic, such as DHCP messages, need to travel beyond the broadcast domain. Not every VLAN maintains its own DHCP server. A centrally managed DHCP server can provide DHCP to multiple VLANs by configuring a DHCP relay agent. A router programmed to support a relay agent receives the message and creates a message of its own to send the specified DHCP traffic beyond the broadcast domain. On some Cisco products, a more robust command, `ip helper-address`, can be configured to create and send helper messages to support several types of UDP traffic, including DHCP, TFTP, DNS, and NetBIOS.

Network engineers value VLANs for their flexibility. They can include ports from more than one switch. Any type of end node can belong to one or more VLANs. VLANs can link

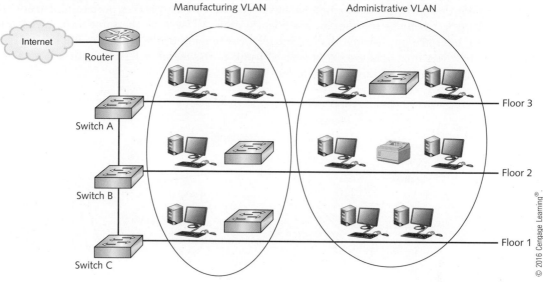

Figure 10-25   A simple VLAN design

geographically distant users over a WAN, and they can create small workgroups within LANs. Reasons for using VLANs include:

- Separating groups of users who need special security or network functions
- Isolating connections with heavy or unpredictable traffic patterns
- Identifying groups of devices whose data should be given priority handling
- Containing groups of devices that rely on legacy protocols incompatible with the majority of the network's traffic
- Separating a very large network into smaller, more manageable subnets

One situation in which a company might want to implement a VLAN is to allow visitors access to minimal network functions—for example, an Internet connection—without allowing the possibility of access to the company's data stored on servers. In another example, companies that use their packet-switched networks to carry telephone calls often group all of the voice traffic on a separate VLAN to prevent this unique and potentially heavy traffic from adversely affecting routine client-server tasks.

A single switch can manage traffic belonging to several VLANs. In fact, one switch's interface can carry the traffic of VLANs configured on multiple switches, thanks to a technique known as trunking. The term *trunk* originated in the telephony field, where it referred to an aggregation of logical connections over one physical connection. For instance, a trunk carried signals for many residential telephone lines in the same neighborhood over one cable. Similarly, in the context of switching, a trunk is a single physical connection between switches through which many logical VLANs can transmit and receive data.

A port on a switch is configured as either an access port or a trunk port. An access port is used for connecting a single node, such as a workstation, that can only exchange information with that switch. For example, a server connected to an access port cannot recognize which VLAN it belongs to, nor can it recognize other VLANs on the same switch. A **trunk port** is the interface on a switch that is capable of managing traffic among multiple VLANs. Thus, a trunk is a link between two switches' trunk ports. Figure 10-26 illustrates how a trunk connects and conveys information about VLANs.

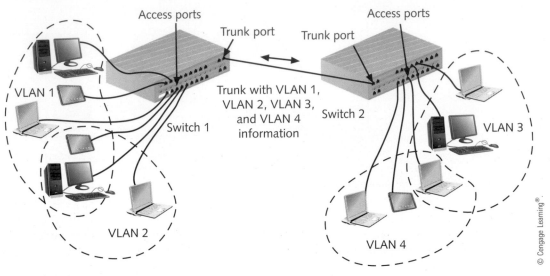

Figure 10-26 Trunk for multiple VLANs

To keep the data belonging to each VLAN separate, each frame of a data transmission is identified with a VLAN identifier, or **tag**, added to its header, according to specifications in the 802.1Q standard. Trunking protocols assign and interpret these tags, thereby managing the distribution of frames through a trunk. The most popular protocol for exchanging VLAN information over trunks is Cisco's **VTP (VLAN trunking protocol)**. VTP allows changes to the VLAN database on one switch, called the **stack master**, to be communicated to all other switches in the network. This provides network administrators with the ability to centrally manage all VLANs by making changes to a single switch. Other switches besides the stack master in the same VTP domain can also communicate VLAN updates, such as the addition of a new VLAN.

A switch is typically preconfigured with one **default VLAN** that includes all its ports (other VLANs might be preconfigured as well, depending on the device and manufacturer). This default VLAN cannot be renamed or deleted. You can create additional VLANs by properly configuring a switch's operating system software. The critical step in creating VLANs is to indicate which VLAN each port belongs to by tagging the VLAN, and ensuring that these tags match on both sides of the trunk. Switches can also manage untagged VLANs, usually called **native VLANs**, which will automatically receive all untagged frames. In addition, you can specify security parameters, filtering instructions (if the switch should not forward any frames from a certain VLAN, for example), performance requirements for certain ports, and network addressing and management options. Options vary according to the switch manufacturer and model. In the Applying Concepts project below, you will have the opportunity to create and configure a VLAN on a Cisco switch.

Once you create a VLAN, you also maintain it via the switch's software. Figure 10-27 illustrates the result of a `show vlan` command on a Cisco switch on a large enterprise-wide network. The `show vlan` command is used to list the current VLANs recognized by a switch, and it is unique to Cisco-brand switches (and a few others that mimic that company's conventions). Other manufacturers' switch software include similar maintenance commands.

Figure 10-27 lists 13 VLANs configured on the network. VLAN number 1 and VLANs 1002 through 1005 are defaults preestablished on the Cisco switch, but not actually used. The first half of the command output shows each VLAN's number, name, status, and which ports belong to it. For example, VLAN number 18, which is named "VLAN0018," is active and contains the ports "Gi1/3" and "Gi2/3." A port called "Gi1/3," in this case, refers to the third port on the first module of this Gigabit Ethernet switch.

The second half of the command output provides additional information about each VLAN, including the type of network it operates on. In this example, all VLANs that are active and not preestablished defaults use Ethernet, which is indicated by the "enet" type. Each VLAN is assigned a different **SAID**, or security association identifier, which indicates to other connectivity devices which VLAN a transmission belongs to. By default, Cisco switches assign a VLAN the SAID of 100,000 plus the VLAN number. Also, in this example each VLAN is configured to transmit and receive frames with a maximum transmission unit (MTU) size of 1500 bytes, which is the default selection. Rarely do network administrators change this variable.

One potential problem in creating VLANs is that by grouping certain nodes, you are not merely including those nodes—you are also excluding another group. This means you can potentially cut off a group from the rest of the network. For example, suppose your company's IT director tells you to assign all executive workstations to their own VLAN, and to configure the network's switch to group these users' computers into a VLAN. After this change, users would be able to exchange data with each other, but they would not be able to download data from the file server or download mail from the mail server, because these servers are not included in their VLAN. To allow different VLANs to exchange data, you need to connect those VLANs with a router or Layer 3 switch.

Another risk with VLANs is the possibility of a hacker crossing VLANs to access sensitive data or to inject harmful software in an attack called VLAN hopping. A **VLAN hopping attack** occurs when an attacker generates transmissions that appear, to the switch, to belong to a protected VLAN. VLAN hopping can be prevented by disabling auto trunking and moving the native VLAN to an unused VLAN, meaning that untagged traffic would essentially run into a dead-end.

It's also important to keep an eye out for signs of incorrect VLAN assignment. This can happen due to a variety of situations, including misconfigurations of the client authentication process in which a VLAN is assigned to the device before the authentication process is complete. Another problematic scenario occurs when ports are incorrectly configured in trunk mode, which is used between switches for trunking, instead of access mode, which is appropriate for user devices.

10

VLAN	Name	Status	Ports
1	default	active	Te1/1, Te1/2, Gi1/5, Gi1/6
			Te2/1, Te2/2, Gi2/5, Gi2/6
			Gi4/3, Gi5/12, Gi6/12, Gi6/19
			Gi8/11, Gi8/19, Gi9/4
5	VLAN0005	active	
13	VLAN0013	active	Gi3/2, Gi3/3, Gi3/4, Gi8/12
14	VLAN0014	active	Gi4/1, Gi4/2, Gi4/4, Gi9/12
16	VLAN0016	active	Gi5/8
18	VLAN0018	active	Gi1/3, Gi2/3
19	VLAN0019	active	Gi5/11, Gi6/11
104	VLAN0104	active	Gi1/4, Gi2/4, Gi3/5, Gi3/6
			Gi4/5, Gi4/6, Gi5/1, Gi5/2
			Gi5/3, Gi5/4, Gi5/5, Gi5/6
			Gi5/7, Gi5/9, Gi5/10, Gi5/13
			Gi5/14, Gi5/15, Gi5/16, Gi5/17
			Gi5/18, Gi5/19, Gi5/20, Gi5/21
			Gi5/22, Gi5/23, Gi5/24, Gi6/1
			Gi6/2, Gi6/3, Gi6/4, Gi6/5
			Gi6/6, Gi6/7, Gi6/9, Gi6/10
			Gi6/13, Gi6/14, Gi6/15, Gi6/16
			Gi6/17, Gi6/18, Gi6/20, Gi6/21
			Gi6/22, Gi6/23, Gi6/24, Gi7/6
			Gi7/8, Gi7/11, Gi7/12, Gi7/19
			Gi8/8, Gi8/24, Gi9/1, Gi9/2
			Gi9/3, Gi9/13
105	VLAN0105	active	Gi7/24, Gi9/5, Gi9/6, Gi9/7
			Gi9/8, Gi9/10, Gi9/11, Gi9/14
			Gi9/16, Gi9/18, Gi9/19, Gi9/20
			Gi9/21, Gi9/22, Gi9/23, Gi9/24
			Gi10/1, Gi10/2, Gi10/4, Gi10/5
			Gi10/6, Gi10/8, Gi10/9, Gi10/10
			Gi10/11, Gi10/12, Gi10/13
			Gi10/14, Gi10/15, Gi10/16
			Gi10/17, Gi10/18, Gi10/19
			Gi10/20, Gi10/21, Gi10/22
			Gi10/23, Gi10/24
106	VLAN0106	active	Gi6/8
107	VLAN0107	active	Gi7/1, Gi7/2, Gi7/3, Gi7/4
			Gi7/5, Gi7/7, Gi7/9, Gi7/10
			Gi7/13, Gi7/14, Gi7/16, Gi7/17
			Gi7/18, Gi7/21, Gi7/22, Gi8/1
			Gi8/2, Gi8/3, Gi8/4, Gi8/5
			Gi8/6, Gi8/7, Gi8/9, Gi8/10
			Gi8/13, Gi8/14, Gi8/16, Gi8/17
			Gi8/18, Gi8/21, Gi8/22
108	VLAN0108	active	Gi7/15, Gi7/20, Gi7/23, Gi8/15
			Gi8/20, Gi8/23
109	VLAN0109	active	
601	VLAN0601	active	
1002	fddi-default	act/unsup	
1003	token-ring-default	act/unsup	
1004	fddinet-default	act/unsup	
1005	trnet-default	act/unsup	

VLAN	Type	SAID	MTU	Parent	RingNo	BridgeNo	Stp	BrdgMode	Trans1	Trans2
1	enet	100001	1500	-	-	-	-	-	0	0
5	enet	100005	1500	-	-	-	-	-	0	0
13	enet	100013	1500	-	-	-	-	-	0	0
14	enet	100014	1500	-	-	-	-	-	0	0
16	enet	100016	1500	-	-	-	-	-	0	0
18	enet	100018	1500	-	-	-	-	-	0	0
19	enet	100019	1500	-	-	-	-	-	0	0
104	enet	100104	1500	-	-	-	-	-	0	0
105	enet	100105	1500	-	-	-	-	-	0	0
106	enet	100106	1500	-	-	-	-	-	0	0
107	enet	100107	1500	-	-	-	-	-	0	0
108	enet	100108	1500	-	-	-	-	-	0	0
109	enet	100109	1500	-	-	-	-	-	0	0
601	enet	100601	1500	-	-	-	-	-	0	0
1002	fddi	101002	1500	-	-	-	-	-	0	0
1003	tr	101003	1500	-	-	-	-	-	0	0
1004	fdnet	101004	1500	-	-	-	ieee	-	0	0
1005	trnet	101005	1500	-	-	-	ibm	-	0	0

Figure 10-27 Result of the show vlan command on a Cisco switch

Source: Cisco Systems, Inc.

Network+
1.1
1.3
2.6
3.2
3.3
4.6

Applying Concepts

Create a VLAN on a Switch

In this project, you will create a VLAN on a Cisco switch using the switch's internetwork operating system (IOS). For this project, you will need a modern switch that runs the Cisco IOS. A used workgroup switch, which can often be purchased for under $150, would be suitable. If you don't have a Cisco switch, you can follow along with the steps to learn about the switch configuration commands. Watching some videos online would also be helpful.

The following steps assume that you have Telnet access to the switch via a network. (If you are working on a Windows 7 or 8.1 computer, you can enable the Telnet client service as follows: Open Control Panel, click Programs, click Turn Windows features on or off, click the Telnet Client check box to select it, and then click OK.) The following steps also assume that you know the access password as well as the enable (administrator) password. To test your new VLAN, you will need a workstation to which you can assign a static IP address. This project uses a workstation running Windows 7 or Windows 8.1, but the steps are essentially the same no matter what operating system your workstation runs.

1. Open the Command Prompt window.

2. At the command prompt, telnet to the switch as follows: type `telnet xx.xx.xx.xx`, where *xx.xx.xx.xx* is your switch's IP address, and then press **Enter**. A password prompt appears.

3. Type the access password and press **Enter**. (The password will not appear on the screen as you type.)

4. Enter privileged mode, which allows you to carry out administrative tasks, as follows: type `enable` and then press **Enter**.

5. At the password prompt, type the enable password and press **Enter**. (The password will not appear on the screen as you type.) The command prompt changes from > to #.

6. Type `show vlan` and press **Enter** to display the currently configured VLANs. If this is a brand-new switch, you should see only the default VLANs, including VLANs 1, 1002, 1003, 1004, and 1005. As you have learned, and as the results of the command will show, all of the switch's ports belong to VLAN 1. In this project, you will create VLAN number 888, assuming that isn't already assigned to a VLAN on your device.

7. Type `configure terminal` and press **Enter**. The prompt changes again, this time to include `config` in parentheses. For example, if the name of your switch is *class1*, the prompt would be `class1(config)#`.

8. Type `vlan 888` and press **Enter**. The prompt changes to include `config-vlan`, as in `class1(config-vlan)#`. You are now ready to configure the VLAN you have established. One of the first things you'll want to do is assign it a name. For this project, you will call the VLAN *lab-a*.

9. Set the VLAN name as follows: type `name lab-a` and then press **Enter**. Note that spaces are not allowed in the VLAN name. The VLAN name is not used by other switches or nodes, but is a convenient reference for network administrators.

10. Type `exit` and press **Enter** to leave VLAN configuration mode. The command prompt changes back to your switch name followed by `config` in parentheses—for example, `class1(config)#`.

11. Type `interface vlan 888` and press **Enter**. The switch's IOS changes to interface configuration mode and the command prompt changes to include `config-if`—for example, `class1(config-if)#`.

12. Type `ip address 10.88.8.1 255.255.255.0` and press **Enter**. This assigns the address 10.88.8.1 and a Class C subnet mask to your VLAN.

13. Type `do show vlan` and press **Enter** to view all VLANs. Verify that the lab-a VLAN now appears in the list. Note that your VLAN currently has no ports associated with it.

    Next, you'll need to choose which ports you want associated with the lab-a VLAN. Follow these steps:

14. To change to the prompt for configuring a physical interface, type `interface Z`, where *Z* is the name of the interface you want to assign to your VLAN, and then press **Enter**. For example, if you wanted to add the first switch port to your VLAN, you might type `interface FastEthernet/0/1`. In this example, FastEthernet represents the switch, /0 represents its first module, and /1 represents the first port on that module. Naming conventions can differ from one model of switch to another, so refer to your switch's documentation for information on identifying interfaces.

15. Type `switchport access vlan 888` and press **Enter**. This assigns the port you specified in Step 14 to VLAN 888.

16. Type `switchport mode access` and press **Enter**. This instructs the switch to treat the host connecting to this port as an access device—for example, a workstation or server—only. In other words, it explicitly rules out the possibility of trunking or connecting to another switch or router via this port.

17. Press **Ctrl+Z** to leave configuration mode.

18. Type `show vlan id 888` and press **Enter** to view the ports assigned to the VLAN you created. Confirm that the port you added in Steps 14 and 15 appears.

19. Type `quit` (or `exit`, if you are working on a Linux or UNIX workstation) and press **Enter** to log off the switch and end your telnet session.

20. To close the Command Prompt window, type `exit` and then press **Enter**.

    Now that you have created a VLAN and associated a port with it, you are ready to test the VLAN's functionality. You will begin by connecting a workstation to the port and assigning that workstation a static IP address of 10.88.8.2. To do this on a computer running Windows 7, follow these steps:

21. Click the **Start** button, type `ncpa.cpl` in the text box, and then press **Enter**. The Network Connections window opens.

22. Right-click the network adapter that is connected to the switch port and choose **Properties**. If the User Account Control window asks if you want to continue, click **Yes**. The Network Adapter Properties dialog box opens.

23. Double-click **Internet Protocol Version 4 (TCP/IPv4)**. The Internet Protocol Version 4 (TCP/IPv4) Properties dialog box opens.

24. Click **Use the following IP address**, then enter **10.88.8.2** for the IP address, **255.255.255.0** for the Subnet mask, and **10.88.8.1** for the Default gateway. Click **OK** to save your changes.

25. Click **OK** to close the Network Adapter Properties dialog box.

26. Close the Network Connections window.

27. Open the Command Prompt window.

28. At the workstation's command prompt, type `ping 10.88.8.1` and press **Enter**. If you receive a "request timed out" message in response to your first attempt, repeat the `ping` command. If the `ping` command receives a response, then you have successfully configured a VLAN and communicated with it.

VLAN configuration can be complex. It requires careful planning to ensure that all users and devices that need to exchange data can do so after the VLANs are in operation. It also requires contemplating how the VLAN switch will interact with other devices. For example, if you want users from different VLANs to be able to communicate, you need to connect those VLANs through a Layer 3 device, such as a router or a higher-layer switch.

STP (Spanning Tree Protocol) and SPB (Shortest Path Bridging)

Suppose you design an enterprise-wide network with several switches interconnected via their uplink ports in a hybrid star-bus topology. To make the network more fault tolerant, you install multiple, or redundant, switches at critical junctures. Redundancy allows data the option of traveling through more than one switch toward its destination and makes your network less vulnerable to hardware malfunctions. For example, if one switch suffers a power supply failure, traffic can reroute through a second switch. Your network might look something like the one pictured in Figure 10-28. (In reality, of course, many more nodes would connect to the switches.)

A potential problem with the network shown in Figure 10-28 has to do with traffic loops. What if a server attached to switch A issues a broadcast frame, which switch A then reissues to all of its ports (other than the port to which the server is attached)? In that case, switch A will issue the broadcast frame to switches B, C, and D, which will then reissue the broadcast frame back to switch A and to each other, and so on, thereby flooding the network. If no mechanism exists to stop this broadcast storm, the high traffic volume will severely impair network performance. To eliminate the possibility of this and other types of traffic loops, switches and bridges use **STP (Spanning Tree Protocol)**.

The first iteration of STP, defined in IEEE standard **802.1D**, functions in the Data Link layer. It prevents traffic loops, also called switching loops, by calculating paths that avoid potential loops and by artificially blocking the links that would complete a loop. In addition, STP can adapt to changes in the network. For instance, if a switch is removed, STP will recalculate the best loop-free data paths between the remaining switches.

STP information is transmitted between switches via **BPDUs (Bridge Protocol Data Units)**. Certain BPDUs are blocked on the type of port serving network hosts, such as workstations and servers, by a **BPDU guard**, which is a software configuration that ensures these devices aren't considered as possible paths. BPDU guards help to enforce STP path rules. They also enhance security because they prevent a rogue, or unsanctioned, switch connected to one of these ports from hijacking the network's STP paths. The BPDU guards block BPDUs from crossing ports that are not configured for connections to switches. Another type of software

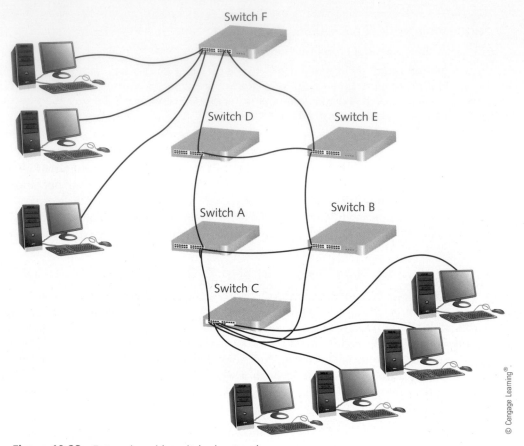

Figure 10-28 Enterprise-wide switched network

configuration, a **BPDU filter**, can be used to disable STP on specific ports. For example, you might use a BPDU filter on the demarc, where the ISP's service connects with a business's network, to prevent the ISP's WAN topology from mixing with the corporate network's topology for the purpose of plotting STP paths.

In the following explanation of STP, you can substitute *switch* wherever the word *bridge* is used. As you have learned, a switch is really just a glorified bridge. STP terminology refers to a Layer 2 device as a *bridge* because STP was designed and created before switches existed.

So how does STP work? First, STP selects a **root bridge**, or master bridge, which will provide the basis for all subsequent path calculations. The term *root bridge* makes sense when you consider the protocol's method, "spanning tree." Only one root bridge exists on a network, and from it a series of logical branches, or data paths, emanate. STP selects the root bridge based on its **BID (Bridge ID)**, which is a combination of a 2-byte priority field and the bridge's MAC address. To begin with, all bridges on the network share the same priority number, and so the bridge with the lowest MAC address becomes the root bridge.

Next, on every other bridge on the network, STP examines the possible paths between that bridge and the root bridge. Then it chooses the shortest of these paths—that is, the path that will carry data to its target fastest. Furthermore, STP stipulates that on any bridge, only one root port, which is the bridge's port that is closest to the root bridge, can forward frames toward the root bridge.

Finally, STP disables links that are not part of the shortest path. To do so, it enables only the lowest-cost port on a segment (link between two bridges), called the designated port, to transmit network traffic. (The ports can, however, continue to receive STP information.) Figure 10-29 illustrates a switched network with certain paths selected and others blocked by STP. In this drawing, root ports, pointing toward the root bridge, are labeled *RP*. Designated ports, pointing downstream from the root bridge, are labeled *DP*. For example, traffic from the root bridge would only be forwarded to switch D via switch B from switch A. Even though switch D is physically connected to switches E and F, STP has limited the logical pathway to go through switch B. If switch B were to fail, STP would choose a different logical pathway for frames destined for switch D.

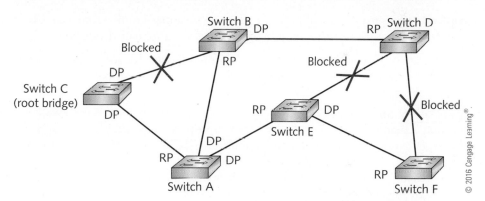

Figure 10-29   STP-selected paths on a switched network. *DP* indicates downstream designated ports, and *RP* indicates upstream root ports.

STP was introduced in the 1980s, and since then, network developers have repeatedly modified it to improve and customize its functioning. The original STP is considered too slow for today's networks. For instance, it could take up to two minutes to detect and account for a link failure. With that kind of lag time, older versions of STP would bog down network transmissions, especially where high-volume, speed-dependent traffic, like telephone or video signals, is involved. Newer versions of STP, such as RSTP (Rapid Spanning Tree Protocol), defined in IEEE's 802.1w standard, and MSTP (Multiple Spanning Tree Protocol), originally defined by the 802.1s standard, can detect and correct for link failures in milliseconds. Other, more current innovations designed to replace STP include TRILL (Transparent Interconnection of Lots of Links), a multipath, link-state protocol (using IS-IS) developed by the IETF, and the similar SPB (Shortest Path Bridging), which is a descendent of STP and is defined in IEEE's 802.1aq standard. Some switch manufacturers, such as Cisco and Extreme Networks, have designed proprietary versions of STP that are optimized to work most efficiently on their equipment.

Protocols designed to replace STP, such as SPB, operate at Layer 3 instead of or in addition to Layer 2, making them more compatible with various types of technologies such as FCoE (discussed in Chapter 4). SPB also differs from earlier iterations of STP in that it keeps all potential paths active while managing the flow of data across those paths to prevent loops. By utilizing all network paths, SPB greatly improves network performance.

When installing switches on your network, you do not need to enable or configure STP (or the more current version that came with your switch). It will come with the switch's operating software and should function smoothly by default and without intervention. However, if you want to designate preferred paths between bridges or choose a special root bridge, for example, STP and its relatives allow you to alter any default prioritization.

Switch Configurations

An **unmanaged switch** provides plug-and-play simplicity with minimal configuration options and has no IP address assigned to it. Unmanaged switches are not very expensive, but their capabilities are limited. **Managed switches**, on the other hand, can be configured via a command-line interface and sometimes can be configured in groups. Usually, they are also assigned IP addresses. VLANs can only be implemented through managed switches.

In Chapter 1, you set up a small network using a consumer-grade, unmanaged switch. Here, you'll learn about some of the configuration options on a managed switch:

- *password security*—It's wise to create a different password for each user who will need to work on the switch. Also, many switches will reject weak passwords, so be sure to choose a strong password for each user.

- *console*—Some switches can be managed by a dashboard in a Web browser or by connecting a **management console**, such as a laptop, to the switch's console port. Other management options include telnetting into the switch's systems, as you saw earlier in this chapter, or accessing the switch by SSH. Telnet and SSH are called **in-band management** systems because they use the existing network and its protocols to interface with the switch. A more-expensive option is an **out-of-band management** system, which can provide on-site infrastructure access when the network is down, or complete remote access in cases of connectivity failures on the network, such as via a cellular signal. Remote configuration on the switch is managed through a **virtual terminal**, or **virtual console**, on the machine at the technician's location.

- *AAA method*—Switches must be configured to use either TACACS+ or RADIUS for authenticating users who are trying to access the switch. Some switches also include a local AAA option.

- *switch port security*—Ports can be configured to filter traffic based on source MAC addresses. Filters are sensitive to VLAN assignments, and violations trigger various protective modes that can also be VLAN specific. One option is to direct traffic from unrecognized MAC addresses to a guest network with limited access to network resources.

- *speed and duplex*—The switch's speed and duplex settings must be configured to match the NIC on the device plugged into that port.

Wireless VLANs

Configuring APs to handle wireless clients on VLANs presents some unique challenges, which have been addressed by tools designed specifically for the wireless VLAN environment.

A large wireless network is often managed by a central wireless controller, also called a Wi-Fi controller or WLAN controller, which provides a central management console for all of the APs in the network. The APs themselves can provide several options, depending on the type of AP implemented. A thick AP is self-contained and can do its job without relying on a higher-level management device. By contrast, thin APs are simple devices that must be configured from the wireless controller's console.

Centralized wireless management is made possible by a lightweight wireless protocol, such as Cisco's proprietary LWAPP (Lightweight Access Point Protocol), or Cisco's newer CAPWAP (Control and Provisioning of Wireless Access Points), both of which direct all wireless frames to the controller by adding extra headers to the frames. The wireless controller can provide centralized authentication for wireless clients, load balancing, and channel management so that neighboring APs don't try to use overlapping channels. The controller also manages AP redundancy by directing wireless traffic to alternate APs when an AP fails. Wireless controllers can also detect the presence of rogue access points by recognizing when an unauthorized AP attempts to connect to the network.

Large numbers of wireless clients, such as you might find at a large corporate office or at a convention center, can overwhelm a single wireless VLAN. The broadcast traffic between so many devices would slow the network to a crawl. The solution is to use several VLANs, with wireless clients balanced across the various VLANs and their respective resources. Wireless controllers make this happen through a feature called VLAN pooling, which is accomplished by grouping multiple VLANs into a single VLAN group, or pool, and then dynamically assigning wireless clients to each successive VLAN in the pool.

10

Troubleshooting VMs and VLANs

Virtual networks resemble physical networks in many aspects. The same concerns regarding addressing, performance, security, and fault tolerance apply. In some cases—for example, when it comes to backups, troubleshooting, and software updates—virtual network management is nearly identical to physical network management. In other cases, management differs only slightly. For example, earlier in this chapter you learned that a DHCP server is included in virtualization software. Running on a host, it dynamically assigns IP addresses for virtual machines in NAT and host-only modes just as a DHCP server on a physical network assigns addresses for its physical clients. However, despite all the similarities between physical and virtual networks, an important difference arises when managing virtual machines in VLANs.

Earlier in the chapter, you learned that VLANs are broadcast domains, logically defined on a physical switch. On a network that uses virtual machines, VLANs will typically include those VMs.

You also know that to create a VLAN you modify a physical switch's configuration. However, to add VMs to a VLAN defined on a physical network, you use the hypervisor to modify a *virtual* switch's configuration. In other words, VMs are not added to a preexisting VLAN on the physical switch that manages that VLAN. Next, let's see how VMs can be incorporated into multiple VLANs.

Applying Concepts

Incorporate VMs into VLANs

Because virtualization programs vary, the steps required and the nomenclature used here will differ depending on what program you use. However, the concepts are the same.

Suppose you work at a small company whose network consists of four VLANs defined on its primary backbone switch. The VLANs subdivide traffic by group as follows: Management, Research, Test, and Public. On the network, they are defined as VLAN 120, VLAN 121, VLAN 122, and VLAN 123, respectively. To consolidate resources, your company is migrating its five physical file servers to virtual file servers on a single host using a VMware program called vSphere. The hypervisor portion of vSphere and the interface that allows you to manage virtual machines and the virtual networks they belong to is called VMware ESXi Server.

1. *Create and configure the VMs*—As you create the five virtual servers on your new host server, you configure each of their vNICs to operate in bridged mode. Furthermore, you decide to assign each virtual server a static IP address. The five new virtual servers are connected to the same virtual switch. By default, each vNIC is assigned a single port, or bridge, on the virtual switch. (If you create multiple vNICs for your servers, each vNIC would connect to a separate port.) Because the vNICs operate in bridged mode, the virtual servers can access the physical network through the host's physical interface. Likewise, nodes on the physical network can access the virtual servers through the host's physical interface.

2. *Install software in each VM*—Next, you install a guest OS and applications on your virtual servers and customize software and NOS parameters.

3. *Add VMs to VLANs*—Finally, you are ready to add the servers to the appropriate VLANs. In this example, suppose all five servers belong to the Management, Research, and Test VLANs, and only one of them belongs to the Public VLAN.

   In VMware, vNICs can be assigned to port groups. Grouping ports allows you to apply certain characteristics to multiple vNICs easily and quickly. Notably, all the vNICs in a port group can be assigned to one VLAN with a single command. For example, the vNICs for all five file servers will be assigned to port groups 120, 121, and 122. The vNIC for one file server will also be assigned to port group 123. Next, you associate each of the port groups with a VLAN. For example, you would associate port group 120 with VLAN 120, port group 121 with VLAN 121, and so on.

   Notice that multiple vNICs can be assigned to a single port group. Also, a single vNIC can be assigned to multiple port groups. (Depending on your network management strategy, however, you might find it simpler to create multiple vNICs so that each vNIC is associated with a different port group, or VLAN.) In other virtualization programs, vNICs are assigned to VLANs by associating them directly with a VLAN number or with a bridge that is, in turn, associated with a VLAN.

4. *Configure the host's NIC in trunking mode*—Earlier in this chapter, you learned that a single physical interface can carry the traffic of multiple VLANs through trunking. Therefore, the host's physical NIC must be configured to operate in trunking mode for VLAN information to pass through. In other words, it must be capable of carrying the traffic of multiple VLANs. Virtualization software refers to the physical NIC, acting as an interface for VLANs, as a trunk.

Now that you have created virtual servers connected to a virtual switch, created port groups on the switch and assigned vNICs to those port groups, associated those port groups with VLANs, and ensured that your host's physical NIC is configured to act as a trunk, all traffic tagged for VLAN 120 will be transmitted to all five file servers, for example, and all traffic tagged for VLAN 123 will only be seen by one file server.

Figure 10-30 illustrates this example of multiple virtual servers connected to multiple VLANs.

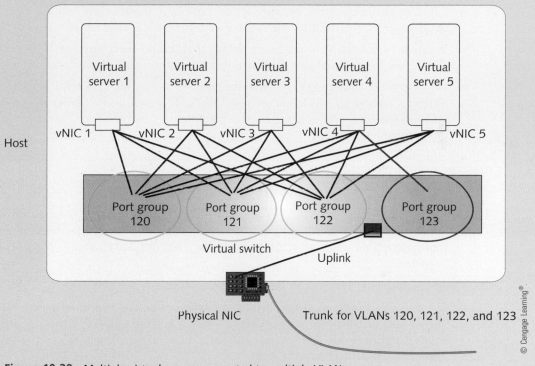

Figure 10-30 Multiple virtual servers connected to multiple VLANs

The virtual network for a company that manages multiple virtual file servers and multiple VLANs would likely be more complicated than the example described in this section. For instance, as a network administrator, you might ensure high performance by using two physical NICs on the host and associating a virtual server's vNIC with both. You might instruct the virtualization software to balance loads between multiple vNICs on a busy server. You might create multiple virtual switches on the host to further separate traffic. You might even create duplicates of your virtual servers on a second physical host to ensure availability. For now, however, it is enough to understand the essential concepts of using VLANs in a combined virtual and physical network.

Chapter Summary

Segmentation and Subnetting

- Separating traffic by subnets or VLANs helps enhance security, improve network performance, and simplify troubleshooting.

- Adhering to the classful addressing model limits flexibility in determining the number of possible hosts in a single network.

- CIDR notation takes the network ID or a host's IP address and follows it with a forward slash (/), followed by the number of bits that are used for the network ID.

- To create a subnet, you must borrow bits that would represent host information in classful addressing and use those bits instead to represent network information.

- Each network class reserves a different number of bits for network information and a different number of bits for host information. Therefore, the number of possible hosts and subnets on a network will vary depending on your network class and the way you implement subnets.

- Supernetting allows you to combine contiguous networks that all use the same CIDR block into one supernet.

- To calculate a host's network ID given its IPv4 address and subnet mask, you can follow a logical process of combining bits known as ANDing.

- Subnetting in IPv6 is simpler than subnetting in IPv4. One substantial difference is that unlike IPv4 addressing, IPv6 addressing does not use class information when subnetting.

Virtualization

- For a single computer, virtualization can emulate the hardware, operating system, and/or applications. For networking, virtualization can emulate hardware, including cabling and network devices, and software, including the network operating system and network management systems.

Virtual Network Components

- When you create a VM, you use the virtualization program to assign the VM's software and hardware characteristics. These characteristics can differ completely from those of the host machine.

- VMs can communicate with a virtual switch on the host computer to reach the physical network and, thereby, communicate with physical or virtual routers, other network devices, and other hosts on its own or another network.

- A vNIC using bridged mode accesses a physical network using the host machine's NIC and appears to other nodes as just another client or server connected directly to the network.

- A vNIC using NAT mode relies on the host machine to act as a NAT device.

- In host-only mode, VMs on one host can exchange data with each other and with their host, but they cannot communicate with any nodes beyond the host.

- Sometimes virtual services and devices are implemented for the purpose of redundancy. In the case of routers, VRRP or HSRP is used to assign a virtual IP address to a group of virtual routers.

- In software defined networking (SDN), services are delivered by applications that are managed by a network controller, which also integrates all of the network's virtual and physical devices into one cohesive system.

VLANs and Trunking

- Programmable switches create VLANs by partitioning their ports into groups. In most situations, each VLAN is assigned its own subnet of IP addresses, so that a Layer 3 subnet includes the same group of hosts as does the Layer 2 VLAN.

- Switches and bridges use STP (Spanning Tree Protocol) to help eliminate the possibility of broadcast storms and other types of traffic loops.

- An unmanaged switch provides plug-and-play simplicity with minimal configuration options and has no IP address assigned to it. Managed switches, on the other hand, can be configured via a command-line interface and sometimes can be configured in groups.

- A large wireless network is often managed by a central wireless controller, which provides a central management console for all the APs in a network.

Troubleshooting VMs and VLANs

- In some cases—for example, when it comes to backups, troubleshooting, and software updates—virtual network management is nearly identical to physical network management. However, an important difference arises when managing virtual machines in VLANs. To create a VLAN, you modify a physical switch's configuration. However, to add VMs to a VLAN defined on a physical network, you use the hypervisor to modify a *virtual* switch's configuration.

10

Key Terms

For definitions of key terms, see the Glossary near the end of the book.

802.1aq

802.1D

802.1Q

802.1s

802.1w

access port

ANDing

BID (Bridge ID)

BPDU (Bridge Protocol Data Unit)

BPDU filter

BPDU guard

bridged mode

CAPWAP (Control and Provisioning of Wireless Access Points)

CIDR (Classless Interdomain Routing)

CIDR block

CIDR notation

classful addressing

classless routing

control plane

data plane

default VLAN

designated port

DHCP relay agent

extended network prefix

guest

host

host-only mode

HSRP (Hot Standby Routing Protocol)

Hyper-V

hypervisor

in-band management

`ip helper-address`

KVM (Kernel-based Virtual Machine)

LWAPP (Lightweight Access Point Protocol)

magic number

managed switch

management console

MSTP (Multiple Spanning Tree Protocol)

NAT mode

native VLAN

network controller

network ID

network number

network prefix

OpenFlow

out-of-band management

prefix mask

root bridge

root port

route aggregation

route prefix

route summarization

routing prefix

RSTP (Rapid Spanning Tree Protocol)

SAID (security association identifier)

slash notation

software defined networking (SDN)

SPB (Shortest Path Bridging)

stack master

STP (Spanning Tree Protocol)

supernet

supernet mask

supernetting

tag

thick AP

thin AP

TRILL (Transparent Interconnection of Lots of Links)

trunk port

trunking

unmanaged switch

virtual adapter

virtual appliance

virtual bridge

virtual console

virtual IP address

virtual machine manager

virtual server

virtual switch

virtual terminal

virtual workstation

VirtualBox

virtualization

VLAN (virtual local area network)

VLAN hopping attack

VLAN pooling

VMware

vNIC (virtual network interface card)

VRRP (Virtual Router Redundancy Protocol)

VTP (VLAN trunking protocol)

Wi-Fi controller

wireless controller

WLAN controller

Review Questions

1. How many bits of a Class A IP address are used for host information?

   a. 8 bits

   b. 16 bits

   c. 24 bits

   d. 32 bits

2. What is the formula for determining the number of possible hosts on a network?

   a. $2^n = Y$

   b. $2^n - 2 = Y$

   c. $2^h = Z$

   d. $2^h - 2 = Z$

3. Which of the following is *not* a good reason to subnet a network?

   a. To reduce the number of hosts on the same network

   b. To increase the number of unique networks available

   c. To reduce the number of routing table entries by combining several entries

   d. To segment a network

4. What is the software that allows you to define VMs and manage resource allocation and sharing among them?

    a. Host

    b. Guest

    c. Switch

    d. Hypervisor

5. What virtual, logically defined device operates at the Data Link layer to pass frames between nodes?

    a. Virtual bridge

    b. Virtual firewall

    c. Virtual switch

    d. Virtual router

6. With which network connection type does the VM obtain IP addressing information from its host?

    a. Bridged mode

    b. Managed mode

    c. NAT mode

    d. Host-only mode

7. Which protocol assigns a virtual IP to a group of routers?

    a. VTP

    b. VRRP

    c. SDN

    d. STP

8. While designing your network's VLAN topology, your team has decided to use a centrally managed DHCP server rather than creating a separate DHCP server for each VLAN. What software will you need?

    a. DHCP server

    b. Hypervisor

    c. DHCP relay agent

    d. Subnet mask

9. Which port on a switch manages traffic for multiple VLANs?

    a. Access port

    b. Console port

    c. Serial port

    d. Trunk port

10

10. Telnet and SSH are called _____ systems because they use the existing network and its protocols to interface with the switch.

    a. virtual terminal

    b. management console

    c. in-band management

    d. switch port security

11. What is the network ID with CIDR notation for the IP address 172.16.32.108 with the subnet mask 255.255.255.0?

12. Suppose you have leased two Class C licenses, 115.100.10.0 and 115.100.11.0. You want to use all these Class C IP addresses in one supernet. What is the CIDR notation for this supernet? What is its supernet mask?

13. Suppose your company has leased one Class C license, 120.10.10.0, and wants to sublease the first half of these IP addresses to another company. What is the CIDR notation for the subnet to be subleased? What is the subnet mask for this network?

14. What are four advantages to using virtualization on a network?

15. How does a vNIC get a MAC address?

16. Subnetting operates at Layer _____ while VLANs function at Layer _____.

17. Which VLAN on a switch manages untagged frames?

18. An attacker configures a VLAN frame with two tags instead of just one. The first tag directs the frame to the authorized VLAN. After the frame enters the first VLAN, the switch appropriately removes the tag, then discovers the next tag, and sends the frame along to a protected VLAN, which the attacker is not authorized to access. What kind of attack is this?

19. Why is a BPDU filter needed at the demarc point?

20. Only one _____ exists on a network using STP.

Hands-On Projects

Project 10-1: Calculate Subnets

In this chapter, you subnetted a Class C private network into six subnets. In this project, you work with a Class B private network. Complete the steps as follows:

1. Your employer is opening a new location, and the IT director has assigned you the task of calculating the subnet numbers for the new LAN. You've determined that you need 50 subnets for the Class B network beginning with the network ID 172.20.0.0. How many host bits will you need to use for network information in the new subnets?

2. After the subnetting is complete, how many unused subnets will be waiting on hold for future expansion, and how many possible hosts can each subnet contain?

3. What is the new subnet mask?

4. Complete the following table:

Subnet number	Extended network prefix	Range of host addresses	Broadcast address
1	172.20.0.0	172.20.0.1 through 172.20.3.254	
2	172.20.4.0	through 172.20.7.254	
3		172.20.8.1 through	172.20.11.255
4			
5			
...	...	...	...
50			

5. What is the CIDR notation for this network?

6. What is the broadcast address of the subnet for the host at 172.20.6.139?

7. Is the host at 172.20.11.250 on the same subnet as the host at 172.20.12.3? How do you know?

Project 10-2: Calculate a Supernet

Complete the following steps to practice calculating a supernet:

10

1. Starting with the network ID 192.16.20.0/24, what is the default Class C subnet mask for this network? Write this information both in decimal and in binary.

2. How many additional network bits must be used for host information in order to have about 2000 hosts per supernet? Use the same formula you learned for calculating number of hosts on a subnet. Write the new supernet mask in binary and in decimal notation.

3. What is the CIDR notation for the network ID now?

Project 10-3: Research Subnetting Calculation Shortcuts

Instructors, network technicians, and IT students have developed a plethora of shortcuts, mnemonics, and lock-step methods to calculate subnets. The trick is to find the method that clicks for you. In this project, you will research some of the options these various methods provide, and create your own "cheat sheet" to help prepare you for subnetting on the CompTIA Network+ exam.

1. Start with a search engine and, if you know you prefer videos instead of written instructions, limit your search to videos or images, or conduct your search on youtube.com. Do a search for topics such as "subnetting," "subnetting made easy," "subnetting tutorial," or "subnetting for dummies."

2. Explore at least three different methods of calculating subnets. (You can use the method presented in this book as one of your selections.) Take the time to understand each method, and why it works. List the Web links for each method you evaluated, and make a few general notes about how each method is performed and what you learned from it.

3. Select one of the methods that makes the most sense to you, and list the steps in detail. Imagine that you're tutoring another student in how to calculate subnets, and be sure to include enough detail that the steps would make sense to someone who doesn't already know how to calculate subnets.

4. If the method relies on any mnemonics, lists, diagrams, or formulas, draw those on an index card. Set the card somewhere that you will notice it on a daily basis, and each day for at least a week take a little time to review this mental starting point for subnet calculations. Redraw this information at least three times during the week.

5. Rework the scenario in Project 10-1 using your selected subnetting calculation method. Did you come up with the same numbers? What differences do you notice in the method presented in this book as compared with the method you selected?

Project 10-4: Troubleshoot Subnetting a Small Network

Recall that a subnet or broadcast domain is bound by routers. You can use hosts on a small network to demonstrate some of the problems that might arise when subnetting errors are made. To do this project, you'll need at least two computers connected via a consumer-grade, SOHO (small office/home office) router using a Class C private address range. These instructions are written for Windows 8.1 machines, but can be adapted for other operating systems. Complete the following steps to demonstrate the errors that occur when subnetting:

1. On computer A, open the Command Prompt window and use the **ipconfig** command to determine the computer's IP address, subnet mask, and default gateway. Write down this information. Confirm Internet connectivity by pinging one of Google's DNS servers using the command **ping 8.8.8.8**.

2. On computer B, open the Command Prompt window and use the **ipconfig** command to determine the computer's IP address, subnet mask, and default gateway. Write down this information. Confirm Internet connectivity with the command **ping 8.8.8.8**. Also ping computer A at its IP address to confirm that the two computers can talk to each other.

3. On computer A, right-click **Start**, click **Network Connections**, right-click the active network connection, and then click **Properties**.

4. Under *This connection uses the following items*, double-click **Internet Protocol Version 4 (TCP/IPv4)**, select **Use the following IP address**, and then fill in the following information:

   a. IP address: **10.0.2.3**

   b. Subnet mask: **255.255.255.0**

5. Click **OK**, return to the Command Prompt window and then repeat the **ipconfig** command to confirm the IP address and subnet mask changes. Ping computer B to determine if the two computers can communicate, then ping Google's DNS server to

determine if computer A has Internet connectivity. Was the `ping` command successful on either attempt? Why do you think this is the case?

6. Open the Internet Protocol Version 4 (TCP/IPv4) properties dialog box again. What IP address should the default gateway have? Enter that information and click **OK**.

7. Ping Google's DNS server again to determine if the computer has Internet connectivity. Was the `ping` command successful this time? Why do you think this is the case?

8. On computer B, right-click **Start,** click **Network Connections,** right-click the active network connection, and then click **Properties.**

9. Under *This connection uses the following items,* double-click **Internet Protocol Version 4 (TCP/IPv4),** select **Use the following IP address,** and fill in the following information:

   a. IP address: **10.0.2.5**

   b. Subnet mask: **255.255.255.0**

10. Click **OK,** return to the Command Prompt window, and then repeat the **`ipconfig`** command to confirm the IP address and subnet mask changes. Ping Google's DNS server to determine if the computer has Internet connectivity. Was the `ping` command successful? Why do you think this is the case?

11. On computer B, enter the command **`ping 10.0.2.3`**. Was the `ping` command successful? Why do you think this is the case?

12. What is the network ID of this subnet? What is the CIDR notation for this subnet? What is the broadcast address?

13. Reconfigure both computers to obtain an IP address automatically. Run the **`ipconfig`** command on each computer to confirm these changes, and ping Google's DNS server again to confirm Internet connectivity. Then close all windows.

10

Case Projects

CASE PROJECTS

Case Project 10-1: Design VLANs and Subnets

This project ties together several skills you have studied in this chapter. Suppose you have decided to implement VLANs as a solution for slow network performance on the company network depicted in Figure 10-25. You want two VLANs, one for the Manufacturing Department and one for the Administrative Department. Employees on all three floors of the building work in each department, as shown in the figure. You are authorized to purchase up to four programmable switches to replace existing switches, and you are not authorized to purchase a new router. The current private Class A network ID is 10.0.0.0. You have decided to subnet the VLANs to allow four VLANs, which will give some room for growth in the corporation. Do the following:

1. Draw a diagram of your network design solution, showing in the diagram the location of all programmable switches. Use color or another method to depict VLANs for each department.

2. What is the original subnet mask for the entire large network? What is the subnet mask of each VLAN?

3. If the Manufacturing VLAN uses the first available subnet, what is the network ID of this VLAN? If the Administrative VLAN uses the second available subnet, what is its network ID?

4. What is the range of host IP addresses of the Manufacturing VLAN? Of the Administrative VLAN?

5. Compare your network design solution with another student's design and discuss any differences you see.

CASE PROJECTS

Case Project 10-2: Explore VM Network Configuration Options in Oracle VirtualBox

Earlier in this book, you created at least one VM using Oracle VirtualBox. The instructions for this project are specific to VirtualBox, although they can be adapted to Hyper-V. The instructions also assume you have Windows 8.1 installed on the VM, although again, the steps could be adapted to another OS.

In this project, you will explore the network settings for the VM, practice communicating between the VM and the host machine, and practice communicating between the VM and a host on the Internet. The host computer, which is the physical computer, should be connected to the Internet. Complete the following steps:

1. Open VirtualBox and start the VM.

2. Open the Command Prompt window and use the **ipconfig** command to determine the VM's IPv4 address, subnet mask, and default gateway. Write down this information. Using this information, calculate the CIDR notation.

3. Check the VM's connection to the Internet by pinging one of Google's DNS servers with the command **ping 8.8.8.8**.

4. Open the Command Prompt window on the host computer, the physical PC hosting the VirtualBox VM. Use the **ipconfig** command on the physical PC to determine the host machine's IPv4 address, subnet mask, and default gateway, then calculate this IPv4 address's CIDR notation. Write down this information. How does this information compare with the VM's information? Are these two computers on the same subnet? How do you know?

5. Return to the Oracle VM VirtualBox Manager window. Right-click the VM listing in the left pane and click **Settings**.

6. In the Settings window, click **Network** in the left pane and then make sure the **Adapter 1** tab is selected, as shown in Figure 10-31. Notice in this figure that the adapter is attached to NAT.

7. Click the **Attached to** down arrow, click **Bridged Adapter**, and then click **OK**.

8. Return to the VM's window. You see a message indicating that the VM has detected a network change, and is requesting permission to find PCs and other devices and content on the network. Click **Yes**.

Figure 10-31   The NAT option should be selected

Source: VirtualBox

9. Repeat the **ipconfig** command. What are the IPv4 address, subnet mask, and default gateway now, and what is the CIDR notation? How does this information compare with the host PC's information? Are the two computers on the same subnet now?

10. On the VM, ping Google's DNS server again. Was the ping successful?

11. On the Oracle VM VirtualBox Manager window, return to the **VM's Settings, Network** menu, click the **Attached to** down arrow, click **Internal Network,** and then click **OK.**

12. On the VM, repeat **ipconfig** and ping Google's DNS server again. What changed?

13. On the Oracle VM VirtualBox Manager window, return to the **VM's Settings, Network** menu, click the **Attached to** down arrow, click **Host-only Adapter,** and then click **OK.**

14. On the VM, repeat the **ipconfig** command and then ping Google's DNS server. What changed?

15. Change the VM's Attached to setting to **NAT** and click **OK.** Close all windows on the VM, shut down the VM, and close all windows on the host machine.

## chapter 11

Wide Area Networks

After reading this chapter and completing the exercises, you will be able to:

- Identify a variety of uses for WANs

- Explain different WAN topologies, including their advantages and disadvantages

- Compare the characteristics of WAN technologies, including their switching type, throughput, media, security, and reliability

- Describe several WAN transmission and connection methods, including dial-up, ISDN, T-carriers, frame relay, DSL, broadband cable, broadband over power line, ATM, SONET, MPLS, and Metro Ethernet

- Describe wireless WAN technologies, including 802.16 (WiMAX), HSPA+, LTE, and satellite communications

- Explore common problems with WAN connections and ways to prevent Internet connection problems

On the Job

Several years ago, I was hired for a small project that involved setting up two routers between office locations in separate counties. The plan was to have the routers communicate continuously through a fractional T-1 line so the servers in each office could synchronize with each other. The configuration required two different phone companies to coordinate their services, because neither company offered coverage at both locations.

The work was completed successfully, but after two weeks it was decided that the connection was still too slow between the servers, and the speed of the frac (fractional) T-1 would need to be increased. We contacted both phone companies and arranged for the upgrade.

The next day I got a call from the client saying that the link was down. I went to the nearest of the two offices and found that the router was fine but there was no link to the other router. I got on the phone and called Customer Support at the first phone company. When they checked the connection, they confirmed that the line on their end was configured correctly, but it was not working on the other end. They suggested that I contact the other phone company because they had no control of the line on the other end of the link.

I understood the company's dilemma, but having learned the art of assertive communication, I requested that the technician stay on the phone with me while I called the second company. Once we were able to explain the issue to the second phone company, their technician checked their end of the line, and found that there was indeed a problem on that end.

It turned out that the outage occurred because the second company had created two work orders to process the service change. One order was to disconnect the old service and the other was to upgrade the service to the new speed. The upgrade was completed first before the disconnect. Then the disconnect work order was completed, disconnecting the upgraded service.

The second phone company got the link working again. While I still had technicians from both companies on the phone, I decided to ask the two companies to compare settings. They discovered that several settings were improperly configured, and were able to correct these issues so that the link worked even better than before the outage.

Not only was the connection repaired, but it was improved because the two phone companies communicated with each other.

Steven Fried
Windows System Administrator

In previous chapters, you have learned about basic transmission media, network models, and networking hardware associated with LANs (local area networks). This chapter focuses on WANs (wide area networks), which, as you know, are networks that connect two or more geographically distinct LANs. WANs are significant concerns for organizations attempting to meet the needs of telecommuting workers, global business partners, and Internet-based commerce.

The distance requirements of WANs affect their entire infrastructure, and, as a result, WANs differ from LANs in many respects. To understand the fundamental difference between a LAN and a WAN, think of the hallways and stairs of your house as LAN pathways. These interior passages allow you to go from room to room. To reach destinations outside your house, however, you need to use sidewalks and streets. These public thoroughfares are analogous to WAN pathways—except that WAN pathways are not necessarily public.

This chapter discusses WAN topologies and various technologies used by WANs. It also notes the potential pitfalls in establishing and maintaining WANs.

WAN Essentials

A WAN traverses a significant distance and usually connects LANs. Each of the following scenarios demonstrates a need for a WAN:

- A bank with offices around the state needs to connect those offices to gather transaction and account information into a central database. Furthermore, it needs to connect with global financial clearinghouses to, for example, conduct transactions with other institutions.

- Regional sales representatives for a national pharmaceutical company need to submit their sales figures to a file server at the company's headquarters and receive email from the company's mail server.

- An automobile manufacturer in Detroit contracts out its plastic parts manufacturing to a Delaware-based company. Through WAN links, the auto manufacturer can video-conference with the plastics manufacturer, exchange specification data, and even examine the parts for quality from a remote location.

- A clothing manufacturer sells its products over the Internet to customers throughout the world.

Although all of these businesses need WANs, they might not need the same kinds of WANs. Depending on the traffic load, budget, geographical breadth, and commercially available technology, each might implement a different transmission method. For every business need, a few appropriate WAN connection types might exist. However, many WAN technologies can coexist on the same network.

The following list summarizes the major characteristics of WANs and explains how a WAN differs from a LAN:

- LANs connect nodes, such as workstations, servers, printers, and other devices, in a small geographical area on a single network, whereas WANs use networking devices, such as routers and modems, to connect networks spread over a wide geographical area.

- Both LANs and WANs use the same protocols from Layers 3 and higher of the OSI model. Whereas a LAN always uses packet-switched connections, a WAN can use either circuit-switched or packet-switched connections, although packet-switched connections are more common.

NOTE Recall that, in packet switching, packets belonging to the same data stream may follow different, optimal paths to their destination. As a result, packet switching uses bandwidth more efficiently and allows for faster transmission than if each packet in the data stream had to follow the same path, as in circuit switching. Packet switching is also more flexible than circuit switching because packet sizes may vary.

- LANs and WANs may differ at Layers 1 and 2 of the OSI model in access methods, topologies, and, sometimes, media. For example, the way DSL transmits bits over a WAN differs from the way Ethernet transmits bits over a LAN.
- LANs are mostly owned and operated by the companies that use them. On the other hand, WANs are owned and operated by telecommunications carriers, known as NSPs (network service providers), for example, AT&T, Verizon, Charter, and Comcast. Corporations lease WAN connections from these carriers, often with payments based on the amount of bandwidth actually used.

An organization can lease a private, dedicated line, which is a cable or other telecommunications path that is not shared with other users and has continuously available communications channels, or it can lease a virtual circuit, which, to the customer, logically appears to be a dedicated line, but, physically, can be any configuration through the carrier cloud. Private or dedicated lines are generally more expensive than virtual circuits and come in a variety of types that are distinguished by their capacity and transmission characteristics. One advantage of virtual circuits is that a company can purchase limited bandwidth, and then use the channel only when it needs to transmit data. When that company is not using the channel, it remains available for use by other virtual circuits.

The individual geographic locations or endpoints connected by a WAN are known as WAN sites. A WAN link is a connection between one WAN site (or endpoint) and another site (or endpoint). WAN links can be point-to-point (connects one site to only one other site) or multipoint (connects one site to two or more other sites). Figure 11-1 illustrates the difference between WAN and LAN connectivity.

The customer's endpoint device on the WAN is called the Data Terminal Equipment (DTE), and the carrier's endpoint device for the WAN is called the Data Communications Equipment (DCE). For example, when you connect a home router and a DSL modem to make a DSL connection to an ISP, the router is the DTE and the modem is the DCE. Figure 11-2 shows this setup, with a router and modem used at both the customer and ISP sites. Generally, the DTE is the responsibility of the customer and the DCE is the responsibility of the ISP. The DTE communicates on the

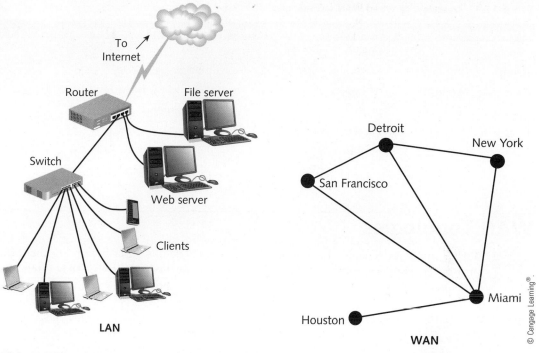

Figure 11-1 Differences in LAN and WAN connectivity

Figure 11-2 A router and modem define the endpoints where a LAN connects to a WAN

LAN, and the DCE communicates on the WAN. Sometimes the DTE and DCE are combined in the same device. For example, a router might have one WAN network adapter that connects to a fiber-optic or frame relay WAN and one LAN network adapter that connects to an Ethernet, twisted-pair LAN.

WAN technologies differ in terms of speed, reliability, cost, distance covered, and security. Also, some are defined by specifications at the Data Link layer, whereas others are defined by specifications at the Physical layer of the OSI model. Table 11-1 provides a high-level view of the various wired WAN technologies discussed in this chapter.

The following section describes different topologies used on WANs.

Table 11-1 Overview of wired WAN technologies

Primary media	Functions at OSI Layer 1	Functions at OSI Layer 2
Copper	Dial-up over PSTN	PPP
Copper	ISDN over PSTN	PPP or frame relay
Copper or fiber optic	T-carriers	PPP, HDLC, frame relay, or ATM
Copper or fiber optic	DSL	PPP, Ethernet, or ATM
Copper and fiber optic	Broadband cable	Broadband cable
Fiber optic	SONET	PPP, frame relay, ATM, MPLS, or Metro Ethernet

© 2016 Cengage Learning®

WAN Topologies

WAN topologies resemble LAN topologies, but their details differ because of the distance they must cover, the larger number of users they serve, and the heavy traffic they often handle. The following sections describe common WAN topologies and special considerations for each.

The CompTIA Network+ exam expects you to know about the bus, ring, star, partial-mesh, and full-mesh WAN topologies.

Bus Topology

A WAN in which each site is directly connected to no more than two other sites in a serial fashion is known as a bus topology WAN. A bus topology WAN is similar to a bus topology LAN in that each site depends on every other site in the network to transmit and receive its traffic. However, bus topology LANs use computers with shared access to one cable, whereas the WAN bus topology connects different locations through point-to-point links.

A bus topology WAN is often the best option for organizations with only a few sites and the capability to use dedicated circuits. Some examples of dedicated circuits include T-1, DSL, and ISDN connections, all of which are detailed later in this chapter. Dedicated circuits make it possible to transmit data regularly and reliably. Figure 11-3 depicts a bus topology WAN using T-1, T-3, and DSL connections.

Ring Topology

In a ring topology WAN, each site is connected to two other sites so that the entire WAN forms a ring pattern, as shown in Figure 11-4. This architecture is similar to the simple ring topology used on a LAN, except that a WAN ring topology connects locations rather than local nodes.

Also, on most modern WANs, a ring topology relies on redundant rings to carry data. Using redundant rings means that a ring topology WAN cannot be taken down by the loss of one site; instead, if one site fails, data can be rerouted around the WAN in a different direction.

adapter was most likely an ISDN router, whereas the terminal equipment could be an Ethernet card in the user's workstation plus, perhaps, a phone.

NOTE The BRI configuration depicted in Figure 11-11 applies to installations in North America only. Because transmission standards differ in Europe and Asia, different numbers of B channels are used in ISDN connections in those regions.

PRI (Primary Rate Interface) used 23 B channels and one 64-Kbps D channel, as represented by the notation 23B+D. PRI was less commonly used by individual subscribers than BRI was, but it could be selected by businesses and other organizations that needed more throughput. As with BRI, the separate B channels in a PRI link could carry voice and data, independently of each other or bonded together. The maximum potential throughput for a PRI connection was 1.544 Mbps.

PRI and BRI connections could be interconnected on a single network. PRI links used the same kind of equipment as BRI links, but required the services of an extra network termination device, called an **NT2 (Network Termination 2)**, to handle the multiple ISDN lines. Figure 11-12 depicts a typical PRI link as it would have been installed in North America.

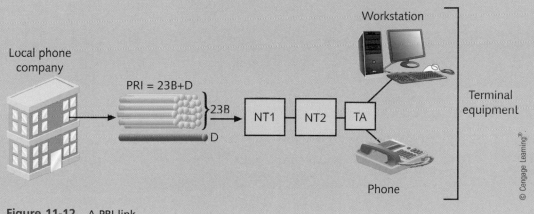

Figure 11-12   A PRI link

T-Carriers

Network+
1.4
7 APPLICATION
6 PRESENTATION
5 SESSION
4 TRANSPORT
3 NETWORK
2 DATA LINK
1 PHYSICAL
Another WAN transmission method that grew from a need to transmit digital data at high speeds over the PSTN is T-carrier technology, which includes T-1s, fractional T-1s, and T-3s. **T-carrier** standards, also called T-CXR standards, specify a method of signaling, which means they belong to the Physical layer of the OSI model. A T-carrier uses TDM (time division multiplexing) over two wire pairs (one for transmitting and one for receiving) to divide a single

channel into multiple channels. For example, multiplexing enables a single T-1 circuit to carry 24 channels, each capable of 64-Kbps throughput; thus, a T-1 has a maximum capacity of 24 × 64 Kbps, or 1.544 Mbps. Each channel may carry data, voice, or video signals. The medium used for T-carrier signaling can be ordinary copper wire, fiber-optic cable, or wireless links.

AT&T developed T-carrier technology in 1957 in an effort to digitize voice signals and thereby enable such signals to travel longer distances over the PSTN. Before that time, voice signals, which were purely analog, were expensive to transmit over long distances because of the number of connectivity devices needed to keep the signal intelligible. In the 1970s, many businesses installed T-1s to obtain more voice throughput per line. In the 1990s, with increased data communication demands, such as Internet access and geographically dispersed offices, T-1s became a popular way to connect WAN sites via leased lines.

The next section describes the various types of T-carriers, and then the chapter moves on to describe T-carrier connectivity.

Types of T-Carriers

A number of T-carrier varieties are available to businesses today, as shown in Table 11-2.

Table 11-2 T-carrier specifications

Signal level	T-carrier	Number of T-1s	Number of channels	Throughput (Mbps)
DS0	—	1/24	1	.064
DS1	T-1	1	24	1.544
DS1C	T-1C	2	48	3.152
DS2	T-2	4	96	6.312
DS3	T-3	28	672	44.736
DS4	T-4	168	4032	274.176
DS5	T-5	240	5760	400.352

© 2016 Cengage Learning®

The speed of a T-carrier depends on its signal level. The term **signal level** refers to the T-carrier's Physical layer electrical signaling characteristics as defined by ANSI standards in the early 1980s. **DS0 (digital signal, level 0)** is the equivalent of one data or voice channel. All other signal levels are multiples of DS0.

You may hear *signal level* and *carrier* terms used interchangeably—for example, DS1 and T-1. In fact, **T-1 (terrestrial carrier level 1)** is the implementation of the DS1 standard used in North America and most of Asia. In Europe, the standard high-speed carrier connections are E-1 and E-3. Like T-1s and T-3s, E-1s and E-3s use time division multiplexing. However, an E-1 allows for 32 channels and offers 2.048-Mbps throughput. An E-3 allows for 512 channels and offers 34.368-Mbps throughput. Using special hardware, T-1s can interconnect with E-1s and T-3s with E-3s for international communications.

As a networking professional, you might work with T-1 or T-3 lines. In addition to knowing their capacity, you should be familiar with their costs and uses. T-1 lines are commonly leased by businesses to connect branch offices or to connect to a carrier, such as an ISP. Because a T-3 provides 28 times more throughput than a T-1, some organizations find that multiple T-1s—rather than a single T-3—can accommodate their throughput needs. For example, suppose a university research laboratory needs to transmit molecular images over the Internet to another university, and its peak throughput need (at any given time) is 10 Mbps. The laboratory would require seven T-1s (10 Mbps divided by 1.544 Mbps equals 6.48 T-1s). Leasing seven T-1s would prove much less expensive for the university than leasing a single T-3.

NETWORK+ EXAM TIP

Recall from Chapter 7 that PPP is a connection protocol used to connect WAN endpoints. The CompTIA Network+ exam covers a version of PPP called Multilink PPP (MLPPP or MLP) that bonds multiple PPP connections to act as a single line and is a type of link aggregation. MLP was originally designed to bond dial-up connections, such as ISDN, but today it is more commonly used for bonding T-1 or T-3 lines.

The cost of T-1s varies from region to region. Leasing a full T-1 might cost anywhere from $200 to $1200 per month in access fees. The longer the distance between the provider (such as an ISP or a telephone company) and the subscriber, the higher a T-1's monthly charge. For example, a T-1 between Houston and New York will cost more than a T-1 between Washington, D.C., and New York. Similarly, a T-1 from a suburb of New York to the city center will cost more than a T-1 from the city center to a business three blocks away.

For small organizations that do not need as much as 1.544-Mbps throughput, a fractional T-1 might be a better option. A fractional T-1 lease allows organizations to use only some of the channels on a T-1 line and be charged according to the number of channels they use. Thus, fractional T-1 bandwidth can be leased in multiples of 64 Kbps. A fractional T-1 is best suited to businesses that expect their traffic to grow and that may require a full T-1 eventually, but can't currently justify leasing a full T-1.

T-3s are more expensive than T-1s and are used by more data-intensive businesses—for example, computer consulting firms that provide online data backups and warehousing for a number of other businesses or large long-distance carriers. The monthly service fee of a T-3 varies based on usage. If a customer uses the full T-3 bandwidth of 45 Mbps, for example, the monthly charges might be as high as $10,000 for a longer-distance connection. Of course, T-carrier costs will vary depending on the service provider, your location, and the distance covered by the T-3.

T-Carrier Connectivity

The approximate costs mentioned previously include monthly access, but not connectivity hardware. Every T-carrier line requires connectivity hardware at both the customer site and the local telecommunications provider's switching facility. Connectivity hardware may be purchased or leased. If your organization uses an ISP to establish and service your T-carrier line, you might lease the connectivity equipment. If you lease the line directly from the local carrier and you anticipate little change in your connectivity requirements over time, however, you might want to purchase the hardware.

11

T-carrier lines require specialized connectivity hardware that cannot be used with other WAN transmission methods. In addition, T-carrier lines require different media, depending on their throughput. In the following sections, you will learn about the physical components of a T-carrier connection between a customer site and a local carrier.

Wiring   As mentioned earlier, the T-carrier system is based on AT&T's original attempt to digitize existing long-distance PSTN lines. T-1 technology can use UTP or STP (unshielded or shielded twisted pair) copper wiring—in other words, plain telephone wire—coaxial cable, microwave, or fiber-optic cable as its transmission media. However, because the digital signals require a clean connection (that is, one less susceptible to noise and attenuation), STP is preferable to UTP. For T-1s using STP, repeaters must regenerate the signal approximately every 6000 feet. Twisted-pair wiring cannot adequately carry the high throughput of multiple T-1s or T-3 transmissions. Thus, for multiple T-1s, fiber-optic cabling is the medium of choice.

Cable Termination   In Chapter 5, you learned how to terminate UTP cable in an RJ-45 connector, the type used for most patch cables on LANs. However, when copper cabling is used to carry T-1 traffic, it terminates in an **RJ-48** connector. RJ-48 and RJ-45 connectors are the same size and contain the same number of pins, but wire pairs used to carry T-1 traffic are terminated differently in an RJ-48, as shown in Figure 11-13. T-1 traffic uses pins 1 and 2 for the receive pair and pins 4 and 5 for the transmit pair.

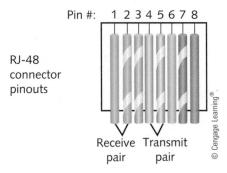

Figure 11-13   T-1 wire terminations in an RJ-48 connector

As with LAN patch cables, T-1 cables can be straight-through, in which case pinouts at both ends match those pictured in Figure 11-13. Straight-through cables might be used at a carrier's facility to connect a patch panel with a T-1 router interface. T-1 crossover cables also exist. In a crossover cable, the transmit and receive pairs are reversed, as shown in Figure 11-14. A T-1 crossover cable could be used to connect two connectivity devices, such as CSUs/DSUs (discussed later) or **WAN interface cards (WICs)** that act as CSU/DSUs.

At the customer's demarc (demarcation point), either inside or outside the building, RJ-48 connectors terminate in a **smart jack**, a type of NIU. In addition to terminating the line, a smart jack functions as a monitoring point for the connection. If the line between the carrier and customer experiences significant data errors, the smart jack will report this fact to the carrier. Technicians can also check the status of the line at the smart jack. Most smart jacks include LEDs associated with transmitted and received signals. For example, a steady

Pin assignments
on Plug A

Pin assignments
on Plug B

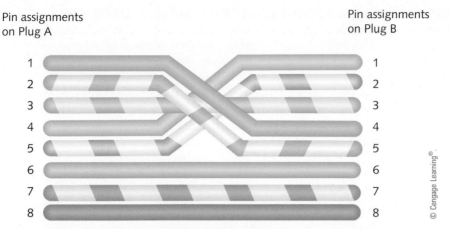

Figure 11-14 T-1 crossover cable terminations

green light on the display indicates no connectivity problems, whereas a flickering light indicates data errors. A power light indicates whether or not the smart jack is receiving any signal. Figure 11-15 shows a smart jack (or network interface) designed to be used with a T-1.

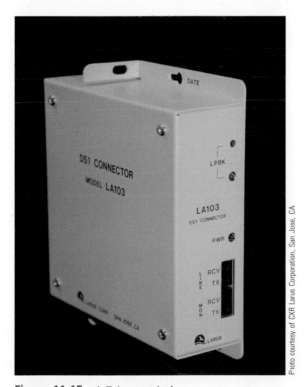

Figure 11-15 A T-1 smart jack

The smart jack is not capable of interpreting data, however. For that, the T-carrier signals depend on a CSU/DSU.

CSU/DSU (Channel Service Unit/Data Service Unit) The DTE or endpoint device for a leased line is a CSU/DSU, which consists of a CSU (channel service unit) and DSU (data service unit). (You might also see the term written in reverse order: DSU/CSU.) The device can be a stand-alone device or an interface card. The CSU provides termination for the digital signal and ensures connection integrity through error correction and line monitoring. The DSU converts the T-carrier frames into frames the LAN can interpret and vice versa. It also connects T-carrier lines with terminating equipment. Finally, a DSU usually incorporates a multiplexer. (In some T-carrier installations, the multiplexer can be a separate device connected to the DSU.)

For an incoming T-carrier line, the multiplexer separates its combined channels into individual signals that can be interpreted on the LAN. For an outgoing T-carrier line, the multiplexer combines multiple signals from a LAN for transport over the T-carrier. After being demultiplexed, an incoming T-carrier signal passes on to devices collectively known as terminal equipment. Examples of terminal equipment include switches, routers, or telephone exchange devices that accept only voice transmissions (such as a telephone switch).

Figure 11-16 shows a stand-alone CSU/DSU.

Courtesy of Kentrox, Inc.

Figure 11-16   A CSU/DSU

Figure 11-17 depicts a typical use of smart jacks, which you'll learn more about later in this chapter, and CSU/DSUs with a point-to-point T-1-connected WAN. In the following sections, you will learn how routers and switches integrate with CSU/DSUs and multiplexers to connect T-carriers to a LAN.

Figure 11-17   A point-to-point T-carrier connection

Terminal Equipment On a typical T-1-connected data network, the DTE or terminal equipment is a router, which translates between different Layer 3 protocols that might be used on the WAN and LAN. The router accepts incoming signals from a CSU/DSU standalone device and, if necessary, translates Network layer protocols, then directs data to its destination exactly as it does on any LAN.

On some implementations, the CSU/DSU is not a separate device, but is an expansion card installed in the router. An integrated CSU/DSU offers faster signal processing and better network performance and is also a less-expensive and lower-maintenance solution than using a separate CSU/DSU device. Figure 11-18 illustrates one way a router with an integrated CSU/DSU can be used to connect a LAN with a T-1 WAN link.

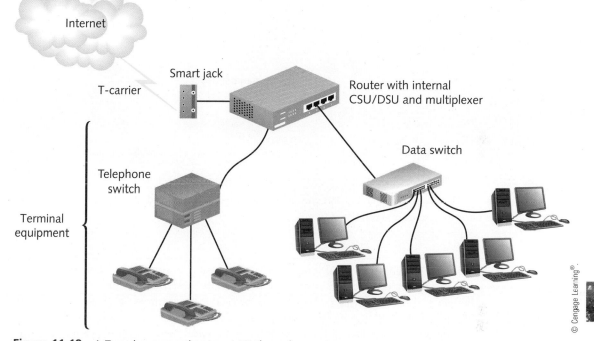

Figure 11-18   A T-carrier connecting to a LAN through a router

Frame Relay

Frame relay is a group of Layer 2 protocols defined by ITU and ANSI in 1984. It was originally designed as a fast packet-switched network over ISDN, although today frame relay is used as the Data Link protocol for various virtual circuit interfaces and media.

The name, *frame relay*, is derived from the fact that data is separated into frames, which are then relayed from one node to another without any verification or processing. Routers establish a virtual circuit and frames carry an identifier, called a **data-link connection identifier (DLCI)**, that routers read to determine which circuit to use for the frame. Therefore, frame relay is a connection-oriented protocol.

Frame relay supports two types of virtual circuits: an **SVC (switched virtual circuit)** or **PVC (permanent virtual circuit)**. SVCs are connections that are established when parties need to transmit, then terminated after the transmission is complete. PVCs are connections that are established before data needs to be transmitted and are maintained after the transmission is complete. Note that in a PVC, the connection is established only between the two points (the sender and receiver); the connection does not specify the exact route the data will travel. For example, an organization might use frame relay for communication among the LANs at each branch office. Each LAN has a PVC from the branch office to the ISP, and SVCs are established as needed for communication among LANs. See Figure 11-19.

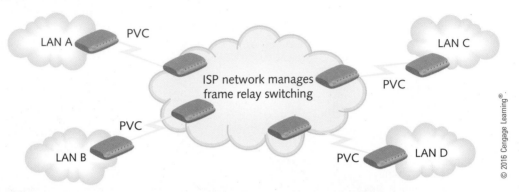

Figure 11-19   Four frame relay PVCs used to establish SVCs as needed for communication among remote LANs in an organization

PVCs are *not* dedicated, individual links. When you lease a frame relay circuit from your local carrier, your contract reflects the endpoints you specify and the amount of bandwidth you require between those endpoints. The service provider guarantees a minimum amount of bandwidth, called the CIR (committed information rate). Provisions usually account for bursts of traffic that occasionally exceed the CIR. When you lease a PVC, you share bandwidth with the other frame relay users on the backbone. PVC links are best suited to frequent and consistent data transmission.

The advantage to leasing a frame relay circuit over leasing a dedicated service is that you pay for only the amount of bandwidth required. Another advantage is that frame relay is less expensive than some other WAN technologies, depending on your location and its network availability. Also, frame relay is a long-established worldwide standard. Although frame relay was first used with various WAN topologies, today, frame relay is primarily used on a backbone WAN that connects two LANs.

DSL (Digital Subscriber Line)

DSL (digital subscriber line) is a WAN connection method introduced by researchers at Bell Laboratories in the mid-1990s. It operates over the PSTN and competes directly with T-1 and broadband cable services. DSL can span only limited distances without the help of repeaters and is, therefore, best suited to the local loop portion of a WAN link. Also, like T-carriers, DSL can support multiple data and voice channels over a single line.

DSL uses data modulation techniques at the Physical layer of the OSI model to achieve extraordinary throughput over regular telephone lines. To understand how DSL and voice signals can share the same line, it's helpful to note that telephone lines carry voice signals over a very small range of frequencies, between 300 and 3300 Hz. This leaves higher, inaudible frequencies unused and available for carrying data. Also recall that in data modulation, a data signal alters the properties of a carrier signal. Depending on its version, a DSL connection may use a modulation technique based on amplitude or phase modulation. However, in DSL, modulation follows more complex patterns than the modulation you learned about earlier in this book. The details of DSL modulation techniques are beyond the scope of this book. However, you should understand that the types of modulation used by a DSL version affect its throughput and the distance its signals can travel before requiring a repeater. The following section describes the different versions of DSL.

Types of DSL

The term xDSL refers to all DSL varieties. The better-known DSL varieties include ADSL (asymmetric DSL), G.Lite (a version of ADSL), HDSL (high bit-rate DSL), SDSL (symmetric or single-line DSL), VDSL (very high bit-rate or data rate DSL), and SHDSL (single-line high bit-rate DSL). In each case, the x in $xDSL$ is replaced by the variety name.

The types of DSL vary according to their throughput rates, data modulation techniques, capacity, and distance limitations, as well as how they use the PSTN. You'll learn about these differences in the following sections.

Symmetrical vs. Asymmetrical DSL types can be divided into two categories: asymmetrical and symmetrical. To understand the difference between these two categories, you must understand the concepts of downstream and upstream data transmission. The term downstream refers to data traveling from the carrier's switching facility to the customer. Upstream refers to data traveling from the customer to the carrier's switching facility.

In some types of DSL, the throughput rates for downstream and upstream traffic differ. In other words, if you were connected to the Internet via a DSL link, you could download images from the Internet more rapidly than you could upload them because the downstream throughput would be greater. A technology that offers more throughput in one direction than in the other is considered asymmetrical. In asymmetrical communications, downstream throughput is higher than upstream throughput. Asymmetrical communication is well suited to users who receive more information from the network than they send to it—for example, people watching movies online or people surfing the Web. ADSL and VDSL are examples of asymmetric DSL.

By contrast, symmetrical technology provides equal capacity for data traveling both upstream and downstream. Symmetrical transmission is suited to users who both upload and download significant amounts of data—for example, a bank's branch office that sends large volumes of account information to the central server at the bank's headquarters and, in turn, receives large amounts of account information from the central server at the bank's headquarters. HDSL, SDSL, and SHDSL are examples of symmetric DSL.

Modulation DSL versions also differ in the type of modulation they use. Some, such as the popular full-rate ADSL and VDSL, create multiple narrow channels in the higher frequency range to carry more data. For these versions, a splitter must be installed at the carrier and at the customer's premises to separate the data signal from the voice signal before it reaches the terminal equipment (for example, the phone or the computer). G.Lite, a slower and less-expensive version of ADSL, eliminates the splitter but requires the use of a filter to prevent high-frequency DSL signals from reaching the telephone. Other types of DSL, such as HDSL and SDSL, cannot use the same wire pair that is used for voice signals. Instead, these types of DSL use the extra pair of wires contained in a telephone cable (that are otherwise typically unused).

Capacity and Maximum Line Length   The types of DSL also vary in terms of their capacity and maximum line length. A VDSL line that carries as much as 52 Mbps in one direction and as much as 16 Mbps in the opposite direction can extend only a maximum of 1000 feet between the customer's premises and the carrier's switching facility. This limitation might suit businesses located close to a telephone company's CO (for example, in the middle of a metropolitan area), but it won't work for most individuals. The most popular form of DSL is **ADSL (asymmetric digital subscriber line)**. The latest version of ADSL is **ADSL2+M** (also called **ADSL Annex M**), which provides a maximum theoretical throughput of 24 Mbps downstream and a maximum of 3.3 Mbps upstream. However, the distance between the customer and the central office affects the actual throughput a customer experiences. Close to the central office, DSL achieves its highest maximum throughput. The farther away the customer's premises, the lower the throughput.

Published distance limitations and throughput can vary from one service provider to another, depending on how far the provider is willing to guarantee a particular level of service. In addition, service providers may limit each user's maximum throughput based on terms of the service agreement. For example, in 2011 AT&T capped the total amount of data transfer allowed for each of its DSL subscribers to 150 GB per month. The company instituted the new policy in response to a dramatic spike in downstream bandwidth usage due to Netflix streaming—in particular, online gaming. In fact, in 2010, Netflix accounted for nearly 30 percent of all downstream Internet traffic requested by fixed users in the United States. Today, many providers cap a subscriber's high-speed data usage, although typically the caps are higher now than the one in this example.

Next, you will learn how DSL connects to a business or residence over the PSTN.

DSL Connectivity

This section follows the path of an ADSL connection from a home computer, through the local loop, to the telecommunications carrier's switching facility. This describes the most common implementation of DSL, although it's important to keep in mind that variations exist.

Suppose you have an ADSL connection at home. One evening you open your Web browser and request the home page of your favorite sports team to find the last game's score. As you know, the first step in this process is establishing a TCP connection with the team's Web server. This initial TCP SYN message leaves your computer's NIC and travels over your home network to a DSL modem. A **DSL modem** is a device that modulates outgoing signals and demodulates incoming DSL signals. Thus, it contains receptacles to connect both to your incoming telephone line and to your computer or network connectivity device.

Because you are using ADSL, the DSL modem also contains a splitter to separate incoming voice and data signals. The DSL modem may be external or internal (as an expansion card, for example) to the computer. If external, it may connect to a computer's NIC via an RJ-45, USB, or wireless interface. If your home network contains more than one computer and you want all computers to share the DSL bandwidth, the DSL modem must connect to a device such as a switch or router, instead of just one computer. In fact, rather than using two separate devices, you could buy a router that combines DSL modem functionalities with the ability to connect multiple computers and share DSL bandwidth. A DSL modem is shown in Figure 11-20.

Figure 11-20   A DSL modem

When your SYN request arrives at the DSL modem, it is modulated according to the ADSL specifications. Then, the DSL modem forwards the modulated signal to your local loop—the lines that connect your home with the rest of the PSTN. For the first stretch of the local loop, the signal continues over four-pair UTP wire. At some distance less than 18,000 feet, it is combined with other modulated signals in a telephone switch, usually at a remote switching facility. (To accept DSL signals, your telecommunications carrier must have newer digital switching equipment. In the few remaining locales where carriers have not updated their switching equipment, DSL service is not available.)

Inside the carrier's remote switching facility, a splitter separates your line's data signal from any voice signals that are also carried on the line. Next, your request is sent to a device called a **DSLAM (DSL access multiplexer)**, which aggregates multiple DSL subscriber lines and connects them to the carrier's CO. Finally, your request is issued from your carrier's network to the Internet backbone, as pictured in Figure 11-21. The request travels over the Internet until it reaches your sports team's Web server. Barring line problems and Internet congestion, the entire journey happens in a fraction of a second. When your team's Web server responds to the SYN message, the data follows the same path, but in reverse.

Telecommunications carriers and manufacturers have positioned DSL as a competitor for T-1 and broadband cable services. The installation, hardware, and monthly access costs for DSL are significantly less than the cost for T-1s, but the cost in comparison with broadband varies widely by location. (At the time of this writing, ADSL costs approximately $35 per month in the United States, though prices vary by speed and location.) Generally speaking, DSL

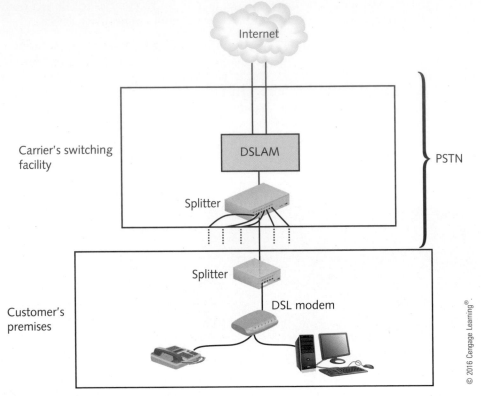

Figure 11-21   A DSL connection

throughput rates, especially upstream, are lower than broadband cable, its main competition among residential customers.

Broadband Cable

While local and long-distance phone companies strive to make DSL the preferred method of Internet access for consumers, cable companies are pushing their own connectivity option. This option, called broadband cable or cable modem access, is based on the coaxial cable wiring used for TV signals and was standardized by an international, cooperative effort orchestrated by CableLabs that yielded DOCSIS (Data Over Cable Service Interface Specification). Such wiring can theoretically transmit as much as 100 Mbps downstream and as much as 20 Mbps upstream. Thus, broadband cable is an asymmetrical technology. However, actual broadband cable throughput is typically limited (or throttled) by the cable companies and further diminished by the fact that physical connections are shared. Customers might be allowed, at most, 10 Mbps downstream and 3 Mbps upstream throughput. During peak times of use, they might see data rates of 3 Mbps downstream and 1 Mbps upstream, for example. The asymmetry of broadband cable makes it a logical choice for users who want to surf the

Web or download data from a network, although the suitable options available in specific areas can vary considerably.

Broadband cable connections require that the customer use a special cable modem, a device that modulates and demodulates signals for transmission and reception via cable wiring. The cable modem must conform to the correct version of DOCSIS supported by the ISP. Most newer cable modems use DOCSIS 3.0 and are backward compatible, but ISPs might charge extra when later modem models are used. Table 11-3 presents the three versions of DOCSIS along with their specifications.

Table 11-3 DOCSIS versions and specifications

Version	Maximum upstream throughput (Mbps)	Maximum downstream throughput (Mbps)	Description
DOCSIS 1.x (1.0 and 1.1)	9	38	Outdated; single channel; throughput was shared among customers
DOCSIS 2.x (2.0 and 2.0 + IPv6)	27	38	Single channel; reduces disparity between upstream and downstream throughputs
DOCSIS 3.x (3.0 and 3.1*)	27 per channel	38 per channel	Multiple channels: minimum of 4, no maximum

© 2016 Cengage Learning®

DOCSIS 3.1 specifications not released at time of printing. Upstream throughput is expected to reach 1 Gbps, and downstream throughput might reach up to 10 Gbps.

Applying Concepts

Determine a Cable Modem's DOCSIS Version

You can determine the DOCSIS version of a cable modem on a SOHO (small office/home office) network with a little detective work. This project requires a SOHO network serviced by broadband cable and a computer (Windows, Linux, or Mac) connected to the network. Complete the following steps to identify the DOCSIS version of a cable modem:

1. Examine the labels on the cable modem to determine the device's manufacturer and model number. In some cases, the DOCSIS version might be printed on one of these labels. If not, continue with the following steps.

2. Research the manufacturer and model number information online. You might find the DOCSIS information while conducting your research. If not, the minimum information you need is the cable modem's default internal IP address (such as 192.168.0.1 or 192.168.100.1) and admin username and password (if there is one).

3. Enter the default internal IP address in a Web browser and log on if necessary. Explore the user interface to locate the cable modem's hardware information. Figure 11-22 shows the hardware information for a cable modem made by ARRIS. What is the DOCSIS version of your cable modem?

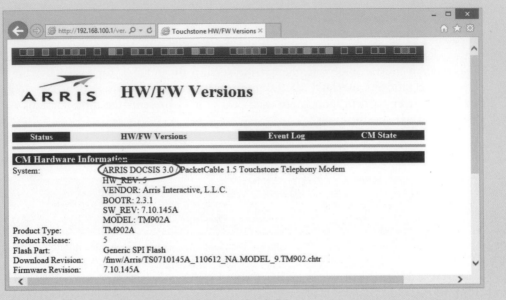

Figure 11-22 This cable modem's DOCSIS version is 3.0

Source: ARRIS

Cable modems operate at the Physical and Data Link layers of the OSI model, and, therefore, do not manipulate higher-layer protocols, such as IP. The cable modem connects to a customer's PC via the NIC's RJ-45, USB, or wireless interface. Alternately, the cable modem could connect to a connectivity device, such as a switch or router, thereby supplying bandwidth to a LAN rather than to just one computer. It's also possible to use a device that combines cable modem functionality with a router; this single device can then provide both the broadband cable connection and the capability of sharing the bandwidth between multiple nodes. Figure 11-23 portrays an example of a cable modem.

Figure 11-23 A cable modem

Before customers can subscribe to broadband cable, the cable company must have the necessary infrastructure. For starters, the cable company must use **HFC (hybrid fiber-coax)**, an expensive fiber-optic link that can support high frequencies, to connect the cable company's offices to a node location near the customer. Either fiber-optic or coaxial cable may connect the node to the customer's business or residence via a connection known as a **cable drop**. All cable drops for the cable subscribers in the same neighborhood connect to the local node. These nodes then connect to the cable company's central office, which is known as its **head-end**. At the head-end, the cable company can connect to the Internet through a variety of means (often via fiber-optic cable) or it can pick up digital satellite or microwave transmissions. The head-end can transmit data to as many as 1000 subscribers, in a one-to-many communication system. Figure 11-24 illustrates the infrastructure of a cable system.

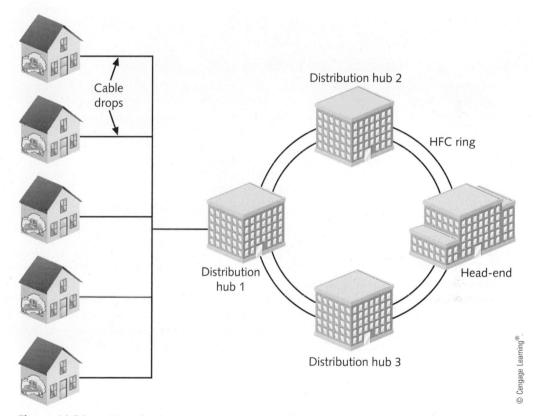

Figure 11-24   Cable infrastructure

Like DSL, broadband cable provides a dedicated and always-up, or continuous, connection that does not require dialing up a service provider. Unlike DSL, broadband cable requires many subscribers to share the same local line, thus raising concerns about security and actual (versus theoretical) throughput. For example, if your cable company supplied you and five of your neighbors with broadband cable services, one of your neighbors could, with some technical prowess, capture the data that you transmit to the Internet. (Modern cable networks provide encryption for data traveling to and from customer premises; however, these encryption schemes can be thwarted.) Moreover, the throughput of a cable line is fixed. As with any fixed resource, the more one claims, the less that is left for others. In other words, the greater the number of users sharing a single line, the less throughput available to each individual user. Cable companies counter this perceived disadvantage by rightly claiming that at some point (for example, at a remote switching facility or at the DSLAM interface), a telecommunications carrier's DSL bandwidth is also fixed and shared among a group of customers.

In the United States, broadband cable access costs approximately $30–$60 per month when bundled with cable TV and/or digital voice services. Broadband cable is less often used in businesses than DSL, primarily because most office buildings do not contain a coaxial cable infrastructure.

Network+ 5.4   Legacy Networking

BPL (Broadband over Power Line)

In addition to coaxial, twisted-pair, and fiber-optic cable, power lines can be used to deliver broadband Internet service. Starting around the year 2000, electric utilities began offering BPL (broadband over power line), or high-speed Internet access, over the electrical grid. The service promised potential for connecting remote users who might not be within reach of DSL or cable services, but who were connected to the power lines, to finally receive high-speed Internet access. BPL is shared among multiple customers, which limits practical throughputs to no more than 1 Mbps. Each customer accesses the network using a modem plugged into an electrical outlet. BPL requires users to be within 2 km of a repeater.

BPL didn't take off as planned, however, and promise for the service's widespread deployment peaked in the mid-2000s. Standards were subjected to opposition from many telecommunications groups and took a long time to develop. Necessary infrastructure upgrades, including numerous repeaters, cost more than anticipated. Also, signals transmitted via power lines are subject to much more noise than those carried by DSL or cable services. And, finally, amateur radio operators who claimed its frequencies interfered with their signals protested the service. Most U.S. utility companies that invested in BPL have abandoned it, despite the fact that IEEE published their BPL standard in 2010, which is simply called IEEE 1901-2010. Installations do exist, however, in some European countries.

NOTE

Power line networks can also be implemented on a LAN with Ethernet over power line, or Ethernet over power (EOP). A home's wiring can be used to transmit Ethernet signals through a pair of power-line adapters, one at each end of the connection, that plug into power outlets. These adapters can provide a network connection in areas of the home that can't receive a reliable Wi-Fi signal.

A somewhat similar technology is Ethernet over HDMI, in which Ethernet signals traverse Ethernet-enabled HDMI cables to connect a TV to the Internet. Not many devices support this technology yet, though, and HDMI by itself does a better job of streaming video.

All of these technologies are now united under the single IEEE 1905.1-2013 standard, operating between Layers 2 and 3, that integrates multiple wired and wireless home networking technologies, including IEEE 1901, IEEE 802.11, and IEEE 802.3.

ATM (Asynchronous Transfer Mode)

Along with frame relay, **ATM (Asynchronous Transfer Mode)** is a WAN technology that functions primarily at Layer 2, the Data Link layer, although its protocols can also reach to Layers 1 and 3. Its ITU standard prescribes both network access and signal multiplexing techniques. **Asynchronous** refers to a communications method in which nodes do not have to conform to any predetermined schemes that specify the timing of data transmissions. In asynchronous communications, a node can transmit at any instant, and the destination node must accept the transmission as it comes. To ensure that the receiving node knows when it has received a complete frame, asynchronous communications provide start and stop bits for each character transmitted. When the receiving node recognizes a start bit, it begins to accept a new character. When it receives the stop bit for that character, it ceases to look for the end of that character's transmission. Asynchronous data transmission, therefore, occurs in random stops and starts.

Like Ethernet, ATM specifies Data Link layer framing techniques. But what sets ATM apart from Ethernet is its fixed packet size. In ATM, a packet is called a cell and always consists of 48 bytes of data plus a 5-byte header. This fixed-sized, 53-byte packet allows ATM to provide predictable network performance. However, recall that a smaller packet size requires more overhead. In fact, ATM's smaller packet size does decrease its potential throughput, but the efficiency of using cells helps compensate for that loss.

Like frame relay, ATM relies on virtual circuits. On an ATM network, switches determine the optimal path between the sender and receiver and then establish this path before the network transmits data. Because ATM packages data into cells before transmission, with each cell traveling separately to its destination, ATM is typically considered a packet-switching technology. At the same time, the use of virtual circuits means that ATM provides the main advantage of circuit switching—that is, a point-to-point connection that remains reliably available to the transmission until it completes. The use of virtual circuits makes ATM a connection-oriented technology.

Establishing a reliable connection allows ATM to guarantee a specific QoS for certain transmissions. ATM networks can supply four QoS levels, from a "best effort" attempt for noncritical data to a guaranteed, real-time transmission for time-sensitive data. This is important for organizations using networks for time-sensitive applications, such as video and audio transmissions. For example, a company depicted in Figure 11-25 might want to use its ATM connection between two offices located at opposite sides of a state to carry voice phone calls with

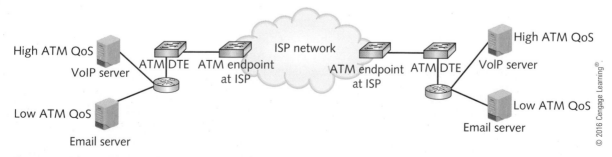

Figure 11-25   QoS can be defined for a point-to-point ATM connection

the highest possible QoS. On the other hand, the company might assign a low QoS to routine email messages exchanged between the two offices.

ATM cells can support multiple types of higher-layer protocols. In addition, the ATM networks can be integrated with Ethernet networks through the use of LANE (LAN Emulation). LANE encapsulates incoming Ethernet frames, then converts them into ATM cells for transmission over an ATM network.

ATM may run over fiber-optic cable or Cat 5 or better UTP or STP cable. When leasing ATM connections, you can choose to pay for only as much throughput as you think you'll need. This also allows you to tailor your desired QoS.

ATM is relatively expensive, is rarely used on small LANs, and is almost never used to connect typical workstations to a network. Although ATM was popular in the 1990s, it's now being replaced by Metro Ethernet, which is a cheaper WAN solution. Where ATM is still used, it's often deployed over the popular SONET WAN technology, discussed next.

SONET (Synchronous Optical Network)

SONET (Synchronous Optical Network) is a high-bandwidth WAN signaling technique developed for fiber-optic cabling by Bell Communications Research in the 1980s, and later standardized by ANSI and ITU. SONET specifies framing and multiplexing techniques at the Physical layer of the OSI model. Its four key strengths are that it can integrate many other WAN technologies, it offers fast data transfer rates, it allows for simple link additions and removals, and it provides a high degree of fault tolerance.

The word *synchronous* as used in the name of this technology means that data being transmitted and received by nodes must conform to a timing scheme. A clock maintains time for all nodes on a network. A receiving node in synchronous communications recognizes that it should be receiving data by looking at the time on the clock.

Perhaps the most important SONET advantage is that it provides interoperability. Before SONET, telecommunications carriers that used different signaling techniques (or even the same technique but different equipment) could not be assured that their networks could communicate. Now, SONET is often used to aggregate multiple T-1s or T-3s. SONET is also used as the underlying technology for ATM transmission. Furthermore, because it can work directly with the different standards used in different countries, SONET has emerged as the best choice for linking WANs between North America, Europe, and Asia. Internationally, SONET is known as SDH (Synchronous Digital Hierarchy).

SONET's extraordinary fault tolerance results from its use of a double-ring topology over fiber-optic cable. In this type of layout, one ring acts as the primary route for data, transmitting in a clockwise direction. The second ring acts as a backup, transmitting data counterclockwise around the ring. If, for example, a backhoe operator severs the primary ring, SONET would automatically reroute traffic to the backup ring without any loss of service. This characteristic, known as self-healing, makes SONET very reliable. (To lower the potential for a single accident to sever both rings, the cables that make up each ring should not lie adjacent to each other.) Figure 11-26 illustrates a SONET ring and its dual-fiber connections.

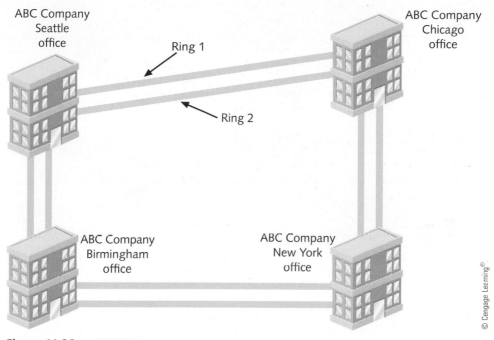

ABC Company
Seattle
office

Ring 1

Ring 2

ABC Company
Chicago
office

ABC Company
Birmingham
office

ABC Company
New York
office

© Cengage Learning®

Figure 11-26   A SONET ring

A SONET ring begins and ends at the telecommunications carrier's facility. In between, it connects an organization's multiple WAN sites in a ring fashion. It may also connect with multiple carrier facilities for additional fault tolerance. Companies can lease an entire SONET ring from a telecommunications carrier, or they can lease part of a SONET ring—for example, a circuit that offers T-1 throughput—to take advantage of SONET's reliability.

At both the carrier and the customer premises, a SONET ring terminates at a multiplexer. A multiplexer combines individual SONET signals on the transmitting end, and another multiplexer separates combined signals on the receiving end. On the transmitting end, multiplexers accept input from different network types (for example, a T-1 line) and format the data in a standard SONET frame. That means that many different devices might connect to a SONET multiplexer, including, for example, a private telephone switch, a T-1 multiplexer, and an ATM data switch. On the receiving end, multiplexers translate the incoming signals back into their original format. Most SONET multiplexers allow for easy additions or removals of connections to the SONET ring, which makes this technology easily adaptable to growing and changing networks. Figure 11-27 shows the devices necessary to connect a WAN site with a SONET ring. This is the simplest type of SONET connection; however, variations abound.

The data rate of a particular SONET ring is indicated by its OC (Optical Carrier) level, a rating that is internationally recognized by networking professionals and standards organizations. OC levels in SONET are analogous to the digital signal levels of T-carriers. Table 11-4 lists the OC levels and their maximum throughput.

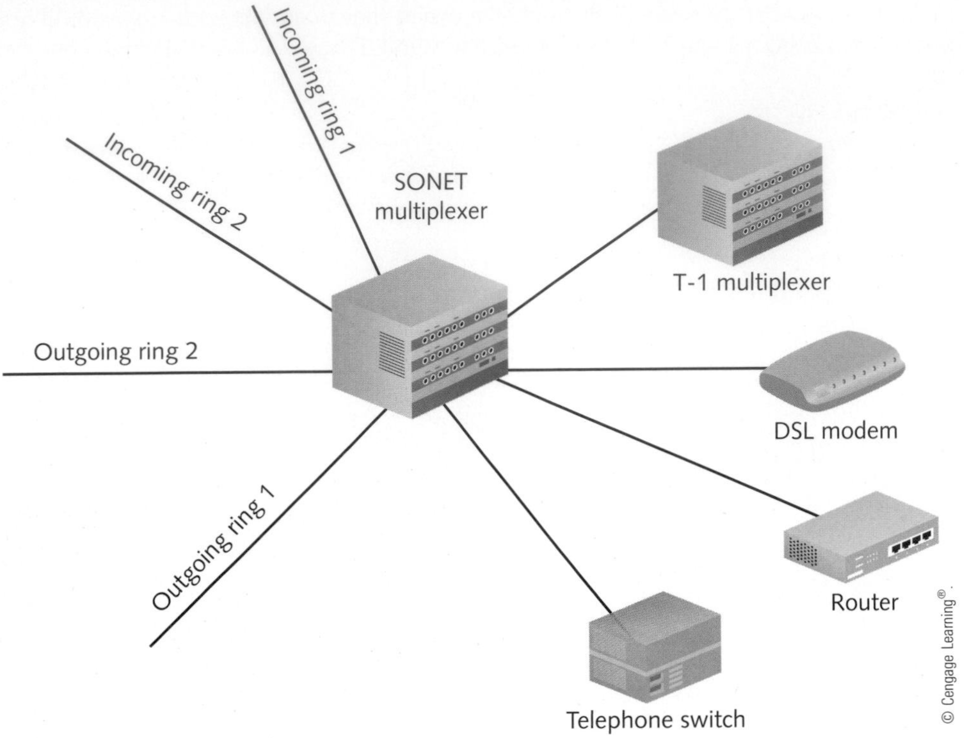

Figure 11-27 SONET connectivity

Table 11-4 **SONET OC levels**

OC level	Throughput (Mbps)	Notes
OC-1	51.84	Base rate.
OC-3	155.52	Popular choice for large businesses. A variant of OC-3 is OC-3c, where the c stands for *concatenated*. OC-3c concatenates three OC-1 lines into a single stream.
OC-12	622.08	Used by ISPs for WAN connections, and by some large enterprises.
OC-24	1244.16	Primarily used by ISPs and large enterprises.
OC-48	2488.32	Primarily used as a regional ISP backbone, and occasionally by very large hospitals, universities, or other major enterprises.
OC-96	4976.64	Primarily used by ISPs.
OC-192	9953.28	Used for Internet backbone connections.
OC-768	39,813.12	Used for Internet backbone connections.

SONET technology is typically not implemented by small or medium-sized businesses because of its high cost. It is commonly used by large companies; long-distance companies linking metropolitan areas and countries; ISPs that want to guarantee fast, reliable access to the Internet; or telephone companies connecting their COs. SONET is particularly suited to audio, video, and imaging data transmission. As you can imagine, given its reliance on fiber-optic cable and its redundancy requirements, SONET technology is expensive to implement.

MPLS (Multiprotocol Label Switching)

In Chapter 9, you learned about MPLS, which uses label switching to enable packet-switched technologies onto circuit-switched networks. MPLS is extremely fast and can handle various types of payloads, including T-carrier, Ethernet, ATM, DSL, and frame relay traffic. For these reasons, it's often used by ISPs on their own networks for moving traffic from one customer site to another, and it's becoming the solution of choice for many enterprises to connect their branch offices. For example, in Figure 11-28, an MPLS cloud within the ISP network manages traffic to and from various sites using a variety of Layer 1 and Layer 2 technologies.

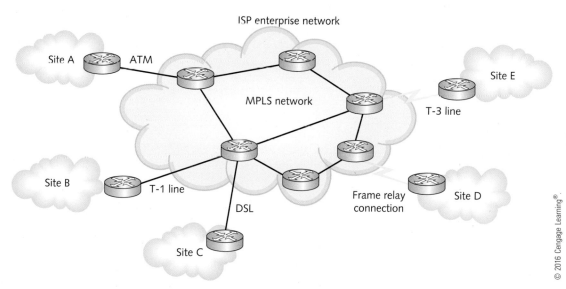

Figure 11-28   An ISP might use an MPLS WAN to move traffic from one customer site to another

© 2016 Cengage Learning®

Metro Ethernet

A growing trend in the ISP offerings for WAN connection services is a fairly recent development in Ethernet technology called Metro Ethernet, or Carrier Ethernet. You've already learned about LAN-based Ethernet. ISPs are now developing ways to send Ethernet traffic across MAN (called Metro Ethernet, or Ethernet MAN) and WAN (called Carrier Ethernet) connections, as standardized by the Metro Ethernet Forum (MEF), which is an alliance of over 220 industry organizations worldwide. Where available, virtual Ethernet networks can be established across other types of networks using technologies such as Ethernet over SONET, Ethernet over MPLS, Ethernet over DSL, and Ethernet over fiber. In metro settings, end-to-end, carrier-grade Ethernet networks can be established via Carrier-Ethernet Transport (CET), which is an Ethernet-based transport solution designed to overcome the inherent weaknesses of implementing Ethernet outside of the LAN environment.

For example, where traditional Ethernet, using STP (Spanning Tree Protocol), forwards frames based on MAC addresses, CET adds a transport label to the frame for forwarding purposes and establishes virtual tunnels, or paths, for frames to follow to their destination. Looking back at Figure 10-29, recall that STP blocks certain paths in order to limit potential pathways. CET, on the other hand, predetermines a pathway and tags frames to follow the specified path, as shown in Figure 11-29.

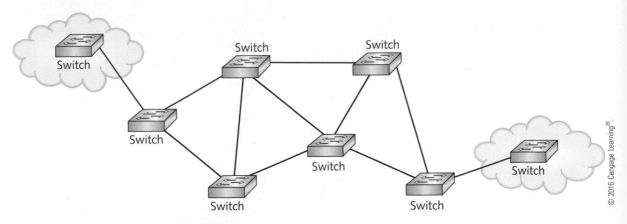

Figure 11-29 CET determines a pathway

Metro Ethernet provides a host of advantages, including:

- *streamlined connections*—Bridging Ethernet LANs with their native Ethernet protocols significantly streamlines the communication processes.

- *cost efficiency*—Metro Ethernet provides higher bandwidth at lower costs than current T-carrier and other options that rely on TDM (such as SONET). Metro Ethernet services at 10 Gbps are available with bandwidths up to 100 Gbps in the works.

- *scalability*—Ethernet services are more easily scaled in finer increments than other high-bandwidth technologies, and can be easily adjusted as subscriber needs change.

- *familiarity*—IT technicians are already familiar with Ethernet protocols and standards, which simplifies maintenance and troubleshooting.

- *hardware*—Ethernet hardware is already widely available and less expensive to obtain the equipment needed for specific situations.

So far in this chapter, you've learned about a wide variety of wired WAN technologies. Similar to LANs, WANs utilize multiple wireless technologies as well, which are covered next.

Wireless WANs

The best 802.11n signal can travel approximately a quarter of a mile. But other types of wireless networks can connect stations over longer distances. For example, in large cities, dozens of surveillance cameras trained on municipal buildings and parks beam video images to a central public safety headquarters. Meanwhile, in developing countries, wireless signals deliver lectures and training videos to students in remote, mountainous regions. In rural areas of the United States, elderly patients at home wear medical monitoring devices, such as blood pressure sensors and blood glucose meters, which use wireless networks to convey information to their doctors hundreds of miles away. Such networks can even alert paramedics in case of an emergency. All of these are examples of wireless WANs. Unlike wireless LANs, wireless WANs are designed for high-throughput, long-distance digital data exchange.

As in asymmetrical wired broadband, on wireless WANs downstream data transmission is typically faster than upstream transmission. Downstream, also called **downlink** in the context of wireless transmission, represents the connection between a carrier's antenna and a client's transceiver—for example, a smartphone. Upstream, also called **uplink** in the context of wireless transmission, refers to the connection between a client's transceiver and the carrier's antenna.

The following sections describe a variety of ways wireless clients can communicate across a city or state.

802.16 (WiMAX)

In 2001, IEEE standardized a wireless technology under its 802.16 (wireless MAN) committee. Since that time, IEEE has released several versions of the 802.16 standard. Collectively, the 802.16 standards are known as WiMAX, which stands for Worldwide Interoperability for Microwave Access, the name of a group of manufacturers, including Intel and Nokia, who banded together to promote and develop 802.16 products and services. WiMAX was envisioned as a wireless alternative to DSL and T-carrier services for homes and businesses. Notable features of this standard include:

- Line-of-sight transmission between two antennas for use with fixed clients or non-line-of-sight transmission between multiple antennas for use with mobile clients

- Use of frequencies in the 2-to-11 GHz range or the 11-to-66 GHz range, either licensed or nonlicensed; most WiMAX installations in the United States use the 2.3-, 2.5-, or 3.65-GHz bands

- Use of MIMO

- Ability to transmit and receive signals up to 50 km, or approximately 30 miles, when antennas are fixed or up to 15 km, or approximately 10 miles, when they are mobile

- QoS provisions

WiMAX provides greater throughput than Wi-Fi and T-1s. Also, its range extends much farther than any of the 802.11 standards. For these reasons, WiMAX is considered more appropriate for use on MANs and CANs. Throughput speeds vary considerably, though, depending upon the type of installation, type of access used (mobile or fixed, line of sight or not), and distance from signal.

WiMAX offers some installation savings and benefits that can be an obstacle to using other broadband services. It is well suited to rural customers, for example, who might be in an area lacking copper or fiber-optic cabling infrastructure. WiMAX also provides network access for mobile computerized devices, including smartphones, laptops, and tablets in metropolitan areas. Finally, WiMAX can act as the backhaul link, or an intermediate connection between subscriber networks and a telecommunications carrier's network. Figure 11-30 illustrates three uses for WiMAX, including a residential customer, mobile users, and a backhaul link.

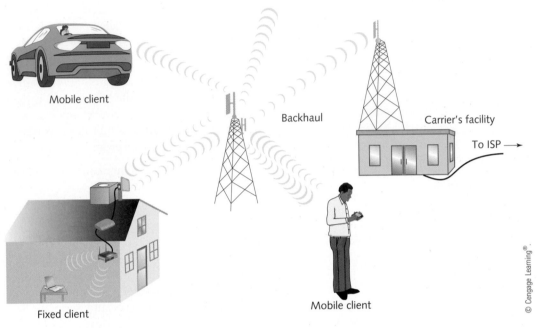

Figure 11-30   WiMAX network

As shown in Figure 11-30, in residential or small business WiMAX, the carrier installs a small antenna on the roof or even inside the building. This antenna is connected to a device similar to a cable or DSL modem for clients to access the LAN. The connectivity device could be incorporated along with the antenna in the same housing or it might be separate. If separate, the device typically attaches to the antenna with coaxial cable. It's often combined with a router. The customer's antenna communicates in a non-line-of-sight fashion with the service provider's antenna. If the service provider's facility is far away, it might use multiple antennas on towers that communicate in a line-of-sight manner, as shown in Figure 11-30. On the left side of Figure 11-31 is a WiMAX antenna used at a customer's location, and on the right side is an external WiMAX modem used to create an Internet connection for a single computer or LAN. Figure 11-32 depicts the type of antenna used by service providers on their towers.

In some installations, as when a WiMAX provider serves a metropolitan area, the customer's antenna and connectivity device are eliminated. Instead, each computer communicates directly via its onboard WiMAX transceiver with an antenna such as the one shown in Figure 11-32.

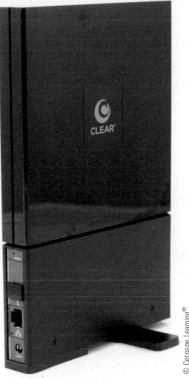

Figure 11-31 WiMAX residential antenna and external WiMAX modem

11

To ISP ⟶

Figure 11-32 WiMAX service provider's antenna

The latest IEEE 802.16 standards, released in 2012, primarily target the needs of MANs, such as a citywide network. One cellular provider, Sprint, had deployed a sizable WiMAX network to service cellular customers. Although Sprint is in the process of dismantling its WiMAX network in favor of LTE (discussed later in this chapter), other WiMAX uses still prevail as legitimate competitors in the wireless marketplace.

A newer version of WiMAX, known as WiMAX Release 2 or just WiMAX 2, is based on the 802.16m standard, and was released in 2011. With higher throughput, less latency, and better support for IP telephony than previous WiMAX versions, 802.16m is positioned to compete favorably with cellular data services in places where fast, cheap deployment is a high priority, such as underdeveloped countries, or in situations where the wireless network is private rather than public, such as in industrial environments (you'll learn more about these large-scale, industrial networks in Chapter 12). And because it is backward compatible with 802.16e equipment, customers and carriers can easily transition to the newer version.

However, WiMAX has received significant competition from quickly evolving cellular data services, described next.

Cellular

Cellular networks were initially designed to provide analog phone service. However, since the first mobile phones became available to consumers in the 1970s, cellular services have changed dramatically. In addition to voice signals, cellular networks now deliver text messages, Web pages, music, and videos to smartphones and handheld devices. This section describes current cellular data technology and explains the role it plays in wide area networking.

To put today's services in context, it's useful to understand that each leap in cellular technology has been described as a new generation. Each successive generation has brought a greater range of services, better quality, and higher throughputs, as described in the following list:

- First-generation, or **1G**, services from the 1970s and 1980s were analog.

- Second-generation, or **2G**, services, which reigned in the 1990s, used digital transmission and paved the way for texting and media downloads on mobile devices. Still, data transmission on 2G systems didn't exceed 240 Kbps.

- Third-generation, or **3G**, services were released in the early 2000s. Data rates rose to 384 Kbps and data (but not voice) communications used packet switching.

- Fourth-generation, or **4G**, services are characterized by an all-IP, packet-switched network for both data and voice transmission. 4G standards, released in 2008, also specify throughputs of 100 Mbps for fast-moving mobile clients, such as those in cars, and 1 Gbps for slow-moving mobile clients, such as pedestrians. WiMAX, though not strictly a cellular-based technology, is considered 4G because of its high-speed, packet-switched characteristics. Later in this section, you will learn about other 3G and 4G systems.

In addition to generation classifications, cellular networks are also grouped by the base technology used to build those networks. Cell phone networks use one of these two competing voice technologies:

- **GSM (Global System for Mobile Communications)** is an open standard that uses digital communication of data that is separated by timeslots on a channel, and is accepted and used worldwide. First introduced with the release of 2G devices, GSM initially only provided voice communications but added data services with the evolution of **GPRS (General Packet Radio Services)** and **Enhanced GPRS (EGPRS)**, also called **EDGE (Enhanced Data rates for GSM Evolution)**. GSM networks require that a cellular device have a **SIM (Subscriber Identity Module) card** that contains a microchip to hold data about the subscription a user has with the cellular carrier.

- **CDMA (Code Division Multiple Access)** differs from GSM in that it spreads a signal over a wider bandwidth so that multiple users occupy the same channel, a technology called **spread-spectrum**. Codes on the packets keep the various calls separated. CDMA networks do not require a SIM card in a cellular device because devices are compared against a white list, which is a database of subscribers that contains information on their subscriptions with the provider.

CDMA was more popular than GSM in the United States for many years, but GSM is overtaking the global market. In fact, there are many parts of the world where only GSM is available.

Although their access methods and features might differ, all cellular networks share a similar infrastructure in which coverage areas are divided into **cells**. Each cell is served by an antenna and its base station, or cell site. At the base station, a controller assigns mobile clients frequencies and manages communication with them. In network diagrams, cells are depicted as hexagons. Multiple cells share borders to form a network in a honeycomb pattern, as shown in Figure 11-33. Antennas are positioned at three corners of each cell, radiating and

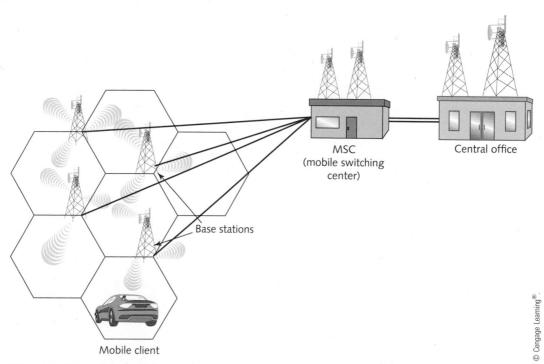

MSC
(mobile switching center)

Central office

Base stations

Mobile client

Figure 11-33 Cellular network

providing coverage over three equidistant lobes. When a client passes from one coverage area to another, his mobile device begins communicating with a different antenna. His communication might change frequencies or even carriers between cells. The transition, which normally happens without the user's awareness, is known as a handoff.

Cell sizes vary from roughly 1000 feet to 12 miles in diameter. The size of a cell depends on the network's access method and the region's topology, population, and amount of cellular traffic. An urban area with dense population and high volume of data and voice traffic might use cells with a diameter of only 2000 feet, their antennas mounted on tall buildings. In sparsely populated rural areas, with antennas mounted on isolated hilltop towers, cells might span more than 10 miles. In theory, the division of a network into cells provides thorough coverage over any given area. In reality, cells are misshapen due to terrain, EMF, and antenna radiation patterns. Some edges overlap and others don't meet up, leaving gaps in coverage.

As shown in Figure 11-33, each base station is connected to an MSC (mobile switching center), also called an MTSO (mobile telecommunications switching office), by a wireless link or fiber-optic cabling. The MSC might be located inside a telephone company's central office or it might stand alone and connect to the central office via another fiber-optic cabling or a microwave link. At the MSC, the mobile network intersects with the wired network. Equipment at an MSC manages mobile clients, monitoring their location and usage patterns, and switches cellular calls. It also assigns each mobile client an IP address. With 4G cellular services, a client's IP address remains the same from cell to cell and from one carrier's territory to another. In 3G cellular services, however, client IP addresses may change when the user transitions to a different carrier's service area. From the switching center, packets sent from cellular networks are routed to wired data networks through the PSTN or private backbones using WAN technologies you learned about earlier in this chapter.

Cellular networking is a complex topic, with rapidly evolving encoding and access methods, changing standards, and innovative vendors vying to dominate the market. This chapter does not detail the various encoding and access methods used on cellular networks. However, to qualify for the CompTIA Network+ certification, you should understand the basic infrastructure of a cellular network and the cellular technologies frequently used for data networking, beginning with HSPA+:

- HSPA+ (High Speed Packet Access Plus) began as a 3G technology released in 2008 that uses MIMO and sophisticated encoding techniques to achieve a maximum 168-Mbps downlink throughput and 22-Mbps uplink throughput in its current release. To achieve such speeds, HSPA+ uses limited channels more efficiently and incorporates more antennas in MIMO transmission. However, faster and more flexible technologies, such as LTE, are overtaking HSPA+ in popularity.

- LTE (Long Term Evolution) is a 4G technology that uses a different access method than HSPA+. The latest version, LTE-Advanced, can theoretically achieve downlink data rates of up to 3 Gbps and uplink rates up to 1.5 Gbps. LTE is currently the fastest wireless broadband service available in the United States. Although Sprint embraced WiMAX early on for its wireless broadband services, other carriers, such as AT&T and Verizon, passed on WiMAX to adopt LTE service.

Satellite

In 1945, Arthur C. Clarke (the author of *2001: A Space Odyssey*) wrote an article in which he described the possibility of communication between manned space stations that continually orbited the Earth. Other scientists recognized the worth of using satellites to convey signals from one location on Earth to another. By the 1960s, the United States was using satellites to transmit telephone and television signals across the Atlantic Ocean. Since then, the proliferation of this technology and reductions in its cost have made satellite transmission appropriate and available for transmitting consumer voice, video, music, and data.

For many years, satellites have been used to transmit live broadcasts of events happening around the world. Satellites are also used to deliver digital television and radio signals, voice and video signals, and cellular and paging signals. More recently, they have become a means of providing data services to mobile clients, such as travelers in flight or on ships at sea, who are beyond the reach of WiMAX, HSPA+, or LTE.

Satellite Orbits Most satellites circle the Earth 22,300 miles above the equator in a geosynchronous orbit. Geosynchronous earth orbit (GEO) means that satellites orbit the Earth at the same rate as the Earth turns. A special case of geosynchronous orbit, called geostationary orbit (because it appears stationary from Earth), stays directly above the equator. This is especially common with communications satellites. Consequently, at every point in their orbit, the satellites maintain a constant distance from a specific point on the Earth's equator. Because satellites are generally used to relay information from one point on Earth to another, information sent to Earth from a satellite first has to be transmitted to the satellite from Earth in an uplink from an Earth-based transmitter to an orbiting satellite. Often, the uplink signal information is scrambled (in other words, its signal is encoded) before transmission to prevent unauthorized interception. At the satellite, a transponder receives the uplink signal, then transmits it to an Earth-based receiver in a downlink. A typical satellite contains 24 to 32 transponders. Each satellite uses unique frequencies for its downlink. These frequencies, as well as the satellite's orbit location, are assigned and regulated by the FCC. Back on Earth, the downlink is picked up by a dish-shaped antenna. The dish shape concentrates the signal so that it can be interpreted by a receiver. Figure 11-34 provides a simplified view of satellite communication.

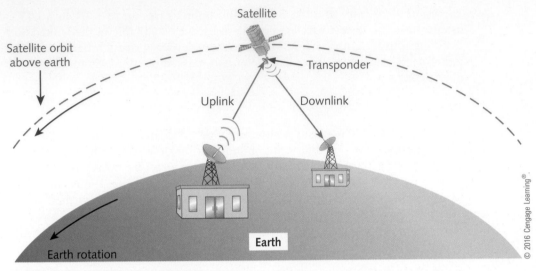

Figure 11-34 Satellite communication

Geosynchronous earth orbiting satellites are the type used by the most popular satellite data service providers. This technology is well established, and is the least expensive of all satellite technology. Also, because many of these satellites remain in a fixed position relative to the Earth's surface, stationary receiving dishes on Earth can be counted on to receive satellite signals reliably, weather permitting.

Satellite Frequencies Satellites transmit and receive signals in any of the following five frequency bands, which are roughly defined as:

- *L-band*—1.5–2.7 GHz
- *S-band*—2.7–3.5 GHz
- *C-band*—3.4–6.7 GHz
- K_u-*band ("K-under band")*—12–18 GHz
- *K-band*—18–27 GHz
- K_a-*band ("K-above band")*—26.5–40 GHz

Within each band, frequencies used for uplink and downlink transmissions differ. This variation helps ensure that signals traveling in one direction (for example, from a satellite to the Earth) do not interfere with signals traveling in the other direction (for example, signals from the Earth to a satellite).

Satellite Internet Services A handful of companies offer high-bandwidth Internet access via GEO satellite links. Each subscriber uses a small satellite antenna and receiver, or satellite modem, to exchange signals with the service provider's satellite network. Clients may be fixed, such as rural dwellers who are too remote for DSL, or mobile subscribers, such as travelers on ocean-going yachts.

Clients are able to exchange signals with satellites as long as they have a line-of-sight path, or an unobstructed view of the sky. To establish a satellite Internet connection, each subscriber must have a dish antenna, which is approximately two feet high by three feet wide, installed in a fixed position. In North America, these dish antennas are pointed toward the Southern Hemisphere (because many geosynchronous satellites travel over the equator). The dish antenna's receiver is connected, via cable, to a modem. This modem uses either a PCI or USB interface to connect with the subscriber's computer.

As with several other wireless WAN technologies, satellite services are typically asymmetrical and bandwidth is shared among many subscribers. Throughputs vary and are controlled by the service provider. Typical downlink rates range from 2 to 3 Mbps and uplink rates reach maybe 1 Mbps. Compared with other wireless WAN options, satellite services are slower and suffer more latency. In addition, client equipment is more expensive than that required by WiMAX, HSPA+, or LTE. Given these drawbacks, satellite data service is preferred only in circumstances that allow few alternatives or in cases where satellite receiving equipment is already installed.

Troubleshooting WAN Issues

 As a network administrator, one of your primary responsibilities is to keep connections to the WAN working well. With this in mind, there are steps you can take to troubleshoot a problem with a WAN connection before contacting your ISP, and preventive measures you can perform to avoid having the problem in the first place.

Company Policies

 Educating users on how to responsibly steward Internet access can go a long way to preventing bandwidth problems. You learned about company security policies in Chapter 8. To manage Internet access, you should consider incorporating the following into your company's security policy:

- *fair access and utilization limits*—A fair access policy is a set of guidelines designed to ensure that users have access to the content they require in order to do their jobs without hogging network resources from other users. Balancing the needs of high-bandwidth users with those of other users, however, requires some finessing of which types of traffic are allowed and to what extent. Traffic critical to business operations should be given high priority. But other network traffic, such as bulk downloads, can be downgraded in priority in the interest of protecting everyone's ongoing access to Internet services.

- *throttling*—One way to limit excessive bandwidth consumption is by throttling bandwidth utilization of a specific user, group of users, type of device, type of traffic, or, as in the case of ISPs, a subscriber to the service. Throttling means to purposely slow down bandwidth utilization or to block additional access once a certain threshold has been reached.

- *blocking*—In some situations, it's helpful to block certain types of traffic entirely. For example, the network administrator might block UDP traffic, video streaming, or mass emails. These preventive measures can help reduce excessive bandwidth utilization, and also help protect the company from legal ramifications and liabilities.

The CompTIA Network+ exam also covers the flip side of the issue of managing Internet traffic. Internet users are increasingly demanding uninhibited access to Internet content, a principle called net neutrality. Many ISPs, governments, and corporations institute some kind of limitations on Internet traffic, while many users, Web content providers, and advocacy organizations are putting pressure on these institutions to change their policies and to both support and enact protective legislation.

Common ISP Problems

Network+
4.8

To troubleshoot ISP problems, you need to know the difference between equipment that belongs to the ISP, and equipment that belongs to the subscriber. Equipment located on the customer's premises, regardless of who owns it and who is responsible for it, is called customer premise equipment (CPE). Equipment belonging to the ISP, despite its location on the customer's premises, should only be serviced by the ISP's technicians, even if it is located on the customer's side of the demarc. Equipment owned by the customer is the responsibility of the customer and will not be serviced by the ISP. The following list describes devices commonly found at or near the demarc:

- *NIU*—Recall that the NIU (also called NID) at the demarc connects the ISP's local loop to the customer's network. A more intelligent version of an NIU is a smart jack, or Intelligent NID (INID), which can provide diagnostic information about the interface. For example, a smart jack might include loopback capabilities. Just like the loopback adapter you use to test a port or cable on your computer, the smart jack can loop the ISP's signal back to the CO for testing. The ISP is responsible for all wiring leading up to the NIU and for the NIU itself. The customer is responsible for everything past the NIU, unless the equipment is owned by the ISP, such as with a line driver, CSU/DSU, or set-top box.

- *line drivers*—Essentially a repeater, a line driver can be installed either on copper lines (in which case, it is called a copper line driver) or fiber lines (in which case, it is called a fiber line driver) to boost the signal across greater distances. The device might be placed on either side of the demarc and, if located on the customer's side, might be owned by either party.

- *CSU/DSU*—Like line drivers, these devices can be owned by either party, depending upon who is responsible for providing this device according to the terms of service. However, the CSU/DSU is typically placed on the customer's side of the demarc, between the demarc and the first router.

When you lose Internet connectivity, a little troubleshooting can help determine the location of the problem and the party responsible for repairing the connection. The following list presents some common issues to look for:

- *interface error*—Misconfigured interfaces, such as an incorrect default gateway or missing DNS server address, can result in interface errors. One possible evaluation technique for bypassing an interface error, which will help to confirm that the interface misconfiguration is the issue, is to switch to a different interface on the same device. For example, if your computer's wired connection is having problems, try connecting to the network using the computer's wireless interface.

- *routing loops*—As you learned in Chapter 3, a routing loop occurs when a message gets stuck in a loop between a limited number of routers without ever reaching its destination. Routing loops are often created when one leg of a route fails, and the remaining routers attempt to compensate by sending transmissions along alternate routes; this, in turn, isolates a network segment from the rest of the network or from Internet access. In Chapter 10, you learned about STP (Spanning Tree Protocol), which functions at Layer 2 to help prevent routing loops. Another method for preventing routing loops is split horizon route advertisement, or simply split horizon. This is a Layer 3 technology employed by distance-vector routing protocols in which a router knows which of its interfaces received a routing update and will not retransmit, or advertise, that same update on the same interface. For example, if Router B learns of a route from a neighboring router, Router A, then Router B will not advertise updates on that route back to Router A.

- *router misconfiguration*—Other router configuration issues to consider when Internet connectivity fails might include blocked ports that should be open, speed or duplex mismatches, incorrect IP address range or subnet mask, incorrect default gateway, and STP issues.

- *DNS issues*—Correct DNS server information—and a functioning DNS server—are critical requirements for enabling Internet access. Computers can be programmed to use DNS servers on a corporate network or the ISP's DNS servers, or alternatively, they can be pointed to public DNS servers such as those run by Google.

- *interference*—Obviously, interference can cause problems with a wireless connection, and in Chapter 5, you learned that interference can wreak havoc with wired connections as well. Intermittent problems, or problems that affect unrelated portions of a network, are common indicators of interference issues.

Applying Concepts
Scenario: Internet Down

11

One evening, you're up late working to meet a fast-approaching deadline when suddenly your Internet connection fails. Much of your work requires Internet access for research, but you belay the panic for a few moments to evaluate the situation:

- You try a couple of different Web sites in your browser, then open a different browser and try a couple of Web sites again. None of the sites will load.

- You check all of the cable connections between your computer and your network's demarc. Everything looks normal.

- You power cycle the modem and router by unplugging both devices from the electrical outlet, waiting a moment, plugging in the modem, waiting for it to establish a connection with the ISP, then plugging in the router.

- You check the Network Connections status on your computer and confirm that you have a functioning connection with your network.

- You try again to navigate to a Web site in your browser, but the page still won't load.

- You open a Command Prompt window and ping one of Google's servers at *8.8.8.8*. The ping works.

- You ping Google's Web site at *google.com*, but this time it doesn't work.

- You pull up an outage reporting Web site for your ISP on your smartphone, and find that a few hundred other people have reported the outage in your area, too.

With a quick adjustment, you get your Internet service functioning again and continue with your work. Which of the following did you do and why?

A. You switched out the Ethernet cable connecting your modem to your router because the cable was damaged.

B. You used `ipconfig` to release the IP address on your computer and get a new one from your network's DHCP service because your computer had a duplicate IP address.

C. You changed the DNS settings on your router to point to Google's DNS servers instead of the DNS servers of your ISP because the ISP's DNS servers were down.

D. You switched to a different ISP because the former ISP's service was unreliable.

E. You replaced the router with a new router you had ready to go, knowing that the old router had already exceeded its life expectancy and had finally ceased to function.

F. You created an ad hoc network with another computer on your network and used that computer's access to the Internet to continue your research because the Wi-Fi radio on your computer had died and will need to be replaced.

G. You performed a factory reset on your modem so it would reinitiate a connection with the ISP.

H. You updated the default gateway on your computer because it was unable to communicate with the router.

I. You restarted your computer because Windows had updates that needed to be installed.

Chapter Summary

WAN Essentials

- Not all businesses need the same kind of WAN. Depending on traffic load, budget, geographical breadth, and commercially available technology, each might implement a different transmission method.

WAN Topologies

- In a bus topology WAN, each site is directly connected to no more than two other sites in a serial fashion.

- In a ring topology WAN, each site is connected to two other sites so that the entire WAN forms a ring pattern.

- In a star topology WAN, a single site acts as the central connection point for several other points.

- A mesh topology WAN incorporates many directly interconnected sites. Because every site is interconnected, data can travel directly from its origin to its destination.

- In a tiered topology WAN, sites connected in star or ring formations are interconnected at different levels, with the interconnection points being organized into layers to form hierarchical groupings.

PSTN (Public Switched Telephone Network)

- Originally, the PSTN carried only analog traffic. All of its lines were copper wires, and switching was handled manually by operators. Today, switching is computer controlled, and nearly all of the PSTN uses digital transmission.

- With a dial-up connection, a user connects her computer, via a modem, to a modem on a distant network and stays connected for a finite period of time.

- ISDN is a legacy technology that is now almost completely phased out. All ISDN connections were based on two types of channels: B channels and D channels. The B channel was the "bearer" channel, employing circuit-switching techniques to carry voice, video, audio, and other types of data over the ISDN connection. The D channel was the "data" channel, employing packet-switching techniques to carry information about the call.

T-Carriers

- Multiplexing enables a single T-1 circuit to carry 24 channels, each capable of 64-Kbps throughput; thus, a T-1 has a maximum capacity of 24 × 64 Kbps, or 1.544 Mbps.

- The speed of a T-carrier depends on its signal level. The signal level refers to the T-carrier's Physical layer electrical signaling characteristics. DS0 (digital signal, level 0) is the equivalent of one data or voice channel.

- Every T-carrier line requires connectivity hardware at both the customer site and the local telecommunications provider's switching facility. Connectivity hardware may be purchased or leased.

- For T-1s using STP, repeaters must regenerate the signal approximately every 6000 feet. Twisted-pair wiring cannot adequately carry the high throughput of multiple T-1s or T-3 transmissions, so fiber-optic cabling is the medium of choice.

- When copper cabling is used to carry T-1 traffic, it terminates in an RJ-48 connector.

- The CSU provides termination for the digital signal and ensures connection integrity through error correction and line monitoring. The DSU converts the T-carrier frames into frames the LAN can interpret and vice versa.

- On a typical T-1 connected data network, the DTE or terminal equipment is a router, which translates between different Layer 3 protocols that might be used on the WAN and LAN.

Frame Relay

- Frame relay was originally designed as a fast packet-switched network over ISDN, although today frame relay is used as the Data Link protocol for various virtual circuit interfaces and media.

DSL (Digital Subscriber Line)

- DSL operates over the PSTN and competes directly with T-1 and broadband cable services.

- In asymmetrical communications, downstream throughput is higher than upstream throughput. Symmetrical technology provides equal capacity for data traveling both upstream and downstream.

- Some versions of DSL, such as ADSL and VDSL, create multiple narrow channels in the higher frequency range to carry more data. For these versions, a splitter must be installed at the carrier and at the customer's premises to separate the data signal from the voice signal before it reaches the terminal equipment (such as a phone or computer).

■ With DSL, the distance between the customer and the central office affects the actual throughput a customer experiences.

■ A DSL modem is a device that modulates outgoing signals and demodulates incoming DSL signals.

Broadband Cable

■ Broadband cable is based on the coaxial cable wiring used for TV signals and was standardized by an international, cooperative effort orchestrated by CableLabs.

BPL (Broadband over Power Line)

■ Signals transmitted via power lines are subject to much more noise than those carried by DSL or cable services.

ATM (Asynchronous Transfer Mode)

■ Like Ethernet, ATM specifies Data Link layer framing techniques. But what sets ATM apart from Ethernet is its fixed packet size.

SONET (Synchronous Optical Network)

■ SONET is a high-bandwidth WAN signaling technique developed for fiber-optic cabling.

MPLS (Multiprotocol Label Switching)

■ MPLS is extremely fast and can handle various types of payloads, including T-carrier, Ethernet, ATM, DSL, and frame relay traffic.

Metro Ethernet

■ ISPs are now developing ways to send Ethernet traffic across MAN (using Metro Ethernet) and WAN (using Carrier Ethernet) connections, as standardized by the Metro Ethernet Forum (MEF).

Wireless WANs

■ As in asymmetrical wired broadband, on wireless WANs, downstream data transmission is typically faster than upstream transmission.

■ Collectively, the 802.16 standards are known as WiMAX, which was envisioned as a wireless alternative to DSL and T-carrier services for homes and businesses.

■ GSM initially only provided voice communications but added data services with the evolution of GPRS and Enhanced GPRS, also called EDGE. Unlike GSM, CDMA networks do not require a SIM card in a cellular device.

■ Satellites are used to transmit live broadcasts of events happening around the world, and to deliver digital television and radio signals, voice and video signals, and cellular and paging signals.

■ Geosynchronous earth orbit means that satellites orbit the Earth at the same rate as the Earth turns.

■ Within each satellite band, frequencies used for uplink and downlink transmissions differ to help ensure that signals traveling in one direction do not interfere with signals traveling in the other direction.

- Clients are able to exchange signals with satellites as long as they have a line-of-sight path, or unobstructed view of the sky.

Troubleshooting WAN Issues

- A fair access policy is based on the premise that users should have access to the content they require in order to do their jobs without hogging network resources from other users.

- Equipment located on the customer's premises, regardless of who owns it and who is responsible for it, is called customer premise equipment (CPE).

Key Terms

For definitions of key terms, see the Glossary near the end of the book.

1G

2G

3G

4G

802.16

802.16m

ADSL (asymmetric digital subscriber line)

ADSL2+M (ADSL Annex M)

advertise

analog modem

asymmetric DSL

asymmetrical

asynchronous

ATM (Asynchronous Transfer Mode)

B channel

backhaul

blocking

bonding

BPL (broadband over power line)

BRI (Basic Rate Interface)

broadband cable

bus topology WAN

cable drop

cable modem

cable modem access

Carrier Detect (CD)

Carrier Ethernet

Carrier-Ethernet Transport (CET)

CDMA (Code Division Multiple Access)

cell

CIR (committed information rate)

CO (central office)

copper line driver

CSU (channel service unit)

CSU/DSU

customer premise equipment (CPE)

D channel

data-link connection identifier (DLCI)

dedicated line

dial-up

DOCSIS (Data Over Cable Service Interface Specification)

downlink

downstream

DS0 (digital signal, level 0)

DSL (digital subscriber line)

DSL modem

DSLAM (DSL access multiplexer)

DSU (data service unit)

E-1

E-3

EDGE (Enhanced Data rates for GSM Evolution)

Enhanced GPRS (EGPRS)

Ethernet MAN

Ethernet over HDMI

Ethernet over power (EOP)

Ethernet over power line

fair access policy

fiber line driver

fractional T-1

frame relay

FTTH (fiber to the home)

FTTP (fiber to the premises)

full-mesh WAN

geostationary orbit

geosynchronous earth orbit (GEO)

GPRS (General Packet Radio Services)

GSM (Global System for Mobile Communications)

guard tone

handoff

head-end

HFC (hybrid fiber-coax)

HSPA+ (High Speed Packet Access Plus)

IEEE 1901-2010

IEEE 1905.1-2013

11

Intelligent NID (INID)

ISDN (Integrated Services Digital Network)

LANE (LAN Emulation)

last mile

line driver

local loop

LTE (Long Term Evolution)

LTE-Advanced

mesh topology WAN

Metro Ethernet

Metro Ethernet Forum (MEF)

MSC (mobile switching center)

MTSO (mobile telecommunications switching office)

Multilink PPP (MLPPP or MLP)

net neutrality

NID (network interface device)

NIU (network interface unit)

NT1 (Network Termination 1)

NT2 (Network Termination 2)

OC (Optical Carrier)

OC-1

OC-12

OC-3

OLT (optical line terminal)

ONU (optical network unit)

partial-mesh WAN

PON (passive optical network)

POTS (plain old telephone service)

PRI (Primary Rate Interface)

PVC (permanent virtual circuit)

ring topology WAN

RJ-48

SDH (Synchronous Digital Hierarchy)

self-healing

signal level

SIM (Subscriber Identity Module) card

smart jack

SONET (Synchronous Optical Network)

split horizon

split horizon route advertisement

spread-spectrum

star topology WAN

SVC (switched virtual circuit)

symmetric DSL

symmetrical

T-1 (terrestrial carrier level 1)

T-3

TA (terminal adapter)

T-carrier

TE (terminal equipment)

throttling

tiered topology WAN

transponder

unmodulated carrier tone

uplink

upstream

virtual circuit

WAN interface card (WIC)

WAN link

WAN site

WiMAX (Worldwide Interoperability for Microwave Access)

WiMAX 2

WiMAX Release 2

xDSL

Review Questions

1. What is the lowest layer of the OSI model at which LANs and WANs support the same protocols?

   a. Layer 2

   b. Layer 3

   c. Layer 4

   d. Layer 5

2. An organization can lease a private _____ that is not shared with other users or a _____ that can be physically configured over shared lines in the carrier's cloud.

   a. permanent virtual circuit (PVC), switched virtual circuit (SVC)

   b. switched virtual circuit (SVC), dedicated line

   c. dedicated line, virtual circuit

   d. switched virtual circuit (SVC), permanent virtual circuit (PVC)

3. Which WAN topology always sends data directly from its origin to its destination?

    a. Bus topology

    b. Ring topology

    c. Star topology

    d. Mesh topology

4. What protocol is used to bond multiple T-1s?

    a. LACP

    b. MLP

    c. TCP/IP

    d. SSH

5. What kind of device can monitor a connection at the demarc but cannot interpret data?

    a. CSU/DSU

    b. NID

    c. NIU

    d. Smart jack

6. What specification defined the standards for broadband cable?

    a. ATM

    b. Digital signal

    c. ANSI

    d. DOCSIS

7. What technology allows a user to access the Internet through the wiring of a home?

    a. Ethernet over HDMI

    b. Broadband over power line

    c. Ethernet over power line

    d. Ethernet over SONET

8. _____ in SONET are analogous to the _____ of T-carriers.

    a. Throughput, digital signal levels

    b. OC levels, digital signal levels

    c. QoS levels, OC levels

    d. OC levels, carrier levels

9. What IEEE committee established WiMAX technologies?

    a. 802.11

    b. 802.3

    c. 802.5

    d. 802.16

10. What method do ISPs use to purposely slow down bandwidth utilization by customers?
    a. Fair access
    b. Throttling
    c. Blocking
    d. Net neutrality

11. List four WAN technologies that are carried over the PSTN.

12. When copper cabling is used to carry T-1 traffic, what kind of connector is used?

13. What two types of virtual circuits does frame relay support?

14. What is the latest version of ADSL?

15. By what name is SONET known internationally?

16. What is the benchmark upstream throughput of 4G services for slow-moving mobile clients?

17. What technology added data services to the GSM standard?

18. What is the fastest wireless broadband service available in the United States?

19. Explain what geosynchronous earth orbit (GEO) is and what it accomplishes.

20. What type of device can loop the ISP's signal back to the CO for testing?

Hands-On Projects

Project 11-1: Research CSU/DSU Devices

Just like you might go shopping for a modem in order to get specific features that you want, you can also shop for a CSU/DSU to meet particular needs when you have a T-1 or T-3 line. In this project, you will research CSU/DSU devices. Complete the following steps to find an appropriate device for each scenario:

1. You've just been hired by a small company that is ready to lease its first fractional T-1 line. Find a Cisco second-generation WIC that can provide a fractional T-1 connection. List the product description details that indicate the WIC you found will meet these requirements, and be sure to include the price and the Web site where you found your device. Find at least three reviews of the product and include that information as well.

2. Your company has grown over the past year, and is ready to upgrade to a full T-1 line. You've also decided to upgrade the router at the same time, so you decide to purchase a router-CSU/DSU bundle. Find a device that includes the router and the CSU/DSU capabilities, and that is rack-mountable. List the product description details that indicate the device you found will meet these requirements, and be sure to include the price and the Web site where you found your device. Find at least one review of the product and include that information as well.

3. Your company has grown even more, and merged with another, larger company. Your new employer is ready to upgrade to a T-3 line. You'll need a new CSU/DSU, and this time you decide to get a dedicated CSU/DSU device. Find a device that includes CSU/DSU capabilities for a full-rate T-3 line and that is rack-mountable. List the product

description details that indicate the device you found will meet these requirements, and be sure to include the price and the Web site where you found your device.

Project 11-2: Develop a Plan to Troubleshoot a WAN Connection

In this project, you'll research suggestions online for troubleshooting Internet connection problems, and develop your own list of procedures to follow the next time you encounter this type of problem.

1. In a Web browser, do a search for tips, tricks, hints, and steps for troubleshooting Internet connection issues. Make a list of ideas from at least three different sources that you can use for future reference.

2. Think about the ideas you've gathered, and consider which steps should be completed first, middle, and last, to narrow down and identify a problem as quickly as possible without a great deal of backtracking. Make sure your troubleshooting steps cover a wide variety of potential problems.

3. Rearrange and edit your list so that the steps would be easy to follow, beginning to end, in a troubleshooting scenario. Explain why you placed the steps in the order you chose, and list one or more potential problems that each step is designed to detect.

Project 11-3: Test for ISP Throttling

Glasnost is a throttle-testing tool that you can run from a Web browser. The only catch is that you must have the current version of Java installed in your browser, but then you can test several different kinds of traffic to determine if your ISP is throttling those types of traffic either during upload or download.

Java is easiest to install in Internet Explorer for Windows computers. A version of Java is also available for Mac computers. The steps for this project will work for either. You must also have Internet access. If you don't currently have Java installed in your browser, complete the following steps:

1. Open your browser and navigate to **java.com,** then download and install the correct version of Java for your computer. If you're using a Windows computer, be sure to select the correct bit version, either 32-bit or 64-bit.

2. After installing Java, close your browser and reopen it to complete installation.

Complete the following steps to test your ISP connection for throttling:

3. In your browser, do a search for the term *glasnost test* and most likely the first result will be the Max Planck Institute Web site. At the time of this writing, the address was broadband.mpi-sws.org/transparency/bttest.php. Click the link to open the test Web site.

4. Scroll down to the box containing the Glasnost tests. At the time of this writing, several Glasnost tests are listed toward the bottom of the Web page. Click to select the **Flash video (e.g., YouTube)** test, then click **Start testing**. If a UAC dialog box appears, click **Run**.

5. The test will run for a few minutes, then produce results on your ISP's service. What upload and download results did you receive? Did you get any notes of explanation or caution?

6. Click the **detailed measurement results of the test here** link. What ports were tested? What was the highest speed measured?

7. Return to the test page and rerun the test using the **HTTP transfer** option. If you get a Java dialog box asking if you want to run the application, click **Run**. What upload and download results did you receive?

8. Click the **detailed measurement results of the test here** link. What ports were tested this time? What was the highest speed measured?

9. Conduct one more test of your choice. List the test you select, then report your upload and download results, as well as the ports tested and the highest speed measured.

10. Conduct the tests again on a different day at a different time of day. Did you get different results? Why do think this might be?

Many IT security experts recommend removing Java from your computer if you don't have a continuing need for it. Therefore, if you installed Java for this project and do not intend to continue using Glasnost, complete the following steps to uninstall Java on a Windows computer (steps will vary for other OSs):

11. Open the Control Panel and click **Uninstall a program**.

12. Select any Java listing, click **Uninstall**, and then click **Yes**.

Case Projects

CASE PROJECTS

Case Project 11-1: Select a WAN Solution for Business Use

Suppose you work for a medium-sized corporation with three offices, one in California, one in Florida, and one in New Jersey. For several years, the company has been using VPNs to connect the offices. As the company has grown, so has the need to share data among the offices, and you have been assigned the task of recommending a more robust WAN solution for transmitting data among offices.

The first task is to identify the applications that will use the WANs:

*   Email, voice, and video transmissions happen during office hours. The company makes heavy use of videoconferencing among the offices.

*   A centralized database resides in the data center at the New Jersey headquarters. Interactivity with the database originates from all three offices.

*   For catastrophic disaster recovery, the company wants to back up the New Jersey database to the Florida data center.

*   Several employees telecommute, and customer service reps access company resources from various off-site locations.

The carrier your company has selected offers private lines, frame relay, ATM, Metro Ethernet, IP VPNs, and L2 MPLS WAN solutions. Answer the following questions about these solutions:

1. Which WAN solution is best suited for customer service reps working at a customer site?

2. Which WAN solution does *not* allow for QoS specifications so that voice and video take precedence over email messaging when competing for bandwidth?

3. Which WAN solution can tunnel frame relay, ATM, and Ethernet traffic, allowing the company to have a consistent backbone service with a variety of WAN solutions?

4. Which WAN solution offers continuous and consistent bandwidth at all times of day and night?

5. Which WAN solution is similar to and has largely replaced frame relay?

6. If you recommend private lines, how many private lines must be installed?

7. Other than the current VPN solution, which WAN solution is likely to require the least amount of hardware changes?

8. List five questions that you need to answer before you can recommend a new WAN solution.

Case Project 11-2: Explore WAN Options in Your Area

Selecting a particular WAN solution because its theoretical maximum speed is faster than another solution's theoretical maximum speed won't help much if your local carrier doesn't actually offer service at that speed. Selecting a WAN solution for a corporation requires familiarity with the options available in your area and their actual performance levels relative to each other. Complete the following steps to evaluate the ISP options available to a business in your area:

1. Compile a list of ISPs in your town or city. If you live in a rural area with few options, select a nearby city with more options so that you'll be able to include some of the private WAN technologies in addition to residential WAN offerings.

2. Check the Web site for each ISP to determine what broadband services they offer in your area, both for residential customers and corporate customers. Include both wired and wireless options. Answer the following questions:

   a. What are their advertised speeds?

   b. How much does each solution cost on a monthly basis?

   c. What installation fees are there, if any?

   d. How far away are you located from their CO? (If you're researching another city besides your own, use a fictional location in that same city.)

   e. What effect will this distance likely have on the actual speeds of each service option?

3. Search online for consumer reviews of each ISP in your list. What kinds of ratings does each ISP receive online?

## chapter 12

Industrial and Enterprise Networking

After reading this chapter and completing the exercises, you will be able to:

- Identify significant components of an industrial control system or SCADA system

- Inventory and manage network assets and identify significant business documents

- Create and follow appropriate change management procedures for major and minor network changes

- Identify significant physical security controls to limit or monitor access to secure areas

- Describe the components of a reliable disaster recovery plan and a defensible incident response plan

On the Job

I used to work for a service provider whose shared network supplied switching, content distribution, and firewall protection for many medium-sized customer Web servers in our data center. We'd assigned one of our best network engineers a project that required a change to every firewall port opening statement on the network. That sort of work did appear on our list of preapproved routine changes, as long as the customer had provided written authorization for the security port opening. However, notifying all customers five days before the change, scheduling the change after hours, and management approval of a change record were not required.

But the network engineer had a complex project in mind. He was going to modify hundreds of lines of configuration at once on a redundant set of network devices that supported dozens of customers, and those lines of configuration were security related. Of course, this wasn't what I'd had in mind when I allowed this activity to be put on the preapproved changes list.

The network engineer had never done this kind of project before, so he mocked it up and tested it in our test lab. The lab maintained equipment and configurations for that purpose, but not a perfect copy of the production system with traffic.

During the middle of the day, the network engineer went ahead and implemented this "routine" change. It took down the whole network, including every one of those dozens of customers, for about 30 minutes. Worse, there was a brief period in which some security rules at the firewall weren't working, exposing some ports.

Today, in networks for which I'm responsible for change management standards, I always include the following caveats for any preauthorization of routine changes:

1. If it's the first time we've done it, it isn't routine.

2. If it's not the version of the change that we do regularly, it isn't routine.

3. If it requires testing before performance, it isn't routine.

The network engineer and I both learned a lot after that change.

Brooke Noelke
CDW Hosting and Managed Services

By now you've learned a great deal about how networks work, how they're constructed, how to keep them secure, and how to troubleshoot network problems. In this chapter, you learn about a special kind of network, an industrial network, such as you might find at a utility company or manufacturing plant, which involves specialized equipment and needs. This chapter also covers the special needs of enterprise networks in large organizations. These organizations often require that network administrators follow a formal change management process when making changes to the network and its computers. Such a system often includes extra documentation and detailed approval and deployment processes. The chapter also discusses some physical security controls that you'll most likely find in larger, enterprise-scale networks, and concludes with information on disaster recovery and forensics.

Industrial Networks

An industrial system is a system of machines, such as an assembly line at a tire manufacturing plant. In the past, industrial systems were totally managed by humans running the machines. Today, many processes are automated by robots, and controlled by computers and their users at a centrally located control center. In these systems, computers must interact with machinery and physical components that are not digital or technical in nature. Types of data these computers must process might include information about manufacturing supplies, production benchmarks, motion, speeds, temperature, water flow, properties of electricity, and potential errors or hazards.

Some industrial systems, such as a public transportation system or a gas pipeline, are spread over a wide geographical area. In that case, the people in charge of managing the system must use the Internet to connect the system's various remote locations. When industrial systems use the Internet for connectivity, these connected devices become part of the greater Internet of Things. Many people consider the Internet of Things (IoT) to be the next generation of the Internet because it connects objects that are not used as computers to the Internet, such as a home thermostat, refrigerator, or security lighting that can be controlled remotely through a Web-based dashboard.

As you can imagine, monitoring and controlling the elements of an industrial network are vitally important. In the next section, you learn about industrial control systems and the networks they require.

Components of an Industrial Control System and SCADA Network

An industrial control system (ICS) is a group of networked computers used to manage a physical system of industrial processes. The physical system might be a single facility, such as an oil refinery, nuclear power plant, or sewage plant, or an infrastructure spread over a wide geographical area, such as a railroad system or natural gas pipeline.

An ICS contains all the components typical for any local network or WAN, including workstations, servers, printers, switches, routers, cabling, and wireless access points. In addition, basic components specific to an ICS are diagrammed in Figure 12-1 and listed here:

- A supervisory control and data acquisition (SCADA) system includes software, servers, and communication channels, and is responsible for acquiring real-time data from the physical system and managing the physical system or presenting the data to humans, who monitor and manage the system. Depending on the situation, a SCADA system might be considered only the supervisory portion of the entire ICS, or the terms *SCADA* and *ICS* might be used interchangeably to describe the entire computerized system.

- Remote terminal units (RTU) are devices installed at key locations in the industrial system, which can sense attributes of the physical system and convert the analog data

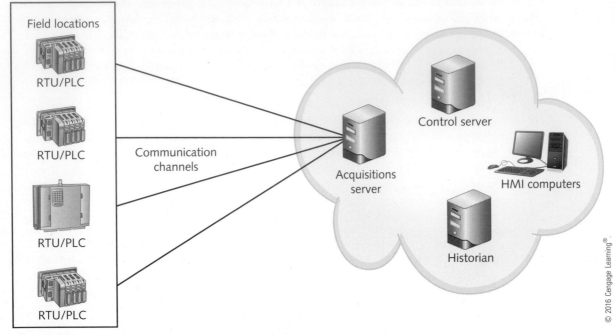

Figure 12-1   Basic components of an ICS or SCADA network

to digital data. For example, an RTU might sense temperature, water depth, humidity, flow through a pipe, pressure on a gasket, or speed of a train. An RTU is considered a field device because it's located within the physical system.

- A **programmable logic controller (PLC)** is a very small dedicated computer capable of converting analog data to digital data; it works in real time, can control machinery, and is a critical component of an industrial control system. See Figure 12-2. Programmers write code that is part of the firmware in a PLC, specific to its dedicated task. For example, the dishwasher in your home contains a PLC that senses the water temperature as the heating element heats up the water and switches the dishwasher to the wash

Figure 12-2   A programmable logic controller is programmed to affect a physical system

cycle when the water is hot enough. A PLC can be embedded in and considered part of an RTU. When an RTU has a suitable PLC embedded, the RTU is capable of not only sensing data, but controlling the physical system. For example, an RTU/PLC in a water processing plant can sense when a water level reaches a certain depth and automatically closes a valve to stop water flow. Any device in an ICS that is motorized and can control the physical system is called an actuator.

- Communication channels, such as satellite, Wi-Fi, the Internet, closed circuits, or PSTN, carry data and control messages between the RTUs and PLCs within the physical system and centralized control centers. When an RTU and PLC are separate devices, the communication channel that connects a PLC to an RTU or to an actuator is called the fieldbus.

NOTE Although the term telemetry can refer to wired communication, generally telemetry is used to refer to a wireless communication that transmits data regarding specific measurements and conditions. For example, a transmitting device carried by a weather balloon uses telemetry to transmit weather data to ground antennas.

- **Human-machine interfaces (HMIs)** are the computers, including hardware and software, that people use to monitor and manage the physical systems.

- Software and ICS servers in an ICS or SCADA system might include:

  ○ An acquisitions server, also called the I/O server, which collects and stores raw data. This server connects to field devices from which it receives raw data and passes that data on to other servers in the SCADA system.

  ○ A supervisory computer or server, which can control the physical system. This server is sometimes called the control server, master terminal unit (MTU), or the SCADA server. (It's called a SCADA server because the term *SCADA* is typically associated with controlling the physical system.)

  ○ The historian, which is a centralized database of collected and analyzed data and control activities. This data is often analyzed to recognize trends in the physical system.

Two methods that an ICS might use to control the physical system are an open loop system and a closed loop system, which are both diagrammed in Figure 12-3 and described here:

- An open loop system, also called an open network, makes decisions based on predetermined expectations, events, and past history of the system without regard for what's currently happening within the system. As an analogy, suppose you can't see a tub that you want to fill with water. You decide to run the water for 10 minutes because, in the past, it has taken 10 minutes to fill the tub. Using ICS and PLC terminology, you are the PLC or controller, the actuator is the water faucet handle, the process is filling the tub, and your turning off the water is a disturbance or change made to the process of filling the tub. (Keep in mind, however, that in a real ICS, the actuator is always motorized.)

12

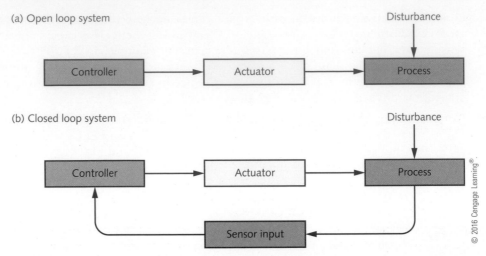

Figure 12-3   An ICS can implement open loop systems or closed loop systems

- A **closed loop system**, also called a **closed network**, makes decisions based on real-time data. To use real-time data for filling the tub, you would need to install a sensor in the tub that sounds an alarm when the water reaches a certain level.

Both types of systems have advantages and disadvantages. For example, if you are using an open loop system, and the tub is already half full, running the water for 10 minutes will flood the room. In that case, you would probably wish that you were using a closed loop system, with a sensor that could give you accurate information about the water level in the tub. On the other hand, if your water level sensor fails you, the water might never get turned off, creating an even worse disaster than running water for only 10 minutes. In that case, the open loop system might seem preferable. In fact, most ICSs employ a combination of open loop and closed loop techniques. For example, you might install a water level sensor to tell you when to turn off the water, and also follow the rule that if you haven't heard the alarm after 10 minutes, you turn off the water anyway.

A closed loop system requires field devices distributed throughout the physical system to monitor many aspects of the system and is called a **distributed control system (DCS)**. In a DCS, control is distributed among these devices and each device is part of a closed loop system. In contrast, a nondistributed system has a single controller at a centralized location.

Securing an ICS/SCADA Network

What if hackers were to gain access to a local electrical grid, chemical manufacturing plant, regional transportation system, or natural gas pipeline? For example, in the year 2000, a man in Queensland, Australia, was denied a job with his local government, and, in retaliation, used radio transmitters to break into the ICS at his local sewage treatment plant and released gallons of raw sewage into nearby rivers and parks. As a network administrator working with an organization that implements an ICS, you need to be aware of the unique security and performance needs of an ICS. Recommended best practices to keep your ICS network secure include:

- Inventory all the connections to your ICS/SCADA network, for example, connections to the corporate network; the Internet; dial-up connections; and connections to vendors, government agencies, and corporate business partners. Disconnect unnecessary connections.

- Segment your ICS/SCADA network from the corporate network. Recall that segmenting a network with VLANs and subnets is covered in Chapter 10.

- Isolate your ICS/SCADA network by deploying a DMZ between the corporate network and the ICS network. Use firewalls between the DMZ networks, the corporate network, and the ICS network, as shown in Figure 12-4. Use strong firewall rules for the firewall that protects the ICS/SCADA network. For example, some ICS implementations don't allow users to log on to the servers in the ICS network from anywhere except from computers physically located on the ICS network.

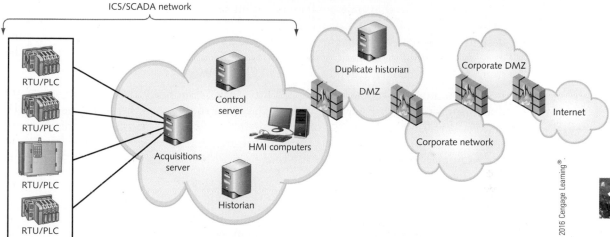

Figure 12-4   Use a DMZ to protect the ICS control network from the corporate network

- Completely disconnect the ICS/SCADA network from the Internet. This technique of physically isolating a network is called an air gap, but isn't possible if the Internet provides communication channels between remote portions of a larger ICS/SCADA network.

- Secure or harden the ICS/SCADA network by implementing strict firewall rules, intrusion detection systems, and physical security controls. Set up around-the-clock incident monitoring.

- For fault tolerance, deploy redundancy as appropriate. Consider redundant RTUs and communication channels to ICS servers. An ICS might have a redundant control center.

- Harden the ICS/SCADA network by strictly controlling access to the network, with encrypted authentication. To enhance security, an ICS network might have its own Windows domain separate from the corporate domain.

- Protect the historian. Personnel working on the corporate network that are not authorized to work on the ICS network might require access to the historian. To allow access without compromising the ICS network, consider placing the historian in the DMZ or, even better, consider duplicating the historian database on a server in the DMZ so that the ICS network and the original historian are not exposed to the corporate network.

- Make sure that vendors responsible for supporting hardware and software on your network fully disclose any backdoor entrance into your network. A backdoor entrance is a way to access a network that bypasses normal authentication. Vendors sometimes build backdoors into a customer's network so they can remotely get in to service their products when normal access fails. This remote access can be a security risk. In some situations, you can disable inbound access and set up a callback system that vendors can use to remotely service their products. Also, don't allow vendors to use proprietary protocols to secure your network because, in general, these secret protocols are easily hacked.

- If the ICS network provides Wi-Fi, consider installing Faraday cages around the Wi-Fi hot spots so that only computers within secured areas of the building can use the hot spots. (A Faraday cage is an enclosure made of a conductive material that is designed to block electromagnetic signals, including Wi-Fi. You can create a Faraday cage by installing metal netting in or on the walls of a building, similar to the situation you read about in Chapter 6's On the Job story.)

- Keep current all documentation needed for configuration management, as this documentation might be critical when responding to any unauthorized access to the system. Perform routine audits of the security policies and technical procedures implemented on your network. (These audits are sometimes called technical audits.) For example, have technicians verify that firewall policies are executed as specified in your documented security policies.

- Keep well-documented and well-maintained backups of the system and its data.

- Clearly define risk management practices and establish risk management teams, with clearly defined roles for each team member. For example, one team essential to a secure ICS network is often called a "red team" and is charged with identifying and evaluating potential attacks on the network and creating disaster recovery plans for each type of attack. (Disaster recovery is discussed later in this chapter.)

- Implement role-based access control (RBAC) to the system. That is, assign each user only the rights and privileges to the system that are necessary for him or her to perform duties based on job description. Educate users regarding social engineering to ensure that all users carefully protect information that might inadvertently give intruders access to the ICS/SCADA network.

ICS networks, as you've seen, present unique challenges. Enterprise-scale networks, which are large networks that support a complex and wide variety of computer systems and networks, present their own challenges. The remainder of this chapter covers network management techniques that, while helpful on smaller networks, are absolutely essential on enterprise-scale networks.

Asset Management and Business Documents

In Chapter 4, you learned about network configuration management, including the importance of maintaining documentation about your network, such as logical and physical network diagrams. Other essential documentation includes asset management documentation; IP address utilization documentation; vendor documentation (such as contact information, warranty information, service agreements, and troubleshooting instructions); and internal operating procedures, policies, and standards.

Other parts of this book cover some of these types of documentation. In this section, you learn about the details of asset management documentation, which is especially important when managing large numbers of devices such as in an enterprise environment, and then you review business documents you might encounter when managing an enterprise network.

Asset Management

The term **asset management** refers to the monitoring and maintaining of all the assets that make up a network. The first step in asset management is to inventory all the components on the network, which include:

- *nodes or hardware devices on the network*—A list of all the nodes on the network should include each device's configuration files, model number, serial number, location on the network, and technical support contact.

- *software*—For each software package purchased by your organization, inventory its version number, vendor, licensing, and technical support contact.

Depending on the needs of your organization, you might require an asset management application that can automatically discover all devices on the network and then save that information in a database, or you might use a simple spreadsheet to save the data. In either case, your asset management records should be comprehensive and accessible to all personnel involved in maintaining or troubleshooting the network. In addition, ensure that the asset management database is regularly updated, either manually or automatically, as changes to network hardware and software occur. The information you retain is useful only while it is current.

Asset management simplifies maintaining and upgrading the network chiefly because you know what the system includes. For example, if you discover that a router purchased two years ago requires an upgrade to its operating system software to fix a security flaw, you need to know how many routers are installed, where they are installed, and whether any have already received the software upgrade. An up-to-date asset management system allows you to avoid searching through old invoices and troubleshooting records to answer these questions.

In addition, asset management documentation provides network administrators with information about the costs and benefits of certain types of hardware or software. For example, if you conclude that 20 percent of your staff's troubleshooting time is spent on one flawed brand of NIC, an asset management system can reveal how many NICs you would need to replace if you chose to replace those cards, and whether it would make sense to replace the entire installed base. Some asset management applications can even track the length of equipment leases and alert network managers when leases will expire.

> **NOTE** The term *asset management* originally referred to an organization's system for keeping tabs on every piece of equipment it owned. This function was usually handled through the Accounting Department. Some of the accounting-related tasks included under the original definition for asset management, such as managing the depreciation on network equipment or tracking the expiration of leases, apply to asset management in networking as well.

Business Documents

Aside from the documentation you create to track network assets and resources, you will also encounter a variety of standard business documents in the course of your work as a network technician. Although you won't likely be held responsible for creating these documents, it's helpful to be familiar with their purpose and structure:

- *RFP*—An **RFP (request for proposal)** is a request to vendors to submit a proposal for a product or service your company wants to purchase. Key parts of an RFP include why your company requires the product or service, how the product or service will be used, how and when the proposals will be evaluated, and a list of items a vendor should include in its proposal (for example, a detailed description of its product or service, technical support, user training, and initial and ongoing costs).

- *MOU*—An **MOU (memorandum of understanding)** documents the intentions of two or more parties to enter into a binding agreement, or contract, and is sometimes used between an informal handshake and the legally binding signatures on contracts. The MOU can be helpful in pushing along contract negotiations and in defining specific concerns of each party, but it is usually not a legally binding document, does not grant extensive rights to either party, provides no legal recourse, and is not intended to provide a thorough coverage of the agreement to come.

- *SOW*—An **SOW (statement of work)** documents in detail the work that must be completed for a particular project, and includes specifics such as tasks, deliverables, standards, payment schedule, and work timeline. An SOW is legally binding, meaning it can be enforced in a court of law.

- *SLA*—An **SLA (service-level agreement)** is a legally binding contract or part of a contract that defines, in plain language and in measurable terms, the aspects of a service provided to a customer, such as the service provided by an ISP. Details specified might include contract duration (minimum or maximum), guaranteed uptime, problem management, performance benchmarks, and termination options.

- *MSA*—An **MSA (master service agreement)** is a contract that defines the terms of future contracts between parties, such as payment terms or arbitration arrangements.

- *MLA*—An **MLA (master license agreement)** grants a license from a creator, developer, or producer, such as a software producer, to a third party for the purposes of marketing, sublicensing, or distributing the product to consumers as a stand-alone product or as part of another product.

It's important to understand the specifics covered—and *not* covered—in a particular document before signing it. For example, although the typical MOU is not intended to serve as a binding contract, there are circumstances under which it could be binding, especially if money is exchanged. Be sure to consult an attorney for advice regarding concerns you might have about any document before you sign it.

Change Management

Network conditions are always in a state of flux. Technology advances, vendors come and go, responsibilities and needs of users change, and attacks from malware and hackers can expose vulnerabilities that require attention. Managing change while maintaining your network's efficiency and availability requires good planning. The following section describes some of the most common types of software and hardware changes, from installing patches to replacing a network backbone. After that, you look at the change management documentation that might be required for an enterprise-scale network.

Software and Hardware Changes

You might be called on to implement the following three types of changes to existing software:

- *patch*—A software **patch** is a correction, improvement, or enhancement to software. It corrects a bug, closes a vulnerability, or adds minor enhancements to only part of the software, leaving most of the code untouched. Microsoft sometimes releases a major group of patches to Windows or a Microsoft application, which it calls a **service pack**.

- *upgrade*—A software **upgrade** is a major change to a software package that enhances the functionality and features of the software, while also correcting bugs and vulnerabilities. When a patch or upgrade is applied to device drivers, it is called a **driver update**.

- *rollback*—A software **rollback**, also called **backleveling** or **downgrading**, is the process of reverting to a previous version of software after attempting to patch or upgrade it.

12

Applying Concepts

Steps to Change Software or Hardware

Although the specifics vary for each type of software or hardware change, the general steps can be summarized as follows:

1. Generally, don't allow patches to be automatically installed in the OS, application, or device. When you're responsible for a computer or network, you need to fully understand the impact of any change before you allow that change.

2. Determine whether the patch or upgrade is necessary. Patches to plug security holes are almost always necessary; however, adding new features or functionality to software might cause more work than it's worth in time and money.

3. Read the vendor's documentation regarding the patch or upgrade to learn its purpose, and make sure you understand how it will affect the system, whether or not it is compatible with current hardware and software, and how to apply or undo the change.

4. Before deploying the patch or upgrade, test it in a testing lab to make sure it acts as expected. A testing lab is a small network that is segmented from the rest of the network, and contains computers, called test beds, that represent the typical hardware and OS configurations in your network, as well as any specialized equipment your company uses (for example, printers, bar-code readers, and biometric devices) that might interact with the proposed new software or hardware. Also determine whether and how the change can be reversed, in case troubles arise. Document your findings.

5. Determine whether the change should apply to some or all users, network segments, or devices. Also decide whether it will be distributed centrally or machine by machine.

6. Schedule the change for completion during off-hours (unless it is an emergency). The time period in which a change will be implemented is called the maintenance window. Everyone responsible for those who might be affected by a disruption in service (for example, the technical staff or directors of user departments) must be informed of and agree to the maintenance window in advance.

7. Immediately before the change is made, announce to system administrators, help desk personnel, and affected users about the change and the maintenance window.

If problems arise as the maintenance is in progress and you realize that you are about to exceed the maintenance window, be sure to inform technical staff and users of the anticipated delay and what to expect.

8. Back up the current system, software, or hardware configuration before making any modifications. You can typically copy the configuration of a router, switch, or server to a USB flash drive, backup media, or network share.

9. If necessary, throughout the maintenance window, prevent users from accessing the system or the part of the system being altered.

10. Keep the installation instructions and vendor documentation handy as you implement the change.

11. After the change is implemented, test the system in real time, even though you've already tested it in the testing lab. Exercise the software as a typical user would. For hardware devices, put a higher load on the device than it would incur during normal use in your organization. Note any unintended or unanticipated consequences of the modification.

12. If the change was successful, reenable access to the system. If it was unsuccessful, revert to the previous version of the software or hardware.

13. Inform system administrators, help desk personnel, and affected users when the change is complete. If you had to reverse it, make this known and explain why.

14. Record your change in the change management system, as described later in this chapter.

Regardless of how hard you try to make hardware and software changes go smoothly, eventually you will encounter a situation when you must backlevel your changes. Although no hard-and-fast rules for backleveling exist, Table 12-1 summarizes some basic suggestions. Bear in mind that you must always refer to the software vendor's documentation to reverse an upgrade. If you must backlevel a network operating system upgrade, you should also consult with experienced professionals about the best approach for your network environment.

Table 12-1 Reversing a software upgrade

Type of upgrade	Options for reversing
Operating system patch	Use the patch's automatic uninstall utility.
Client software upgrade	Use the upgrade's automatic uninstall utility, or reinstall the previous version of the client on top of the upgrade.
Shared application upgrade	Use the application's automatic uninstall utility, or maintain a complete copy of the previous installation of the application and reinstall it over the upgrade.
Operating system upgrade	Prior to the upgrade, make a complete backup of the system; to backlevel, restore the entire system from the backup; uninstall an operating system upgrade only as a last resort.

© 2016 Cengage Learning®

 NOTE When replacing a device or component in a device (for example, a NIC), keep the old component for a while, especially if it is the only one of its kind at your organization. Not only might you need to put it back in the device, but you might also need to refer to it for information.

Change Management Documentation

Network+
2.3
2.5
5.8

Generally, the larger an organization, the more documentation is required when making hardware and software changes. Required processes and how these processes are documented are designed to protect the person making the change, users, managers, and the organization so that changes don't unnecessarily disrupt normal work flow or put undue responsibility for a problem on any one person. Here is a list of what to expect:

1. *Submit a change request document*—Know who in the organization may submit such a document. For example, the lead accountant might be considered the owner of an accounting application and this person is the only one who can request an upgrade to the application. On the other hand, IT personnel can request a security patch be applied to this same application. The change request document might include:

   • The person submitting the change request and the person who must authorize the change (for example, the network administrator is submitting the request and the director of IT must approve it)

   • The type of change (for example, software patch)

12

- Reason for the change (for example, to fix a bug)
- Configuration procedures (for example, an upgraded application might require new data file templates be built, settings defined for an entire department of users, or existing data be converted to a new format)
- Potential impact of the change (for example, 10 users in the Accounting Department will need three hours of training)
- Rollback process (for example, if the new application doesn't work as expected and the Accounting Department head decides it's best to go back to the old way of doing things)
- Notification process (when and how management and users will be informed of the change)
- Timeline for the change

2. *Understand and follow the approval process*—The manager of a department might be able to approve a minor change to an application, hardware device, or OS, whereas major changes might need to go through a review board process. You might be expected to provide additional documentation during this review process. The complexity of the approval process is usually determined by the cost and time involved in making the change, the number of users affected and the potential risk to their work productivity, and the difficulty of rolling back the change. Sometimes a change request is entered into a change management database where many people can access the request, enter supporting documentation and questions, and weigh in on their opinions regarding the change.

Minor changes, such as applying a security patch to an application that involves only a few users, are sometimes made without going through an official change request process, but are usually documented in some way, such as a technician making entries in the change management database before and after the change is made.

3. *The change is project managed*—After a major change is approved, a change coordinator is usually assigned to the project. This coordinator is responsible for shepherding through all aspects of the change including user training; coordinating between departments involved in the change; documenting how and when notification of the change will happen; negotiating with users, management, and the IT Department regarding the authorized downtime for the change to happen; communicating with management regarding any unforeseen problems that arise during the change; and managing the budget for the change. Technicians and the network administrator work closely with the change coordinator during the change process.

4. *Provide additional documentation*—Depending on the organization, other required documentation might include testing documentation (for example, test data, testing scenarios, and software and hardware used for the testing), step-by-step procedures for applying the change, vendor documentation and vendor contact information, and locations of configuration backups and of backups that will be used in the

event of a rollback. A network administrator will pay particular attention to update his or her own documentation regarding the network, including updating the network map you learned about in Chapter 4. These network documentation updates might include:

- Network configuration (for example, the network was segmented with three new VLANs and subnets added)

- IP address utilization (for example, the IP address ranges used in the three new subnets)

- Additions to the network (for example, new routers and switches were installed to accommodate new VLANs to handle additional network traffic)

- Physical location changes (for example, 20 workstations, a switch, and two printers were moved to a different building on the corporate campus)

5. *Close the change*—After the change is implemented and tested and users have settled into the change without problems, the change is officially closed. Sometimes the change coordinator will call a debriefing session where all involved can evaluate how well the change went and what can be done to improve future changes.

Physical Security Controls

Network+
3.4

You studied network risk management in Chapter 7, along with several issues that are common to every network. An important element in network security that is especially relevant to large networks is the challenge of restricting physical access to all of its critical components. Only trusted networking staff should have access to secure computer rooms, data rooms, network closets, storage rooms, entrance facilities, and locked equipment cabinets. Furthermore, only authorized staff should have access to the premises, such as offices and data centers, where these rooms are located. If computer rooms are not locked, intruders may steal equipment or sabotage software or hardware. For example, a malicious visitor could slip into an unsecured computer room and take control of a server where an administrator is logged on, then steal data or reformat the server's hard drive. Although a security policy defines who has access to the computer room, locking the locations that house networking equipment is necessary to keep unauthorized individuals out. Many larger organizations have highly sophisticated door access controls, as described here:

- *keypad or cipher locks*—Locks may be either physical or electronic. Electronic keypads, for example, can reduce the inherent risk of lost keys. Changing the code regularly can also help increase security. Cipher locks (one brand name is Cypher Lock) are physical or electronic locks requiring a code to open the door. Cipher locks are not designed for physical security, such as on an outside door, so much as for the purpose of controlling access to an area, such as an indoor data room, by logging who comes and goes, enabling or disabling unescorted entry, scheduling open access times, and even responding to access made under duress (with a special hostage code that trips an alarm when entered). Figure 12-5 shows one example of a cipher lock.

© iStockphoto/richterfoto.

Figure 12-5 A cipher lock can document who enters an area and when

- *access badges*—Many large organizations require authorized employees to wear electronic access badges, or **smart cards**. These badges can be programmed to allow their owner access to some, but not all, rooms in a building. Figure 12-6 depicts a typical badge access security system. Some badges, such as the one in Figure 12-7, are actually **proximity cards** (also called **prox cards**), which do not require direct contact with a proximity reader in order to be detected. In fact, a reader can be concealed inside a wall or other enclosure and requires very little maintenance. With a typical range of about 5–10 cm, the card can be detected even while it's still inside a wallet or purse, or

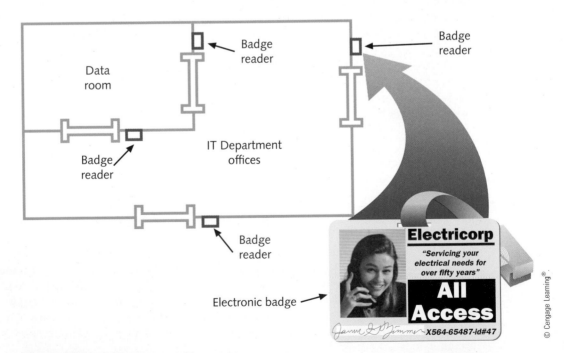

© Cengage Learning®

Figure 12-6 Badge access security system

© gifted/Shutterstock.com.

Figure 12-7 A proximity card does not require physical contact with a proximity reader

it can be incorporated or duplicated in a key fob. Passive cards, similar to NFC tags, collect power from the reader's power field in order to transmit data. Active cards, on the other hand, contain an internal lithium battery and provide a greater range (up to 150 m), which makes these cards ideal for long-range applications such as security gates or tollbooths.

- *biometrics*—A more expensive physical security solution involves biorecognition access, in which a device scans an individual's unique physical characteristics, called biometrics, such as the color patterns in his iris or the geometry of his hand, to verify his identity. Organizations may use biometric devices to regulate entrance through physical barriers to their campuses, such as gates, fences, walls, or landscaping. See Figure 12-8.

© iStockphoto/Auttachod.

Figure 12-8 Fingerprint scanner

- *mantraps*—Some organizations increase security of access-controlled areas with mantraps. A mantrap consists of two doors on either end of a small entryway where the first door must close before the second door can open. A separate form of identification might be required for each door, such as a badge for the first door and a fingerprint scan for the second door, and in some cases, the mantrap can lock both sets of doors in order to detain a suspect attempting unauthorized access. A mantrap might be monitored by a security guard, and might even include metal detectors, X-ray machines, or AIT machines, such as those used by the TSA at airports. **AIT (advanced imaging technology) machines** use millimeter-wave scanners, which emit radio waves similar to those emitted by cell phones, to indicate on cartoonlike images any areas of concern to security personnel. See Figure 12-9 for an example of this image.

© sahua d/Shutterstock.com.

Figure 12-9   Results of an AIT scan

Many IT departments use video surveillance systems, called **closed-circuit TV (CCTV)**, to monitor activity in secured rooms. IP cameras can be placed in data centers, computer rooms, data rooms, and data storage areas, as well as facility entrances. IT technicians might also be called upon to install and service a video surveillance system for the entire company (see Figure 12-10). A central security office might display several camera views at once, or it might switch from camera to camera. The video footage generated from these cameras is contained within a secure segment of the network, and is usually saved for a period of time in case it's needed later in a security breach investigation or prosecution.

As with other security measures, the most important way to ensure physical security is to plan for it. You can begin your planning by asking questions related to physical security checks in your security audit. Relevant questions include the following:

- Which rooms contain critical systems or data and must be secured?

- Through what means might intruders gain access to the facility, computer room, data room, network closet, or data storage areas (including doors, windows, adjacent rooms, ceilings, large vents, temporary walls, hallways, and so on)?

- How and to what extent are authorized personnel granted entry? (Do they undergo background or reference checks? Is their need for access clearly justified? Are their hours of access restricted? Who ensures that lost keys or ID badges are reported?)

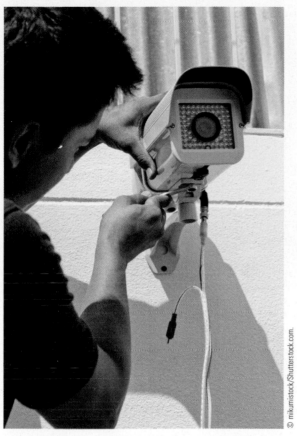

© mikumistock/Shutterstock.com.

Figure 12-10 IT personnel might be responsible for the installation and maintenance of a CCTV network

- Are employees instructed to ensure security after entering or leaving secured areas (for example, by not propping open doors)?

- Are authentication methods (such as ID badges) difficult to forge or circumvent?

- Do supervisors or security personnel make periodic physical security checks?

- Are all combinations, codes, or other access means to computer facilities protected at all times, and are these combinations changed frequently?

- Do you have a plan for documenting and responding to physical security breaches?

Also consider what you might stand to lose if someone salvaged computers you discarded. To guard against the threat of information being stolen from a decommissioned hard drive, you can run a specialized drive sanitizer program to not only delete the hard drive's contents but also make file recovery impossible. Alternatively, you can remove the hard drive from the computer and erase its contents using a magnetic hard drive eraser called a **degausser**, as shown in Figure 12-11. Some security professionals even advise physically destroying a hard drive by pulverizing or melting it to be certain data is unreadable.

Figure 12-11   Use a degausser to sanitize a magnetic hard drive or tape

Troubleshooting and Response Policies

Despite every precaution, disasters and security breaches do happen. Training and preparation can make all the difference in your company's ability to respond and adapt to these situations.

Disaster Recovery

Disaster recovery is the process of restoring your critical functionality and data after an outage that affects more than a single system or a limited group of users. Disaster recovery must take into account the possible extremes, such as an enterprise-wide outage, not just relatively minor outages, failures, security breaches, or data corruption.

Disaster Recovery Planning A disaster recovery plan accounts for the worst-case scenarios, from a far-reaching hurricane to a military or terrorist attack. It should identify a disaster recovery team, sometimes called the red team, with an appointed coordinator. It should also provide contingency plans for restoring or replacing computer systems, power, telephone systems, and paper-based files. The goal of a disaster recovery plan is to ensure business continuity, which is the ability of the company to continue doing business with the least amount of interruption possible. Sections of the plan related to computer systems should include the following:

- Contact names and phone numbers for emergency coordinators who will execute the disaster recovery response in case of disaster, as well as roles and responsibilities of other staff.
- Details on which data and servers are being backed up, how frequently backups occur, where backups are kept (off-site), and, most important, how backed-up data can be recovered in full.

- Details on network topology, redundancy, and agreements with national service carriers, in case local or regional vendors fall prey to the same disaster.

- Regular strategies for testing the disaster recovery plan.

- A plan for managing the crisis, including regular communications with employees and customers. Consider the possibility that regular communications modes (such as phone lines) might be unavailable.

Having a comprehensive disaster recovery plan lessens the risk of losing critical data in case of extreme situations, and also makes potential customers and your insurance providers look more favorably on your organization.

Disaster Recovery Contingencies
An organization can choose from several options for recovering from a disaster. The options vary by the amount of employee involvement, hardware, software, planning, and investment each involves. They also vary according to how quickly they will restore network functionality in case a disaster occurs. As you would expect, every contingency plan necessitates a site other than the building where the network's main components normally reside. An organization might maintain its own disaster recovery sites—for example, by renting office space in a different city—or contract with a company that specializes in disaster recovery services to provide the alternate site. Disaster recovery contingencies are commonly divided into three categories: cold site, warm site, and hot site.

- A cold site is a place where the computers, devices, and connectivity necessary to rebuild a network exist, but they are not appropriately configured, updated, or connected. Therefore, restoring functionality from a cold site could take a long time. For example, suppose your small business network consists of a file and print server, mail server, backup server, Internet gateway/DNS/DHCP server, 25 clients, four printers, a router, a switch, two access points, and a connection to your local ISP. At your cold site, you might store four server computers on which your company's NOS is not installed, and that do not possess the appropriate configurations and data necessary to operate in your environment. The 25 client machines stored there might be in a similar state. In addition, you might have a router, a switch, and two access points at the cold site, but these might also require configuration to operate in your environment. Finally, the cold site would not necessarily have Internet connectivity, or at least not the same type as your network uses. Supposing you followed good backup practices and stored your backup media at the cold site, you would then need to restore operating systems, applications, and data to your servers and clients; reconfigure your connectivity devices; and arrange with your ISP to have your connectivity restored to the cold site. Even for a small network, this process of rebuilding your network could take weeks.

- A warm site is a place where the computers, devices, and connectivity necessary to rebuild a network exist, with some pieces appropriately configured, updated, or connected. For example, a service provider that specializes in disaster recovery might maintain a duplicate of each of your servers in its data center. You might arrange to have the service provider update those duplicate servers with your backed-up data on the first of each month because updating the servers daily is much more expensive. In that case, if a disaster occurs in the middle of the month, you would still need to

12

update your duplicate servers with your latest weekly or daily backups before they could stand in for the downed servers. Recovery using a warm site can take hours or days, compared with the weeks a cold site might require. Maintaining a warm site costs more than maintaining a cold site, but not as much as maintaining a hot site.

- A hot site is a place where the computers, devices, and connectivity necessary to rebuild a network exist, and all are appropriately configured, updated, and connected to match your network's current state. For example, you might use server mirroring to maintain identical copies of your servers at two WAN locations. In a hot site contingency plan, both locations would also contain identical connectivity devices and configurations, and thus be able to stand in for the other at a moment's notice. As you can imagine, hot sites are expensive and potentially time consuming to maintain. For organizations that cannot tolerate downtime, however, hot sites provide the best disaster recovery option.

Forensics

Network+
2.3
3.7

Every security policy should include a response policy, which specifically defines the characteristics of an event that qualifies as a formal incident and the steps that should be followed as a result. Qualifying incidents might include a break-in, fire, weather-related emergency, hacking attack, discovery of illegal content or activity on an employee's computer, or a malware outbreak. This policy is written with the intent of keeping people safe; protecting sensitive data; ensuring business continuity and integrity; and collecting data to determine what went wrong, who is responsible, and what actions should be taken in the future to prevent similar damage.

In some cases, the data being collected might be presented in a court of law for the purpose of prosecuting an instigator of illegal activity. In this case, data must be carefully collected according to industry best practices so that it will stand up to the scrutiny of the court. Some of the forensic data available for analysis can be damaged or destroyed if improperly handled. Ideally, one or more first responders would take charge. First responders are the people with training and/or certifications that prepare them to handle evidence in such a way as to preserve its admissibility in court. However, it's critical that every IT technician in a company know how to safeguard sensitive information, logged data, and other legal evidence until the first responder or incident response team can take over the collection of evidence.

eDiscovery, or electronic discovery, can reveal a great deal of information, called ESI (electronically stored information) or active data, contained on a computer's hard drives and storage media, such as calendars, email, and databases. Computer forensics is a process of investigating deeper data on a computer and will essentially autopsy the computer to discover hidden data, such as deleted files and file fragments, and who has accessed that data and when. This hidden information is called ambient data.

A response policy should detail the following steps:

1. *Determine if escalation is necessary*—The first step in responding to an incident is to determine whether the event requires escalation—that is, if it should be recognized as

something other than a normal problem faced by IT technicians. Each company will have its own criteria for which incidents require escalation, as well as its own chain of command for notification purposes. Make sure you're familiar with your company's requirements.

2. *Secure the area*—To prevent contamination of evidence, each device involved must be isolated. This means it should be disconnected from the network (remove the Ethernet cable or disable the Wi-Fi antenna) and secured, to ensure that no one else has contact with it until the response team arrives. Ideally, you should leave the device running without closing any programs or files. Different OSs require different shutdown procedures to preserve forensic data, so the shutdown process should be left to incident response experts. However, if a destructive program is running that might be destroying evidence, the fastest and safest solution is to unplug the power cord from the back of the machine (not just from the wall). Treat the entire work area as a crime scene. In some cases, such as with a physical break-in, an entire room, or possibly multiple rooms, must be secured to protect the evidence.

3. *Document the scene*—Creating a defensible audit trail is one of the highest priorities in the forensics process. An audit trail is a system of documentation that makes it possible for a third party to inspect evidence later and understand the flow of events. A defensible audit trail is an audit trail that can be justified and defended in a court of law. Document everything you or your team does, noting the time and the reason for each action. For example, if you unplugged the machine because a virus was wiping the hard drive, document the time and describe the symptoms you observed that led you to unplug the machine. Also make a list of everyone found in the area and their access to the computer in question. Make sure no one else enters the area until the response team arrives, and don't leave the area unattended even for a few moments.

4. *Monitor evidence and data collection*—Record all items collected for evidence. Take care to preserve all evidence in its original state. Do not attempt to access any files on a computer or server being collected for evidence, as this action alters a file's metadata and could render it inadmissible in court.

NOTE Another situation in which your company might be required to collect, secure, and monitor custody of computer equipment or data is after receiving a legal hold notification. A legal hold is a court order to preserve data for the purposes of an investigation. Upon receipt of a legal hold notification, a company is required to activate a defensible policy for the preservation of the data. In other words, the company must be able to justify its actions in a court of law. All relevant activities must be documented, and certain best practices should be followed to prevent any destruction of protected evidence. It's important to formulate a plan of action in case of a legal hold notification, before you receive such a notification. Doing so can prevent serious missteps in evidence preservation.

5. *Protect the chain of custody*—All collected data must be carefully processed and tracked so it does not leave official hands at any point in the forensics process. Typically, documentation used to track chain of custody describes exactly what the evidence is, when it was collected, who collected it, its condition, and how it was secured. If at any point in the process you have custody of evidence, be sure to sign off on a chain of custody

document, and obtain a signature from the next person in line when you hand over custody of the evidence.

6. *Monitor transport of data and equipment*—Generally, the incident response team is responsible for transporting all evidence to the forensics lab or other authority. Every item should be carefully documented so that the exact same configuration can be replicated in the lab. The response team might even have the capability to do a hot seizure and removal, which means they can use specialized devices that transfer a computer from one power source to another without shutting down the computer. This can be especially critical if it's possible that the computer or its data will become inaccessible after power is turned off—perhaps because a password is unknown or data is currently in memory.

7. *Create a report*—Be prepared to report on all activities that you observed or participated in during the course of the incident response. It's best to take notes along the way, and to write your report in full as soon as possible after the event while it's still fresh on your mind. All of this information will likely be included in the final forensics report, so it's important to be thorough and accurate.

The response policy should identify the members of a response team, all of whom should clearly understand the security policy, risks to the network, and security measures that have already been implemented. The responsibilities assigned to each team member should be clearly spelled out, and the team should regularly rehearse their roles by participating in security threat drills. Suggested team roles include the following:

- *dispatcher*—The person on call who first notices or is alerted to the problem. The dispatcher notifies the lead technical support specialist and then the manager. He or she also creates a record for the incident, detailing the time it began, its symptoms, and any other pertinent information about the situation. The dispatcher remains available to answer calls from clients or employees or to assist the manager.

- *manager*—The team member who coordinates the resources necessary to solve the problem. If in-house technicians cannot handle the incident, the manager finds outside assistance. The manager also ensures that the security policy is followed and that everyone within the organization is aware of the situation. As the response ensues, the manager continues to monitor events and communicate with the public relations specialist.

- *technical support specialist*—The team member who focuses on only one thing: solving the problem as quickly as possible. After the situation has been resolved, the technical support specialist describes in detail what happened and helps the manager find ways to avert such an incident in the future. Depending on the size of the organization and the severity of the incident, this role may be filled by more than one person.

- *public relations specialist*—If necessary, this team member learns about the situation and the response and then acts as official spokesperson for the organization to the public or other interested parties.

After resolving a problem, the team reviews what happened, determines how it might have been prevented, and then implements measures designed to prevent future problems. However, a security policy alone can't guard against intruders. Network administrators must also attend to physical, network design, and NOS vulnerabilities, as described earlier in this book.

Chapter Summary

Industrial Networks

■ An industrial system is a system of machines, such as an assembly line at a tire manufacturing plant. These systems produce data where computers and machinery must interact with physical components that are not digital or technical in nature.

■ An industrial control system (ICS) is a group of networked computers used to manage a physical system of industrial processes. Besides the devices typical to any network, an ICS network includes a SCADA system, RTUs, PLCs, HMIs, and ICS servers.

■ For best security, isolate an ICS/SCADA network by deploying a DMZ between the corporate network and the ICS network. Use firewalls between the DMZ networks, the corporate network, and the ICS network. If possible, completely isolate the ICS/SCADA network from the Internet.

Asset Management and Business Documents

■ When managing all the assets that make up a network, the first step is to inventory all the components on the network. Your asset management records should be comprehensive and accessible to all personnel who may become involved in maintaining or troubleshooting the network.

■ You should be familiar with the following standard business documents: RFP, MOU, SOW, SLA, MSA, and MLA. It's important to understand the specific items covered—and *not* covered—in a particular document before signing it. For example, although the typical MOU is not intended to serve as a binding contract, there are circumstances under which it could be binding, especially if money is exchanged.

Change Management

■ Managing change while maintaining your network's efficiency and availability requires good planning.

■ The three types of changes to existing software you might be called upon to implement include patches, upgrades or updates, and rollbacks. Before deploying the change, test the patch or upgrade in your testing lab to make sure it acts as expected.

■ The complexity of a change approval process is usually determined by the cost and time involved in making the change, the number of users affected, the potential risk to their work productivity, and the difficulty of rolling back the change.

Physical Security Controls

■ A security policy defines who has access to the computer room. To prevent unauthorized access, locking the locations that house networking equipment is necessary. Many larger organizations have highly sophisticated door access controls, such as cipher locks, proximity readers, biometric devices, and mantraps.

Troubleshooting and Response Policies

- Disaster recovery must take into account the possible extremes, such as an enterprise-wide outage, not just relatively minor outages, failures, security breaches, or data corruption.

- A disaster recovery plan should identify a disaster recovery team, sometimes called the red team, with an appointed coordinator. It should also provide contingency plans for restoring or replacing computer systems, power, telephone systems, and paper-based files. The goal of a disaster recovery plan is to ensure business continuity, which is the ability of the company to continue doing business with the least amount of interruption possible.

- Every contingency plan necessitates a site other than the building where the network's main components normally reside. An organization might maintain its own disaster recovery sites, or contract with a company that specializes in disaster recovery services to provide an alternate site.

- Some forensic data available for analysis can be damaged or destroyed if improperly handled. Ideally, one or more first responders would take charge. First responders are the people with training and/or certifications that prepare them to handle evidence in such a way as to preserve its admissibility in court. However, it's critical that every IT technician in a company know how to safeguard sensitive information, logged data, and other legal evidence until the first responder or incident response team can take over the collection of evidence.

Key Terms

For definitions of key terms, see the Glossary near the end of the book.

acquisitions server	closed network	fieldbus
active card	closed-circuit TV (CCTV)	first responder
active data	cold site	historian
actuator	computer forensics	hot seizure and removal
AIT (advanced imaging technology) machine	degausser	hot site
	disaster recovery	human-machine interfaces (HMI)
ambient data	distributed control system (DCS)	I/O server
asset management	downgrading	ICS server
backleveling	driver update	industrial control system (ICS)
biometrics	eDiscovery	industrial system
biorecognition access	electronic discovery	Internet of Things (IoT)
business continuity	ESI (electronically stored information)	legal hold
chain of custody		maintenance window
cipher lock	Faraday cage	mantrap
closed loop system	field device	

master terminal unit (MTU)

MLA (master license agreement)

MOU (memorandum of understanding)

MSA (master service agreement)

open loop system

passive card

patch

programmable logic controller (PLC)

prox card

proximity card

remote terminal unit (RTU)

RFP (request for proposal)

rollback

service pack

SLA (service-level agreement)

smart card

SOW (statement of work)

supervisory control and data acquisition (SCADA)

telemetry

testing lab

upgrade

warm site

Review Questions

1. Which ICS component senses attributes of the physical system and converts analog data to digital data, but cannot control the physical system?

   a. SCADA

   b. RTU

   c. PLC

   d. HMI

2. Which server controls the physical system in an ICS system?

   a. Acquisitions server

   b. I/O server

   c. MTU

   d. Historian

3. What should you place between the corporate network and the ICS network?

   a. VLAN

   b. Dial-up connection

   c. Redundant RTUs

   d. DMZ

4. Which business document fills the gap between an informal handshake and the legally binding signatures on contracts?

   a. SLA

   b. SOW

   c. MOU

   d. RFP

5. Your company has developed a Web site that includes a small program that collects real-time data on mortgage rates in specific geographic areas, and uses that information to calculate mortgage payment amounts based on the user's inputted data. The program was written by an independent software developer, who has granted your company a license to incorporate the program into your Web site for your customers' use. Which document was used?

   a. SLA

   b. MLA

   c. RFP

   d. SOW

6. Your team is in the process of implementing what you thought would be a relatively minor update to the NOS. You've hit a small but time-consuming snag, and it's now obvious that the update won't be completed until about an hour after your maintenance window passes. What should you do immediately?

   a. Consult the vendor documentation.

   b. Roll back the update and try again later.

   c. Bring the system back online and allow users to access any services that are available.

   d. Inform technical staff and users of the problem and what to expect.

7. Which of the following cards contains an internal lithium battery?

   a. Smart card

   b. Active card

   c. Passive card

   d. Proximity card

8. Which type of disaster recovery site is the most expensive?

   a. Hot site

   b. Ambient site

   c. Warm site

   d. Cold site

9. What process ensures that exact duplicates of servers are available if needed in the event of a disaster?

   a. Business continuity

   b. Server mirroring

   c. Network redundancy

   d. Contingency plan

10. While troubleshooting a network connection issue on a corporate workstation, you've just discovered that the workstation has been used for illegal gambling activities. You've notified your supervisor, and she said she's on her way to collect the computer for an investigation. While you're waiting for your supervisor to arrive, what should you do?

    a. Play games on the computer to pass the time.

    b. Close all running programs.

    c. Start investigating browser history.

    d. On a separate device or on a sheet of paper, make notes on everything that you've seen and done so far.

11. Industrial systems become part of the IoT when _____.

12. What is the primary difference between an open loop system and a closed loop system?

13. Which network components should be documented in asset management documentation?

14. A service pack is a collection of _____.

15. What is the basic process for backleveling an operating system upgrade?

16. How can a mantrap provide multifactor authentication?

17. What kind of device erases the contents of a magnetic hard drive?

18. What kind of information can computer forensics recover that eDiscovery cannot?

19. While upgrading a sales rep's corporate desktop computer, you notice some HR files for several coworkers from several different departments. You're pretty sure the sales rep shouldn't have access to this information, so you call your supervisor for assistance. He says he's on his way. Should you shut down the computer? Why or why not?

20. When your supervisor arrives, she has a document with her for you to sign, indicating the condition of the computer, how you kept it secure while you waited for her, and the transfer of responsibility for the computer from you to her. What kind of document is it?

12

Hands-On Projects

Project 12-1: Update Windows

On a Windows 7 or Windows 8.1 system, follow these steps to update Windows:

1. To open Control Panel in Windows 7, click **Start**, **Control Panel**. In Windows 8.1, right-click **Start** and click **Control Panel**.

2. In the Control Panel window in Category view, click **System and Security**, and then click **Windows Update**. The Windows Update window appears.

3. By default, Windows automatically downloads and installs updates. To change this setting, click **Change settings** in the left pane.

4. Under Important updates, select **Download updates but let me choose whether to install them**. Click **OK**.

5. In the left pane of the Windows Update window, click **Check for updates**. Windows checks for available updates. In Figure 12-12, Windows Update indicates that one important update and four optional updates are available. Your screen will probably look different.

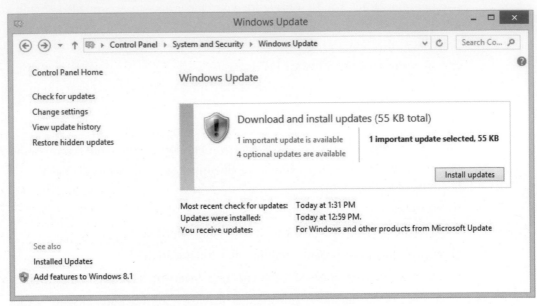

Figure 12-12   Windows 8.1 shows available updates ready to install

Source: Microsoft LLC

6. If you have updates to install, click the link for important updates or the link for optional updates to view these updates. Figure 12-13 shows the Windows Update

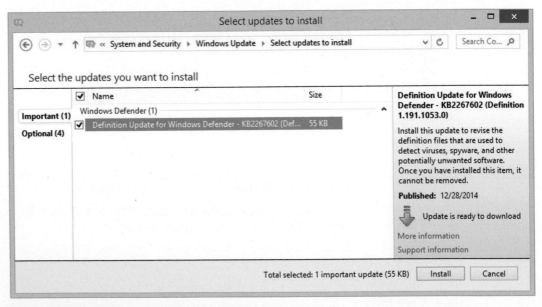

Figure 12-13   Information about an important Windows update

Source: Microsoft LLC

window after one important update was selected. Information in the right pane explains the update. For example, in Figure 12-13, the right pane explains that you cannot roll back the update once it is installed.

7. In the left pane, click **Optional** to view the optional updates. By default, optional updates are not selected for installation.

8. Make sure the important and optional updates you want to install are selected. On the Select updates to install window (see Figure 12-13), click **Install** to install all the important and optional updates you've selected. Follow directions on screen to install the updates. You might need to restart your computer to complete the installation.

9. Sometimes Microsoft holds back updates until others are installed. To check for more updates, reopen Windows Update, and then click **Check for updates**. If you find important updates, install them.

10. In an enterprise environment, Windows updates are usually carefully monitored and controlled by IT personnel, but for school and home computers, it's best to allow Windows to handle important updates automatically. To configure Windows Update to automatically download and install important updates, click **Change settings**.

11. Under Important updates, select **Install updates automatically (recommended)** and click **OK**.

Project 12-2: Update and Roll Back Device Drivers

Using a Windows 7 or Windows 8.1 computer, follow these steps to open the Device Manager window, update the device drivers for the NIC, and then roll back the drivers:

1. To open Device Manager in Windows 7, click **Start**, right-click **Computer**, click **Properties**, and then, in the System window, click **Device Manager**. In Windows 8.1, right-click **Start** and click **Device Manager**.

2. Double-click the **Network adapters** group to expand it and then right-click the Ethernet adapter. In Figure 12-14, the Ethernet adapter is Intel(R) 82579V Gigabit Network Connection, but your adapter might have a different name. Click **Properties** from the shortcut menu. The Properties dialog box for the adapter appears. See Figure 12-15a.

The tabs you see on the Properties box for a NIC depend on the features of the NIC.

3. Click the **Driver** tab (see Figure 12-15b). You can use this tab to update drivers, and, in some cases, roll back a driver update, depending on whether or not the Roll Back

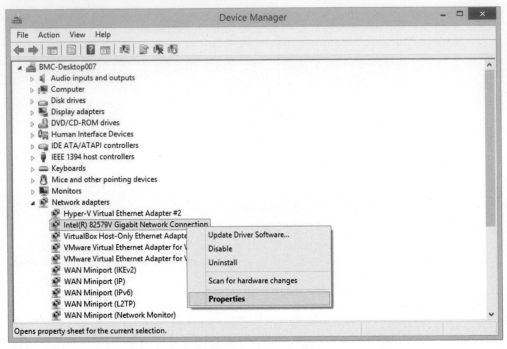

Figure 12-14 Open the Properties dialog box for the wired network adapter

Source: Microsoft LLC

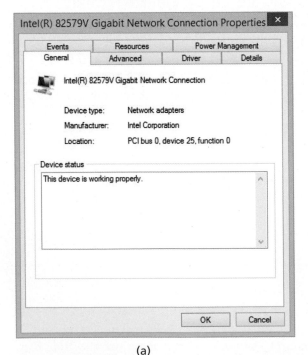

(a)

(b)

Figure 12-15 General tab and Driver tab of the network adapter Properties dialog box

Source: Microsoft LLC

Driver button is grayed out. In Figure 12-15b, the Roll Back Driver button is grayed out, indicating there is no driver update available to roll back.

4. Click **Update Driver**, and then click **Search automatically for updated driver software**. Windows searches for updates to the drivers. If it finds updates, follow directions on screen to install the updates. You might need to restart your computer.

5. If updates are found and installed, open the Device Manager window again, open the Properties dialog box for your network adapter, and then roll back the driver update.

Project 12-3: Research Disaster Recovery Solutions

HANDS-ON PROJECTS

Many companies offer DRaaS (disaster recovery as a service) solutions for all types of IT-related problems. These solutions might include basics, such as off-site storage and access to virtual servers during recovery, or more expensive (but more convenient) options such as single-file recovery (the ability to recover a single file at a time rather than an entire drive) and customizable backup schedules. In this project, you research two different disaster recovery solutions and compare the features, cost, and reviews for each.

Complete the following steps:

1. Use a search engine to search for companies that provide disaster recovery solutions, and select two of these solutions. The more thorough the information provided on the company Web site, the easier your research will be.

2. For each of your selections, find answers to at least three of the following five questions:

   - What are the key features?
   - Where would the company store your data? In other words, in what geographic areas are their servers located?
   - What kind of encryption does the company use?
   - Which standards are the services compliant with: HIPAA? PCI? SOX?
   - Who audits the company and their disaster recovery services?

3. Find reviews for both solutions. Summarize feedback from at least three customers about these solutions.

Case Projects

Case Project 12-1: Research Document Samples and Templates

CASE PROJECTS

If you are ever called on to create, modify, or evaluate a business document, document samples and templates can be of great help. Do the following to research the many document samples and templates available on the Web:

1. Search the Web for an MOU sample or template. What are the sections in the document? Save a sample MOU or save the link to an MOU.

2. Microsoft Office offers many online templates. If you have Office installed on your computer, use it to search for an SOW template. If you don't have Office installed, find an SOW sample or template on the Web. What are the names of the sections in the document?

3. An SLA is often used to define the technical support that a supplier of a product or server will provide a client. Search the Web and save or print the link to a sample SLA that contains these elements:

   • Uptime (the time that a supplier guarantees the client can use the product or service)

   • Response time (the time it takes for the supplier to respond to a support request made by the client)

   • Penalties (what will happen if the supplier regularly does not meet the first two commitments)

CASE PROJECTS

Case Project 12-2: Explore Computer Forensics Investigations

As a network technician, you'll be better prepared to spot security compromises if you're already familiar with issues that have affected other networks in the past. In this project, you research three computer forensics investigations.

Complete the following steps:

1. Using a search engine, find articles, blogs, or videos discussing three different computer forensics cases. Identifying information might have been changed to protect privacy, but be sure the cases are actual cases, not just theoretical ones. Document your source or sources for each case.

2. Answer the following questions for each case:
   • How was the problem discovered?
   • What clues initiated the investigation?
   • What crime was committed or suspected?
   • What evidence was collected using computer forensics?
   • Were there any significant mistakes made in collecting this evidence?
   • What was the final outcome of the case?

CompTIA Network+ N10-006 Certification Exam Objectives

This book covers material related to all of the CompTIA Network+ examination objectives for exam N10-006, which were released by CompTIA (the Computing Technology Industry Association) in 2015. The official list of objectives is available at CompTIA's Web site, *comptia.org*. For your reference, the following tables list each exam objective and the chapter of this book that explains the objective, plus the amount of the exam that will cover each certification domain. Each objective belongs to one of five domains (or main categories) of networking expertise. For example, comparing and contrasting different 802.11 standards belongs to Objective 5.3 in the "Industry standards, practices, and network theory" domain, which accounts for 16% of the exam's content.

Domain	% of Examination
1.0 Network architecture	22%
2.0 Network operations	20%
3.0 Network security	18%
4.0 Troubleshooting	24%
5.0 Industry standards, practices, and network theory	16%
Total	100%

Domain 1.0 Network Architecture—22% of Examination

Objective	Chapter	Section
1.1 Explain the functions and applications of various network devices		
• Router	3	Routers and How They Work
• Switch	10	VLANs and Trunking
• Multilayer switch	3	Routers and How They Work
• Firewall	8	Security in Network Design

Objective	Chapter	Section
• HIDS	8	Security in Network Design
• IDS/IPS	8	Security in Network Design
• Access point (wireless/wired)	4 6	NICs and Ethernet Wi-Fi WLAN (Wireless LAN) Architecture
• Content filter	8	Security in Network Design
• Load balancer	9	Troubleshooting Network Integrity and Availability
• Hub	4	NICs and Ethernet
• Analog modem	11	PSTN (Public Switched Telephone Network)
• Packet shaper	9	Monitoring and Managing Network Traffic
• VPN concentrator	7	Remote Access
1.2 Compare and contrast the use of networking services and applications		
• VPN	7	Remote Access
○ Site to site/host to site/host to host	7	Remote Access
○ Protocols	7	Remote Access
■ IPsec	7	Encryption Techniques, Protocols, and Utilities
■ GRE	7	Remote Access
■ SSL VPN	7	Encryption Techniques, Protocols, and Utilities
■ PTP/PPTP	7	Remote Access
• TACACS/RADIUS	7	Authentication Protocols
• RAS	7	Remote Access
• Web services	7	Cloud Computing
• Unified voice services	9	Unified Communications Technologies
• Network controllers	10	Virtual Network Components
1.3 Install and configure the following networking services/applications		
• DHCP	2	How IP Addresses Are Formatted and Assigned
○ Static vs dynamic IP addressing	2	Overview of Addressing on Networks
○ Reservations	2	How IP Addresses Are Formatted and Assigned
○ Scopes	2	How IP Addresses Are Formatted and Assigned
○ Leases	2	Overview of Addressing on Networks
○ Options (DNS servers, suffixes)	10	Segmentation and Subnetting
○ IP helper/DHCP relay	10	VLANs and Trunking
• DNS	2	How Host Names and Domain Names Work
○ DNS servers	2	How Host Names and Domain Names Work
○ DNS records (A, MX, AAAA, CNAME, PTR)	2	How Host Names and Domain Names Work
○ Dynamic DNS	2	How Host Names and Domain Names Work

Objective	Chapter	Section
• Proxy/reverse proxy	8	Security in Network Design
• NAT	2	How IP Addresses Are Formatted and Assigned
○ PAT	2	How IP Addresses Are Formatted and Assigned
○ SNAT	2	How IP Addresses Are Formatted and Assigned
○ DNAT	2	How IP Addresses Are Formatted and Assigned
• Port forwarding	7	Encryption Techniques, Protocols, and Utilities
1.4 Explain the characteristics and benefits of various WAN technologies		
• Fiber	5 11	Fiber-Optic Cable SONET (Synchronous Optical Network)
○ SONET	11	SONET (Synchronous Optical Network)
○ DWDM	5	Transmission Basics
○ CWDM	5	Transmission Basics
• Frame relay	11	Frame Relay
• Satellite	11	Wireless WANs
• Broadband cable	11	Broadband Cable
• DSL/ADSL	11	DSL (Digital Subscriber Line)
• ISDN	11	PSTN (Public Switched Telephone Network)
• ATM	11	ATM (Asynchronous Transfer Mode)
• PPP/Multilink PPP	7 11	Remote Access T-Carriers
• MPLS	9 11	QoS (Quality of Service) Assurance MPLS (Multiprotocol Label Switching)
• GSM/CDMA	11	Wireless WANs
○ LTE/4G	11	Wireless WANs
○ HSPA+	11	Wireless WANs
○ 3G	11	Wireless WANs
○ Edge	11	Wireless WANs
• Dialup	11	PSTN (Public Switched Telephone Network)
• WiMAX	11	Wireless WANs
• Metro-Ethernet	11	Metro Ethernet
• Leased lines	11	T-Carriers
○ T-1	11	T-Carriers
○ T-3	11	T-Carriers
○ E-1	11	T-Carriers
○ E-3	11	T-Carriers
○ OC3	11	SONET (Synchronous Optical Network)
○ OC12	11	SONET (Synchronous Optical Network)
• Circuit switch vs packet switch	9	Unified Communications Technologies

Objective	Chapter	Section
1.5 Install and properly terminate various cable types and connectors using appropriate tools		
• Copper connectors	5	Twisted-Pair Cable
○ RJ-11	5	Twisted-Pair Cable
○ RJ-45	5	Twisted-Pair Cable
○ RJ-48C	5	Twisted-Pair Cable
○ DB-9/RS-232	5	Twisted-Pair Cable
○ DB-25	5	Twisted-Pair Cable
○ UTP coupler	5	Twisted-Pair Cable
○ BNC coupler	5	Transmission Basics
○ BNC	5	Transmission Basics
○ F-connector	5	Transmission Basics
○ 110 block	4	Network Equipment in Commercial Buildings
○ 66 block	4	Network Equipment in Commercial Buildings
• Copper cables	5	Twisted-Pair Cable
○ Shielded vs unshielded	5	Twisted-Pair Cable
○ CAT3, CAT5, CAT5e, CAT6, CAT6a	5	Twisted-Pair Cable
○ PVC vs plenum	4	Network Equipment in Commercial Buildings
○ RG-59	5	Transmission Basics
○ RG-6	5	Transmission Basics
○ Straight-through vs crossover vs rollover	5	Twisted-Pair Cable
• Fiber connectors	5	Fiber-Optic Cable
○ ST	5	Fiber-Optic Cable
○ SC	5	Fiber-Optic Cable
○ LC	5	Fiber-Optic Cable
○ MTRJ	5	Fiber-Optic Cable
○ FC	5	Fiber-Optic Cable
○ Fiber coupler	5	Fiber-Optic Cable
• Fiber cables	5	Fiber-Optic Cable
○ Single mode	5	Fiber-Optic Cable
○ Multimode	5	Fiber-Optic Cable
○ APC vs UPC	5	Fiber-Optic Cable
• Media converters	5	Twisted-Pair Cable
○ Single mode fiber to Ethernet	5	Fiber-Optic Cable
○ Multimode fiber to Ethernet	5	Fiber-Optic Cable
○ Fiber to coaxial	5	Fiber-Optic Cable
○ Single mode to multimode fiber	5	Fiber-Optic Cable

Objective	Chapter	Section
• Tools	5	Troubleshooting Cable Problems
○ Cable crimpers	5	Twisted-Pair Cable
○ Punch down tool	4	Network Equipment in Commercial Buildings
○ Wire strippers	5	Twisted-Pair Cable
○ Snips	5	Twisted-Pair Cable
○ OTDR	5	Troubleshooting Cable Problems
○ Cable certifier	5	Troubleshooting Cable Problems
1.6 Differentiate between common network topologies		
• Mesh	1 11	Networking Hardware and Physical Topologies WAN Topologies
○ Partial	1 11	Networking Hardware and Physical Topologies WAN Topologies
○ Full	1 11	Networking Hardware and Physical Topologies WAN Topologies
• Bus	1 11	Networking Hardware and Physical Topologies WAN Topologies
• Ring	1 11	Networking Hardware and Physical Topologies WAN Topologies
• Star	1 11	Networking Hardware and Physical Topologies WAN Topologies
• Hybrid	1	Networking Hardware and Physical Topologies
• Point-to-point	1	How Networks Are Used
• Point-to-multipoint	1	How Networks Are Used
• Client-server	1	Controlling Network Access
• Peer-to-peer	1	Controlling Network Access
1.7 Differentiate between network infrastructure implementations		
• WAN	1	Networking Hardware and Physical Topologies
• MAN	1	Networking Hardware and Physical Topologies
• LAN	1	Networking Hardware and Physical Topologies
• WLAN	6	Wi-Fi WLAN (Wireless LAN) Architecture
○ Hotspot	6	Wi-Fi WLAN (Wireless LAN) Architecture
• PAN	1 6	Networking Hardware and Physical Topologies Characteristics of Wireless Transmissions
○ Bluetooth	6	Characteristics of Wireless Transmissions
○ IR	6	Characteristics of Wireless Transmissions
○ NFC	6	Characteristics of Wireless Transmissions

Objective	Chapter	Section
• SCADA/ICS	12	Industrial Networks
○ ICS server	12	Industrial Networks
○ DCS/closed network	12	Industrial Networks
○ Remote terminal unit	12	Industrial Networks
○ Programmable logic controller	12	Industrial Networks
• Medianets	9	QoS (Quality of Service) Assurance
○ VTC	9	Unified Communications Technologies
▪ ISDN	11	PSTN (Public Switched Telephone Network)
▪ IP/SIP	9	Unified Communications Technologies
1.8 Given a scenario, implement and configure the appropriate addressing schema		
• IPv6	2	Overview of Addressing on Networks
○ Auto-configuration	2	How IP Addresses Are Formatted and Assigned
▪ EUI 64	2	How IP Addresses Are Formatted and Assigned
▪ DHCP6	2	How IP Addresses Are Formatted and Assigned
▪ Link local	2	How IP Addresses Are Formatted and Assigned
▪ Address structure	2	How IP Addresses Are Formatted and Assigned
▪ Address compression	2	How IP Addresses Are Formatted and Assigned
▪ Tunneling 6to4, 4to6	2	How IP Addresses Are Formatted and Assigned
▪ Teredo, miredo	2	How IP Addresses Are Formatted and Assigned
• IPv4	2	Overview of Addressing on Networks
○ Address structure	2	How IP Addresses Are Formatted and Assigned
○ Subnetting	10	Segmentation and Subnetting
○ APIPA	2	How IP Addresses Are Formatted and Assigned
○ Classful A, B, C, D	2	How IP Addresses Are Formatted and Assigned
○ Classless	10	Segmentation and Subnetting
• Private vs public	2	How IP Addresses Are Formatted and Assigned
• NAT/PAT	2	How IP Addresses Are Formatted and Assigned
• MAC addressing	2	Overview of Addressing on Networks
• Multicast	2	How IP Addresses Are Formatted and Assigned
• Unicast	2	How IP Addresses Are Formatted and Assigned
• Broadcast	2	How IP Addresses Are Formatted and Assigned
• Broadcast domains vs collision domains	4	NICs and Ethernet
1.9 Explain the basics of routing concepts and protocols		
• Loopback interface	2	How IP Addresses Are Formatted and Assigned
• Routing loops	3	Routers and How They Work

Objective	Chapter	Section
• Routing tables	3	Routers and How They Work
• Static vs dynamic routes	3	TCP/IP Core Protocols
• Default route	3	Routers and How They Work
• Distance vector routing protocols	3	Routers and How They Work
◦ RIP v2	3	Routers and How They Work
• Hybrid routing protocols	3	Routers and How They Work
◦ BGP	3	Routers and How They Work
• Link state routing protocols	3	Routers and How They Work
◦ OSPF	3	Routers and How They Work
◦ IS-IS	3	Routers and How They Work
• Interior vs exterior gateway routing protocols	3	Routers and How They Work
• Autonomous system numbers	3	Routers and How They Work
• Route redistribution	3	Routers and How They Work
• High availability	9	Troubleshooting Network Integrity and Availability
◦ VRRP	10	Virtual Network Components
◦ Virtual IP	10	Virtual Network Components
◦ HSRP	10	Virtual Network Components
• Route aggregation	10	Segmentation and Subnetting
• Routing metrics	3	Routers and How They Work
◦ Hop counts	3	Routers and How They Work
◦ MTU, bandwidth	3	Routers and How They Work
◦ Costs	3	Routers and How They Work
◦ Latency	3	Routers and How They Work
◦ Administrative distance	3	Routers and How They Work
◦ SPB	10	VLANs and Trunking
1.10 Identify the basic elements of unified communication technologies		
• VoIP	1 9	How Networks Are Used Unified Communications Technologies
• Video	1 9	How Networks Are Used Unified Communications Technologies
• Real time services	9	Unified Communications Technologies
◦ Presence	9	Unified Communications Technologies
◦ Multicast vs unicast	9	Unified Communications Technologies
• QoS	1 9	How Networks Are Used QoS (Quality of Service) Assurance
◦ DSCP	9	QoS (Quality of Service) Assurance
◦ COS	9	QoS (Quality of Service) Assurance

Objective	Chapter	Section
• Devices	9	Unified Communications Technologies
○ UC servers	9	Unified Communications Technologies
○ UC devices	9	Unified Communications Technologies
○ UC gateways	9	Unified Communications Technologies
1.11 Compare and contrast technologies that support cloud and virtualization		
• Virtualization	10	Virtualization
○ Virtual switches	10	Virtual Network Components
○ Virtual routers	10	Virtual Network Components
○ Virtual firewall	10	Virtual Network Components
○ Virtual vs physical NICs	10	Virtual Network Components
○ Software defined networking	10	Virtual Network Components
• Storage area network	4	Network Equipment in Commercial Buildings
○ iSCSI	4	Network Equipment in Commercial Buildings
○ Jumbo frame	4	NICs and Ethernet
○ Fibre Channel	4	Network Equipment in Commercial Buildings
○ Network attached storage	4	Network Equipment in Commercial Buildings
• Cloud concepts	7	Cloud Computing
○ Public IaaS, SaaS, PaaS	7	Cloud Computing
○ Private IaaS, SaaS, PaaS	7	Cloud Computing
○ Hybrid IaaS, SaaS, PaaS	7	Cloud Computing
○ Community IaaS, SaaS, PaaS	7	Cloud Computing
1.12 Given a set of requirements, implement a basic network		
• List of requirements	4	Network Equipment in Commercial Buildings
• Device types/requirements	4 6	Network Equipment in Commercial Buildings Implementing a WLAN
• Environment limitations	4 6	Managing Power Sources and the Environment Characteristics of Wireless Transmissions
• Equipment limitations	4	Troubleshooting Network Devices
• Compatibility requirements	4	NICs and Ethernet
• Wired/wireless considerations	4 6	Troubleshooting Network Devices Characteristics of Wireless Transmissions *and* Wi-Fi WLAN (Wireless LAN) Architecture
• Security considerations	4 6 7	Managing Power Sources and the Environment Implementing a WLAN *and* 802.11 Wireless Network Security Encryption Techniques, Protocols, and Utilities

Domain 2.0 Network Operations—20% of Examination

Objective	Chapter	Section
2.1 Given a scenario, use appropriate monitoring tools		
• Packet/network analyzer	2	How Ports and Sockets Work
• Interface monitoring tools	9	Monitoring and Managing Network Traffic
• Port scanner	8	Security Risks
• Top talkers/listeners	9	Monitoring and Managing Network Traffic
• SNMP management software	9	Monitoring and Managing Network Traffic
○ Trap	9	Monitoring and Managing Network Traffic
○ Get	9	Monitoring and Managing Network Traffic
○ Walk	9	Monitoring and Managing Network Traffic
○ MIBS	9	Monitoring and Managing Network Traffic
• Alerts	9	Monitoring and Managing Network Traffic
○ Email	9	Monitoring and Managing Network Traffic
○ SMS	9	Monitoring and Managing Network Traffic
• Packet flow monitoring	9	Monitoring and Managing Network Traffic
• SYSLOG	9	Monitoring and Managing Network Traffic
• SIEM	8	Security in Network Design
• Environmental monitoring tools	4	Managing Power Sources and the Environment
○ Temperature	4	Managing Power Sources and the Environment
○ Humidity	4	Managing Power Sources and the Environment
• Power monitoring tools	4	Managing Power Sources and the Environment
• Wireless survey tools	6	Implementing a WLAN
• Wireless analyzers	6	Troubleshooting Wireless LANs
2.2 Given a scenario, analyze metrics and reports from monitoring and tracking performance tools		
• Baseline	9	Fundamentals of Network Management
• Bottleneck	9	Monitoring and Managing Network Traffic
• Log management	9	Monitoring and Managing Network Traffic
• Graphing	9	Fundamentals of Network Management
• Utilization	9	Fundamentals of Network Management
○ Bandwidth	9	Monitoring and Managing Network Traffic
○ Storage	9	Monitoring and Managing Network Traffic
○ Network device CPU	9	Monitoring and Managing Network Traffic

Objective	Chapter	Section
○ Network device memory	9	Monitoring and Managing Network Traffic
○ Wireless channel utilization	6	Characteristics of Wireless Transmissions
• Link status	9	Monitoring and Managing Network Traffic
• Interface monitoring	9	Monitoring and Managing Network Traffic
○ Errors	9	Monitoring and Managing Network Traffic
○ Utilization	9	Monitoring and Managing Network Traffic
○ Discards	9	Monitoring and Managing Network Traffic
○ Packet drops	9	Monitoring and Managing Network Traffic
○ Interface resets	9	Monitoring and Managing Network Traffic
○ Speed and duplex	4	NICs and Ethernet
2.3 Given a scenario, use appropriate resources to support configuration management		
• Archives/backups	9	Troubleshooting Network Integrity and Availability
• Baselines	9	Fundamentals of Network Management
• On-boarding and off-boarding of mobile devices	6	Implementing a WLAN
• NAC	8	Security in Network Design
• Documentation	12	Asset Management and Business Documents
○ Network diagrams (logical/physical)	4	Troubleshooting Network Devices
○ Asset management	12	Asset Management and Business Documents
○ IP address utilization	12	Asset Management and Business Documents
○ Vendor documentation	12	Asset Management and Business Documents
○ Internal operating procedures/policies/standards	12	Asset Management and Business Documents
2.4 Explain the importance of implementing network segmentation		
• SCADA systems/Industrial control systems	12	Industrial Networks
• Legacy systems	9	Fundamentals of Network Management
• Separate private/public networks	8	Security in Network Design
• Honeypot/honeynet	8	Security in Network Design
• Testing lab	12	Change Management
• Load balancing	9	Troubleshooting Network Integrity and Availability
• Performance optimization	9	Monitoring and Managing Network Traffic
• Security	8	Security Risks
• Compliance	9	Fundamentals of Network Management

Objective	Chapter	Section
2.5 Given a scenario, install and apply patches and updates		
• OS updates	12	Change Management
• Firmware updates	1	The Seven-Layer OSI Model
• Driver updates	12	Change Management
• Feature changes/updates	12	Change Management
• Major vs minor updates	12	Change Management
• Vulnerability patches	12	Change Management
• Upgrading vs downgrading	12	Change Management
○ Configuration backup	12	Change Management
2.6 Given a scenario, configure a switch using proper features		
• VLAN	10	VLANs and Trunking
○ Native VLAN/Default VLAN	10	VLANs and Trunking
○ VTP	10	VLANs and Trunking
• Spanning tree (802.1d)/rapid spanning tree (802.1w)	10	VLANs and Trunking
○ Flooding	10	VLANs and Trunking
○ Forwarding/blocking	10	VLANs and Trunking
○ Filtering	10	VLANs and Trunking
• Interface configuration	10	VLANs and Trunking
○ Trunking/802.1q	10	VLANs and Trunking
○ Tag vs untag VLANs	10	VLANs and Trunking
○ Port bonding (LACP)	9	Troubleshooting Network Integrity and Availability
○ Port mirroring (local vs remote)	8	Security in Network Design
○ Speed and duplexing	4	NICs and Ethernet
○ IP address assignment	10	Virtual Network Components
○ VLAN assignment	10	VLANs and Trunking
• Default gateway	2	Overview of Addressing on Networks
• PoE and PoE+ (802.3af, 802.3at)	5	Twisted-Pair Cable
• Switch management	10	VLANs and Trunking
○ User/passwords	10	VLANs and Trunking
○ AAA configuration	10	VLANs and Trunking
○ Console	10	VLANs and Trunking
○ Virtual terminals	10	VLANs and Trunking
○ In-band/Out-of-band management	10	VLANs and Trunking
• Managed vs unmanaged	10	VLANs and Trunking

Objective	Chapter	Section
2.7 Install and configure wireless LAN infrastructure and implement the appropriate technologies in support of wireless capable devices		
• Small office/home office wireless router	6	Wi-Fi WLAN (Wireless LAN) Architecture *and* 802.11 Wireless Network Security
• Wireless access points	6	Wi-Fi WLAN (Wireless LAN) Architecture
○ Device density	6	Characteristics of Wireless Transmissions
○ Roaming	6	Wi-Fi WLAN (Wireless LAN) Architecture
○ Wireless controllers	10	VLANs and Trunking
■ VLAN pooling	10	VLANs and Trunking
■ LWAPP	10	VLANs and Trunking
• Wireless bridge	6	Implementing a WLAN
• Site surveys	6	Implementing a WLAN
○ Heat maps	6	Implementing a WLAN
• Frequencies	6	Characteristics of Wireless Transmissions
○ 2.4 Ghz	6	Characteristics of Wireless Transmissions
○ 5.0 Ghz	6	Characteristics of Wireless Transmissions
• Channels	6	Characteristics of Wireless Transmissions
• Goodput	6	Characteristics of Wireless Transmissions
• Connection types	6	Wi-Fi WLAN (Wireless LAN) Architecture
○ 802.11a-ht	6	Wi-Fi WLAN (Wireless LAN) Architecture
○ 802.11g-ht	6	Wi-Fi WLAN (Wireless LAN) Architecture
• Antenna placement	6	Implementing a WLAN *and* Troubleshooting Wireless LANs
• Antenna types	6	Characteristics of Wireless Transmissions
○ Omnidirectional	6	Characteristics of Wireless Transmissions
○ Unidirectional	6	Characteristics of Wireless Transmissions
• MIMO/MUMIMO	6	Wi-Fi WLAN (Wireless LAN) Architecture
• Signal strength	6	Characteristics of Wireless Transmissions *and* Wi-Fi WLAN (Wireless LAN) Architecture
○ Coverage	6	Implementing a WLAN
○ Differences between device antennas	6	Wi-Fi WLAN (Wireless LAN) Architecture
• SSID broadcast	6	Implementing a WLAN
• Topologies	6	Wi-Fi WLAN (Wireless LAN) Architecture
○ Adhoc	6	Wi-Fi WLAN (Wireless LAN) Architecture
○ Mesh	6	Wi-Fi WLAN (Wireless LAN) Architecture
○ Infrastructure	6	Wi-Fi WLAN (Wireless LAN) Architecture

Objective	Chapter	Section
• Mobile devices	6	Characteristics of Wireless Transmissions
○ Cell phones	6	Characteristics of Wireless Transmissions
○ Laptops	6	Wi-Fi WLAN (Wireless LAN) Architecture
○ Tablets	6	Implementing a WLAN
○ Gaming devices	6	Characteristics of Wireless Transmissions
○ Media devices	6	Characteristics of Wireless Transmissions

Domain 3.0 Network Security—18% of Examination

Objective	Chapter	Section
3.1 Compare and contrast risk related concepts		
• Disaster recovery	12	Troubleshooting and Response Policies
• Business continuity	12	Troubleshooting and Response Policies
• Battery backups/UPS	4	Managing Power Sources and the Environment
• First responders	12	Troubleshooting and Response Policies
• Data breach	8	Security Assessment
• End user awareness and training	8	Security Risks
• Single point of failure	9	Troubleshooting Network Integrity and Availability
○ Critical nodes	9	Troubleshooting Network Integrity and Availability
○ Critical assets	9	Troubleshooting Network Integrity and Availability
○ Redundancy	9	Troubleshooting Network Integrity and Availability
• Adherence to standards and policies	8	Security Risks
• Vulnerability scanning	8	Security in Network Design
• Penetration testing	8	Security in Network Design
3.2 Compare and contrast common network vulnerabilities and threats		
• Attacks/threats	8	Security Risks
○ Denial of service	8	Security Risks
■ Distributed DoS	8	Security Risks
□ Botnet	8	Security Risks
□ Traffic spike	8	Security Risks
□ Coordinated attack	8	Security Risks

Objective	Chapter	Section
■ Reflective/amplified	8	Security Risks
□ DNS	8	Security Risks
□ NTP	8	Security Risks
□ Smurfing	8	Security Risks
■ Friendly/unintentional DoS	8	Security Risks
■ Physical attack	8	Security Risks
□ Permanent DoS	8	Security Risks
○ ARP cache poisoning	8	Security Risks
○ Packet/protocol abuse	8	Security Risks
○ Spoofing	8	Security Risks
○ Wireless	6	802.11 Wireless Network Security
■ Evil twin	6	802.11 Wireless Network Security
■ Rogue AP	6	Wi-Fi WLAN (Wireless LAN) Architecture *and* Implementing a WLAN
■ War driving	6	802.11 Wireless Network Security
■ War chalking	6	802.11 Wireless Network Security
■ Bluejacking	6	Characteristics of Wireless Transmissions
■ Bluesnarfing	6	Characteristics of Wireless Transmissions
■ WPA/WEP/WPS attacks	6	802.11 Wireless Network Security
○ Brute force	7	Encryption Techniques, Protocols, and Utilities
○ Session hijacking	8	Security Risks
○ Social engineering	8	Security Risks
○ Man-in-the-middle	8	Security Risks
○ VLAN hopping	10	VLANs and Trunking
○ Compromised system	8	Security Risks
○ Effect of malware on the network	8	Troubleshooting Malware Risks and Infections
○ Insider threat/malicious employee	8	Security Risks
○ Zero day attacks	8	Security Risks
● Vulnerabilities	8	Security Risks
○ Unnecessary running services	8	Security Risks
○ Open ports	8	Security Risks
○ Unpatched/legacy systems	8	Security Risks
○ Unencrypted channels	8	Security Risks
○ Clear text credentials	8	Security Risks
○ Unsecure protocols	8	Security Risks
■ TELNET	8	Security Risks

Objective	Chapter	Section
■ HTTP	8	Security Risks
■ SLIP	8	Security Risks
■ FTP	8	Security Risks
■ TFTP	8	Security Risks
■ SNMPv1 and SNMPv2	8	Security Risks
○ TEMPEST/RF emanation	8	Security Risks
3.3 Given a scenario, implement network hardening techniques		
• Anti-malware software	8	Troubleshooting Malware Risks and Infections
○ Host-based	8	Troubleshooting Malware Risks and Infections
○ Cloud/server-based	8	Troubleshooting Malware Risks and Infections
○ Network-based	8	Troubleshooting Malware Risks and Infections
• Switch port security	10	VLANs and Trunking
○ DHCP snooping	8	Security Risks
○ ARP inspection	8	Security Risks
○ MAC address filtering	10	VLANs and Trunking
○ VLAN assignments	10	VLANs and Trunking
■ Network segmentation	10	VLANs and Trunking
• Security policies	8	Effective Security Policies
• Disable unneeded network services	8	Security Risks
• Use secure protocols	7	Encryption Techniques, Protocols, and Utilities
○ SSH	7	Encryption Techniques, Protocols, and Utilities
○ SNMPv3	9	Monitoring and Managing Network Traffic
○ TLS/SSL	7	Encryption Techniques, Protocols, and Utilities
○ SFTP	7	Encryption Techniques, Protocols, and Utilities
○ HTTPS	7	Encryption Techniques, Protocols, and Utilities
○ IPsec	7	Encryption Techniques, Protocols, and Utilities
• Access lists	8	Security in Network Design
○ Web/content filtering	8	Security in Network Design
○ Port filtering	8	Security in Network Design
○ IP filtering	8	Security in Network Design
○ Implicit deny	8	Security in Network Design
• Wireless security	6	802.11 Wireless Network Security
○ WEP	6	802.11 Wireless Network Security
○ WPA/WPA2	6	802.11 Wireless Network Security
■ Enterprise	6	802.11 Wireless Network Security
■ Personal	6	802.11 Wireless Network Security

Objective	Chapter	Section
o TKIP/AES	7	Authentication Protocols
o 802.1x	7	Authentication Protocols
o TLS/TTLS	7	Encryption Techniques, Protocols, and Utilities
o MAC filtering	6	802.11 Wireless Network Security
• User authentication	7	Authentication Protocols
o CHAP/MSCHAP	7	Authentication Protocols
o PAP	7	Authentication Protocols
o EAP	7	Authentication Protocols
o Kerberos	7	Authentication Protocols
o Multifactor authentication	7	Authentication Protocols
o Two-factor authentication	7	Authentication Protocols
o Single sign-on	7	Authentication Protocols
• Hashes	7	Encryption Techniques, Protocols, and Utilities
o MD5	7	Encryption Techniques, Protocols, and Utilities
o SHA	7	Encryption Techniques, Protocols, and Utilities
3.4 Compare and contrast physical security controls		
• Mantraps	12	Physical Security Controls
• Network closets	12	Physical Security Controls
• Video monitoring	12	Physical Security Controls
o IP cameras/CCTVs	12	Physical Security Controls
• Door access controls	12	Physical Security Controls
• Proximity readers/key fob	12	Physical Security Controls
• Biometrics	12	Physical Security Controls
• Keypad/cipher locks	12	Physical Security Controls
• Security guard	12	Physical Security Controls
3.5 Given a scenario, install and configure a basic firewall		
• Types of firewalls	8	Security in Network Design
o Host-based	8	Security in Network Design
o Network-based	8	Security in Network Design
o Software vs hardware	8	Security in Network Design
o Application aware/context aware	8	Security in Network Design

Objective	Chapter	Section
○ Small office/home office firewall	8	Security in Network Design
○ Stateful vs stateless inspection	8	Security in Network Design
○ UTM	8	Security in Network Design
• Settings/techniques	8	Security in Network Design
○ ACL	8	Security in Network Design
○ Virtual wire vs routed	8	Security in Network Design
○ DMZ	8	Security in Network Design
○ Implicit deny	8	Security in Network Design
○ Block/allow	8	Security in Network Design
■ Outbound traffic	8	Security in Network Design
■ Inbound traffic	8	Security in Network Design
○ Firewall placement	8	Security in Network Design
■ Internal/external	8	Security in Network Design
3.6 Explain the purpose of various network access control models		
• 802.1x	7	Authentication Protocols
• Posture assessment	8	Security Assessment
• Guest network	6	802.11 Wireless Network Security
• Persistent vs non-persistent agents	8	Security in Network Design
• Quarantine network	8	Security in Network Design
• Edge vs access control	8	Security in Network Design
3.7 Summarize basic forensic concepts		
• First responder	12	Troubleshooting and Response Policies
• Secure the area	12	Troubleshooting and Response Policies
○ Escalate when necessary	12	Troubleshooting and Response Policies
• Document the scene	12	Troubleshooting and Response Policies
• eDiscovery	12	Troubleshooting and Response Policies
• Evidence/data collection	12	Troubleshooting and Response Policies
• Chain of custody	12	Troubleshooting and Response Policies
• Data transport	12	Troubleshooting and Response Policies
• Forensics report	12	Troubleshooting and Response Policies
• Legal hold	12	Troubleshooting and Response Policies

Domain 4.0 Troubleshooting—24% of Examination

Objective	Chapter	Section
4.1 Given a scenario, implement the following network troubleshooting methodology		
• Identify the problem	1	Troubleshooting Network Problems
○ Gather information	1	Troubleshooting Network Problems
○ Duplicate the problem, if possible	1	Troubleshooting Network Problems
○ Question users	1	Troubleshooting Network Problems
○ Identify symptoms	1	Troubleshooting Network Problems
○ Determine if anything has changed	1	Troubleshooting Network Problems
○ Approach multiple problems individually	1	Troubleshooting Network Problems
• Establish a theory of probable cause	1	Troubleshooting Network Problems
○ Question the obvious	1	Troubleshooting Network Problems
○ Consider multiple approaches	1	Troubleshooting Network Problems
▪ Top-to-bottom/bottom-to-top OSI model	1	Troubleshooting Network Problems
▪ Divide and conquer	1	Troubleshooting Network Problems
• Test the theory to determine cause	1	Troubleshooting Network Problems
○ Once theory is confirmed, determine next steps to resolve problem	1	Troubleshooting Network Problems
○ If theory is not confirmed, re-establish new theory or escalate	1	Troubleshooting Network Problems
• Establish a plan of action to resolve the problem and identify potential effects	1	Troubleshooting Network Problems
• Implement the solution or escalate as necessary	1	Troubleshooting Network Problems
• Verify full system functionality and if applicable implement preventative measures	1	Troubleshooting Network Problems
• Document findings, actions, and outcomes	1	Troubleshooting Network Problems
4.2 Given a scenario, analyze and interpret the output of troubleshooting tools		
• Command line tools	2 3	Overview of Addressing on Networks Troubleshooting Router Issues
○ ipconfig	2	Overview of Addressing on Networks
○ netstat	3	Troubleshooting Router Issues
○ ifconfig	2	Tools for Troubleshooting IP Address Problems
○ ping/ping6/ping -6	2	Tools for Troubleshooting IP Address Problems
○ tracert/tracert -6/traceroute6/traceroute -6	3	Troubleshooting Router Issues
○ nbtstat	3	Troubleshooting Router Issues

Objective	Chapter	Section
○ nslookup	2	Tools for Troubleshooting IP Address Problems
○ arp	3	TCP/IP Core Protocols
○ mac address lookup table	3	TCP/IP Core Protocols
○ pathping	3	Troubleshooting Router Issues
• Line testers	5	Troubleshooting Cable Problems
• Certifiers	5	Troubleshooting Cable Problems
• Multimeter	5	Troubleshooting Cable Problems
• Cable tester	5	Troubleshooting Cable Problems
• Light meter	5	Troubleshooting Cable Problems
• Toner probe	5	Troubleshooting Cable Problems
• Speed test sites	6	Characteristics of Wireless Transmissions
• Looking glass sites	3	Routers and How They Work
• WiFi analyzer	6	Troubleshooting Wireless LANs
• Protocol analyzer	2	How Ports and Sockets Work
4.3 Given a scenario, troubleshoot and resolve common wireless issues		
• Signal loss	6	Troubleshooting Wireless LANs
• Interference	6	Characteristics of Wireless Transmissions
• Overlapping channels	6	Troubleshooting Wireless LANs
○ Mismatched channels	6	Troubleshooting Wireless LANs
• Signal-to-noise ratio	6	Characteristics of Wireless Transmissions
• Device saturation	6	Troubleshooting Wireless LANs
• Bandwidth saturation	6	Troubleshooting Wireless LANs
• Untested updates	6	Troubleshooting Wireless LANs
• Wrong SSID	6	Troubleshooting Wireless LANs
• Power levels	6	Troubleshooting Wireless LANs
• Open networks	6	802.11 Wireless Network Security
• Rogue access point	6	Wi-Fi WLAN (Wireless LAN) Architecture
• Wrong antenna type	6	Troubleshooting Wireless LANs
• Incompatibilities	6	Troubleshooting Wireless LANs
• Wrong encryption	6	Troubleshooting Wireless LANs
• Bounce	6	Characteristics of Wireless Transmissions
• MIMO	6	Wi-Fi WLAN (Wireless LAN) Architecture
• AP placement	6	Implementing a WLAN
• AP configurations	10	VLANs and Trunking
○ LWAPP	10	VLANs and Trunking
○ Thin vs thick	10	VLANs and Trunking

Objective	Chapter	Section
• Environmental factors	6	Characteristics of Wireless Transmissions
○ Concrete walls	6	Characteristics of Wireless Transmissions
○ Window film	6	Characteristics of Wireless Transmissions
○ Metal studs	6	Characteristics of Wireless Transmissions
• Wireless standard–related issues	6	Characteristics of Wireless Transmissions
○ Throughput	6	Characteristics of Wireless Transmissions
○ Frequency	6	Characteristics of Wireless Transmissions
○ Distance	6	Characteristics of Wireless Transmissions
○ Channels	6	Characteristics of Wireless Transmissions
4.4 Given a scenario, troubleshoot and resolve common copper cable issues		
• Shorts	5	Troubleshooting Cable Problems
• Opens	5	Troubleshooting Cable Problems
• Incorrect termination (mismatched standards)	5	Troubleshooting Cable Problems
○ Straight-through	5	Troubleshooting Cable Problems
○ Crossover	5	Troubleshooting Cable Problems
• Cross-talk	5	Troubleshooting Cable Problems
○ Near end	5	Troubleshooting Cable Problems
○ Far end	5	Troubleshooting Cable Problems
• EMI/RFI	5	Troubleshooting Cable Problems
• Distance limitations	5	Troubleshooting Cable Problems
• Attenuation/Db loss	5	Troubleshooting Cable Problems
• Bad connector	5	Troubleshooting Cable Problems
• Bad wiring	5	Troubleshooting Cable Problems
• Split pairs	5	Troubleshooting Cable Problems
• Tx/Rx reverse	5	Troubleshooting Cable Problems
• Cable placement	4	Network Equipment in Commercial Buildings
• Bad SFP/GBIC - cable or transceiver	5	Fiber-Optic Cable
4.5 Given a scenario, troubleshoot and resolve common fiber cable issues		
• Attenuation/Db loss	5	Troubleshooting Cable Problems
• SFP/GBIC - cable mismatch	5	Fiber-Optic Cable
• Bad SFP/GBIC - cable or transceiver	5	Fiber-Optic Cable
• Wavelength mismatch	5	Troubleshooting Cable Problems
• Fiber type mismatch	5	Troubleshooting Cable Problems
• Dirty connectors	5	Troubleshooting Cable Problems
• Connector mismatch	5	Troubleshooting Cable Problems

Objective	Chapter	Section
• Bend radius limitations	5	Fiber-Optic Cable
• Distance limitations	5	Troubleshooting Cable Problems
4.6 Given a scenario, troubleshoot and resolve common network issues		
• Incorrect IP configuration/default gateway	2	Tools for Troubleshooting IP Address Problems
• Broadcast storms/switching loop	10	VLANs and Trunking
• Duplicate IP	2	Tools for Troubleshooting IP Address Problems
• Speed and duplex mismatch	4	NICs and Ethernet
• End-to-end connectivity	7	Troubleshooting Cloud Computing and Remote Access
• Incorrect VLAN assignment	10	VLANs and Trunking
• Hardware failure	3 4	Troubleshooting Router Issues Network Equipment in Commercial Buildings
• Misconfigured DHCP	2	Tools for Troubleshooting IP Address Problems
• Misconfigured DNS	2	Tools for Troubleshooting IP Address Problems
• Incorrect interface/interface misconfiguration	3 4	Troubleshooting Router Issues Troubleshooting Network Devices
• Cable placement	4	Network Equipment in Commercial Buildings
• Interface errors	3	Troubleshooting Router Issues
• Simultaneous wired/wireless connections	6	Troubleshooting Wireless LANs
• Discovering neighboring devices/nodes	3	Troubleshooting Router Issues
• Power failure/power anomalies	4	Managing Power Sources and the Environment
• MTU/MTU black hole	3	Troubleshooting Router Issues
• Missing IP routes	3	Troubleshooting Router Issues
• NIC teaming misconfiguration	9	Troubleshooting Network Integrity and Availability
○ Active-active vs active-passive	9	Troubleshooting Network Integrity and Availability
○ Multicast vs broadcast	9	Troubleshooting Network Integrity and Availability
4.7 Given a scenario, troubleshoot and resolve common security issues		
• Misconfigured firewall	8	Security in Network Design
• Misconfigured ACLs/applications	8	Security in Network Design
• Malware	8	Troubleshooting Malware Risks and Infections
• Denial of service	8	Security Risks
• Open/closed ports	8	Security Risks
• ICMP–related issues	8	Security Risks
○ Ping of death	8	Security Risks
○ Unreachable default gateway	4	Troubleshooting Network Devices

Objective	Chapter	Section
• Unpatched firmware/OSs	8	Security Risks
• Malicious users	8	Security Risks
○ Trusted	8	Security Risks
○ Untrusted users	8	Security Risks
○ Packet sniffing	9	Monitoring and Managing Network Traffic
• Authentication issues	7	Authentication Protocols *and* Troubleshooting Cloud Computing and Remote Access
○ TACACS/RADIUS misconfigurations	7	Authentication Protocols *and* Troubleshooting Cloud Computing and Remote Access
○ Default passwords/settings	7	Troubleshooting Cloud Computing and Remote Access
• Improper access/backdoor access	8	Security Risks
• ARP issues	8	Security Risks
• Banner grabbing/OUI	8	Security Risks
• Domain/local group configurations	8	Security in Network Design
• Jamming	8	Security Risks
4.8 Given a scenario, troubleshoot and resolve common WAN issues		
• Loss of internet connectivity	11	Troubleshooting WAN Issues
• Interface errors	11	Troubleshooting WAN Issues
• Split horizon	11	Troubleshooting WAN Issues
• DNS issues	11	Troubleshooting WAN Issues
• Interference	11	Troubleshooting WAN Issues
• Router configurations	11	Troubleshooting WAN Issues
• Customer premise equipment	11	Troubleshooting WAN Issues
○ Smart jack/NIU	11	T-Carriers
○ Demarc	11	T-Carriers
○ Loopback	11	Troubleshooting WAN Issues
○ CSU/DSU	11	T-Carriers
○ Copper line drivers/repeaters	11	Troubleshooting WAN Issues
• Company security policy	11	Troubleshooting WAN Issues
○ Throttling	11	Troubleshooting WAN Issues
○ Blocking	11	Troubleshooting WAN Issues
○ Fair access policy/utilization limits	11	Troubleshooting WAN Issues
• Satellite issues	11	Wireless WANs
○ Latency	11	Wireless WANs

Domain 5.0 Industry Standards, Practices, and Network Theory—16% of Examination

Objective	Chapter	Section
5.1 Analyze a scenario and determine the corresponding OSI layer		
• Layer 1 - Physical	1	The Seven-Layer OSI Model
• Layer 2 - Data link	1	The Seven-Layer OSI Model
• Layer 3 - Network	1	The Seven-Layer OSI Model
• Layer 4 - Transport	1	The Seven-Layer OSI Model
• Layer 5 - Session	1	The Seven-Layer OSI Model
• Layer 6 - Presentation	1	The Seven-Layer OSI Model
• Layer 7 - Application	1	The Seven-Layer OSI Model
5.2 Explain the basics of network theory and concepts		
• Encapsulation/de-encapsulation	1	The Seven-Layer OSI Model
• Modulation techniques	5	Transmission Basics
○ Multiplexing	5	Transmission Basics
○ De-multiplexing	5	Transmission Basics
○ Analog and digital techniques	5	Transmission Basics
○ TDM	5	Transmission Basics
• Numbering systems	Apx B	Numbering Systems
○ Binary	Apx B	Manual Conversions
○ Hexadecimal	Apx B	Manual Conversions
○ Octal	Apx B	Manual Conversions
• Broadband/base band	5	Transmission Basics
• Bit rates vs baud rate	5	Transmission Basics
• Sampling size	9	Monitoring and Managing Network Traffic
• CSMA/CD and CSMA/CA	4 6	NICs and Ethernet Wi-Fi WLAN (Wireless LAN) Architecture
• Carrier detect/sense	11	PSTN (Public Switched Telephone Network)
• Wavelength	5	Transmission Basics
• TCP/IP suite	3	TCP/IP Core Protocols
○ ICMP	3	TCP/IP Core Protocols
○ UDP	3	TCP/IP Core Protocols
○ TCP	3	TCP/IP Core Protocols
• Collision	4	NICs and Ethernet

Objective	Chapter	Section
5.3 Given a scenario, deploy the appropriate wireless standard		
• 802.11a	6	Wi-Fi WLAN (Wireless LAN) Architecture
• 802.11b	6	Wi-Fi WLAN (Wireless LAN) Architecture
• 802.11g	6	Wi-Fi WLAN (Wireless LAN) Architecture
• 802.11n	6	Wi-Fi WLAN (Wireless LAN) Architecture
• 802.11ac	6	Wi-Fi WLAN (Wireless LAN) Architecture
5.4 Given a scenario, deploy the appropriate wired connectivity standard		
• Ethernet standards	5	Twisted-Pair Cable
○ 10BaseT	5	Twisted-Pair Cable
○ 100BaseT	5	Twisted-Pair Cable
○ 1000BaseT	5	Twisted-Pair Cable
○ 1000BaseTX	5	Twisted-Pair Cable
○ 10GBaseT	5	Twisted-Pair Cable
○ 100BaseFX	5	Fiber-Optic Cable
○ 10Base2	5	Transmission Basics
○ 10GBaseSR	5	Fiber-Optic Cable
○ 10GBaseER	5	Fiber-Optic Cable
○ 10GBaseSW	5	Fiber-Optic Cable
○ IEEE 1905.1-2013	11	Broadband Cable
■ Ethernet over HDMI	11	Broadband Cable
■ Ethernet over power line	11	Broadband Cable
• Wiring standards	5	Twisted-Pair Cable
○ EIA/TIA 568A/568B	5	Twisted-Pair Cable
• Broadband standards	11	Broadband Cable
○ DOCSIS	11	Broadband Cable
5.5 Given a scenario, implement the appropriate policies or procedures		
• Security policies	8	Effective Security Policies
○ Consent to monitoring	8	Effective Security Policies
• Network policies	8	Effective Security Policies
• Acceptable use policy	8	Effective Security Policies
• Standard business documents	12	Asset Management and Business Documents
○ SLA	12	Asset Management and Business Documents
○ MOU	12	Asset Management and Business Documents
○ MSA	12	Asset Management and Business Documents
○ SOW	12	Asset Management and Business Documents

Objective	Chapter	Section
5.6 Summarize safety practices		
• Electrical safety	1	Staying Safe When Working with Networks and Computers
○ Grounding	1	Staying Safe When Working with Networks and Computers
• ESD	1	Staying Safe When Working with Networks and Computers
○ Static	1	Staying Safe When Working with Networks and Computers
• Installation safety	1	Staying Safe When Working with Networks and Computers
○ Lifting equipment	1	Staying Safe When Working with Networks and Computers
○ Rack installation	1	Staying Safe When Working with Networks and Computers
○ Placement	1	Staying Safe When Working with Networks and Computers
○ Tool safety	1	Staying Safe When Working with Networks and Computers
• MSDS	1	Staying Safe When Working with Networks and Computers
• Emergency procedures	1	Staying Safe When Working with Networks and Computers
○ Building layout	1	Staying Safe When Working with Networks and Computers
○ Fire escape plan	1	Staying Safe When Working with Networks and Computers
○ Safety/emergency exits	1	Staying Safe When Working with Networks and Computers
○ Fail open/fail close	1	Staying Safe When Working with Networks and Computers
○ Emergency alert system	1	Staying Safe When Working with Networks and Computers
• Fire suppression systems	1	Staying Safe When Working with Networks and Computers
• HVAC	1	Staying Safe When Working with Networks and Computers
5.7 Given a scenario, install and configure equipment in the appropriate location using best practices		
• Intermediate distribution frame	4	Network Equipment in Commercial Buildings
• Main distribution frame	4	Network Equipment in Commercial Buildings
• Cable management	4	Network Equipment in Commercial Buildings
○ Patch panels	4	Network Equipment in Commercial Buildings

Objective	Chapter	Section
• Power management	4	Managing Power Sources and the Environment
○ Power converters	4	Managing Power Sources and the Environment
○ Circuits	4	Managing Power Sources and the Environment
○ UPS	4	Managing Power Sources and the Environment
○ Inverters	4	Managing Power Sources and the Environment
○ Power redundancy	4	Managing Power Sources and the Environment
• Device placement	4	Network Equipment in Commercial Buildings
• Air flow	4	Network Equipment in Commercial Buildings
• Cable trays	4	Network Equipment in Commercial Buildings
• Rack systems	4	Network Equipment in Commercial Buildings
○ Server rail racks	4	Network Equipment in Commercial Buildings
○ Two-post racks	4	Network Equipment in Commercial Buildings
○ Four-post racks	4	Network Equipment in Commercial Buildings
○ Free-standing racks	4	Network Equipment in Commercial Buildings
• Labeling	4	Network Equipment in Commercial Buildings
○ Port labeling	4	Network Equipment in Commercial Buildings
○ System labeling	4	Network Equipment in Commercial Buildings
○ Circuit labeling	4	Network Equipment in Commercial Buildings
○ Naming conventions	4	Network Equipment in Commercial Buildings
○ Patch panel labeling	4	Network Equipment in Commercial Buildings
• Rack monitoring	4	Network Equipment in Commercial Buildings
• Rack security	4	Network Equipment in Commercial Buildings
5.8 Explain the basics of change management procedures		
• Document reason for a change	12	Change Management
• Change request	12	Change Management
○ Configuration procedures	12	Change Management
○ Rollback process	12	Change Management
○ Potential impact	12	Change Management
○ Notification	12	Change Management
• Approval process	12	Change Management
• Maintenance window	12	Change Management
○ Authorized downtime	12	Change Management
• Notification of change	12	Change Management
• Documentation	12	Change Management
○ Network configurations	12	Change Management
○ Additions to the network	12	Change Management
○ Physical location changes	12	Change Management

Objective	Chapter	Section
5.9 Compare and contrast the following ports and protocols		
• 80 HTTP	2	How Ports and Sockets Work
• 443 HTTPS	7	Encryption Techniques, Protocols, and Utilities
• 137-139 NetBIOS	2 3	How Ports and Sockets Work Troubleshooting Router Issues
• 110 POP	2	How Ports and Sockets Work
• 143 IMAP	2	How Ports and Sockets Work
• 25 SMTP	2	How Ports and Sockets Work
• 5060/5061 SIP	9	Unified Communications Technologies
• 2427/2727 MGCP	9	Unified Communications Technologies
• 5004/5005 RTP	9	Unified Communications Technologies
• 1720 H.323	9	Unified Communications Technologies
• TCP	3	TCP/IP Core Protocols
○ Connection-oriented	1	The Seven-Layer OSI Model
• UDP	3	TCP/IP Core Protocols
○ Connectionless	1	The Seven-Layer OSI Model
5.10 Given a scenario, configure and apply the appropriate ports and protocols		
• 20, 21 FTP	1	How Networks Are Used
• 161 SNMP	2 9	How Ports and Sockets Work Monitoring and Managing Network Traffic
• 22 SSH	7	Encryption Techniques, Protocols, and Utilities
• 23 Telnet	2	How Ports and Sockets Work
• 53 DNS	2	How Ports and Sockets Work
• 67, 68 DHCP	2	How Ports and Sockets Work
• 69 TFTP	2	How Ports and Sockets Work
• 445 SMB	2	How Ports and Sockets Work
• 3389 RDP	7	Encryption Techniques, Protocols, and Utilities

Numbering Systems

Network+
5.2 In Chapter 2, you learned that the binary numbering system has two digits (0 and 1), the octal numbering system has eight digits (0 through 7), and the hexadecimal numbering system has 16 digits (0, 1, 2, 3, 4, 5, 6, 7, 8, 9, A, B, C, D, E, and F). Table B-1 shows how to count in each numbering system.

Table B-1 Counting in four numbering systems

Decimal	Binary	Octal	Hex	Decimal	Binary	Octal	Hex
0	0	0	0	11	1011	13	B
1	1	1	1	12	1100	14	C
2	10	2	2	13	1101	15	D
3	11	3	3	14	1110	16	E
4	100	4	4	15	1111	17	F
5	101	5	5	16	10000	20	10
6	110	6	6	17	10001	21	11
7	111	7	7	18	10010	22	12
8	1000	10	8	19	10011	23	13
9	1001	11	9	20	10100	24	14
10	1010	12	A	21	10101	25	15

You need to be familiar with converting numbers between numbering systems when you're working with either IPv4 or IPv6 addressing. You probably won't see the octal system used much. However, you will often need to convert back and forth among the binary, decimal, and hexadecimal systems.

NETWORK+ EXAM TIP The CompTIA Network+ exam expects you to be familiar with the octal, hex, and binary numbering systems.

Converting between numbering systems can be done by hand, or by using a scientific calculator, such as the one available with any of the Windows operating systems. You will not be allowed to use a calculator during the CompTIA Network+ exam, so learning how to convert these numbering systems manually will help prepare you for taking the exam.

Manual Conversions

As you saw in Chapter 10, you need to know how to convert decimal to binary numbers and back in order to calculate subnets. Recall that an IPv4 address is made up of four binary octets. For example, the IPv4 address 192.168.89.0 in binary is: 11000000.10101000.01011001.00000000

When converting 8-bit binary numbers, such as the octets in an IPv4 address, you work with 2 raised to the power of 0 (2^0) through 2 raised to the power of 7 (2^7). Recall that a power tells you how many times to multiply a number by itself. For example, 2 to the 5th power (2^5) means $2 \times 2 \times 2 \times 2 \times 2$, which equals 32. Figure B-1 is your starting point for converting between decimal and binary numbering systems. In this figure, the powers of 2 are arranged so that the smallest value (2^0) is on the right, because this is where the smallest value bit is located in an 8-bit octet (such as 11011001—the 1 on the far right has a smaller place value than the 1 on the far left). The largest value (2^7) is on the left. That is, each power of 2 represents one digit in a binary, 8-bit octet, starting with 2^0 on the right and ending with 2^7 on the left.

2^7	2^6	2^5	2^4	2^3	2^2	2^1	2^0

Figure B-1   Arrange the powers of 2 with the largest on the left and the smallest on the right
© 2016 Cengage Learning®.

In the rest of this appendix, you will use the basic structure of Figure B-1 as you learn to convert between decimal and binary numbering systems.

Decimal to Binary

Suppose you're converting an IPv4 address, 192.168.1.25, from decimal to binary. One of the 8-bit octets in the address is the decimal number 25. Complete the following steps to calculate the conversion for this octet:

1. First, on a scratch sheet of paper write the powers of 2, as shown in Figure B-1. Remember to begin with 2^0 on the right and 2^7 on the left. Fill in the values of each power of 2, as shown in Figure B-2.

$2^7 = 128$	$2^6 = 64$	$2^5 = 32$	$2^4 = 16$	$2^3 = 8$	$2^2 = 4$	$2^1 = 2$	$2^0 = 1$

Figure B-2   It's very helpful to have the first eight powers of 2 memorized
© 2016 Cengage Learning®.

The powers of 2 are easy to remember if you practice counting from the bottom up. Don't be embarrassed to count the powers of 2 on your fingers if you find that helpful. Raise a finger each time you use a 2. The total number of fingers raised tells you which power you're on. For example, 2 times 2 is 4 (that's two 2s and two fingers, or 2^2), times 2 is 8 (now three 2s and three fingers, or 2^3), times 2 is 16 (now four 2s and four fingers, or 2^4), and so on. The first bit was 2^0, so 2^7 is as high as you'll need to go for an 8-bit binary number.

2. Now you can easily select the correct power of 2 to use in the next step. Keep in mind that, just like when playing blackjack, you want to get the closest power of 2 to the target decimal number (in this case, 25) as you can without going over. For example, 2^5 ($2 \times 2 \times 2 \times 2 \times 2$) is 32, and that's too big. 2^4 ($2 \times 2 \times 2 \times 2$), however, is 16, so that's a good place to start because it's the largest power of 2 without going over the target number of 25.

3. Fill in the next row of your conversion chart to calculate the 8-bit binary equivalent of the decimal number 25, as shown in Figure B-3. The first three digits from the left will be 0s because, as you already discovered, any power of 2 above 2^4 is too big to fit into the decimal number 25. However, place a 1 under 2^4 because the value of 2^4, which is 16, fits once inside the original decimal number 25. This fills in the first four digits of your 8-bit binary number.

$2^7 = 128$	$2^6 = 64$	$2^5 = 32$	$2^4 = 16$	$2^3 = 8$	$2^2 = 4$	$2^1 = 2$	$2^0 = 1$
0	0	0	1	?	?	?	?

Figure B-3 Insert 0 for each power of 2 that is larger than the number you are converting to binary
© 2016 Cengage Learning®.

4. For each binary digit you filled in, you subtract its decimal value from the original decimal number 25 minus whatever you've already used up. Take a look at Figure B-4. You did not use 2^7 (which equals 128), so you subtract 0 from 25, which still leaves 25. You also did not use 2^6 or 2^5, so you subtract 0 from 25 for each of these digits. However, you did use 2^4 (which equals 16), so you subtract 16 from 25, and that leaves 9 more to go.

$2^7 = 128$	$2^6 = 64$	$2^5 = 32$	$2^4 = 16$	$2^3 = 8$	$2^2 = 4$	$2^1 = 2$	$2^0 = 1$
0	0	0	1	?	?	?	?
$25 - 0 = 25$	$25 - 0 = 25$	$25 - 0 = 25$	$25 - 16 = 9$				

Figure B-4 Subtract the largest possible power of 2 from the number you're converting to binary

© 2016 Cengage Learning®.

5. Figure B-5 shows the rest of the calculation. For each digit, if its value fits in the number you're working with at that point, you use a 1 for that digit. If it doesn't fit, you use a 0. $2^3 = 8$, which is small enough to fit into the 9 you have available, leaving 1 (take 8 from 9) left over. 2^2 and 2^1 are both too big for that remainder, so you put 0s in those slots. But you can use up the rest of the remainder with 2^0. (Remember that any number raised to the power of 0 is 1.) This gives you the results shown in Figure B-5.

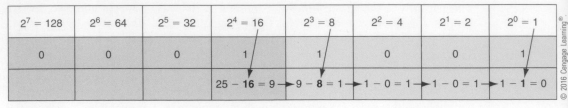

$2^7 = 128$	$2^6 = 64$	$2^5 = 32$	$2^4 = 16$	$2^3 = 8$	$2^2 = 4$	$2^1 = 2$	$2^0 = 1$
0	0	0	1	1	0	0	1
			$25 - 16 = 9 \rightarrow$	$9 - 8 = 1 \rightarrow$	$1 - 0 = 1 \rightarrow$	$1 - 0 = 1 \rightarrow$	$1 - 1 = 0$

Figure B-5 Continue subtracting powers of 2 from the remainder of the previous step

Now you see that the decimal number 25 converts to 00011001 in 8-bit binary. Try calculating the binary values for each of the other three octets in the IP address 192.168.1.25.

This is a pretty simple way to convert decimal to binary, and can be done on a scratch sheet of paper without needing a calculator or a lot of space to write. You can use a similar process to convert a hexadecimal number to a binary number. Because of the way that binary and hexadecimal numbers relate to one another mathematically, you can treat each group of 4 binary bits as a single hexadecimal digit. That means an 8-bit binary number always converts to a 2-digit ($8 \div 4 = 2$) hexadecimal number.

Hexadecimal to Binary

Suppose you need to convert the hexadecimal number FE80 to a binary number. (Before you attempt this, it's helpful to review Table B-1, which shows how to count in hexadecimal.) Can you predict how many digits this binary number will have?

1. Start with the first character in the hexadecimal number: F. This conversion is easiest to calculate if you convert each digit to decimal first, and then convert to binary. So F in hexadecimal equals the decimal number 15. You can figure this out by counting up to 9, then count by letters after you pass 9, as shown in Figure B-6.

Hex	0	1	2	3	4	5	6	7	8	9	A	B	C	D	E	F
Dec	0	1	2	3	4	5	6	7	8	9	10	11	12	13	14	15

Figure B-6 The hexadecimal numbering system uses letters beyond the value of 9 for a total of 16 single-digit values

© 2016 Cengage Learning®.

2. Next convert this decimal value to its corresponding binary value. Note that 15 is the largest possible decimal value of a 4-bit binary number, so decimal 15 equals binary 1111. You could also calculate this value by following the steps in the "Decimal to Binary" section earlier in this appendix, as shown in Figure B-7.

$2^3 = 8$	$2^2 = 4$	$2^1 = 2$	$2^0 = 1$
1	1	1	1
$15 - 8 = 7$	$7 - 4 = 3$	$3 - 2 = 1$	$1 - 1 = 0$

Figure B-7 Subtract powers of 2 from the remainder of the previous step

Note that you only need four digits here because, as you'll recall, you're converting each digit of the hexadecimal number into four binary digits.

3. The next digit in the original hexadecimal number is E. E in hexadecimal is 1 less than F, so you can save a little time by simply subtracting 1 from the decimal value of F: $15 - 1 = 14$. You can also skip ahead to the binary calculation and perform the same calculation: $1111 - 1 = 1110$.

4. The next hexadecimal digit is 8, which is the same as 8 in decimal. Both are 1000 in binary (that's one 2^3, which equals 8, and no other powers of 2), as shown in Figure B-8.

$2^3 = 8$	$2^2 = 4$	$2^1 = 2$	$2^0 = 1$
1	0	0	0
$8 - 8 = 0$	$0 - 0 = 0$	$0 - 0 = 0$	$0 - 0 = 0$

Figure B-8   Once the remainder reaches zero, no more powers of 2 are needed

5. 0 is the same in all three numbering systems. Therefore, you can now see in Figure B-9 that FE80=1111 1110 1000 0000.

Hexadecimal	F	E	8	0
Decimal	15	14	8	0
Binary	1111	1110	1000	0000

Figure B-9   Each hexadecimal digit is individually converted to a 4-bit binary number
© 2016 Cengage Learning®.

Binary to Hexadecimal

You can do this process in reverse to convert from a smaller base (such as binary) to a larger base (such as hexadecimal). Convert 1011 1001 from binary to hexadecimal, calculating each group of 4 bits separately, as follows:

1. Begin with the first 4 bits, 1011. Using the first four powers of 2, calculate the value of each bit if and only if there is a 1 in that bit, as shown in Figure B-10.

1	0	1	1
$2^3 = 8$	0	$2^1 = 2$	$2^0 = 1$

Figure B-10   Insert a power of 2 for each bit containing a one
© 2016 Cengage Learning®.

2. Add up the values for each power of 2 that is included: $8+2+1=11$

3. Now do the same calculations for the second 4 bits, as shown in Figure B-11.

1	0	0	1
$2^3 = 8$	0	0	$2^0 = 1$

Figure B-11   Remember to reuse the four smallest powers of 2

© 2016 Cengage Learning®.

Then add the values: $8 + 1 = 9$

4. You have now converted the binary numbers 1011 and 1001 to the decimal numbers 11 and 9, respectively. The problem is that you can only write one hexadecimal digit for each set of 4 binary bits. So the decimal value of 11 is written as a B in hexadecimal, and the decimal value of 9 can still be written as a 9 in hexadecimal. See Figure B-12.

Binary	1	0	1	1	1	0	0	1
Decimal	8 + 0 + 2 + 1				8 + 0 + 0 + 1			
	11				9			
Hexadecimal	B				9			

© 2016 Cengage Learning®

Figure B-12   Continue to treat each set of four binary digits separately until the conversion to hexadecimal is complete

To practice working with each numbering system, create a table similar to Table B-1 and count for each of the four numbering systems (decimal, binary, octal, and hex) beginning with decimal 22, going through decimal 40.

Conversion with a Calculator

You won't be allowed to use a calculator during the CompTIA Network+ exam, but when calculating conversions on the job, using a calculator can make the task much simpler. Take, for example, the decimal number 131. Complete the following steps to convert it to a binary number using the Windows Calculator:

1. On a Windows computer, open the Calculator program from the Start menu (Windows 7) or Start screen (Windows 8.1). In Windows 8.1, be sure to use the desktop Calculator program, not the Start screen's Calculator app.

2. Click **View**, and then click **Programmer**. Verify that the Dec option button is selected.

3. Type **131**, and then click the **Bin** option button. The binary equivalent of the decimal number 131, which is 10000011, appears in the display window. You can reverse this process to convert a binary number to a decimal number.

NOTE   Note that if the binary number yielded by the calculator is less than eight digits, you will need to insert leading 0s to complete the octet. For example, enter the decimal number 89 and convert it to binary. The calculator shows only seven digits: 1011001. To make this an octet, you'll need to write it as 01011001 (with an extra 0 at the beginning).

If you're connected to the Internet and using a Web browser, you can quickly convert binary and decimal numbers using Google calculator:

1. Go to **google.com,** and then type the number you want to convert, along with the desired format, in the search text box. For example, to convert the decimal number 131 into binary form, type **131 in binary,** and then press **Enter.** You see the following result: 131=0b10000011. The prefix "0b" (that's a zero, not the letter O) indicates that the number is in binary format. Notice that Google assumes a number is in decimal form unless stated otherwise.

2. To convert a binary number into decimal form, type 0b (again, that's the number zero, not the letter O) before the binary number. For example, entering **0b10000011 in decimal** returns the decimal number 131.

In Chapter 10, you practice converting between binary, decimal, and hexadecimal numbers while calculating subnets. To best prepare yourself for the CompTIA Network+ exam, consider performing all of these calculations manually and using the calculator only to check your results. If your manual calculations don't match the calculator's computations, make sure you investigate carefully to see where you made a mistake until your calculations are consistently correct.

appendix C

Visual Guide to Connectors

Throughout this book, you learned about several different cabling and connector options that may be used on networks. Some, such as RJ-45 connectors, are very common, whereas others, such as MT-RJ connectors, are used only on high-speed optical networks. So that you can compare such connectors and ensure that you understand their differences, this appendix compiles drawings of the connectors and a brief summary of their uses in two simple tables (see Tables C-1 and C-2). You must be familiar with the most popular types of connectors to qualify for CompTIA's Network+ certification. You can find more details about these connectors and the networks on which they are used in Chapters 5 and 11.

Table C-1 Copper connectors and their uses

Specification	Male connector (front view)	Male connector (side view)	Female receptacle (front view)	Application
BNC				Used with coaxial cable for broadband cable connections; also used on old Ethernet networks such as Thinnet
F-connector				Used on coaxial cable suitable for use with broadband video and data applications; more common than BNC connectors
DB-9				One of the RS-232 standard connectors used in serial connections

Table C-1 Copper connectors and their uses (*continued*)

Specification	Male connector (front view)	Male connector (side view)	Female receptacle (front view)	Application
DB-25				One of the RS-232 standard connectors used in serial connections
RJ-11 (registered jack 11)				Used on twisted-pair cabling for telephone systems (and some older twisted-pair networks)
RJ-45 (registered jack 45) and RJ-48 (registered jack 48)				Used on twisted-pair cabling for Ethernet (RJ-45) and T-carrier (RJ-48) connections
USB (Universal Serial Bus)				Used to connect external peripherals, such as modems, mice, audio players, NICs, cameras, and smartphones

Table C-2 Fiber connectors and their uses

Specification	Male connector (front view)	Male connector (side view)	Female receptacle (front view)	Application
ST (straight tip), usually multimode				Uses a bayonet locking mechanism; one of the first commercially available fiber connectors
SC (subscriber connector or standard connector)				Widely used; has a snap-in connector
LC (local connector), single-mode				Most common 2.5-mm ferrule; available in full-duplex mode

Table C-2   Fiber connectors and their uses (*continued*)

Specification	Male connector (front view)	Male connector (side view)	Female receptacle (front view)	Application
MT-RJ (Mechanical Transfer Register Jack), multimode				Most common MMF; contains two strands of fiber per ferrule to provide full-duplex signaling
FC (ferrule connector)				Not commonly used; has a screw-on mechanism

CompTIA Network+ Practice Exam

The following exam contains questions that are similar in content and format to the questions you will encounter on CompTIA's Network+ N10-006 certification exam, released in 2015. This practice exam consists of 100 questions, all of which are multiple choice. Some questions have more than one correct answer. The number of questions on each topic reflects the weighting that CompTIA assigned to these topics in its exam objectives. To simulate taking the CompTIA Network+ certification exam, allow yourself 90 minutes to answer all of the questions.

1. Which of the following does *not* accurately describe TACACS+ in comparison to RADIUS?

   a. TACACS+ relies on TCP, not UDP, at the Transport layer.

   b. TACACS+ is typically installed on a router or switch, rather than on a server.

   c. TACACS+ encrypts all information transmitted for AAA rather than just the password.

   d. TACACS+ was developed for proprietary use on Cisco products.

   e. TACACS+ operates as a software application on a remote access server.

2. Your network manager has purchased a dozen new access points and all are configured to use the new 802.11ac standard in the 5-GHz band. These access points will be backward-compatible with older access points that run which of the following standards? (Choose all that apply.)

   a. 802.11g

   b. 802.11n

   c. 802.11b

   d. Bluetooth

   e. None of the above

3. Which of the following figures reflects the type of physical topology commonly used on a 100Base-T network?

a.

b.

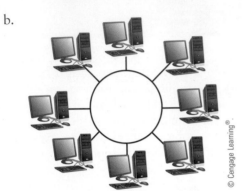

c.

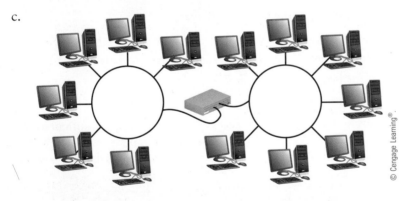

d.

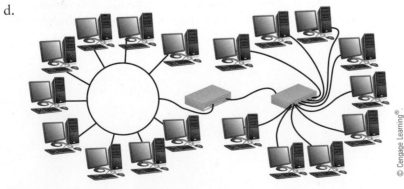

e.

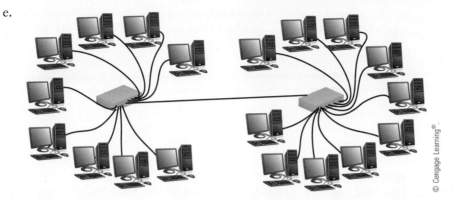

4. You have installed and configured two virtual Web servers and a virtual mail server on a physical server. What networking mode will you assign to each server's vNIC to ensure that the virtual machines' hosts on the Internet can access the virtual machines?

    a. NAT

    b. Bridged

    c. Host-only

    d. Internal

    e. Grouped

5. Your organization contracts with a cloud computing company to store all of its data. The company promises 99.99% uptime. If it lives up to its claims, for how many minutes each year can you expect your data to be unavailable?

    a. Less than 448 minutes

    b. Less than 99 minutes

    c. Less than 52 minutes

    d. Less than 14 minutes

    e. Less than 6 minutes

6. You are rearranging nodes on your Gigabit Ethernet network. Due to a necessarily hasty expansion, you have decided to supply power to a wireless router in a makeshift data room using PoE. What is the minimum cabling standard you must use to connect this wireless router to the network's backbone?

    a. RG-6

    b. RG-59

    c. Cat 5e

    d. SMF

    e. Cat 6

7. To ensure that your private network is always protected, you decide to install three redundant firewalls. Which of the following would allow you to assign the same IP address to all three?

    a. SMTP

    b. CARP

    c. SNMPv3

    d. IMAP

    e. NTP

8. You are a networking technician in a radiology clinic, where physicians use the network to transmit and store patients' diagnostic results. Shortly after a new wing, which contains X-ray and MRI (magnetic resonance imaging) machines, is added to the building, computers in that area begin having intermittent problems saving data to the file server. After you have gathered information, identified the symptoms, questioned users, and determined what has changed, what is your next step in troubleshooting this problem?

    a. Establish a plan of action to resolve the problem.

    b. Escalate the problem.

    c. Document findings, actions, and outcomes.

    d. Establish a theory of probable cause.

    e. Determine the next steps to resolve the problem.

9. You are part of a team participating in a posture assessment of your company's WAN. Which of the following tools or strategies will help you gain a broad understanding of your network's vulnerabilities?

    a. MIB

    b. War chalking

    c. Nmap

    d. WPA cracking

    e. PGP

10. You work for an ISP. Several of your customers have called to complain about the slow response from a popular Web site. You suspect that network congestion is at fault. Which TCP/IP utility would help you determine where the congestion is occurring?

    a. FTP

    b. Nslookup

    c. Nbtstat

    d. Tracert

    e. Telnet

11. Which of the following WAN topologies is the most fault tolerant?

    a. Full mesh

    b. Bus

    c. Peer-to-peer

    d. Ring

    e. Hierarchical

12. Which of the following is a valid MAC address?

    a. C3:00:50:00:FF:FF

    b. 153.101.24.3

    c. ::9F53

    d. FE80::32:1CA3:B0E2

    e. D0:00:00:00

13. What type of network could use the type of connector shown below?

    a. 100Base-FX

    b. 100Base-TX

    c. 10Base-T

    d. 1000Base-T

    e. 10Base-2

14. Your organization has just ordered its first T-1 connection to the Internet. Prior to that, your organization relied on a DSL connection. Which of the following devices must you now have that your DSL connection didn't require?

    a. Modem

    b. CSU/DSU

    c. Switch

    d. Hub

    e. Router

15. Which of the following wireless standards provides an entirely IP-based, packet-switched network for both voice and data transmissions? (Choose two.)

    a. LTE

    b. 802.16e

    c. 802.16m

    d. HSPA+

    e. 802.11n

16. You have created a new Web server on a computer running the Linux operating system. Which of the following programs will generate messages when modules don't load correctly or services encounter errors?

    a. Event Viewer

    b. IDS/IPS

    c. Packet Sniffer

    d. Network Monitor

    e. Syslog

17. You have been asked to provide a connectivity solution for a shuttle-bus system at a large theme park. The owners of the park want a wireless network that reaches all parking lots and drop-off points throughout the park's 2.4-square-mile campus. Each shuttle is to be equipped with a wireless antenna to provide real-time pick-up and drop-off directives to each driver. The park owners plan to install their own base station antennas in order to have complete control of the amount and type of traffic traversing the WAN, but they are very concerned about the cost of equipment installation. Considering the needs and priorities of the theme park owners, what is the best solution for this client?

    a. Metro Ethernet

    b. 802.11n

    c. NFC

    d. 802.11ac

    e. WiMAX

18. You want to add the five virtual machines that exist on your host machine to the Staff VLAN at your office. Which of the following must your host machine's NIC support?

    a. CSMA/CA

    b. Channel bonding

    c. MIMO

    d. Trunking

    e. OSPF

19. You have just rearranged the access points on your small office network. Now a group of employees complains that they cannot reliably get their workstations to connect with a new 802.11ac access point. You have confirmed that the workstations are using the correct SSID, security type, and passphrase. You have also confirmed that the access point is on and functioning properly because when you stand in the computer room where it's located, you can connect to the access point from your smartphone. Which of the following is likely preventing the other users' workstations from associating with the new access point?

    a. The users are attempting to log on using incorrect user IDs.

    b. The workstations are located beyond the access point's range.

    c. The workstations are set to use 802.11g.

    d. The users have turned off their wireless antennas.

    e. The workstations' wired NICs are causing addressing conflicts with their wireless NICs.

20. Which of the following wireless security techniques uses RADIUS and AES?

    a. WEP

    b. WPA

    c. WPA2

    d. WPA-Enterprise

    e. WPA2-Enterprise

21. You are the network administrator for a large university whose network contains nearly 10,000 workstations, over 100 routers, 80 switches, and 2000 printers. You are researching a proposal to both upgrade the routers and switches on your network and at the same time improve the management of your network. To make automating network management easier, what type of protocol must the new routers and switches support?

    a. TFTP

    b. SMTP

    c. NNTP

    d. ICMP

    e. SNMP

22. In the process of troubleshooting an intermittent performance problem with your network's Internet connection, you attempt to run a tracert test to microsoft.com. The tracert response displays the first 12 hops in the route, but then presents several "Request timed out" messages in a row. What is the most likely reason for this?

    a. Your network's ISP is experiencing connectivity problems.

    b. The Internet backbone is experiencing traffic congestion.

    c. Your client's TCP/IP service limits the `tracert` command to a maximum of 12 hops.

    d. Your IP gateway failed while you were attempting the tracert test.

    e. Microsoft's network is bounded by firewalls that do not accept incoming ICMP traffic.

23. What is the network ID for a network that contains the group of IP addresses from 194.73.44.10 through 194.73.44.254 and is not subnetted?

    a. 194.1.1.1

    b. 194.73.0.0

    c. 194.73.44.1

    d. 194.73.44.255

    e. 194.73.44.0

24. Which of the following 10-gigabit technologies has the longest maximum segment length?

    a. 10GBase-SR

    b. 10GBase-ER

    c. 10GBase-T

    d. 10GBase-LW

    e. 10GBase-SW

25. Recently, your company's WAN experienced a disabling DDoS attack. Which of the following devices could detect such an attack and prevent it from affecting your network in the future?

    a. A honeypot

    b. SIEM

    c. HIPS

    d. Nmap

    e. NIPS

26. In NAT, how does an IP gateway ensure that outgoing traffic can traverse public networks?

    a. It modifies each outgoing frame's Type field to indicate that the transmission is destined for a public network.

    b. It assigns each outgoing packet a masked ID via the Options field.

    c. It interprets the contents of outgoing packets to ensure that they contain no client-identifying information.

    d. It replaces each outgoing packet's Source address field with a public IP address.

    e. It modifies the frame length to create uniformly sized frames, called cells, which are required for public network transmission.

27. You have purchased an access point capable of exchanging data via the 802.11n or 802.11ac wireless standard. According to these standards, what is the maximum distance, in meters, from the access point that wireless stations can travel and still reliably exchange data with the access point?

    a. 20

    b. 75

    c. 100

    d. 400

    e. 550

28. Which of the following functions does SIP perform on a VoIP network? (Choose all that apply.)

    a. Determines the locations of endpoints

    b. Provides call waiting and caller ID services

    c. Prioritizes calls for any single endpoint in a queue

    d. Establishes sessions between endpoints

    e. Encrypts VoIP signals before they are transmitted over the network

29. You suspect that a machine on your network with the host name PRTSRV is issuing excessive broadcast traffic on your network. What command can you use to determine this host's IP address?

    a. `netstat PRTSRV`

    b. `ipconfig PRTSRV`

    c. `nslookup PRTSRV`

    d. `ifconfig PRTSRV`

    e. `nbtstat PRTSRV`

30. Which of the following allows a protocol analyzer on your network's backbone switch to monitor all the traffic on a VLAN?

    a. Trunking

    b. Port mirroring

    c. Looping

    d. Spanning Tree Protocol

    e. Caching

31. What element of network management systems operates on a managed device, such as a router?

    a. MIB

    b. Polling

    c. Agent

    d. Nmap

    e. Caching

32. Your company is experiencing a growth spurt and is ready to invest in a more sophisticated disaster recovery plan. Currently the only backup plan consists of a few spare computers in a storage closet, with data on the servers duplicated weekly to an off-site backup service. The owners of the company have committed to acquiring additional servers to duplicate critical servers in their current network, and they want the servers to be configured identically to the servers now in use. The new servers will be stored at an off-site data center, and updated every time the on-site servers are updated. What type of disaster recovery site is your company creating?

    a. Hot site

    b. Ambient site

    c. Site survey

    d. Warm site

    e. Looking glass site

33. Which of the following is a single sign-on authentication method?

    a. IPsec

    b. EAPoL

    c. SSL

    d. Kerberos

    e. CHAP

34. You are a network administrator for a WAN that connects two regional insurance company offices—the main office and a satellite office—to each other by a T-3. The main office is also connected to the Internet using a T-3. This T-3 provides Internet access for both offices. To ensure that your private network is not compromised by unauthorized access through the Internet connection, you install a firewall between the main office and the Internet. Shortly thereafter, users in your satellite office complain that they cannot access the file server in the main office, but users in the main office can still access the Internet. What two things should you check?

    a. Whether the firewall has been configured to run in promiscuous mode

    b. Whether the firewall is placed in the appropriate location on the network

    c. Whether the firewall has been configured to allow access from IP addresses in the satellite office

    d. Whether the firewall has been configured to receive and transmit UDP-based packets

    e. Whether the firewall has been configured to allow Internet access over the main office's T-3

35. What is one function of a VPN concentrator?

    a. To prioritize traffic on a VPN

    b. To consolidate multiple VPNs into a single, larger VPN

    c. To cache a VPN's frequently requested content

    d. To establish VPN tunnels

    e. To collect traffic from multiple VLANs into a VPN

36. While troubleshooting a workstation connectivity problem, you type the following command: `ping 127.0.0.1`. The response indicates that the test failed. What can you determine about that workstation?

    a. Its network cable is faulty or not connected to the wall jack.

    b. Its TCP/IP stack is not installed properly.

    c. Its IP address has been prevented from transmitting data past the default gateway.

    d. Its DHCP settings are incorrect.

    e. Its DNS name server specification is incorrect.

37. You are a support technician working in a data closet in a remote office. You suspect that a connectivity problem is related to a broken RJ-45 plug on a patch cable that connects a switch to a patch panel. You need to replace that connection, but you forgot to bring an extra patch cable. You decide to install a new RJ-45 connector to replace the broken RJ-45 connector. What two tools do you need to successfully accomplish this task?

   a.   Punch-down tool

   b.   Crimping tool

   c.   Wire stripper

   d.   Cable tester

   e.   Multimeter

38. In IPv6, which of the following is the loopback address?

   a.   1.0.0.1

   b.   127:0:0:0:0:0:0:1

   c.   FE80::1

   d.   ::1

   e.   127.0.0.1

39. Which two of the following devices operate only at the Physical layer of the OSI model?

   a.   Hub

   b.   Switch

   c.   Router

   d.   Bridge

   e.   Repeater

40. Which of the following is a reason for using subnetting?

   a.   To facilitate easier migration from IPv4 to IPv6 addressing

   b.   To enable a network to use DHCP

   c.   To limit broadcast domains

   d.   To reduce the likelihood for user error when modifying TCP/IP properties

   e.   To reduce the number of routing table entries

41. Which of the following is often used to secure data traveling over VPNs that use L2TP?

   a.   PPTP

   b.   PPoE

   c.   Kerberos

   d.   SSH

   e.   IPsec

42. Which two of the following routing protocols offer fast convergence time and can be used on interior or border routers?

    a. RIP

    b. RIPv2

    c. OSPF

    d. BGP

    e. EIGRP

43. At the beginning of the school year, students at your school must configure their computers and other devices to obtain trusted access to the student portion of the school's network. What is this process called?

    a. Authenticating

    b. Remote wiping

    c. Backleveling

    d. Onboarding

    e. Updating

44. Which signaling protocol is modeled after HTTP and is limited to IP networks?

    a. H.323

    b. RTCP

    c. SIP

    d. MGCP

    e. RTP

45. Due to popular demand from employees who need to roam from one floor of your office building to another, you are expanding your wireless network. You want to ensure that mobile users enjoy uninterrupted network connectivity without having to reconfigure their workstations' wireless network connection settings. Which of the following variables must you configure on your new access points to match the settings on existing access points?

    a. Administrator password

    b. Scanning rate

    c. SSID

    d. IP address

    e. Signal strength

46. Which transport protocol and TCP/IP port does telnet use?

    a. UDP, port 23

    b. TCP, port 21

    c. UDP, port 22

    d. TCP, port 23

    e. UDP, port 21

47. What is the purpose of an AAAA resource record in your DNS zone file?

    a. It identifies a host's IPv4 address.

    b. It identifies a host's IPv6 address.

    c. It identifies a host's MAC address.

    d. It identifies a mail server address.

    e. It indicates an alternate name for the host.

48. What protocol is used to transfer mail between a Sendmail server and a Microsoft Exchange server?

    a. SMTP

    b. SNMP

    c. IMAP4

    d. POP3

    e. TFTP

49. What would the command `route del default gw 192.168.5.1 eth1` accomplish on your Linux workstation?

    a. Delete the default gateway's route to the host whose IP address is 192.168.5.1

    b. Remove the assignment of IP address 192.168.5.1 from the eth1 interface

    c. Remove the workstation's route to the default gateway whose IP address is 192.168.5.1

    d. Add a route from the workstation to the default gateway whose IP address is 192.168.5.1

    e. Remove the designation of default gateway, but keep the route for the host whose IP address is 192.168.5.1

50. Your 100Base-T network is wired following the TIA/EIA 568B standard. As you make your own patch cable, which wires do you crimp into pins 1 and 2 of the RJ-45 connector?

    a. White with green stripe and green

    b. White with brown stripe and brown

    c. White with blue stripe and blue

    d. White with red stripe and red

    e. White with orange stripe and orange

51. A regional bank manager asks you to help with an urgent network problem. Because of a sudden and severe network performance decline, the manager worries that the bank's network might be suffering a DoS attack. Viewing which of the following types of network documentation would probably give you the quickest insight into what's causing this problem?

    a. Wiring schematic

    b. Firewall log

    c. Logical network diagram

    d. The main file server's system log

    e. Physical network diagram

52. You have connected to your bank's home page. Its URL begins with "https://." Based on this information, what type of security can you assume the bank employs for receiving and transmitting data to and from its Web server?

    a. Kerberos

    b. SSL

    c. IPsec

    d. L2TP

    e. Packet-filtering firewall

53. What is the function of protocols and services at the Network layer of the OSI model?

    a. To manage the flow of communications over a channel

    b. To add segmentation and assembly information

    c. To encode and encrypt data

    d. To add logical addresses and properly route data

    e. To apply electrical pulses to the wire

54. Which of the following utilities could you use to log on to a UNIX host?

    a. NTP

    b. ARP

    c. Ping

    d. SSH

    e. SNMP

55. While attempting to load a video to YouTube.com, the operation freezes and the upload fails. Which characteristic of the connection is being affected?

    a. Signaling

    b. Signal-to-noise ratio

    c. Throughput

    d. Goodput

    e. Attenuation

56. As a networking professional, you might use a multimeter to do which of the following? (Choose all that apply.)

    a. Determine where the patch cable for a specific server terminates on the patch panel

    b. Verify that the amount of resistance presented by terminators on coaxial cable networks is appropriate

    c. Check for the presence of noise on a wire (by detecting extraneous voltage)

    d. Confirm that a fiber-optic cable can transmit signals from one node to another

    e. Validate the processing capabilities of a new router

57. **A virtual switch includes several virtual ports, each of which can be considered a:**
    a. Virtual repeater
    b. Virtual router
    c. Virtual gateway
    d. Virtual hub
    e. Virtual bridge

58. **What is the default subnet mask for the following IP address: 154.13.44.87?**
    a. 255.255.255.255
    b. 255.255.255.0
    c. 255.255.0.0
    d. 255.0.0.0
    e. 0.0.0.0

59. **Which of the following diagrams illustrates a SONET network?**
    a.

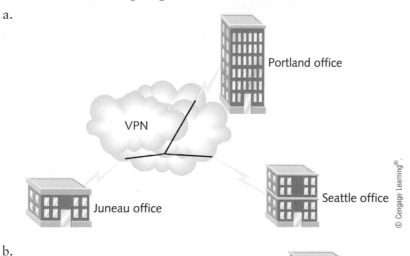

    b.

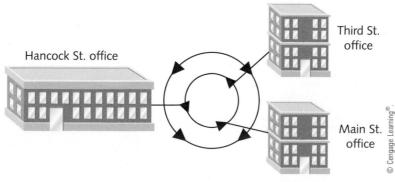

c.

 Archer St. office

 Third St. office

 Main St. office

Hancock St. office

d.

Hancock St. office

 Third St. office

 Main St. office

Archer St. office

Oak St. office

 Pine St. office

e.

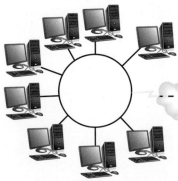

Juneau office

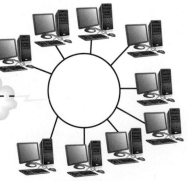

Portland office

60. **How do most modern FTP servers prevent FTP bounce attacks?**

   a. They will not issue data to hosts other than the client that originated the request.

   b. They will deny requests to ports 21 or 22.

   c. They will not allow anonymous logons.

   d. They require clients to communicate using SSH.

   e. They maintain an access list to determine which clients are legitimate.

61. **At what layer of the TCP/IP model is routing information interpreted?**

   a. Physical layer

   b. Data Link layer

   c. Network layer

   d. Application layer

   e. Transport layer

62. **You work for a soft drink company where the temperature of the sodas must be monitored before the drinks are bottled. What device does this industrial network require that can detect this information but is not capable of adjusting the thermostat of the food processing equipment in reaction to temperature changes?**

   a. PLC

   b. MTU

   c. RTU

   d. Actuator

   e. HMI

63. **You have been asked to help improve network performance on a store's small office network, which relies on two switches, two access points, and a router to connect its 18 employees to the Internet and other store locations. You decide to determine what type of traffic the network currently handles. In particular, you're interested in the volume of unnecessary broadcast traffic that might be bogging down shared segments. Which of the following tools will help you identify the percentage of traffic that comprises broadcasts?**

   a. Butt set

   b. OTDR

   c. Protocol analyzer

   d. Multimeter

   e. Cable tester

64. A colleague calls you for help with his home office Internet connection. He is using an 802.11n access point/router connected to a DSL modem. The access point/router's private IP address is 192.168.1.1 and it has been assigned an Internet routable IP address of 76.83.124.35. Your friend cannot connect to any resources on the Internet using his new Windows workstation. You ask him to run the `ipconfig` command and read the results to you. He says his workstation's IP address is 192.168.1.3, the subnet mask is 255.255.255.0, and the default gateway address is 192.168.1.10. What do you advise him to do next?

   a. Display his DNS information.

   b. Change his gateway address.

   c. Change his subnet mask.

   d. Try pinging the loopback address.

   e. Use the `tracert` command to contact the access point/router.

65. You are setting up a new Windows 8.1 client to connect with your LAN, which relies on DHCP. You made certain that the client has the TCP/IP protocol installed and is bound to its NIC. Which of the following must you do next to ensure that the client obtains correct TCP/IP information via DHCP?

   a. Make certain the client's computer name and host name are identical.

   b. Enter the client's MAC address in the DHCP server's ARP table.

   c. Make sure the Client for Microsoft Networks service is bound to the client's NIC.

   d. Enter the DHCP server address in the Windows 8.1 TCP/IP configuration.

   e. Nothing; in Windows 8.1, the DHCP option is selected by default, and the client will obtain IP addressing information upon connecting to the network.

66. Which OSI layer(s) operate differently in wired versus wireless network connections?

   a. Layers 5, 6, and 7

   b. Layers 1, 2, and 3

   c. Layer 1

   d. Layer 2

   e. Layers 1 and 2

67. Which of the following devices separates broadcast domains?

   a. Hub

   b. Switch

   c. Bridge

   d. Repeater

   e. Router

68. Which one of the following media is most resistant to EMI?

    a. Coaxial cable

    b. UTP cable

    c. STP cable

    d. Fiber-optic cable

    e. Microwave

69. In the following figure, if router B suffers a failure, how will this failure affect nodes 1 through 9?

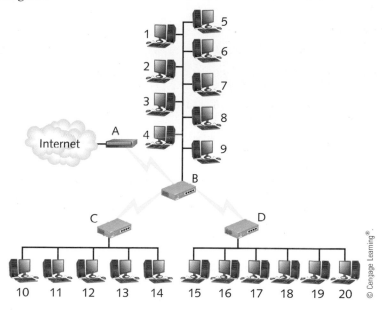

    a. They will only be unable to access the Internet.

    b. They will be unable to access the Internet and *either* nodes 10 through 14 or 15 through 20.

    c. They will be unable to access the Internet, and all other nodes on the LAN.

    d. They will be unable to access the Internet and nodes 10 through 20.

    e. Their connectivity will not be affected.

70. Which of the following routing protocols has the poorest convergence time?

    a. RIP

    b. EIGRP

    c. OSPF

    d. BGP

    e. IGRP

71. Which of the following ports would be used during a domain name lookup?

    a. 22

    b. 23

    c. 53

    d. 110

    e. 443

72. Suppose you have created six subnets on your network, which leases a group of Class C IPv4 addresses. What subnet mask must you specify in your clients' configurations to adhere to your subnetting scheme?

    a. 255.255.255.6

    b. 255.255.255.128

    c. 255.255.255.192

    d. 255.255.255.224

    e. 255.255.255.0

73. Which of the following protocols encapsulates data for transmission over VPNs?

    a. CHAP

    b. SNMP

    c. L2TP

    d. SFTP

    e. MPLS

74. You are configuring a DHCP server. Which of the following variables refers to the range of IP addresses that you will make available to all nodes on a segment?

    a. Scope

    b. Lease

    c. Zone

    d. Prefix

    e. Period

75. Which of the following wireless networking standards can reliably transmit data the farthest?

    a. LTE

    b. WiMAX

    c. 802.11b

    d. 802.11c

    e. 802.11n

76. How does STP (Spanning Tree Protocol) prevent or stop broadcast storms?

   a. It examines the source IP address field in each broadcast packet and temporarily blocks traffic from that address.

   b. It enables routers to choose one set of best paths and ensures that alternate paths are used only when the best paths are obstructed.

   c. It enables switches to calculate paths that avoid potential loops and artificially blocks the links that would complete a loop.

   d. It enables firewalls to keep access lists that name hosts known for high-volume broadcast traffic and block those hosts from transmitting to the network.

   e. It helps routers define the boundaries of a broadcast domain.

77. Which of the following standards describes a security technique, often used on wireless networks, in which a port is prevented from receiving traffic until the transmitter's credentials are verified by an authentication server?

   a. EAPoL

   b. SSH

   c. SSL

   d. Kerberos

   e. MS-CHAP

78. If a Windows workstation is configured to use DHCP, but cannot find a DHCP server, it will assign itself an address and subnet mask. Which of the following IPv4 addresses might it assign itself?

   a. 129.0.0.1

   b. 255.255.255.255

   c. 123.45.67.89

   d. 169.254.1.120

   e. 987.65.432.1

79. Suppose your Windows laptop's wireless network adapter is configured to use the 802.11n wireless networking standard. Also, suppose a café you visit has an 802.11ac access point. Assuming you have the correct SSID and logon credentials, what will happen when you attempt to associate with the café's wireless network?

   a. Your wireless networking client will be able to see the access point, but will be unable to associate with it.

   b. Your wireless networking client will not be able to see the access point.

   c. Your wireless networking client will be able to see the access point and attempt to associate with it, but the incompatible frequencies will prevent successful authentication.

   d. Your wireless networking client will be able to see the access point and attempt to associate with it, but the incompatible security techniques will prevent successful authentication.

   e. Your wireless networking client will be able to see the access point and successfully associate with it.

80. **Routers use IGMP to:**

   a. Identify nodes belonging to a multicast group

   b. Communicate with other routers about the best path between nodes

   c. Reserve bandwidth for priority transmissions, ensuring high QoS

   d. Filter out potentially harmful packets

   e. Predict the expected round-trip time of a packet over a WAN

81. **A virtual PBX would provide your organization with which of the following services?**

   a. Data storage in the cloud

   b. VoIP call connection

   c. Expedited Internet routing

   d. QoS guarantees for video streaming

   e. Load balancing for WAN connections

82. **You work for a large fashion design firm. Because of a recent TV promotion, your company has received national recognition. At the same time, your WAN has received more security threats. To help fend off these threats, you decide to implement an IPS/IDS. Following is a simplified network diagram that represents your private network and its public network connection. Where on this diagram would you place the IPS/IDS device?**

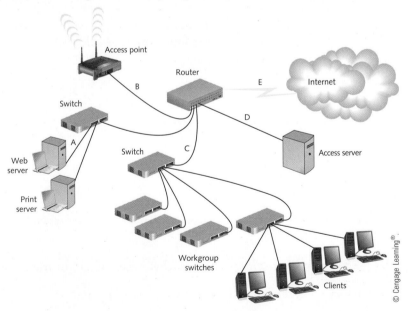

83. An implementation of multiple 5-GHz APs that talk to each other in order to obtain 802.11n-type speeds is accomplished with what unofficial wireless standard?

    a. 802.11a-ht

    b. 802.11g-ht

    c. 802.11ac

    d. Super G

    e. 802.11i

84. A user watching a YouTube video over the Internet is an example of what type of communication?

    a. Unicast

    b. Multicast

    c. Broadcast

    d. Point-to-multipoint

    e. Multipoint-to-point

85. You are configuring a connection between two backbone switches, and you want to make sure the connection doesn't fail or become overwhelmed by heavy traffic. Which of the following techniques would help you achieve both aims?

    a. Round-robin DNS

    b. CARP

    c. Clustering

    d. Trunking

    e. NIC teaming

86. Using RIPv2, what is the maximum number of hops a packet can take between its source and its destination?

    a. 3

    b. 5

    c. 10

    d. 15

    e. 18

87. Which of the following QoS techniques enables packet-switched technologies to travel over traditionally circuit-switched connections?

    a. ATM

    b. SONET

    c. MPLS

    d. Frame relay

    e. Clustering

88. **What kind of management does SSH provide for a switch?**

    a. Remote configuration

    b. Management console

    c. In-band management

    d. Virtual terminal

    e. KVM

89. **How many bits are in an IPv6 address?**

    a. 16

    b. 32

    c. 64

    d. 128

    e. 256

90. **Which of the following makes use of channel bonding to maximize throughput?**

    a. Bluetooth

    b. Satellite

    c. 802.11g

    d. 802.11n

    e. WiMAX

91. **The following graph, which represents traffic activity for an ISP's client, indicates that the ISP is utilizing what traffic-shaping technique?**

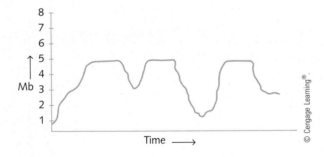

    a. Traffic policing

    b. Caching

    c. Load balancing

    d. Access list controls

    e. Fault tolerance

92. Your organization is reassessing its WAN connections to determine how much more bandwidth it will need to purchase in the next five years. As a network administrator, which of the following data can you share that will help management make the right decision?

    a. Wiring schematic

    b. Logical network diagram

    c. Syslogs

    d. Baselines

    e. Physical network diagram

93. If an organization follows structured cabling standards, where would its demarc be located?

    a. Entrance facility

    b. Work area

    c. IDF

    d. Cross-connect facility

    e. Backbone

94. You are helping to troubleshoot a recurring problem related to obtaining and keeping a DHCP-distributed IP address on a colleague's Windows 7 workstation. What application would allow you to configure the workstation to tally these errors and send you an email message every time such a problem occurred?

    a. Network and Internet Connections

    b. System Logger

    c. PuTTY

    d. System Manager

    e. Event Viewer

95. You are creating a new Linux server as a virtual machine on your Windows 8.1 workstation. Which of the following commands will tell you the IP address that is assigned to your virtual server?

    a. `ipconfig/all` at the Windows command prompt

    b. `ifconfig -a` at the Linux server's shell prompt

    c. `ethtool -a` at the Linux server's shell prompt

    d. `ip addr` at the Windows command prompt

    e. `ipconfig -a` at the Linux server's shell prompt

96. In IPv6 addressing, which of the following prefixes indicates that an address belongs to a multicast group?

    a. 00FF

    b. 1F3E

    c. FF02

    d. 0001

    e. FEC0

97. Suppose your WAN contains a segment that relies on the 10GBase-EW standard. Which of the following transmission technologies might it use?

   a. SONET

   b. Satellite

   c. Broadband cable

   d. DSL

   e. Metro Ethernet

98. The software on a firewall you recently installed on your network examines each incoming packet. Based on a set of criteria, including source IP address, source and destination ports, and protocols, it blocks or allows traffic. What type of system is this? (Choose all that apply.)

   a. Content-filtering firewall

   b. Stateful firewall

   c. Stateless firewall

   d. Packet-filtering firewall

   e. Application layer firewall

99. Ethernet and ATM both specify Data Link layer framing techniques. How do they differ?

   a. Ethernet uses CRC fields to confirm the validity of the frame, whereas ATM uses no error detection.

   b. Ethernet uses variably sized packets, whereas ATM uses fixed-sized cells.

   c. Ethernet uses synchronous transmission, whereas ATM uses asynchronous transmission.

   d. Ethernet uses frame headers, whereas ATM does not.

   e. Ethernet offers no guarantee of timely delivery, whereas ATM ensures that packets are delivered within 10 ms.

100. What STP configuration ensures that a laptop connected to a switch cannot alter the STP paths on the network?

   a. BPDU filter

   b. BPDU guard

   c. Root bridge

   d. BID

   e. Designated port

Glossary

1000Base-LX A Physical layer standard for networks that specifies 1-Gbps transmission over fiber-optic cable using baseband transmission. 1000Base-LX is a common fiber version of Gigabit Ethernet and can run on either single-mode or multimode fiber. The *LX* represents its reliance on long wavelengths of 1300 nanometers.

1000Base-SX A Physical layer standard for networks that specifies 1-Gbps transmission over fiber-optic cable using baseband transmission. 1000Base-SX runs on multimode fiber. The *SX* represents its reliance on short wavelengths of 850 nanometers.

1000Base-T A Physical layer standard for achieving 1 Gbps over UTP. 1000Base-T achieves its higher throughput by using all four pairs of wires in a Cat 5 or better twisted-pair cable to both transmit and receive signals. 1000Base-T also uses a different data encoding scheme than that used by other UTP Physical layer specifications.

1000Base-TX A Physical layer standard for networks that achieves 1 Gbps over Cat 6 or better cabling using only two pairs of wires.

100Base-FX A largely outdated Physical layer standard for networks that specifies baseband transmission, multimode fiber cabling, and 100-Mbps throughput. 100Base-FX is the fiber version of Fast Ethernet.

100Base-T A Physical layer standard for networks that specifies baseband transmission, twisted-pair cabling, and 100-Mbps throughput. 100Base-T networks have a maximum segment length of 100 meters and use the star topology. 100Base-T is also known as Fast Ethernet.

10Base2 *See* Thinnet.

10Base-T A Physical layer standard for networks that specifies baseband transmission, twisted-pair media, and 10-Mbps throughput. 10Base-T networks have a maximum segment length of 100 meters and rely on a star topology.

10GBase-ER A Physical layer standard for achieving 10-Gbps data transmission over single-mode, fiber-optic cable. In 10GBase-ER, the *ER* stands for *extended reach*. This standard specifies a star topology and segment lengths up to 40,000 meters.

10GBase-EW A variation of the 10GBase-ER standard that is specially encoded to operate over SONET-based WAN links.

10GBase-LR A Physical layer standard for achieving 10-Gbps data transmission over single-mode, fiber-optic cable using wavelengths of 1310 nanometers. In 10GBase-LR, the *LR* stands for *long reach*. This standard specifies a star topology and segment lengths up to 10,000 meters.

10GBase-LW A variation of the 10GBase-LR standard that is specially encoded to operate over SONET-based WAN links.

10GBase-SR A Physical layer standard for achieving 10-Gbps data transmission over multimode fiber using wavelengths of 850 nanometers. 10GBase-SR is designed to work with LANs. The maximum segment length for 10GBase-SR can reach up to 300 meters, depending on the fiber core diameter and modal bandwidth used.

10GBase-SW A variation of the 10GBase-SR standard that is specially encoded to operate over SONET-based WAN links.

10GBase-T A Physical layer standard for achieving 10-Gbps data transmission over twisted-pair cable. Described in its 802.3an standard, IEEE specifies Cat 6 or Cat 7 cable as the appropriate medium for 10GBase-T. The maximum segment length for 10GBase-T is 100 meters.

10-Gigabit Ethernet *See* 10GBase-T.

110 block A type of punch-down block designed to terminate Cat 5 or better twisted-pair wires and typically used to handle data connections rather than telephone connections. The numeral *110* refers to the model number of the earliest blocks.

1G The first generation of mobile phone services, popular in the 1970s and 1980s, which were entirely analog.

2.4-GHz band The range of radio frequencies from 2.4 to 2.4835 GHz. The 2.4-GHz band, which allows for 11 unlicensed channels in the United States (or up to 14 channels in other countries), is used by WLANs that follow the popular 802.11b and 802.11g standards. However, it is also used for cordless telephone and other transmissions, making the 2.4-GHz band more susceptible to interference than the 5-GHz band.

2G Second-generation mobile phone service, popular in the 1990s. 2G was the first standard to use digital transmission, and as such, it paved the way for texting and media downloads on mobile devices.

3G Third-generation mobile phone service, released in the early 2000s, that specifies throughputs of 384 Kbps and packet switching for data (but not voice) communications.

4G Fourth-generation mobile phone service that is characterized by an all-IP, packet-switched network for both data and voice transmission. 4G standards, released in 2008, also specify throughputs of 100 Mbps for fast-moving mobile clients, such as those in cars, and 1 Gbps for slow-moving mobile clients, such as pedestrians.

4to6 A tunneling protocol that enables transmission of IPv4 packets over an IPv6 network.

5-GHz band A range of frequencies that comprises four frequency bands: 5.1 GHz, 5.3 GHz, 5.4 GHz, and 5.8 GHz. It consists of 24 unlicensed bands, each 20-MHz wide. The 5-GHz band is used by WLANs that follow the 802.11a, 802.11n, and 802.11ac standards.

66 block A type of punch-down block designed to terminate telephone connections. The numeral 66 refers to the model number of the earliest blocks.

6to4 The most common tunneling protocol that enables travel of IPv6 packets over IPv4 networks. IPv6 addresses intended to be used by this protocol always begin with the prefix 2002::/16.

802.11a The IEEE standard for a wireless networking technique that uses multiple frequency bands in the 5-GHz frequency range and provides a theoretical maximum throughput of 54 Mbps. 802.11a's higher throughput, compared with 802.11b, is attributable to its use of higher frequencies, its unique method of modulating data, and more available bandwidth.

802.11ac The IEEE standard for a wireless networking technique that exceeds benchmarks set by earlier standards by increasing its useful bandwidth and amplitude. 802.11ac is the first Wi-Fi standard to approach Gigabit Ethernet capabilities. 802.11ac APs function more like a switch in that they can handle multiple transmissions at one time over the same frequency spectrum. This new standard is being deployed in three waves with Wave 1 devices already available on the market.

802.11a-ht An adaptation of 802.11a technology that allows older access points to emulate higher 802.11n-like speeds. The *ht* stands for *high throughput* and is accomplished by improvements such as DIDO (distributed-input distributed-output), in which multiple access points work together, or channel bonding.

802.11b The IEEE standard for a wireless networking technique that uses DSSS (direct-sequence spread spectrum) signaling in the 2.4–2.4835-GHz frequency range (also called the 2.4-GHz band). 802.11b separates the 2.4-GHz band into 14 overlapping 22-MHz channels and provides a theoretical maximum of 11-Mbps throughput.

802.11g The IEEE standard for a wireless networking technique designed to be compatible with 802.11b while using different data modulation techniques that allow it to reach a theoretical maximum capacity of 54 Mbps. 802.11g, like 802.11b, uses the 2.4-GHz frequency band.

802.11g-ht An adaptation of 802.11g technology that allows older access points to emulate higher 802.11n-like speeds. The *ht* stands for *high throughput* and is accomplished by improvements such as DIDO (distributed-input distributed-output), where multiple access points work together, or channel bonding.

802.11i The IEEE standard for wireless network encryption and authentication that uses the EAP authentication method, strong encryption, and dynamically assigned keys, which are different for every transmission. 802.11i specifies AES encryption and weaves a key into each packet.

802.11n The IEEE standard for a wireless networking technique that may issue signals in the 2.4-GHz or 5-GHz band and can achieve actual data throughput between 65 Mbps and 600 Mbps. It accomplishes this through several means, including MIMO, channel bonding, and frame aggregation. 802.11n is backward compatible with 802.11a, b, and g.

802.16 The IEEE standard for broadband wireless metropolitan area networking (also known as WiMAX). 802.16 networks may use frequencies between 2 GHz and 66 GHz. Their antennas may operate in a line-of-sight or non-line-of-sight manner and cover 50 kilometers (or approximately 30 miles). 802.16 connections can achieve a maximum throughput of 70 Mbps, though actual throughput diminishes as the distance between transceivers increases. Several 802.16 standards exist. Collectively, they are known as WiMAX.

802.16m Also known as WiMAX 2, the IEEE standard for a version of 802.16 that achieves theoretical throughputs of 330 Mbps with lower latency and better quality for VoIP applications than previous WiMAX versions. 802.16m has been approved as a true 4G technology.

802.1aq The IEEE standard that describes SPB (Shortest Path Bridging) and that evolved from STP (Spanning Tree Protocol).

802.1D The IEEE standard that describes, among other things, bridging and STP (Spanning Tree Protocol).

802.1Q The IEEE standard that specifies how VLAN and trunking information appears in frames and how switches and bridges interpret that information.

802.1s The IEEE standard that describes MSTP (Multiple Spanning Tree Protocol), which evolved from STP (Spanning Tree Protocol).

802.1w The IEEE standard that describes RSTP (Rapid Spanning Tree Protocol), which evolved from STP (Spanning Tree Protocol).

802.1X A vendor-independent IEEE standard for securing transmission between nodes according to the transmission's port, whether physical or logical. 802.1X, also known as EAPoL, is commonly used with RADIUS authentication and is the authentication standard followed by wireless networks using 802.11i.

802.3ae The IEEE standard that describes 10-Gigabit Ethernet technologies, including 10GBase-SR, 10GBase-SW, 10GBase-LR, 10GBase-LW, 10GBase-ER, and 10GBase-EW.

802.3af The IEEE standard that specifies a way of supplying electrical power over twisted-pair Ethernet connections, also known as PoE (Power over Ethernet). 802.3af requires Cat 5 or better UTP or STP cabling and uses power sourcing equipment to supply current over a wire pair to powered devices.

802.3at The IEEE standard that improves upon the older 802.3af by supplying more power over Ethernet connections. Whereas PoE supplies about 15.4 watts for standard PoE devices, PoE+ provides about 25.5 watts.

A

A (Address) record A type of DNS data record that maps the IPv4 address of an Internet-connected device to its domain name.

AAA (authentication, authorization, and accounting) A category of protocols that establish a client's identity, authorize a user for certain privileges on a system or network, and keep an account of the client's system or network usage.

AAAA (authentication, authorization, accounting, and address) record A type of DNS data record that maps the IPv6 address of an Internet-connected device to its domain name.

AC (alternating current) Electrical power flow on a circuit that continually switches direction.

acceptable use policy *See* AUP.

access control list *See* ACL.

access list *See* ACL.

access point *See* AP.

access port The interface on a switch used for an end node. Devices connected to access ports are unaware of VLAN information.

ACL (access control list) A list of statements used by a router to permit or deny the forwarding of traffic on a network based on one or more criteria.

acquisitions server An ICS server that collects and stores raw data. This server connects to field devices from which it receives the raw data and passes that information on to other servers in the SCADA system.

active card A proximity card that contains an internal lithium battery to provide a greater range (up to 150 m). These cards are ideal for long-range applications such as security gates or tollbooths.

active data *See* ESI.

Active Directory *See* AD.

Active Directory Domain Services *See* AD DS.

active scanning A method used by wireless stations to detect the presence of an access point. In active scanning, the station issues a probe to each channel in its frequency range and waits for the access point to respond.

active-active mode A link aggregation configuration in which both connections are active as a matter of course. If one link fails, the other maintains the connection.

active-passive mode A link aggregation configuration in which only one connection is used at a time, with the other being a passive connection that is only activated if the first connection fails.

actuator Any device in an ICS that is motorized and can control the physical system.

AD (Active Directory) The centralized directory database that contains user account information and security for the entire group of computers on a network.

AD (administrative distance) A number indicating a protocol's reliability, with lower values being given higher priority. This assignment can be changed by a network administrator when one protocol should take precedence over a previously higher-rated protocol on a network.

AD DS (Active Directory Domain Services) The Active Directory service that manages the process that allows a user to sign on to a network from any computer on the network and get access to the resources that Active Directory allows.

ad hoc WLAN A type of wireless LAN in which stations communicate directly with each other (rather than using an access point).

Address record *See* A record (which is IPv4) or AAAA record (which is IPv6).

Address Resolution Protocol *See* ARP.

address translation The process of substituting a private IP address used by computers on a private network with the public IP address of a gateway device or router when these computers need access to other networks or the Internet.

administrative distance *See* AD.

ADSL (asymmetric digital subscriber line) The most popular variation of DSL. The latest version of ADSL, ADSL2+M, offers more throughput when data travels downstream than when data travels upstream.

ADSL Annex M *See* ADSL2+M.

ADSL2+M The latest version of ADSL. ADSL2+M provides a maximum theoretical throughput of 24 Mbps downstream and a maximum of 3.3 Mbps upstream.

Advanced Encryption Standard *See* AES.

advanced imaging technology machine *See* AIT machine.

advanced persistent threat *See* APT.

advertise To transmit a routing update between routers.

AES (Advanced Encryption Standard) A private key encryption algorithm that uses a sophisticated family of ciphers along with multiple stages of data transformation.

AF (Assured Forwarding) One of two DiffServ forwarding specifications. AF allows routers to assign data streams one of several prioritization levels, but it provides no guarantee that, on a busy network, messages will arrive on time or in sequence. AF is specified in the DiffServ field in an IPv4 packet.

agent A software routine that collects data about a managed device's operation or compliance with security benchmarks, and provides this information to a network management application.

AH (authentication header) In the context of IPsec, a type of encryption that provides authentication of the IP packet's data payload through public key techniques.

airflow In a chassis, the path along which air from a cool air source is conducted, past equipment to cool it, and then out of the rack. Typically, air moves from front to back. Clutter in the rack should be minimized to prevent airflow blockages.

AIT (advanced imaging technology) machine A security device similar to an X-ray machine that uses millimeter-wave scanners, which emit radio waves similar to those emitted by cell phones, to indicate on cartoonlike images any areas of concern to security personnel.

algorithm A set of rules that tells a computer how to accomplish a particular task. For example, a computer uses an algorithm to create an encryption key.

alias A nickname for a host.

alien cross-talk Electromagnetic interference induced on one cable by signals traveling over a nearby cable.

alternating current *See* AC.

AM (amplitude modulation) A modulation technique in which the amplitude of the carrier signal is modified by the application of a data signal.

ambient data Hidden data on a computer, such as deleted files and file fragments, as well as information about who has accessed that data and when.

American Registry for Internet Numbers *See* ARIN.

American Wire Gauge *See* AWG.

amplification attack An attack instigated using small, simple requests that trigger very large responses from the target. DNS, NTP, ICMP, and SNMP lend themselves to being used in these kinds of attacks.

amplifier A device that increases the voltage, or strength, of an analog signal.

amplitude A measure of a signal's strength at a given point in time.

amplitude modulation *See* AM.

analog modem *See* modem.

analog signal A signaling method in which electromagnetic waves vary infinitely and continuously, and appear as a wavy line when graphed over time.

analog telephone adapter *See* ATA.

ANDing A logical process of combining bits. In ANDing, a bit with a value of 1 combined, or ANDed, with another bit having a value of 1 results in a 1. A bit with a value of 0 ANDed with any other bit (either 0 or 1) results in a 0.

Angle Polished Connector *See* APC.

anycast address A type of IPv6 address that represents a group of interfaces, any one of which (and usually the first available of which) can accept a transmission. At this time, anycast addresses are not designed to be assigned to hosts, such as servers or workstations, but rather to routers.

Anything as a Service *See* XaaS.

AP (access point) A device used on wireless LANs that accepts wireless signals from multiple nodes and retransmits them to the rest of the network. APs can connect a group of nodes with a network or two networks with each other. They may use unidirectional or omnidirectional antennas.

APC (Angle Polished Connector) The latest advancement in ferrule technology that uses the principles of reflection to its advantage by placing the end faces of the highly polished ferrules at an angle to each other, thus reducing the effect of back reflection.

API (application programming interface) call The process an application uses to make a request of the OS.

APIPA (Automatic Private IP Addressing) A service available on computers running one of the Windows operating systems that automatically assigns the computer's network interface a link-local IP address. In IPv4, this address is in the range of 169.254.0.1 through 169.254.255.254. IPv6 does not use APIPA, but a similar address type, the unicast link-local address with the prefix FE80::/10, is used instead.

application aware A feature that enables a firewall to monitor and limit the traffic of specific applications, including the application's vendor and digital signature.

Application Control An NGFW (Next Generation Firewall) feature that gives a firewall some level of application awareness functionality, meaning the firewall can monitor and limit the traffic of specific applications, including the application's vendor and digital signature.

Application layer The seventh layer of the OSI model. Application layer protocols enable software programs to negotiate formatting, procedural, security, synchronization, and other requirements with the network.

application programming interface call *See* API call.

application service provider (ASP) *See* SaaS.

application-specific integrated circuit *See* ASIC.

APT (advanced persistent threat) A network attack that continues undetected for a long period of time. These attacks are successful because the intent is to clandestinely steal data rather than damage network resources.

archive bit A file attribute that can be checked (or set to "on") or unchecked (or set to "off") to indicate whether the file needs to be archived. An operating system checks a file's archive bit when it is created or changed.

ARIN (American Registry for Internet Numbers) A non-profit corporation that manages the distribution of public IP addresses for the North American region, including the United States, Canada, and several small islands, countries, and territories in that region (including in the Caribbean). ARIN also services Antarctica.

ARP (Address Resolution Protocol) A core protocol in the TCP/IP suite that belongs in the Network layer of the OSI model. ARP obtains the MAC (physical) address of a host, or node, and then creates a local database that maps the MAC address to the host's IP (logical) address.

ARP cache *See* ARP table.

ARP cache poisoning An attack in which attackers use fake ARP replies to alter ARP tables in a network.

ARP table A database of records that maps MAC addresses to IP addresses. The ARP table is stored on a computer's hard disk where it is used by the ARP utility to supply the MAC addresses of network nodes, given their IP addresses.

AS (authentication service) In Kerberos terminology, the process that runs on a KDC (Key Distribution Center) to initially validate a client that is logging on.

AS (autonomous system) A group of networks, often on the same domain, that are operated by the same organization.

ASCII A character encoding system consisting of 128 characters.

ASIC (application-specific integrated circuit) A specialized microchip designed to provide customized features to a specific application.

ASN (autonomous system number) A globally unique number that identifies an autonomous system. ASNs work similarly to IP addresses that identify individual nodes on a network. Each ASN now consists of 32 bits instead of 16 bits, and they are assigned by IANA.

ASP (application service provider) *See* SaaS.

asset management The process of collecting and storing data on the number and types of software and hardware assets in an organization's network. The data collection is automated by electronically examining each network node from a server.

association In the context of wireless networking, the communication that occurs between a station and an access point to enable the station to connect to the network via that access point.

Assured Forwarding *See* AF.

asymmetric digital subscriber line *See* ADSL.

asymmetric DSL Any version of DSL in which downstream throughput is higher than upstream throughput.

asymmetric encryption A type of encryption (such as public key encryption) that uses a different key for encoding data than is used for decoding the cipher text.

asymmetrical The characteristic of a transmission technology that affords greater bandwidth in one direction (either from the customer to the carrier, or vice versa) than in the other direction.

asynchronous A transmission method in which data being transmitted and received by nodes do not have to conform to any timing scheme. In asynchronous communications, a node can transmit at any time and the destination node must accept the transmission as it comes.

Asynchronous Transfer Mode *See* ATM.

ATA (analog telephone adapter) An internal or externally attached adapter that converts analog telephone signals into packet-switched voice signals and vice versa.

ATM (Asynchronous Transfer Mode) A WAN technology functioning primarily at Layer 2 (although its protocols can also reach Layers 1 and 3) that was originally conceived in the early 1980s at Bell Labs and standardized by the ITU in the mid-1990s. ATM delivers data using fixed packets, called cells, that each consist of 48 bytes of data plus a 5-byte header. ATM relies on virtual circuits and establishes a connection before sending data. The reliable connection ensured by ATM allows network managers to specify QoS levels for certain types of traffic.

attenuation The loss of a signal's strength as it travels away from its source.

Augmented Category 6 *See* Cat 6a.

Augmented Category 7 *See* Cat 7a.

AUP (acceptable use policy) A portion of the security policy that explains to users what they can and cannot do, and penalties for violations. It might also describe how these measures protect the network's security.

authentication The process of comparing and matching a client's credentials with the credentials in a client database to enable the client to log on to the network.

authentication header *See* AH.

authentication protocol A set of rules that governs how servers authenticate clients. Several types of authentication protocols exist.

authentication service *See* AS.

authentication, authorization, and accounting *See* AAA.

authenticator In Kerberos authentication, the user's time stamp encrypted with the session key. The authenticator is used to help the service verify that a user's ticket is valid.

authoritative server The authority on computer names and their IP addresses for computers in their domains.

automatic failover In the event of a component failure, the ability of a redundant component to immediately assume the duties of the failed component.

Automatic Private IP Addressing *See* APIPA.

autonomous system *See* AS.

autonomous system number *See* ASN.

availability How consistently and reliably a file, device, or connection can be accessed by authorized personnel.

AWG (American Wire Gauge) A standard rating that indicates the diameter of a wire, such as the conducting core of a coaxial cable.

B

B channel In ISDN, the channel that employs circuit-switching techniques to carry voice, video, audio, and other types of data over the ISDN connection; sometimes called the bearer channel.

back reflection The return of a light signal back into the fiber that is transmitting the signal. Back reflection is measured as optical loss in dB (decibels).

backbone The central conduit of a network that connects network segments and significant shared devices (such as routers, switches, and servers) and is sometimes referred to as "a network of networks."

backdoor A software security flaw that can allow unauthorized users to gain access to a system. Legacy systems are particularly notorious for leaving these kinds of gaps in a network's overall security net.

backhaul An intermediate connection between subscriber networks and a telecommunications carrier's network.

backleveling *See* rollback.

backplane A synonym for *motherboard*, often used in the context of switches and routers.

backup A copy of data or program files created for archiving or safekeeping.

bandwidth (1) The amount of traffic, or data transmission activity, on a network. (2) A measure of the difference between the highest and lowest frequencies that a medium can transmit.

banner-grabbing attack An attack in which hackers transmit bogus requests (or, sometimes, successful requests) for connection to servers or applications in order to harvest useful information to guide their attack efforts.

base station *See* AP.

base 2 number system *See* binary number system.

base 8 number system *See* octal number system.

baseband A form of transmission in which digital signals are sent through direct current pulses applied to a wire. This direct current requires exclusive use of the wire's capacity, so baseband systems can transmit only one signal, or one channel, at a time. Every device on a baseband system shares a single channel.

baseline A record of how a network operates under normal conditions (including its performance, error statistics, utilization rate, and so on). Baselines are used for comparison when conditions change.

Basic Rate Interface *See* BRI.

basic service set *See* BSS.

basic service set identifier *See* BSSID.

baud rate (Bd) For analog transmissions, a measurement of throughput and bandwidth that is determined by symbols transmitted per second. A symbol is a voltage, frequency, pulse, or phase change in the analog transmission. Also called modulation rate or symbol rate.

Bd *See* baud rate.

beacon frame In the context of wireless networking, a frame issued by an access point to alert other nodes of its existence.

bend radius The radius of the maximum arc into which a cable can be looped without impairing data transmission. Generally, a twisted-pair cable's bend radius is equal to or greater than four times the diameter of the cable.

Berkeley Internet Name Domain *See* BIND.

BERT (bit-error rate test) A test that measures the bit-error rate of a transmission, which is the percentage of bits with errors in a transmission.

best path The most efficient route from one node on a network to another, as calculated by a router. Under optimal network conditions, the best path is the most direct path between two points. However, when traffic congestion, segment failures, and other factors create obstacles, the most direct path might not be the best path.

best-effort protocol *See* connectionless protocol.

BGP (Border Gateway Protocol) Dubbed the "protocol of the Internet," this path-vector routing protocol is the only current EGP and is capable of considering many factors in its routing metrics.

BID (Bridge ID) A combination of a 2-byte priority field and a bridge's MAC address, used in STP (Spanning Tree Protocol) to select a root bridge.

binary number system A system that uses 1s and 0s to encode information.

BIND (Berkeley Internet Name Domain) The most popular DNS server software. BIND is free, open source software that runs on Linux, UNIX, and Windows platforms.

biometrics Unique physical characteristics of an individual, such as the color patterns in his iris or the geometry of his hand.

biorecognition access A method of authentication in which a device scans an individual's unique physical characteristics, such as the color patterns in her iris or the geometry of her hand, to verify the user's identity.

bit A single pulse in the digital encoding system that can have one of only two values: 0 or 1.

bit rate In digital transmissions, a measurement of throughput and bandwidth that is expressed as bits transmitted per second.

bit-error rate test *See* BERT.

blackout A complete power loss.

BLE (Bluetooth low energy) Also called Bluetooth Smart, a new version of Bluetooth that provides a range comparable to the earlier version of Bluetooth, but that consumes less power. BLE devices are also cheaper than earlier Bluetooth devices.

block ID *See* OUI.

blocking A preventive measure on a network that can help reduce excessive bandwidth utilization, and also help protect a company from legal ramifications and liabilities, by preventing certain types of traffic from entering or exiting the network.

bluejacking An attack in which a Bluetooth connection is used to send unsolicited data.

bluesnarfing An attack in which a Bluetooth connection is used to download data from a device without the owner's permission.

Bluetooth A low-power wireless technology that provides close-range communication between devices such as PCs, smartphones, tablets, and accessories. Bluetooth operates in the radio band of 2.4 GHz to 2.485 GHz and hops between frequencies within that band (up to 1600 hops/sec) to help reduce interference.

Bluetooth low energy *See* BLE.

BNC (Bayonet Neill-Concelman, or British Naval Connector) A standard for coaxial cable connectors named after its coupling method and its inventors.

BNC connector A coaxial cable connector type that uses a turn-and-lock (or bayonet) style of coupling. It may be used with several coaxial cable types, including RG-6 and RG-59.

BNC coupler A coupler designed to connect two coaxial cables.

bonding The process of combining more than one B channel of an ISDN line to increase throughput. For example, BRI's two 64-Kbps B channels are bonded to create an effective throughput of 128 Kbps.

boot A plastic cover designed to protect the strands at the end of a cable where the strands enter a connector.

Boot Protocol *See* BootP.

boot sector virus A virus that positions its code on the boot sector of a computer's hard disk so that, when the computer boots up, the virus runs in place of the computer's normal system files. Boot sector viruses are commonly spread from external storage devices to hard disks.

BootP (Boot Protocol or Bootstrap Protocol) An IP network protocol that automatically boots a system and assigns an IP address without user involvement.

Bootstrap Protocol *See* BootP.

Border Gateway Protocol *See* BGP.

border router A router that connects an autonomous system with an outside network—for example, the router that connects a business to its ISP.

bot Short for *robot*, a program that runs automatically. Bots can spread viruses or other malicious code between users in a chat room by exploiting the IRC protocol.

botnet A group of computers requisitioned in coordinated DDoS attacks without the owners' knowledge or consent.

bounce *See* reflection.

BPDU (Bridge Protocol Data Unit) A type of network message that transmits STP information between switches.

BPDU filter A software configuration that can be used to disable STP on specific ports, such as the port leading to the network's demarc. A BPDU filter prevents access to network links that should not be considered when plotting STP paths in a network.

BPDU guard A software configuration on a switch's access ports that blocks certain types of BPDUs from being sent to or received by the devices, such as workstations and servers, connected to these ports. A BPDU guard is necessary because network hosts should not be considered as possible paths to other destinations.

BPL (broadband over powerline) High-speed Internet access delivered over the electrical grid.

braiding A braided metal shielding used to insulate some types of coaxial cable.

BRI (Basic Rate Interface) A variety of ISDN that uses two 64-Kbps bearer channels and one 16-Kbps data channel, as summarized by the notation 2B+D.

Bridge ID *See* BID.

Bridge Protocol Data Unit *See* BPDU.

bridged mode A type of network connection in which a vNIC accesses a physical network using the host machine's NIC. In other words, the virtual interface and the physical interface are bridged. The bridged vNIC, however, obtains its own IP address, default gateway, and subnet mask information from the physical LAN's DHCP server.

broadband A form of transmission in which signals are modulated as radio frequency analog pulses with different frequency ranges. Unlike baseband, broadband technology does not involve binary encoding. The use of multiple frequencies enables a broadband system to operate over several channels and, therefore, carry much more data than a baseband system.

broadband cable A method of connecting to the Internet over a cable network. In broadband cable, computers are connected to a cable modem that modulates and demodulates signals for transmission and reception via cable wiring.

broadband over powerline *See* BPL.

broadcast domain Logically grouped network nodes that can communicate directly via broadcast transmissions. By default, switches and repeating devices, such as hubs, extend broadcast domains. Routers and other Layer 3 devices separate broadcast domains.

brownout A momentary decrease in voltage, also known as a *sag*. An overtaxed electrical system may cause brownouts, recognizable as a dimming of the lights.

brute force attack An attempt to discover an encryption key or password by trying numerous possible character combinations until the correct combination is found. Usually, a brute force attack is performed rapidly by a program designed for that purpose.

BSS (basic service set) In IEEE terminology, a group of stations that share an access point.

BSSID (basic service set identifier) In IEEE terminology, the identifier for a BSS (basic service set).

buffer overflow A memory problem in which a buffer's size is forced beyond its allotted space, causing the operating system to save data in adjacent memory areas. Older operating systems are vulnerable to buffer overflows.

bus topology A topology in which a single cable connects all nodes on a network without intervening connectivity devices.

bus topology WAN A WAN in which each location is connected to no more than two other locations in a serial fashion.

business continuity The ability of a company to continue doing business with the least amount of interruption possible after a major outage or other disaster.

C

CA (call agent) *See* MGC.

CA (certificate authority) An organization that issues and maintains digital certificates as part of the Public-key Infrastructure (PKI).

cable checker *See* continuity tester.

cable crimper *See* crimping tool.

cable drop The fiber-optic or coaxial cable that connects a neighborhood cable node to a customer's house.

cable modem A device that modulates and demodulates signals for transmission and reception via cable wiring.

cable modem access *See* broadband cable.

cable performance tester A troubleshooting tool that tests cables for continuity, but can also measure cross-talk, attenuation, and impedance; identify the location of faults; and store or print cable testing results. Also called line tester, certifier, or network tester.

cable tester A device that tests cables for one or more of the following conditions: continuity, segment length, distance to a fault, attenuation along a cable, near-end cross-talk, and termination resistance and impedance. Cable testers may also issue pass/fail ratings for wiring standards or store and print cable testing results.

cable tray A tray, usually made of metal, built into equipment racks, office desks, or along the ceiling to help collect cables into a single track.

caching The local storage of frequently needed files that would otherwise be obtained from an external source.

caching-only server A nonauthoritative name server that exists merely to resolve names for clients. When it receives a request for information that is not stored in its DNS cache, it will then query the company's authoritative name server.

CALEA (Communications Assistance for Law Enforcement Act) A U.S. federal regulation that requires telecommunications carriers and equipment manufacturers to provide for surveillance capabilities. CALEA was passed by Congress in 1994 after pressure from the FBI, which worried that networks relying solely on digital communications would circumvent traditional wiretapping strategies.

call agent *See* MGC.

call tracking system A software program used to document technical problems and their resolutions; also known as help desk software.

CAM (channel access method) A categorical form of multiplexing that allows multiple devices to share the same communication channel. FDM, TDM, WDM, CSMA/CD, and CSMA/CA are all types of CAM technology.

campus area network *See* CAN.

CAN (campus area network) A network of connected LANs within a limited geographical area, such as the buildings on a university campus.

canonical name The true name of a server, such as *www.example.com*, as opposed to one of many alias names a server might have, such as *ns1.example.com*.

Canonical Name record *See* CNAME record.

captive portal page The first page displayed by a client's browser when the client connects to a guest network. This page usually requires the user to agree to a set of terms and conditions before gaining further access to the guest network.

CAPWAP (Control and Provisioning of Wireless Access Points) A proprietary protocol created by Cisco to replace LWAPP. Both LWAPP and CAPWAP make centralized wireless management possible, and both direct all wireless frames to the wireless controller by adding extra headers to the frames.

CARP (Common Address Redundancy Protocol) A protocol that allows a pool of computers or interfaces to share one or more IP addresses. CARP improves availability and can contribute to load balancing among several devices, including servers, firewalls, or routers.

Carrier Detect *See* CD.

Carrier Ethernet A WAN technology that sends Ethernet traffic across long-distance WAN connections.

Carrier Sense Multiple Access with Collision Avoidance *See* CSMA/CA.

Carrier Sense Multiple Access with Collision Detection *See* CSMA/CD.

Carrier-Ethernet Transport *See* CET.

Cat or CAT (computer and telephone) *See* category.

Cat 3 (Category 3) An outdated form of UTP that contained four wire pairs and could carry up to 10 Mbps, with a possible bandwidth of 16 MHz. Cat 3 was used for 10-Mbps Ethernet or 4-Mbps token ring networks.

Cat 5 (Category 5) A form of UTP that contains four wire pairs and supports up to 100-Mbps throughput and a 100-MHz signal rate. Required minimum standard for Fast Ethernet.

Cat 5e (Enhanced Category 5) A higher-grade version of Cat 5 wiring that contains high-quality copper, offers a high twist ratio, and uses advanced methods for reducing cross-talk. Enhanced Cat 5 can support a signaling rate of up to 350 MHz, more than triple the capability of regular Cat 5, and a maximum throughput of 1 Gbps, making it the required minimum standard for Gigabit Ethernet.

Cat 6 (Category 6) A twisted-pair cable that contains four wire pairs, each wrapped in foil insulation. Additional foil insulation can cover the bundle of wire pairs, and a fire-resistant plastic sheath might cover the second foil layer. The foil insulation provides excellent resistance to cross-talk and enables Cat 6 to support a signaling rate of 250 MHz and throughput up to 10 Gbps.

Cat 6a (Augmented Category 6) A higher-grade version of Cat 6 wiring that further reduces attenuation and cross-talk, and allows for potentially exceeding traditional network segment length limits. Cat 6a is capable of a 500-MHz signaling rate and can reliably transmit data at multigigabit per second rates.

Cat 7 (Category 7) A twisted-pair cable that contains multiple wire pairs, each separately shielded then surrounded by another layer of shielding within the jacket. Cat 7 can support up to a 600-MHz signal rate. But because of its extra layers, it is less flexible than other forms of twisted-pair wiring.

Cat 7a (Augmented Category 7) A higher-grade version of Cat 7 wiring that will possibly support up to 100-Gbps throughput and up to 1000-MHz signal rate. ISO standards for Cat 7a cabling are still being drafted and simulations conducted.

catastrophic failure A failure that destroys a component beyond use.

category A term used to refer to a type of twisted-pair cable. All of the category cables fall under the TIA/EIA 568 standard.

Category 3 *See* Cat 3.

Category 5 *See* Cat 5.

Category 6 *See* Cat 6.

Category 7 *See* Cat 7.

CCTV (closed-circuit TV) A video surveillance system that monitors activity in secured areas.

CD (Carrier Detect) On some modems, a light that indicates the modem has detected another modem's carrier tone on the line and the connection has been established.

CDMA (Code Division Multiple Access) A cellular standard that uses spread-spectrum technology, in which a signal is spread over a wide bandwidth so that multiple users can occupy the same channel. A cellular device on a CDMA network does not require a SIM card because, on a CDMA network, devices are compared against a white list, which is a database of subscribers that contains information on their subscriptions with the provider.

cell (1) A packet of a fixed size. In ATM technology, a cell consists of 48 bytes of data plus a 5-byte header. (2) In a cellular network, an area of coverage serviced by an antenna and its base station.

central office *See* CO.

central processing unit *See* CPU.

certificate authority *See* CA.

certifier *See* cable performance tester.

CET (Carrier-Ethernet Transport) An Ethernet-based transport solution designed to overcome the inherent weaknesses of implementing Ethernet outside of a LAN environment.

chain of custody Documentation that describes evidence, including when it was collected, who collected it, its condition, and how it was secured and transferred from one responsible party to the next.

challenge A random string of text issued from one computer to another in some forms of authentication. A challenge is used, along with the password (or other credential), in a response to verify the computer's credentials.

Challenge Handshake Authentication Protocol *See* CHAP.

Challenge-Response Authentication Mechanism—Message Digest 5 *See* CRAM-MD5.

channel access method *See* CAM.

channel bonding In the context of 802.11n and 802.11ac wireless technology, the combination of two adjacent 20-MHz frequency bands to create one 40-MHz frequency band that can carry more than twice the amount of data that a single 20-MHz band could. 802.11ac products also support 80-MHz channel bonding by merging four 20-MHz channels, and some products can provide 160-MHz channels. Channel bonding is recommended for use only in the 5-GHz range because this band has more available channels and suffers less interference than the 2.4-GHz band.

channel service unit *See* CSU.

CHAP (Challenge Handshake Authentication Protocol) An authentication protocol that operates over PPP and also encrypts usernames and passwords for transmission. During CHAP's three-way handshake, the server sends the client a randomly generated string of characters. The client sends a new string in response to the server while the server concatenates the user's password with a challenge and creates its own string. The server then compares its encrypted string of characters with the encrypted string received from the client to determine the client's authenticity.

checksum A method of error checking that determines if the contents of an arriving data unit match the contents of the data unit sent by the source.

CIA (confidentiality, integrity, and availability) triad A three-tenet, standard security model describing the primary ways that encryption protects data. Confidentiality ensures that data can only be viewed by its intended recipient or at its intended destination. Integrity ensures that data was not modified after the sender transmitted it and before the receiver picked it up. Availability ensures that data is available to and accessible by the intended recipient when needed.

CIDR (Classless Interdomain Routing) An IP addressing and subnetting method in which network and host information is manipulated without adhering to the limitations imposed by traditional network class distinctions. CIDR is also known as classless routing or supernetting. Older routing protocols, such as RIP, are not capable of interpreting CIDR addressing schemes.

CIDR block In CIDR notation, the forward slash plus the number of bits used for the network ID. For example, the CIDR block for 199.34.89.0/22 is /22.

CIDR notation A shorthand method for denoting the distinction between network and host bits in an IP address.

CIFS (Common Internet File System) A file access protocol. CIFS runs over TCP/IP and is the cross-platform version of SMB used between Windows, UNIX, and other operating systems.

cipher A mathematical code used to scramble data into a format that can be read only by reversing the cipher—that is, by deciphering, or decrypting, the data.

cipher lock A physical or electronic lock requiring a code to open the door.

cipher text The unique data block that results when an original piece of data (such as text) is encrypted (for example, by using a key).

CIR (committed information rate) The guaranteed minimum amount of bandwidth selected when leasing a frame relay circuit. Frame relay costs are partially based on CIR.

circuit-switched A type of switching in which a connection is established between two network nodes before they begin transmitting data. Bandwidth is dedicated to this connection and remains available until users terminate the communication between the two nodes.

Cisco console cable *See* rollover cable.

cladding The glass or plastic shield around the core of a fiber-optic cable. Cladding reflects light back to the core in patterns that vary depending on the transmission mode. This reflection allows fiber to bend around corners without impairing the light-based signal.

Class A A license for a single octet in an IPv4 address range. For example, the Class A license for 119 would acquire 119.0.0.0 through 119.255.255.255 IP addresses.

Class B A license for the first two octets in an IPv4 address range. For example, the Class B license for 150.100 would acquire 150.100.0.0 through 150.100.255.255 IP addresses.

Class C A license for the first three octets in an IPv4 address range. For example, the Class C license for 200.80.15 would acquire 200.80.15.0 through 200.80.15.255 IP addresses.

Class of Service *See* CoS.

classful addressing An IP addressing convention that adheres to network class distinctions, in which the first 8 bits of a Class A address, the first 16 bits of a Class B address, and the first 24 bits of a Class C address are used for network information.

Classless Interdomain Routing *See* CIDR.

classless routing *See* CIDR.

CLI (command-line interface) A graphic-free user interface, such as the Command Prompt program in Windows, where technicians can enter commands more quickly and with more flexibility than in a GUI (graphical user interface) environment.

client_hello In the context of SSL encryption, a message issued from the client to the server that contains information about what level of security the client's browser is capable of accepting and what type of encryption the client's browser can decipher. The client_hello message also establishes a randomly generated number that uniquely identifies the client and another number that identifies the SSL session.

client-server application Data or a service requested by one computer from another.

client-server network model A network where resources are managed by the NOS via a centralized directory database.

client-to-site VPN A type of VPN in which clients, servers, and other hosts establish tunnels with a private network using a VPN gateway at the edge of the private network. Each remote client on a client-to-site VPN must run VPN software to connect to the VPN gateway, and a tunnel is created between them to encrypt and encapsulate data. This is the type of VPN typically associated with remote access.

closed-circuit TV *See* CCTV.

closed loop system One of two methods that an ICS might use to control the physical system. In a closed loop system, decisions are made based on real-time data. Also called a closed network.

closed network *See* closed loop system.

cloud backup A technique in which data is backed up to a central location over the Internet.

cloud computing The flexible provision of data storage, applications, or services to multiple clients over a network. Cloud computing consolidates resources and is elastic, metered, self-service, multiplatform, and available on demand.

CNAME (Canonical Name) record A type of DNS data record that holds alternative names for a host.

CO (central office) The location where a local or long-distance telephone service provider terminates and interconnects customer lines.

coarse wavelength division multiplexing *See* CWDM.

coaxial cable A type of cable that consists of a central metal conducting core, which might be solid or stranded and is often made of copper, surrounded by an insulator, a braided metal shielding (called braiding), and an outer cover (called the sheath or jacket). Coaxial cable, called "coax" for short, was the foundation for Ethernet networks in the 1980s. Today it's used to connect cable Internet and cable TV systems.

Code Division Multiple Access *See* CDMA.

cold site A place where the computers, devices, and connectivity necessary to rebuild a network exist, but are not appropriately configured, updated, or connected to match the network's current state.

cold spare A duplicate component that is not installed, but can be installed in case of a failure.

collector A computer that gathers event messages from generators.

collision (1) In Ethernet networks, the interference of one node's data transmission with the data transmission of another node sharing the same segment. (2) In the context of hashing, a problem that occurs when the input of two different data sets result in the same hash value.

collision domain The portion of an Ethernet network in which collisions could occur if two nodes transmit data at the same time. Today, switches and routers separate collision domains.

command-line interface *See* CLI.

committed information rate *See* CIR.

Common Address Redundancy Protocol *See* CARP.

Common Internet File System *See* CIFS.

Communications Assistance for Law Enforcement Act *See* CALEA.

community cloud A deployment model in which shared and flexible data storage, applications, or services are shared between multiple organizations, but not available publicly. Organizations with common interests, such as regulatory requirements, performance requirements, or data access needs might share resources in this way.

company-ID *See* OUI.

computer and telephone (CAT) *See* category.

computer forensics The process of investigating deeper data on a computer, essentially performing an autopsy on the computer to discover hidden data, such as deleted files and file fragments, and who has accessed that data and when.

computer name *See* FQDN.

confidentiality, integrity, and availability triad *See* CIA triad.

configuration management The collection, storage, and assessment of information related to the versions of software installed on every network device and every device's hardware configuration.

connection-oriented protocol A type of Transport layer protocol that requires the establishment of a connection between communicating nodes before it will transmit data.

connectionless protocol A type of Transport layer protocol that services a request without requiring a verified session and without guaranteeing delivery of data.

connectivity device One of several types of specialized devices that allows two or more networks or multiple parts of one network to connect and exchange data.

connector The piece of hardware that connects a wire to a network device, be it a file server, workstation, switch, or printer.

consent to monitoring A document designed to make employees aware that their use of company equipment and accounts can be monitored and reviewed as needed for security purposes.

console port The type of port on a router used to communicate with the router itself, such as when making programming changes to the device.

content switching *See* load balancing.

content-filtering firewall A firewall that can block designated types of traffic from entering a protected network based on application data contained within packets.

context aware An NGFW (Next Generation Firewall) feature that enables a firewall to adapt to various applications, users, and devices.

continuity tester An instrument that tests whether voltage (or light, in the case of fiber-optic cable) issued at one end of a cable can be detected at the opposite end of the cable. A continuity tester can indicate whether the cable will successfully transmit a signal. Also called cable checker or cable tester.

Control and Provisioning of Wireless Access Points *See* CAPWAP.

control plane The process of decision making, such as routing, blocking, and forwarding, that is performed by protocols.

convergence The use of data networks to carry voice, video, and other communications services in addition to data.

convergence time The time it takes for a router to recognize a best path in the event of a change or network outage.

copper line driver A line driver installed on copper lines.

core A cable's central component, designed to carry a signal. The core of a fiber-optic cable, for example, consists of one or several glass or plastic fibers. The core of a coaxial copper cable consists of one large or several small strands of copper.

CoS (Class of Service) Quality control techniques performed at Layer 2 on Ethernet frames. Most often, CoS is used to more efficiently route Ethernet traffic between VLANs.

coupler A simple kind of connector that passes data through a homogenous connection without any modification.

CPE (customer premise equipment) Any equipment located on the customer's premises, regardless of who owns it or who is responsible for it.

CPU (central processing unit) The component of a computer that performs almost all data processing for the computer.

CRAM-MD5 (Challenge-Response Authentication Mechanism—Message Digest 5) An authentication mechanism built on the MD5 algorithm that provides some additional security when communicating over an unencrypted connection. The server initiates a challenge, the client hashes a response with a secret key, and the server compares the client's response to its own calculations.

CRC (cyclic redundancy check) An algorithm (or mathematical routine) used to verify the accuracy of data contained in a data frame.

crimping The process of fixing wires at the end of a cable inside a connector in order to terminate the cable.

crimping tool A tool used to attach a connector onto the end of a cable, causing the internal RJ-45 pins to pierce the insulation of the wires, thus creating contact between the conductors at each wire. Also called a cable crimper.

crossover cable A twisted-pair patch cable in which the termination locations of the transmit and receive wires on one end of the cable are reversed as compared with the other end. A crossover cable is used to connect a PC to a PC, a switch to a switch, or a PC to a router.

cross-talk A type of interference caused by signals traveling on nearby wire pairs infringing on another pair's signal.

CSMA/CA (Carrier Sense Multiple Access with Collision Avoidance) A network access method used on 802.11 wireless networks. In CSMA/CA, before a node begins to send data, it checks the medium. If it detects no transmission activity, it waits a brief, random amount of time, and then sends its transmission. If the node does detect activity, it waits a brief period of time before checking the channel again. CSMA/CA does not eliminate, but minimizes, the potential for collisions.

CSMA/CD (Carrier Sense Multiple Access with Collision Detection) A network access method specified for use by IEEE 802.3 (Ethernet) networks. In CSMA/CD, each node waits its turn before transmitting data to avoid interfering with other nodes' transmissions. If a node's NIC determines that its data has been involved in a collision, it immediately stops transmitting. Next, in a process called jamming, the NIC issues a special 32-bit sequence that indicates to the rest of the network nodes that its previous transmission was faulty and that those data frames are invalid. After waiting, the NIC determines if the line is again available; if it is available, the NIC retransmits its data.

CSU (channel service unit) A device used with T-carrier technology that provides termination for the digital signal and ensures connection integrity through error correction and line monitoring. Typically, a CSU is combined with a DSU in a single device, a CSU/DSU.

CSU/DSU A combination of a CSU (channel service unit) and a DSU (data service unit) that serves as the connection point for a T-1 line at the customer's site. Most modern CSU/DSUs also contain a multiplexer. A CSU/DSU may be a separate device or an expansion card in another device, such as a router.

customer premise equipment *See* CPE.

CWDM (coarse wave division multiplexing) A multiplexing technique used over single-mode or multimode fiber-optic cable in which each signal is assigned a different wavelength for its carrier wave. In CWDM, channels are spaced more widely apart than in DWDM to allow for the use of cheaper transceiver equipment.

cyclic redundancy check *See* CRC.

D

D channel In ISDN, the channel that employs packet-switching techniques to carry information about the call, such as session initiation and termination signals, caller identity, call forwarding, and conference calling signals. Sometimes called the data channel.

DAI (dynamic ARP inspection) A security feature on a switch that monitors ARP messages in order to detect faked ARP messages.

data breach Unauthorized access or use of sensitive data.

data frame An 802.11 frame type that is responsible for carrying data between stations. Two other frame types include management frames, which are involved in association and reassociation, and control frames, which are related to medium access and data delivery.

data leak prevention or data loss prevention *See* DLP.

Data Link control *See* DLC.

Data Link layer The second layer in the OSI model. The Data Link layer, also called the Link layer, bridges the networking media with the Network layer. Its primary function is to divide the data it receives from the Network layer into frames that can then be transmitted by the Physical layer.

Data Link layer address *See* MAC (media access control) address.

Data Over Cable Service Interface Specification *See* DOCSIS.

data plane The actual contact made between physical devices and data transmissions as these messages traverse a network.

data service unit *See* DSU.

datagram A UDP message.

data-link connection identifier *See* DLCI.

dB (decibel) A unit of sound intensity, signal attenuation, SNR, or antenna gain.

DB-9 connector A type of connector with nine pins that's used in serial communication and conforms to the RS-232 standard.

DB-25 connector A type of connector with 25 pins that's used in serial communication and conforms to the RS-232 standard.

DC (direct current) The flow of electrical power at a steady rate in only one direction.

DCS (distributed control system or distributed computer system) A network of field devices in a closed loop system that are distributed throughout the physical system to monitor many aspects of the system.

DDNS (Dynamic DNS) A method of dynamically updating DNS records for a host. DDNS monitoring software reports IP address changes to the DDNS service, which automatically updates DNS records.

DDoS (distributed DoS) attack An attack in which multiple hosts simultaneously flood a target host with traffic, rendering the target unable to function.

DD-WRT Open source, Linux-based firmware that can be installed on routers or access points to expand their capabilities.

dead zone A gap in Wi-Fi coverage.

decapsulation Removing a header or trailer from a lower OSI layer.

decibel *See* dB.

dedicated line A continuously available link or service that is leased through another carrier. Examples of dedicated lines include ADSL, T-1, and T-3.

default gateway The gateway device that nodes on the network turn to first for access to the outside world.

default route A backup route, usually to another router, used when a router cannot determine a path to a message's destination.

default VLAN A preconfigured VLAN on a switch that includes all of the switch's ports and cannot be renamed or deleted. The switch might be preconfigured with other VLANs as well, depending on the device and manufacturer.

degausser A magnetic hard drive eraser.

delay-sensitive Transmissions that will suffer significantly compromised user experiences if portions of the transmission are delayed, such as with voice and video transmissions.

demarc *See* demarcation point.

demarcation point (demarc) The point of division between a telecommunications service carrier's network and a building's internal network.

demilitarized zone *See* DMZ.

demultiplexer (demux) A device that separates multiplexed signals once they are received and regenerates them in their original form.

demux *See* demultiplexer.

denial-of-service attack *See* DoS attack.

dense wavelength division multiplexing *See* DWDM.

designated port The port on a segment (which is the link between two bridges) that provides the shortest path to a specific destination. Only the designated port on a segment can transmit network traffic because STP disables links that are not part of the shortest path.

device driver The software that enables an attached device, such as a NIC or mouse, to communicate with the computer's operating system.

device ID *See* extension identifier.

DHCP (Dynamic Host Configuration Protocol) An Application layer protocol in the TCP/IP suite that manages the dynamic distribution of IP addresses on a network. Using DHCP to assign IP addresses can nearly eliminate duplicate-addressing problems.

DHCP relay agent A DHCP configuration that provides DHCP service to multiple VLANs. The relay agent receives a DHCP-related message, then creates its own message to send the specified DHCP traffic beyond the broadcast domain.

DHCP scope The predefined range of addresses that can be leased to any network device on a particular segment.

DHCP snooping A security feature on switches whereby DHCP messages on the network are checked and filtered.

DHCP6 *See* DHCPv6.

DHCPv6 The version of DHCP used with IPv6. DHCPv6 uses port number 546 for client-to-server communications and port number 547 for server-to-client communications.

dial-up A type of connection in which a user connects to a distant network from a computer and stays connected for a finite period of time. Most of the time, the term *dial-up* refers to a connection that uses a PSTN line.

dictionary attack A technique in which attackers run a program that tries a combination of a known user ID and, for a password, every word in a dictionary to attempt to gain access to a network.

differential backup A backup method in which only data that has changed since the last full or incremental backup is copied to a storage medium even if earlier differential backups have been made, and in which that same information is marked for subsequent backup, regardless of whether it has changed. In other words, a differential backup does not uncheck the archive bits for files it backs up.

Differentiated Service *See* DiffServ.

Differentiated Services Code Point *See* DSCP.

diffraction In the context of wireless signal propagation, the phenomenon that occurs when an electromagnetic wave encounters an obstruction and splits into secondary waves. The secondary waves continue to propagate in the direction in which they were split. If diffracted wireless signals were visible, they would appear to be bending around the obstacle. Objects with sharp edges—including the corners of walls and desks—cause diffraction.

DiffServ (Differentiated Service) A technique for ensuring QoS by prioritizing traffic, taking into account all types of network traffic, not just the time-sensitive services such as voice and video. DiffServ places-information in the DiffServ field in an IPv4 packet. In IPv6 packets, DiffServ uses a similar field known as the Traffic Class field. This information indicates to network routers how the data stream should be forwarded.

digital certificate A small file containing verified identification information about the user and the user's public key. Digital certificates are issued and maintained by a certificate authority, which attaches its own digital signature to the digital certificate to validate the certificate.

digital PBX *See* IP-PBX.

digital signal A signaling method composed of pulses of precise, positive voltages and zero voltages. Unlike analog signals, there is nothing infinite or continuous about a digital signal because it is inherently either on or off.

digital signal, level 0 *See* DS0.

digital subscriber line *See* DSL.

direct current *See* DC.

direct sequence spread spectrum *See* DSSS.

DirectAccess A service embedded in Windows Server 2008 R2, 2012, and 2012 R2 that can automatically authenticate remote users and computers to the Windows domain and its corporate network resources.

directional antenna *See* unidirectional antenna.

disaster recovery The process of restoring critical functionality and data to a network after an enterprise-wide outage that affects more than a single system or a limited group of users.

discard Short for *discarded packet*, which is a packet that arrives at its destination but is then deliberately rejected because issues such as buffer overflow, latency, bottlenecks, or other forms of network congestion delayed the packet beyond its usable time frame.

dissolvable agent *See* nonpersistent agent.

distance-vector routing protocol The simplest type of routing protocols; used to determine the best route for data based on the distance to a destination. Some distance-vector routing protocols only factor in the number of hops to the destination, while others take into account latency and other network traffic characteristics.

distributed computer system *See* DCS.

distributed control system *See* DCS.

distributed database model A database model in which data is distributed over multiple servers. In the case of DNS, for example, the records for host names and IP addresses are stored on thousands of servers around the globe so that DNS will not fail catastrophically if one or a handful of servers experience errors.

distributed DoS attack *See* DDoS attack.

distributed reflector DoS attack *See* DRDoS attack.

DLC (Data Link control) A service provided at the Data Link layer to manage frames, including error detection and flow control.

DLCI (data-link connection identifier) A field in a frame relay frame that routers read to determine which circuit to use for the frame.

DLP (data leak prevention) A security technique that uses software to monitor confidential data, track data access and ownership, and provide additional layers of security for sensitive data.

DMZ (demilitarized zone) An area on the perimeter of a network that is surrounded by two firewalls—an external firewall that is more porous to allow more types of access, and an internal firewall that is more hardened to provide greater protection to the internal network. DNS servers and Web servers are typically placed in the DMZ.

DNAT (Dynamic Network Address Translation) A type of address translation in which a gateway has a pool of public IP addresses that it is free to assign to a local host whenever the local host makes a request to access the Internet.

DNS (Domain Name System or Domain Name Service) A hierarchical way of tracking domain names and their addresses, devised in the mid-1980s. The DNS database does not rely on one file or even one server, but rather is distributed over several key computers across the Internet to prevent

catastrophic failure if one or a few computers go down. DNS is a TCP/IP service that belongs to the Application layer of the OSI model.

DNS cache A database on a computer that stores information about IP addresses and their associated host names. DNS caches can exist on clients as well as on name servers.

DNS server A server that contains a database of TCP/IP host names and their associated IP addresses. A DNS server supplies a resolver with the requested information. If it cannot resolve the IP address, the query passes to a higher-level DNS server.

DNS spoofing An attack in which an outsider forges name server records to falsify his host's identity.

DNS zone A portion of the DNS namespace for which one organization is assigned authority to manage.

DOCSIS (Data Over Cable Service Interface Specification) An international, cooperative effort orchestrated by Cable-Labs that standardized broadband cable service.

domain In the context of Windows Server NOSs, a group of users, servers, and other resources that share account and security policies through a Windows Server NOS.

domain local group A group of workstations that is centrally managed via Active Directory for the entire network.

domain name The last two parts of an FQDN, such as *mycompany.com*. Usually, a domain name is associated with the company's name and its type of organization, such as a university or military unit.

Domain Name Service *See* DNS.

Domain Name System *See* DNS.

DoS (denial-of-service) attack An attack in which a system becomes unable to function because it has been inundated with requests for services and can't respond to any of them. As a result, all data transmissions are disrupted.

downgrading *See* rollback.

downlink In the context of wireless transmission, the connection between a carrier's antenna and a client's transceiver—for example, a smartphone.

downstream A term used to describe data traffic that flows from a carrier's facility to the customer. In asymmetrical communications, downstream throughput is usually much higher than upstream throughput. In symmetrical communications, downstream and upstream throughputs are equal.

DRDoS (distributed reflector DoS) attack A DoS attack bounced off of uninfected computers, called reflectors, before being directed at the target. This is achieved by spoofing the source IP address in the attack to make it look like all of the requests for response are being sent by the target, then all of the reflectors send their responses to the target, thereby flooding the target with traffic.

driver *See* device driver.

driver update A patch or upgrade applied to a device driver.

drop To discard a packet at its destination because issues such as buffer overflow, latency, bottlenecks, or other forms of network congestion delayed the packet beyond its usable time frame.

DS0 (digital signal, level 0) The equivalent of one data or voice channel in T-carrier technology, as defined by ANSI Physical layer standards. All other signal levels are multiples of DS0.

DSCP (Differentiated Services Code Point) The first 6 bits of the 8-bit DiffServ field in an IPv4 packet. DSCP indicates to network routers how the data stream should be forwarded.

DSL (digital subscriber line) A dedicated WAN technology that uses advanced data modulation techniques at the Physical layer to achieve high throughput over regular phone lines. DSL comes in several different varieties, the most common of which is Asymmetric DSL (ADSL).

DSL access multiplexer *See* DSLAM.

DSL modem A device that demodulates an incoming DSL signal, extracting the information and passing it to the data equipment (such as telephones and computers), and modulates an outgoing DSL signal.

DSLAM (DSL access multiplexer) A connectivity device located at a telecommunications carrier's office that aggregates multiple DSL subscriber lines and connects them to a larger carrier or to the Internet backbone.

DSSS (direct sequence spread spectrum) A modulation technique that, like other spread-spectrum technologies, distributes lower-level signals over several frequencies simultaneously. DSSS transmissions are especially resistant to jamming and background noise.

DSU (data service unit) A device used in T-carrier technology that converts T-carrier frames into frames the LAN can interpret and vice versa. Typically, a DSU is combined with a CSU in a single device, a CSU/DSU.

dual-stacked A type of network that supports both IPv4 and IPv6 traffic.

duplex *See* full-duplex.

DWDM (dense wavelength division multiplexing) A multiplexing technique used over single-mode or multi-mode fiber-optic cable in which each signal is assigned a different wavelength for its carrier wave. In DWDM, little space exists between carrier waves to achieve extraordinary high capacity.

dynamic ARP inspection *See* DAI.

dynamic ARP table entry A record in an ARP table that is created when a client makes an ARP request that cannot be satisfied by data already in the ARP table.

Dynamic DNS *See* DDNS.

Dynamic Host Configuration Protocol *See* DHCP.

dynamic IP address An IP address that is assigned to a device upon request and may change when the DHCP lease expires or is terminated. BOOTP and DHCP are two ways of assigning dynamic IP addresses.

Dynamic Network Address Translation *See* DNAT.

dynamic port TCP/IP ports in the range of 49,152 through 65,535, which are open for use without requiring administrative privileges on a host or approval from IANA.

dynamic routing A method of routing that automatically calculates the best path between two networks and accumulates this information in a routing table. If congestion or failures affect the network, a router using dynamic routing can detect the problems and reroute data through a different path. Modern networks primarily use dynamic routing.

E

E-1 A digital carrier standard used in Europe that offers 32 channels and a maximum of 2.048-Mbps throughput.

E-3 A digital carrier standard used in Europe that offers 512 channels and a maximum of 34.368-Mbps throughput.

EAP (Extensible Authentication Protocol) An extension to the PPP protocol suite that provides the framework for authenticating clients and servers. It does not perform encryption or authentication on its own, but rather works with other encryption and authentication schemes to verify the credentials of clients and servers.

EAP over LAN *See* 802.1X.

EAPoL (EAP over LAN) *See* 802.1X.

EDGE (Enhanced Data rates for GSM Evolution) *See* EGPRS.

eDiscovery The process of collecting information from a computer's hard drive and storage media.

EDNS (extension mechanism for DNS) A mechanism that expands DNS parameters, thereby increasing the protocol's functionality.

EF (Expedited Forwarding) One of two DiffServ forwarding specifications. EF assigns each data stream a minimum departure rate from a given node. This technique circumvents delays that slow normal data from reaching its destination on time and in sequence. EF information is inserted in the DiffServ field of an IPv4 packet.

EGP (exterior gateway protocol) A type of routing protocol used by border routers and exterior routers to distribute data outside of autonomous systems. BGP is the only modern example of an exterior gateway protocol.

EGPRS (Enhanced GPRS) A technology added to GSM to provide data services on a cellular network. EGPRS is an improvement over the earlier GPRS.

EIA (Electronic Industries Alliance) A former trade organization composed of representatives from electronics manufacturing firms across the United States that sets standards for electronic equipment and lobbies for legislation favorable to the growth of the computer and electronics industries. EIA was dissolved in 2011 and its responsibilities transferred to ECA (Electronic Components, Assemblies, Equipment & Supplies Association), but the standards brand name, EIA, will continue to be used.

elastic A characteristic of cloud computing that means services can be quickly and dynamically—sometimes even automatically—scaled up or down.

electric circuit A medium for the transfer of electrical power over a closed loop.

electromagnetic interference *See* EMI.

electronic discovery *See* eDiscovery.

Electronic Industries Alliance *See* EIA.

electronically stored information *See* ESI.

electrostatic discharge *See* ESD.

elevated command prompt window A command prompt window with administrative privileges.

emergency alert system A system that typically generates loud noise and flashing lights in response to a fire. The system might also be able to send alert messages to key personnel or make networkwide announcements.

EMI (electromagnetic interference) A type of interference that can be caused by motors, power lines, televisions, copiers, fluorescent lights, or other sources of electrical activity.

emission security *See* EmSec.

EmSec (emission security) The implementation of TEMPEST, which is a specification created by the NSA to define protection standards against RF emanation.

Encapsulating Security Payload encryption *See* ESP encryption.

encapsulation The process of adding a header to the data inherited from the layer above.

encrypted virus A virus that is encrypted to prevent detection.

encryption The use of an algorithm to scramble data into a format that can be read only by reversing the algorithm—that is, by decrypting the data—to keep the information private.

encryption device Computers or specialized adapters inserted into other devices, such as routers or servers, that perform encryption.

endpoint In SIP terminology, any client, server, or gateway communicating on the network.

endpoint security vulnerability An inherent vulnerability at the time data is accessed, stored, or otherwise manipulated in its unencrypted form at an endpoint of use, such as when a password is entered on a user's smartphone.

end-to-end connectivity A connection that allows two endpoints to communicate with each other through an established session that is not dependent upon intermediate devices directing each hop for each transmission, such as when establishing a TLS session. Failed authentication and incompatible encryption methods can both prevent the end-to-end connectivity required for a secure connection.

Enhanced Category 5 *See* Cat 5e.

Enhanced Data rates for GSM Evolution (EDGE) *See* EGPRS.

Enhanced GPRS *See* EGPRS.

entrance facility The location where an incoming network service (whether phone, Internet, or long-distance service) enters a building and connects with the building's backbone cabling.

EOP (Ethernet over power or Ethernet over power line) An Ethernet LAN connection implemented over the electrical wiring in a building using a pair of power-line adapters, one at each end of the connection, that plug into power outlets.

ESD (electrostatic discharge) The transfer of electrical charge between two bodies, such as when a technician touches a computer component.

ESI (electronically stored information) Information stored on a computer's hard drive and storage media, such as calendars, email, and databases.

ESP (Encapsulating Security Payload or (Network+) encapsulated security packets) encryption In the context of IPsec, a type of encryption that provides authentication of the IP packet's data payload through public key techniques. In addition, ESP also encrypts the entire IP packet for added security.

ESS (extended service set) A group of access points and associated stations (or basic service sets) connected to the same LAN.

ESSID (extended service set identifier) A special identifier shared by BSSs that belong to the same ESS.

Ethernet II The Ethernet frame type developed by Digital Equipment Corporation, Intel, and Xerox (collectively called DIX), before the IEEE began to standardize Ethernet. Ethernet II is distinguished from other Ethernet frame types in that it contains a 2-byte type field to identify the upper-layer protocol contained in the frame. It supports TCP/IP and other higher-layer protocols.

Ethernet MAN *See* Metro Ethernet.

Ethernet over HDMI A technology that transmits Ethernet signals over Ethernet-enabled HDMI cables to connect multimedia equipment, such as a TV, to the Internet.

Ethernet over power *See* EOP.

Ethernet over power line *See* EOP.

Ethernet port The type of port used to create LANs through a router. Ethernet ports allow for network communications on a LAN.

ethtool A UNIX or Linux utility that allows a technician to view or modify NIC settings.

EUI-64 (Extended Unique Identifier-64) The IEEE standard defining 64-bit physical addresses. In the EUI-64 scheme, the OUI portion of an address is 24 bits in length. A 40-bit extension identifier makes up the rest of the physical address, for a total of 64 bits.

event log The service on Windows-based operating systems that records events; also, the ongoing record of such events.

Event Viewer A GUI application that allows users to easily view and sort events recorded in the event log on a computer running a Windows-based operating system.

Everything as a Service *See* XaaS.

evil twin An exploit in which a rogue access point masquerades as a legitimate access point, using the same SSID and potentially other identical settings.

Expedited Forwarding *See* EF.

exploit In the context of network security, the act of taking advantage of a vulnerability.

extended digital subscriber line *See* XDSL.

extended network prefix The combination of an IP address's network ID and subnet information. By interpreting the address's extended network prefix, a device can determine the subnet to which an address belongs.

extended service set *See* ESS.

extended service set identifier *See* ESSID.

Extended Unique Identifier-64 *See* EUI-64.

Extensible Authentication Protocol *See* EAP.

eXtensible Markup Language *See* XML.

extension identifier A unique set of characters assigned to each NIC by its manufacturer. In the traditional, 48-bit physical addressing scheme, the extension identifier is 24 bits long. In EUI-64, the extension identifier is 40 bits long.

extension mechanism for DNS *See* EDNS.

exterior gateway protocol *See* EGP.

exterior router A router that directs data between autonomous systems, for example, routers used on the Internet's backbone.

F

fading A variation in a wireless signal's strength as a result of some of the electromagnetic energy being scattered, reflected, or diffracted after being issued by the transmitter.

fail close System default that denies access during a system or network failure.

fail open System default that allows access during a system or network failure.

failure A deviation from a specified level of system performance for a given period of time. A failure occurs when something doesn't work as promised or as planned.

fair access policy A set of guidelines designed to ensure that users have access to the content they require in order to do their jobs without hogging network resources from other users.

far end cross-talk *See* FEXT.

Faraday cage An enclosure made of conductive material that is designed to block electromagnetic signals, including Wi-Fi.

Fast Ethernet A type of Ethernet network that is capable of 100-Mbps throughput. 100Base-T and 100Base-FX are both examples of Fast Ethernet.

fault The malfunction of one component of a system. A fault can result in a failure.

fault management The detection and signaling of device, link, or component faults.

fault tolerance (1) Techniques that allow data storage or other operations to continue in the event of a failure or fault of one of its components, for example, storing redundant data on multiple storage devices in the event one device fails. (2) A system's ability to continue performing despite an unexpected hardware or software malfunction.

FC (ferrule connector or fiber channel) A connector with a 2.5-mm ferrule that is used with single-mode, fiber-optic cable.

FC (Fibre Channel) A distinct network transmission method that relies on fiber-optic media and its own proprietary protocol. Fibre Channel is capable of over 5-Gbps throughput.

F-connector A connector used to terminate coaxial cable used for transmitting television and broadband cable signals.

FCS (frame check sequence) The field in a frame responsible for ensuring that data carried by the frame arrives intact. It uses an algorithm, such as CRC, to accomplish this verification.

FDM (frequency division multiplexing) A type of multiplexing that assigns a unique frequency band to each communications subchannel. Signals are modulated with different carrier frequencies, then multiplexed to simultaneously travel over a single channel.

ferrule The extended tip of a fiber-optic cable connector that encircles the fiber strand to keep it properly aligned and ensure that it makes contact with the receptacle in a jack or other connector.

ferrule connector *See* FC.

FEXT (far end cross-talk) Cross-talk measured at the far end of the cable from the signal source.

FHSS (frequency hopping spread spectrum) A wireless signaling technique in which a signal jumps between several different frequencies within a band in a synchronization pattern known to the channel's receiver and transmitter.

fiber channel *See* FC.

fiber coupler A simple fiber connector that can be used to connect like terminations, such as when joining two shorter cables to make a longer one. Some fiber couplers can also combine signals from multiple lines into a single line.

fiber line driver A line driver installed on a fiber-optic cable.

fiber to the home *See* FTTH.

fiber to the premises *See* FTTP.

fiber type mismatch A problem created by mismatching fiber core types, such as when connecting an SMF cable to an MMF cable.

fiber-optic cable A form of cable that contains one or several glass or plastic fibers in its core. Data is transmitted via a pulsing light sent from a laser or light-emitting diode (LED) through the central fiber (or fibers). Fiber-optic cables offer significantly higher throughput than copper-based cables. They may be single-mode or multimode and typically use wave-division multiplexing to carry multiple signals.

Fibre Channel *See* FC.

field device A device located within the physical portion of an industrial system.

fieldbus The communication channel that connects a PLC to an RTU (when these are separate devices) or to an actuator.

file server A specialized server that enables clients to share applications and data across the network.

file services The functions of a file server that allow users to share data files, applications, and storage areas.

File Transfer Protocol *See* FTP.

File Transfer Protocol Secure or (Network+) File Transfer Protocol Security *See* FTPS.

file-infector virus A virus that attaches itself to executable files. When the infected executable file runs, the virus copies itself to memory. Later, the virus attaches itself to other executable files.

fire suppression system Any system designed to combat the outbreak of a fire. A fire suppression system might include an emergency alert system, fire extinguishers, emergency power-off switch, and/or a suppression agent such as a foaming chemical or water.

firewall A device (either a router or a computer running special software) that selectively filters or blocks traffic between networks.

first responder A person with training or certifications in handling evidence in such a way as to preserve its admissibility in court.

flashing An attack in which an Internet user sends commands to another Internet user's machine that cause the screen to fill with garbage characters. A flashing attack causes the user to terminate her session.

flow A sequence of packets issued from one source to one or many destinations. Routers interpret flow information to ensure that packets belonging to the same transmission arrive together. Flow information may also help with traffic prioritization.

flow control A method of gauging the appropriate rate of data transmission based on how fast the recipient can accept data.

FM (frequency modulation) A method of data modulation in which the frequency of the carrier signal is modified by the application of the data signal.

four-post rack An equipment rack consisting of four vertical side posts to which equipment is attached via brackets incorporated in the posts.

FQDN (fully qualified domain name) A host name plus domain name that uniquely identifies a computer or location on a network.

fractional T-1 An arrangement that allows a customer to lease only some of the channels on a T-1 line.

fragmentation A Network layer service that subdivides packets into smaller packets when those packets exceed the maximum size for the network.

frame The entire Data Link layer message, including the header, payload, and trailer.

frame aggregation In the context of 802.11n and 802.11ac wireless networking, a technique for combining multiple data frames into one larger frame called an A-MSDU (Aggregated Mac Service Data Unit) or A-MPDU (Aggregated Mac Protocol Data Unit). Both approaches combine multiple frames to reduce overhead. 802.11ac actually uses A-MPDU for all transmissions by default.

frame check sequence *See* FCS.

frame relay A digital, packet-switched WAN technology whose protocols operate at the Data Link layer. The name is derived from the fact that data is separated into frames, which are then relayed from one node to another without any verification or processing. A frame relay customer chooses the amount of bandwidth he requires and pays for only that amount.

frequency The number of times that a wave's amplitude cycles from its starting point, through its highest amplitude and its lowest amplitude, and back to its starting point over a fixed period of time, expressed in cycles per second, or hertz (Hz).

frequency division multiplexing *See* FDM.

frequency hopping A process performed by some wireless devices to help reduce interference by quickly hopping between frequencies within a given band of frequencies. Bluetooth, for example, performs up to 1600 hops/sec within the radio band of 2.4 GHz to 2.485 GHz.

frequency hopping spread spectrum *See* FHSS.

frequency modulation *See* FM.

friendly attack *See* unintentional DoS attack.

FTP (File Transfer Protocol) An Application layer protocol used to send and receive files via TCP/IP. FTP uses port 20 for data and port 21 for file transfer control information.

FTP bounce An attack in which an FTP client specifies a different host's IP address and port number for the requested data's destination. By commanding the FTP server to connect to a different computer, a hacker can scan the ports on other hosts and transmit malicious code. To thwart FTP bounce attacks, most modern FTP servers will not issue data to hosts other than the client that originated the request.

FTPS (File Transfer Protocol Secure or (Network+) File Transfer Protocol Security) A version of FTP that incorporates the TLS and SSL protocols for added security.

FTTH (fiber to the home) A service in which a residential customer is connected to his carrier's network with fiber-optic cable.

FTTP (fiber to the premises) A service in which a residential or business customer is connected to his carrier's network using fiber-optic cable.

full backup A backup in which all data on all servers is copied to a storage medium, regardless of whether the data is new or changed. A full backup unchecks the archive bit on files it has backed up.

full-duplex A type of transmission in which signals may travel in both directions over a medium simultaneously; also called, simply, duplex.

full-mesh WAN A version of the mesh topology WAN in which every site is directly connected to every other site. Full-mesh WANs are the most fault-tolerant type of WAN.

fully qualified domain name *See* FQDN.

fully qualified host name (FQHN) *See* FQDN.

G

gateway A computer, router, or other device that a host uses to access another network. Gateways perform connectivity, session management, and data translation, so they must operate at multiple layers of the OSI model.

gateway of last resort The router on a network that accepts all unroutable messages from other routers.

gateway router *See* border router.

GBIC (Gigabit interface converter) A standard type of modular interface designed in the 1990s for Gigabit Ethernet connections. GBICs may contain RJ-45 or fiber-optic cable ports (such as LC, SC, or ST). They are inserted into a socket on a connectivity device's backplane. Pronounced *jee-bick*.

Gbps (Gigabits per second) A unit for measuring data transfer rate.

General Packet Radio Services *See* GPRS.

generator A computer that is monitored by a syslog-compatible application and that issues event information.

Generic Routing Encapsulation *See* GRE.

GEO (geosynchronous earth orbit) The orbit of a satellite that maintains a constant distance from a point on the equator at every point in its orbit.

geostationary orbit A special case of geosynchronous orbit in which the satellite stays directly above the equator and appears stationary from Earth. Geostationary orbit satellites are the type used to provide satellite Internet access.

geosynchronous earth orbit *See* GEO.

ghost A frame that is not actually a data frame, but rather an aberration caused by a device misinterpreting stray voltage on the wire. Unlike true data frames, ghosts have an invalid pattern at the beginning of the frame pattern.

giant A packet that exceeds the medium's maximum packet size. For example, any Ethernet packet that is larger than 1518 bytes (or 1522 bytes for VLAN packets) is considered a giant.

Gigabit Ethernet A type of Ethernet network that is capable of 1000-Mbps, or 1-Gbps, throughput. Requires Cat 5e or higher cabling.

Gigabit interface converter *See* GBIC.

Gigabits per second *See* Gbps.

global account A user's domain-level account, also called a global username or network ID, which is assigned by the network administrator and is kept in Active Directory.

global address *See* global unicast address.

Global System for Mobile Communications *See* GSM.

global unicast address An IPv6 address that can be routed on the Internet. These addresses are similar to public IPv4 addresses. Most global addresses begin with the prefix 2000::/3, although other prefixes are being released.

GNU Privacy Guard *See* GPG.

goodput The throughput experienced at the application level, such as the quality of a video feed or the speed of a Web page loading in the browser.

gpedit.msc *See* Group Policy.

GPG (GNU Privacy Guard) An encryption software program that provides an alternative to PGP.

GPRS (General Packet Radio Services) A technology added to GSM to provide data services on a cellular network.

GRE (Generic Routing Encapsulation) A tunneling protocol developed by Cisco that is used to transmit PPP data frames through a VPN tunnel. GRE encapsulates PPP frames to make them take on the temporary identity of IP packets at Layer 3. To the WAN, messages look like inconsequential IP traffic.

grounding Connecting a device directly to the earth so that, in the event of a short, the electricity flows into the earth rather than out of control through the device.

Group Policy (gpedit.msc) A Windows utility that is used to control what users can do and how the system can be used. Group Policy works by making entries in the Registry, applying scripts to Windows start-up, shutdown, and logon processes, and affecting security settings.

GSM (Global System for Mobile Communications) An open standard that uses digital communication of data, which is separated by time slots on a channel. GSM is accepted and used worldwide to provide cellular service.

guard tone A tone at a particular frequency that indicates a calling modem has successfully contacted another modem on the other end.

guest In the context of virtualization, a virtual machine operated and managed by a virtualization program.

guest network A separate wireless network created through a Wi-Fi router or access point to protect a private network while still providing guests with access to the Internet.

H

H.225 A Session layer call signaling protocol defined as part of ITU's H.323 multiservice network architecture. H.225 is responsible for call or videoconference setup between nodes

on a VoIP or video-over-IP network, indicating node status and requesting additional bandwidth and call termination.

H.245 A Session layer control protocol defined as part of ITU's H.323 multiservice network architecture. H.245 is responsible for controlling a session between two nodes. For example, it ensures that the two nodes are communicating in the same format.

H.248 *See* Megaco.

H.323 A signaling protocol used to make a connection between hosts prior to communicating multimedia data. H.323 has largely been replaced by SIP, which is easier to use.

H.323 gatekeeper The nerve center for networks that adhere to H.323. Gatekeepers authorize and authenticate terminals and gateways, manage bandwidth, and oversee call routing, accounting, and billing. Gatekeepers are optional on H.323 networks.

H.323 gateway On a network following the H.323 standard, a gateway that provides translation between network devices running H.323 signaling protocols and devices running other types of signaling protocols (for example, SS7 on the PSTN).

H.323 terminal On a network following the H.323 standard, any node that provides audio, visual, or data information to another node.

H.323 zone A collection of H.323 terminals, gateways, and MCUs that are managed by a single H.323 gatekeeper.

hacker Traditionally, a person who masters the inner workings of computer hardware and software in an effort to better understand them. More generally, an individual who gains unauthorized access to systems or networks with or without malicious intent.

hacking The act of finding a creative way around a problem, increasing functionality of a device or program, or otherwise manipulating resources beyond their original intent.

half-duplex A type of transmission in which signals may travel in both directions over a medium, but in only one direction at a time.

half-rack An equipment rack that is about half the height of the standard rack. Standard racks measure 42U, but half-racks are typically 18U–22U tall.

handoff The transition that occurs when a cellular network client moves from one antenna's coverage area to another.

handshake protocol One of several protocols within SSL, and perhaps the most significant. As its name implies, the handshake protocol allows the client and server to authenticate (or introduce) each other and establishes terms for how they securely exchange data during an SSL session.

hardening technique A measure taken to help mitigate security risks to a network.

hardware address *See* MAC (media access control) address.

hashed data Data that has been transformed through a particular algorithm that generally reduces the amount of space needed for the data. Hashing data is nearly impossible, mathematically, to reverse.

HDLC (High-Level Data Link Control) A group of Layer 2 protocols that can provide either connection-oriented or connectionless service for data transfer between nodes.

HDMI (High Definition Multimedia Interface) A proprietary standard connector used primarily for video or audio data transfer.

head-end A cable company's central office, which connects cable wiring to many nodes before it reaches customers' sites.

header An area at the beginning of a payload where protocols add their own control information.

Health Insurance Portability and Accountability Act *See* HIPAA.

heat map A map of Wi-Fi signals and other electromagnetic noise in a specific location.

heating, ventilation, and air conditioning system *See* HVAC system.

hertz *See* Hz.

heuristic scanning A type of virus scanning that attempts to identify malware by discovering malware-like behavior.

hex number *See* hexadecimal number.

hexadecimal number A number written in the base 16 numbering system, which uses the 16 numerals 0, 1, 2, 3, 4, 5, 6, 7, 8, 9, A, B, C, D, E, and F.

HFC (hybrid fiber-coax) A link that consists of fiber cable connecting the cable company's offices to a node location near the customer and fiber or coaxial cable connecting the node to the customer's house. HFC upgrades to existing cable wiring are required before older TV cable systems can provide Internet access.

hidden node problem A situation on a wireless network in which a node on one side of a coverage area is too far apart from and therefore invisible to nodes on the other side of the coverage area. This situation prevents nodes from collaborating to prevent collisions.

HIDS (host-based intrusion detection system) A type of intrusion detection that runs on a single computer, such as a client or server, to alert about attacks against that one host.

High Definition Multimedia Interface *See* HDMI.

High Speed Packet Access Plus *See* HSPA+.

high throughput *See* HT.

High-Level Data Link Control *See* HDLC.

highly available A network that is functional a high percentage of time per year, such as 99.99 percent of the time (as opposed to just 99.9 percent of the time).

HIPAA (Health Insurance Portability and Accountability Act) A federal regulation in the United States, enacted in 1996. One aspect of this regulation addresses the security and privacy of medical records, including those stored or transmitted electronically.

HIPS (host-based intrusion prevention system) A type of intrusion prevention that runs on a single computer, such as a client or server, to intercept and help prevent attacks against that one host.

historian An ICS server that stores a centralized database of collected and analyzed data and control activities. This data is often analyzed to recognize trends in the physical system.

HMI (human-machine interface) A computer, including hardware and software, that technicians use to monitor and manage physical systems in an industrial system.

honeynet A network of honeypots.

honeypot A decoy system isolated from legitimate systems and designed to be vulnerable to security exploits for the purposes of learning more about hacking techniques or nabbing a hacker in the act.

hop A term used to describe each trip a unit of data takes from one connectivity device to another. Typically, *hop* is used in the context of router-to-router communications.

hop limit The number of times that an IPv6 packet can be forwarded by routers on the network; similar to the TTL field in IPv4 packets.

horizontal wiring The wiring that connects workstations to the closest data closet.

host (1) Any computer or device on a network that provides a resource such as an application or data. (2) In the context of virtualization, the physical computer on which virtualization software operates and manages guests.

host name The first part of an FQDN, such as www or ftp, which identifies the individual computer on the network.

host table *See* hosts file.

host-based firewall A firewall that only protects the computer on which it's installed.

host-based intrusion detection system *See* HIDS.

host-based intrusion prevention system *See* HIPS.

hosted virtual desktop *See* HVD.

host-only mode A type of network connection in which VMs on a host can exchange data with each other and with their host, but they cannot communicate with any nodes beyond the host. In other words, the vNICs never receive or transmit data via the host machine's physical NIC.

In host-only mode, as in NAT mode, VMs use the DHCP service in the host's virtualization software to obtain IP address assignments.

hosts file A text file that associates TCP/IP host names with IP addresses. On a UNIX- or Linux-based computer, hosts is found in the /etc directory. On a Windows-based computer, it is found in the %systemroot%\system32\ drivers\etc folder.

host-to-host VPN A type of VPN in which two computers create a VPN tunnel directly between them. Both computers must have the appropriate software installed, and they can't serve as a gateway to other hosts on their respective networks.

host-to-site VPN *See* client-to-site VPN.

hot seizure and removal The use of a specialized device that transfers a computer from one power source to another without the need to shut down the computer.

hot site A place where the computers, devices, and connectivity necessary to rebuild a network exist, and all are appropriately configured, updated, and connected to match a network's current state.

hot spare A duplicate component already installed in a device that can assume the original component's functions in case that component fails.

Hot Standby Router Protocol *See* HSRP.

hot spot An area that is within range of a wireless network providing access to the Internet.

hot-swappable The feature of a component that allows it to be installed or removed without disrupting operations.

HSPA+ (High Speed Packet Access Plus) A 3G mobile wireless technology released in 2008 that uses MIMO and sophisticated encoding techniques to achieve a maximum 168-Mbps downlink throughput and 22-Mbps uplink throughput in its current release. HSPA+ uses limited channels more efficiently than earlier technologies and incorporates more antennas in MIMO transmission. However, faster and more flexible technologies, such as LTE, are overtaking HSPA+ in popularity.

HSRP (Hot Standby Router Protocol) Cisco's proprietary standard, similar to VRRP, that assigns a virtual IP address to a group of routers. At first, messages routed to the virtual IP address are handled by the active router. If the active router fails, standby routers stand in line to take over responsibility for the virtual IP address.

HT (high throughput) A relative term indicating more efficient data transfer.

HTTP (Hypertext Transfer Protocol) An Application layer protocol that formulates and interprets requests between Web clients and servers. HTTP uses the TCP port number 80.

HTTP over Secure Sockets Layer *See* HTTPS.

HTTP Secure *See* HTTPS.

HTTPS (HTTP over Secure Sockets Layer or HTTP Secure) The URL prefix that indicates that a Web page requires its data to be exchanged between client and server using SSL or TLS encryption. HTTPS uses the TCP port number 443.

hub An outdated connectivity device that belongs to the Physical layer of the OSI model and retransmits incoming data signals to its multiple ports.

human-machine interface *See* HMI.

HVAC (heating, ventilation, and air conditioning) system A system that controls the environment in a data center, including the temperature, humidity, airflow, and air filtering.

HVD (hosted virtual desktop) A desktop operating environment hosted virtually on a different physical computer from the one the user interacts with.

hybrid cloud A deployment model in which shared and flexible data storage, applications, or services are made available through a combination of other service models into a single deployment, or a collection of services connected within the cloud. In the real world, the hybrid cloud infrastructure is a common result of transitory solutions.

hybrid fiber-coax *See* HFC.

hybrid routing protocol A routing protocol that exhibits characteristics of both distance-vector and link-state routing protocols.

hybrid topology A physical topology that combines characteristics of more than one simple physical topology.

Hypertext Transfer Protocol *See* HTTP.

Hyper-V Microsoft's virtualization software package. Hyper-V was first available with Windows Server 2008, and is now available in some 64-bit versions of Windows 8.1 as well.

hypervisor The element of virtualization software that manages multiple guest machines and their connections to the host (and by association, to a physical network). A hypervisor is also known as a virtual machine manager.

Hz (Hertz) A unit of frequency. One Hz equals one wave cycle per second.

I

I/O server *See* acquisitions server.

IaaS (Infrastructure as a Service) A service model in which hardware services are provided virtually, including network infrastructure devices such as virtual servers.

IANA (Internet Assigned Numbers Authority) A nonprofit, U.S. government-funded group that was established at the University of Southern California and charged with managing IP address allocation and the Domain Name System. The oversight for many of IANA's functions was given to ICANN in 1998; however, IANA continues to perform Internet addressing and Domain Name System administration.

ICA (Independent Computing Architecture) A proprietary protocol used by Citrix's XenApp and other products to standardize data transfer between servers and clients.

ICANN (Internet Corporation for Assigned Names and Numbers) The nonprofit corporation currently designated by the U.S. government to maintain and assign IP addresses.

ICMP (Internet Control Message Protocol) A core protocol in the TCP/IP suite that notifies the sender that something has gone wrong in the transmission process and that packets were not delivered.

ICMPv6 The version of ICMP used with IPv6 networks. ICMPv6 performs the functions that ICMP, IGMP, and ARP perform in IPv4. It detects and reports data transmission errors, discovers other nodes on a network, and manages multicasting.

ICS (Internet Connection Sharing) The use of one device's Internet connection to provide Internet connectivity to one or more other devices.

ICS (industrial control system) A group of networked computers used to manage a physical system of industrial processes.

ICS server A server in an ICS or SCADA system that might include an acquisitions server, which collects and stores raw data, a supervisory server, which controls the physical system, or a historian, which is a centralized database of collected and analyzed data and control activities.

IDF (intermediate distribution frame) A junction point between the MDF and concentrations of fewer connections—for example, those that terminate in a data closet.

IDS (intrusion detection system) A dedicated device or software running on a workstation, server, or switch, which might be managed from another computer on the network, and is used to monitor network traffic and create alerts when suspicious activity happens within the network.

IEEE (Institute of Electrical and Electronics Engineers) A professional society that develops national and international standards in a variety of technical areas.

IEEE 1901-2010 A standard that defines the broadband over powerline technology.

IEEE 1905.1-2013 A standard operating between Layers 2 and 3 that integrates multiple wired and wireless networking technologies, such as IEEE 1901, IEEE 802.11, and IEEE 802.3.

IETF (Internet Engineering Task Force) An organization that sets standards for how systems communicate over the Internet (for example, how protocols operate and interact).

ifconfig A TCP/IP configuration and management utility used with UNIX and Linux systems.

IGMP (Internet Group Management Protocol or Internet Group Multicast Protocol) A Network layer protocol used on IPv4 networks to manage multicast transmissions. Routers use IGMP to determine which nodes belong to a multicast group, and nodes use IGMP to join or leave a multicast group.

IGP (interior gateway protocol) A type of routing protocol, such as OSPF and IS-IS, used by interior routers and border routers within autonomous systems.

IKE (Internet Key Exchange) One of two services in the key management phase of creating a secure IPsec connection. IKE negotiates the exchange of keys, including authentication of the keys. It uses UDP and usually runs on port 500.

IMAP (Internet Message Access Protocol) A mail retrieval protocol that improves on the shortcomings of POP. The most current version of IMAP is version 4 (IMAP4). The single biggest advantage IMAP4 has relative to POP is that it allows users to store messages on the mail server, rather than always having to download them to the local machine.

IMAP4 (Internet Message Access Protocol, version 4) The most commonly used form of the Internet Message Access Protocol (IMAP).

impedance The resistance that contributes to controlling an electrical signal. Impedance is measured in ohms.

implicit deny An ACL rule which ensures that any traffic the ACL does not explicitly permit is denied by default.

in-band management A switch management option, such as Telnet, that uses the existing network and its protocols to interface with a switch.

inbound traffic Data received by a device on its way into a network.

incremental backup A backup in which only data that has changed since the last full or incremental backup is copied to a storage medium. After backing up files, an incremental backup unchecks the archive bit for every file it has saved.

Independent Computing Architecture *See* ICA.

industrial control system *See* ICS (industrial control system).

industrial system A system of machines, such as an assembly line at a manufacturing plant.

information technology *See* IT.

infrared *See* IR.

Infrastructure as a Service *See* IaaS.

infrastructure WLAN A type of WLAN in which stations communicate with an access point and not directly with each other.

INID (Intelligent NID) *See* smart jack.

Initial Sequence Number *See* ISN.

initialization vector *See* IV.

Institute of Electrical and Electronics Engineers *See* IEEE.

Integrated Services Digital Network *See* ISDN.

integrity The assurance that a network's programs, data, services, devices, and connections have not been altered without authorization. To ensure a network's integrity, it must be protected from anything that might render it unusable, such as corruption, tampering, natural disasters, and viruses.

integrity checking A method of comparing the current characteristics of files and disks against an archived version of these characteristics to discover any changes. The most common example of integrity checking involves using a checksum, though this tactic might not prove effective against malware with stealth capabilities.

Intelligent NID *See* smart jack.

intelligent switch A switch with configuration capabilities.

Intelligent Transportation System *See* ITS.

interface A network connection made by a node or host on a network.

interface error An error that is reported when a logical (not physical) connection between a node and a network is malfunctioning. They can be prompted by any number of problems, including interface misconfiguration.

interface ID The last 64 bits, or four blocks, of an IPv6 address that uniquely identify the interface on the local link.

interface monitor A tool that can monitor traffic at a specific interface between a server or client and the network, but not the entire network.

interior gateway protocol *See* IGP.

interior router A router that directs data between networks within the same autonomous system.

intermediate distribution frame *See* IDF.

Intermediate System to Intermediate System *See* IS-IS.

International Telecommunication Union *See* ITU.

Internet Assigned Numbers Authority *See* IANA.

Internet Connection Sharing *See* ICS (Internet Connection Sharing).

Internet Control Message Protocol *See* ICMP.

Internet Corporation for Assigned Names and Numbers *See* ICANN.

Internet Engineering Task Force *See* IETF.

Internet Group Management Protocol *See* IGMP.

Internet Group Multicast Protocol *See* IGMP.

Internet Key Exchange *See* IKE.

Internet Message Access Protocol *See* IMAP.

Internet Message Access Protocol, version 4 *See* IMAP4.

Internet Network Information Center *See* InterNIC.

Internet of Things *See* IoT.

Internet Protocol *See* IP.

Internet Protocol Security *See* IPsec.

Internet Protocol version 4 *See* IPv4.

Internet Protocol version 6 *See* IPv6.

Internet Relay Chat *See* IRC.

Internet SCSI *See* iSCSI.

Internet Security Association and Key Management Protocol *See* ISAKMP.

Internet service provider *See* ISP.

Internet telephony The provision of VoIP-based telephone service over the Internet.

internetwork To traverse more than one LAN segment and more than one type of network through a router.

InterNIC (Internet Network Information Center) More recently known as the Network Information Center (NIC), a predecessor to ARIN in the oversight and management of multiple Internet resources, such as IP address allocation in North America.

Intra-Site Automatic Tunnel Addressing Protocol *See* ISATAP.

intrusion detection system *See* IDS.

intrusion prevention system *See* IPS.

inverter A device that converts DC electrical energy to AC electrical energy. Better inverters will also condition the power, which helps protect sensitive electronic equipment from power fluctuations.

IoT (Internet of Things) Considered to be the next generation of the Internet because it provides Internet connectivity to objects that are not used as computers, such as a home thermostat or security lighting.

IP (Internet Protocol) A core protocol in the TCP/IP suite that operates in the Network layer of the OSI model and provides information about how and where data should be delivered. IP is the subprotocol that enables TCP/IP to internetwork.

IP address A unique Network layer address assigned to each node on a TCP/IP network. IPv4 addresses consist of 32 bits divided into four octets, or bytes. IPv6 addresses are composed of eight 16-bit fields, for a total of 128 bits.

ip helper-address A Cisco command that can be configured to create and send helper messages to support several types of UDP traffic, including DHCP, TFTP, DNS, and NetBIOS.

IP phone *See* IP telephone.

IP spoofing An attack in which an outsider obtains internal IP addresses and then uses those addresses to pretend that he has authority to access a private network from the Internet.

IP telephone A telephone used for VoIP on a TCP/IP-based network. IP telephones are designed to transmit and receive only digital signals.

IP telephony *See* VoIP.

ipconfig The utility used to display TCP/IP addressing and domain name information in the Windows client operating systems.

IP-PBX A private switch that accepts and interprets both analog and digital voice signals (although some IP-PBXs do not accept analog lines). It can connect with both traditional PSTN lines and data networks. An IP-PBX transmits and receives IP-based voice signals to and from other network connectivity devices, such as a router or gateway.

IPS (intrusion prevention system) A dedicated device or software running on a workstation, server, or switch, that stands between the attacker and the network or host, and can prevent traffic from reaching the protected network or host.

IPsec (Internet Protocol Security) A Layer 3 protocol that defines encryption, authentication, and key management for TCP/IP transmissions. IPsec is an enhancement to IPv4 and is native to IPv6. IPsec is unique among authentication methods in that it adds security information to the header of all IP packets.

IPv4 (Internet Protocol version 4) The Internet Protocol standard released in the 1980s and still commonly used on modern networks. It specifies 32-bit addresses composed of four octets.

IPv6 (Internet Protocol version 6) A standard for IP addressing that is gradually replacing the current IPv4. Most notably, IPv6 uses a newer, more efficient header in its packets and allows for 128-bit source and destination IP addresses, which are usually written as eight blocks of hexadecimal numbers, such as 2001:0DB8:0B80:0000:0000:00D3:9C5A:00CC.

IR (infrared) A mostly outdated wireless technology that requires an unobstructed line of sight between the transmitter and receiver.

IRC (Internet Relay Chat) A protocol that enables users running special IRC client software to communicate instantly with other participants in a chat room on the Internet.

ISAKMP (Internet Security Association and Key Management Protocol) One of two services in the key management phase of creating a secure IPsec connection. ISAKMP works within the IKE process to establish policies for managing the keys.

ISATAP (Intra-Site Automatic Tunnel Addressing Protocol) A tunneling protocol that enables transmission of IPv6 packets over IPv4 networks. This protocol works only on a single organization's intranet.

iSCSI (Internet SCSI) A Transport layer protocol used by SANs that runs on top of TCP to allow fast transmission over LANs, WANs, and the Internet.

ISDN (Integrated Services Digital Network) An international standard that uses PSTN lines to carry digital signals. It specifies protocols at the Physical, Data Link, and Transport layers of the OSI model. ISDN lines may carry voice and data signals simultaneously.

IS-IS (Intermediate System to Intermediate System) A link-state routing protocol that uses a best-path algorithm similar to OSPF's. IS-IS was originally codified by ISO, which referred to routers as "intermediate systems," thus the protocol's name. Unlike OSPF, IS-IS is designed for use on interior routers only.

ISN (Initial Sequence Number) The sequence number in the first SYN message in a three-way handshake. The ISN appears to be random, but in reality, it is calculated by a specific, clock-based algorithm, which varies by operating system.

ISP (Internet service provider) A company that provides Internet connectivity.

IT (information technology) The study or use of computers and other telecommunications equipment.

iterative query A DNS query that does not demand a resolution, which means the server provides the information only if it already has that information available.

ITS (Intelligent Transportation System) Innovations in transit and traffic management.

ITU (International Telecommunication Union) A United Nations agency that regulates international telecommunications and provides developing countries with technical expertise and equipment to advance their technological bases.

IV (initialization vector) The initial, arbitrary number used to randomize the encryption process. Also called a nonce.

iwconfig A command-line utility for viewing and setting wireless interface parameters on Linux and UNIX workstations.

J

jabber A device that handles electrical signals improperly, usually affecting the rest of the network. A network analyzer will detect a jabber as a device that is always retransmitting, effectively bringing the network to a halt. A jabber usually results from a bad NIC. Occasionally, it can be caused by outside electrical interference.

jamming An attack on a wireless network in which an attacker creates a high volume of illegitimate wireless traffic and overwhelms the wireless network.

jumbo frame A setting on Ethernet network devices that allows the creation and transmission of extra-large frames, as high as 9198 bytes, depending on the type of Ethernet architecture used.

K

Kbps (Kilobits per second) A unit for measuring data transfer rate.

KDC (Key Distribution Center) In Kerberos terminology, the server that issues keys to clients during initial client authentication.

Kerberos A cross-platform authentication protocol that uses key encryption to verify the identity of clients and to securely exchange information after a client logs on to a system. It is an example of a private key encryption service.

Kernel-based Virtual Machine *See* KVM.

key A series of characters that is combined with a block of data during that data's encryption. To decrypt the resulting data, the recipient must also possess the key.

Key Distribution Center *See* KDC.

key management The method whereby two nodes using key encryption agree on common parameters for the keys they will use to encrypt data.

key pair The combination of a public and private key used to encrypt and then decipher data using public key encryption.

keyboard video mouse switch *See* KVM.

Kilobits per second *See* Kbps.

knowledge base A collection of accumulated insights and solutions to the problems encountered on a particular network.

KVM (Kernel-based Virtual Machine) An open source virtualization package designed for use with Linux systems.

KVM (keyboard video mouse) switch A device that connects the equipment in a rack to a single console to provide a central control portal for all devices on the rack.

L

L2F (Layer 2 Forwarding) A VPN protocol similar to PPTP that was developed by Cisco.

L2TP (Layer 2 Tunneling Protocol) A VPN tunneling protocol that encapsulates PPP data for use on VPNs. L2TP is based on Cisco technology and is standardized by the IETF. It is distinguished by its compatibility with different manufacturers' equipment; its ability to connect between clients, routers, and servers alike; and its ability to connect nodes belonging to different Layer 3 networks.

LACP (Link Aggregation Control Protocol) A protocol currently defined by IEEE's 802.1AX standard that dynamically coordinates communications between two hosts.

LAN (local area network) A network of computers and other devices that typically is confined to a relatively small space, such as one building or even one office. Each node on a LAN can communicate directly with others on the same LAN.

LAN Emulation *See* LANE.

LANE (LAN Emulation) A method for transporting token ring or Ethernet frames over ATM networks. LANE encapsulates incoming Ethernet or token ring frames, then converts them into ATM cells for transmission over an ATM network.

last mile *See* local loop.

latency The delay between the transmission of a signal and its receipt.

Layer 2 Forwarding *See* L2F.

Layer 2 switch The least intelligent type of switch because it is nonprogrammable. Layer 2 switches are incapable of transmitting messages outside of the LAN.

Layer 2 Tunneling Protocol *See* L2TP.

Layer 3 switch A switch capable of interpreting Layer 3 data and works much like a router in that it supports the same routing protocols and makes routing decisions.

Layer 4 switch A switch capable of interpreting Layer 4 data, which means it can perform advanced filtering, keep statistics, and provide security functions.

LC (local connector) The most common 1.25-mm ferrule connector, which is used with single-mode, fiber-optic cable.

LDAP (Lightweight Directory Access Protocol) A standard protocol for accessing network directories.

LEC (local exchange carrier) A local telephone company.

LED (light-emitting diode) A cool-burning, long-lasting technology that creates light by the release of photons as electrons move through a semiconductor material.

legal hold A court order to preserve data for the purposes of an investigation. Upon receipt of a legal hold notification, a company is required to activate a defensible policy for the preservation of the data.

light meter *See* OPM.

light-emitting diode *See* LED.

Lightweight Access Point Protocol *See* LWAPP.

Lightweight Directory Access Protocol *See* LDAP.

line driver Essentially a repeater, a device placed on either side of the demarc that boosts the signal across greater distances.

line of sight *See* LOS.

line tester *See* cable performance tester.

link Any local area network (LAN) bounded by routers.

link aggregation The seamless combination of multiple network interfaces or ports to act as one logical interface.

Link Aggregation Control Protocol *See* LACP.

Link layer *See* Data Link layer.

Link layer switch *See* Layer 2 switch.

link local address An IP address that is automatically assigned by an operating system to allow a node to communicate over its local subnet if a routable IP address is not available. ICANN has established the range of 169.254.0.0 through 169.254.254.255 as potential link-local IPv4 addresses. IPv6 link-local addresses begin with the prefix FE80::/10.

link local unicast address An IPv6 address that can be used for communicating with nodes in the same link. These addresses are similar to IPv4's autoconfigured APIPA addresses and begin with the prefix FE80::/10.

link-state routing protocol A type of routing protocol that enables routers to share information beyond neighboring routers, after which each router can independently map the network and determine the best path between itself and a message's destination node.

live streaming video A video feed issued directly from the source to the user as the camera captures it.

LLC (Logical Link Control) A sublayer in the OSI model residing at the upper end of the Data Link layer.

load balancer A device that distributes traffic intelligently among multiple computers.

load balancing The distribution of traffic over multiple components or links to optimize performance and fault tolerance.

local account A Windows access account that works only on that one computer.

local area network *See* LAN.

local connector *See* LC.

local exchange carrier *See* LEC.

local link *See* link.

local loop The part of a phone system that connects a customer site with a telecommunications carrier's switching facility.

logic bomb A malicious program designed to start when certain conditions are met.

Logical Link Control *See* LLC.

logical topology A characteristic of network transmission that reflects the way in which data is transmitted between nodes. A network's logical topology may differ from its physical topology.

Long Term Evolution *See* LTE.

looking glass site A Web site that provides access to a looking glass server, which processes queries generated by ping, traceroute, tracert, or BGP to remotely report network routing information from its network or Web site.

loopback adapter *See* loopback plug.

loopback address An IP address reserved for communicating from a node to itself, used mostly for troubleshooting purposes. The IPv4 loopback address is always cited as 127.0.0.1, and the IPv6 loopback address is ::1.

loopback interface A computer's connection with itself.

loopback plug A connector used for troubleshooting that plugs into a port (for example, a serial, parallel, or RJ-45 port) and crosses over the transmit line with the receive line, allowing outgoing signals to be redirected back into the computer for testing.

LOS (line of sight) A wireless signal or path that travels directly in a straight line from its transmitter to its intended receiver. This type of propagation maximizes distance for the amount of energy used and results in reception of the clearest possible signal.

loss-tolerant Transmissions that can tolerate occasional loss of data without compromising the user experience.

LTE (Long Term Evolution) A 4G cellular network technology that, in its latest version (called LTE-Advanced), achieves downlink data rates of up to 3 Gbps and uplink rates of up to 1.5 Gbps. AT&T and Verizon have adopted LTE for their high-speed wireless data networks.

LTE-Advanced The latest version of LTE, achieving theoretical downlink rates of up to 3 Gbps and uplink rates up to 1.5 Gbps.

lure A decoy system that, when attacked, can provide unique information about hacking behavior.

LWAPP (Lightweight Access Point Protocol) A wireless protocol created by Cisco that makes centralized wireless management possible. LWAPP directs all wireless frames to the wireless controller by adding extra headers to the frames, but it is also considered a lightweight protocol because the headers are relatively small.

M

MAC (media access control or (Network+) medium access control) The process by which devices determine which device may access the network at any given time.

MAC address A 48- or 64-bit network interface identifier that includes two parts: the OUI, assigned by IEEE to the manufacturer, and the extension identifier, a unique number assigned to each NIC by the manufacturer.

MAC address filtering *See* MAC filtering.

MAC address lookup table An online database that correlates manufacturers with their respective OUIs.

MAC filtering A security measure that prevents an AP or a switch from authenticating any device whose MAC address is not listed by the network administrator as an approved device.

macro virus A virus that takes the form of a macro (such as the kind used in a word-processing or spreadsheet program), which may execute when the program is in use.

magic number In the context of calculating subnets, the difference between 256 and the interesting octet (any octet in the subnet whose value is something other than 0 or 255). The magic number can also be calculated by raising 2 to the power of the number of bits in the host portion of the subnet mask using the formula 2^h=magic number. The magic number can be used to calculate the network IDs in all the subnets of the larger network.

Mail Exchanger record *See* MX record.

main cross connect *See* MDF.

main distribution frame *See* MDF.

maintenance window The time period in which a change is expected to be implemented.

malware A program or piece of code designed to intrude upon or harm a system or its resources.

MAN (metropolitan area network) A network of connected LANs within a limited geographical area, such as multiple city government buildings around a city's center.

managed device Any network node monitored by the NMS. The device might contain several objects that can be managed, including components such as a processor, memory, hard disk, or NIC, or intangibles such as performance or utilization.

managed switch A switch that can be configured via a command-line interface and sometimes can be configured in groups. Usually, they are assigned their own IP addresses. VLANs can only be implemented through managed switches.

management console A workstation, such as a laptop, that is connected to a switch's console port and allows for changes to be made to a switch's configurations.

Management Information Base *See* MIB.

man-in-the-middle attack *See* MitM attack.

mantrap An entryway to an access-controlled area that consists of two doors on either end of the entryway. The first door must close before the second door can open. A separate form of identification might be required for each door, and in some cases both sets of doors can be locked to detain a suspect attempting unauthorized access.

master license agreement *See* MLA.

master name server *See* primary name server.

master service agreement *See* MSA.

master terminal unit *See* MTU (master terminal unit).

master zombie An upper-layer host in a botnet.

material safety data sheet *See* MSDS.

maximum transmission unit *See* MTU (maximum transmission unit).

Mbps (Megabits per second) A unit for measuring data transfer rate.

MBps (Megabytes per second) A unit for measuring data transfer rate.

MCU (multipoint control unit) A computer that provides support for multiple H.323 terminals (for example, several workstations participating in a videoconference) and manages communication between them. An MCU is also known as a video bridge.

MD5 (Message Digest algorithm 5) The most recent version of the MD (Message Digest) hash. MD5 uses 128-bit hash values to replace data with values computed according to the hash algorithm. Inherent flaws in the MD5 design have compromised the security of this hash function. It is still in widespread use; however, it's usually only enabled alongside the more secure SHA hash.

MDF (main distribution frame) Also known as the main cross connect, the first point of interconnection between an organization's LAN or WAN and a service provider's facility.

MDI (media dependent interface) A connector used with twisted-pair wiring on an Ethernet network.

MDIX (media dependent interface crossover) A crossover version of MDI connector that connects similar devices.

Mechanical Transfer Registered Jack *See* MT-RJ.

media access control *See* MAC.

Media Access Control address *See* MAC (Media Access Control) address.

media converter A device that enables networks or segments running on different media to interconnect and exchange signals.

media dependent interface *See* MDI.

media dependent interface crossover *See* MDIX.

media gateway A gateway capable of accepting connections from multiple devices (for example, IP telephones, traditional telephones, IP fax machines, traditional fax machines, and so on) and translating analog signals into packetized, digital signals, and vice versa.

Media Gateway Control Protocol *See* MGCP.

media gateway controller *See* MGC.

medianet A network that has been optimized for media transmissions.

medium access control *See* MAC.

MEF (Metro Ethernet Forum) An alliance of over 220 industry organizations worldwide that standardizes Metro Ethernet and Carrier Ethernet technologies.

Megabits per second *See* Mbps.

Megabytes per second *See* MBps.

Megaco A protocol used between media gateway controllers and media gateways. Megaco is poised to replace MGCP on modern converged networks, as it supports a broader range of network technologies, including ATM. Also known as H.248.

memorandum of understanding *See* MOU.

mesh topology WAN A type of WAN in which several sites are directly interconnected. Mesh WANs are highly fault tolerant because they provide multiple routes for data to follow between any two points.

mesh WLAN A wireless network in which multiple APs work as peer devices on the same network, thereby providing more fault-tolerant network access to clients.

Message Digest algorithm 5 *See* MD5.

metasploit A penetration-testing tool that combines known scanning techniques and exploits to explore potentially new types of exploits.

Metro Ethernet A WAN technology that sends Ethernet traffic across MAN connections.

Metro Ethernet Forum *See* MEF.

metropolitan area network *See* MAN.

MFA (multifactor authentication) An authentication process that requires the client to provide two or more pieces of information. The three categories of authentication factors are knowledge (something you know), possession (something you have), and inherence (something you are).

MGC (media gateway controller) A computer that manages multiple media gateways and facilitates the exchange of call control information between these gateways. It also manages and disseminates information about the paths that voice or video signals take between gateways. Also called a call agent (CA).

MGCP (Media Gateway Control Protocol) A protocol used for communication between media gateway controllers and media gateways.

MIB (Management Information Base) A database used in network management that contains a list of objects managed by the NMS and their descriptions as well as data about each object's performance.

Microsoft Challenge Handshake Authentication Protocol *See* MS-CHAP.

Microsoft Challenge Handshake Authentication Protocol, version 2 *See* MS-CHAPv2.

MIMO (multiple input-multiple output) In the context of 802.11n wireless networking, the ability for access points to use multiple antennas in order to issue multiple signals to stations, thereby multiplying the signal's strength and increasing their range and data-carrying capacity. Because the signals follow multipath propagation, they must be phase-adjusted when they reach their destination.

mini GBIC *See* SFP.

Miredo A third-party software that provides Teredo service on UNIX and Linux systems.

MitM (man-in-the-middle) attack An attack that relies on intercepted transmissions. It can take one of several forms, but in all cases a person redirects or captures secure data traffic while in transit.

MLA (master license agreement) A contract that grants a license from a creator, developer, or producer, such as a software producer, to a third party for the purposes of marketing, sublicensing, or distributing the product to consumers as a stand-alone product or as part of another product.

MLA (multilateral agreement) A contract between three or more parties.

MLP (Multilink PPP) A version of PPP that bonds multiple PPP connections to act as a single line and that is a type of link aggregation. MLP was originally designed to bond dial-up connections, such as ISDN, but today it is more commonly used for bonding T-1 and T-3 lines.

MLPPP (Multilink PPP) *See* MLP.

MMF (multimode fiber) A type of fiber-optic cable containing a core that is usually 50 or 62.5 microns in diameter, over which many pulses of light generated by a laser or light-emitting diode (LED) travel at different angles.

mobile switching center *See* MSC.

mobile telecommunications switching office (MTSO) *See* MSC.

modal bandwidth A measure of the highest frequency of signal a multimode fiber-optic cable can support over a specific distance. Modal bandwidth is measured in MHz-km.

modem A device that modulates digital signals from a computer into analog signals at the transmitting end for transmission over telephone lines, and demodulates analog signals into digital signals at the receiving end so a computer can read the received transmission.

modulation A technique for formatting signals in which one property of a simple carrier wave is modified by the addition of a data signal during transmission.

MOU (memorandum of understanding) A document presenting the intentions of two or more parties to enter into a binding agreement, or contract. The MOU is usually not a legally binding document (although there are exceptions), does not grant extensive rights to either party, provides no legal recourse, and is not intended to provide a thorough coverage of the agreement to come.

MPLS (multiprotocol label switching) A type of switching that enables multiple types of Layer 3 protocols to travel over any one of several connection-oriented Layer 2 protocols. One of its benefits is the ability to use packet-switched technologies over traditionally circuit-switched networks. MPLS can also create end-to-end paths that act like circuit-switched connections.

MSA (master service agreement) A contract that defines terms of future contracts.

MSC (mobile switching center) A carrier's facility to which multiple cellular base stations connect. An MSC might be located inside a telephone company's central office or it might stand alone and connect to the central office via fiber-optic cabling or a microwave link. Equipment at an MSC manages mobile clients, monitoring their location and usage patterns, and switches cellular calls. It also assigns each mobile client an IP address.

MS-CHAP (Microsoft Challenge Handshake Authentication Protocol) An authentication protocol provided with Windows operating systems that uses a three-way handshake to verify a client's credentials and encrypts passwords with a challenge text.

MS-CHAPv2 (Microsoft Challenge Handshake Authentication Protocol, version 2) An authentication protocol provided with Windows operating systems that follows the CHAP model, but uses stronger encryption, uses different encryption keys for transmission and reception, and requires mutual authentication between two computers.

MSDS (Material Safety Data Sheet) Instructions provided with dangerous substances that explain how to properly handle these substances and how to safely dispose of them.

MSTP (Multiple Spanning Tree Protocol) As described in IEEE's 802.1s standard, a version of the Spanning Tree Protocol that can detect and correct for network changes much more quickly.

MT-RJ (Mechanical Transfer-Registered Jack) The most common type of connector used with multimode fiber-optic cable.

MTSO (mobile telecommunications switching office) *See* MSC.

MTU (master terminal unit) A supervisory computer or server in an ICS or SCADA system that controls the physical system. Also called the control server or the SCADA server.

MTU (maximum transmission unit) The largest IP packet size in bytes allowable by routers in a path without fragmentation and excluding the frame size.

MTU black hole A problem that occurs when a router receives a message that is too large for the next segment's MTU. The router returns an ICMP error message to the sender, but the error message is not returned correctly. From the sender's perspective, messages are lost for no apparent reason.

multicast address A type of IPv6 address that represents multiple interfaces, often on multiple nodes. An IPv6 multicast address begins with the following hexadecimal field: FF0x, where x is a character that identifies the address's group scope.

multicast distribution A client-server model with one server and many clients.

multicasting A means of transmission in which one device sends data to a specific group of devices (not necessarily the entire network segment) in a point-to-multipoint fashion.

multifactor authentication *See* MFA.

multilateral agreement *See* MLA.

Multilink PPP *See* MLP.

multimeter A simple instrument that can measure multiple characteristics of an electric circuit, including its resistance, voltage, and impedance.

multimode fiber *See* MMF.

multipath The characteristic of wireless signals that follow a number of different paths to their destination (for example, because of reflection, diffraction, and scattering).

multiple input-multiple output *See* MIMO.

Multiple Spanning Tree Protocol *See* MSTP.

multiplexer (mux) A device that separates a medium into multiple channels and issues signals to each of those subchannels.

multiplexing A form of transmission that allows multiple signals to travel simultaneously over one medium.

multipoint control unit *See* MCU.

multiprotocol label switching *See* MPLS.

multi-tenant A feature of cloud computing in which multiple customers share storage locations or services without knowing it.

multiuser MIMO *See* MU-MIMO.

MU-MIMO (multiuser MIMO) In the context of 802.11ac wireless networking, the ability for access points to use multiple antennas in order to issue multiple signals to different stations at the same time, thereby reducing congestion and contributing to faster data transmission. MU-MIMO will become available with Wave 2 802.11ac products.

mutual authentication An authentication scheme in which both computers verify the credentials of each other. For example, the client authenticates the server just as the server authenticates the client.

mux *See* multiplexer.

MX (Mail Exchanger) record A type of DNS data record that identifies a mail server and that is used for email traffic.

N

NAC (network access control) A technology solution that balances the need for network access with the demands of network security by employing a set of rules, called network policies, to determine the level and type of access granted to a device when it joins a network. NAC authenticates and authorizes devices by verifying that the device complies with predefined security benchmarks, such as whether the device has certain system settings, or whether it has specific applications installed.

name resolution The process of discovering the IP address of a host when the FQDN is known.

name server *See* DNS server.

name space lookup *See* nslookup.

namespace The entire collection of Internet IP addresses and their associated names distributed over DNS name servers worldwide.

nanometer *See* nm.

NAS (network attached storage) A specialized storage device or group of storage devices that provides centralized fault-tolerant data storage for a network. NAS depends on traditional network transmission methods such as Ethernet.

NAT (Network Address Translation) A technique in which IP addresses used on a private network are assigned a public IP address by a gateway when accessing a public network.

NAT mode A type of network connection in which a vNIC relies on the host machine to act as a NAT device. In other words, the VM obtains IP addressing information from its host, rather than a server or router on the physical network. To accomplish this, the virtualization software acts as a DHCP server.

National Institute of Standards and Technology *See* NIST.

native VLAN An untagged VLAN on a switch that will automatically receive all untagged frames. Options for native VLANs vary according to the switch manufacturer and model.

nbtstat (NetBIOS over TCP/IP Statistics) A TCP/IP troubleshooting utility that provides information about NetBIOS names and their IP addresses. If you know the NetBIOS name of a workstation, you can use nbtstat to determine its IP address.

NCP (Network Control Protocol) An obsolete ARPANET protocol that provides remote access and data transfer.

near end cross-talk *See* NEXT.

near-far effect A problem on a wireless network in which a client can receive a signal from a high-powered AP near the edge of the AP's range, but the return signal from the client is not reliably strong enough to reach the AP.

near-field communication *See* NFC.

neighbor Two or more nodes on the same link.

neighbor discovery A process whereby routers learn about all of the devices on their networks. On IPv4 networks, this process is managed by ARP with help from ICMP. On IPv6 networks, NDP (Neighbor Discovery Protocol) automatically detects neighboring devices and automatically adjusts when nodes fail or are removed from the network.

Nessus A penetration testing tool from Tenable Security that performs sophisticated vulnerability scans to discover information about hosts, ports, services, and software.

net neutrality A principle whereby Internet users demand uninhibited access to Internet content.

NetBEUI (network basic input/output extended user interface) An extension of NetBIOS that provides standardization for the frame format used during data transport on small networks. Pronounced *net-booey*.

NetBIOS (network basic input/output system) A protocol that runs in the Session and Transport layers of the OSI model and associates NetBIOS names with workstations. NetBIOS allows old applications designed for out-of-date NetBIOS networks to work on TCP/IP networks.

NetBIOS over TCP/IP *See* NetBIOS.

NetBIOS over TCP/IP Statistics *See* nbtstat.

NetBT (NetBIOS over TCP/IP) *See* NetBIOS.

netstat A TCP/IP troubleshooting utility that displays statistics and details about TCP/IP components and connections on a host. It also displays ports, which can signal whether services are using the correct ports.

network A group of computers and other devices (such as printers) that are connected by and can exchange data via some type of transmission media, such as a cable, a wire, or the atmosphere.

network access control *See* NAC.

network adapter *See* NIC.

Network Address Translation *See* NAT.

network attached storage *See* NAS.

network basic input/output extended user interface *See* NetBEUI.

Network Control Protocol *See* NCP.

network controller (1) In the context of virtualization, a central console that manages virtual devices, services, and appliances. For example, the newest, not-yet-released Windows Server will provide a Network Controller role for managing both physical and virtual network infrastructure. (2) Sometimes used to refer to a device's NIC or network adapter.

network diagram A graphical representation of a network's devices and connections.

Network File System or (Network+) Network File Service *See* NFS.

network ID The portion of an IP address common to all nodes on the same network or subnet.

network interface card *See* NIC.

network interface device (NID) *See* NIU.

network interface unit *See* NIU.

network key A key (or character string) required for a wireless station to associate with an access point using WEP.

Network layer The third layer in the OSI model. The Network layer, sometimes called the Internet layer, is responsible for moving messages from one node to another until they reach the destination host.

network management The assessment, monitoring, and maintenance of all aspects of a network.

network management agent A software routine that collects information about a device's operation and provides that data to the NMS.

network management system *See* NMS.

network mapping The process of discovering and identifying the devices on a network.

network monitor A software-based tool that monitors traffic on the network from a server or workstation attached to the network. Network monitors typically can interpret up to Layer 3 of the OSI model.

Network News Transfer Protocol *See* NNTP.

network number *See* network ID.

network operating system *See* NOS.

network policy A rule or set of rules that determines the level and type of access granted to a device when it joins a network.

network prefix *See* network ID.

network segmentation A network arrangement in which some portions of the network have been separated from the rest of the network in order to protect some resources while granting access to other resources.

network service provider *See* NSP.

network services The resources a network makes available to its users, including applications and the data provided by these applications.

network tap A monitoring device installed inline with network traffic. A network tap usually has three ports: two ports to send and receive all traffic and a third port that mirrors the traffic, sending it to a computer running monitoring software in promiscuous mode.

Network Termination 1 *See* NT1.

Network Termination 2 *See* NT2.

Network Time Protocol *See* NTP.

network virus A virus that propagates itself via network protocols, commands, messaging programs, and data links. Although all viruses could theoretically travel across network connections, network viruses are specially designed to attack network vulnerabilities.

network-based firewall A firewall configured and positioned to protect an entire network.

network-based intrusion detection system *See* NIDS.

network-based intrusion prevention system *See* NIPS.

NEXT (near end cross-talk) Cross-talk that occurs between wire pairs near the source of a signal.

Next Generation Firewall *See* NGFW.

NFC (near-field communication) A form of radio communication that transfers data wirelessly over very short distances (usually 10 cm or less).

NFC (Network File System or (Network+) Network File Service) A network service that enables file access between remote computers.

NFC tag A small, inexpensive device that uses NFC technology to store and transmit data to another device, such as a smartphone; the data might include contact information, showtime details, meeting arrangements, or an equipment label, or it could be a command to launch an app, change device settings, or navigate to a Web page. NFC tags require no power source other than the receiving device's power field. Also called a smart tag.

NGFW (Next Generation Firewall) A firewall innovation that includes advanced, built-in features, including Application Control, IDS and/or IPS functionality, user awareness, and context awareness.

NIC (network interface card) The device that enables a workstation to connect to the network and communicate with other computers. NICs are manufactured by several different companies and come with a variety of specifications that are tailored to the workstation's and the network's requirements. NICs are also called network adapters.

NIC teaming A type of link aggregation in which two or more NICs work in tandem to handle traffic to and from a single node.

NID (network interface device) *See* NIU.

NIDS (network-based intrusion detection system) A type of intrusion detection that protects an entire network and is situated at the edge of the network or in a network's protective perimeter, known as the DMZ (demilitarized zone). Here, it can detect many types of suspicious traffic patterns.

NIPS (network-based intrusion prevention system) A type of intrusion prevention that protects an entire network and is situated at the edge of the network or in a network's DMZ.

NIST (National Institute of Standards and Technology) A nonregulatory agency of the U.S. Department of Commerce that sets many technology standards.

NIU (network interface unit) The point at which PSTN-owned lines terminate at a customer's premises. The NIU is usually located at the demarc.

nm (nanometer) A microscopic unit of distance.

Nmap A scanning tool designed to assess large networks quickly and provide comprehensive, customized information about a network and its hosts. Nmap, which runs on virtually any modern operating system, is available for download at no cost at nmap.org.

NMS (network management system) A server or workstation hosting software that serves as a central collection point and management interface for data collected on networked devices.

NNTP (Network News Transport Protocol) A protocol used by newsgroups on a network to share news articles between servers or clients.

node Any computer or other device on a network that can be addressed on the local network.

nonpersistent agent Agent software that remains on a device long enough to verify compliance and complete authentication, and then uninstalls. Devices might be required to periodically reinstall the agent to complete the authentication process again.

NOS (network operating system) The software that runs on a server and enables the server to manage data, users, groups, security, applications, and other networking functions. The most popular network operating systems are UNIX, Linux, and Microsoft Windows Server.

nslookup A TCP/IP utility that allows a technician to query the DNS database from any computer on the network and find the host name of a network node by specifying its IP address, or vice versa. This ability is useful for verifying that a host is configured correctly and for troubleshooting DNS resolution problems.

NSP (network service provider) A carrier that provides long-distance (and often global) connectivity between major data-switching centers across the Internet. AT&T, Verizon, and Sprint are all examples of network service providers in the United States. Customers, including ISPs, can lease dedicated private or public Internet connections from an NSP.

NT1 (Network Termination 1) A device used on ISDN networks that connects the incoming twisted-pair wiring with the customer's ISDN terminal equipment.

NT2 (Network Termination 2) An additional connection device required on PRI to handle the multiple ISDN lines between the customer's network termination connection and the local phone company's wires.

NTP (Network Time Protocol) A simple Application layer protocol in the TCP/IP suite used to synchronize the clocks of computers on a network. NTP depends on UDP for Transport layer services.

O

OC (Optical Carrier) An internationally recognized rating that indicates throughput rates for SONET connections.

OC-1 The base rate of a SONET ring's potential throughput, providing a maximum 51.84 Mbps.

OC-12 SONET throughput service used by ISPs for WAN connections, and by some large enterprises. OC-12 provides a maximum 622.08 Mbps.

OC-3 A popular throughput rate for SONET services, providing a maximum 155.52 Mbps.

Occupational Safety and Health Administration *See* OSHA.

octal number system A system founded on using eight numbers (0 through 7) to encode information.

octet One of the 4 bytes that are separated by periods and together make up an IPv4 address.

offboarding The reverse process of onboarding, involving the removal of programs that gave a device special permissions on the network.

offline UPS *See* standby UPS.

OLT (optical line terminal) A device located at the carrier's endpoint of a passive optical network. An OLT contains multiple optical ports, or PON interfaces, and a splitter that subdivides the capacity of each port into up to 32 logical channels, one per subscriber.

omnidirectional antenna A type of antenna that issues and receives wireless signals with equal strength and clarity in all directions. This type of antenna is used when many different receivers must be able to pick up the signal, or when the receiver's location is highly mobile.

onboard network port A port that is integrated into a computer's motherboard.

onboarding A process of configuring clients for wireless access to a network.

online UPS A power supply that uses the AC power from the wall outlet to continuously charge its battery, while providing power to a network device through its battery.

ONU (optical network unit) In a passive optical network, the device near the customer premises that terminates a carrier's fiber-optic cable connection and distributes signals to multiple endpoints via fiber-optic cable, in the case of FTTP, or via copper.

open circuit A circuit in which necessary connections are missing, such as occurs when a wire breaks.

open loop system One of two methods that an ICS might use to control the physical system. In an open loop system, decisions are made based on predetermined expectations, events, and past history of the system without regard for what's currently happening within the system. Also called an open network.

Open Shortest Path First *See* OSPF.

open source The term that describes software whose code is publicly available for use and modification.

Open Systems Interconnection reference model *See* OSI reference model.

OpenFlow A protocol that serves as a common language in SDN (software defined networking) to bridge the gap between virtualized service applications and a network's physical devices, ensuring that the applications make decisions rather than the devices themselves operating independently from the virtualized services.

OpenSSH An open source version of the SSH suite of protocols.

OpenVPN An open source VPN software that is available for multiple platforms. OpenVPN requires more effort to set up than software embedded in the OS, but it is extremely adaptable and generally more secure than other options.

operating system *See* OS.

OPM (optical power meter) A device that measures the amount of light power transmitted on a fiber-optic line. Also called laser power meter or light meter.

Optical Carrier *See* OC.

optical line terminal *See* OLT.

optical loss The degradation of a light signal on a fiber-optic network as it travels away from its source.

optical network unit *See* ONU.

optical power meter *See* OPM.

optical time domain reflectometer *See* OTDR.

Organizationally Unique Identifier *See* OUI.

OS (operating system) Software that controls a computer.

OSHA (Occupational Safety and Health Administration) The main federal agency charged with regulating safety and health in the workplace.

OSI (Open Systems Interconnection) reference model A model for understanding and developing computer-to-computer communication developed in the 1980s by ISO. It divides networking functions among seven layers: Physical, Data Link, Network, Transport, Session, Presentation, and Application.

OSPF (Open Shortest Path First) An IGP and link-state routing protocol that makes up for some of the limitations of RIP and can coexist with RIP on a network.

OTDR (optical time domain reflectometer) A performance testing device for use with fiber-optic networks. An OTDR works by issuing a light-based signal on a fiber-optic cable and measuring the way in which the signal bounces back (or reflects) to the OTDR. Based on the type of return light signal, an OTDR can accurately measure the length of the fiber; determine the location of faulty splices, breaks, bad or mismatched connectors, or bends; and measure attenuation over the cable.

OUI (Organizationally Unique Identifier) A 24-bit character sequence assigned by IEEE that appears at the beginning of a network interface's physical address and identifies the NIC's manufacturer.

outbound traffic Traffic attempting to exit a LAN.

out-of-band management A switch management option that provides on-site infrastructure access when the network is down or complete remote access in cases of connectivity failures on the network, such as via a cellular signal, in order to interface with a switch.

P

P2P (peer-to-peer) *See* peer-to-peer network model.

PaaS (Platform as a Service) A service model in which various platforms are provided virtually, enabling developers to build and test applications within virtual, online environments tailored to the specific needs of a project.

packet The entire Network layer message, which includes the segment (TCP) or datagram (UDP) from the Transport layer, plus the Network layer header.

packet analyzer *See* protocol analyzer.

Packet Internet Groper *See* ping.

packet loss The loss of packets due to an unknown protocol, unrecognized port, network noise, or some other anomaly. Lost packets never arrive at their destination.

packet shaper *See* traffic shaper.

packet shaping *See* traffic shaping.

packet sniffer *See* network tap.

packet-switched A type of switching in which data is broken into packets before being transported. In packet switching, packets can travel any path on the network to their destination because each packet contains a destination address and sequencing information.

packet-filtering firewall A router (or a computer installed with software that enables it to act as a router) that examines the header of every packet of data that it receives to determine whether that type of packet is authorized to continue to its destination.

paired A term used to describe two Bluetooth devices that are communicating with each other. Pairing is achieved by turning on the Bluetooth antenna for each device (if it is not on by default), making the devices discoverable, and entering a PIN if required.

PAN (personal area network) A network of personal devices, such as a cell phone, laptop, and Bluetooth printer.

PAP (Password Authentication Protocol) A simple authentication protocol that operates over PPP. Using PAP, a client issues its credentials in a request to authenticate, and the server responds with a confirmation or denial of authentication after comparing the credentials with those in its database. PAP is not very secure and is, therefore, rarely used on modern networks.

partial-mesh WAN A version of a mesh topology WAN in which only critical sites are directly interconnected and secondary sites are connected through star or ring topologies. Partial mesh WANs are less expensive to implement than full-mesh WANs.

passive card A proximity card that collects power from a proximity reader's power field in order to transmit data to the reader. The typical range is about 5 to 10 cm.

passive optical network *See* PON.

passive scanning In the context of wireless networking, the process by which a station listens to several channels within a frequency range for a beacon frame issued by an access point.

Password Authentication Protocol *See* PAP.

PAT (Port Address Translation) A form of address translation that assigns a separate TCP port number to each ongoing conversation, or session, between a local host and an Internet host.

patch A correction, improvement, or enhancement to part of a software application, often distributed at no charge by software vendors to fix a bug in their code or to add slightly more functionality.

patch cable A relatively short section (usually between 3 and 25 feet) of cabling with connectors on both ends.

patch panel A wall- or rack-mounted panel where cables converge in one location.

pathping A Windows utility that combines the functionality of the tracert and ping utilities to provide deeper information about network issues along a route; similar to UNIX's mtr command.

payload Data that is passed between applications or utility programs and the operating system, and includes control information.

Payment Card Industry Data Security Standard *See* PCI DSS.

PBX (private branch exchange) A telephone switch used to connect and manage an organization's voice calls.

PC (personal computer) A freestanding computer designed for user productivity.

PC (Physical Contact) An early generation of ferrule that has a curved tip, which allows the two fibers to meet more closely than a flat surface would.

PCI DSS (Payment Card Industry Data Security Standard) A set of security guidelines created by the PCI Security Standards Council to protect credit card data and transactions, such as segmenting the parts of a network that have access to sensitive financial information from parts that are more vulnerable to compromise.

PCP (Priority Code Point) A 3-bit field in an Ethernet frame's header that is employed in CoS (class of service) configurations on VLANs. CoS works by setting these bits to one of eight levels ranging from 0 to 7, which indicates to the switch the level of priority the message should be given if the port is receiving more traffic than it can forward at any one time.

PD (powered device) On a network using Power over Ethernet, a node that receives power from power sourcing equipment.

PDoS (permanent DoS) attack An attack on a device that attempts to alter the device's management interface to the point where the device is irreparable.

PDU (protocol data unit) A unit of data at any layer of the OSI model.

peer-to-peer network model A network in which every computer can communicate directly with every other computer. By default, no computer on a peer-to-peer network has more authority than another. However, each computer can be configured to share only some of its resources and keep other resources inaccessible to other nodes on the network.

penetration testing A process of scanning a network for vulnerabilities and investigating potential security flaws.

performance management The ongoing assessment of how well network links, devices, and components keep up with the demands made on them.

permanent DoS attack *See* PDoS attack.

permanent virtual circuit *See* PVC.

persistent agent Agent software that is permanently installed on a device and that can provide robust security measures such as remote wipe, virus scanning, and mass messaging.

personal area network *See* PAN.

personal computer *See* PC.

personal protective equipment *See* PPE.

PGP (Pretty Good Privacy) A key-based encryption system for email that uses a two-step verification process.

phase A point or stage in a wave's progress over time.

phishing A practice in which a person attempts to glean access or authentication information by posing as someone who needs that information.

physical address *See* MAC (media access control) address.

physical attack *See* PDoS attack.

Physical Contact *See* PC.

Physical layer The lowest, or first, layer of the OSI model. The Physical layer is responsible only for sending bits via a wired or wireless transmission.

physical topology The physical layout of the media, nodes, and devices on a network. A physical topology does not specify device types, connectivity methods, or addressing schemes. Physical topologies are categorized into three fundamental shapes: bus, ring, and star. These shapes can be mixed to create hybrid topologies.

ping (Packet Internet Groper) A TCP/IP troubleshooting utility that can verify that TCP/IP is installed, bound to the NIC, configured correctly, and communicating with the network. Ping uses ICMP to send echo request and echo reply messages that determine the validity of an IP address.

ping -6 The version of the ping utility used on Windows computers that run IPv6.

ping of death An attack in which a buffer overflow condition is created by sending an ICMP packet that exceeds the maximum 65,535 bytes, often resulting in a system crash. Today's systems, however, are designed to resist these attacks.

ping6 The version of the ping utility used on Linux computers that run IPv6.

pinout The pin numbers and color-coded wire assignments determined by the TIA/EIA standard used when terminating a cable or installing a jack. The two standards defined for Ethernet, for example, are TIA/EIA 568A and TIA/EIA 568B.

PKI (Public-key Infrastructure) The use of certificate authorities to associate public keys with certain users.

plain old telephone service (POTS) *See* PSTN.

platform The operating system, the runtime libraries or modules the OS provides to applications, and the hardware on which the OS runs.

Platform as a Service *See* PaaS.

PLC (programmable logic controller) A very small dedicated computer in an industrial system that is capable of converting analog data to digital data. The PLC works in real time, can control machinery, and is a critical component of the ICS (industrial control system).

plenum The area above the ceiling tile or below the subfloor in a building.

PoE (Power over Ethernet) A method of delivering current, usually 15.4 watts, to devices using Ethernet connection cables.

PoE+ A method of delivering more current (25.5 watts) than PoE does to devices using Ethernet connection cables.

Point to Point *See* PTP.

Pointer record *See* PTR record.

point-to-multipoint model A communications arrangement in which one transmitter issues signals to multiple receivers. The receivers may be undefined, as in a broadcast transmission, or defined, as in a nonbroadcast transmission.

point-to-point model A data transmission that involves one transmitter and one receiver.

Point-to-Point Protocol *See* PPP.

Point-to-Point Tunneling Protocol *See* PPTP.

polling A network management application's regular collection of data from managed devices.

polymorphic virus A type of virus that changes its characteristics (such as the arrangement of its bytes, size, and internal instructions) every time it is transferred to a new system, making it harder to identify.

polyvinyl chloride *See* PVC.

PON (passive optical network) A network in which a carrier uses fiber-optic cabling to connect with multiple endpoints— for example, many businesses on a city block. The word *passive* applies because in a PON no repeaters or other connectivity devices intervene between a carrier and its customer.

POP (Post Office Protocol) An Application layer protocol used to retrieve messages from a mail server. When a client retrieves mail via POP, messages previously stored on the mail server are downloaded to the client's workstation, and then deleted from the mail server.

POP3 (Post Office Protocol, version 3) The most commonly used form of the Post Office Protocol.

Port Address Translation *See* PAT.

port authentication A technique in which a client's identity is verified by an authentication server before a port, whether physical or logical, is opened for the client's Layer 3 traffic. *See also* 802.1X.

port bonding *See* link aggregation.

port forwarding The process of redirecting traffic from its normally assigned port to a different port, either on the client or server. In the case of using SSH, port forwarding can send data exchanges that are normally insecure through encrypted tunnels.

port mirroring A monitoring technique in which one port on a switch is configured to send a copy of all its traffic to a second port.

port number The address on a host where an application makes itself available to incoming data.

port scanner Software that searches a server, switch, router, or other device for open ports, which can be vulnerable to attack.

port-based authentication *See* port authentication.

Post Office Protocol *See* POP.

Post Office Protocol, version 3 *See* POP3.

posture assessment An assessment of an organization's security vulnerabilities. Posture assessments should be performed at least annually and preferably quarterly—or sooner if the network has undergone significant changes. For each risk found, it should rate the severity of a potential breach, as well as its likelihood of happening.

POTS (plain old telephone service) *See* PSTN.

power converter A device that changes the form of electrical energy in some way. Four common types are inverter, rectifier, transformer, and voltage regulator.

Power over Ethernet *See* PoE.

power redundancy The provision of a backup power source, such as a generator.

power sourcing equipment *See* PSE.

powered device *See* PD.

PPE (personal protective equipment) Wearable equipment such as goggles that might be required in the workplace to increase safety of workers.

PPP (Point-to-Point Protocol) A Layer 2 communications protocol that enables a workstation to connect to a server using a serial connection such as dial-up or DSL. PPP can support multiple Network layer protocols, can encrypt transmissions (although PPP encryption is considered weak by today's standards), and can use an authentication protocol such as PAP or CHAP to authenticate a client to the remote system.

PPP over Ethernet *See* PPPoE.

PPPoE (PPP over Ethernet) PPP running over an Ethernet network.

PPTP (Point-to-Point Tunneling Protocol) A Layer 2 protocol developed by Microsoft that encapsulates PPP data frames for transmission over VPN connections. PPTP supports the encryption, authentication, and access services provided by RRAS. It is simple, but less secure than more modern tunneling protocols.

preamble The field in an Ethernet frame that signals to the receiving node that data is incoming and indicates when the data flow is about to begin.

prefix mask The usually optional slash notation at the end of an IPv6 address that indicates the number of bits used by the network prefix.

presence The indication of a user's availability through states set by the user (such as *online*, *away*, *busy*, or *invisible*) or by predetermined conditions (such as the time of day or a user's location).

Presentation layer The sixth layer of the OSI model. Protocols in the Presentation layer are responsible for reformatting, compressing, and/or encrypting data in a way that the application on the receiving end can read.

pre-shared key *See* PSK.

Pretty Good Privacy *See* PGP.

prefix mask Slash notation used on an IPv6 address to indicate the number of bits used for network information.

PRI (Primary Rate Interface) A type of ISDN that uses 23 bearer channels and one 64-Kbps data channel, represented by the notation 23B+D.

primary name server An authoritative name server that is queried first on a network when resolution of a name that is not already cached is requested. Also called master name servers.

Primary Rate Interface *See* PRI.

principal In Kerberos terminology, a user or client.

print services The network service that allows printers to be shared by several users on a network.

Priority Code Point *See* PCP.

private branch exchange *See* PBX.

private cloud A deployment model in which shared and flexible data storage, applications, or services are managed on and delivered via an organization's own network, or established virtually for a single organization's private use.

private IP address IP addresses that can be used on a private network but not on the Internet. IEEE recommends the following IP address ranges for private use: 10.0.0.0 through 10.255.255.255; 172.16.0.0 through 172.31.255.255; and 192.168.0.0 through 192.168.255.255.

private key encryption A type of key encryption in which the sender and receiver use a key to which only they have access. Also known as symmetric encryption.

private port A port assigned by a network administrator that is different from the well-known port number normally used for that service.

probe (1) A repeated trial message transmitted by the tracert and traceroute utilities to trigger routers along a route to return specific information about the route. (2) In 802.11 wireless networking, a type of frame issued by a station during active scanning to find nearby access points. (3) *See* tone locator.

programmable logic controller *See* PLC.

promiscuous mode The feature of a network adapter that allows it to pick up all frames that pass over the network—not just those destined for the node served by the card.

protocol A standard method or format for communication between network devices. For example, some protocols ensure that data is transferred in sequence and without error from one node on the network to another. Other protocols ensure that data belonging to a Web page is formatted to appear correctly in a Web browser window. Still others encode passwords and keep data transmissions secure.

protocol analyzer A software package or hardware-based tool that can capture and analyze data on a network. Protocol analyzers are more sophisticated than network monitoring tools, as they can typically interpret data up to Layer 7 of the OSI model.

protocol data unit *See* PDU.

prox card *See* proximity card.

proximity card A smart card that does not require direct contact with a proximity reader in order to be detected and read.

proxy server (1) A network host that runs a proxy service. Proxy servers are also called gateways. (2) On a SIP network, a server that accepts requests for location information from user agents, then queries the nearest registrar server on behalf of those user agents. If the recipient user agent is in the SIP proxy server's domain, then that server will also act as a go-between for calls established and terminated between the requesting user agent and the recipient user agent.

proxy service A software application on a network host that acts as an intermediary between the external and internal

networks, screening all incoming and outgoing traffic and providing one address to the outside world, instead of revealing the addresses of internal LAN devices.

PSE (power sourcing equipment) On a network using Power over Ethernet, the device that supplies power to end nodes.

PSK (pre-shared key) An authentication method for WPA or WPA2 that provides an alternative to 802.1X.

PSTN (Public Switched Telephone Network) The network of lines and carrier equipment that provides telephone service to most homes and businesses. Now, except for the local loop, nearly all of the PSTN uses digital transmission. Its traffic is carried by fiber-optic or copper twisted-pair cable, microwave, and satellite connections.

PTP (Point to Point) Might be used to refer to PPTP, but more often refers to point-to-point network topology (such as point-to-point remote access) or to Precision Time Protocol (a protocol that syncs clocks on a network).

PTR (Pointer) record A type of DNS data record that is used for reverse lookups, to provide a host name when the IP address is known.

public cloud A deployment model in which shared and flexible data storage, applications, or services are managed centrally by service providers and delivered over public transmission lines, such as the Internet. Rackspace and Amazon (with its EC2 offering) are leading public cloud service providers.

public IP address An IP address that is valid for use on public networks, such as the Internet. An organization assigns its hosts public addresses from the range of addresses assigned to it by Internet numbering authorities.

public key encryption A form of key encryption in which data is encrypted using two keys: One is a key known only to a user (that is, a private key), and the other is a key associated with the user and that can be obtained from a public source, such as a public key server. Public key encryption is also known as asymmetric encryption.

public key server A publicly available host (such as an Internet host) that provides free access to a list of users' public keys (for use in public key encryption).

Public Switched Telephone Network *See* PSTN.

Public-key Infrastructure *See* PKI.

punch-down tool A pointed tool used to insert twisted-pair wire into receptors in a punch-down block to complete a circuit.

PVC (permanent virtual circuit) A point-to-point connection over which data may follow any number of different paths, as opposed to a dedicated line that follows a predefined path. PVCs are established before data needs to be transmitted and are maintained after the transmission is complete. Frame relay technology uses PVCs.

PVC (polyvinyl chloride) A flame-resistant material used to manufacture cable jackets because it produces less smoke than regular cable coating materials.

Q

QoS (quality of service) The result of specifications for guaranteeing data delivery within a certain period of time after their transmission.

quality of service See QoS.

quarantine network A network segment that is situated separately from sensitive network resources and might limit the amount of time a device can remain connected to the network. A quarantine network provides a relatively safe holding place for devices that do not meet compliance requirements or that are indicated to have been compromised.

R

rack An open or enclosed cabinet that holds network devices such as switches, routers, servers, and/or patch panels.

rack system Mounting hardware for network equipment that helps optimize the use of square footage in equipment rooms and helps ensure adequate spacing, access, and ventilation for those devices.

rack unit See U (rack unit).

radiation pattern The relative strength over a three-dimensional area of all the electromagnetic energy an antenna sends or receives.

radio frequency emanation See RF emanation.

radio frequency interference See RFI.

RADIUS (Remote Authentication Dial-In User Service) A popular protocol for providing centralized AAA (authentication, authorization, and accounting) for multiple users. RADIUS runs over UDP and can use one of several authentication protocols.

RADIUS server A server that offers centralized authentication services to a network's access server, VPN server, or wireless access point via the RADIUS protocol.

range The geographical area in which signals issued from an antenna or wireless system can be consistently and accurately received.

range extender A device that increases a wireless signal's range by repeating the signal from a different broadcast point.

Rapid Spanning Tree Protocol See RSTP.

RARP (Reverse Address Resolution Protocol) An obsolete protocol used by network clients to request an IP address.

RAS (remote access server) A server that runs communications services that enable remote users to log on to a network and grant privileges to the network's resources. Also known as an access server.

RAS (Remote Access Service) The dial-up networking software provided with Microsoft Windows 95, 98, NT, and 2000 client operating systems. Beginning with Windows 2000, RAS was replaced by RRAS (Routing and Remote Access Service).

RDP (Remote Desktop Protocol) An Application layer protocol that uses TCP/IP to transmit graphics and text quickly over a remote client-host connection. RDP also carries session, licensing, and encryption information.

Real Time Streaming Protocol See RTSP.

real transfer time See RTT.

real-time services Time-sensitive services provided over a network, such as telephone conversations and videoconferences, where data is transferred as it is created.

Real-time Transport Control Protocol See RTCP.

Real-time Transport Protocol See RTP.

reassociation In the context of wireless networking, the process by which a station establishes a connection with (or associates with) a different access point.

Recommended Standard 232 See RS-232.

rectifier A device that converts AC electrical energy to DC electrical energy. The power supply in a laptop or desktop computer contains a rectifier to convert AC to DC.

recursive query A DNS query that demands a resolution or the response that the information can't be found.

redirect server On a SIP network, a server that accepts and responds to requests from user agents and SIP proxy servers for location information on recipients that belong to external domains.

redundancy The use of more than one identical component, device, or connection for storing, processing, or transporting data. Redundancy is intended to eliminate single points of failure and is the most common method of achieving fault tolerance.

reflection In the context of wireless signaling, the phenomenon that occurs when an electromagnetic wave encounters an obstacle and bounces back toward its source. A wireless signal will bounce off objects whose dimensions are large compared with the signal's average wavelength.

reflective attack See DRDoS attack.

reflector An uninfected computer used in a DDoS attack where the computer is tricked into responding to a bogus request for a response, prompting the computer to send a response to the attacker's target.

regeneration The process of retransmitting a digital signal. Regeneration, unlike amplification, repeats the pure signal, with none of the noise it has accumulated.

registered jack 11 *See* RJ-11.

registered jack 45 *See* RJ-45.

registered port The TCP/IP ports in the range of 1024 to 49,151. These ports can be used by network users and processes that are not considered standard processes. Default assignments of these ports must be registered with IANA.

registrar server On a SIP network, a server that maintains a database containing information about the locations (network addresses) of each user agent in its domain. When a user agent joins a SIP network, it transmits its location information to the SIP registrar server.

remote access A method for connecting and logging on to a server, LAN, or WAN from a workstation that is in a different geographical location.

remote access server *See* RAS (remote access server).

Remote Access Service *See* RAS (Remote Access Service).

remote-access VPN *See* client-to-site VPN.

remote application An application that is installed and executed on a server, and is presented to a user working at a client computer.

Remote Authentication Dial-In User Service *See* RADIUS.

Remote Desktop A feature of Windows operating systems that allows a computer to act as a remote host and be controlled from a client also running Windows.

Remote Desktop Protocol *See* RDP.

Remote Desktop Services A feature of Windows Server 2008 and later editions of Windows Server that allows technicians to manage remote applications.

remote shell *See* RSH.

remote terminal unit *See* RTU.

remote wipe A security procedure that clears a device of all important information, permissions, and programs without having physical access to the device.

repeater A device used to regenerate a digital signal in its original form. Repeaters operate at the Physical layer of the OSI model.

request for proposal *See* RFP.

Request to Send/Clear to Send *See* RTS/CTS.

reservation A static IP address assigned by DHCP.

resolver A DNS client that requests information from DNS name servers.

resource record The element of a DNS database stored on a name server that contains information about TCP/IP host names and their addresses.

Reverse Address Resolution Protocol *See* RARP.

reverse DNS lookup A function that finds the host name of a device whose IP address is known.

reverse proxy A host that provides services to Internet clients from servers on its own network. The reverse proxy provides identity protection for the server rather than the client. Reverse proxies are particularly useful when multiple Web servers are accessed through the same public IP address.

RF (radio frequency) emanation A condition created by the leaking of radio or electrical signals from computer equipment. These signals can carry a surprising amount of information, which can be intercepted by a third party and used for his own purposes.

RFI (radio frequency interference) A kind of electromagnetic interference that can be generated by broadcast signals from radio or TV antennas.

RFP (request for proposal) A document requesting that vendors submit a proposal for a product or service that a company wants to purchase.

RG-6 (radio guide 6) A type of coaxial cable with an impedance of 75 ohms and an 18 AWG core conductor. RG-6 is used for television, satellite, and broadband cable connections.

RG-8 A type of coaxial cable characterized by a 50-ohm impedance and a 10 AWG core conductor. RG-8 provided the medium for the first Ethernet networks and was called Thicknet.

RG-58 A type of coaxial cable characterized by a 50-ohm impedance and a 24 AWG core conductor. RG-58 was a popular medium for Ethernet LANs in the 1980s and was called Thinnet, which is more flexible and easier to handle and install than Thicknet.

RG-59 A type of coaxial cable characterized by a 75-ohm impedance and a 20 or 22 AWG core conductor, usually made of braided copper. Less expensive but suffering greater attenuation than the more common RG-6 coax, RG-59 is used for relatively short connections.

ring topology A network layout in which each node is connected to the two nearest nodes so that the entire network forms a circle. Data is transmitted in one direction around the ring. Each workstation accepts and responds to packets addressed to it, then forwards the other packets to the next workstation in the ring.

ring topology WAN A type of WAN in which each site is connected to two other sites so that the entire WAN forms a ring pattern.

RIP (Routing Information Protocol or (Network+) Routing Internet Protocol) The oldest routing protocol that is still widely used, RIP is a distance-vector protocol that uses hop count as its routing metric and allows up to only 15 hops. Compared with other, more modern, routing protocols, RIP is slower and less secure.

RIPv2 (Routing Information Protocol version 2) An updated version of the original RIP routing protocol that generates less broadcast traffic and functions more securely than its predecessor. However, RIPv2's packet forwarding is still limited to a maximum 15 hops.

Rivest, Shamir, Adleman *See* RSA.

RJ-11 (registered jack 11) The standard connector used with unshielded twisted-pair cabling (usually Cat 3) to connect analog telephones.

RJ-45 (registered jack 45) The standard connector used with shielded twisted-pair and unshielded twisted-pair cabling.

RJ-48 A standard for terminating wires in an 8-pin connector. It's similar to RJ-45, but pins 1 and 2 serve as the receive pair, and pins 4 and 5 serve as the transmit pair. RJ-48 is the preferred connector type for T-1 connections that rely on twisted-pair wiring.

RJ-48C The standard connector used with T-1 or ISDN lines. The number *48* refers to the pinout standard, and the letter indicates the wiring or mounting method used; in this case, the C indicates this jack is flush with the surface.

roaming In wireless networking, the process that describes a station moving between BSSs without losing connectivity.

rogue access point An unauthorized access point in the same vicinity as a legitimate network. The rogue access point might be illegitimately connected to the authorized network, or it might access the Internet through its own WAN connection. Similarly, rogue access points are sometimes set up by naïve users who don't realize the inherent risk, or might be created by hackers with ill intent.

rollback The process of reverting to a previous version of a software application after attempting to patch or upgrade it.

rollover cable A twisted-pair patch cable in which all of the wires are reversed on one end of the cable as compared with the other end without regard to how they are paired. A rollover cable is used to connect a computer to the console port of a router. Also called Yost cable or Cisco console cable.

root bridge The single bridge on a network selected by STP to provide the basis for all subsequent path calculations. Also called master bridge.

root port The port on a bridge that is closest to the root bridge. On any bridge, the root port is the only port that can forward frames toward the root bridge.

root server A DNS server maintained by ICANN and IANA that is an authority on how to contact the top-level domains, such as those ending with .com, .edu, .net, .us, and so on. ICANN oversees the operation of 13 clusters of root servers around the world.

round-robin DNS A method of increasing name resolution availability by pointing a host name to a list of multiple IP addresses in a DNS zone file. After pointing a client to one IP address in the list, DNS will point the next client that requests resolution for the same domain name to the next IP address in the list, and so on.

round-trip time *See* RTT.

route aggregation A supernet configuration implemented for the purpose of reducing the number of routing table entries by combining several entries, one for each network, into one entry that represents multiple networks.

route command A command-line tool that shows a host's routing table.

route prefix The prefix in an IPv6 address that identifies a route. Because route prefixes vary in length, slash notation is used to define them. For example, the route prefix indicated by 2608:FE10::/32 includes all subnets whose prefixes begin with 2608:FE10 and, consequently, all interfaces whose IP addresses begin with 2608:FE10.

route redistribution A complex, manual process in which route information from one routing protocol is adapted to another routing protocol's specifications.

route summarization *See* route aggregation.

router A Layer 3 device that uses logical addressing information to direct data between two or more networks and can help find the best path for traffic to get from one network to another.

Routing and Remote Access Service *See* RRAS.

routing cost A value assigned to a particular route as judged by the network administrator; the more desirable the path, the lower its cost.

Routing Information Protocol *See* RIP.

Routing Information Protocol version 2 *See* RIPv2.

routing loop A problem that happens when a message gets stuck in a loop between a limited number of routers without ever reaching its destination.

routing metric Properties of a route used by routing protocols to determine the best path to a destination when various paths are available. Routing metrics may be calculated using any of several variables, including hop count, bandwidth, delay, MTU, cost, and reliability.

routing prefix In an IPv6 address, the first four blocks (or 64 bits) that identify the network and serve as the network ID. Also called network prefix.

routing protocol The means by which routers communicate with each other about network status. Routing protocols determine the best path for data to take between networks.

routing table A database stored in a router's memory that maintains information about the location of hosts and best paths for forwarding packets to them.

RRAS (Routing and Remote Access Service) The software included with Windows operating systems that enables a server to act as a router, firewall, and remote access server. Using RRAS, a server can provide network access to multiple remote clients. Beginning with Windows Server 2008 R2 and Windows 7 (Enterprise or Ultimate), RRAS now works in conjunction with DirectAccess to enable always-on remote connections while also allowing VPN connections to the network.

RS-232 (Recommended Standard 232) A Physical layer standard for serial communications, as defined by TIA/EIA.

RSA (Rivest, Shamir, Adleman) An encryption algorithm.

RSH (remote shell) Software that enables a user to run shell commands from another user's account. RSH has mostly been replaced by SSH.

RSTP (Rapid Spanning Tree Protocol) As described in IEEE's 802.1w standard, a version of the Spanning Tree Protocol that can detect and correct for network changes much more quickly.

RTCP (Real-time Transport Control Protocol) A companion protocol to RTP that provides feedback on the quality of a call or videoconference to its participants.

RTP (Real-time Transport Protocol) An Application layer protocol used with voice and video transmission. RTP operates on top of UDP and provides information about packet sequence to help receiving nodes detect delay and packet loss. It also assigns packets a time stamp that corresponds to when the data in the packet was sampled from the voice or video stream. This time stamp helps the receiving node synchronize incoming data.

RTP Control Protocol *See* RTCP.

RTS/CTS (Request to Send/Clear to Send) An exchange in which a source node requests the exclusive right to communicate with an access point and the access point confirms that it has granted that request.

RTSP (Real Time Streaming Protocol) A protocol used to create and manage media sessions.

RTT (round-trip time or real transfer time) The length of time it takes for a packet to go from sender to receiver, then back from receiver to sender. RTT is usually measured in milliseconds.

RTU (remote terminal unit) A device installed at a key location in an industrial system, which can sense attributes of the physical system and convert this analog data to digital data.

RU (rack unit) *See* U (rack unit).

runt An erroneously shortened packet.

S

S/N (signal-to-noise ratio) *See* SNR.

SA (security association) The relationship created between two devices for the purposes of establishing a secure connection. SA is integral to the functioning of IPsec.

SaaS (Software as a Service) A service model in which applications are provided through an online user interface and are compatible with a multitude of devices and operating systems.

sag *See* brownout.

SAID (security association identifier) Part of a VLAN configuration that indicates to other connectivity devices which VLAN a transmission belongs to. By default, Cisco switches assign a VLAN the SAID of 100,000 plus the VLAN number (such as 100,000+12).

Samba An open source software package that provides complete Windows-style file- and printer-sharing capabilities.

SAN (storage area network) A distinct network of storage devices that communicate directly with each other and with other networks. A SAN uses a proprietary network transmission method such as Fibre Channel rather than a traditional network transmission method such as Ethernet.

SC (subscriber connector or standard connector) A connector with a 2.5-mm ferrule that is used with single-mode, fiber-optic cable.

SCADA (supervisory control and data acquisition) A network that includes software, servers, and communication channels. SCADA is responsible for acquiring real-time data from a physical system and managing the physical system or presenting the data to humans, who monitor and manage the system.

scalable The property of a network that allows you to add nodes or increase its size easily.

scanning The process by which a wireless station finds an access point. *See also* active scanning and passive scanning.

scattering The diffusion, or the reflection in multiple directions, of a wireless signal that results from hitting an object that has small dimensions compared with the signal's wavelength. Scattering is also related to the roughness of the surface a wireless signal encounters. The rougher the surface, the more likely a signal is to scatter when it hits that surface.

scope ID *See* zone ID.

SCP (Secure Copy Protocol) A method for copying files securely between hosts. SCP is part of the OpenSSH package, which comes with modern UNIX and Linux operating systems. Third-party SCP applications are available for Windows-based computers.

SDH (Synchronous Digital Hierarchy) The international equivalent of SONET.

SDLC (software development life cycle) The time it takes to plan, create, test, and deploy a program or application.

SDN (software defined networking) The virtualization of network services in which a network controller manages these services instead of the services being directly managed by the hardware devices involved.

SDP (Session Description Protocol) A standard for creating multimedia sessions.

SDSL (symmetric digital subscriber line) A variation of DSL that provides equal throughput both upstream and downstream between the customer and the carrier.

secondary name server A name server that can take the place of a primary name server to resolve names and addresses on a network. Secondary name servers poll primary name servers to ensure that their zone information is identical. Also called slave name servers.

secure channel A channel secured by IPsec where data is encrypted and then transmitted. Either AH (authentication header) encryption or ESP (Encapsulating Security Payload) encryption may be used.

Secure Copy Protocol *See* SCP.

Secure File Transfer Protocol *See* SFTP.

Secure Hash Algorithm *See* SHA.

Secure Shell *See* SSH.

Secure Socket Tunneling Protocol *See* SSTP.

Secure Sockets Layer *See* SSL.

security association *See* SA.

security association identifier *See* SAID.

security audit An assessment of an organization's security vulnerabilities performed by an accredited network security firm.

Security Information and Event Management *See* SIEM.

security policy (configuration) A configuration programmed into an operating system or firewall that defines the conditions that must be met in order for a device or transmission to be given access to a network or computing resource.

security policy (document) A document or plan that identifies an organization's security goals, risks, levels of authority, designated security coordinator and team members, responsibilities for each team member, and responsibilities for each employee. In addition, it specifies how to address security breaches.

security token A device or piece of software used for authentication that stores or generates information, such as a series of numbers or letters, known only to its authorized user.

segment (1) A unit of data that results from subdividing a larger protocol data unit. (2) A part of a network. Usually, a segment is composed of a group of nodes that share the same communications channel for all their traffic.

self-healing A characteristic of dual-ring topologies that allows them to automatically reroute traffic along the backup ring if the primary ring becomes severed.

sequence number A chronological number that TCP attaches to each segment so the destination host can, if necessary, reorder segments as they arrive.

Serial Line Internet Protocol *See* SLIP.

server rail Slides mounted directly on a rack to make equipment access easier for technicians to service the equipment without completely removing devices from the rack.

server_hello In the context of SSL encryption, a message issued from the server to the client that confirms the information the server received in the client_hello message. It also agrees to certain terms of encryption based on the options the client supplied. Depending on the Web server's preferred encryption method, the server may choose to issue the browser a public key or a digital certificate at this time.

Server Message Block *See* SMB.

service-level agreement *See* SLA.

service pack A major group of patches to a Windows or Microsoft application.

service set identifier *See* SSID.

Session Description Protocol *See* SDP.

session hijacking attack An attack in which a session key is intercepted and stolen so that an attacker can take control of a session. One type of session hijacking attack that relies on intercepted transmissions is a man-in-the-middle (MitM) attack.

Session Initiation Protocol *See* SIP.

session key In the context of Kerberos authentication, a key issued to both the client and the server by the authentication service that uniquely identifies their session.

Session layer The fifth layer in the OSI model. The Session layer describes how data between applications is synced and recovered if messages don't arrive intact at the receiving application.

SFP (small form-factor pluggable) transceiver A standard hot-swappable network interface used to link a connectivity device's backplane with fiber-optic or copper cabling. SFPs are known as mini GBICs because they perform a similar function as GBICs, but have a smaller profile. Current SFP standards enable them to send and receive data at up to 10 Gbps.

SFP GBIC *See* SFP.

SFP+ A type of SFP that can send and receive data at rates of up to 10 Gbps.

SFTP (Secure File Transfer Protocol) A protocol available with the proprietary version of SSH that copies files between hosts securely. Like FTP, SFTP first establishes a connection with a host and then allows a remote user to browse directories, list files, and copy files. Unlike FTP, SFTP encrypts data before transmitting it.

SGCP (Simple Gateway Control Protocol) A predecessor to MGCP that was used in VoIP systems.

SHA (Secure Hash Algorithm) A hash algorithm designed by the NSA to eliminate the inherent weaknesses of the older MD5 hash, especially via its increased resistance to collisions, although the added security requires more time to perform the hashing process. This original version of SHA, later dubbed SHA-0, used a 160-bit hash function.

SHA-1 The first, slightly modified revision of SHA.

SHA-2 The second revision of SHA, also designed by the NSA, which supports a variety of hash sizes, the most popular of which are SHA-256 and SHA-512.

SHA-256 An implementation of SHA-2 using a 256-bit hash.

SHA-3 The most recent iteration of SHA. It was developed by private designers for a public competition in 2012. SHA-3 is very different in design from SHA-2, even though it uses the same 256- and 512-bit hash lengths.

SHA-512 An implementation of SHA-2 using a 512-bit hash.

sheath The outer cover, or jacket, of a cable.

shell prompt Another term for the UNIX command interpreter.

shield *See* braiding.

shielded twisted pair *See* STP.

short circuit An unwanted connection, such as when exposed wires touch each other.

Short Message Service *See* SMS.

Shortest Path Bridging *See* SPB.

SIEM (Security Information and Event Management) Software that can be configured to evaluate data logs from IDS, IPS, firewalls, and proxy servers in order to detect significant events that require the attention of IT staff according to predefined rules.

signal level An ANSI standard for T-carrier technology that refers to its Physical layer electrical signaling characteristics. DS0 is the equivalent of one data or voice channel. All other signal levels are multiples of DS0.

signaling The exchange of information between the components of a network or system for the purposes of establishing, monitoring, or releasing connections as well as controlling system operations.

signaling protocol A protocol that makes an initial connection between hosts but that does not actually participate in data exchange.

Signaling System 7 *See* SS7.

signal-to-noise ratio *See* SNR.

signature scanning The comparison of a file's content with known malware signatures (unique identifying characteristics in the code) in a signature database to determine whether the file is dangerous.

SIM (Subscriber Identity Module) card A microchip installed in a cellular device to hold data about the subscription a user has with the cellular carrier. GSM networks require that a cellular device have a SIM card.

Simple Gateway Control Protocol *See* SGCP.

Simple Mail Transfer Protocol *See* SMTP.

Simple Network Management Protocol *See* SNMP.

Simple Network Management Protocol version 1 *See* SNMPv1.

Simple Network Management Protocol version 2 *See* SNMPv2.

Simple Network Management Protocol version 3 *See* SNMPv3.

simplex A type of transmission in which signals may travel in only one direction over a medium.

single mode fiber *See* SMF.

single sign-on *See* SSO.

SIP (Session Initiation Protocol) A set of Application layer signaling and control protocols for multiservice, packet-based networks. SIP is used to make an initial connection between hosts for transferring multimedia data.

site survey In the context of wireless networking, an assessment of client requirements, facility characteristics, and coverage areas to determine an access point arrangement that will ensure reliable wireless connectivity within a given area.

site-to-site VPN A type of VPN in which VPN gateways at multiple sites encrypt and encapsulate data to exchange over tunnels with other VPN gateways. Meanwhile, clients, servers, and other hosts on a site-to-site VPN communicate with the VPN gateway.

SLA (service-level agreement) A legally binding contract or part of a contract that defines, in plain language and in measurable terms, the aspects of a service provided to a customer. Specific details might include contract duration, guaranteed uptime, problem management, performance benchmarks, and termination options.

slash notation *See* CIDR notation.

slave name server *See* secondary name server.

slave zombie A lower-layer host in a botnet.

SLIP (Serial Line Internet Protocol) An obsolete Layer 2 communications protocol that enabled a workstation to connect to a server using a serial connection such as dial-up or DSL. SLIP did not support encryption and could carry only IP traffic. SLIP was replaced by PPP.

small form-factor pluggable transceiver *See* SFP transceiver.

small office/home office network *See* SOHO network.

smart card An electronic access badge.

smart jack An intelligent type of NIU located at the customer's demarc that can provide diagnostic information about the interface.

smart tag *See* NFC tag.

SMB (Server Message Block) A protocol for communications and resource access between systems, such as clients and servers. SMB was first used by earlier Windows OSs for file sharing on a network. UNIX uses a version of SMB in its Samba software. The cross-platform version of SMB used between Windows, UNIX, and other operating systems is called the CIFS (Common Internet File System) protocol.

SMF (single mode fiber) A type of fiber-optic cable with a narrow core of 8 to 10 microns in diameter that carries light pulses along a single path from one end of the cable to the other end. Data can be transmitted faster and for longer distances on single mode fiber than on multimode fiber. However, single mode fiber is more expensive.

SMS (Short Message Service) A service that transmits text messages.

SMTP (Simple Mail Transfer Protocol) The Application layer TCP/IP subprotocol responsible for moving messages from one email server to another.

smurf attack A threat to networked hosts in which the host is flooded with broadcast ping messages. A smurf attack is a type of denial-of-service attack.

SNAT (Static Network Address Translation) A type of address translation in which a gateway assigns the same public IP address to a host each time it makes a request to access the Internet.

snips A synonym for scissors.

SNMP (Simple Network Management Protocol) An Application layer protocol in the TCP/IP suite used to monitor and manage devices on a network.

SNMP response message A response from a managed device's agent to the NMS providing requested information.

snmpget A command sent from the NMS to a managed device's agent to retrieve data from the device.

snmpgetnext A command sent from the NMS to a managed device's agent to retrieve data from the next sequential row in the MIB data table.

snmptrap A command used to program a device's agent to detect certain abnormal conditions and prompt the generation of SNMP trap messages, where the agent sends the NMS unsolicited data once the specified conditions are met.

SNMPv1 (Simple Network Management Protocol version 1) The original version of SNMP, released in 1988. Because of its limited features, it is rarely used on modern networks.

SNMPv2 (Simple Network Management Protocol version 2) The second version of SNMP, which improved on SNMPv1 with faster performance and slightly better security, among other features.

SNMPv3 (Simple Network Management Protocol version 3) A version of SNMP similar to SNMPv2, but with authentication, validation, and encryption for messages exchanged between managed devices and the network management console. SNMPv3 is the most secure version of the protocol.

snmpwalk A command issued from an NMS to a managed device to request a sequence of snmpgetnext requests in order to walk through multiple sequential rows in an MIB data table.

SNR (signal-to-noise ratio) The proportion of noise to the strength of a signal.

SOA (Start of Authority) A record in a DNS zone about that zone and records within it.

social engineering The act of manipulating social relationships to circumvent network security measures and gain access to a system.

socket A logical address consisting of a host's IP address and the port number of an application running on the host with a colon separating the two values. For example, if a host has an IP address of 10.43.3.87, the socket address for Telnet running on that host is 10.43.3.87:23.

softphone A computer configured to act like an IP telephone. Softphones present the caller with a graphical representation of a telephone dial pad and can connect to a network via any wired or wireless method.

Softswitch *See* MGC.

Software as a Service *See* SaaS.

software defined networking *See* SDN.

software development life cycle *See* SDLC.

SOHO (small office/home office) network A network consisting of fewer than 10 workstations.

solution A robust word that refers to a product, service, or combination of products and services. The term is commonly used in technology because these products and services often exist specifically to solve problems, and the solution often includes extra features, such as ongoing customer service. Examples include *VoIP solutions*, a *transportation management solution*, or a *CRM (customer relationship management) solution*.

SONET (Synchronous Optical Network) A high-bandwidth WAN signaling technique that specifies framing and multiplexing techniques at the Physical layer of the OSI model. Its four key strengths are that it can integrate many other WAN technologies, it offers fast data transfer rates, it allows for simple link additions and removals, and its double ring of fiber-optic cable provides a high degree of fault tolerance.

SOW (statement of work) A document that details the work that must be completed for a particular project, including specifics such as tasks, deliverables, standards, payment schedule, and work timeline. An SOW is legally binding, meaning it can be enforced in a court of law.

Spanning Tree Protocol *See* STP.

SPB (Shortest Path Bridging) As described in IEEE's 802.1aq standard, a descendent of the Spanning Tree Protocol that can detect and correct for network changes much more quickly.

spectrum analyzer A software tool that assesses the characteristics (for example, frequency, amplitude, and the effects of interference) of wireless signals.

speed and duplex mismatch A problem that occurs when neighboring devices are using different speed or duplex configurations and results in failed transmissions.

speed test site A Web site that can measure upload and download speeds to help determine how a connection's throughput is affecting goodput.

SPI (stateful packet inspection) The inspection by a firewall of each incoming packet to determine whether it belongs to a currently active connection.

split DNS An implementation of DNS where internal and external DNS queries are handled by different DNS servers or by a single DNS server that is specially configured to keep internal and external DNS zones separate.

split horizon A method for preventing routing loops. This Layer 3 technology is employed by distance-vector routing protocols to ensure that a router knows which of its interfaces received a routing update so the router will not retransmit that same update back on the same interface.

split horizon route advertisement *See* split horizon.

split pair A problem created when wires from different twisted pairs in twisted-pair cable are improperly yoked

together, rather than wiring twisted pairs together according to the appropriate pinout.

split-horizon DNS *See* split DNS.

spoofing The act of impersonating fields of data in a transmission, such as when a source IP address is impersonated in a DRDoS attack.

spread-spectrum A type of wireless transmission used in CDMA technology in which lower-level signals are distributed over several frequencies simultaneously. Spread-spectrum transmission is more secure than narrowband.

SPS (standby power supply) *See* standby UPS.

SS7 (Signaling System 7) A set of standards established by the ITU for handling call signaling on circuit-switched portions of the PSTN (Public Switched Telephone Network).

SSH (Secure Shell) A connection utility that provides authentication and encryption. With SSH, you can securely log on to a host, execute commands on that host, and copy files to or from that host. SSH encrypts data exchanged throughout the session.

SSID (service set identifier) A unique character string used to identify an access point on an 802.11 network.

SSL (Secure Sockets Layer) A method of encrypting TCP/IP transmissions—including Web pages and data entered into Web forms—en route between the client and server using public key encryption technology.

SSL session In the context of SSL encryption, an association between the client and server that is defined by an agreement on a specific set of encryption techniques. An SSL session allows the client and server to continue to exchange data securely as long as the client is still connected to the server. SSL sessions are established by the SSL handshake protocol.

SSL VPN A VPN that is configured to support SSL transmissions to and from services running on its protected network. An SSL VPN is typically created and supported by software running on a VPN concentrator.

SSO (single sign-on) A form of authentication in which a client signs on once to access multiple systems or resources.

SSTP (Secure Socket Tunneling Protocol) A proprietary Microsoft protocol, first available with Windows Vista, though it is also available for Linux and some other operating systems (but not Apple products).

ST (straight tip) A connector with a 2.5-mm ferrule that is used with single-mode, fiber-optic cable.

stack master A single switch that hosts the VLAN database for all switches on a network.

standard connector *See* SC.

standby power supply *See* standby UPS.

standby UPS A power supply that provides continuous voltage to a device by switching virtually instantaneously to the battery when it detects a loss of power from the wall outlet. Upon restoration of the power, the standby UPS switches the device back to AC power.

star topology A physical topology in which every node on the network is connected through a central device.

star topology WAN A type of WAN in which a single site acts as the central connection point for several other points. This arrangement provides separate routes for data between any two sites; however, if the central connection point fails, the entire WAN fails.

star-bus topology A hybrid topology in which groups of workstations are connected in a star fashion to connectivity devices that are networked via a single bus.

Start of Authority *See* SOA.

stateful firewall A firewall capable of a stateful inspection, in which it examines an incoming packet to determine whether it belongs to a currently active connection and is, therefore, a legitimate packet.

stateful packet inspection *See* SPI.

stateless firewall A firewall that manages each incoming packet as a stand-alone entity without regard to currently active connections. Stateless firewalls are faster than stateful firewalls, but are not as sophisticated.

statement of work *See* SOW.

static ARP table entry A record in an ARP table that someone has manually entered using the ARP utility. Static ARP table entries remain the same until someone manually modifies them with the ARP utility.

static electricity An electrical charge at rest. When that charge is transferred between two bodies, it creates an electrostatic discharge, or ESD.

static IP address An IP address that is manually assigned to a device and remains constant until it is manually changed.

Static Network Address Translation *See* SNAT.

static routing A technique in which a network administrator programs a router to use specific paths between networks. Because it does not account for occasional network congestion, failed connections, or device moves, and requires manual configuration, static routing is not optimal.

static teaming A configuration in which both the switch and the host are configured to handle a division of labor between redundant links according to particular rules but without the ability to compensate for errors.

station An end node on a network; used most often in the context of wireless networks.

statistical multiplexing A method of multiplexing in which each node on a network is assigned a separate time slot for transmission, based on the node's priority and need.

stealth virus A type of virus that hides itself to prevent detection. Typically, stealth viruses disguise themselves as legitimate programs or replace part of a legitimate program's code with their destructive code.

storage area network *See* SAN.

STP (shielded twisted pair) A type of copper-based cable containing twisted-pair wires that are not only individually insulated, but are also surrounded by a shielding made of a metallic substance such as foil.

STP (Spanning Tree Protocol) A switching protocol defined in IEEE 802.1D. STP operates in the Data Link layer to prevent traffic loops by calculating paths that avoid potential loops and by artificially blocking links that would complete a loop. Given changes to a network's links or devices, STP recalculates its paths.

straight tip *See* ST.

straight-through cable A twisted-pair patch cable in which the wire terminations in both connectors follow the same scheme.

streaming video A service in which video signals are compressed and delivered over the Internet in a continuous stream so that a user can watch and listen even before all the data has been transmitted.

structured cabling A method for uniform, enterprise-wide, multivendor cabling systems specified by the TIA/EIA 568 Commercial Building Wiring Standard. Structured cabling is based on a hierarchical design using a high-speed backbone.

subchannel One of many distinct communication paths established when a channel is multiplexed or modulated.

subnet A smaller network within a larger network in which all nodes share a network addressing component and a fixed amount of bandwidth.

subnet ID The 16 bits, or one block, in an IPv6 address that can be used to identify a subnet on a large corporate network.

subnet mask In IPv4 addressing, a 32-bit number that helps one computer find another by indicating what portion of an IP address is the network portion and what portion is the host portion.

subscriber connector *See* SC.

Subscriber Identity Module card *See* SIM card.

subscription model A service model in which software is provided by subscription. The software might be accessed through a Web portal or might be downloaded and installed on a local computer. Downloadable software is available in formats that are compatible with multiple OSs, and the license might provide for installation on multiple devices.

supernet In IPv4, a type of subnet that is created by moving the subnet boundary to the left instead of the right and using bits that normally would be reserved for network information instead of using bits reserved for host information.

supernet mask A 32-bit number that, when combined with a device's IPv4 address, indicates the kind of supernet to which the device belongs. Whereas the subnet mask moves the network prefix to the right, the supernet mask moves the network prefix to the left, thereby taking up fewer digits than the related classful network prefix.

supernetting *See* CIDR.

supervisory control and data acquisition *See* SCADA.

surge A momentary increase in voltage caused by distant lightning strikes, solar flares, or electrical problems.

surge protector A device that directs excess voltage away from equipment plugged into it and redirects it to a ground, thereby protecting the equipment from harm.

SVC (switched virtual circuit) A logical, point-to-point connection that relies on switches to determine the optimal path between sender and receiver. SVCs are established when parties need to transmit, then terminated after the transmission is complete. Frame relay technology uses SVCs.

switch A connectivity device that logically subdivides a network into smaller, individual collision domains. A switch operates at the Data Link layer of the OSI model and can interpret MAC address information to determine whether to filter (discard) or forward packets it receives.

Switch Dependent Mode A configuration that accomplishes NIC teaming with a single switch.

Switch Independent Mode A configuration in which NICs are teamed to multiple switches, which can be nonintelligent switches.

switched virtual circuit *See* SVC.

switching A component of a network's logical topology that determines how connections are created between nodes on the network.

symmetric DSL *See* SDSL.

symmetric encryption A method of encryption that requires the same key to encode the data as is used to decode the cipher text.

symmetrical A characteristic of transmission technology that provides equal throughput for data traveling both upstream and downstream and is suited to users who both upload and download significant amounts of data.

Synchronous Digital Hierarchy *See* SDH.

Synchronous Optical Network *See* SONET.

syslog A standard for generating, storing, and processing messages about events on a system. Syslog describes methods for detecting and reporting events and specifies the format and contents of messages.

system log On a computer running a UNIX or Linux operating system, the record of monitored events, which can range in priority from 0 to 7 (where "0" indicates an emergency situation and "7" simply points to information that might help in debugging a problem). You can view and modify system log locations and configurations in the file /etc/syslog.conf on most systems (on some systems, this is the /etc/rsyslog.conf file).

T

T-1 (terrestrial carrier level 1) A digital carrier standard used in North America and most of Asia that provides 1.544-Mbps throughput and 24 channels for voice, data, video, or audio signals. T-1s rely on time division multiplexing and may use shielded or unshielded twisted pair, coaxial cable, fiber optics, or microwave links.

T-3 A digital carrier standard used in North America and most of Asia that can carry the equivalent of 672 channels for voice, data, video, or audio, with a maximum data throughput of 44.736 Mbps (typically rounded up to 45 Mbps for purposes of discussion). T-3s rely on time division multiplexing and require either fiber-optic or microwave transmission media.

TA (terminal adapter) A device used to convert digital signals into analog signals for use with ISDN phones and other analog devices. TAs are sometimes called ISDN modems, although they are not actually modems.

TACACS+ (Terminal Access Controller Access Control System Plus) A Cisco proprietary protocol for AAA (access, authentication, and authorization). Like RADIUS, TACACS+ may use one of many authentication protocols. Unlike RADIUS, TACACS+ relies on TCP at the Transport layer instead of UDP, allows for separation of the AAA services, encrypts all information transmitted for AAA, and is typically installed on a router or switch rather than on a server.

tag A VLAN identifier added to a frame's header according to specifications in the 802.1Q standard.

tagged An Ethernet frame that is addressed to a specific VLAN.

T-carrier Standards that specify a method of signaling using TDM (time division multiplexing) over two wire pairs to divide a single channel into multiple channels, which enables digital data to be transmitted at high speeds over the PSTN. T-carrier standards are also called T-CXR standards, and include T-1s, fractional T-1s, and T-3s.

TCP (Transmission Control Protocol) A core protocol of the TCP/IP suite that makes a connection with the end host, checks whether data is received, and resends it if it is not.

TCP/IP (Transmission Control Protocol/Internet Protocol) A suite of networking protocols that includes TCP, IP, UDP, and many others. TCP/IP provides the foundation for data exchange across the Internet.

TDM (time division multiplexing) A method of multiplexing that assigns a time slot in the flow of communications to every node on the network and, in that time slot, carries data from that node.

TDR (time domain reflectometer) A high-end instrument for testing the qualities of a cable. It works by issuing a signal on a cable and measuring the way in which the signal bounces back (or reflects) to the TDR. Many performance testers rely on TDRs.

TE (terminal equipment) The end nodes (such as computers and printers) served by the same connection (such as an ISDN, DSL, or T-1 link).

Telco Short for *telephone company*.

Telecommunications Industry Association *See* TIA.

telemetry A term that sometimes refers to wired communication, but generally refers to wireless communication that transmits data regarding specific measurements and conditions, such as weather data transmitted from a weather balloon to ground antennas.

Telnet A terminal emulation protocol used to log on to remote hosts using the TCP/IP protocol.

TEMPEST A specification created by the NSA to define protection standards against RF emanation, which when implemented are called EmSec (emission security).

Temporal Key Integrity Protocol *See* TKIP.

Teredo A tunneling protocol, named after the Teredo worm, that enables transmission of IPv6 packets over IPv4 networks. IPv6 addresses intended to be used by this protocol begin with the prefix 2001::/32.

Terminal Access Controller Access Control System Plus *See* TACACS+.

terminal adapter *See* TA.

terminal equipment *See* TE.

Terminal Services A feature of Windows Server editions prior to Windows Server 2008 that allows technicians to manage remote applications.

terrestrial carrier level 1 *See* T-1.

testing lab A small network that is segmented from the rest of the network, and contains computers that represent the typical hardware and OS configurations on the larger network as well as any specialized equipment used by the company, for the purpose of testing a patch or upgrade before deployment.

TFTP (Trivial File Transfer Protocol) A TCP/IP Application layer protocol that is seldom used by humans. Computers commonly use it as they are booting up to request configuration files from another computer on the local network. Unlike FTP, TFTP relies on UDP at the Transport layer using port 69.

TGS (Ticket-Granting Service) In Kerberos terminology, an application separate from the AS (authentication service) that runs on the KDC and issues Ticket-Granting Tickets to clients so that they need not request a new ticket for each new service they want to access.

TGT (Ticket-Granting Ticket) In Kerberos terminology, a ticket that enables a user to be accepted as a validated principal by multiple services.

thick AP A self-contained AP that can do its job without relying on a higher-level management device.

Thicknet An outdated IEEE Physical layer standard for achieving a maximum of 10-Mbps throughput over coaxial copper cable. Thicknet was also known as 10Base5. Its maximum segment length is 500 meters, and it relies on a bus topology.

thin AP A simple AP that must be configured from the wireless controller's console in order to function.

Thinnet An outdated IEEE Physical layer standard for achieving 10-Mbps throughput over coaxial copper cable. Thinnet was also known as 10Base2. Its maximum segment length is 185 meters, and it relies on a bus topology.

three-way handshake A three-step process in which Transport layer protocols establish a connection between nodes. The three steps are: Node A issues a SYN packet to node B, node B responds with SYN-ACK, and node A responds with ACK.

throttling One way to limit excessive bandwidth consumption of a specific user, group of users, type of device, type of traffic, or (as in the case of ISPs) a subscriber to the service. Throttling means to purposely slow down bandwidth utilization or to block additional access once a certain threshold has been reached.

throughput The amount of data that a medium transmits during a given period of time. Throughput is usually measured in megabits (1,000,000 bits) per second, or Mbps.

Thunderbolt Apple's proprietary competitor to the USB port. Thunderbolt can be used to connect several types of external peripheral devices to Mac computers.

TIA (Telecommunications Industry Association) A subgroup of the former EIA that focuses on standards for information technology, wireless, satellite, fiber optics, and telephone equipment. EIA was dissolved in 2011 and its responsibilities transferred to ECA (Electronic Components, Assemblies, Equipment & Supplies Association), but the standards brand name, EIA, will continue to be used. Probably the best known standards to come from the TIA/EIA alliance are its guidelines for how network cable should be installed in commercial buildings, known as the "TIA/EIA 568-B Series."

ticket In Kerberos terminology, a temporary set of credentials that a client uses to prove that its identity has been validated by the authentication service.

Ticket-Granting Service *See* TGS.

Ticket-Granting Ticket *See* TGT.

tiered topology WAN A type of WAN in which sites that are connected in star or ring formations are interconnected at different levels, with the interconnection points being organized into layers to form hierarchical groupings.

time division multiplexing *See* TDM.

time domain reflectometer *See* TDR.

Time to Live *See* TTL.

Time to Live field A field in a DNS resource record that identifies how long the record should be saved in a cache on a server. This field is included in zone transfers.

time-shifted video A broadcast that is delayed by a few minutes to allow for editing processes and licensing concerns.

TKIP (Temporal Key Integrity Protocol) An encryption key generation and management scheme used by 802.11i.

TLD (top-level domain) The last part of an FQDN and the highest-level category used to distinguish domain names—for example, .org, .com, and .net. A TLD is also known as the domain suffix.

TLS (Transport Layer Security) A version of SSL standardized by the IETF (Internet Engineering Task Force). TLS uses slightly different encryption algorithms than SSL, but otherwise is very similar to the most recent version of SSL.

TMS (transportation management system) Software that tracks inventory as it is transported between locations, such as between a warehouse and a storefront.

tone generator A small electronic device that issues a signal on a wire pair. When used in conjunction with a tone locator, it can help locate the termination of a wire pair.

tone locator A small electronic device that emits a tone when it detects electrical activity on a wire pair. When used in conjunction with a tone generator, it can help locate the termination of a wire pair.

toner *See* tone generator.

toner and probe kit A two-piece tool that includes both a tone generator and a tone locator. Used together, they can help locate the termination of a wire pair.

toner probe *See* toner and probe kit.

top listener A host that receives an inordinate amount of data.

top talker A host that sends inordinate amounts of data.

top-level domain *See* TLD.

topology How the parts of a whole fit together.

TOS (Type of Service) A field in an IPv4 header that currently serves as the DSCP field and the ECN (Explicit Congestion Notification) field.

traceroute A TCP/IP troubleshooting utility available in Linux, UNIX, and OS X systems that sends UDP messages to a random port on the destination node to trace the path from one networked node to another, identifying all intermediate hops between the two nodes.

tracert A Windows utility that uses ICMP echo requests to trace the path from one networked node to another, identifying all intermediate hops between the two nodes.

traffic policing A traffic-shaping technique in which the volume or rate of traffic traversing an interface is limited to a predefined maximum.

traffic shaper Software running on a router, multilayer switch, gateway, server, or even a client workstation that can prioritize traffic according to protocol, IP address, user group, DiffServ flag (in an IP packet), VLAN tag, service, or application.

traffic shaping Manipulating certain characteristics of packets, data streams, or connections to manage the type and amount of traffic traversing a network or interface at any moment.

trailer Control information attached to the end of a packet by the Data Link layer protocol.

transformer A device that changes the voltage of AC electrical energy, such as when the power over the main line from the electric company is transformed before being delivered to a house.

Transmission Control Protocol *See* TCP.

Transmission Control Protocol/Internet Protocol *See* TCP/IP.

Transparent Interconnection of Lots of Links *See* TRILL.

transponder The equipment on a satellite that receives an uplinked signal from Earth, amplifies the signal, modifies its frequency, then retransmits it (in a downlink) to an antenna on Earth.

Transport layer The fourth layer of the OSI model. The Transport layer is responsible for transporting Application layer payloads from one application to another.

Transport Layer Security *See* TLS.

transportation management system *See* TMS.

TRILL (Transparent Interconnection of Lots of Links) A multipath, link-state protocol (using IS-IS) developed by the IETF and designed to replace STP.

trip hazard Items such as extension cords or tools lying on the ground in walkways that can cause someone to stumble.

Trivial File Transfer Protocol *See* TFTP.

Trojan horse A program that disguises itself as something useful, but actually harms your system.

trunk port The interface on a switch capable of managing traffic from multiple VLANs. A trunk is a link configured between two switches' trunk ports.

trunking The aggregation of multiple logical connections in one physical connection between connectivity devices. In the case of VLANs, a trunk allows two switches to manage and exchange data between multiple VLANs.

TTL (Time to Live) Indicates the maximum duration that an IPv4 packet can remain on the network before it is discarded. Although this field was originally meant to represent units of time, on modern networks it represents the number of times a packet can still be forwarded by a router, or the maximum number of router hops remaining.

TTLS (Tunneled Transport Layer Security) A variant of TLS that provides authentication like SSL/TLS, but does not require a certificate for each user. Instead, TTLS authenticates the server end of the connection by certificate, and users are authenticated by password only or some other legacy method.

tunnel A secured, virtual connection between two nodes on a VPN.

Tunneled Transport Layer Security *See* TTLS.

tunneling The process of encapsulating one type of protocol in another. Tunneling is the way in which higher-layer data is transported over VPNs by Layer 2 protocols.

twist ratio The number of twists per meter or foot in a twisted-pair cable.

twisted-pair A type of cable similar to telephone wiring that consists of color-coded pairs of insulated copper wires, each with a diameter of 0.4 to 0.8 mm. Every two wires are twisted around each other to form pairs, and all the pairs are encased in a plastic sheath.

two-factor authentication An authentication process in which clients must supply two pieces of information to verify their identity and gain access to a system.

two-post rack An equipment rack consisting of two vertical side posts to which equipment is attached via brackets incorporated in the posts.

Tx/Rx reverse A problem caused by mismatched pinout standards, resulting in near end cross-talk.

Type of Service *See* TOS.

U

U (rack unit) The industry-standard unit for measuring rack height. Standard racks are 42U tall—about 6 feet. Most rack-mountable computers are 1U–4U high, whereas a server may only require 1U.

UC (unified communications) The centralized management of multiple types of network-based communications, such as voice, video, fax, and messaging services.

UC gateway *See* media gateway.

UDP (User Datagram Protocol) A core protocol in the TCP/IP suite that does not guarantee delivery because it does not first make the connection before sending data or check to confirm that data is received.

Ultra Polished Connector *See* UPC.

UNC (Universal Naming Convention) Notation that identifies files or peripheral devices shared on a network.

unicast address A type of IPv6 address that represents a single node on a network.

unidirectional antenna A type of antenna that issues wireless signals along a single direction, or path. Also called a directional antenna.

unified communications *See* UC.

unified messaging *See* UC.

Unified Threat Management *See* UTM.

unified voice services VoIP when used in cloud-based PBX systems.

Uniform Resource Locator *See* URL.

unintentional DoS attack A DoS situation that is created unintentionally and without malicious intent, such as when a Web site is flooded with an unexpectedly high amount of shopping traffic during a flash sale.

uninterruptible power supply *See* UPS.

Universal Naming Convention *See* UNC.

Universal Serial Bus *See* USB.

unmanaged switch A switch that provides plug-and-play simplicity with minimal configuration options and has no IP address assigned to it. Unmanaged switches are inexpensive, but their capabilities are limited.

unmodulated carrier tone *See* guard tone.

unshielded twisted pair *See* UTP.

UPC (Ultra Polished Connector) A type of ferrule in which the tip has been highly polished, thereby increasing the efficiency of the connection.

upgrade A significant change to an application's existing code, typically designed to improve functionality or add new features while also correcting bugs and vulnerabilities.

uplink In the context of wireless transmission, the connection between a client's transceiver and a carrier's antenna.

UPS (uninterruptible power supply) A battery-operated power source directly attached to one or more devices and to a power supply (such as a wall outlet) that prevents undesired fluctuations of the wall outlet's AC power from harming the device or interrupting its services.

upset failure Damage that can shorten the life of a component and/or cause intermittent errors.

upstream A term used to describe data traffic that flows from a customer's site to a carrier's facility. In asymmetrical communications, upstream throughput is usually much lower than downstream throughput. In symmetrical communications, upstream and downstream throughputs are equal.

uptime The duration or percentage of time a system or network functions normally between failures.

URL (Uniform Resource Locator) A string of text that uniquely identifies a file available on a network.

USB (Universal Serial Bus) A connector used for peripheral devices.

user agent In SIP terminology, any node that initiates or responds to SIP requests.

user agent client In SIP terminology, end-user devices such as workstations, tablet computers, smartphones, or IP telephones. A user agent client initiates a SIP connection.

user agent server In SIP terminology, a server that responds to user agent clients' requests for session initiation and termination.

user awareness An NGFW (Next Generation Firewall) feature that adapts a firewall's configuration to the class of a specific user or user group.

User Datagram Protocol See UDP.

UTF-8 An 8-bit character encoding system that includes ASCII and is the most common character encoding system used today.

UTM (Unified Threat Management) A security strategy that combines multiple layers of security appliances and technologies into a single safety net.

UTP (unshielded twisted pair) A type of copper-based cable that consists of one or more insulated twisted-pair wires encased in a plastic sheath. As its name implies, UTP does not contain additional shielding for the twisted pairs. As a result, UTP is both less expensive and less resistant to noise than STP.

UTP coupler A connector that can connect two UTP cables to each other. This is helpful when needing to lengthen a cable without installing a new, longer cable.

V

VA (volt-ampere) A measure of electrical power. A volt-ampere, or volt-amp, is the product of the voltage and current (measured in amps) of the electricity on a line.

variable digital subscriber line See VDSL.

VDSL (very-high-bit-rate digital subscriber line or (Network+) variable digital subscriber line) A variety of DSL that provides higher throughput than its predecessor, ADSL.

vertical cross connect Part of a network's backbone that supplies connectivity between a building's floors. For example, vertical cross connects might connect an MDF and an IDF or IDFs and data closets within a building.

very-high-bit-rate digital subscriber line See VDSL.

video bridge Hardware or software that manages multiple audiovisual sessions so that participants can see and hear each other.

video over IP Any type of video service, including IPTV, videoconferencing, and streaming video, that delivers video signals over packet-switched networks using the TCP/IP protocol suite.

video phone A type of phone that includes a screen and can decode compressed video and interpret transport and signaling protocols necessary for conducting videoconference sessions.

video teleconference See VTC.

videoconferencing The real-time reception and transmission of images and audio among two or more locations.

video-on-demand See VoD.

vim text editor The text editing utility in Linux that allows a technician to make changes to text files, such as when editing the IP address range for a DHCP server.

virtual adapter See vNIC.

virtual appliance An image that includes the appropriate operating system, software, hardware specifications, and application configuration necessary for a prepackaged solution to run properly on a virtual machine.

virtual bridge An interface connecting a vNIC with a virtual or physical network, or a port on a virtual switch.

virtual circuit A connection between network nodes that, although based on potentially disparate physical links, logically appears to be a direct, dedicated link between those nodes.

virtual console See virtual terminal.

virtual IP address An IP address that can be shared by a group of routers.

virtual local area network See VLAN.

virtual machine manager See hypervisor.

virtual network connection See VNC.

virtual network interface card See vNIC.

virtual private network See VPN.

Virtual Router Redundancy Protocol *See* VRRP.

virtual server A server that exists as a virtual machine, created and managed by virtualization software on a host, or physical, computer.

virtual switch A logically defined device that is created and managed by virtualization software and that operates at the Data Link layer to pass frames between nodes. Ports on a virtual switch connect virtual machines with a network, whether virtual or physical, through the host's physical NIC.

virtual terminal A machine at the technician's location that provides for remote configuration of a switch.

virtual wire mode A firewall installation in which the firewall is transparent to surrounding nodes, as if it were just part of the network transmission media.

virtual workstation A workstation that exists as a virtual machine, created and managed by virtualization software on a host, or physical, computer.

VirtualBox A virtualization software platform from Oracle.

virtualization The emulation of all or part of a computer or network.

virus A program that replicates itself to infect more computers, either through network connections when it piggybacks on other files or through exchange of external storage devices, such as USB drives, passed among users. Viruses might damage files or systems or simply annoy users by flashing messages or pictures on the screen or by causing the keyboard to beep.

VLAN (virtual local area network) A network within a network that is logically defined by grouping ports on a switch so that some of the local traffic on the switch is forced to go through a router. A VLAN can consist of any type of network node in any geographic location and can incorporate nodes connected to different switches.

VLAN hopping attack An attack in which the attacker generates transmissions that appear, to the switch, to belong to a protected VLAN.

VLAN pooling A feature on wireless controllers that groups multiple VLANs into a single VLAN group, or pool, and then dynamically assigns wireless clients to each successive VLAN in the pool.

VLAN trunking protocol *See* VTP.

VMware A vendor that supplies the most popular types of workstation and server virtualization software. Used casually, the term *VMware* may also refer to the virtualization software distributed by the company.

VNC (virtual network connection) Software that provides remote access and control of another computer.

vNIC (virtual network interface card) A logically defined network interface associated with a virtual machine.

VoD (video-on-demand) A service in which a video stored as an encoded file is delivered to a viewer upon his request.

Voice over IP *See* VoIP.

VoIP (Voice over IP) The provision of telephone service over a packet-switched network running the TCP/IP protocol suite.

voltage regulator A device that maintains a constant voltage level for either AC or DC electrical energy.

volt-ampere *See* VA.

VPN (virtual private network) A virtual connection between a client and a remote network, two remote networks, or two remote hosts over the Internet or other types of networks, to remotely provide network resources. VPNs can be created through the use of software or combined software and hardware solutions.

VPN concentrator A specialized device that authenticates VPN clients, establishes tunnels for VPN connections, and manages encryption for VPN transmissions.

VPN gateway A device that sits at the edge of a LAN to establish and maintain a secure VPN connection. Each gateway is a router or remote access server with VPN software installed, and encrypts and encapsulates data to exchange over the tunnel. Meanwhile, clients, servers, and other hosts on the protected LANs communicate through the VPN gateways as if they were on the same, private network and do not have to run special VPN software.

VRRP (Virtual Router Redundancy Protocol) A standard that assigns a virtual IP address to a group of routers. At first, messages routed to the virtual IP address are handled by the master router. If the master router fails, backup routers stand in line to take over responsibility for the virtual IP address.

VTC (video teleconference) An application that allows people to communicate in video and voice.

VTP (VLAN trunking protocol) Cisco's protocol for exchanging VLAN information over trunks. VTP allows one switch on a network to centrally manage all VLANs.

vulnerability A weakness of a system, process, or architecture that could lead to compromised information or unauthorized access to a network.

W

WAN (wide area network) A network that spans a long distance and connects two or more LANs.

WAN interface card *See* WIC.

WAN link A point-to-point connection between two nodes on a WAN.

WAN site An individual geographic location or endpoint connected by a WAN.

WAP (wireless access point) *See* AP.

war chalking The use of chalk to draw symbols on a sidewalk or wall within range of an access point. The symbols, patterned after marks that hobos devised to indicate hospitable places for food or rest, indicate the access point's SSID and whether it's secured.

war driving The act of driving around an area while running a laptop configured to detect and capture wireless data transmissions.

warehouse management system *See* WMS.

warm site A place where the computers, devices, and connectivity necessary to rebuild a network exist, though only some are appropriately configured, updated, or connected to match the network's current state.

wavelength The distance between corresponding points on a wave's cycle, expressed in meters or feet. Wavelength is inversely proportional to frequency.

wavelength division multiplexing *See* WDM.

wavelength mismatch A problem created when transmissions are optimized for one type of cable, such as SMF, but sent over a different type of cable, such as MMF.

WDM (wavelength division multiplexing) A multiplexing technique in which each signal on a fiber-optic cable is assigned a different wavelength, which equates to its own subchannel. Each wavelength is modulated with a data signal. In this manner, multiple signals can be simultaneously transmitted in the same direction over a length of fiber.

Web caching A technique in which Web pages are stored at an ISP or locally, either on a host or network, and then delivered to requesters more quickly than if they had been obtained from the original source.

Web services *See* cloud computing.

Webcast A streaming video, either on demand or live, that is delivered via the Web.

well-known ports The TCP/IP port numbers 0 to 1023, so named because they were long ago assigned by Internet authorities to popular services (for example, FTP and Telnet), and are, therefore, well known and frequently used.

WEP (Wired Equivalent Privacy) A key encryption technique for wireless networks that uses keys both to authenticate network clients and to encrypt data in transit.

WEP attack A security exploit in which a hacker uses a program to discover a WEP key.

WEP cracking *See* WEP attack.

WIC (WAN interface card) A specialized NIC that can act as a CSU/DSU in order to connect a device directly to a WAN.

wide area network *See* WAN.

Wi-Fi (wireless fidelity) The IEEE standards and their amendments, extensions, and corrections for wireless networking.

Wi-Fi analyzer *See* wireless analyzer.

Wi-Fi controller *See* wireless controller.

Wi-Fi Protected Access *See* WPA.

Wi-Fi Protected Setup *See* WPS.

wildcard mask A variation of a network address that specifies a network segment (group of IP addresses) by using 0s in bits that must match the network address and 1s in bits that can hold any value. Wildcard masks are used in ACL statements to dictate which traffic can or cannot pass through.

WiMAX (Worldwide Interoperability for Microwave Access) *See* 802.16.

WiMAX 2 *See* 802.16m.

WiMAX Release 2 *See* 802.16m.

Windows Internet Name Service *See* WINS.

WINS (Windows Internet Name Service) A predecessor to DNS on Windows networks.

wire stripper A tool designed to pull the protective covering off the inside wires of a cable without damaging the wires themselves.

Wired Equivalent Privacy *See* WEP.

wireless A type of signal made of electromagnetic energy that travels through the air.

wireless access point *See* AP.

wireless analyzer Software that can evaluate Wi-Fi network availability as well as help optimize Wi-Fi signal settings or help identify Wi-Fi security threats.

wireless bridge An access point used to create remote wired access to a network. The throughput demands of a wireless bridge can be significantly higher than typical Wi-Fi clients.

wireless controller A central management console for all of the APs on a network.

wireless gateway An AP that provides routing functions and is used as a gateway.

wireless local area network *See* WLAN.

wireless mesh network *See* mesh WLAN.

wireless PAN *See* WPAN.

Wireless Protected Access *See* WPA.

wireless router An AP that provides routing functions.

wireless spectrum A continuum of electromagnetic waves used for data and voice communication. The wireless spectrum (as defined by the FCC, which controls its use) spans frequencies between 9 KHz and 300 GHz. Each type of wireless service can be associated with one area of the wireless spectrum.

wiring schematic A graphical representation of a network's wired infrastructure.

WLAN (wireless local area network) A LAN that uses wireless connections for some or all of its transmissions.

WLAN controller *See* wireless controller.

WMN (wireless mesh network) *See* mesh WLAN.

WMS (warehouse management system) Software that manages the resources in a warehouse.

Worldwide Interoperability for Microwave Access (WiMAX) *See* 802.16.

worm A program that runs independently and travels between computers and across networks. Although worms do not alter other programs as viruses do, they can carry viruses.

WPA (Wi-Fi Protected Access or Wireless Protected Access) A wireless security method that dynamically assigns every transmission its own key.

WPA attack A security exploit in which a hacker uses a program to intercept a WPA key as it is communicated between stations and access points.

WPA cracking *See* WPA attack.

WPA2 A wireless security method that improves upon WPA by using a stronger encryption protocol called AES.

WPA2-Enterprise An authentication scheme for Wi-Fi networks that combines WPA2 with RADIUS.

WPA-Enterprise An authentication scheme for Wi-Fi networks that combines WPA with RADIUS.

WPAN (wireless PAN) A purely wireless version of a PAN.

WPS (Wi-Fi Protected Setup) A user-friendly—but not very secure—security setting available on some consumer-grade APs. Part of the security involves requiring a PIN in order to access the AP's settings or to associate a new device with the network. The PIN can be easily cracked through a brute force attack, so this PIN feature should be disabled if possible.

WPS attack A security exploit in which a WPS PIN is discovered by means of a brute force attack, giving the attacker access to the network's WPA2 key. The PIN feature in WPS should be disabled if possible.

www World Wide Web.

X

XaaS (Anything as a Service, or Everything as a Service) A type of cloud computing in which the cloud can provide any combination of functions depending on a client's exact needs, or assumes functions beyond networking including, for example, monitoring, storage, applications, and virtual desktops.

xDSL The term used to refer to all varieties of DSL.

XDSL (extended digital subscriber line) A variety of DSL that provides DSL services to locations outside the normal DSL service area.

Xen Virtualization software by Citrix.

XFP A type of SFP that can send and receive data at rates of up to 10 Gbps.

XML (eXtensible Markup Language) An alternative to HTML that provides rules for formatting documents.

Y

Yost cable *See* rollover cable.

Z

zero configuration *See* zeroconf.

zeroconf (zero configuration) An automatically configured IP network.

zero-day attack *See* zero-day exploit.

zero-day exploit An exploit that takes advantage of a software vulnerability that hasn't yet become public, and is known only to the hacker who discovered it. Zero-day exploits are particularly dangerous because the vulnerability is exploited before the software developer has the opportunity to provide a solution for it.

zipcord cable A relatively short fiber-optic cable in which two strands are arranged side by side in conjoined jackets, enabling full-duplex communication.

zombie A computer used without the owner's knowledge in a coordinated attack.

zombie army *See* botnet.

zone file A text file associated with a DNS zone that contains resource records identifying domains and their IP addresses.

zone ID A % sign and a number at the end of an IPv6 address that is used to identify the link the computer belongs to.

zone transfer In DNS, the act of copying a primary name server's zone file to the secondary name server to ensure that both contain the same information.

Index